William Hanson

**Geographical encyclopaedia of New South Wales**

Including the counties, towns, and villages within the colony

William Hanson

**Geographical encyclopaedia of New South Wales**
*Including the counties, towns, and villages within the colony*

ISBN/EAN: 9783337270148

Printed in Europe, USA, Canada, Australia, Japan

Cover: Foto ©Andreas Hilbeck / pixelio.de

More available books at **www.hansebooks.com**

Published by Authority of the Government of New South Wales for
the World's Columbian Exposition, Chicago, 1893.

# GEOGRAPHICAL ENCYCLOPÆDIA

OF

# NEW SOUTH WALES,

INCLUDING THE

COUNTIES, TOWNS, AND VILLAGES, WITHIN THE COLONY,

WITH

THE SOURCES AND COURSES OF THE RIVERS AND THEIR TRIBUTARIES.
PORTS, HARBOURS, LIGHT-HOUSES, AND MOUNTAIN RANGES.
POSTAL, MONEY ORDER AND TELEGRAPH OFFICES, AND SAVINGS BANKS.
THE RAILWAYS AND STATIONS ON EACH LINE.
THE PUBLIC SCHOOLS, AND THE COUNTY IN WHICH EACH SCHOOL IS LOCATED.

WITH A MAP, AND DIAGRAM OF LIGHT-HOUSES ON THE COAST.

By WILLIAM HANSON, A.L.S., LOND.
*(Formerly Government Printer of New South Wales),*
AUTHOR OF "THE PASTORAL POSSESSIONS OF NEW SOUTH WALES."

Sydney:
CHARLES POTTER, GOVERNMENT PRINTER, PHILLIP-STR
1892.
[*Registered under the Copyright Act, 1879.*]
[12s. 6d.]

# Dedicated

(BY PERMISSION)

## TO HIS EXCELLENCY
### The Right Honorable Victor Albert George,
## EARL OF JERSEY,

A MEMBER OF HER MAJESTY'S MOST HONORABLE PRIVY COUNCIL,
KNIGHT GRAND CROSS OF THE MOST DISTINGUISHED ORDER OF ST. MICHAEL
AND ST. GEORGE,
GOVERNOR AND COMMANDER-IN-CHIEF OF
THE COLONY OF NEW SOUTH WALES AND ITS DEPENDENCIES,
ETC., ETC.,

By His Excellency's Faithful Servant,

WM. HANSON.

*February, 1892.*

# TABLE OF CONTENTS.

MAP OF NEW SOUTH WALES (Facing Title Page).

DIAGRAM OF LIGHTHOUSES ON THE COAST (Ditto).

| | PAGE. |
|---|---|
| DEDICATION | iii |
| PREFACE ... | vii |
| ALPHABETICAL ARRANGEMENT FROM A TO Z | 1–402 |
| Grouped as follows :— | |
| COUNTIES IN THE COLONY ... | 89 |
| ,, ,, EASTERN DIVISION | 90–116 |
| ,, ,, CENTRAL DIVISION | 117–135 |
| ,, ,, WESTERN DIVISION | 136–149 |
| MOUNTAIN RANGES .. | 275-278 |
| PORTS, HARBOURS, LIGHTHOUSES, AND RIVERS ON THE COAST | 317-331 |
| PORT JACKSON AND ITS WHARFS AND DOCKS | 321-327 |
| PUBLIC SCHOOLS IN EASTERN DIVISION | 333–344 |
| ,, CENTRAL DIVISION | 344–346 |
| ,, WESTERN DIVISION ... | 346 |
| RAILWAYS, TRAMWAYS, AND TELEGRAPH LINES ... | 350-352 |
| RIVERS—THEIR SOURCES AND COURSES | 357-383 |

# GEOGRAPHICAL ENCYCLOPÆDIA

OF

## NEW SOUTH WALES.

## A

ABATTOIRS (*Co. Cumberland*), about 3 miles W. of the General Post Office, and is the principal slaughtering place for the city and suburbs of Sydney. Mail, three times daily, and telegraph office. Situate on a portion of Balmain, and formerly known as Glebe Island.

ABBEYGREEN (*Co. Northumberland*), a small settlement on the banks of the river Hunter, a few miles from the township of Singleton.

ABBOTSBURY (*Co. Cumberland*), a rural settlement, situated in the parish of Melville, to the N.W. of Liverpool.

ABERCROMBIE (*Co. Georgiana*), a postal receiving-office, 194 miles W. of Sydney, with daily mail. The nearest railway station is Lyndhurst, 22 miles, on the Blayney and Murrumburrah line. It is an alluvial gold working, about 14 miles N. of the village of Bigga.

ABERCROMBIE RIVER (*Co. Georgiana*). [*See* "RIVERS."]

ABERDEEN (*Co. Brisbane*), a postal village, 185 miles N. of Sydney, with daily mail. Money-order, telegraph offices, and Government savings bank. A railway station on the northern line. The district is an agricultural and pastoral one, with some rich flats of cultivation ground.

ABERFOYLE (*Co. Clarke*), a small settlement on the N. bank of the river of that name, 400 miles N. of Sydney.

ABERFOYLE RIVER (*Co. Clarke*). [*See* "RIVERS."]

ABERGLASSLYN (*Co. Northumberland*), a postal receiving-office, 123 miles N. of Sydney, with mail twice a week. The nearest railway station is West Maitland, 6 miles, on the northern line. A rich rural district on the south bank of the Hunter River.

ACACIA (*Co. Yancowinna*), a post-office, 813 miles W. of Sydney, with daily mail. Situated between Silverton and Broken Hill.

ACACIA CREEK (*Co. Buller*), a post-office, 470 miles N. of Sydney, with mail twice a week. On the extreme northern boundary of the territory, and to the N. of Maryland.

ACRES BILLABONG (*Co. Rankin*), a series of lagoons, having their rise in Greenough's Range, and flowing into the river Darling, in 31° S. lat.

ADAMINABY (*Co. Wallace*), a post-office, 295 miles S. of Sydney, with mail twice a week. Money-order and telegraph offices, and Government savings bank. The nearest railway station is Cooma, 80 miles, on the Goulburn and Cooma line. The district is auriferous.

ADAMS PEAK (*Co. Northumberland*), situated on the W. bank of the Wollombi Brook, in the parish of Dalton, near the junction of Drew's Creek, in the Hunter Range.

ADAMSTOWN (*Co. Northumberland*), a post-office, 104 miles N. of Sydney, with daily mail. Money-order and telegraph offices, and Government savings bank. A railway station on the northern line. It is a municipal district, governed by eight aldermen and a mayor, situated in the parish of Newcastle, and is a coal-mining district, with a population of about 2,000.

ADELONG (*Co. Wynyard*), a postal town, 308 miles S. of Sydney, with daily mail. Money-order and telegraph offices, and Government savings bank. The nearest railway station is Gundagai, 23 miles on the Cootamundra and Gundagai line. The district is a mining one, and within a proclaimed gold-field.

ADELONG CREEK (*Co. Wynyard*), an important auriferous stream, flowing through the Adelong gold-fields, and the township of Adelong, and falling into the Murrumbidgee River, about 5 miles S. of Gundagai.

ADELONG CROSSING PLACE (*Co. Wynyard*), a postal township, 297 miles S. of Sydney, with daily mail. Situated on the Adelong Creek, about 3 miles from its junction with the Murrumbidgee River. The district is highly productive, and it is within a proclaimed gold-field. The nearest railway station is Gundagai, 11 miles, on the Cootamundra and Gundagai line.

AILSA (*Co. Bligh*), an agricultural hamlet on the Krui River, about 117 miles N.W. of Maitland, and 16 miles E. of Cassilis.

AINSLIE MOUNT (*Co. Murray*), situated about 8 miles N. of Queanbeyan, at the head of M'Laughlin's Creek. It is a lofty peak, 500 feet above the level of the surrounding limestone plains.

AIRDS (*Co. Cumberland*), is bounded on the N.W. side by Bunburry Creek, Minto, and Upper Minto, on the W. side by the Nepean River, and on the E. by George's River.

ALBERMARLE (*Co. Livingston*), a township, 880 miles W. of Sydney, on the banks of the Darling, near Menindie.

ALBERT LAKE (*Co. Wynyard*), an extensive fresh-water lake to the S. of Wagga Wagga, and to the E. of the southern railway line, and S. of Wagga Wagga.

ALBERT TOWN (*Co. Cumberland*), a township reserve in the parish of Willoughby, on the Middle Harbour of Port Jackson.

ALBION (*Co. Yancowinna*), a proclaimed village, 830 miles W. of Sydney, on the South Australian border.

ALBION PARK (*Co. Camden*), a postal town on the southern coast, 61 miles S. of Sydney, with daily mail, money-order and telegraph offices, and Government savings bank ; a railway station on the South Coast and Illawarra line; situated near the Macquarie River, and within a short distance of Lake Illawarra, and is a most productive farming and dairy district. It lies in the immediate neighbourhood of the southern coal-fields.

ALBURY (*Co. Goulburn*), a postal town, 386 miles S. of Sydney, with daily mail therefrom ; telegraph and money-order offices, and Government savings bank. Albury is the border town between Victoria and New South Wales, situated on the river Murray, and on the main southern line of railway to Melbourne and Adelaide. It is distant 386 miles S. of Sydney, and 205 miles N.E. of Melbourne, the capital of Victoria, and possesses all the accommodation necessary for a large and populous city, and its commercial requirements are well supplied. The vine is successfully cultivated here, and the vignerons of the district occupy an European reputation for their wine-producing excellencies. Albury has a fine piece of land reserved as a botanical garden, in which a monument to Mr. Hamilton Hume, of the Hovell and Hume exploration, in commemoration of the discovery of the Upper Murray River, has been erected. It is governed by a borough council, consisting of eight aldermen and a mayor, incorporated under the Municipalities Act of 1858. Supreme Court sittings, quarter sessions, and district courts are held here periodically. Population of district, about 6,000.

ALBURY RACECOURSE (*Co. Goulburn*), 384 miles S. of Sydney, and 2 miles from the town of Albury. It is a railway station on the southern line.

ALEXANDRIA (*Co. Cumberland*), a suburban municipality, proclaimed a borough in 1868, situated on the Botany Road, in the parish of the same name. It is governed by eleven aldermen and a mayor. The borough is divided into four wards, viz., east ward, west ward, south ward, and Beaconsfield ward. It is a populous district, lying between Waterloo and Macdonaldtown. There is a mail twice a day from Sydney ; money-order and telegraph offices, Government savings bank, and delivery by letter-carrier. Population, about 8,000.

ALFRED TOWN (*Co. Wynyard*), a postal receiving-office, 319 miles S. of Sydney, with mail three days a week.

ALGOMERA CREEK (*Co. Dudley*), a southern tributary of the Nambucera River, flowing through good cedar country.

ALICE (*Co. Drake*), a small agricultural settlement, situated about 16 miles S. of Tabulam, at the junction of the Alice Creek and the Clarence River.

ALICE CREEK (*Co. Richmond*), a tributary of the Clarence River, falling into it at the township of Alice.

ALICETON (*Co. Northumberland*), a post-office, 132 miles N. of Sydney, with mail twice a week.

ALICKTOWN (*Co. Ashburnham*), a postal office, 313 miles W. of Sydney, with mail twice a week. Money-order office and Government savings bank. The nearest railway station is Molong, 7½ miles, on the Orange and Molong service, western line.

ALIONAYONYIGA CREEK (*Co. Argyle*), a small stream flowing into Lake George, taking its rise in the western slope of the Australian Alps.

ALIONAYONYIGA MOUNT (*Co. Argyle*), a peak of the Australian Alps, lying N.E. of Kenny's Point on Lake George, and attains an altitude of 1,500 feet above the level of the lake.

ALISON (*Co. Durham*), a post-office, 160 miles N. of Sydney, with mail three days a week.

ALISON'S SIDING (*Co. Cooper*), a railway station, 386 miles to the W. of Sydney, on the south-western line—Junee Junction to Hay service.

ALLANDALE (*Co. Northumberland*), a post-office, 126 miles N. of Sydney, with mail twice a week; a railway station on the northern line.

ALLAN'S CREEK (*Co. Fitzroy*), a small eastern tributary of the Don Dorrigo River.

ALLAN'S MOUNT (*Co. Cunningham*), a lofty mountain on the plains, about 10 miles N. of the Lachlan River.

ALLEN'S CREEK (*Co. Hardinge*), an eastern tributary of the Gwydir River.

ALLJOE'S CREEK (*Co. Townsend*), an arm of the Edward River at Deniliquin.

ALLPON CREEK (*Co. Clarence*), a southern tributary of the Clarence River, flowing into the main stream at South Grafton.

ALLYNBROOK (*Co. Durham*), a post-office, 152 miles N. of Sydney, with mail three times a week. The nearest railway station is West Maitland, 32 miles, on the northern line.

ALLYN MOUNT (*Co. Durham*), situated about 16 miles N. of the village of Eccleston, is a peak of the Mount Royal Range, at the head of the Allyn River.

ALLYN RIVER (*Co. Durham*). [*See* "RIVERS."]

ALMA (*Co. Yancowinna*), a proclaimed township, 840 miles W. of Sydney, on the South Australian border.

ALMA (*Co. Wellington*), a township, distant 21 miles from Wellington. The nearest railway station is Wellington, 27 miles, on western line.

ALNWICK (*Co. Durham*), a small agricultural village near the township of Raymond Terrace. The district abounds in coal.

ALSTONVILLE (*Co. Rous*), a post and telegraph office, 367 miles N. of Sydney, with mail twice a week.

ALTAI LAKE (*Co. Yantara*), is one of a series of lakes in the same county, in the extreme N.W. of the Colony.

ALTCAR (*Co. Cadell*), a postal receiving-office, 583 miles S. of Sydney, with mail twice a week.

ALTOLKA (*Co. Yantara*), situate about 600 miles N.W. of Sydney, and about 60 miles S. of the Queensland boundary.

ALUM CREEK (*Co. Clarence*), a northern tributary of the Clarence River, flowing into the main stream at Grafton.

ALUM CREEK (*Co. Cowley*), a tributary of the Upper Murrumbidgee River rising in the eastern slopes of Mount Phillips.

AMAROO (*Co. Wellington*), a postal receiving-office, 208 miles W. of Sydney, with daily mail. A railway station on the western line.

AMERICAN CREEK (*Co. Camden*) is a beautiful stream, flowing from the coast range, opposite Wollongong, 66 miles S. of Sydney. There is a considerable development of kerosene shale in this creek. The seam is about 1 foot 9 inches in thickness.

AMOSFIELD (*Co. Clive*), on the Herding-yard Creek, 462 miles N. of Sydney, in a tin-bearing district. The nearest railway station is Tenterfield, 33 miles, on the northern line.

AMUNGERIE (*Co. Lincoln*), a township, 220 miles N.E. of Sydney, on the Coolbaggie Creek, near Dubbo.

AMYOT MOUNT (*Co. Ashburnham*), a most distinguishable mountain lying between Goobank Creek and the Lachlan River.

ANA BRANCH CREEK (*Co. Courallie*), a watercourse flowing into the Gwydir River and the Goonal Swamp.

ANA BRANCH CREEK (*Co. Wentworth*), the western mouth of the Darling River, on the N.W. of the township of Wentworth.

ANDERSON'S CREEK (*Co. Murchison*), a small northern tributary of the Cabbadah Creek.

ANDREW CREEK (*Co. Tongowoko*), a creek having its flow from Mount Poole, on the Queensland boundary.

ANDRUCO (*Co. Wentworth*), a township situate on the Darling River, near the town of Wentworth.

ANDULBRY (*Co. Napier*), a township to the N.W. of Sydney, on the Castlereagh River.

ANGLEDOOL (*Co. Narran*), a post-office, 557 miles to the N. of Sydney, with mail twice a week, money-order and telegraph offices. The nearest railway station is Narrabri, 190 miles, on the north-western line.

ANGOURIE POINT (*Co. Clarence*), a rocky headland, 4 miles S. of the entrance to the Clarence River.

ANGULA CREEK (*Co. Murchison*), a southern auriferous tributary of the Gwydir River, flowing into the Bingera gold-fields.

ANNANDALE (*Co. Cumberland*), is an immediate suburb of Sydney, on the Parramatta road, beyond the University. It is within the municipal district of Leichhardt, and is a populous neighbourhood, with tramway communication to the city. The nearest railway station is Petersham, 1 mile, on the suburban line.

ANN RIVER (*Co. Gresham*), an auriferous stream flowing through the Oban diggings into the Sara River. [*See* "RIVERS."]

ANTILL'S CREEK *(Co. Murray)*, a drainage creek flowing into Molonglo Plains and the Primrose Valley Creek.

ANTONIO CREEK *(Co. Westmoreland)*, a tributary of the Solitary Creek, rising on the eastern slopes of the Blue Mountain Range, S. of Mount Lambie.

ANVIL CREEK *(Co. Northumberland)*, a tributary of Black Creek, flowing through the village of Greta. The nearest railway station is Greta, 1 mile, on the northern line.

APPIN *(Co. Cumberland)*, a postal town, 42 miles S. of Sydney. Telegraph and money-order offices; mail daily from Sydney. The Sydney Nepean water supply flows through the district. The nearest railway station is Campbelltown, 10 miles, on the southern line.

APPLE-TREE FLAT *(Co. Wellington)*, a township, 202 miles W. of Sydney. The nearest railway station is Mudgee, 12 miles, on the Wallerawang and Mudgee service, western line.

APPLE-TREE FLAT *(Co. Roxburgh)*, a township, 150 miles W. of Sydney. The nearest railway station is Mudgee, 12 miles, on the Wallerawang and Mudgee line.

APPLE-TREE HILL *(Co. Waljeers)*, lying to the N.W. of the county of Oxley, on the Lower Lachlan. It is a low-lying hill, covered with stunted timber.

APPLE-TREE HILL *(Co. Waljeers)*, situated on the Lower Lachlan River, lying to the N.W. of the township of Oxley.

APSLEY *(Co. Bathurst)*, a village, 245 miles W. of Sydney, with railway station, on the western line.

APSLEY FALLS *(Co. Vernon)*, a very extensive series of waterfalls on the Apsley River, about 16 miles S.E. of Walcha. First discovered by Oxley.

APSLEY MOUNT DIGGINGS *(Co. Bathurst)*, a gold-producing district near Evans' Plains.

APSLEY RANGE *(Co. Hawes)*, a lofty range to the E. from the New England Range, near Walcha. The highest peak attaining an elevation of 3,800 feet above the sea-level.

APSLEY RIVER *(Co. Vernon)*. [See "RIVERS."]

AQUILA MOUNT *(Co. Wellington)*, a spur of the Stoney Creek Range, at the head of the Muckerwa Creek, about 3 miles from the Ironbark diggings.

ARABLE CREEK *(Co. Wallace)*, a tributary of the Wullwye River, falling into it near Wullwye Hill.

ARAKOON *(Co. Macquarie)*, a postal town, 336 miles N. of Sydney, with money-order and telegraph offices, and Government savings bank. Mail five times a week.

ARALUEN (*Co. St. Vincent*), a postal village, 196 miles S. of Sydney, with money-order and telegraph offices, and Government savings bank. Daily mail from Sydney. The nearest railway station is Tarago, 39 miles, on Cooma line. The district is an alluvial mining one, and comprises the whole extent of the Araluen Valley, extending for a distance of about 16 miles, including the Upper and Lower Waterfall, Crown Flat, and Mundinalong, and several other diggings in its course. The nearest places are Major's Creek, 4 miles, and Braidwood, 16 miles distant.

ARALUEN CREEK (*Co. St. Vincent*), an auriferous tributary of the Moruya River, rising near the township of Elrington, flowing through the Araluen diggings.

ARANAIN CREEK (*Co. Clarence*), a tributary of the Coldstream River, flowing through good agricultural land.

ARAPOOL HILL (*Co. Beresford*), a lofty hill at the head of Arable Creek, on the road from Cooma to Eden, and about 7 miles from the former.

ARBUTHNOT VALLEY (*Liverpool Plains*) is a low-lying flat on the E. side of Warrabungle Range.

ARDGOWRIE POINT (*Co. Clarence*), situate 323 miles to the N. of Sydney, on the E. seaboard.

ARDING (*Co. Sandon*), a post-office, 351 miles N. of Sydney, with mail twice a week.

ARGENTON (*Co. Gough*), a postal receiving-office, 471 miles N. of Sydney, with mail once a week.

ARGENT'S WELL (*Co. Raleigh*), a post-office, 370 miles N. of Sydney, with mail twice a week.

ARGOON (*Co. Boyd*), a postal town, 459 miles S. of Sydney. Mail three times a week. The nearest railway station is Jerilderie, 35 miles, on the southern line.

ARGYLE, a county in the Eastern Division of the Colony. [*See* "COUNTIES."]

ARIAH MOUNT (*Co. Cooper*), a solitary hill, lying between the Lachlan and Murrumbidgee Rivers.

ARKSTONE (*Co. Bathurst*), a postal receiving-office, 167 miles W. of Sydney, with mail once a week.

ARMATREE, a village, 129 miles from Mudgee, the nearest railway station on the Wallerawang and Mudgee line.

ARMIDALE (*Co. Sandon*), 30° 36′ S. lat., 157° 22′ E. long., is an ecclesiastical city, situated in the parishes of Armidale and Butler, 359 miles N. of Sydney, with daily mail, telegraph and money-order offices, and Government savings bank. Situated on the great northern railway, 266 miles from the city of Newcastle, and 364 miles from Brisbane, the capital of Queensland, and is the central town of the New England District. Armidale has long been incorporated under the Municipalities Act, and is governed by eight aldermen and a mayor. The public and commercial buildings are of the most substantial character. The surrounding country is elevated and mountainous, the height above mean sea-level being 3,278 feet. The soil is rich and productive, and the yield of cereals is usually highly satisfactory, and the pastoral holdings are of an important character. The area of the city and suburban lands comprise about 11,400 acres. Sittings of the supreme court, quarter sessions, and district courts are held here periodically. Population, about 3,000.

ARMIDALE GULLY (*Co. Sandon*), a postal receiving-office, 380 miles N. of Sydney, with mail once a week.

ARNCLIFFE (*Co. Cumberland*), a postal suburb, 7 miles S. of Sydney, with daily mail therefrom. Telegraph and money-order offices, Government savings bank, and delivery by letter-carrier. A railway station on the Illawarra and South Coast line.

ARRAWARRANG VALLEY (*Co. Buccleuch*), a mountain gorge at the head of the Mungola Creek, a tributary of the Tumut River. Cliffs of water-worn marble abound in this valley. The marble is either white or red, and there are several stalactitic caverns of great beauty.

ARRAWATTA, a county partly in the Eastern and Central Divisions of the Colony. [*See* "COUNTIES."]

ARRAWATTA CREEK (*Co. Arrawatta*), a tributary of the Severn River, flowing through good agricultural land from Wellingrove to Warialda, near the junction of the Strathbogie Road.

ARROWSMITH MOUNT (*Co. Evelyn*), the highest peak of the Grey Range, and attains an elevation of 2,000 feet above the level of the sea. Situate on the South Australian border.

ARTHUR MOUNT (*Co. Durham*), a high mountain a few miles S. of Muswellbrook.

ARTHUR MOUNT (*Co. Gordon*), a high hill on the west bank of the Bell River, at its confluence with the Macquarie, near Wellington.

ARTHUR'S CREEK (*Co. Roxburgh*), an auriferous stream, rising in the Limekiln Range, and flowing N. through the Palmer's or Oakey Creek gold-fields into the Turon River at Dulabree.

ARTHUR'S STATION (*Co. Wellington*), a gold-mining working on the Turon diggings, about 7 miles from the township of Sofala.

ARTHURVILLE (*Co. Gordon*), a post-office, 265 miles W. of Sydney, with mail twice a week. The nearest railway station is Wellington, 17 miles, on the western line. Situated on the Little River, with good agricultural land on its banks.

ARUMPO (*Co. Wentworth*), a township to the W. of Sydney, on the boundary-line of Taila county.

ASHBURNHAM, a county partly in the Eastern and Central Divisions of the Colony. [*See* "COUNTIES."]

ASHBY (*Co. Clarence*), an agricultural village lying on the N. bank of the Clarence River, near the entrance to Broadwater, and opposite the Rocky Mouth Creek. The soil is very good.

ASHFIELD (*Co. Cumberland*), a populous and prosperous suburb of the city of Sydney, in the parish of Concord and Petersham, situated on the main southern and western lines of railway, 5 miles from the General Post Office, with money-order and telegraph offices, Government savings bank, and delivery by letter-carriers three times daily. The soil of the district is rich, and its conveniences to the metropolis are such that it has become a favourite place of residence for merchants and others having their business in the city. The population of Ashfield is about 2,000, and was incorporated a borough in 1871, under the Municipalities Act, with eight aldermen and a mayor as a governing body.

ASHFORD (*Co. Arrawatta*), is a post town, 508 miles N. of Sydney, with the mail twice a week. The nearest railway station on the northern line is Glen Innes, 65 miles. Situated on the Frazer Creek, the Macintyre River being 7 miles W. The district is an agricultural and pastoral one.

ASH ISLAND (*Co. Northumberland*), situated in the lower part of the Hunter River, about 3 miles from the city of Newcastle, and opposite the town of Hexham. It is about 5 miles in length and 2 miles in width. This island, together with Mosquito and some other small islands, divide the stream of the Hunter into two parts, called respectively the North and South Channels, the former being the one used by steamers.

ASHLEY (*Co. Clarence*), a postal receiving-office, 403 miles N. of Sydney. Mail twice a week.

ATTUNGA (*Co. Parry*), a post-office, 266 miles N. of Sydney. Daily mail from Sydney. The nearest railway station is Tamworth, 16 miles, on the northern line.

ATTUNGA SPRINGS (*Co. Parry*), a post-office, 294 miles N. of Sydney, with daily mail. The nearest railway station is Tamworth, 16 miles, on the northern line.

AUBURN (*Co. Cumberland*), a postal village, 12 miles S. of Sydney, with daily mail. Telegraph and money-order offices, Government savings bank, and delivery by letter-carrier. A railway station on the southern line.

AUBURN VALE CREEK (*Co. Hardinge*), a tributary of Cope's Creek, rising near Inverell, situated about 16 miles from Borthwick.

AUCKLAND (*Co. Durham*), a small agricultural village a short distance to the W. of Singleton, on the Hunter River, at the junction of Rix's Creek.

AUCKLAND, a county in the Eastern Division of the Colony. [*See* "COUNTIES."]

AUSTINMER (*Co. Camden*), a postal village, 39 miles S. of Sydney, with daily mail. A railway station on the Illawarra and South Coast line.

AVISFORD (*Co. Wellington*), a post-office, 190 miles W. of Sydney, with mail four times a week, situated on the Meroo Creek, about 20 miles from Mudgee, and is a purely gold-mining district. The nearest railway station is Mudgee, 10 miles, on the western line.

AVOCA (*Co. Wentworth*), a township, 760 miles to the S.W. of Sydney, on the banks of the ana branch of the Darling River.

AVON RIVER (*Co. Gloucester*). [See "RIVERS."]

AWABA (*Co. Northumberland*), a postal receiving-office, 84 miles N. of Sydney, with daily mail. A railway station on the Sydney and Newcastle line.

AYTON HILLS (*Co. Auckland*), a range of low hills, 20 miles S. of the township of Eden.

# B

BAAN BAA (*Co. White*), a post-office, 328 miles N. of Sydney, with daily mail. A railway station on north-western line.

BABBAGE MOUNT (*Co. Tongowoko*), a solitary hill N.W. of the Darling River, between the Barrier and Grey Ranges.

BABBINBOON MOUNT (*Co. Buckland*), a volcanic hill S.E. of the township of Carroll.

BABBY WERRILAK (*Co. Murchison*), a small alluvial diggings in the Bingara gold-fields, about 4 miles from Bingera.

BACK CREEK (*Co. Bathurst*), a tributary of Brown's Creek, flowing in the parish of Bringellet.

BACK CREEK (*Co. Ashburnham*), a small eastern tributary of the Goobang Creek.

BACK CREEK (*Co. Goulburn*), a northern tributary of the Billabung Creek, draining some swampy country to the W. of Billabung.

BACK CREEK (*Co. Harden*), a tributary of the head of the Demondrille Creek, rising to the S. of Burrangong gold-fields, in the parish of Wilkie.

BACK CREEK (*Co. King*), a northern tributary of the Pudman Creek, rising in the Burrowa Plains.

BACK CREEK (*Co. Rous*), a small tributary of the Leycester Creek.

BACK CREEK (*Co. Wallace*), a small tributary of the Upper Murrumbidgee River, rising on the southern slope of Mount Phillips.

BACK FOREST CREEK (*Co. King*), a small drainage creek of the Burrowa Plains, flowing into the Forest Creek.

BADGER BRUSH (*Co. Roxburgh*), a tract of agricultural land, situated in the parish of Cullen Bullen, to E. of the Kirconnell gold-fields.

BADGER CREEK (*Co. Cumberland*), a small western tributary of the upper part of South Creek.

BADGERY'S SIDING (*Co. Camden*), a railway siding, 91 miles from Sydney, on the southern line.

BADJORY SWAMP (*Co. Wellesley*), a small marshy flat to the S. of the township of Catheart, and draining into the Coolombrook River.

BAERAMI (*Co. Durham*), a post-office, 209 miles N. of Sydney, with mail three days a week. The nearest railway station is Muswellbrook, 30 miles, on the northern line.

BAGNELL LAGOONS (*Co. Goulburn*), a series of lagoons lying in a swampy flat, between the Murray River and the Bagnell Range.

BAGNELL RANGE (*Co. Goulburn*), a range lying to the W. of Albury, and near the Murray River.

BAGO CREEK (*Co. Wynyard*), an eastern tributary of Tarcutta Creek, flowing into the main stream near the village of Bago.

BAGO HILL (*Co. Wynyard*), a peak in Mane's Range, lying on the N. of the Bago reserve, and on the W. side of the track from the Upper Murray to Gundagai.

BAGOWA (*Co. Fitzroy*), a township, 150 miles N. of Sydney, near the eastern seaboard.

BAJIMBA MOUNTAIN (*Co. Clive*), a chain of hills to the S. of Tenterfield, on the E. of the great northern railway.

BAKALONG MOUNT (*Co. Wellesley*), a high ridge on the Bongolong Creek, about 10 miles S. of Bombala.

BAKER'S CREEK (*Co. Gloucester*), a small tributary of the Belbora Creek.

BAKER'S CREEK (*Co. Hardinge*), an auriferous western tributary of the upper part of the Gwydir River, rising in the N.W. slope of Mount Lowry, and flowing into the main stream to the E. of Mount Drummond.

BAKER'S FLAT (*Co. Gordon*), a small flat on the Newrea Creek, about 12 miles S. of Wellington, and 4 miles S. of Newrea.

BAKER'S PEAK (*Co. Clarke*), a peak of the New England range on the Guyra River, about 14 miles from Falconer.

BAKER'S SWAMP (*Co. Wellington*), a post-office, 219 miles W. of Sydney, with mail twice a week. The nearest railway station is Springs, 8 miles, on the western line.

BALALA (*Co. Gordon*), a postal town, 351 miles N. of Sydney, with mail three times a week. The nearest railway station is Uralla, 11 miles, on the northern line.

BALANAFAD (*Co. Murray*), a postal receiving-office, 215 miles S. of Sydney, with mail three times a week. The nearest railway station is Bungendore, 31 miles, on the Cooma line.

BALARAMBONE MOUNTAIN (*Co. Booroondarra*), a solitary mount to the S.W. of Cobar, in the W. interior.

BALD BLAIR (*Co. Sandon*), a township, 440 miles N. of Sydney. The nearest railway station is Guyra, 7 miles, on the northern line.

BALD CREEK (*Co. Parry*), an eastern tributary of the head of the Muluerindie River, fed by the Cobrabald and running creeks.

BALD HILL *(Co. Argyle)*, a lofty peak to the N.W. of the village of Mutmutbilly.

BALD HILL *(Cos. Dampier and Murray)*, a lofty range of hills running on both sides of the Shoalhaven River, to the head of Wiaubene Creek.

BALD HILLS *(Co. Bathurst)*, two prominent hills to the S.W. of Bathurst, about 2 miles distant.

BALD HILL CREEK *(Co. Harden)*, a western tributary of the Jugiong Creek, falling into it at Bagolong.

BALD HILL CREEK *(Co. Wellington)*, a small auriferous tributary of the Tambaroora Creek, and flowing through the Tambaroora gold-fields.

BALD NOB *(Co. Sandon)*, a lofty peak in the parish of Eastlake, at the head of Graves' Creek.

BALD NOB *(Co. Sandon)*, a post-office, 433 miles N. of Sydney, with mail three times a week. The nearest railway station is Glen Innes, 10 miles, on the northern line.

BALD NOB CREEK *(Co. Gough)*, is a small northern tributary of the Mitchell River.

BALD or SNOWY MOUNTAIN *(Cos. Wallace and Selwyn)*, a part of the Muniong Range lying between the counties of Wallace on the E. and Selwyn on the W. These mountains run nearly N. and S. and attain the greatest elevation in New South Wales, rising nearly to the level of perpetual snow, reaching an altitude of over 7,000 feet above the sea level, Mount Kosciusco being the highest peak. The Bald Mountains extend from the southern part of the range northward to Granderra or Kiandra.

BALDERODGERY *(Co. Gordon)*, a post-office 258 miles W. of Sydney, with mail three days a week.

BALENGARA *(Co. Macquarie)*, a small agricultural settlement on the Wilson River, 12 miles above Port Macquarie.

BALFOUR MOUNT *(Co. Burnett)*, a peak lying on the W. bank of Oxley's Creek, about 12 miles N.E. of Warialda.

BALGOWLAH *(Co. Cumberland)*, a postal township 11 miles N. of Sydney, with daily mails, situated on the N. harbour of Port Jackson, in the parish of Manly.

BALLAGREEN CREEK *(Co. Ewenmar)*, a western tributary to the Castlereagh River.

BALLALABA *(Co. Murray)*, a post-office, 215 miles S. of Sydney, with mail three times a week. Tarago is the nearest railway station 20 miles on the Cooma line. Situated on the Shoalhaven River, 16 miles S. from Braidwood.

BALLALA CREEK *(Co. Courallie)*, a tributary of the head of the Gilgil River.

BALLAST POINT *(Co. Cumberland)*, the western head of Waterview Bay, Balmain. Good sandstone quarries are worked at this point and in the neighbourhood.

BALLINA (*Co. Richmond*), is a postal town, 364 miles N. of Sydney, with mail per steamers. Telegraph and money-order offices and Government savings bank. Incorporated a municipal district in 1883, with five aldermen and a mayor. Ballina is situated at the mouth of the Richmond River, and is the seaport town about 4 miles S. of Lennox Heads, 85 miles by water to Lismore and 30 miles by land. Population, about 750.

BALLOO ARM (*Co. Buccleuch*), a tributary of the head of Gooburragandra River in an almost inaccessible country to the N. of the Bogong Ranges.

BALLOW MOUNTAIN (*Co. Buller*), a high peak in the dividing range on the extreme northern boundary of the Colony.

BALL'S HEAD (*Co. Cumberland*), a bold rocky headland on the North Shore of Port Jackson, opposite to Goat Island, on the Parramatta River.

BALMAIN (*Co. Cumberland*), a suburb of Sydney, situated in the parish of Petersham, on the western side of Darling Harbour, is a branch of the General Post Office, with all the conveniences of the head office, both in telegraphic and postal arrangements. With Government savings bank, and money-order office, and delivery by letter-carriers. Balmain is an important suburb of the city, having many miles of frontage to the waters of Port Jackson, and manufactories of large proportions are carried on in iron and wood. Mort's Dry Dock and ship-building yards are situated in Waterview Bay. Ship-builders, engineers, boiler-makers, carpenters, &c., form the bulk of the population. It is separated from Sydney by Darling Harbour. The transit communication is amply supplied by steam-ferries, as well as by vehicular traffic landwards; and every convenience for the residents is afforded by such. Balmain was incorporated a borough in 1860, under the Municipalities Act, and is governed by ten aldermen and a mayor. Population, about 46,000.

BALMORAL (*Co. Camden*), a post-office, 65 miles S. of Sydney, with daily mail. A railway station on the southern line.

BALRANALD (*Co. Caira*), is a postal town, 574 miles S. of Sydney, with post, telegraph and money-order offices, and Government savings bank. The nearest railway station is Hay, 120 miles, on the south-western line. Balranald is an important town in a purely pastoral district and possesses all the public conveniences to be found in this flourishing part of New South Wales. It is situated on the Murrumbidgee River, and about 18 miles from its junction with the Murray, the former river being navigable for any of the steamers so long as the navigation of the other is practicable. Talbitt's crossing-place, on the Wakool River, is distant about 25 miles S.E. Balranald was incorporated a municipal district in 1882, and is governed by five aldermen and a mayor. Quarter sessions and district courts are held here periodically. Population of district, about 16,000.

BAMBO CREEK (*Co. Dampier*), a small northern tributary of the Tuross River falling into it about 8 miles S.W. of Coila.

BANAR SWAMP (*Co. Gipps*), a large swamp in the centre of the county and to the S. of the Lachlan.

BANDALLA CREEK (*Co. Argyle*), a small tributary of the Windellama Creek.

BANDALLA CREEK (*Co. Gowan*), a tributary of the Castlereagh River, rising in Mount Cowany, in the Warrabungle Range, flowing through the villages of Uraldabinia and Larron.

BANDAMORA CREEK (*Co. Roxburgh*), an eastern tributary of the Round Swamp Creek, flowing through ground suitable for agricultural purposes.

BANDON GROVE (*Co. Durham*), a postal township, 164 miles to the N. of Sydney, with mail three times a week. Morpeth is the nearest railway station on the northern line, 44 miles, situated on the E. bank of Chichester River, at its junction with the Williams. The nearest town is Dungog, distant about 7 miles.

BANFIELD (*Co. Gloucester*), an agricultural settlement on the Williams River, about 7 miles N. of the township of Clarence Town.

BANGALORE (*Co. Argyle*), a railway station, 113 miles S. of Sydney, on the Goulburn-Cooma line.

BANGALORE CREEK (*Co. Argyle*), a small tributary of the Mulwarree Ponds, flowing through the rich pastoral country of the Goulburn Plains.

BANGALORE GAP (*Co. Argyle*), a passage through the ranges between Goulburn and Braidwood.

BANGANDAN (*Co. Wynyard*), an agricultural settlement, about 7 miles N.W. from the township of Adelong.

BANG-BANG CREEK (*Co. Monteagle*), a tributary of the Crowther Creek, falling into it at the township of Koorawatha.

BANGO CREEK (*Co. King*), a tributary of the Yass River and flowing into it about 5 miles from the township of Yass.

BANKS' CAPE (*Co. Cumberland*), the N. head of the entrance to Botany Bay.

BANKSTOWN (*Co. Cumberland*), a post-office, 12 miles S. of Sydney, with mail twice daily. A railway station on the suburban lines.

BANNABY (*Co. Georgiana*), a post-office, 175 miles S. of Sydney, with mail three times a-week. The nearest railway station is Goulburn, 41 miles, on the southern line.

BANNOO RIVER (*Co. Macquarie*). [*See* "RIVERS."]

BANTRY BAY (*Co. Cumberland*), one of the many branches of the head of Middle Harbour.

BARABOOL PLAINS (*Co. Baradine*), situate on the western slopes of Liverpool Plains, between Baradine Creek and the Namoi River.

BARA CREEK (*Co. Phillip*), a northern tributary of Lawson Creek, in the western slopes of the Australian Alps, flowing past the foot of Mount Bara.

BARADINE (*Co. Baradine*), a post-office, 390 miles N. of Sydney, with mail five days a week. Telegraph and money-order offices. The nearest railway station is Gunnedah, 111 miles, on the north-western line.

BARADINE, a county in the Central Division of the Colony. [See "COUNTIES."]

BARADINE CREEK (*Co. Baradine*), a southern tributary of the Namoi River, rising in the Warrabungle Ranges. The road from Coonabarrabran to Walgett runs alongside this creek for a considerable distance.

BARAMA MOUNT (*Co. Leichhardt*), is a peak 3,600 feet above the sea-level, in the Warrabungle Range, situated about 10 miles from Coonabarrabran.

BARA MOUNT (*Co. Phillip*), situate about 10 miles N. of the township of Mudgee, on the west branch of Bara Creek, a spur of the Blue Mountain Range.

BARATTA, or TEN MILE WATERHOLES (*Co. Wakool*), a pastoral hamlet, lying between Moulamein and Deniliquin, about 35 miles from the former, and 37 miles from the latter.

BARBERGAL (*Co. Lincoln*), an agricultural settlement, about 15 miles N.E. of the township of Dubbo.

BARBER'S CREEK (*Co. Camden*), a postal receiving-office. 110 miles S. of Sydney, with a mail daily; a railway station on the southern line. Barber's Creek rises to the E. of Marulan, and flows into Shoalhaven River.

BARBER'S GAP (*Co. Harden*), situated at the head of the Oak Creek, in the parish of Talmo.

BARBORAH CREEK (*Co. Northumberland*), a small tributary of the Mangrove Creek near its source.

BARCOM GLEN (*Co. Cumberland*), adjoining the eastern boundary of the City of Sydney. Glenmore Road passes through the beautiful " Vale of Lacroza," from Old South Head Road to New South Head Road, across Rushcutters' Bay.

BARE HILL (*Co. Wellesley*), a peak of the South Coast Range, about 12 miles to the S. of Bombala.

BARELLAN (*Co. Cooper*), a rural settlement, 400 miles S.W. of Sydney. The nearest railway station is Whitton, on the south-western line.

BARGO (*Co. Camden*), a post-office, 62 miles S. of Sydney, with mail twice a week. It takes its name from the well-known Bargo Brush, situated on the Bargo River, between the townships of Picton and Mittagong. The nearest railway station is Picton, 10 miles, on the southern line.

BARGO RIVER (*Co. Camden*). [See "RIVERS."]

BARIGAN CREEK (*Co. Bligh*), a fine stream rising in the Dividing Range near Dabee, and flowing into the Wollar Creek.

BARLOW'S CREEK (*Co. Hardinge*), a tributary of the upper part of the Gwydir, near the village of Abingdon.

BARMEDMAN (*Co. Bland*), a post-office, 317 miles S. of Sydney, with money-order and telegraph offices and Government savings bank. Mail five times a week. The nearest railway station is Cootamundra, 57 miles, on the southern line.

BARNARD RIVER (*Cos. Gloucester and Macquarie*). [*See* "RIVERS."]

BARNATO (*Co. Booroondurra*), a township, 600 miles W. of Sydney, and to the W. of Cobar.

BARNEY DOWNS (*Co. Clive*), a tract of fine pastoral land lying at the head of the Demon and Cataract Rivers, to the E. of Tenterfield over the range.

BARNEY'S HILL (*Co. Gresham*), a high, detached hill, on the Boyd River, near the junction of the Guy Fawkes River.

BARONIA CREEK (*Co. Gloucester*), a small drainage creek flowing into Port Stephens on its northern shore.

BARONNE CREEK (*Co. Gowen*), an eastern tributary of the Castlereagh River, flowing W. through the Baronne Plains.

BARONNE PLAINS (*Co. Leichhardt*), situated on the E. bank of the Castlereagh River, to the S. of Coonamble, is a large tract of open flat, pastoral country.

BAROO CREEK (*Co. Gough*), a small northern tributary of the Mitchell River.

BAROONGANGIE CREEK (*Co. Young*), a creek flowing across the country to the W. of Wilcannia.

BARRABA (*Co. Darling*), a postal town, 339 miles N. of Sydney, with mail daily, money-order and telegraph offices, and Government savings bank. The nearest station is Tamworth, 60 miles, on the northern line, situated on the Manilla River, Bell's Mountain lying 5 miles N., and Ironbark Creek flowing into the Manilla River 7 miles below the township. The district is agricultural and pastoral.

BARRABA CREEK (*Co. Darling*), a small S. tributary of the Manilla Creek, flowing through pastoral country into the river at the township of Barraba.

BARRAGON (*Co. Phillip*), a postal village, 227 miles W. of Sydney, situated on the creek of the same name on the road from Dungaree to Merriwa. Mail from Sydney three times a week. The nearest railway station is Mudgee, 42 miles, on the northern line.

BARRAHINEBIN (*Co. Northumberland*), a large swamp, lying 9 miles from Newcastle.

BARRAMI CREEK (*Co. Hunter*), a southern tributary of the Goulburn River.

BARRANJUEY HEAD (*Co. Cumberland*), a post and telegraph office, 27 miles S. of Sydney, with mail twice a week. Is a rocky peninsular forming the southern head of Broken Bay.

BARRATTA (*Co. Townsend*), a township on the banks of the Kyalite or Edward River, to the N.E. of Deniliquin.

BARRENGARRY (*Co. Camden*), a post-office, 99 miles S. of Sydney, with a daily mail. Is the name of a high peak in the Illawarra Ranges, attaining an elevation of 2,500 feet above the sea-level. The nearest railway station is Moss Vale, 19 miles, on the southern line.

BARREN GROUND (*Co. Camden*), a small rural settlement, 95 miles S. of Sydney. The nearest railway station is Moss Vale, 9 miles, on the southern line.

BARREN JACK (*Co. Harden*), a mountain, lying on the N. bank of the Murrumbidgee River, near the junction of the Goodradigbee River, and about 10 miles S. of the town of Bookham.

BARREN JUMBO (*Co. Dampier*), situated at the head of the Tuross River, is a lofty, bare, rocky peak in the Main Dividing Range.

BARREN MOUNTAIN (*Co. Fitzroy*), an E. spur of the E. range, running out at Coff on the Eastern seaboard.

BARRINGTON (*Co. Gloucester*), a post town, 181 miles N. of Sydney, with a daily mail. The nearest railway station is Hexham, 69 miles, on the northern line. The river is a fine stream rising near the head of the Manning.

BARRINGUN (*Co. Irrara*), a post town, 593 miles west of Sydney, with mail twice a week, money-order and telegraph offices. The nearest railway station is Bourke, 90 miles, on the western line.

BARRONA, a county in the Western Division of the Colony. [*See* "COUNTIES."]

BARRY (*Co. Bathurst*), a postal receiving-office, 179 miles W. of Sydney, with mail three times a week.

BARTUNGA HEAD (*Co. Dampier*), a sandstone promontory standing out from the coast opposite Mount Dromedary, about half-way between the Tuross and Bega Rivers.

BARUTTA (*Co. Killara*), a township on the banks of the Paroo River in the far western interior.

BARWANG (*Co. Harden*), a post-office, 236 miles south of Sydney, with mail twice a week. The nearest railway station is Harden, 10 miles, on the southern line.

BARWANG CREEK (*Co. Harden*), a tributary of the head of Spring Creek, between the Burrowa and Cunningham Plains.

BARWON OR UPPER DARLING RIVER (*Cos. Yandu and Cowper*). [*See* "RIVERS."]

BASALTIC COLUMN (*Co. Hawes*), a lofty and steep basaltic hill in the New England Range, on the road from the Manning River to Walcha, about 20 miles from Nowendoc.

BASIN CREEK (*Co. Goulburn*), a fine mountain stream flowing into the river Murray, a few miles E. of Dora.

BASS POINT (*Co. Camden*), a rocky promontory on the S. coast, to the N. of Shellharbour and to the S. of the Illawarra Lake.

B

BATEMAN'S BAY (*Co. St. Vincent*), a postal town, 200 miles to the S. of Sydney, with daily mail, telegraph and money-order offices and Government savings bank. The nearest railway station is Tarago, 70 miles, on the Cooma line. Situated on the southern coast, and the estuary of the Clyde River. The nearest townships are Nelligen, 14 miles, and Mornya, 20 miles.

BATH'S CREEK (*Co. Bathurst*), a small tributary on the head of the Queen Charlotte Vale Creek, in the parish of Ponsonby.

BATHURST (*Co. Bathurst*) (34° 28' S. lat., 149° 38' E. long.), is an ecclesiastical city in the parish of the same name, 144 miles west of Sydney, with daily mail, telegraph and money-order offices and Government savings bank. Situated on the S. bank of the Macquarie River and on the Great Western Railway, with almost a direct line to Melbourne, via the Blayney and Murrumburra line. It is in the eastern division of the pastoral holdings, and is the grand emporium for nearly the whole of the western interior. Governor Macquarie named the town Bathurst in 1815, in honor of Lord Bathurst, the then Secretary of State for the colonies. The city is laid out in wide streets, and is undoubtedly the finest of all the inland towns of the colony. The district is rich in its agricultural, pastoral, and mining productions, and it possesses the great advantage of a ready market for all its products both in Sydney and Melbourne. The extent of cultivated land is very great, and large and wealthy estates have been formed in the surrounding country in consequence. As a wheat-growing district it is proverbial for the high quality of its grain. The substantial buildings, both private and public, in and around Bathurst, testify to the energy and wealth of its inhabitants. The area of the city and suburban lands comprise about 6,200 acres. Bathurst was incorporated a municipality in 1862, and is governed by eleven aldermen and a mayor. Sittings of the supreme court, quarter sessions, and district courts are held at Bathurst periodically. Population, 8,000.

BATHURST, a county in the Eastern Division of the Colony. [*See* "COUNTIES."]

BATHURST (*Co. Cumberland*), is the name of one of the original districts of the county of Cumberland, in the parish of Rooty Hill; bounded on the S. by Prospect Hill and Melville districts; on the N.W. sides by the South Creek to the bridge; and on the N.E. side by the Windsor and Toongabbee roads.

BATHURST LAKE (*Co. Argyle*).—Lake Bathurst was discovered by Hume in 1817. It lies 10 miles E. from Lake George, being separated by the Dividing Range which passes between the lakes, and is a fine sheet of water amid the fertile plains of the table-land 2,000 feet above the sea-level. It lies about 20 miles S. of the city of Goulburn, and 1½ miles E. of the township of Tarago. The water in it is slightly brackish.

BATHURST PLAINS (*Cos. Bathurst and Roxburgh*).—These extensive plains when first sighted by Wentworth and his small party of explorers, gave cheering hopes to them of the fertility of the soil they were approaching, and which was so soon to be realised. The plains are about 20 miles in length and 8 miles wide, containing about 120 square miles of naturally cleared land, the surrounding forest country being generally very thinly timbered, and are traversed in the direction of its length by the river Macquarie, which pursues a meandering course. These plains are upwards of 2,100 feet above the sea-level, an elevation which compensates for 10 degrees of latitude.

BATLOW (*Co. Wynyard*), a post-office, 333 miles S. of Sydney, with mail twice a week. Telegraph and money-order offices, and Government savings bank.

BATTERY POINT (*Co. Cumberland*).—This is a well-known point in the city of Sydney, on the S. side of Port Jackson, situated between Farm Cove and Sydney Cove. The Circular Quay is built round on the E. and N. points, and the sea-wall is continued around to the Botanical Gardens; and the harbour entrance to Government House is from this point.

BAULKHAM HILLS (*Co. Cumberland*), a postal village, 20 miles to the W. of Sydney, with a mail daily. The nearest railway station is Parramatta, 14 miles on the suburban line. It lies on the road from Parramatta to Windsor and Pitt Town, and about 5 miles from the former place. The cultivation of the orange is carried on very successfully and profitably in this district.

BAW BAW (*Co. Argyle*), a village, 140 miles S. of Sydney to the W. of Goulburn.

BAY VIEW (*Co. Cumberland*), a postal town, 19 miles N. of Sydney, between Manly and Newport, with daily mail.

BEABULA (*Co. Sturt*), a railway station, 436 miles from Sydney, on the S.W. line.

BEACONSFIELD (*Co. Cumberland*), a suburb of the city of Sydney, 1 mile from Burwood station, on the suburban line.

BEARDY PLAINS (*Co. Gough*), a tract of fine pastoral country to the N.E. of Glen Innes, consisting of undulating downs well grassed and watered by the Beardy waters and its tributaries.

BEARDY WATERS (*Co. Gough*), a fine stream rising in the western slopes of the Australian Alps, flowing N. for about 30 miles into the Severn River at Ranger's Valley. It crosses the main road and telegraph line from Sydney to Brisbane at Yarrowford, about half way between Glen Innes and Severn. The Rocky Ponds and Furrucubad Creeks empty their waters into this stream to the N.E. of Glen Innes.

BEAR HILL (*Co. Gough*), a post-office, 426 miles N. of Sydney, with mail twice a week. The nearest railway station is Guyra, 40 miles, on the northern line.

BEAUFORT (*Co. Gough*), a post-office, 428 miles N. of Sydney, with mail therefrom daily. The nearest railway station is Glen Innes, 6 miles, on the northern line.

BECKETT CATARACT (*Co. Vernon*), the name of one of the waterfalls on the Apsley River, lying 12 miles S.E. of Walcha.

BECOURT (*Co. Gordon*), a township, 230 miles N.W. of Sydney, near the Bell River.

BECTIVE (*Co. Inglis*), a small township reserve, 14 miles N.W. of Tamworth, on the Peel River, the nearest railway station being West Tamworth, 15 miles.

BEDDING GROUND (*Co. Wellesley*), a tract of country lying on the Bombala River, about 8 miles W. of Bombala.

BEDGEREBONG (*Co. Cunningham*), a postal receiving-office, 294 miles N.W. of Sydney, with mail twice a week. The nearest railway station is Borenore, 80 miles, on the western line.

BEDHAM CREEK (*Co. Northumberland*), a small tributary of the lower end of the Mangrove Creek.

BEECHWOOD (*Co. Macquarie*), a post-office, 295 miles N. of Sydney, with mail three days a week, and telegraph office. The nearest railway station is Hexham, 187 miles, on the northern line.

BEECROFT (*Co. Cumberland*), a post-office, 16 miles N. of Sydney, with daily mail. A railway station on the Sydney and Newcastle line.

BEECROFT HEAD (*Co. St. Vincent*), a prominent headland on the coast, to the N. of Jervis Bay.

BEEMARANG MOUNT (*Co. Cook*), the loftiest peak of the Blue Mountain Range. It is 4,100 feet above the sea-level.

BEEMERY (*Co. Clyde*), a township, on the banks of the Barwon River, near Mount Druitt.

BEEMERY (*Co. Clyde*), a township, on the Bogan River, at its confluence with the Barwon River.

BEE MOUNTAIN (*Co. Robinson*), a solitary high mount to the S. of Cobar.

BEGA (*Co. Auckland*), a postal town, 316 miles S. of Sydney, with daily mail, money-order and telegraph offices, and Government savings bank. The nearest railway station is Tarago, on the Cooma line, 80 miles. Situated on the banks of the Bemboka, at the junction of the Brogo, the two forming the Bega River. At about 5 miles N. the Mumbulla Mountain rises to a height of about 2,000 feet above the sea-level, and the Walumla Peak line about 14 miles distant S. The district is a purely agricultural and pastoral one, and dairy operations are carried out within it on a very extensive scale, and a ready market is found in Sydney for the produce of the district. Bega was incorporated a municipal district in 1883, governed by eight aldermen and a mayor. Quarter sessions and district courts are held periodically at Bega. The population is about 2,000.

BEGA RIVER (*Cos. Dampier and Auckland*). [*See* "RIVERS."]

BELALIE (*Co. Culgoa*), a township on the extreme northern boundary between Queensland and this Colony.

BELARBIGILL (*Co. Lincoln*), a post-office, 288 miles N.W. of Sydney, with mail twice a week. The nearest railway station is Dubbo, 10 miles, on the western line.

BELAR CREEK (*Co. Gowen*), a western tributary of the upper part of the Castlereagh River, taking its rise in the Warrabungle Ranges.

BELARINGAR (*Co. Oxley*), a railway station, 349 miles W. of Sydney, on the western line.

BELARINGAR CREEK (*Co. Oxley*), a small tributary of the Macquarie River, near Nevertire, on the western railway.

BELARINGAR CREEK (*Co. Oxley*), a tributary of the Gunningbar Creek, rising near the W. bank of the Macquarie River.

BELBORA CREEK (*Co. Gloucester*), a southern tributary of the Manning River, receiving the waters of the Millbrook and Baker's Creeks.

BELERADA CREEK (*Co. Bathurst*), a small eastern tributary of the Lewis Ponds Creek flowing into it near the Belerada Pass.

BELERADA PASS (*Co. Bathurst*), a pass over the lower end of Lewis Ponds Creek, on the road from Ophir to Tambaroora.

BELFORD (*Co. Northumberland*), a post-office, 138 miles N. of Sydney, with daily mail. A railway station on northern line. Situated within 3 miles of the Hunter, on the Jump-up Creek, and is an agricultural district.

BELGAMILL CREEK (*Co. Ashburnham*), a small southern tributary of the Billabong Creek.

BELGRAVIA (*Co. Wellington*), a post-office, 209 miles W. of Sydney, with mail twice a week.

BELL (*Co. Cook*), a post-office, 83 miles W. of Sydney, with daily mail and telegraph office. A railway station on the western line.

BELLABULLA CREEK (*Co. Denison*), a tributary of the Tuppal Creek, near the Tocumwal, on the road from Albury to Deniliquin.

BELLALABA CREEK (*Co. Murray*), a tributary of the head of the Molonglo River, rising in the western slope of the Australian Alps.

BELLA-LEPPA CREEK (*Co. Bligh*), a western tributary of the Krui River.

BELLAMBI (*Co. Camden*), a postal village, 44 miles S. of Sydney, with daily mail. A railway station on the Illawarra and South Coast line.

BELLAMBI (*Co. Camden*), on the Southern Coast, about 4 miles N. of Wollongong. The first jetty for the shipment of coal was erected here by the late Mr. Thos. Hale, who opened a coal-mine at Bulli.

BELLBROOK, a postal town, 345 miles N. of Sydney, with mail three times a week and telegraph office. The nearest railway station is Hexham, 158 miles, on the northern line.

BELL CREEK (*Co. Roxburgh*), a western tributary of the Tanwarra Creek, rising in the Wattle Flat Gold-field.

BELLINGER (*Co. Raleigh*), a proclaimed village, 370 miles to the N. of Sydney, on the Bellinger River.

BELLINGER HEADS (*Co. Raleigh*), a post-office, 363 miles to the N. of Sydney, with mail three times a week.

BELLINGER RIVER (*Co. Raleigh*). [*See* "RIVERS."]

BELLOURI CREEK (*Co. Gordon*), a western tributary of the Wambangalong Creek.

BELL RIVER (*Co. Wellington and Gordon*). [*See* "RIVERS."]

BELL'S CREEK (*Co. Gloucester*), an eastern tributary of the head of the Hunter River.

BELL'S CREEK (*Co. St. Vincent*), a post-office, 190 miles S. of Sydney, with a daily mail. The nearest railway station is Tarago, 29 miles, on the Cooma line. This creek is a small auriferous tributary of the Araluen Creek, flowing into it near the road from Braidwood to Moruya.

BELL'S MOUNTAIN (*Co. Darling*), a lofty peak of the Mundewar range of mountains, lying about 10 miles S. from Cobborah.

BELL'S PEAK (*Co. Wellesley*), a lofty peak, about 9 miles S. of Nimitybelle.

BELLTREES (*Cos. Durham and Brisbane*), a pastoral district, 15 miles S.W. of Moorau and 20 miles E. of Scone.

BELMONT (*Co. Northumberland*), a post-office, 112 miles N. of Sydney, with daily mail, money-order and telegraph offices, and Government savings bank. The nearest railway station is Newcastle, 15 miles, on the northern line.

BELMONT FOREST (*Co. King*), a rural settlement, 10 miles from Gunning station, on the southern line.

BELMORE (*Co. Cumberland*), a post-office, 10 miles S. of Sydney, with daily mail. The nearest railway station is Ashfield, 5 miles, on the suburban line.

BELOKA CREEK (*Co. Wallace*), a southern tributary of the Snowy River, falling into it at Buckley's Crossing-place.

BELUBULA GOLD-FIELD (*Co. Bathurst*), the westerly extensions thereof are in the parish of Hampton, Belubula River.

BELUBULA RIVER (*Co. Bathurst*). [*See* "RIVERS."]

BEMA CREEK (*Co. St. Vincent*), an eastern tributary of the Dena, or upper part of the Moruya River.

BENANDARA (*Co. St. Vincent*), a postal receiving-office, 207 miles S. of Sydney, with mail once a week.

BENANDARA CREEK (*Co. St. Vincent*), a stream rising near the township of Currowan, and flowing into the sea by a wide estuary near Point Upright.

BENANEE (*Co. Taila*), a swampy lagoon on the N. bank of the Murray River, about 8 miles N.E. of the township of Euston.

BENANEE LAKE (*Co. Taila*), a large lake on the S. side of the Murray River, near Euston.

BENARBA, a county in the Central Division of the Colony. [*See* "COUNTIES."]

BEN BULLEN (*Co. Cook*), a post-office, 121 miles W. of Sydney, with a daily mail. A railway station on the Mudgee line.

BEN BULLEN SWAMP (*Co. Roxburgh*), a tract of swampy land at the head of the Turon River. The village of Cullen Bullen lies about 4 miles to the S.W.

BENCANYA LAKE (*Co. Mootwingee*), one of a series of lakes to the E. of the Coko range of mountains, near the south-western border.

BENDEELA (*Co. Camden*), a postal receiving-office, 110 miles S. of Sydney, with mail twice a week. The nearest railway station is Moss Vale, 24 miles, on the southern line.

BENDEMEER (*Co. Inglis*), a postal town, 273 miles N. of Sydney, with mail three times a week, money-order and telegraph offices. The nearest railway station is Moonbi, 17 miles, on the northern line. It is a mountainous and gold-bearing district, situated on the Mulucrindie River, near Moonbi.

BENDICK MURRELL (*Co. Monteagle*), a postal receiving-office, 268 miles S. of Sydney, with mail twice a week. A railway station on the southern line.

BENDOLBAH (*Co. Durham*), a post-office, 162 miles N. of Sydney, with mail three times a week. The nearest railway station is Morpeth, 42 miles, on the northern line.

BENEREE GOLD-FIELD (*Co. Bathurst*), situated in the parish of Beneree, at Osborne's paddock. Proclaimed 15th November, 1870.

BENEREE LAGOON (*Co. Bathurst*), a large sheet of fresh water, lying in the parish of Beneree, about 7 miles S. of the township of Orange.

BENEREMBAH (*Co. Cooper*), a railway station, 394 miles S. of Sydney, on the south-western line.

BENGALLA (*Co. Arrawatta*), a township on the Dumaresq River, adjoining the boundary of Queensland.

BENGALLA (*Co. Arrawatta*), a village, 568 miles N. of Sydney. The nearest railway station is Glen Innes, 145 miles, on the northern line.

BEN LOMOND (*Co. Sandon*), is a postal receiving-office, 403 miles N. of Sydney, with a mail twice a week. A railway station on the southern line.

BEN LOMOND MOUNT (*Co. Sandon*), the highest point of that part of the dividing range known as the New England Range, on the main northern road from Armidale to Glen Innes, and about 16 miles N. of the township of Falconer.

BEN LOMOND RAILWAY STATION (*Co. Sandon*), a post-office, 400 miles N. of Sydney, with daily mail. A station on the northern line.

BENLY (*Co. Brisbane*), a village in this county.

BERADY CREEK (*Co. Gloucester*), a small tributary of the southern mouth of the Manning River.

BERAGO CREEK *(Co. Wellington)*, a fine stream rising in the ranges lying between the Meroo gold-fields and the township of Mudgee, about 10 miles S.W. of the latter.

BERESFORD, a county in the Eastern Division of the Colony. [*See* "COUNTIES."]

BERGALIA *(Co. Dampier)*, a post-office, 204 miles S. of Sydney, with a daily post. The nearest station is Tarago, 47 miles, on the Cooma line.

BERGEN-OP-ZOOM CREEK *(Co. Vernon)*, a western tributary of the Ohio Creek, joining it about 6 miles N. of Walcha.

BERICO CREEK *(Co. Gloucester)*, a southern tributary of the Gloucester River.

BERIGAN CREEK *(Co. Denison)*, a creek flowing in the country to the S. of Jerilderie.

BERKLEY *(Co. Camden)*, an agricultural settlement, about 6 miles distant from the township of Wollongong.

BERMAGUI *(Co. Dampier)*, a postal village, 246 miles S. of Sydney, with mail four times a week. The nearest railway station is Tarago, 26 miles on the Cooma line.

BERNANA PLAINS *(Co. Bligh)*, a tract of fine pastoral country, lying at the lower end of the Coolaburragundy River, N.E. of Cobborah.

BEROWRA *(Co. Cumberland)*, a railway station, 28 miles N. of Sydney, on the Hawkesbury line.

BEROWRA CREEK *(Co. Cumberland)*, a proclaimed village, with a small creek falling into Broken Bay on its southern side.

BERRAWINNIA *(Co. Irrara)*, a village on the E. bank of the Paroo River, on the Queensland border.

BERRELLAN *(Co. St. Vincent)*, a postal receiving-office, 128 miles S. of Sydney, with daily mail. The nearest railway station is Moss Vale, 30 miles on the southern line.

BERRENDERRY CREEK *(Co. Bligh)*, a small western tributary of the head of the Krui River.

BERRIDALE *(Co. Wallace)*, a post-office, 278 miles S. of Sydney, with mail three times a week; money-order and telegraph offices. The nearest railway station is Cooma, 20 miles on the Goulburn and Cooma line.

BERRIGAN *(Co. Denison)*, a post-office, 442 miles S. of Sydney, with mail three times a week. The nearest railway station is Jerilderie, 20 miles, on the south-western line.

BERRIMA *(Co. Camden)*, a postal town, 92 miles S. of Sydney, with daily mail, money-order and telegraph offices, and Government savings bank. The nearest railway station is Moss Vale, 5 miles on the southern line. Situated on the Wingecarribee River, at an altitude of about 2,300 feet above the sea-level, the Jellore Mountain being distant about 10 miles. Berrima is an agricultural district, and coal with other valuable minerals abounds within it. One of the gaols of the Colony is built here.

BERRIMA COLLIERY (*Co. Camden*), a postal receiving-office, 92 miles S. of Sydney, with mail three times a week.

BERRIMA RANGE (*Co. Wallace*), is a high mountain, lying in the south-west corner of the county, near the Victorian boundary line.

BERRY (*Co. Camden*), a post-office 87 miles S. of Sydney, with daily mail. Telegraph and money-order offices, Government savings bank, and delivery by letter-carrier. The nearest railway station is Kiama, 20 miles on the Illawarra and south coast line.

BERRY'S BAY (*Co. Cumberland*), a well-known bay on the N. shore of the harbour, between Ball's Head and Blue's Point.

BETEALWEEN MOUNT (*Co. Phillip*), a high peak on the Blue Mountain Range, at the head of the Molarben Creek, and about 9 miles N.W. of Barigan.

BETEATWEEN HILL (*Co. Phillip*), is a spur of the Liverpool Range.

BETHUNGRA (*Co. Clarendon*), a postal village, 268 miles S. of Sydney, with daily mail, money-order and telegraph offices and Government savings bank. A railway station on the southern line.

BETHUNGRA CREEK (*Co. Clarendon*), an eastern tributary of the Billabong Creek flowing through the township of the same name.

BETHUNGRA MOUNT (*Cos. of Harden and Clarendon*), a lofty mountain, about 9 miles south-west of Cootamundra, on the W. side of Muttama Creek.

BEVENDALE, a post-office, 189 miles S. of Sydney, with mail once a week therefrom.

BEXCOURT (*Co. Wellington*), an agricultural settlement on the Bell River, at the junction of the Native Dog Creek.

BEXHILL (*Co. Rous*), a post town, 364 miles N. of Sydney with mail, by Clarence and Richmond River steamers.

BEXLEY (*Co. Cumberland*), a post-office 9 miles to the S. of Sydney, with daily mail. The nearest railway station is Rockdale, one mile on the Illawarra and South Coast line.

BIALA CREEK (*Co. King*), a drainage creek, the N.E. of the Gap Plains, flowing into the Lampton Creek.

BIBBENLUKE (*Co. Wellesley*), a postal village, 302 miles S. of Sydney, with mail four times a week. The nearest railway station is Cooma, 46 miles on the Goulburn and Cooma line.

BIBBENLUKE MOUNT (*Co. Wellesley*), a hill lying on the Bombala River, about 7 miles S. of Bombala.

BIDEE CREEK (*Co. St. Vincent*), a small tributary of the upper end of the Endrick River, falling into it above Nerriga.

BIDGEMWINGEE (*Co. King*), an agricultural settlement, lying about 5 miles from the township of Burrowa, in an easterly direction.

BIGBAJA HILL (*Cos. Beresford and Dampier*), a lofty peak at the head of the Bigbaja River, attaining an elevation of 4,000 feet above the sea level.

BIGBAJA RIVER (*Co. Beresford*). [*See* "RIVERS."]

BIGGA (*Co. Georgiana*), a postal village, 199 miles S. of Sydney, with a mail three times a week; nearest railway station is Goulburn, 65 miles on the southern line. It is situated in an agricultural and pastoral district, on the upper branch of the Lachlan River.

BIG HILL (*Co. Cowley*), a lofty detached peak, lying on the W. bank of the Murrumbidgee River, opposite the confluence of the Molonglo River.

BIG HILL (*Co. Harden*), a high hill lying in the parish of Talmo and on the N. bank of the Murrumbidgee River, about 10 miles S.W. of Bookham.

BIG HILL (*Co. Camden*), a post-office, 127 miles S. of Sydney, with mail three times weekly. The nearest railway station, Marulan, 15 miles, on the southern line.

BIG SWAMP (*Co. Goulburn*), a tract of marshy ground, on the Murray River, to the W. of Jingellic township Reserve.

BIG SWAMP CREEK (*Co. Goulburn*), a drainage creek from the swamp, lying to the W. of Jingellic township, and flowing into the river Murray.

BILLABONG CREEK (*Co. Clarendon*), a northern tributary of the Murrumbidgee River, rising about 6 miles N.W. of the township of Bethunga. It is fed by the Mitta Mitta and Bethunga Creeks.

BILLABONG CREEK (*Co. Ashburnham*), an eastern tributary of the Goobang Creek, lying to the N.E. of the Lachlan gold-fields.

BILLABONG GOLD-FIELDS (*Co. Ashburnham*).—These gold-fields, situated at Goobong and Billibong Creeks, were proclaimed on the 4th July, 1866, and extended on the 16th April, 1872.

BILLABUNG (*Co. Goulburn*), a small village, lying on the Billabung Creek, 7 miles E. of the township of Germanton.

BILLABUNG CREEK (*Cos. Wakool and Townshend*), a long and important creek flowing through and with its tributaries draining the extensive flat pastoral country which lies between the Murrumbidgee on the N. and W., the Murray on the S., and the Mane's Range on the E., and, after a meandering course of 250 miles, empties itself into the Edward River at Moulamein.

BILLEROY, a postal town, 410 miles W. of Sydney, with mail therefrom once a week.

BILLIPALLULA MOUNT (*Co. Buccleugh*), a lofty hill, lying about 10 miles inland from Tumut in a north-easterly direction.

BILLONG CREEK (*Co. Cook*), a small western tributary of the Hawkesbury River.

BILOELA (*Co. Cumberland*), 3 miles W. of Sydney, with daily mail therefrom, situated on Cockatoo Island, on the Parramatta River, opposite Balmain.

BIMBERRI MOUNT (*Co. Cowley*), a high peak of the Murrumbidgee Range, lying near the head of Goodradigbee River.

BIMBI (*Co. Monteagle*), a post-office, 328 miles S. of Sydney, with mail twice a week. The nearest railway station is Young, 40 miles, on the southern line.

BIMMEL MOUNT (*Co. Auckland*), a solitary mountain, situated on the coast, a few miles S. of Panbula, and forming a prominent land-mark for vessels making Twofold Bay.

BINALONG (*Co. Harden*), a post-office, 208 miles S. from Sydney, with daily mail, money-order and telegraph offices, and Government savings bank; a railway station on the southern line. It lies on the Bangullen Creek and on the road from Murrumboola to Yass.

BINBEN MOUNT (*Co. Phillip*), a high peak of the Blue Mountain Range, lying on the S.E. corner of the county, at the head of the Cudgegong River.

BINDA (*Co. King*), a postal village, 171 miles to the S. of Sydney, with mail three times a week, telegraph and money-order offices; nearest railway station, Goulburn, 39 miles, on the southern line. Situated on the Binda Creek on the line of road between that place and Tuena.

BINDA CREEK (*Co. King*), a small northern tributary of the Crookwell River. It flows in the N. part of the Yass Plains, and falls into the main stream at the township of Binda.

BINDA CREEK (*Co. Westmoreland*), a small eastern tributary of the Fish River, rising in the eastern slope of the Blue Mountain Range.

BINDA CREEK (*Co. St. Vincent*), is a small eastern tributary of the Shoalhaven River, falling into it near the confluence of the Corang.

BINDOGRANDA (*Co. Ashburnham*), a post-office, 257 miles W. of Sydney, with daily mail. The nearest railway station is Molong, 43 miles, on the western line.

BINDOGRANDI CREEK (*Co. Ashburnham*), a small tributary of the Billabong Creek, flowing S., about 10 miles, through rugged pastoral country.

BINDOWRY MOUNT (*Co. Wellington*), a solitary peak on the N. bank of the Grattai Creek, E. of its confluence with the Meroo Creek.

BINGA BINGE POINT (*Co. Dampier*), a rocky headland, standing boldly out into the sea, about 6 miles N. of the entrance to the Tuross River.

BINGARA (*Co. Murchison*), a postal town in the parishes of Bingara and Molroy, 352 miles to the N. of Sydney, with daily mail, money-order and telegraph offices, and Government savings bank; nearest railway station Tamworth, 100 miles, on the northern line, situated on the confluence of the Gwydir River and Bingera Creek. The district is agricultural, pastoral, and mining. Bingara was incorporated a municipal district in 1889 with five aldermen and a mayor. Quarter sessions and district courts are held here periodically. The population is about 600.

BINGARA CREEK (*Co. Murchison*), an auriferous stream flowing alongside the road from Cobbadah to Bingara, and falling into the Gwydir at the latter township.

BINGHAM (*Co. Georgiana*), a township reserve lying on the Isabella River, 15 miles N. from the township of Bolong.

BINGLEBURRA (*Co. Cumberland*), a postal receiving-office, 156 miles N. of Sydney, with mail once a week.

BINJURA LAGOONS (*Co. Beresford*), the name of two lagoons, lying about 2 miles N. of Cooma on the road to Bunyan and Queanbeyan.

BINNAWAY (*Co. Gowen*), a post-office, 316 miles W. of Sydney, with mails therefrom twice a week. The nearest railway station is Mudgee, 105 miles, on the western line.

BINNI CREEK (*Co. Bathurst*), a tributary of the Wangoola Creek, falling into it about 3 miles N. of the township of Cowra.

BINYAH (*Co. Cooper*), a township on the Mirrool Creek, near Cave Hill.

BIRAGAMBIL (*Co. Phillip*), a village situated on the W. bank of the Cudgegong River, 176 miles from Sydney on the main road, *via* Mudgee to Dubbo.

BIRD ISLAND (*Co. Northumberland*), lying between Bungaree Norah and Pier Head, a small rocky inlet in the Cabbage Tree Harbour.

BIRD'S EYE CORNER (*Co. Cumberland*). [*See* "MENANGLE."]

BIRIE RIVER (*Co. Narran*). [*See* "RIVERS."]

BIRKENHEAD (*Co. Cumberland*), a village on the Five Dock estate, in the parish of Concord, about 9 miles from Sydney and 3 from the Ashfield railway station. It is within the municipal district of Five Dock.

BIRREBORLA CREEK (*Co. Buckland*), an eastern tributary of the Yarramanbah Creek flowing through the Australian Agricultural Company's grant of 249,000 acres.

BISHOP'S BRIDGE (*Co. Northumberland*), a post-office, 102 miles N. of Sydney, with mail twice a week, situated in the parish of Allandale, on the Bishop's Bridge Creek, in a good agricultural district. The nearest railway station is Farley, 4 miles, on the southern line.

BITTANGABBEE HEADS (*Co. Auckland*), a rocky promontory jutting boldly out into the sea, about 12 miles from Twofold Bay and 5 miles N. of Green Cape.

BLACK BOB'S CREEK (*Co. Camden*), a small stream flowing through the Wombat Brush into the Wingecarribee River.

BLACKBURN COVE (*Co. Cumberland*), a small indentation on the E. side of Double Bay.

BLACK CREEK (*Co. Buccleugh*), an eastern boundary of the Tumut River, rising in the western slope of Blowering Range. Also a small drainage creek flowing through agricultural land at Bogong into the Tumut River.

BLACK CREEK (*Co. Northumberland*), a small southern tributary of the Hunter River, rising near Cessnock; a good agricultural district. There are also good beds of coal in the neighbourhood.

BLACK CREEK (*Co. Wynyard*), a small auriferous creek flowing into the Adelong Creek.

BLACKFELLOW'S CREEK (*Co. Westmoreland*), a tributary of Cox's River, rising in Mount Werong.

BLACK FLAT CREEK (*Co. Auckland*), a northern tributary of the Bemboka River.

BLACKGUARD GULLY CREEK (*Co. Monteagle*), an auriferous tributary of the head of the Burranjong Creek, flowing into the township of Young.

BLACK HEAD (*Co. Camden*), a bold rocky promontory, jutting out into the sea at Gerringong.

BLACK HEAD ISLAND (*Co. Gloucester*), the name given to three small rocks, lying off the coast between Port Stephens on the S. and Treachery Head on the N.

BLACKHEATH (*Co. Cook*), a postal village, 73 miles W. of Sydney, with daily mail, money-order, and telegraph office and Government savings bank. Railway station on the western line. Situated on a plateau of the Blue Mountain Range, about 14 miles from the township of Hartley, attaining a height of 3,400 feet above sea-level.

BLACKHEATH CREEK (*Co. Westmoreland*), an eastern tributary of Cox's River, rising in the magnificent rocky plateau of Blackheath, in the Blue Mountain Range.

BLACK HILL CREEK (*Co. Bathurst*), a small tributary of the Rocky Bridge Creek.

BLACK HILLS AND GULLY SWAMP GOLD-FIELD (*Co. Bathurst*), situated in the parish of Somers, about 19 square miles. At Cooming Creek, Mandurama Ponds, and Fell-timber Creek. Proclaimed 23rd January, 1874.

BLACKMAN'S CREEK (*Co. Georgiana*), a tributary of the Abercrombie River, flowing through a swampy country. S.W. of the Tuena gold-fields.

BLACKMAN'S CROWN (*Co. Roxburgh*), a lofty peak of the Blue Mountain Range, in the parish of Bandamora, near the head of the Turon River, and about 6 miles N. of Cullen Bullen.

BLACKMAN'S POINT (*Co. Roxburgh*), a post-office, 278 miles N. of Sydney, with daily mail.

BLACKMAN'S SWAMP (*Co. Wellington*), a track of swampy land on the E. of the township of Ophir, in the parish of March.

BLACKMAN'S SWAMP CREEK (*Co. Bathurst*), rising in the N.E. slopes of the Canobolas Mountains, flowing through the township of Orange.

BLACK MOUNTAIN (*Co. Roxburgh*), a post-office, 356 miles to the N. of Sydney, with daily mail. A railway station on the northern line.

BLACKNOTE MOUNT (*Co. Sandon*), a spur of the dividing range, in the parish of Blacknote, about 20 miles S.E. of Uralla.

BLACK POINT (*Co. Camden*), a bold, rocky projection on the sea-coast, to the S. of Gerringong.

BLACK RANGE (*Co. Goulburn*), a range of high hills, in the parish of Mungabarina, about 5 miles N. of the township of Albury.

BLACK RANGE (*Co. Harden*), a high, rugged range of hills, in the parish of Bowring, about 7 miles S.W. of the town of Bowring.

BLACK RANGE (*Co. Goulburn*), a post-office, 390 miles S. of Sydney, with mail three times a week.

BLACK RANGE CREEK (*Co. Harden*), a small creek, S. of Bogolong, falling into the Talmo Creek.

BLACK RANGE GOLD-FIELD (*Co. Goulburn*), lies within the watershed of the Bungambraweth Creek, near Albury. Proclaimed, 31st December, 1861.

BLACK RANGE GOLD-FIELD EXTENSION (*Co. Goulburn*). The easterly extension comprises the gold-fields on Crown lands in the parishes of Albury and Mungabarina; on the W. by the eastern boundary of the Black Range gold-field, as proclaimed on the 31st December, 1861. The north-easterly extension comprises about 1,000 acres, in the parish of Mungabarina. Proclaimed, 20th May, 1873.

BLACK ROCK (*Co. Wellington*), situated on the E. bank of the Bell River, in the parish of Newrea. The district is an agricultural and pastoral one. The nearest railway station is Wellington, 10 miles, on the western line.

BLACK ROCK (*Co. Beresford*), a rocky hill on the road from Bunyan to Nimitabel, on the W. side of the Rock Flat Creek.

BLACK SPRING CREEK (*Co. Bathurst*), a small tributary of the Coombing Creek, in the parish of Shaw. Sandstone, also a small auriferous eastern tributary of the lower end of Lewis Ponds Creek, in the parish of Aberfoil.

BLACK SPRING CREEK (*Co. Parry*), an eastern tributary of the Mulucrindie River.

BLACK SPRING CREEK (*Co. Wynyard*), a tributary of the Yaven-Yaven Creek, to the S. of the Murrumbidgee River.

BLACK SPRINGS (*Co. Roxburgh*), a post-office, 152 miles W. of Sydney, with mail twice a week. The nearest railway station is Tarana, 22 miles, on the western line.

BLACK SWAMP CREEK (*Co. Roxburgh*), a creek on the Kirkconnell gold-fields, draining into the Lucky Swamp.

BLACKTOWN (*Co. Cumberland*), a post-office, 22 miles W. of Sydney, with daily mail. Telegraph and money-order offices. A station on the Great Western Railway, in the parish of Prospect, 3 miles S. of the Eastern Creek.

BLACKVILLE (*Co. Buckland*), a postal town, 272 miles N. of Sydney, with mail three days a week. Telegraph and money-order offices. The nearest railway station is Quirindi, 55 miles, on the northern line.

BLACKWALL (*Co. Richmond*), an agricultural and cedar-cutting settlement, situated on the Richmond River, 75 miles S.E. of the township of Lismore.

BLACKWALL (*Co. Cumberland*), a postal town, 58 miles N. of Sydney, with daily mail. Telegraph and money-order offices, and Government savings bank. The nearest railway station is Gosford, 6 miles, on the Sydney and Newcastle line.

BLACKWALL POINT (*Co. Cumberland*), forming the western head of Five Dock and the eastern head of Fig-tree Bays, is a rocky promontory on the S. side of the Parramatta River.

BLACKWATER CREEK (*Co. Phillip*), a tributary of the head of the Weddin Brook, rising in Mount Coricudgy, and flowing N. about 16 miles.

BLACKWATTLE COVE (*Co. Cumberland*), situate between Pyrmont and the Glebe, on the S.W. side of the City of Sydney; the Blackwattle Creek flows into the head of the Cove.

BLACKWATTLE CREEK (*Co. Cumberland*), forms the boundary between the Glebe and Ultimo.

BLACKWILLOW CREEK (*Co. Wellington*), an eastern tributary of the Macquarie River, and falls into it near the Burrandong gold-fields.

BLACKWOOD PEAK (*Albert District*), a peak of the Grey Range.

BLAIR'S HILL (*Co. Gough*), a peak of the New England Range, lying about 2 miles W. of Stonehenge.

BLAKE BROOK (*Co. Clarence*), a postal town, 362 miles N. of Sydney, with mail per Clarence and Richmond steamers.

BLAKEHURST (*Co. Cumberland*), a suburban post-office, 9 miles from Sydney, with daily mail therefrom.

BLAKENEY CREEK (*Co. King*), a drainage creek flowing through the Yass Plains in a westerly direction into the upper part of the Lachlan River. The nearest railway station is Gunning, 25 miles, on the southern line.

BLAKE'S RIVER (*Co. Fitzroy*). [*See* "RIVERS."]

BLAND, a county, partly in the Eastern and Central Divisions of the Colony. [*See* "COUNTIES."]

BLAND CREEK. (*Co. Harden*), a small eastern tributary of the Murrumboola Creek, flowing through Cunningham's Plains.

BLANDFORD (*Co. Brisbane*), a post-office, 188 miles N. of Sydney, with daily mail and telegraph office. Railway station on the northern line. Situated on the Page River and Warland's Creek, about 3 miles N. of Murrurundi.

BLAXLAND (*Co. Cook*), a railway station, 42 miles from Sydney, on the western line.

BLAXLAND, a county in the Western Division of the Colony. [*See* "COUNTIES."]

BLAXLAND MOUNT (*Co. Cook*), a lofty peak of the Blue Mountain Range, attaining an elevation of 3,256 feet above the sea-level.

BLAXLAND VALLEY (*Co. Northumberland*), a grassy, low-lying tract of grazing country, in the parish of Blaxland.

BLAXLAND'S CREEK (*Co. Fitzroy*), a fine stream rising to the S. of Grafton, and flowing S.W. into the Nymboi River at Nymboida.

BLAXLAND'S SWAMP (*Co. Westmoreland*), a tract of swampy agricultural country, lying on Lockyer's line of road, between Hartley and Bathurst.

BLAYNEY (*Co. Bathurst*), a postal village, in the parishes of Napier, Errol, and Lindsay, 166 miles W. of Sydney, with daily mail, money-order and telegraph offices, Government savings bank, and delivery by letter-carrier; also railway station on the western line. The district is an agricultural, pastoral, and mining one. Blayney was incorporated a municipal district in 1882, with seven aldermen and a mayor. The population is about 1,000.

BLIGH, a county in the Eastern Division of the Colony. [*See* "COUNTIES."]

BLIND CREEK (*Co. Buccleugh*), a tributary of the Adjungbilli Creek, rising in the Kangaroo Hill, and falling into the Tumut River.

BLIN'S RIVER (*Co. Richmond*), a local name given to the upper part of the Clarence River.

BLOWERING (*Co. Buccleugh*), a post-office, 336 miles S. of Sydney, with mail once a week. The nearest railway station is Gundagai, 48 miles, on the southern line.

BLOWERING CREEK (*Co. Buccleugh*), a small eastern tributary of the Tumut River, rising in the Blowering Mountain.

BLOWERING (OR BOGONG) MOUNTAINS (*Co. Buccleugh*), an eastern spur of the Tumut Range of mountains, almost inaccessible, and covered with snow for many months in the year.

BLUE'S BAY (*Co. Cumberland*). [*See* "BERRY'S BAY."]

BLUE GUM CREEK (*Co. Cumberland*), a small eastern tributary of the upper end of the Lane Cove River.

BLUE GUM FLAT (*Co. Northumberland*), a tract of fine land near the township of Gosford.

BLUE MOUNTAIN (*Co. Sandon*), a detached peak in the parish of Lawrence, on the E. side of the road from Port Macquarie to Armidale, about 18 miles S.E. of Uralla.

BLUE MOUNTAIN RANGE (*Cos. Cook, Roxburgh, and Westmoreland*). The Blue Mountains are so named from the appearance they present from a distance. They form the Great Dividing Range, stretching from the Liverpool Range to Lake Burra Burra, S. of the thirty-fourth parallel. Its course, though generally southerly, is very irregular, and though 150 miles from the sea at starting, its average distance is not more than 70 miles. In the middle part of their course the Blue Mountains consist of two ranges, running nearly parallel, and separated by a deep, narrow valley. The western range exceeds the eastern in altitude: "Narrow, gloomy, and profound, the stupendous rents in these mountains are enclosed between gigantic walls of sandstone and rock, sometimes receding from, sometimes frightfully overhanging, the dark bed of the ravine, and its black silent eddies, or its foaming torrents of water." To the early settlers in the Colony the rugged nature of the Blue Mountains long interposed an impassable barrier between the coast and the interior. A passage was first discovered in 1813, twenty-five years after the first settlement of the Colony. The average height of this portion of the great dividing chain is about 3,300 feet above sea-level. The highest point is probably Beemarang, 4,100 feet, at the head of Campbell's River, a little to the N. of the thirty-fourth parallel. The whole mass consists of ferruginous sandstone.

BLUE NOBBY (*Co. Burnett*), a prominent solitary peak, lying on the W. bank of Oxley's Creek, and near the road from Warialda to Bengalla, about 25 miles S. of the latter place.

BLUE PEAK (*Co. Beresford*), a lofty peak of the Monaro Range, about 4 miles E. of the township of Bunyan, and on the E. bank of the Flat Rock Creek.

BLUE'S POINT (*Co. Cumberland*), native name, Warung. This is a well-known point, jutting out from the north shore of Port Jackson, and situated in the W. part of St. Leonards, opposite Sydney. This point derives its name from an old inhabitant, William Blue, a coloured man.

BLUFF ROCK (*Co. Clive*), a railway station, 470 miles N. of Sydney, on the northern line.

BLUFF, THE (*Co. Clive*), a prominent hill on the road from Severn to Tenterfield, about 10 miles S. of the latter place.

BOALATLEY (*Co. Dampier*), a village to the S. of Sydney, in this county.

BOATHARBOUR (*Co. Rous*), a post-office, 374 miles N. of Sydney, with mail three times a week, money-order and telegraph offices. The nearest railway station is Hexham, 262 miles, on the northern line. Quarter sessions and district courts are held here periodically.

BOAT-HARBOUR CREEK (*Co. Rous*), a small tributary of the north arm of the Richmond River.

BOB HIGGINS CREEK (*Co. Westmoreland*), a small tributary of the Wollondilly River, flowing into it near Burragorang.

c

BOBBARA MOUNT (*Co. Harden*), a lofty peak, lying at the S. end of a range of mountains, situated about 3 miles N.W. of the township of Binalong.

BOBBERA MOUNT (*Co. Murray*), a steep, narrow range of mountains, lying to the E. of Jingery Mountains.

BOBBY'S HOLE (*Co. Manara*), one of a series of waterholes in this county, in the far West.

BOBIALLA CREEK (*Co. Bligh*), a western tributary of the Bow Creek.

BOBOYAN FLAT (*Co. Cowley*), situated to the W. of the Murrumbidgee River, near Clinton.

BOB'S CREEK (*Co. Gresham*), a small tributary of the Sara River, rising in Mount Mitchell, to the N. of the Obau diggings.

BOB'S CREEK (*Co. Wellington*), a small, auriferous, western tributary of the Molong River.

BOBUNDARA CREEK (*Co. Wallace*), a northern tributary of the Snowy River, rising in the eastern slope of Mount Jinnybruthera.

BOBUNDARA HILL (*Co. Wallace*).—This hill lies about 8 miles E. of Buckley's Crossing-place, on the W. bank of the Bobundara Creek.

BOBUNDARAH (*Co. Beresford*), a post-office, 294 miles S. of Sydney, with mail twice a week. The nearest railway station is Cooma, 21 miles, on the Goulburn and Cooma line. Situated on the Bobundarah Creek, the Snowy River flowing 12 miles distant.

BOCO ROCK (*Co. Wellington*), a rocky peak on the Boco Creek, to the W. of Nimmitabel.

BOCOBLE MOUNT (*Co. Wellington*), a remarkable hill situated at the head of the Cudgegong and Four-mile Creeks, on the S. bank of the Cudgegong River, 3½ miles W. of Cudgegong township, and 14 miles of Mudgee.

BOCOCO CREEK (*Co. Dudley*), a small northern tributary of the Macleay River.

BODALDURA CREEK (*Co. Wellington*), an auriferous eastern tributary of the Bell River.

BODALLA (*Co. Dampier*), a postal village, 257 miles to the S. of Sydney, with daily mail, money-order and telegraph offices, and Government savings bank. The nearest railway station is Tarago, 55 miles, on Goulburn and Cooma line. The district is agricultural and pastoral, and the soil is very fertile. Large dairy operations are carried on here, and the late Mr. T. S. Mort's extensive manufactory of cheese for the Sydney market is situated on the Comerang estate on the Tuross River.

BOGABILLA (*Co. Stapylton*), a postal village, 490 miles N. of Sydney, with mail therefrom twice a week. The nearest railway station is Glen Innes, 150 miles, on the northern line.

BOGAN GATE (*Co. Ashburnham*), a postal receiving-office, 299 miles W. of Sydney, with mail twice a week. The nearest railway station is Borenore, 99 miles, on the Orange and Molong line.

BOGAN RIVER (*Cos. Bligh and Wellington.*) [*See* "RIVERS."]

BOGANDILLAN LAGOON (*Co. Gipps*), a small swampy waterhole on the Manna Creek, situated between Lake Cowal and the Lachlan River, about 30 miles S.E. of Condobolin.

BOGEE (*Co. Roxburgh*), a small alluvial gold-diggings on the Capertee River, near the township of Rylstone.

BOGGABRI (*Co. Pottinger*), a postal town, 318 miles N. of Sydney, with daily mail, money-order and telegraph offices, and Government savings bank. A railway station on the northern line. Situated on the upper end of the Boco Creek, about 8 miles W. of Merriwa, on the road to Mudgee.

BOGGY CREEK (*Co. Jamison*), a small agricultural hamlet in the neighbourhood of the Namoi River, a short distance from the township of Narrabri.

BOGGY CREEK (*Liverpool Plains*), a small drainage creek, supposed to flow into the Ghean Creek.

BOGGY CREEK (*Co. Bourke*), a postal receiving-office, 319 miles S. of Sydney, with daily mail. A railway station on the south-western line.

BOGGY FLAT (*Co. Durham*), a post-office, 155 miles N. of Sydney, with mail three times a week. The nearest railway station is Singleton, 7 miles, on the northern line.

BOGLEDI CREEK (*Co. Baradine*), a western tributary of the head of the Baradine Creek, rising in Mount Boreable, in the Warrabungle Range, and flowing N. about 35 miles into the main stream at the township of Baradine.

BOGOLARE WATERFALL (*Co. Harden*), a cataract on Barber's Creek, under Hunt's Look-out Hill, about 2½ miles S. of Bookham.

BOGOLONG (*Co. Harden*), a small township reserve, situated on the Bogolong Creek, about 8 miles W. of Yass.

BOGOLONG CREEK (*Co. Harden*), a small eastern tributary of the head of the Jugiong Creek, falling into it at the township of Bogolong.

BOGONG PEAKS (*Co. Buccleuch*), are two high peaks, divided by a narrow gully, in an almost inaccessible country to the S.W. of Tumut. These peaks are covered with snow for many months in the year.

BOGREE (*Co. Courallie*), a township to the extreme N. of the Colony, near the Queensland border.

BOIGA CREEK (*Co. Wellington*), a small auriferous stream, flowing in the Louisa Creek gold-fields, about 7 miles S. of Windeyer.

BOIGA CREEK GOLD-FIELD (*Co. Wellington*).—It forms part of the Tuena gold-field, proclaimed on the 31st August, 1865.

BOIGA CREEK (*Co. Wellington*), a small auriferous northern tributary of the Pyramul Creek.

BOIGA MOUNT (*Co. Wellington*), a lofty peak on the Louisa Creek gold-field, at the head of the Boiga Creek, about 6 miles from the township of Windeyer.

BOKHARA CREEK (*Co. Narran*), a small watercourse connecting the Mogila Creek with the Bokhara River, on the border of Queensland.

BOKHARA RIVER (*Co. Narran*). [*See* "RIVERS."]

BOLAIRA HILL (*Co. Wallace*), a detached peak, lying in the parish of Bolaira, near the junction of the Goorudee Rivulet with the Murrumbidgee.

BOLAIRA SWAMP (*Co. Wallace*), situated at the western foot of Bolaira Hill, and formed by the flow of the Gorudee Rivulet, and flows into the Murrumbidgee River.

BOLARO (*Co. Durham*), a postal receiving-office, 277 miles N. of Sydney, with mail twice a week. The nearest railway station is Dubbo, 48 miles, on the railway line.

BOLIVIA (*Co. Clive*), a post-office, 455 miles N. of Sydney, with daily mail, money-order and telegraph offices, and Government savings bank. A railway station on the northern line.

BOLONG (*Co. Camden*), is a postal village, 128 miles S. of Sydney, with a daily mail, situated on the N. bank of the Shoalhaven River. The district is an agricultural one, the nearest place being Nowra, 3 miles S. A vein of coal crops out above ground at intervals along the face of the Cambewarra Range to the north.

BOLONG (*Co. Georgiana*), a township situate in Phil's Creek. The nearest railway station is Picton, on the southern line.

BOLONG RIVER (*Co. Georgiana*). [*See* "RIVERS."]

BOLTON VALE (*Co. Westmoreland*), a postal receiving office, 143 miles W. of Sydney, with mail twice a week.

BOLUMBON MOUNT (*Co. Macquarie*), a peak of the Hastings Range, on the S. bank of the Hastings River.

BOLWARRA (*Co. Durham*), a rich agricultural district on the northern bank of the Hunter River, about 8 miles N.W. from Morpeth.

BOMADARY (*Co. Camden*), an agricultural village on the estate of the Messrs. Berry, of Shoalhaven. The nearest railway station is Moss Vale, 42 miles, on southern line. Situated on the N. side of the Shoalhaven River, about 4 miles from the village of Numba.

BOMBALA (*Co. Wellesley*), a postal town, 312 miles S. of Sydney, with mail five days weekly. Money-order and telegraph office and Government savings bank. The nearest railway station is Cooma, 53 miles, on the Goulburn-Cooma line. Situated on the Bombala River, being 1 mile S., and the Black Lake about 6 miles N. The district is a pastoral and agricultural one. Courts of quarter sessions and district courts are held here periodically.

BOMBALA RIVER (*Co. Wellesley*). [*See* "RIVERS."]

BOMBI POINT (*Co. Northumberland*), a rocky promontory, forming the outer north head of Broken Bay.

BOMEN (*Co. Wynyard*), a post-office, 300 miles S. of Sydney, with daily mail, money-order and telegraph offices, and Government savings bank. A railway station on the southern line.

BONARD CREEK (*Co. Wellington*), a small auriferous tributary of the Eagle Beagle Creek, 3 miles W. of Burrendong.

BONDI (*Co Cumberland*), a postal suburb, 5 miles from the City of Sydney, with daily mail and delivery by letter-carriers. It is a very favorite suburb, having tram accommodation. Many wealthy citizens resort to it for villa residences. It is beautifully situated on the sea-coast.

BONDI BAY (*Co. Cumberland*), a fine open bight in the coast, having a shallow sandy beach, exposed to the heavy ground swell from the ocean, and therefore useless as a place of shelter for vessels. The north head of this bay, known as Ben Buckler, lies about 4 miles S. of the entrance to Port Jackson, the bay being about half-a-mile across, and its south head being a rocky point known as the Boot. Bondi Bay lies about 4 miles from the centre of the City of Sydney, and is a very favourite place of resort for picnic parties. The aquarium is a very great attraction to all classes of visitors.

BONDI PEAK (*Co. Auckland*), a high hill, on the creek of the same name, on the road from Gipps' Land, *via* the Genoa River, about 7 miles N. of the Dividing Range.

BONGALONG (*Co. Harden*), a railway station, 267 miles S. of Sydney, on the Cootamundra and Gundagai line.

BONG-BONG (*Co. Camden*), is a hamlet, 30 miles S.W. of Sydney, with railway station on the southern line. Situated on the Wingecarribee Creek, about 5 miles from Berrima, 2 miles from Bowral, and 8 miles from Kangaloon. A purely pastoral and agricultural district, and for which the soil and climate are admirably adapted.

BONGONGALONG CREEK (*Co. Harden*), is a small western tributary of the Muttama Creek.

BONGONGO (*Co. Buccleuch*), a postal-receiving office, 223 miles S. of Sydney, with mail once a week.

BONNYRIGG (*Co. Cumberland*), a post-office, 26 miles S. of Sydney, with a daily mail.

BONSHAW (*Co. Gough*), a postal village, 419 miles N. of Sydney, with mail twice a week. The nearest railway station is Glen Innes, 113 miles, on the northern line.

BOOBORA LAGOON (*Co. Stapylton*), an extensive lagoon to the S. of the Macintyre River, on the border of Queensland.

BOOGOOYON (*Co. Stapylton*), a township on the banks of the Macintyre River, near Queensland border.

BOOK-BOOK (*Co. Wynyard*), a group of three detached peaks, lying to the E. of Livingstone Gully, W. of the Kyamba Creek, and about 22 miles S. of Wagga Wagga.

BOOKHAM (*Co. Harden*), a postal village, 206 miles S. of Sydney, with mail three times a week. The nearest railway station is Bowning, 12 miles, on the southern line.

BOOLAMBAYTE (*Co. Gloucester*), a post-office, 157 miles to the N. of Sydney, with mail three times a week. The nearest railway station is Hexham, 52 miles, on the northern line.

BOOLEMDILE MOUNT (*Co. Leichhardt*), a lofty peak of the Warrabungle Range, about 8 miles W. of Coonabarabran.

BOOLIGAL (*Co. Nicholson*), a postal village, 505 miles S.W. of Sydney, with mail three times a week. Money-order and telegraph offices. The nearest railway station is Hay, 50 miles, on the southern line.

BOOLKA LAKE (*Co. Evelyn*), a large lake on the South Australian border, running into Pack Saddle Creek.

BOOLOLAGUNG MOUNT (*Co. Rous*), is a peak of the Macpherson Range, on the boundary between New South Wales and Queensland, about 8 miles W. of Point Danger.

BOOLOOMBAGO (*Co. Gloucester*), a small hamlet, in the parish of the same name. Situated on the creek, and the W. border of the Myall Lakes. Stroud is 28 miles to the west.

BOOLULTA (*Co. Fitzgerald*), a township in the extreme W. of the Colony.

BOOMERA CREEK (*Co. Napier*), a western tributary of the Turrabeill Creek, flowing into the main stream in Bowen Plains.

BOOMEY (*Co. Wellington*), a postal town, 233 miles W. of Sydney, with daily mail. The nearest railway station is Molong, 8 miles, on the western line.

BOOMI CREEK (*Co. Murchison*), a small western tributary of the Noocera Creek, rising in the Nundawar Range, and flowing about 20 miles.

BOOMI RIVER (*Co. Benarba*), a branch of the Macintyre River, flowing out of it at Boolonga. After a course of 70 miles it falls into the Barwon.

BOONABILLA VALLEY (*Co. Durham*), a deep valley, lying between Mount Carrow and Cobrabald, about 25 miles N. from Bandon Grove.

BOONAL (*Co. Stapylton*), a township on the Whalan, a tributary of the Dumaresq River, on the Queensland border.

BOONBOURONBI MOUNT (*Co. Courallie*), a lofty and precipitous peak of the Nundawar Range, about 36 miles N.E. of Narrabri.

BOONDI LAKE (*Co. Auckland*), a small saline lagoon, situate about 1 mile S. of Wallagoot Lake, and 7 miles S.E. of Bega.

BOONOO BOONOO (*Co. Buller*), a postal receiving office, 486 miles, to the N. of Sydney, with a mail twice a week.

BOONOO BOONOO GOLD-FIELD (*Co. Buller*), an alluvial diggings, on the road from Tenterfield to Queensland, about 10 miles from Maryland.

BOONOO BOONOO RIVER (*Co. Buller*). [*See* "RIVERS."]

BOORAH CREEK DIGGINGS (*Co. Murchison*), a small alluvial gold working, in the Bingera gold-fields, 6 miles S. of the township of Bingera.

BOORAL (*Co. Gloucester*), a postal village, 114 miles N. of Sydney, with daily mail. The nearest railway station is Hexham, 27 miles, on the northern line. A small agricultural hamlet, situated at the head of the navigation of the Karuah River, about half-way between Stroud and Gloucester.

BOORANGALLEN PONDS (*Co. King*), a stream rising in the western slope of the Australian Alps, near Mutmutbilly, crossing the Yass Road into Diamond Creek.

BOORE CREEK (*Co. Ashburnham*), a northern tributary of the Bourimbla Creek, rising on the W. of the Conoblis, and flowing S.W.

BOOREL (*Co. Gloucester*), a small agricultural settlement on the Karuah River, 7 miles from Stroud.

BOOROLONG CREEK (*Co. Hardinge and Sandon*), an auriferous northern tributary of the Rocky River, rising in a western spur of the Australian Alps, to the N. of the parish of Exmouth, on the road from Armidale to Falconer.

BOOROOBAN (*Co. Waradgery*), a postal town, 480 miles S.W. of Sydney, with mail five days a week. The nearest railway station is Hay, 30 miles, on the south-western line.

BOOROOBELLE MOUNT (*Co. Nandewar*), a peak of the Peel Range, lying on the N. bank of the Namoi River, about 1 mile N. of the township of Carroll.

BOOROOK (*Co. Clive*), a township, 570 miles N. of Sydney. The nearest railway station is Tenterfield, 32 miles, on the northern line.

BOOROOK AND LUNATIC GOLD-FIELD (*Co. Buller and Clive*), bounded on the N. from the confluence of the Cataract and Clarence Rivers, by a line W. to the Great Dividing Range.

BOOROOLONG CREEK (*Co. Sandon*), is an auriferous N. tributary of the Rocky River, flowing through the village of Borolong.

BOOROOLONG (*Co. Sandon*), a postal receiving-office, 384 miles N. of Sydney, with mail three days a week. The nearest railway station is Black Mountain, 9 miles, on the northern line.

BOOROONDARRA MOUNTAIN (*Co. Yanda*), a very high mount to the S.E. of the Darling River.

BOOROONDARRA, a county in the Western Division of the Colony. [*See* "COUNTIES."]

BOOTH HILL (*Co. Cowley*), a high peak lying to the W. of the Naas Valley, about 12 miles W. of Michelago.

BOOTHTOWN (*Co. Cumberland*), a village, 25 miles W. of Sydney. The nearest railway station is Rooty Hill, 6 miles, on the western line.

BOOYAMURRA PLAINS (*Co. Napier*), a tract of pastoral land situate on the Coolaburragungy River, and in the southern part of the district of Liverpool Plains.

BORAH CREEK (*Co. Darling*), a western tributary of the Manilla River, rising in and flowing through good pastoral country N.E. of Gulligal.

BORAH CREEK (*Co. White*), the eastern head or tributary of the Brigalow Creek, near the village of Borambulla, to its junction with the Yanimba Creek.

BORAMBIL (*Co. Bligh*), postal receiving-office, 254 miles N. of Sydney, with mail four days a week. The nearest railway station is Orange or Borenore, on the western line.

BORAMBIL CREEK (*Cos. Bligh and Buckland*), an eastern tributary of the Conadilly River, rising in the western slope of the Australian Alps, near Doughboy Hollow.

BOREABLE MOUNT (*Co. Leichhardt*), a lofty peak of the Arbuthnot or Warrabungle Range, about 10 miles from Coonabarrabran.

BOREE CREEK (*Co. Urana*), a postal receiving-office, 415 miles S. of Sydney, with mail twice a week.

BOREE HOLLOW CREEK (*Co. Wellington*), a small auriferous western tributary of the Molong River.

BOREE SWAMP (*Co. Northumberland*), a tract of marshy land on the Big and Little Boree Creeks, 10 miles from Wollombi township.

BOREHOLE (*Co. Northumberland*), situate about 2 miles from Newcastle, a mining village occupied by miners principally.

BORENORE (*Co. Wellington*), a post-office, 198 miles W. of Sydney, with daily mail, money-order office, and Government savings bank. A railway station on the western line.

BORERI CREEK (*Co. Rous*), a small tributary of the N. arm of the Richmond River.

BORIMBADAL (*Co. St. Vincent*), a small southern tributary of the Shoalhaven River.

BORO (*Co. Argyle*), a postal village, 165 miles S. of Sydney, with daily mail. The nearest railway station is Tarago, 5 miles, on southern line, situated on the Boro Creek, Lake George lying W. 12 miles, and Lake Bathurst N. 8 miles distant. The district is an agricultural one, forming the southern part of the celebrated Goulburn Plains.

BORO FLAT (*Co. Argyle*), a tract of flat agricultural land, lying between the Boro Creek and the Shoalhaven River, near the villages of Larbert and Marlow. This flat forms the S.E. part of the Goulburn Plains.

BORONGA (*Co. Stapylton*), a township on the banks of the Macintyre River, on the Queensland border.

BOSH'S CREEK (*Co. Wellington*), a northern tributary of the Coolamin Creek, rising in the Mullion's Range, and flowing E. past the foot of Mount Coolamin.

BOTANY (*Co. Cumberland*), a postal suburb, 5 miles S. of Sydney, with daily mail, money-order and telegraph offices, and delivery by letter-carriers. Situated on Cook's River and the north shore of Botany Bay—the former lying W., the latter S. by W., and George's River S., 6 miles distant. It is one of the most favourite resorts of pleasure parties from Sydney, being celebrated for the beauty of its situation and of the surrounding scenery. The tramway, which now conveys vast numbers of citizens to this favoured spot, has in some measure disturbed the quiet of former years, but gives enjoyment to larger numbers. Botany was incorporated a borough in 1888, divided into three wards, viz., Cook Ward, Banks Ward, and Booralee Ward, under eight aldermen and a mayor. The population is about 2,250.

BOTANY BAY (*Co. Cumberland*), a fine capacious harbour, the entrance to which lies about 9 miles S. to that of Port Jackson. The N. head of Botany Bay, Cape Banks, is in 34° S. lat., 151° 16′ E. long. It is the first spot touched at by Captain Cook, when he discovered the eastern coast of Australia, on the 28th April, 1770; early on the morning of which day he anchored under the S. shore, about 2 miles within the entrance, abreast of a small native village, consisting of six or eight huts. The first person buried at Botany Bay was Forbes Sutherland, a native of the Orkneys, and one of the seamen belonging to the crew of Captain Cook, who died on the 30th April, 1770, and was, on the 1st of May, carried on shore, and buried near a small fresh-water creek, and from that circumstance Captain Cook called the point, which the land forms on that part of the bay, Sutherland Point. The name of Botany Bay conferred upon the comparatively barren coast, where Cook and Banks first landed, is a permanent proof of the rich field of botanical specimens which the latter met with there. The harbour of Botany Bay is about 5 miles long from N. to S., and 6 miles in width from E. to W., and receives the waters of Cook's and George's Rivers. A brass plate on the cliffs marks the spot where Captain Cook first landed, which, together with a simple monument erected to the memory of La Perouse, contributes to give an intellectual interest to the scene.

BOTANY NORTH (*Co. Cumberland*), is the northern portion of Botany proper, and was proclaimed a borough in 1888, under the Municipalities Act. It is situated between Botany and Waterloo, and is governed by eight aldermen and a mayor. The population is about 2,000.

BOTOBOLAR CREEK (*Co. Phillip*), a tributary of the head of Barrigan Creek.

BOTTLE AND GLASS (*Co. Cumberland*), the name applied to two remarkable rocks standing at the W. head of Vaucluse Bay, near the entrance to Port Jackson, and nearly opposite Watson's Bay.

BOTTLE CREEK (*Co. Rous*), a small eastern tributary of the head of the Clarence River, flowing through a scrubby pastoral country.

BOUGH-YARD CREEK (*Co. Buccleuch*), a small tributary of the upper end of Bungle Creek.

BOUNDARY CREEK (*Co. Goulburn*), a small western tributary of Woomargama Creek, having its rise in the Little Yambla Range.

BOUNDARY CREEK (*Co. Gresham*), a small southern tributary of the Aberfoyle River.

BOURBAH (*Co. Leichhardt*), a post-office, 364 miles W. of Sydney, with mail three times weekly. The nearest railway station is Nevertire, 67 miles, on the western line.

BOURIMBLA CREEK (*Co. Ashburnham*), an eastern tributary of Byrne's Creek, rising in the Canobolas Mountains, and flowing W., through rugged scrubby country about 25 miles. It is fed by Spring, Boorem, Oakey, and Bowen Creeks.

BOURKE, a county in the Central Division of the Colony. [*See* "COUNTIES."]

BOURKE (*Cos. Cooper and Gunderbooka*), a postal town, in the parishes of Davidson, East Bourke, Bourke, and Bullamunter, 503 miles W. of Sydney, with daily mail, money-order, and telegraph offices, Government savings bank, and delivery by letter-carriers. It is the terminus of the Great Western Railway, and is situated on the Darling River, 7 miles below the confluence of the Bogan with that river, 20 miles below the confluence of the Culgoa, and 40 miles above the Warrego. Bourke derives its name from the fort which was built by Major Mitchell, as a means of defence against the blacks, and which is situated about 6 miles below the present township. This place was reached by Mitchell on the 25th of May, 1835, in his expedition in search of the ultimate destination of the Darling River, the expedition in which Cunningham was murdered by the blacks. The district in which Bourke is situated is the western pastoral district of the Colony, and is a strictly pastoral one, and is unsurpassed in the variety and luxuriance of its pasturage, the grassy plains being intersected by immense belts of valuable salt bush. To the N. of the township good specimens of gold have been obtained, but the country has yet to be properly prospected and developed. Dubbo lies about 300 miles S.E., Menindie 300 miles S.W., Brewarrina 70 miles N.E., Walgett about 150 miles E., and Wentworth about 520 miles S.W., distant from Bourke. Between the two latter named places, however, steamers ply for a great portion of the year up the Darling, supplying this enormous district with stores, chiefly from South Australia, and taking produce in return. The diversion of the traffic by opening the Great Western Railway to the Port of Sydney has affected a great and beneficial change in the commerce of Fort Bourke. The river abounds with choice fish and innumerable wild fowl are found in numbers on the vast plains of the district. Bourke was proclaimed a municipal district in 1878 under the Municipalities Act, and is governed by eight aldermen and a mayor. Quarter sessions and district courts are held here periodically. The population is about 3,500.

BOURKE ISLAND (*Co. Cumberland*), a small rocky islet lying in Long Cove, about three quarters of a mile S.W. from the Parramatta River.

BOURKE TOWN (*Co. Cumberland*), a rural village selected on the Five Dock Road, in the parish of Concord, and is a fruit and vegetable producing district. It is 3 miles N. of Ashfield, and 9 miles W. from Sydney.

BOW (*Co. Brisbane*), a postal receiving-office, 235 miles N. of Sydney, with mail therefrom three days a week. The nearest railway station is Muswellbrook, 57 miles on the northern line.

BOWAN PARK (*Co. Ashburnham*), a post-office, 227 miles W. of Sydney, with mail three days weekly. The nearest railway station is Borenore, 22 miles on the western line.

BOWAN CREEK (*Co. Ashburnham*), a tributary of Bourimble Creek, rising in the broken country W. of the Canobolas.

BOWBOWRING CREEK (*Co. Cumberland*), a small tributary of the Bunbury Curran Creek, rising near the township of Narellan.

BOWENFELLS (*Co. Cook*), a postal village, 97 miles W. of Sydney, with daily mail, money-order and telegraph offices, and Government savings bank. A railway station on the western line, situated at an elevation of 2,921 feet above sea-level, and is within 4 miles of the Bowenfells station. The surrounding country is exceedingly mountainous and rugged.

BOWEN'S CREEK (*Co. Cook*), a tributary or branch of the Wollangambi Creek, rising in Mount Tomah.

BOWEN'S ISLAND (*Co. St. Vincent*), a small sandy patch lying at the entrance of Jervis Bay, 20 miles S. of Nowra.

BOWLING ALLEY POINT (*Co. Parry*), postal and mining township, 316 miles N. of Sydney, with mail three times a week. The nearest railway station is Tamworth, on the northern line. Situated on the Peel River, 7 miles S. of the township of Nundle. The banks of the Peel River are fertile alluvial flats, and highly cultivated, and to the W. extend large pastoral plains.

BOWMAN (*Co. Gloucester*), a township. 177 miles N. of Sydney, on the Bowman River, a tributary of the Manning River.

BOWMAN (*Co. Gloucester*), a village to the N. of Sydney. The nearest railway station is Hexham, on the northern line.

BOWMAN'S RIVER (*Co. Gloucester*). [*See* "RIVERS."]

BOWNA (*Co. Goulburn*), a postal village, 398 miles S. of Sydney, with daily mail, money-order and telegraph offices. The grape-vine and tobacco are extensively cultivated in the district.

BOWNA CREEK (*Co. Goulburn*), a creek rising in the eastern slope joining the western slope of the boundary of the county of Goulburn, and falls into the river Murray, about 10 miles E. of Albury.

BOWNING (*Co. Harden*), a postal village, 194 miles to the S. of Sydney, with daily mail, money-order and telegraph offices, and Government savings bank. A railway station on the southern line, about 4 miles N.W. of Yass, situated on the Bowning Creek, between Burrowa and Yass Plains.

BOWNING CREEK (*Co. Harden*), a northern tributary of the Yass River, falling into that river after a southern course of about 12 miles. It crosses the Yass and Gundagai road, at the township of Bowning.

BOWNING HILL (*Co. Harden*), a hill of some eminence overhanging the town of Bowning on the S.E. side. This hill is a bold round elevation, 7 miles distant from Yass.

BOWRAL (*Co. Camden*), a postal village in the parishes of Mittagong and Berrima, 80 miles S. of Sydney, with daily mail, money-order and telegraph offices. and Government savings bank. A railway station on the southern line, about 3 miles from Mittagong. Bowral was incorporated a municipal district in 1886, with eight aldermen and a mayor. The population is about 8,000.

BOWRAVILLE (*Co. Raleigh*), a postal village, 349 miles N. of Sydney, with mail three times a week, money-order and telegraph offices. The nearest railway station is Hexham, on the northern line.

BOXRIDGE (*Co. Wellington*), a post-office, 180 miles W. of Sydney, with mail twice a week. The nearest railway-station is Bathurst, 24 miles, on the western line.

BOYD, a county in the Central Division of the Colony. [*See* "COUNTIES."]

BOYD RIVER (*Co. Gresham*). [*See* "RIVERS."]

BOYD, OR LITTLE RIVER GOLD-FIELD (*Co. Gresham*), commencing on the left bank of the Boyd, or Little River, at a point half-a-mile easterly from Winter Vale House. The eastern extension thereof is situated at the junction of the Boyd or Little River with the Nymboi River.

BOYD'S CREEK (*Co. Gresham*). a small tributary of the Boyd River, falling into it near its junction with the Nymboi River.

BRACE MOUNT (*Co. Phillip*), a lofty detached mountain, about 2 miles E. of Dabee.

BRADLEY'S HEAD (*Co. Cumberland*), native name Burroggy, a bold narrow promontory of high land, standing out more than half a mile from the mainland, on the northern shore of Port Jackson, opposite Double Bay.

BRAEFIELD (*Co. Buckland*), a railway station on the northern line, 232 miles N. of Sydney.

BRAIDWOOD (*Co. St. Vincent*), is an important postal town, 189 miles S. of Sydney, with daily mail, money-order and telegraph offices, Government savings bank, and delivery by letter-carrier. Courts of quarter sessions and district courts are held here periodically. The nearest railway station is Tarago, on the Goulburn line. Situated on the Tillimatong Creek, the Shoalhaven River being 5 miles distant at the nearest point. The district is both agricultural and pastoral, gold-mining, chiefly alluvial, being also carried on to a great extent in the neighbourhood. The surrounding country is undulating, and consists of a fine agricultural district, the soil being especially suited to the growth of wheat. Braidwood is a flourishing town doing a large business, it being the principal town in the southern gold-field district, and supplying the whole of the surrounding country with stores.

BRAIDWOOD AND BROULEE, an incorporated district in the county of St. Vincent, and embraces the greater portion of that county, and the east portion of the county of Murray.

BRAMAH CREEK (*Co. King*), a western tributary of the upper part of the Lachlan River, rising in the N.E. of Burrowa.

BRANCH CREEK (*Co. Brisbane*), a western tributary or head of the Hunter River.

BRANXTON (*Co. Durham*), a postal village, 110 miles to the N. of Sydney, with daily mail, money-order and telegraph offices, Government savings bank, a railway station on the northern line. Situated on the Anvil and Black Creeks, the Hunter River flowing within 4 miles S., and the Tanjorin mountain standing 7 miles distant in the same direction. Branxton is principally an agricultural district; being, however, within a coal-field, mining is extensively carried on at Anvil Creek, the coal obtained at the mines there being amongst the best in the Colony.

BRASFORT (*Co. Cook*), a proclaimed village on the S. of the Great Western Railway.

BRASFORT (*Co. Cook*), to the W. of Sydney, on Cox's River, and to the S. of the western line of railway.

BRASS WATER (*Co. Gloucester*), a noble sheet of water at the head of the Myall River, above Port Stephen.

BRASSI (*Co. Townsend*), a proclaimed village near Deniliquin.

BRASSIL CREEK (*Co. Murray*), a small tributary of the Murrumbidgee River, rising in the S.E. part of Yass Plains.

BRAWLIN (*Co. Harden*), a postal town, 262 miles S. of Sydney, with daily mail. A station on the southern line.

BREAD AND BUTTER FLAT CREEK (*Co. Roxburgh*), a small tributary of the Clear Creek, rising in the Limekilns Hill.

BREAD AND BUTTER FLAT (*Co. Roxburgh*), an auriferous flat, forming part of the Cheshire Creek gold-fields, and lying south-west of the Limekilns.

BREADALBANE (*Co. Argyle*), a postal village, 149 miles S. of Sydney, with daily mail, telegraph and money-order offices, and Government savings bank; railway station on the southern line. The district is agricultural and pastoral, and lies within 15 miles of the Currawang copper-mines.

BREADALBANE PLAINS (*Co. Argyle*), a tract of fine undulating country lying in the western part of the county and to the N. of Lake George. The surrounding country is flat and elevated, and is well known as the Breadalbane Plains.

BREAKFAST CREEK (*Co. Georgiana*), a small drainage creek, flowing into the scrubby swamp formed by the overflow of the lower part of the Mulgowrie Creek.

BREAKFAST CREEK (*Co. Northumberland*), a small northern tributary of the lower end of the Hawkesbury River.

BREDBO (*Co. Beresford*), a postal receiving-office, 230 miles S. of Sydney, with daily mail. A railway station on the Goulburn and Cooma line.

BREDBO RIVER (*Co. Beresford*). [See "Rivers."]

BREEBONG (*Co. Gowen*), a township to the W. of Sydney, 98 miles, from Mudgee, on the western line.

BREEKIN MOUNT (*Co. Durham*), a high hill, lying to the S.E. of Gresford at a distance of 4 miles.

BREEZA (*Co. Buckland*), a postal town, with railway station on northern line, 268 miles N. of Sydney, with daily mail, money-order and telegraph offices, situated on the Mooki or Corradilly River, the Breeza mountain lying immediately W., and within the township reserve of 9 square miles. The district is almost entirely pastoral.

BRELSFORD (*Co. Fitzroy*), a proclaimed village, on the border of Raleigh and Fitzroy.

BRENDA (*Co. Culgoa*), a settlement on the N. bank of the Culgoa River, close to the Queensland boundary. The nearest railway station is Byrock, 130 miles on the western line.

BRENDA (*Co. Clarence*), a postal receiving-office, 556 miles N. of Sydney, with mail once a week. A small agricultural village in the Clarence River district.

BREWARRINA (*Co. Clyde*), a postal town, 527 miles W. of Sydney, with mail three days a week, money-order and telegraph offices, and Government savings bank. The nearest railway station is Byrock, 75 miles on the western line. Situate on the Darling River, a few miles from the township of Bourke.

BREWONGLE (*Co. Westmoreland*), a postal town, 135 miles W. of Sydney, with telegraph office, and a daily mail. A railway station on the western line.

BRIDGEMAN (*Co. Northumberland*), a postal village, 133 miles N. of Sydney, with mail twice a week. The nearest railway station is Singleton, 10 miles, on northern line.

BRIGALOW CREEK (*Co. White*), is a stream flowing from the S. through fine rich pastoral country into the Namoi River, about 5 miles N.W. of Narrabri.

BRINDABELLA (*Co. Murray*), a postal village, 239 miles S. of Sydney, with mail twice a week. The nearest railway station is Queanbeyan, 44 miles, on the Goulburn and Cooma line.

BRINDINGABBA (*Co. Irrara*), a township in the county, on the Queensland border.

BRINGAGEE (*Co. Cooper*), a postal receiving-office, 404 miles S. of Sydney, with mail five times a week. A railway station on Junee Junction line.

BRINGELLY (*Co. Cumberland*), a postal village, 40 miles S. of Sydney, with daily mail, with money-order office. Nearest railway station is Liverpool, 15 miles, on southern line, situated at the Bringelly cross roads, on the Great Southern Road, between Penrith and Camden. The Nepean River flows about 5 miles W., and South Creek about 2 miles E. The district is principally agricultural, consisting mainly of dairy and cultivation farms. There is also some fine pastoral country in the district. The surrounding country is undulating, well grassed and timbered.

BRISBANE, a county in the Eastern Division of the Colony. [*See* "COUNTIES."]

BRISBANE VALLEY (*Co. Westmoreland*), the name of an alluvial diggings, about 7 miles W. of the township of Oberon.

BRISBANE VALLEY CREEK (*Co. Westmoreland*), a small eastern tributary of the Stony Creek, flowing along the Brisbane Valley.

BRISBANE VALLEY AND NATIVE DOG CREEK GOLD-FIELDS (*Cos. of Bathurst, Georgiana, and Westmoreland*), situated on Campbell's River, the Macquarie and the Fish Rivers. Proclaimed 31st August, 1865.

BRISBANE WATER (*Co. Northumberland*), an inlet of the sea forming a fine harbour, and being the N. arm of Broken Bay. The navigation is impeded by several small islands, the principal of which is known as Mangrove Island. The township of Gosford is situated at the northern extremity of the harbour of Brisbane Water.

BROAD MEADOW (*Co. Northumberland*), a village, 99 miles N. of Sydney. A railway station on the Sydney and Newcastle line.

BROADWATER (*Co. Clarence*), a postal village, 342 miles N. of Sydney, with mail per Clarence steamers, money-order, telegraph offices, and Government savings bank. An expansion of the debouchure into the Clarence River near the towns of Ashby and Maclean, and is in the form of a large lake, and being studded with islets, gives a picturesque aspect to the scenery.

BROADWATER (*Co. Gloucester*), an expansion of the Myall River, forming the S. portion of the sheet of water known as the Myall Lake.

BROADWATER, THE (*Co. Northumberland*), the name applied to Brisbane Water Harbour, and also to Clocides Bay.

BROCKLEHURST (*Co. Lincoln*), a postal village, 286 miles to the W. of Sydney, with mail three times a week. The nearest railway station is Dubbo, 5 miles, on western line.

BROCKLEY (*Co. Clarke*), a postal receiving-office, 399 miles N. of Sydney, with mail therefrom once a week.

BROGAN'S CREEK (*Co. Roxburgh*), a rural hamlet, 141 miles W. of Sydney. A railway station on the western line.

BROGDEN MOUNT (*Co. Cooper*), a lofty solitary mountain, on the Mirool Creek, to the N. of the Murrumbidgee River, in the Lachlan district, On 6th June, 1816, Mr. Cunningham, the botanist and explorer, planted some acorns, peach-stones, and quince-seeds, being the anniversary of the King's Birthday.

BROGO (*Co. Auckland*), a postal village, 246 miles S. of Sydney, with mail daily. The nearest railway station, is Cooma, 84 miles, on Cooma line.

BROGO RIVER (*Co. Auckland*). [*See* "RIVERS."]

BROKE (*Co. Northumberland*), a postal village, 161 miles N. of Sydney, with daily mail, money-order and telegraph offices. The nearest railway station is Singleton, on northern line, situated on the Wollombi Brook or Cockfighters' Creek, the Yellow Rock Mountain being about 2 miles distant. The district is an agricultural and pastoral one.

BROKEN BAGHO (*Co. Macquarie*), a mountain of considerable elevation to the S.E. of the hamlet of Huntingdon, and on the banks of the Hastings River, about 16 miles from its mouth.

BROKEN BAY (*Co. Cumberland and Northumberland*), is the estuary of the Hawkesbury River, and may be said to extend in a westerly direction for about 14 miles. It was discovered by Captain Cook, and was afterwards explored by Governor Phillip, in March, 1788, when Pittwater was first discovered. Broken Bay is a fine wide harbour, rendered comparatively useless, however, by a sand-bar stretching across its mouth. This bay lies 16 miles to the northward of Port Jackson, and is easily made out when coming from the southward, Barranjuey Head being a penisular head, 310 feet above sea-level. The entrance to the bay is about 2 miles wide, between Barranjuey and Hawke Heads, both of which may be approached within ½ a mile. There are several coves in Pittwater where vessels may conveniently lighten and careen.

BROKEN DAM (*Co. Wynyard*), a postal receiving-office, 359 miles S. of Sydney, with mail twice a week.

BROKEN HILL (*Co. Yancowinnia*), a postal town, in the parishes of Alma, Soudan, Nadbuck, Picton, and Balaira, 941 miles W. of Sydney, with mail daily; money-order and telegraph offices, Government savings bank. The nearest railway station is Hay, 425 miles, on the south-western line. Broken Hill was incorporated a municipal district in 1888, with eleven aldermen and a mayor, sittings of the supreme court, quarter sessions, and district courts, are held here periodically. The population is about 16,000. The great silver-fields are in this county.

BROKEN POT CREEK (*The Gwydir*), a small arm of the Moom Creek, draining swampy land to the W. of Burrandon.

BROLGON (*Co. Ashburnham*), a fine stream flowing S.W. through the Brolgon Plains into the Goobung Creek.

BROMBEE (*Co. Phillip*), a postal receiving-office, 163 miles W. of Sydney. Mail six days a week.

BRONGONG CREEK (*Co. Urana*), a creek tributary to the Urana Creek, rising in Mount Galore, flowing through flat, swampy, pastoral country.

BRONTE (*Co. Argyle*), a postal receiving-office, 167 miles S. of Sydney, with mail three times a week.

BROOKFIELD (*Co. Durham*), a postal village, 122 miles N. of Sydney, with mail three days a week. The nearest railway station is Morpeth on northern line, situated on the Williams River, 3 miles N.W. of the Wallarobba Hill, and midway between Clarencetown and Dungog.

BROOKLYN (*Co. Cumberland*), a post-office, 36 miles N. of Sydney, with daily mail, telegraph and money-order offices.

BROOK'S CREEK (*Co. Murray*), a small auriferous tributary of Shinglehouse Creek, rising on the W. of Lake George.

BROOKE'S FLAT (*Co. Northumberland*), an agricultural settlement, about 7 miles E. of East Maitland.

BROOKVALE (*Co. Cumberland*), a postal receiving-office, 9 miles S. of Sydney, with daily mail.

BROOMAN (*Co. St. Vincent*), a post-office, 175 miles S. of Sydney, with mail once a week.

BROTHERS, THE (*Co. Bathurst*). two small hills, on the road to Ophir, about 6 miles S.E. of the latter place.

BROTHERS, THE (*Co. Beresford*) are three lofty and conspicuous mountains, in the Monaro Range, at the head of the Cooma Back Creek, in the undulating plain country to the S. of Cooma, of which township The Brothers are about 8 miles S.

BROTHERS' CREEK (*Co. Beresford*), a small western tributary of the Cooma Creek, within the town boundary of Cooma.

BROTHERS' LAKE (*Co. Beresford*), a large water-hole in the hilly country to the S.W. of The Brothers' Mountain. It is supposed to be caused by springs from underneath the trap rock of the locality.

BROUGHTON (*Co. Cumberland*), a village, in the parish of Petersham, situated on the E. side of Long Cove, between Garryowen and Balmain Road, about 6 miles W. of Sydney, and 1 mile N. of Petersham.

BROUGHTON ISLES (*Co. Gloucester*) are a cluster of islands lying off the coast. The southern extremity of these Isles bears about N.E. 7 miles from Yacaba Head over Cabbage-tree Island.

BROUGHTON VILLAGE (*Co. Camden*), a postal village, 81 miles S. of Sydney, with daily mail. The nearest railway station is Moss Vale, on the southern line. It was incorporated a municipal district in 1871, and is governed by five aldermen and a mayor. The population is about 700.

BROUGHTON'S CREEK (*Co. Camden*), adjoins Broughton Village, and was incorporated a municipal district in 1878, with seven aldermen and a mayor. The population is about 1,400. Situated on Broughton's Creek, in the parishes of Broughton, Camberra, and Wallaya. The Shoalhaven River being about 6 miles S., and numerous small creeks flowing S.E. down the many ravines and gullies in the mountains into the creek. The locality is mountainous. The district is an agricultural one, but both coal and copper are to be found along the face of the mountains abundantly. Broughton's Creek is admitted by all who visit it to be one of the prettiest spots on the coast.

BROUGHTON'S CREEK (*Co. Camden*), a small northern tributary of the mouth of the Shoalhaven River, rising in the Cambewarra Range, and flowing in a S.W. direction, for about 10 miles through good cultivated land.

BROULEE (*Co. St. Vincent*), a small agricultural township, a few miles N. of Moringa, celebrated for the excellence of the potato grown there. Situated on the N.E. portion of the Monaro pastoral district, about 2 miles S. of Point Upright.

BROWNLOW HILL (*Co. Camden*), a postal village, 45 miles S. of Sydney, with mail three days a week. The nearest railway station is Camden, 5 miles, on southern line. An agricultural village, situated on the Nepean River, near the junction of Mount Hunter Creek, 5 miles N.W. from Camden, and 8 miles N.E. of the Oaks.

D

BROWN'S CREEK (*Co. Bathurst*), a small tributary of Perrier's Creek, rising in the parish of Culville. Also a small tributary or head of the Queen Charlotte Vale Creek, which is fed by the Back Creek.

BROWN'S CREEK (*Co. Bathurst*), a post-office, 178 miles W. of Sydney, with mail three days each week. The nearest railway station is Blayney, 6 miles, on western line.

BROWN'S MOUNTAIN (*Co. Beresford*), a small settlement, 310 miles S. of Sydney. The nearest railway station is Cooma, 50 miles, on the Goulburn and Cooma line.

BROWNSVILLE (*Co. Camden*), a post-office, 73 miles S. of Sydney, with daily mail. The nearest railway station is Dapto, 1 mile on the South Coast line.

BRUCEDALE (*Co. Wynyard*), a postal receiving-office, 315 miles S. of Sydney, with mail twice a week. The nearest railway station is Bomen, 1 mile, on southern line.

BRUNDAH CREEK (*Co. Monteagle*), a post-office, 295 miles S. of Sydney, with mail twice a week. The nearest railway station is Young, 46 miles, on southern line.

BRUNGLE (*Co. Buccleuch*), a post-office, 299 miles S. of Sydney, with mail twice a week. The nearest railway station is Gundagai, 19 miles, on southern line.

BRUNGLE CREEK (*Co. Buccleuch*), a small eastern tributary of the Tumut River, rising in the Wyangle hills, and flows N.W., about 12 miles past Kiley's Hill.

BRUNSWICK (*Co. Rous*), a postal town, 340 miles S. of Sydney, with mail, per Clarence and Richmond steamers; telegraph and money-order offices, and Government savings bank.

BRUNSWICK RIVER (*Co. Rous.*) [*See* "RIVERS."]

BRUSH GROVE (*Co. Clarence*), a postal village, 338 miles N. of Sydney, with mail, per steamers; money-order and telegraph offices, Government savings bank.

BRUSH ISLAND (*Co. St. Vincent*), a small rocky islet, to the N. of Kiola Point, about a mile from the land.

BRUSHY HILL (*Co. Brisbane*), a postal township, 188 miles to the N. of Sydney, with mail twice each week. The nearest railway station is Aberdeen, 7 miles on the northern line.

BRYAN'S GAP (*Co. Clive*), a post-office, 486 miles N. of Sydney, with mail twice each week.

BUBBAH-BUBBAH SWAMP (*Co. Northumberland*), a tract of flat swampy ground, near Stingaree Point, at the fall of the Dora Creek into Lake Macquarie.

BUBBERMORE CREEK (*Co. Narran*), a small tributary of the Birie River, flowing into it near the junction of that and the Culgoa River.

BUBURBA CREEK (*Co. Argyle*), a small tributary of the Windellama Creek

BUCCA BUCCA (*Co. Clarence*), a postal receiving-office, 398 miles N. of Sydney, with mail, per steamer, via Grafton.

BUCCAN PLAINS (*Co. Narromine*), a small tract of open pastoral country, on the Macquarie River, about 40 miles from Dubbo.

BUCCARUMBI (*Co. Gresham*), a township, 478 miles N. of Sydney, on the Nymboi River.

BUCCLEUCH, a county in the Eastern Division of the Colony. [*See* "COUNTIES."]

BUCHANAN (*Co. Northumberland*), a postal village, 123 miles N. of Sydney, with mail three days a week. The nearest railway station is East Maitland, 8 miles, on northern line.

BUCKENBOWRA CREEK (*Co. St. Vincent*) is a stream, rising near the township of Bolaro, and flowing into Bateman's Bay.

BUCKIMBE (*Co. Rankin*), a township, on the W. bank of the Darling River, below Killara.

BUCKIMBE (*Co. Rankin*), a township on the banks of the Darling, to the S. of Killara.

BUCKINBAR CREEK (*Co. Gordon*), an eastern tributary of the Little River.

BUCKINBAR REEF GOLD-FIELD (*Co. Gordon*), situated on Little River, above the confluence of Wandawandory Creek with that river.

BUCKLAND, a county partly in the Eastern and Central Divisions of the Colony. [*See* "COUNTIES."]

BUCKLEY'S CROSSING PLACE (*Co. Wallace*), a postal village, 291 miles S. of Sydney, with mail three days a week. The nearest railway station is Cooma, 30 miles, on the Goulburn and Cooma line. Situated on the Snowy River, near the junction of the Wullwye and Barnes' Creek, and is the only crossing over the Snowy River for several miles. It lies on the road from Cooma to Gippsland. The district is partly agricultural, but mostly pastoral.

BUDAWANG RANGE (*Co. St. Vincent*), a chain of elevated peaks, extending in a general N. and S. direction. The most prominent elevation is Mount Budawang, which attains a height of 3,800 feet above the sea-level.

BUDD LAKE (*Co. Narromine*), a lagoon, formed by the expansion of a western arm of the Macquarie River.

BUDGEE BUDGEE (*Co. Phillip*), a post-office, 201 miles W. of Sydney, with mail twice a week. The nearest railway station is Mudgee, 7 miles on western line.

BUDGINNIGI MOUNT (*Co. Goulburn*), a detached hill, in the parish of Yambla, 10 miles N. of Albury.

BUDJONG CREEK (*Co. Argyle*), a small tributary of the upper part of the Windellama Creek.

BUDY CREEK (*Co. Wellington*), a small tributary of the Waurdong Creek, in the Louisa Creek gold-field.

BUENA VISTA (*Co. Cumberland*), a post-office, on the Military Road, North Sydney, 5¼ miles N. of Sydney, with mail daily.

BUGGABUDDA (*Co. Ewenmar*), a township to the W. of Sydney, lying midway between the Macquarie and Castlereagh Rivers.

BUGGAMBIL MOUNT (*Co. Bourke*), a solitary hill, on the vast plain between the Lachlan and Murrumbidgee Rivers.

BUGGIL (*Co. Leichhardt*), a rural settlement, 398 miles W. of Sydney. The nearest railway station is Dubbo, 122 miles, on the western line.

BUGILBONE (*Co. Barradine*), a post-office, 422 miles N. of Sydney, with mail twice a week.

BUKKULLA (*Co. Arrawatta*), a post-office, 493 miles N. of Sydney, with mail twice a week. The nearest railway station is Glen Innes, 55 miles, on the northern line.

BULAHDELAH (*Co. Gloucester*), a postal town, 155 miles N. of Sydney, with mail three times a week. Money and telegraph offices, Government savings bank. The nearest railway station is Hexham, 47 miles, on the northern line.

BULBARARING LAKE (*Co. Northumberland*), a small lagoon or inlet of the sea, about 1 mile square, and having a sand-bank or island in its centre. The N. part of the lake is called Moore's Lagoon, and is about 2 miles E. of Kincumber.

BULEAWAY MOUNT (*Co. Leichhardt*), a lofty peak of the Warrabungle Range.

BULGA (*Co. Durham*), a postal town, 202 miles N. of Sydney, with mail three times a week. The nearest railway station is Singleton, 14 miles, on the northern line.

BULGANDRAMINE (*Co. Gordon*), a post-office, 287 miles W. of Sydney, with mail twice a week. The nearest railway station is Dubbo, 44 miles, on the western line.

BULGAR CREEK (*Co. Murray*), a small eastern tributary of the Upper Murrumbidgee River, flowing W. about 7 miles through undulating pastoral country.

BULGEROI (*Co. Nandewar*), a postal receiving-office, 410 miles N. of Sydney, with mail twice a week.

BULL PLAIN (*Co. Hume*), a post-office, 449 miles S. of Sydney, with mail once a week. The nearest railway station is Albury, 72 miles, on the southern line.

BULLA (*Co. Monteagle*), a proclaimed village to the N. of Young.

BULLA (*Co. Monteagle*), a township, 266 miles S. of Sydney, near Young, on the Murrumburrah and Blayney railway.

BULLABALKIT MOUNT (*Co. White*), a mountain in the district of Liverpool Plains, near the Namoi River. It consists principally of granular felspar and partly of concretionary porphyry, the concretions being mottled red and white.

BULLAGREEN (*Co. Gregory*), a postal receiving-office, 381 miles W. of Sydney, with mail twice a week.

BULLAHDELAH MOUNT (*Co. Gloucester*).—This mountain is situated about three-quarters of a mile E., and the Myall Lakes 6 miles W. by bush track, from the township of Bullahdelah.

BULLAMALITA CREEK (*Co. Argyle*), a southern tributary of the Wollondilly River, flowing in a northerly direction into the main stream, 8 miles S.W. of the township of Goulburn.

BULLANAMINS, one of the old districts of the county of Cumberland, bounded on the N. by the Sydney and Parramatta Road, from Iron Cove Creek to Blackwattle Swamp bridge; on the E. side by a S. line to Botany Bay; on the S. side by Cook's River; on the W. Liberty Plains district.

BULLAROORA (*Co. Leichhardt*), a township on the Marabo Creek, a tributary of the Castlereagh River, to the N. of Coonamble.

BULLATALE CREEK (*Co. Cadell*), a small creek flowing into the Edward River, near its junction with the Tuppal Creek, and about 3 miles S.E. of Deniliquin.

BULLENBOIG (*Co. Cooper*), a postal receiving-office, 339 miles S.W. of Sydney, with mail three times a week.

BULLENBUNG CREEK (*Co. Mitchell*), a southern tributary of the Murrumbidgee River, rising in the Doodlo Swamp. It is fed by the Yerong Creek, and is crossed by the telegraph line from Wagga Wagga to Deniliquin, near the junction of that creek with the main stream.

BULLENGARA (*Co. Macquarie*), a high solitary peak, lying on the S. bank of Wilson's River and to the S. of Rollins Plains. About 16 miles N.W. of Port Macquarie.

BULLER—A county in the Eastern Division of the Colony. [*See* "COUNTIES."]

BULLEWA (*Co. Jamison*), a stream rising in Mount Lindsay, in the Nundewar Range, and flowing S. through rich alluvial flats. It is fed by the Eula Creek, and falls into the Namoi River, about 8 miles S.E. of Narrabri.

BULLI (*Co. Camden*), a postal town, 39 miles S. of Sydney, with daily mail from Sydney, money-order and telegraph offices, and Government savings bank, a railway station on the Illawarra and South-coast line. It is a coal-mining district, large exportation of coal taking place from it.

BULLIAMY (*Co. Waradgery*), a township on the Murrumbidgee River, near its confluence with the Lachlan River, to the W. of Hay.

BULLOCK CREEK (*Co. Gresham*), a small southern tributary of the Aberfoyle River.

BULLOCK CREEK (*Co. Kennedy*), a small western tributary of the Bogan River, rising in flat sandy plains, and flowing N.E.

BULLOCK CREEK (*Co. Monteagle*), a small eastern tributary of the upper part of the Burrangong Creek.

BULLOCK HILL (*Co. Harden*), a rocky hill lying in a small group in the parish of Illalong, S.E. of the township of Binalong.

BULLOCK ISLAND (*Co. Northumberland*), a large Island on the S. side of the Hunter River, about a mile above the town of Newcastle and separated from the mainland by a narrow channel called Throsby's Creek. On the N.W. point of this Island is the quarantine ground for the port of Newcastle.

BULLONMONG (*Co. Wentworth*), a township on the E. bank of the Darling River, above the township of Wentworth.

BULL'S CAMP (*Co. Cook*), situated on the Great Western Road, 50 miles W. from Sydney. Bull's Camp derives its name from Captain Bull, having had his principal camp and residence there whilst in charge of a large convict gang making the road over the Blue Mountains to Bathurst. The camp is situated at an altitude of about 2,000 feet above sea-level.

BULL'S PEAK (*Co. Selwyn*), a high Peak in the Muniong Range, near the N. head of Tooma River, and about 20 miles N. of Mount Kosciusco. The surrounding country is very broken.

BULMAROO CREEK (*Co. Murray*), a fine stream rising in the western slope of the Australian Alps, and flowing N.W. about 20 miles through good pastoral country into the S.E. of Lake George.

BULPUNGA (*Co. Tara*), a township on the W. bank of the Ana branch of the Darling River.

BUMADERY (*Co. Camden*), a small agricultural settlement in the parish of the same name, situated on the N. bank of the Shoalhaven River.

BUMBERRA CREEK (*Co. Camden*), a small northern tributary of the Shoalhaven River, flowing through good cultivated land.

BUMBERRY (*Co. Ashburnham*), a post-office, 250 miles W. of Sydney, with mail daily. The nearest railway station is Molong, 34 miles, on the western line.

BUMBLE (*Co. Courallie*), a post-office, 390 miles N. of Sydney, with daily mail. The nearest railway station is Narrabri, 50 miles, on the north-western line.

BUMBO CREEK (*Co. Dampier*), a northern tributary of the Tuross River, flowing on the W. of Coila by a very tortuous course for about 50 miles into the main stream of Urobodalla

BUMBOLEE CREEK (*Co. Buccleuch*), an eastern tributary of the Tumut River, rising in Clear Hill, and flowing about 16 miles W. into the main stream, 2 miles N. of the township of Tumut.

BUMBURRA (*Co. Barrona*), a township on the Ana branch of the Paroo River.

BUN BUCKLEY CREEK (*Co. Bligh*), a small tributary of the Cudgegong River.

BUNABUCKBUCK SWAMP (*Co. Wynyard*), a long tract of swampy land on the banks of the Adelong Creek to the N.W. of the township.

BUNBURRY CURRAN CREEK (*Co. Cumberland*), a small western tributary of George's River.

BUNDANOON (*Co. Camden*), a postal town, 95 miles S. of Sydney, with daily mail, money-order and telegraph offices, and Government savings bank. A railway station on the southern line.

BUNDANOON CREEK (*Co. Camden*), a northern tributary of the Kangaroo, rising near the road from Berrima to Goulburn, about 20 miles S. of the former place.

BUNDARRA (*Co. Hardinge*), a postal town, 393 miles N. of Sydney, with mail four times a week, money-order and telegraph offices, and Government savings bank. The nearest railway station is Uralla, 45 miles, on the northern line. Situated on the Bundarra River and Clark's Creek, the Namoi and Macintyre Rivers being 30 miles S.

BUNDARRA RIVER (*Cos. Murchison and Hardinge*), the name of the upper part of the Gwydir River. During flood-time this river is frequently 150 yards wide and 40 feet deep.

BUNDELLA (*Co. Buckland*), a post-office, 296 miles N. of Sydney, with mail three days a week. The nearest railway station is Quirindi, 46 miles, on the northern line.

BUNDURE (*Co. Urana*), a railway station, 391 miles S.W. of Sydney, on the Junee and Jerilderie line.

BUNGA HEAD (*Co. Dampier*), a rocky promontory, standing boldly out into the sea, about 10 miles N. of the entrance to the Bega River.

BUNGALABEN MOUNT (*Co. Northumberland*), a peak in the Hunter Range, in the parish of Moruben, on the E. bank of the M'Donald River, and about 18 miles S.E. of Wollombi.

BUNGALAL CREEK (*Co. Harden*), a northern tributary of the Jugiong Creek, rising to the N. of Binalong, and flowing in a S.W. direction through that township. It is an agricultural district.

BUNGALEE CREEK (*Co. Camden*), a small northern tributary of the lower part of the Shoalhaven River, flowing through good cultivation country.

BUNGAMBRAWARTHA CREEK (*Co. Hume*), a small creek rising in the low ranges to the N. of Albury, and flowing in a northerly direction into a small swampy lake of the same name.

BUNGAMBRAWARTHA LAKE (*Co. Hume*), a small swampy lake to the N. of the Binalong Creek, near the crossing of the Bowna and Urana roads. It is fed by the creek of the same name, and its overflow falls into the Billabong Creek.

BUNGAMBRAWATHA CREEK (*Co. Goulburn*), a small creek rising in the Spring Hill and flowing S. through the township of Albury into the Murray River.

BUNGARBY *(Co. Wellesley)*, a postal receiving-office, 306 miles S. of Sydney, with mail once a week.

BUNGAWALBIN *(Co. Clarence)*, a postal receiving-office, 345 miles N. of Sydney, on the Clarence River. Mail six days a week by steamers to Harwood Island and Woodburn.

BUNGAWALBIN *(Co. Clarence)*, a postal receiving-office, 345 miles to the N. of Sydney, with mail twice a week per Clarence River steamers.

BUNGEE PEAK *(Co. Wellesley)*, a lofty peak, attaining the height of 3,000 feet above sea-level on the S. bank of the M'Laughlin River, about 20 miles S. of Nimitybelle.

BUNGENDORE *(Co. Murray)*, a postal village, 177 miles S. of Sydney, with daily mail. Money-order and telegraph offices, and Government savings bank. On the Cooma line of railway with station there. Situated on the Turalla Creek, 40 miles S.W. of Goulburn. The Gibraltar Mountain is 1 mile to the E. of Bungendore. Near to its summit is a cave of granite formation, said to have been the hiding place of the notorious bushranger Jackey-Jackey. Lake George is 4 miles N. The district is agricultural and pastoral.

BUNGINBAR CREEK *(Co. Richmond)*, a small northern tributary of the Clarence River, flowing through country suitable for agricultural pursuits.

BUNGONIA *(Co. Argyle)*, a postal town and money-order office, 120 miles S. of Sydney, with daily mail. The nearest railway station is Marulan, 12 miles, on the southern line. Situated on the Bungonia Creek, between Goulburn and Braidwood. There are four creeks flowing within a short distance of the town, viz., the Bungonia, Jacqua, Spring Pond, and Jerrara, all tributaries to the Shoalhaven River.

BUNGONIA CREEK *(Co. Argyle)*, a small tributary to the Jerrara Creek, flowing through the township of Bungonia.

BUNGOWANNAH *(Co. Goulburn)*, a post-office, 398 miles S. of Sydney, with mail twice a week. The nearest railway station is Albury, 10 miles, on the southern line.

BUNGWALL FLAT *(Co Gloucester)*, a post-office, 169 miles N. of Sydney, with mail three times a week, money-order and telegraph offices, and Government savings bank. The nearest railway station is Hexham, 67 miles, on the northern line.

BUNIANA CREEK *(Co. Argyle)*, a small tributary the Pejar Creek.

BUNJA MOUNT *(Co. Cooper)* a solitary hill on the vast plain between the Lachlan and Murrumbid e Rivers.

BUNNABY *(Co. Argyle)*, an gricultural settlement, situated about 8 miles N.E. of Taralga.

BUNNABY CREEK *(Co. Argyle)*, a mall stream, flowing from the W. into the Wollondilly River, in the north- n part of the country.

BUNNALONG SWAMP *(Co. Northumberland)*, a tract of swampy ground on the N. bank of the Dorah Creek, near Stingaree Point.

BUNNAN (*Co. Brisbane*), a post-office, 187 miles N. of Sydney, with mail three days a week. The nearest railway station is Scone, 20 miles, on the northern line.

BUNNUM PIC (*Co. Camden*), a remarkable point on the perpendicular cliff which trends Burragorong, between the Wollondilly and Nattai Rivers, 76 miles from Sydney.

BUNYAN (*Co. Beresford*), a post-office, 259 miles S. of Sydney, with daily mail therefrom. Situated on the Cooma Creek, about 4 miles E. of the Murrumbidgee. A railway station on the Goulburn and Cooma line.

BURAJA (*Co. Hume*), a proclaimed village in the county.

BURAMANGULA MOUNT (*Co. Lincoln*), a high hill, lying about 8 miles N.E. of the township of Wellington.

BURANGYLONG CREEK (*Co. Georgiana*), a northern tributary of Thompson's Creek, rising to the S.W. of Rockley, and flowing with the main stream near Bombah, on the Tuena gold-fields.

BURBONG (*Co. Murray*), a proclaimed village in the county.

BURBONG (*Co. Murray*), a proclaimed village, 188 miles S. of Sydney. A railway station on the Goulburn and Cooma line.

BURBURGATE (*Co. Nandewar*), a township on the banks of the Namoi River, to the N.E. of Gunnedah.

BURGAN BUNGY MOUNT (*Co. Bligh*), a peak to the N.W. of the confluence of the Macquarie and Cudgegong Rivers.

BURIMMA MOUNT (*Co. Wellesley*), a small hill on the road from Bombala to Catchcart.

BURKETOWN (*Co. Cumberland*), a village about 9 miles from Sydney, on the Parramatta Road, and within the municipal district of Five Dock, of which it forms part.

BURKE'S CREEK (*Co. Mitchell*). [*See* "PULLETOP CREEK."]

BURKE'S CREEK (*Co. St. Vincent*). [*See* "UPPER ARALUEN."]

BURMAGUEE HEAD (*Co. Dampier*), a rocky promontory, standing boldly into the sea. Situated about half-way between, or 20 miles distant from, the Bega and Tuross Rivers.

BURNERINGEE (*Co. Wentworth*), a township on the E. bank of the Ana branch of the Darling River, to the S. of Lake Milkenya.

BURNETT, a county in the Central Division of the Colony. [*See* "COUNTIES."]

BURNS (*Co. Yancowinna*), a proclaimed township, 850 miles to the W. of Sydney.

BURNS (*Co. Selwyn*), a rural settlement, 374 miles S. of Sydney, 65 miles from the Wagga Wagga railway station, on the southern line.

BURNS' LAKES (*Co. Wellesley*), a chain of small lakes in the bold undulating pastoral plains to the W. of the Comalong Creek, and S. of Mount Cooper.

BURNS' HILL (*Co. Wellesley*), a small peak about half a mile S. of the township of Bombala. The road to Gippsland passes under the W. of the hill.

BURNT YARDS (*Co. Wellington*), a postal receiving-office, 212 miles W. of Sydney, with mail twice a week. The nearest railway station is Carcoar, 8 miles on the southern line.

BURONONRY MOUNT (*Co. Roxburgh*), a peak in the Blue Mountain Range, about 4 miles S.E. of Dabee.

BURR CREEK (*Co. Tongowoko*), a stream rising in the S. of the Grey Range and flowing in a S.E. direction.

BURRA (*Co. Beresford*), a postal receiving-office, 239 miles S. of Sydney, with mail once a week.

BURRA BURRA CREEK (*Co. Georgiana*), a southern tributary of the upper part of the Abercrombie River, rising in the western slopes of the Australian Alps, flowing in a northerly direction.

BURRA BURRA LAKE (*Co. Argyle*), a small sheet of fine fresh water, to the W. of the Dividing Range, to the N. of Teralga, and about 16 miles S.E. of Boloug.

BURRA CREEK (*Co. Dampier*), a small southern tributary of the Moruya River, flowing into it about 12 miles from its mouth.

BURRA CREEK (*Co. Murray*), a western tributary of the Queanbeyan River, flowing N.E. through a flat pastoral country, between Colinton and Queanbeyan.

BURRA CREEK (*Co. Selwyn*), a tributary of the Tumberumba Creek, rising in Mane's Range, and flowing S.W. into Tumberumba Creek.

BURRA CREEK GOLD-FIELD (*Co. Selwyn*), is a south-easterly extension of the Tumbarumba Creek gold-field, at Burra Creek. 72 square miles.

BURRABA (*Co. Wellington*), a southern tributary of Campbell's Creek, falling into it at the township of Windeyer, and flowing to the E. of the Louisa Creek gold-fields. It is fed by the Nuggetty Gully and Kingarragan Creeks.

BURRADOO (*Co. Camden*), a post-office, 81 miles S. of Sydney, with a daily mail. A railway station on the southern line.

BURRADULLA CREEK (*Co. Wellington*), a tributary of the Cudgegong Creek, flowing into it near the township of Mudgee.

BURRAGA (*Co. Georgiana*), a postal village, 183 miles W. of Sydney, with mail three days a week, money-order office, and Government savings bank. The nearest railway station is George's Plains, 46 miles, on western line.

BURRAGATE (*Co. Auckland*), a proclaimed village, to the N. of Eden.

BURRAGATE (*Co. Auckland*), a township, 350 miles S. of Sydney, to the S. of Pambula.

BURRAGORANG (*Co. Camden*), a postal village, 54 miles S. of Sydney, with mail three days a week. The nearest railway station is Picton, 30 miles on the southern line. The district is entirely an agricultural one. In the neighbourhood of Burragorang are two villages known as The Oaks and Vanderville. The Wollondilly flows through the township.

BURRAGORANG VALLEY (*Co. Camden*), a long, narrow valley between the Merrigong Range and the Blue Mountains, with only one pass into it, and that a very precipitous one. It runs N. and S. along the banks of the Warragamba River, 58 miles from Sydney. The scenery in this valley is of the most magnificent character.

BURRAGURRA MOUNT (*Co. Northumberland*), a peak in the Hunter Range, in the parish of Lockyer, and about 14 miles S.S.W. of Wollombi.

BURRALOW CREEK (*Co. Cook*), a small northern tributary of the Grose River.

BURRAM BURRAM CAVE (*Co. Bligh*), a limestone chasm in the earth, situated on the hill of the same name, on the N. bank of the Macquarie River, near the confluence of the Dreel Creek.

BURRAM BURRAM MOUNT (*Co. Bland*), a solitary hill lying in the vast plain between the Lachlan and Macquarie Rivers.

BURRAM BURRAM MOUNT (*Co. Bligh*), a high solitary mountain on the N. bank of the Macquarie River, and 4 miles E. of Wellington.

BURRAMBURRANGAL MOUNT (*Co. Bathurst*), a lofty hill, about 15 miles west of Carcoar.

BURRAMUNDARA MOUNTAIN (*Co. Wallace.*) [*See* "BERRIMA RANGE."]

BURRAMUNGEE MOUNT (*Co. Wallace*). [*See* "RAM'S HEAD."]

BURRAN-BURRAN CAVE (*Co. Wellington*), a remarkable cavern in the limestone on the Gillory Creek. Its principal chamber is about 720 feet in length, 130 feet wide, and 100 feet in the centre.

BURRANGONG CREEK (*Co. Monteagle*), an auriferous stream rising in the Burrangong gold-fields, to the S. of the township of Young, and flowing N. and N.W. through that place into a large swamp, which drains into the Yeo Yeo Creek.

BURRANGONG GOLD-FIELD (*Co. Harden and Monteagle*), is an alluvial digging on the S.W. gold-fields, and on the Burrangong Creek, to the N.E of the township of Young.

BURRANGUBUGGE CREEK (*Co. Wallace*), a small mountain creek at the head of the Snowy River.

BURRAWANG (*Co. Camden*), a postal village, 96 miles S. of Sydney, with daily mail, money-order and telegraph offices, and Government savings bank. The nearest railway station is Moss Vale, 10 miles, on the southern line. The district is very mountainous, and combined with innumerable waterfalls, gives a charm almost indescribable. The principal mountains are the Barrangarry and the Kangaroo, about 2,500 feet above the sea-level. These mountains run from E. to W., and form a semi-circular precipitous range of rocks dividing this table-land from the Illawarra district. The various creeks and rivers running S. and W. unite and form several waterfalls. The district is well watered, and the fertility of the soil produces every kind of cereals and fruits in abundance.

BURRAWERRE POINT (*Co. St. Vincent*), a rocky promontory, running boldly out into the sea, and forming the S. head of the entrance to Bateman's Bay.

BURRAWINDRA CREEK (*Co. King*), a southern tributary of the Crookwell River, rising in Mount Windnella.

BURRENDONG (*Co. Wellington*), a postal village, 256 miles W. of Sydney, with mail three times a week. The nearest railway station is Stuart Town, 20 miles, on the western line. Situated on the Macquarie River, Oaky, Spring, and Devil's Hole Creeks, all running into that river, which is surrounded by a chain of mountains known as the Barrendong Ranges.

BURRIE (*Co. Wentworth*), a township on the W. bank of the Darling River, to the N. of Wentworth.

BURRIER (*Co. St. Vincent*), a postal village, 142 miles S. of Sydney, with mail twice a week. The nearest railway station is Moss Vale, 40 miles on the southern line, situated on the Shoalhaven River. The district is entirely agricultural; gold has, however, been found in the neighbourhood. The nearest place is Nowra, about 13 miles east.

BURRIL LAKE (*Co. St. Vincent*), a beautiful expanse of salt water, about 7 miles long and 1 mile broad, and is fed on its W. side by the Burril Creek. Situated about 2½ miles S. of Ulladulla.

BURRILL (*Co. St. Vincent*), an agricultural settlement near the coast, about 3 miles S. of Ulladulla.

BURRILL CREEK (*Co. Gloucester*), a small tributary of the Manning River. It is fed by several local creeks.

BURRILL CREEK (*Co. Narramine*), is a small southern tributary of the Ten-mile Creek, flowing N.W. across the road from Obley and Bexcourt to Condoblin.

BURRILL CREEK (*Co. St. Vincent*), a small creek flowing into the Burrill Lake at its head.

BURRIMBUCO MOUNT (*Co. Wellesley*), a peak of the S. coast range, to the S.E. of Bombala, about 10 miles distant.

BURRINGBAR (*Co. Rous*), a postal receiving-office, to the N. of Sydney, with mail twice a week, per Clarence and Richmond River steamers.

BURROWA (*Co. King*), a postal town, 226 miles S. of Sydney, with daily mail, money-order, and telegraph offices, and Government savings bank. The district is a rich pastoral and agricultural one, situated on the Burrowa River, in the parishes of Boorowa, Gunnary, Getyngalong, and Murrungal. There are two beautiful volcanic hills near the township, Big and Little Carramumbola. The nearest railway station is Binalong, 16 miles, on the southern line. Burrowa was incorporated a municipal district in 1888, and is governed by five aldermen and a mayor. Quarter sessions and districts courts are held here periodically. The population is about 3,000.

BURROWA FLAT CREEK (*Co. Harden*), a small tributary of the head of the Spring Creek, in the parish of Nurung, flowing S.W.

BURROWA PLAINS (*Co. King*), a tract of fine pastoral country, between the Burrowa River on the W. and the Pudman Creek on the E.

BURROWA RIVER (*Co. Monteagle, Harden, and King*). [*See* "RIVERS."]

BURRUMBUTTOCK (*Co. Goulburn*), a postal village, 406 miles S. of Sydney, with mail three times a week. The nearest railway station is Albury, 18 miles on the southern line.

BURRUNDULLA (*Co. Phillip*), an agricultural settlement to the E. of the township of Mudgee, distant about 3 miles.

BURSTEMS (*Co. Lincoln*), a rural settlement, 288 miles W. of Sydney, and 10 miles from Dubbo, the nearest railway station on the western line.

BURWOOD (*Co. Cumberland*), a suburban post-office, with money-order and telegraph offices, Government savings bank, and delivery twice a a day by letter-carrier. A pleasant roadside village and railway station in the parish of Concord, about 7 miles westward of the city, of which it forms one of the most attractive suburbs. Situated about 1 mile S. of the Parramatta River, and 2 miles from the villages of Ashfield and Enfield, and half a mile from the village of Longbottom. There is a large population in Burwood, and very many fine residences have been erected there. Burwood was incorporated a borough in 1874, under the Municipalities Act, and is governed by eight aldermen and a mayor. The population is about 5,550.

BURWOOD (*Co. Northumberland*), a village near Hexham, on the road and railway between Newcastle and Maitland.

BUSHRANGERS' HILL (*Co. Westmoreland*), a solitary peak on the road from Bathurst to Goulburn, about 5 miles N. of Swatchfield.

BUSHRANGERS' HILL (*Co. Gordon*), a rugged mountain on the E. bank of the Little River, about 10 miles W. of Wellington.

BUTCHERS' BLOCK (*Co. Cumberland*), a large mass of sandstone on the Lane Cove River, near Onion's Point.

BUTCHERS' CREEK (*Co. Westmoreland*), a tributary of Cox's River, rising in Mount Werong, and flowing N.W. through rugged country.

BUTHEROO CREEK (*Co. Napier*), an eastern tributary of the upper part of the Castlereagh River, rising in the Boogamurra Plains, flowing W. past the village of Buthero.

BUTLER'S CREEK (*Co. Auckland*), a small northern tributary of the Bemboka River.

BUTLER'S FALLS (*Co. Gordon*), the name given to a fall on the Macquarie River, about 3 miles S.E. of Dubbo.

BUTTERWICK (*Co. Durham*), an agricultural settlement, about 8 miles distant from Maitland.

BYANGUN (*Co. Rous*), a postal receiving-office, 400 miles N. of Sydney, mail by Clarence and Richmond River steamers.

BYE (*Co. Cowper*), a proclaimed village in this county.

BYGGOLEER MOUNT (*Co. Darling*), a solitary hill on the vast plains between the Lachlan and Murrumbidgee Rivers, and a few miles S. of Condobolin.

BYGOO MOUNT (*Co. Cooper*), a hill between the Lachlan and Murrumbidgee Rivers.

BYJERKEM'S WATERHOLE (*Co. Farnell*), a large waterhole on the border of South Australia.

BYLONG (*Co. Phillip*), a postal village, 186 miles W. of Sydney, with mail three days a week. Nearest railway station is Rylstone, 37 miles on the western line.

BYLONG CREEK (*Co. Phillip*), a southern tributary of the Goulburn River, flowing in a northerly direction along the W. side of the road from Dabee to Boggabri.

BYNG (*Co. Bathurst*), a postal town, 188 miles W. of Sydney, with mail three times a week. The nearest railway station is Millthorpe, 10 miles on the western line.

BYNG CREEK (*Co. Bathurst*), a western tributary of the upper part of Lewis' Ponds, and flowing into the main stream at the township of Byng.

BYRNE'S CREEK (*Co. Georgiana*), a small eastern tributary of the Burongylong Creek, draining the country to the north of the Tuena gold-fields.

BYRNE'S CREEK (*Co. Ashburnham*), a stream flowing through good pastoral country to the N.W. of Orange and the Nangar and Eugowra Valley.

BYROCK (*Co. Cowper*), a postal village, 455 miles W. of Sydney, with daily mail, money-order and telegraph offices, Government savings bank. A railway station on the western line.

BYRON (*Co. Arrawatta*), a Government township, situated about 140 miles N.W. of the township of Inverell.

BYRON BAY (*Co. Rous*), a postal village, 405 miles N. of Sydney, with telegraph office, and mails per Clarence and Richmond River steamers and Tweed River steamers.

BYRON CAPE BAY (*Co. Rous*), situated about a mile to the W. of Cape Byron the land is low, and taking a S.W. bend forms a bay, in which coasters and small vessels may find shelter from the N.W., S., and S.W. gales, and in some measure protected from easterly gales by a ledge of rocks to the N. from the cape.

BYRON CAPE (*Co. Rous*), a rocky promontory, being the easternmost point of Australia, projecting about 2 miles from the lowland, and visible from 24 to 27 miles. The position of the cape is in lat. 28° 38′ S., long. 153° 38′ E.

BYRON CREEK (*Co. Arrawatta*), a western tributary of the Macintyre River, flowing through the fertile Byron Plains.

BYRON MOUNT (*Co. Murray*), a lofty peak in the ranges lying to the W. of Lake George, and on the E. bank of M'Laughlin's Creek.

BYRON PLAINS (*Co. Arrawatta*), the name given to a tract of good pastoral land, to the N.W. of the township of Byron, and on the W. bank of the Macintyre River.

# C

CABBAGE-TREE (*Co. Durham*), an agricultural settlement, about 9 miles N. of Raymond Terrace.

CABBAGE-TREE BAY (*Co. Cumberland*), a securely sheltered bay at the S. end of Manly Beach Bay and fully exposed to the heavy ground swell of the ocean. It lies between the high rocky cliffs about a mile to the North Head and the Curl Curl Head. The southern part of the bay is sheltered by a spur of rocky land and is available for boats.

CABBAGE-TREE HARBOUR (*Co. Northumberland*), an open sandy bight, lying between Bungaree Head on the S. and the Pier Head on the N., and between the opening to the Tuggerah Beach Lake and Lake Macquarie.

CABBAGE-TREE ISLAND (*Co. Durham*), off the entrance to Port Stephens. There are three islands; the northernmost and largest, named Cabbage-Tree Island, lies at about 1 mile to the N.E. of Yacaaba Head and shelters Providence Bay. The other two islands are bare rocks, the S. and largest of which is called by the natives Boondelbah.

CABLE'S SIDING (*Co. Camden*), a railway station, 102 miles S. of Sydney, on southern line.

CABRAMATTA (*Co. Cumberland*), a postal village, 20 miles S. of Sydney, with mail therefrom twice daily, money-order and telegraph offices, and Government savings bank. A railway station on the southern line.

CABRAMATTA CREEK (*Co. Cumberland*), a western tributary of George's Creek, rising near the village of Cabramatta.

CADELL, a county in the Central Division of the Colony. [*See* "COUNTIES."]

CADIA (*Co. Bathurst*), a postal village, 192 miles to the W. of Bathurst, with mail three times a week, and money-order office. The nearest railway station is Millthorpe, 10 miles, on western line, situated on the Cadiangullong Rivulet, and on an E. spur of the Canobolas Mountains, the watershed draining into the Belubula River.

CADIANGULLONG (*Co. Bathurst*), a northern tributary of the Belubula Creek, rising in the S. of the Canobolas cluster of hills, flowing S. through good agricultural and pastoral land.

CADIGAL CREEK (*Co. Wallace*), a small southern tributary of the Murrumbidgee River, flowing in the Dry Plains past the W. of Bolairs Hill.

CAIDMURRA (*Co. Benarba*), a township on the E. bank of the Barwon River, on the Queensland border.

CAIRA, a county partly in the Central and Western Divisions of the Colony. [*See* "COUNTIES."]

CAIRNCROP MOUNT (*Co. Macquarie*), a point on the Hastings Range, between the Hastings and Wilson Rivers, and about 20 miles E.N.E. of Port Macquarie.

CALATHORA CREEK (*Co. Jamison*), a small drainage creek, flowing S.W. into the Namoi River, and crossing the Narrabri and Moree Road.

CALEWATTA RIVER (*Warrego District*), one of the native names of the river Darling.

CALEY'S REPULSE (*Co. Cook*), a spot in the Blue Mountains, where the explorer Caley turned back disheartened at his failure in crossing the range. It is marked by a cairn of stones, which he erected at that place.

CALGA (*Co. Leichhardt*), a township to the S.E. of Coonamble, to the N.W. of Sydney.

CALLAN PARK (*Co. Cumberland*), is within the municipal district of Leichhardt. The principal lunatic asylum of the Colony is here located.

CALLAWAROI (*Co. Narran*), a township on the E. bank of the Barwon River, to the N.W. of Sydney.

CALOOLA (*Co. Bathurst*), a postal village, 170 miles, W. of Sydney, with mail three days weekly. The nearest railway station is Newbridge, 6 miles, on western line, situated on the Caloola Creek, the Three Brothers Mountains being situated about 5 miles S.W. from the town, and are the highest in the district.

CALOOLA CREEK GOLD-FIELD (*Co. Bathurst*), including Caloola Creek, Queen Charlotte's Vale Ponds, and Back Creek gold-fields. Is the western head of Queen Charlotte Vale Creek, rising in the range known as the Three Brothers, and flowing N.W. through good country.

CALORE MOUNT (*Co. Northumberland*), a peak in the Hunter Range, in parish of Moruben, on the E. bank of the Macdonald River, and about 18 miles S.E. of Wollundi.

CAMARA MOUNT (*Co. Raleigh*), a triple-peaked mountain at the head of the Mulla Mulla Creek, and on the road from Kempsey to Grafton.

CAMBALONG CREEK (*Co. Wellesley*), a northern tributary of the Bombala River, rising in Mount Cooper, and flowing in a southerly direction.

CAMBERWELL (*Co. Durham*), a postal village, 156 miles N. of Sydney, with daily post. The nearest railway station is Glennie's Creek, 2 miles, on the northern line, situated about 2 miles from the junction of the Falbrook and the Hunter Rivers. The district is chiefly pastoral. There are coal-seams in the neighbourhood, but too great a distance from water-carriage to be of much value.

CAMBEWARRA (*Co. Camden*), a postal village, 120 miles S. of Sydney, with daily mail, money-order and telegraph offices. The nearest railway station is Moss Vale, 31 miles, on the southern line.

CAMBEWARRA RANGE (*Co. Camden*), a chain of hills forming the eastern edge of the table-land, which runs inland from the N. of the lower end of the Shoalhaven River. It is the source of the Kangaroo River and several small creeks, the principal of which is Broughton's Creek. It forms the S. part of the Illawarra Range.

CAMDEN, a county in the Eastern Division of the Colony. [*See* "COUNTIES."]

CAMDEN (*Co. Camden*), an important town, 40 miles S. of Sydney, with mail twice each day. There is a tram-line from Campbelltown to Camden, running in conjunction with the main southern line of railway, situated on the S.E. bank of the Nepean River, and about 4 miles N. of the Razor Back Range of mountains. The features of the surrounding country are remarkably pleasing, and it resembles some of the finest parts of England. Agriculture and horticulture are extensively followed in the district. The vineyards of Camden Park, Wivenhoe, Maryland, Kirkham, and Macquarie Grove yield superior wine, which is much prized by connoisseurs. The Menangle viaduct and high-level bridge crosses the Nepean River, close to Camden; and the Sydney water-works passes through the district. Camden was proclaimed a municipal district in 1889, with eight aldermen and a mayor. The population is about 1,500.

CAMDEN HAVEN (*Co. Macquarie*), a postal village, 264 miles N. of Sydney, with mail three times a week. It is a beautiful bay or inlet from the ocean, the entrance lying about 20 miles S. of Port Macquarie, and consists of two separate lakes or lagoons, the one to the W. being called Queen's Lake and that to the S. Wilson Taylor's Lake. The name of Camden Haven was given by Oxley, who discovered Port Macquarie, and who named it after Lord Camden. The surrounding country is generally good land, much of it being available for agriculture.

CAMDEN HAVEN POINT (*Co. Macquarie*), a postal village, 261 miles N. of Sydney, with daily mail and money-order office. The nearest railway station is Hexham, 149 miles, on the northern line.

CAMERA HILL (*Co. Cumberland*), situated at Manly Beach (now called Brighton), between the ocean beach and the bay. It was a favourite resort of visitors to Manly Beach before it was excluded to the public by private purchase, as many other lovely spots have become invaded in this favoured locality from the same cause.

E

CAMERON CREEK (*Co. Gough*), a southern tributary of the Severn River, rising on the N. of the Waterloo Plains, and flowing N. about 12 miles through good land, much of which is suitable for cultivation.

CAMERON'S CREEK (*Co. Hardinge*), a western tributary of the west end of the Gwydir River, rising in the northern slope of Mount Lowry, and flowing N.E. across the Bendemeer and Inverell road about 16 miles.

CAMP COVE (*Co. Cumberland*), a small sandy bight in the inner S. head of Port Jackson, about a quarter of a mile S.S.W. of the point, and about a quarter of a mile N. of the village of Watson's Bay. This is the head-quarters of the pilots, the famous look-out at the Gap enabling them to see vessels approaching the harbour in all directions seaward. It is also a very favourite place for picnic and fishing parties.

CAMP CREEK (*Co. Georgiana*), an eastern tributary of the Copperhannia Creek, rising near the road from Rockley to Bombah, about 5 miles N. of the latter place.

CAMPBELL CREEK (*Albert District*), a stream rising in the Barrier Range and flowing in a westerly direction.

CAMPBELL'S CREEK (*Co. Durham*), a small tributary of the head of the Goorangoola Creek.

CAMPBELL'S CREEK (*Co. Wellington*), a small mining hamlet situated on the creek, whence it derives its name, and forms part of the Louisa Creek Diggings. The country is essentially an alluvial mining one.

CAMPBELL'S (or JUGIONG) CREEK (*Co. Wellington*), an auriferous southern tributary of the upper part of the Moree Creek, rising in the W. of Mount Beroble, and flowing N.W. into the main stream of the township of Windeyer.

CAMPBELL'S RIVER (*Cos. Bathurst and Westmoreland*). [See "RIVERS."]

CAMPBELLFIELDS (*Co. Cumberland*), on the southern line of railway, 31 miles from Sydney. It is a pleasant suburb of Campbelltown, and is situated a few miles to the northward of it. Minto is the name of the railway station, 9 miles to the south of Liverpool.

CAMPBELLTOWN (*Co. Camden*), an important postal town, 34 miles S. of Sydney, with money-order and telegraph offices, postal delivery twice each day by letter carriers, and Government savings bank. The junction of the tramway to Camden takes place here, and trams run in conjunction with the trains on the southern line. Campbelltown is situated in the parish of St. Peter's on the Bunbury Curran Creek, and 1½ mile S. of Badgally Hill, and from which a really magnificent view is obtained. It is a most perfect panorama; and on a clear day objects can be seen all round to the extent of the horizon. It is well deserving a visit. Campbelltown was proclaimed a municipal district in 1882, with eight aldermen and a mayor. Courts of quarter sessions and district courts are held here periodically. The population is about 800.

CAMPERDOWN (*Co. Cumberland*), a postal suburb of the city, 2½ miles S.W. of Sydney, with money-order and telegraph offices, Government savings bank, and delivery by letter-carriers twice each day. Situated in the parish of Petersham, on the Parramatta and Cook's River Roads, and on Johnson's and Orphan School Creeks. The Sydney University and the affiliated colleges are situated within the municipality. Camperdown was proclaimed a municipality in 1870, with eight aldermen and a mayor. The population is about 3,000.

CAMPSIE (*Co. Durham*), an agricultural village, on the N. bank of the Allyn River, near Torybrun estate, about 8 miles N. of the township of Paterson. The district is a purely agricultural one. The soil is very good, and produces large crops of grain and potatoes.

CANADIAN LEAD (*Co. Phillip*), a postal village, 197 miles W. of Sydney, with money-order office, and a daily mail. The nearest railway station is Mudgee, 17 miles, on the western line.

CANBELEGO, a county, partly in the Central and Western Divisions of the Colony. [*See* " COUNTIES."]

CANBERRA (*Co. Murray*), a post-office, 214 miles S. of Sydney, with mail three days a week *via* Yass, and three days a week *via* Queanbeyan. The nearest railway station is Queanbeyan, 7 miles, on the southern line.

CANDELO (*Co. Auckland*), a postal town, 258 miles S. of Sydney, with daily mail, money-order and telegraph offices, and Government savings bank. The nearest railway station is Cooma, 70 miles, on the Cooma line.

CANDELO CREEK (*Co. Auckland*), a southern tributary of the Bemboka River, about 12 miles S.E. of Bega. It flows through the village of Candelo, and has good agricultural land upon its banks.

CANGAR GOLD-FIELD (*Cos. Drake and Gresham*), situated on the Mitchell Creek at Cangar.

CANLEY VALE (*Co. Cumberland*), a postal village, 19 miles S. of Sydney, with daily mail, situated on the southern line of railway, with a station.

CANNONBAR (*Co. Oxley*), a postal village, 393 miles W. of Sydney, with mail twice a week, telegraph and money-order offices, and Government savings bank. The nearest railway station is Nyngan, 18 miles, on the western line. Situated on the Bogan, at its junction with the Bogan River. The district is exclusively pastoral.

CANN'S PLAINS CREEK (*Co. Parry*), an auriferous tributary of the Peel River, joining it at Bowling Alley Point diggings.

CANOBLAS (*Co. Wellington*), a post-office, 196 miles W. of Sydney, with mail twice a week. The nearest railway station is Orange, 3½ miles, on the western line.

CANOBLAS MOUNTAINS, THE (*Cos. Wellington, Bathurst, and Ashburnham*).—These mountains attain a height of 4,610 feet above sea-level, and form a most conspicuous object at a great distance. They are a group in the Macquarie Range, known as Towac. Booree-noir, Gowadth, and Cowragora. From the towns of Orange, Ophir, Blayney, and Carcoar they are very imposing. The Canoblas lie on the S. of the road from Orange to Molong. Copper abounds in these mountains.

CANOMODINE CREEK (*Co. Ashburnham*), a tributary of the Cargo Creek. flowing from the S.W. of the Canoblas Mountains in a S.E. direction about 20 miles.

CANOWINDRA (*Co. Ashburnham*), a postal village, 217 miles W. of Sydney, with daily mail therefrom. Money-order and telegraph offices, Government savings bank. The nearest railway station is Cowra, 20 miles, on the western line. Situated on the north bank of the Belubula River, 10 miles N.E. from the Lachlan River.

CANTERBURY (*Co. Cumberland*), a postal hamlet, 6 miles S. of Sydney. Money-order and telegraph offices, Government savings bank, and delivery by letter-carriers three times daily. The nearest railway station is Ashfield, 1 mile, on the southern and western lines. It is situated in the parishes of Petersham, Concord, and St. George, and was proclaimed a municipal district in 1879, with eight aldermen and a mayor.

CAPERTEE (*Co. Roxburgh*), a postal village, 127 miles W. of Sydney, with daily mail therefrom. Money-order and telegraph offices. Situated on the Western Mudgee line of railway, and has a station at Capertee.

CAPERTEE RIVER (*Co. Roxburgh*). [*See* "RIVERS."]

CAPOOMPETA (*Co. Drake*), a mountain, lying about 16 miles N.E. of Severn or Dundee, which attains an elevation of 4,730 feet above sea-level, in the New England Range.

CAPPABELLA (*Co. Goulburn*), a creek rising in Mane's Range, near the township reserve of Cappabella, and flowing S.W. into the Jingellec, at Jingellec. It is crossed by the track from Albury to Cooma and Twofold Bay.

CAPTAIN KING'S CREEK (*Co. Westmoreland*), an eastern tributary of the Stony Creek, flowing to the N. of Mount Stroud.

CAPTAIN'S FLAT (*Co. Murray*), a post-town, 201 miles S. of Sydney, with daily mail. The nearest railway station is Bungendore, 28 miles, on the Cooma line.

CARABOST (*Co. Wynyard*), a postal receiving-office, 377 miles S. of Sydney, with mails three times a week. The nearest railway station is Gundagai, 87 miles, on the southern line.

CARABOST CREEK (*Co. Wynyard*), a small western tributary of the Umutbee Creek, draining the boggy country to the N.E. of Billabong township.

CARCOAR (*Co. Bathurst*), a postal town, 180 miles to the W. of Sydney, with daily mail, money-order and telegraph offices, and Government savings bank; a railway station on the western line. Situated on the Belubula River, in the parish of Errol, about 8 miles from Mount Macquarie, a high peak having snow on its summit nearly the whole of the winter months. Carcoar was proclaimed a municipal district in 1878, with five aldermen and a mayor. Courts of quarter sessions and district courts are held here periodically. The population is about 600.

CARDIFF (*Co. Northumberland*). a railway station, 94 miles N. of Sydney, on the Sydney and Newcastle line.

CAREEL BAY (*Co. Cumberland*), a small bay on the east side of Pittwater, containing deep water and secure anchorage.

CAREENING COVE (*Co. Cumberland*), a beautiful little bay running E. and W. on the North Shore, next to Neutral Bay, and nearly opposite Pinchgut.

CARGELLICO LAKE GOLD-FIELD (*Co. Dowling*), situated on Cargellico Lake, Lachlan District.

CARGELLICO (*Co. Dowling*), a proclaimed village, situate on Lake Cargellico, on the S. of the Lachlan River.

CARGI PONDS (*Co. Narromine*), a chain of water-holes lying to the S.W. of Hervey's Range; it flows N.W. into the head of the Bogan River, near the crossing-place of the Obley and Condobolin Road.

CARGO (*Co. Ashburnham*), a postal town, 217 miles W. of Sydney, with daily mail, money-order and telegraph offices, Government savings bank. The nearest railway station is Cargo Road, on the Molong branch of western line.

CARGO CREEK (*Co. Ashburnham*), a northern tributary of the Belubula River, falling into it about 10 miles above Canowindra.

CARGO GOLD-FIELDS (*Co. Ashburnham*).—The western extension comprises 68 square miles, and the southerly extension 10 square miles.

CARINDA (*Co. Oxley*), a post-office, 429 miles W. of Sydney, with mail twice a week. The nearest railway station is Nevertire, 110 miles, on the western line.

CARLINGFORD (*Co. Cumberland*), a postal village, 15 miles W. of Sydney, with daily mail. A railway station on the Sydney and Newcastle line.

CARLOS GAP (*Co. Roxburgh*), a railway station, 136 miles W. of Sydney, on the western line.

CARLTON (*Co. Cumberland*), a suburb, 8 miles S. of Sydney. A station on the Illawarra and South Coast railway.

CARLYLE'S CREEK (*Co. Inglis*), an auriferous tributary of the Mulucrindie River, rising in the western slope of the Australian Alps, flowing to the N. of Bendemeer.

CARLYLE'S GULLY (*Co. Inglis*), on the road from Bendemeer to Armidale, about 6 miles N. of the former place, and on the Spring Creek. The nearest railway station is Walcha Road, on the northern line.

CARNSDALE (*Co. Hume*), a postal village, 434 miles S. of Sydney, with mail once a week. The nearest railway station to it is Gerogery, 30 miles, on the southern line.

CAROWERY CREEK (*Co. Gloucester*), a tributary of the Williams River fed by the Farm Creek.

CARRABEAN (*Co. Gloucester*), the native name of Port Stephens.

CARRAMUMBOLA MOUNT (*Co. King*), two remarkable hills on the Burrowa Plains, close to the township of that name. The larger mount is seen from a great distance; it is a beautiful mount covered with verdure, well timbered with large trees, park-like, and no scrub.

CARRANGAL MOUNT (*Co. Murray*), a mount of the Cullarin Range, attaining a height of 3,058 feet above the sea-level.

CARRATHOOL (*Co. Waradgery*), a postal village, 419 miles S.W. of Sydney, with mail five days a week, money-order and telegraph offices, and Government savings bank. A railway station on the south-western line.

CARRAWA (*Co. Georgiana*), a proclaimed village on the creek of that name.

CARRAWA CREEK (*Co. Georgiana*), a drainage creek from the swampy country S.E. of Rockley, flowing into the head of Burangylong Creek.

CARRAWOBBITY (*Co. Ashburnham*), a postal receiving-office, 279 miles W. of Sydney, with mail twice a week. The nearest railway station is Borenore, 77 miles, on the western line.

CARRICK (*Co. Argyle*), a postal village, 122 miles S. of Sydney, with mail daily. A station on the Great Southern line.

CARRINGTON (*Co. Gloucester*), an agricultural settlement, lying on the N. shore of Port Stephens and formerly the head quarters of the Australian Agricultural Company.

CARRINGTON (*Co. Northumberland*), a postal town, 103 miles N. of Sydney, with daily mail, telegraph and money-order offices, Government savings bank, and delivery by letter-carrier. One mile from Honeysuckle Point railway station on northern line. Proclaimed a municipal district in 1887, with eight aldermen and a mayor as a governing body.

CARROLL (*Co. Buckland*), a postal town, 315 miles N. of Sydney, with daily mail, money-order and telegraph offices, and Government savings bank. The nearest railway station is Gunnedah, 12 miles, on the northern line; situated on the Namoi River, about 5 miles below the confluence of that and the Peel River.

CARROLL CREEK (*Co. Buckland*), a drainage creek, flowing into the lower end of the Conadilly River from the east.

CARROW BROOK (*Co. Durham*), a postal receiving-office, 173 miles N. of Sydney, with mail therefrom twice a week. The Brook is an eastern tributary of the head of the Falbrook, rising in Mount Carrow and flowing south.

CARROW MOUNT (*Co. Durham*), a peak of the Mount Royal Range, lying at the head of Carrow Brook, and on the W. bank of the Paterson River.

CARR'S ISLAND (*Co. Clarence*), a small island in the Clarence River, on the W. of the town of Grafton.

CARSON'S SIDING (*Co. Cook*), a railway station, 115 miles N.W. of Sydney, on the Mudgee branch of the northern line.

CART-ROAD CREEK (*Co. Harden*), a small tributary of Calmo Creek, falling into it near Bookham.

CARTWRIGHT'S CREEK (*Co. King*), a stream rising to the W. of Crookwell township, and flowing W. into the Wheeo Creek at the township of Wheeo.

CARVANBA (*Co. Rous*), a proclaimed village in the county.

CARWELL (*Co. Roxburgh*), a proclaimed village on the creek of the same name.

CARWELL CREEK (*Co. Roxburgh*), a southern tributary of the upper part of the Cudgegong Creek.

CASINO (*Co. Richmond*), a postal town, 385 miles N. of Sydney, with money-order and telegraph offices, Government savings banks, and delivery by letter-carriers; mails by Clarence River steamers. Situated on the S. arm, on the main stream, of the Richmond River, 40 miles from the confluence with the N. arm, and to the S. about 40 miles distant from the Macpherson Range. The district is solely an agricultural and pastoral one. Casino was proclaimed a municipal district in 1880, with eight aldermen and a mayor. Population about 1,500. Courts of quarter sessions and district courts are held here periodically.

CASSELL'S CREEK (*Co. Harden*), a small tributary at the head of Murrimboola Creek.

CASSILIS (*Co. Bligh*), a postal village, 223 miles N. of Sydney, with daily mail, money-order and telegraph offices, Government savings bank. The nearest station is Muswellbrook, 90 miles, on the northern line. Cassilis is situated on the right bank of the Munmurray River, about 10 miles from the Krui River, and 9 miles from the Talbragar River, and within 8 miles of the dividing range. The district is a purely pastoral one.

CASTLE DOYLE (*Co. Sandon*), a postal receiving-office, 368 miles N. of Sydney, with mail once a week.

CASTLE FORBES (*Co. Northumberland*), an agricultural settlement on the Hunter River, near the township of Singleton.

CASTLE HILL (*Co. Cumberland*), a postal village, 21 miles W. of Sydney, with daily mail. The nearest railway station is Parramatta, 6 miles, on the western line. One of the original districts of the county; bounded on the S.W. and N.W. by Upper Nelson district, on the S. by Toongabbee, and Field of Mars district, and on the E. by Oxley district.

CASTLE MOUNTAIN (*Co. Buckland*), a post-office, 221 miles to the N. of Sydney, with mail daily. The nearest railway station is Quirindi, 9 miles, on the northern line.

CASTLEREAGH (*Co. Cumberland*), a postal village, 40 miles W. of Sydney, with daily mail. The nearest railway station is Penrith, 5 miles, on the western line. Situated in the parish of Castlereagh, about a mile to the E. of the Nepean River, the land being composed of rich alluvial soil. The Blue Mountains lie to the W., running parallel with the Nepean River.

CASTLEREAGH RIVER (*Co. Bligh*). [*See* "RIVERS."]

CATARACT RIVER (*Co. Buller*). [*See* "RIVERS."]

CATARACT RIVER (*Cos. Cumberland and Camden.* [*See* "RIVERS."]

CATARACT (*Co. Camden*) a village, 45 miles S. of Sydney. The nearest railway station is Douglas Park, 4 miles, on the southern line.

CATHCART (*Co. Wellesley*), a postal village, 322 miles S. of Sydney, with mail twice a week, and by steamers *via* Eden and Merimbula. The nearest railway station is Cooma, 62 miles, on the Cooma branch of the southern line. Situated on a stream of water running in a southerly direction through Taylor's Flat, called the Coollumbooka Creek.

CATHERINE HILL BAY (*Co. Northumberland*), a postal village, 104 miles N. of Sydney, with daily mail and money-order office.

CATHILL CREEK (*Co. Gloucester*), a small southern tributary of the Gloucester River.

CATOMBUL CREEK (*Co. Gordon*), a western tributary of the Bell River, rising in the Catombul Mountains, and flowing into the main stream to the N. of Newrea; also a tributary of the head of the Buckinbar Creek.

CATOMBULS (*Co. Gordon*), a chain of lofty mountains, lying on the W. side of the Bell River, and on the road from Wellington to Orange, about 10 miles S. of the latter place. From that point, the N. Catombul, the range runs about 6 miles in a southerly direction, where it turns to the E. about 2 miles. The principal peaks are the N. and S. Catombuls, in which the Catombul Creek takes its rise.

CATTAI CREEK (*Co. Gloucester*), a postal receiving-office, 243 miles N. of Sydney, with mail twice a week.

CATTAI CREEK (*Co. Cumberland*), a fine stream rising near Pennant Hills, and flowing in a north-westerly direction across the road from Windsor to Maitland into the Hawkesbury River below Pitt Town. There is a smaller creek a little further on known as little Cattai.

CAVAN (*Co. Cowley*), a post-office, 207 miles S. of Sydney, with mail once a week. The nearest railway station to it is Yass, 20 miles, on the southern line.

CAVAN CAVES (*Co. Cowley*), situated on the W. bank of the Murrumbidgee River, about 20 miles S. of Yass. They form a series of chasms in a low range of limestone hills.

CAVE CREEK (*Co. Wellington*), a postal receiving-office, 207 miles W. of Sydney, with mail three times a week.

CAVEEN CREEK (*Co. Harden*), a postal receiving-office, 207 miles W. of Sydney, with mail once a week. The nearest railway station is Orange, 15 miles, on the western line.

CAVE FLAT (*Co. Harden*), a tract of good pastoral land, on the N. bank of the Murrumbidgee, near the junction of the Goodradigbee. There are several caverns in a limestone hill, about the centre of the flat.

CAWATTIE (*Co. Bourke*), a village, 309 miles S. of Sydney. The nearest railway station is Coolaman, 23 miles, on the south-western line.

CAWATTIE MOUNT (*Co. Bourke*), a high solitary mount to the S. of Merrool Creek.

CAWDOR (*Co. Camden*), a rural settlement on the Camden estate, lying on the old Southern Road, about 2½ miles S. of the township of Camden.

CAWLEY'S CREEK (*Co. Cumberland*), a village, 27 miles S. of Sydney. The nearest railway station is Waterfalls, 2 miles, on the Illawarra and South Coast line.

CAWNDILLA LAKE (*Co. Menindie*), situate about 30 miles S.W. of Menindie, is a large shallow lake, formed by the overflow of the Darling, and fed by a branch of that river called Laidley's Ponds.

CAYALAL MOUNT (*Co. Courallie*), situate about 36 miles N.W. of Narrabri, and W. of the Horton River, is a lofty and precipitous peak of the Nundawar range.

CEDAR BRUSH GAP (*Co. Buckland*), situated between Mounts Tinagroo on the E. and Towarri on the W., in an opening in the Liverpool Range, through which the road from Scone to Warrah passes.

CEDAR CREEK (*Co. Northumberland*), a tributary of the Wollombi Brook, falling into it above Wollombi.

CEDAR CREEK (*Co. Westmoreland*), a small tributary of Cox's River, rising in Pulpit Hill, and flowing S. about 16 miles through rugged brush country.

CEDAR PARTY CREEK (*Co. Macquarie*), a postal village, 238 miles N. of Sydney, with mail four times a week.

CENTRAL COLO (*Co. Cumberland*), a postal village, 38 miles W. of Sydney, with post every Saturday. The nearest railway station is Windsor, 28 miles, on the Richmond line.

CENTRAL MACDONALD (*Co. Cumberland*), a postal village, 68 miles W. of Sydney, with mail four times a week. The nearest railway station is Hawkesbury, 20 miles, on the Sydney and Newcastle line.

CENTRAL RALEIGH (*Co. Raleigh*), a postal receiving-office, 377 miles N. of Sydney, with mail twice a week per steamer, *via* Fernmount.

CESSNOCK (*Co. Northumberland*), a postal village, 114 miles N. of Sydney, with mail three times a week. The nearest railway station is Farley, 16 miles, on the northern line. Situated in the parish of Polkolbin, on the Black Creek, in the district of the Hunter.

CHAELUNDI MOUNT (*Co. Gresham*), is a solitary mountain in the broken country near the junction of the Aberfoyle and Guy Fawkes Rivers, about 40 miles E. of Falconer.

CHAMBERS (*Co. Bathurst*), a proclaimed village on the creek of the same name.

CHAMBERS' CREEK (*Co. Bathurst*), a village, 25 miles from Bathurst, on the southern railway line.

CHAMBERS CREEK GOLD-FIELDS (*Co. Bathurst*), is a goldfield, known as the southerly extension to the Macquarie River and Chambers Creek gold-fields.

CHAMBIGNE CREEK GOLD-FIELDS (*Cos. Gresham and Fitzroy*), situated at the Nymboi River.

CHANDLER RIVER (*Co. Sandon*). [See " RIVERS."]

CHANDLER'S CREEK (*Co. Gresham*), is a small tributary of the Boyd River.

CHANDLER'S PEAK (*Co. Clarke*), is a lofty peak of the New England Range, lying about 12 miles S.E. of Falconer, and on the E. bank of the Gyra River. It attains an altitude of upwards of 4,000 feet, by the measurement of the Rev. W. B. Clarke. The Guyra Station, on the Great Northern line, 383 miles from Sydney, is the nearest railway station.

CHANDLER'S PEAK (*Co. Clive*), a village, 12 miles from Guyra, on the northern line.

CHAPMAN (*Co. Dudley*), a small agricultural settlement lying on the Coolambooka River, about 7 miles N. of Kempsey.

CHARCOAL (*Co. Camden*), a roadside village in the district of Wollongong, situated on the Charcoal Creek, the Cordeaux River being on the W., the Fig Tree Creek on the N., and Mullet Creek on the S. Mounts Keira and Kembla are conspicuous objects. Wollongong and Dapto are each about 4 miles distant. The nearest railway station is Dapto, on the Illawarra line.

CHARCOAL CREEK (*Co. Camden*), a small creek crossing the road from Dapto to Wollongong, at the village of Charcoal, it falls into the Tom Thumb Lagoon. The nearest railway station is Campbelltown, 36 miles, on southern line.

CHARLESTOWN (*Co. Northumberland*), a postal town 87 miles N. of Sydney, with mail daily, telegraph and money-order office, and Government savings bank. The nearest railway station is Adamstown, 2 miles, on the northern line.

CHARLEYONG (*Co. Northumberland*), a postal village, 201 miles S. of Sydney, with mail twice a week. The nearest railway station is Tarago, 44 miles, on the southern line.

CHATON MOUNT (*Co. King*), a lofty peak of the Cullarin Range, lying about 8 miles N. of Gundaroo, 6½ miles N.E. of the Yass River, and 10 miles S.W. of Collector. It attains an elevation of 3,000 feet above the level of the sea.

CHATSBURY (*Co. Argyle*), a postal village, 143 miles S. of Sydney, with mail daily therefrom.

CHATSWOOD (*Co. Cumberland*), a postal village, about 5 miles N. of Sydney, with a daily mail. It is part of the district of St. Leonards, the branch northern line *via* Hornsby passing through it where there is a station.

CHATSWORTH ISLAND (*Co. Clarence*), a post-office, 320 miles N. of Sydney with mail by every steamer to the Clarence. Money-order and telegraph offices, and Government savings bank. It is situated on an estuary of the Clarence River.

CHEESEMAN'S CREEK (*Co. Ashburnham*), a postal village, 209 miles W. of Sydney, with mail daily. The nearest railway station is Borenore, 7 miles, on the western branch line.

CHERRY-TREE HILL (*Co. Bathurst*), an auriferous district, lying about 1 mile E. of Evans' Plains.

CHERRY-TREE HILL (*Co. Roxburgh*), a peak in the Blue Mountain Range, about 1 mile N.E. of Sofala, and 3 miles S.E. of Keene's Swamp.

CHESHIRE CREEK (*Co. Roxburgh*), is within a proclaimed goldfield. It is an eastern tributary of the Winburndale Rivulet, rising in the Limekiln Hill, and flowing W. through the Cheshire Creek gold-field.

CHESNEY LAKE (*Co. Barrona*), a large lake in the centre of this county, and to the N. of the salt lakes.

CHICHESTER RIVER (*Co. Gloucester*). [*See* "RIVERS."]

CHIDOWLA (*Co. King*), a postal receiving-office, 210 miles S. of Sydney, with mail once a week. The nearest railway station is Bowning, 24 miles, on the southern line.

CHILCOTT'S CREEK (*Co. Buckland*), a tributary of the head of the Borambil Creek. Rising in the western slope of the Australian Alps, near Mount Temi, and flowing through rugged country in a westerly direction.

CHIMNEY POT (*Co. Buller*), on the New England Range, about 18 miles N.W. of Tenterfield, and is a very conspicuous object on the road to Drake and Tabulam.

CHINA GULLY CREEK (*Co. Monteagle*), an auriferous tributary of the Burrangong Creek, flowing into it at the township of Forbes.

CHINDERA (*Co. Rous*), a township, 450 miles N. of Sydney, and to the S. of Point Danger, on the N. boundary-line of the colony.

CHINDERAH (*Co. Rous*), a proclaimed village, 372 miles N. of Sydney.

CHIPPENDALE (*Co. Cumberland*), an important division, so named within the City of Sydney, lying between Parramatta-street and Redfern, on the western side of the railway line.

CHOWDER HEAD AND BAY (*Co. Cumberland*), situated on the N. shore of Port Jackson, opposite Shark Point, about 2 miles S.W. of the entrance. Chowder Bay is one of the many pretty spots in Port Jackson.

CHRISTMAS CREEK (*Co. Dudley*), a fine northern tributary of the Macleay River, falling into it at Frederickton, and flowing through rich agricultural land.

CHURCHYARD CREEK (*Co. Murchison*), a western tributary of the Gwydir River, rising in a rugged auriferous country.

CIRCUIT FLAT (*Co. Northumberland*), situated about 15 miles S. of Wollombi, between Mounts Manning and Lockyer, on the old North Road from Sydney to Maitland.

CIRCUS POINT (*Co. Wellington*), situated about 4 miles from the township of Sofala, is auriferous, and forms part of the Turon diggings.

CLAIRVILLE (*Co. Cumberland*), situated about 9 miles W. of Sydney, in the parishes of St. George and Bankstown. It is also known by the name of Punchbowl.

CLANDULLA (*Co. Roxburgh*), a lofty mount on the Blue Mountain Range, lying on the E. side of the road from Bowenfels to Rylstone, *via* the Capertee River.

CLARE (*Co. Manara*), a township, in the far W. of the Colony.

CLARENCE, a county in the Eastern Division of the Colony. [*See* "COUNTIES."]

CLARENCE MOUNT (*Co. Cook*), a lofty peak, attaining a height of 3,500 feet above the sea-level, in the Blue Mountain Range.

CLARENCE RIVER HEADS (*Co. Clarence*), situated at the mouth of the Clarence River, 300 miles N. of Sydney, communication to and from which is by steamer. The country generally is not fertile. The flats along the river bank, however, are of good alluvial soil, and are highly cultivated.

CLARENCE RIVER (*Cos. Clarence, Richmond, Drake, Butler, and Rous*). [*See* "RIVERS."]

CLARENCE TOWN (*Co. Durham*), a postal town, 140 miles to the N. of Sydney, with daily mail, money-order and telegraph offices, and Government savings bank. The nearest railway station is Morpeth, 18 miles, on the northern line. Situated on the W. bank of the Williams River, in the parish of Uffington. The tobacco plant flourishes here, and considerable quantities of tobacco enter into consumption produced in the district.

CLARENCE TUNNEL (*Co. Cook*), a postal village, 88 miles W. of Sydney, with a daily mail, situated on the western railway, and has a siding to that line.

CLARENDON, a county partly in the Central and Eastern Divisions of the Colony. [*See* "COUNTIES."]

CLARENDON (*Co. Cumberland*), a railway station on the Windsor and Richmond line, 35 miles W. of Sydney.

CLAREVAL (*Co. Gloucester*), a postal receiving-office, 153 miles N. of Sydney, with daily mail.

CLAREVAULX (*Co. Gough*), 433 miles N. of Sydney, with mail four times a week. The nearest railway station is Glen Innes, 8 miles, on the northern line.

CLARKE, a county in the Eastern Division of the Colony. [*See* "COUNTIES."]

CLARKE'S CREEK (*Co. Wellington*), situated on and forms part of Louisa Creek diggings. The district is essentially a mining one.

CLARKE'S CREEK (*Co. Hardinge*), an eastern tributary of the Gwydir River, formed by the Moredun and Limestone Creeks. It flows through rugged auriferous country.

CLARKE'S ISLAND, native name, BILLONGOBAH (*Co. Cumberland*), one of the islands in Port Jackson, opposite and to the N. of Darling Point.

CLARKSON'S CROSSING (*Co. Gloucester*), a postal village, with money-order office, 211 miles N. of Sydney, with mail three times a week.

CLEAR CREEK (*Co. Roxburgh*), a postal town, 154 miles W. of Sydney, with mail therefrom twice a week. The creek is an eastern tributary of the Winburndale Rivulet, rising in the Limekilns Hills, and is within a gold-field of that name. The nearest railway station is Bathurst, 12 miles, on the western line.

CLEAR HILL (*Co. Buccleuch*), a high peak lying in the rugged mountainous country to the E. of the Tumut.

CLEAR HILL (*Co. Wynyard*), a peak lying to the W. of the Tumut River, and the head of the eastern arm of the Adelong Creek. Also a peak on the E. bank of the Yaven-Yaven Creek.

CLEARED HILL (*Co. Roxburgh*), a peak in the Blue Mountains, on the N. side of the Turon River, about 3 miles N. of the township of Cullen Bullen.

CLEAR MOUNT (*Co. Cowley*), a lofty and prominent peak, about 4 miles S.W. of Clinton, situate on the W. bank of the Murrumbidgee River.

CLIFFORD'S CREEK (*Co. Georgiana*), a small creek running into the Reedy Creek at Flowerdale, 7 miles from Laggan.

CLIFTON (*Co. Cumberland*), a postal village, 37 miles to the S. of Sydney, with daily mail, money-order and telegraph office, and Government savings bank. A railway station on the Illawarra and South Coast line.

CLIVE, a county in the Eastern Division of the Colony. [*See* "COUNTIES."]

CLIVE (*Co. Clive*), a postal town, 469 miles N. of Sydney, with mail therefrom once a week.

CLOCIDES BAY (*Co. Northumberland*), an eastern arm of the harbour of Brisbane Water. The township of Kincumber is situated in the eastern arm of this bay, and the district is finely timbered.

CLOUD'S CREEK (*Co. Fitzroy*), a small tributary of the head of the Nymboi River.

CLOVER CREEK (*Co. Cowper*), an eastern tributary of the Darling River, rising in the northern part of Dunlop's Range, and flowing N.W. about 8 miles through tolerably good pastoral country.

CLUNES (*Co. Rous*), a postal village, 370 miles N. of Sydney, with telegraph office, and mail by Clarence and Richmond River steamers.

CLUNIE MOUNT (*Co. Buller*), a peak of the Macpherson Range, lying at the head of Pinnacle Creek.

CLYBUCCA CREEK (*Co. Dudley*), a small northern tributary of the mouth of the Macleay River, draining the overflow of the Clybucca Swamp.

CLYBUCCA (*Co. Dudley*), a postal village, 323 miles N. of Sydney, with mail three days a week.

CLYDE (*Co. Cumberland*), a suburban village, 13 miles to the S. of Sydney, on the main southern line.

CLYDE, a county partly in the Central and Western Divisions of the Colony. [*See* "COUNTIES."]

CLYDE RIVER (*Co. St. Vincent*). [*See* "RIVERS."]

CLYWDD, VALE OF (*Co. Cook*).—This beautiful valley is situated at the base of Mount York, and near the town of Hartley. It is watered by Cox's River and the river Lett.

COAL RIDGE (*Co. Clarence and Drake*), a range of low hills, lying on the W. of the county of Clarence, and the E. of the county of Drake.

COALDALE (*Co. Clarence*), a small agricultural hamlet, situated on Whiteman's Creek, about 20 miles N.W. of Grafton.

COBAR (*Co. Robinson*), a postal town, 495 miles to the W. of Sydney, with mail three times a week, money-order and telegraph offices, and Government savings bank, and delivery by letter-carrier. The nearest railway station is Nyngan, 80 miles on the western line. Cobar was proclaimed a municipal district in 1884, with eight aldermen and a mayor. The population is about 3,000. Courts of quarter sessions and district courts are held here periodically. The railway from Nyngan to Cobar is nearly completed.

COBARGO (*Co. Beresford*), a postal village, 296 miles S. of Sydney, with daily mail, money-order and telegraph offices, and Government savings bank. The nearest railway station is Cooma, 91 miles, on the southern line *via* Cooma.

COBBADAH (*Co. Murchison*), a postal village, 351 miles N. of Sydney, with daily mail. The nearest railway station is Tamworth, 72 miles, on the northern line.

COBBADAH CREEK (*Co. Murchison*), an eastern tributary of the Horton River, rising to the N. of Barraba, and flowing through the town of Cobbadah.

COBBITTY (*Co. Cumberland*), situated 43 miles S. of Sydney, on the river Nepean. It is a very pretty village in the celebrated Cowpasture district. Mail daily from Sydney. The branch southern line of tramway to Camden passes through the district. The nearest station is Narellan, 5 miles distant.

COBBON HILL (*Co. Wallace*), a high peak lying on the E. of the road from Cooma to Gipps Land, about 8 miles from Jindabyne.

COBBORA (*Co. Lincoln*), a postal town, 329 miles W. of Sydney, with mail twice a week. Money-order and telegraph offices, and Government savings bank. The nearest railway station is Mudgee, on the western line. It is situated on the Talbragar River.

COBRABALD CREEK (*Co. Parry*), a northern tributary of the Bald Creek, rising in Walcha Hill.

COBRABALD MOUNT (*Co. Durham*), stands near the head of the Paterson River, attaining an altitude of over 3,000 feet above the sea-level.

COBUL CREEK (*Co. Wakool*), a small tributary of the Wakool River, rising to the S. of Jegur township.

COCHRANE CREEK (*Co. Wakool*), a postal-receiving office, 530 miles S. of Sydney, with mail therefrom once a week. The nearest railway station is Jerilderie, 102 miles, on the south-western line.

COCHRANE LAKE (*Co. Northumberland*), a small lagoon or inlet of the sea. Situated about 1 mile of the township of Kincumber.

COCKABUTTA (*Co. Bligh*), a village reserve, situated on the Talbragar River, 20 miles S.W. of Cassilis.

COCKATOO ISLAND (*Co. Cumberland*), a well-known island lying in the Parramatta River, abreast of Balmain, formerly used as a penal establishment and now a reformatory for juvenile offenders. The Government dry dock, known as the Fitzroy and Sutherland Dock, for cleaning and repairing men-of-war and the largest ships afloat, is on the island.

COCKBURN RIVER (*Co. Inglis.*) [*See* "RIVERS."]

COCKEJEDONG CREEK (*Co. Urana*), a small northern tributary of the Billabong Creek, conveying the overflow of Lake Urana with that creek.

COCKLE CREEK (*Co. Northumberland*), a post-office, 91 miles N. of Sydney, with daily mail. A railway station on the Sydney and Newcastle line.

COCKWHY CREEK (*Co. St. Vincent*), a tributary of the Clyde River rising near Kioloa Point.

COCO CREEK (*Co. Roxburgh*), a tributary of the Capertee, or upper portion of the Colo River, rising in the northern slope of the Blackman's Crown.

COCOMINGLA (*Co. Bathurst*), postal-receiving office, 218 miles W. of Sydney, with daily mail.

CODRINGTON (*Co. Richmond*), a postal town, 355 miles N. of Sydney, with mail *per* Clarence River steamer. Situated on the S. arm of the Richmond River, 10 miles S. of Lismore.

COFF'S HARBOUR (*Co. Fitzroy*), a postal village, 429 miles N. of Sydney, with mail by steamer to Grafton.

COFF'S HARBOUR (*Co. Fitzroy*), a postal receiving-office, 429 miles N. of Sydney, with mail per Grafton steamer.

COGGANS (*Co. Phillip*), a village reserve, situated on the Goulburn River, S.E. of Cassilis.

COGHLAN MOUNT (*Co. Harden*), situated about 1 mile from Cootamundra, is a lofty hill well timbered but lightly grassed.

COILA (*Co. Dampier*), a small agricultural settlement, about 8 miles S. of Moruya.

COLANE (*Co. Gregory*), a postal village, 402 miles W. of Sydney, with mail once a week. The nearest railway station, Nyngan, 29 miles, on the western line.

COLDSTREAM (*Co. Clarence*), a postal village, 342 miles N. of Sydney, with mail by Clarence River steamers. The river of this name is a fine stream, rising in Mount Kremnoss, flowing N. into the Clarence, opposite Woodford Island.

COLE CREEK (*Co. Harden*), a small western tributary of the Cunningham Creek, near Mallana Gold-fields.

COLIGON CREEK (*Co. Townsend*), a branch of the Edward River, flowing into the Neimur.

COLINTON (*Co. Beresford*), a postal village, 225 miles S. of Sydney, with mail daily. A railway station on the Cooma line.

COLITON (*Co. Cumberland*), an agricultural settlement, situate on the South Creek, about 2 miles from the township of St. Mary's.

COLLARINDABRI (*Co. Finch*), a post-office, 517 miles N. of Sydney, with mail therefrom twice a week. The nearest railway station is Narrabri, 120 miles, on the north-western line.

COLLAROY (*Co. Brisbane*), an agricultural settlement, lying about 10 miles E. of Cassilis.

COLLECTOR (*Co. Argyle*), a postal town, 150 miles S. of Sydney, with daily mail. Money-order office. The nearest railway station is Breadalbane, 11 miles, on the Cooma line. Situated on a creek of that name, near Lake George.

COLLEY CREEK (*Co. Buckland*), a small northern tributary of Borambi Creek.

COLLIE (*Co. Ewenmar*), a postal village, 349 miles W. of Sydney, with mail twice a week. The nearest railway station is Dubbo, 66 miles, on the northern line. It is an exclusively pastoral district.

COLLINGULLIE (*Co. Wynyard*), a receiving-office, 325 miles S. of Sydney, with mail three times weekly. The nearest railway station is Wagga Wagga, 15 miles, on the southern line.

COLLINS' FLAT (*Co. Argyle*), a tract of fine land, situate on the road from Marulan to Bungonia.

COLLY BLUE (*Co. Buckland*), a postal village, 278 miles N. of Sydney, with mail twice a week and money-order office. The nearest railway station is Quirindi, 46 miles, on the northern line.

COLO (*Co. Cook*) is a rich agricultural district, situate on the river of that name, 66 miles S.E. of Sydney. The nearest railway station is Richmond, 26 miles, on the Windsor line.

COLO RIVER (*Cos. Roxburgh and Cook*). [*See* "RIVERS."]

COLO VALE (*Co. Cook*), a postal village, 72 miles S. of Sydney, with daily mail. A railway station on the southern line.

COLOMBO CREEK (*Co. Auckland*), a small southern tributary of the upper part of the Bemboka River.

COLOMBO (*Co. Auckland*), a proclaimed village in that county.

COLOMBO CREEK (*Co. Urana*), a water-course flowing through flat pastoral country in the counties of Mitchell and Urana, and connecting the Yanko and Billabong Creeks.

COLONG MOUNT (*Co. Westmoreland*), a remarkable square-tipped mount, lying at the head of the Joorland and Butcher's Creeks, and about 10 miles S.E. of Burragorang.

COLTWANG (*Co. Tarla*), a township on the N. bank of the Murray River, above Euston.

COLYER'S CREEK (*Co. Beresford*), a small tributary creek of the Upper Murrumbidgee River, rising S. of the township of Clinton, running along the E. side of the road from Cooma to Queanbeyan.

COMARA CREEK (*Co. Dudley*), a small northern tributary of the Macleay River.

COMATAWA RANGE (*Co. Wynyard*), lying to the W. of the Minbargo Creek and S. of Umutbee. Mount Flint is the principal peak in this range.

COMBOYNE MOUNT (*Co. Macquarie*), a high point in the Hastings Range, about 30 miles S.W. of Port Macquarie.

COMBEROY ROAD (*Co. Cook*), a postal town, 55 miles W. of Sydney, with mail twice a week.

COME-BY-CHANCE (*Co. White*), a postal village, 410 miles N. of Sydney, with mail three times a week.

COMERONG (*Co. St. Vincent*), a postal village, 131 miles S. of Sydney, with mail three times a week.

COMO (*Co. Cumberland*), a post-office, 13 miles S. of Sydney, with daily mail. A railway station on the Illawarra and South Coast line.

COMOBELLA (*Co. Wellington*), a postal village, 264 miles W. of Sydney, with mail twice each week. The nearest railway station is Wellington, 12 miles, on the western line.

CONADILLY (*Cos. Buckland and Pottinger*). [*See* " RIVERS."]

CONARGO (*Co. Townsend*), a postal town, with money-order and telegraph office, 458 miles S. of Sydney. The nearest railway station is Jerelderie, 35 miles, on the southern line. Situated on the Billabong Creek, near the Ten-mile and Yanko Creeks.

CONCORD (*Co. Cumberland*), one of the original districts of the county, is now a populous suburb of the city of Sydney, with the trunk line of railway, with all its divergences, passing through the district, possessing all the conveniences incidental to a very thriving population. Burwood station, 2 miles, is the most frequented by the residents. Concord was proclaimed a municipal district in 1883, with five aldermen and a mayor. The population is about 2,500.

CONDOBOLIN (*Co. Cunningham*), a postal town, with money-order and telegraph offices, and Government savings bank, 310 miles W. of Sydney, with daily mail. The nearest railway station is Cowra, 120 miles, on the branch line Molong to Orange. Situated on the Lachlan River, on the road from Forbes to Balranald.

CONDOLE CREEK (*Co. Clarence*), a small northern tributary of the Sandon River.

CONGAI CREEK (*Co. Inglis*), an eastern tributary of the Mulnerindie River, flowing through the village of Congai, about 12 miles E. of Bendemeer.

CONGAI DIGGINGS (*Co. Inglis*), a small alluvial gold working, situate about 7 miles from the township of Bendemeer.

CONGEWAI (*Co. Northumberland*), an agricultural settlement, about 12 miles distant from Millfield.

CONGI (*Co. Sandon*), a village, 320 miles N. of Sydney. The nearest railway station is Walcha Road, 4 miles, on the northern line.

CONGOLA LAKE (*Co. St. Vincent*) is an arm of the sea, to the N. of Ulladulla. The Green Island lies opposite its entrance. The N. basin of this lake is exceedingly picturesque, and is frequented by large numbers of aquatic fowl.

CONGUDANG MOUNT (*Co. Wellington*), a peak in the rugged hilly country to the N. of the Merinda gold-fields, and lying on the S. bank of the Cudgegong River.

CONJOLA (*Co. St. Vincent*), a postal village, 151 miles S. of Sydney, with mail daily. The nearest railway station is Moss Vale, 43 miles, on the southern line.

CONNAUGHTMAN'S CREEK (*Co. Harden*), a tributary of the Cunningham Creek, to the S. of the Burrangong gold-field, and flowing S.E. about 20 miles.

F

CONNOR'S CREEK (*Co. Darling*), a small northern tributary of the Manilla River, flowing into that river at Barraba.

CONROY'S CREEK (*Co. Harden*), a small stream in the Black Range, flowing into the Stoney Creek.

CONSTITUTION HILL (*Co. Cumberland*), a well known hill, on the S. side of Botany old road, and known now as Mount Rennie, and part of Moore Park.

COOBA (*Co. Clarendon*), a postal receiving-office, 334 miles S. of Sydney, with mail twice a week.

COOBA BULGA CREEK (*Co. Bligh*), a tributary of the head of Munmurra Creek.

COOBANGOOLA CREEK (*Co. Baradine*), a small eastern tributary of the Baradine Creek.

COOGEE (*Co. Cumberland*), a delightful sea-side resort enjoyed by the citizens of Sydney and visitors generally of the surrounding districts. Trams run every twenty minutes from the Metropolis, and there is a large resident population. About 4 miles from the post-office, with frequent postal delivery, and every convenience attached to an extensive suburban community.

COOK, a county in the Eastern Division of the Colony. [*See* "COUNTIES."]

COOK ISLAND (*Co. Rous*), a small rocky islet, lying off the coast between Point Danger and Fingal Point.

COOK MUNICIPALITY (*Co. Cumberland*), lies W. of Sydney, and between the Municipalities of Newtown, Camperdown, and the Glebe. Proclaimed 13th November, 1862.

COOKABURRA CREEK (*Co. Oxley*), a small drainage into the head of the Beleringe Creek.

COOKARDINIA (*Co. Goulburn*), a postal village, 370 miles S. of Sydney, with mails three times a week. The nearest railway station is Culcairn (12 miles) on the southern line.

COOKBUNDOON CREEK (*Co. Cowley*), a small eastern tributary of the Goodradigbee River, joining it at the crossing of the road from Yass to Kiandra, about 10 miles south of its confluence with the Murrumbidgee.

COOKBUNDOON RIVER (*Co. Georgiana*). [*See* "RIVERS."]

COOKOOK RANGE (*Co. Goulburn*), a chain of bold granite ranges lying to the S. of the Billabong Reserve, and to the E. of the village of Germanton.

COOKOOMINGALA CREEK (*Co. Monteagle*), a western tributary of the Burrowa River, flowing to the N.E. of the Burrangong gold-fields and E. of Wanbanumba.

COOKOPIE PONDS (*Co. Narromine*), a chain of water-holes, rising to the E. of the Goonamble Hill, and flowing N.W. into the Bogan River.

COOK'S RIVER (*Co. Cumberland*), a fine stream flowing into the head of the N. arm of Botany Bay, where an excellent tidal dam is constructed across its mouth.

COOK'S VALE CREEK GOLD-FIELD (*Co. Georgiana*), near the Abercrombie Gold-field. Proclaimed 31st August, 1865.

COOK'S VALE (*Co. Georgiana*), an agricultural settlement, lying on the Cook's Vale Creek.

COOK'S VALE CREEK (*Co. Georgiana*), an auriferous southern tributary of the Abercrombie River, north-east of Binda, flowing into the Tuena gold-fields, about 4 miles S.E. of Bombah.

COOKY'S FLAT (*Co. Wellington*), a small alluvial and quartz diggings on the Burrendong gold-fields.

COOLA CREEK (*Co. Clarence*), a small western tributary of the Coldstream River, flowing through good agricultural land.

COOLABAH (*Co. Canbelego*), a postal village, 424 miles W. of Sydney, with daily mail therefrom. A railway station on the western line.

COOLABERN MOUNT (*Co. Northumberland*), a high peak in the Hunter Range, lying on the S. bank of the Wollombi Creek, about 2 miles from the township of Wollombi.

COOLABURRAGUNDY RIVER (*Cos. Napier and Bligh*). [See "RIVERS."]

COOLAC (*Co. Harden*), a postal village, 276 miles S. of Sydney, with daily mail, money-order and telegraph offices. A railway station on the southern line.

COOLAH (*Co. Napier*), a postal village, 246 miles N. of Sydney, with mail therefrom four times a week, money-order and telegraph offices. The nearest railway station is Mudgee, 70 miles, on the Great Western line. The district is an agricultural and pastoral one. The soil is rich and well watered by springs and heavily timbered.

COOLAMIGAL CREEK (*Co. Roxburgh*), a southern tributary of the Turon River, rising in the eastern slope of the Limekiln Range.

COOLAMIN CREEK (*Co. Wellington*), a small western tributary of the Macquarie River, rising in the Mullion's Range.

COOLAMIN MOUNT (*Co. Wellington*), a peak on the eastern side of the road from Ophir to Stoney Creek gold-field, and at the head of Bosh's Creek.

COOLAMON (*Co. Bourke*), a postal village, 309 miles S. of Sydney, with mail therefrom five times a week, money-order and telegraph offices, and Government savings bank. A railway station on the Junee branch of the Southern line.

COOLANGATTA (*Co. St. Vincent*), a postal village, 124 miles S. of Sydney, with daily mail. The nearest railway station is Moss Vale, 40 miles, on the southern line.

COOLANGATTA MOUNTAIN (*Co. St. Vincent*), a peak of the Shoalhaven Range, rising to the height of 1,000 feet above the sea-level, situate about 3 miles N.E. of the Village of Numba.

COOLANGUBRA MOUNT (*Co. Auckland*), situated at the head of Mahratta Creek, about 16 miles S.E. of the township of Bombala, is the highest peak on the South Coast Range, attaining an elevation of 3,712 feet above the sea-level.

COOLAWINE CREEK (*Co. Northumberland*), a small tributary of the Wollombi Brook, falling into it a short distance above Wollombi.

COOLONGOLOOK (*Co. Gloucester*), a postal town, 167 miles to the N. of Sydney, with mail twice a week. The nearest railway station is Hexham, 66 miles, on the northern line.

COOLOOMBUTTA CREEK (*Co. Dudley*), a small eastern tributary of the Christmas Creek.

COOLOON (*Co. Rous*), a proclaimed village in the county.

COOLRINDONG HILL (*Co. Beresford*), situated on the W. side of the road from Gipps Land to Cooma, and the N. of the road from Kiandra to the same place. It is a lofty peak to the N. of the Monaro Range of mountains.

COOLRINGDON CREEK (*Co. Wallace*), is the name of the eastern branch of the Wambrook Creek.

COOLUMBALO CREEK (*Co. Bathurst*), an eastern tributary of the Lewis Ponds, flowing past the village reserve of that name.

COOLUMBALO MOUNT (*Co. Bathurst*), a high hill lying about 6 miles S. of the Ophir Diggings.

COOLUMBOOKA RIVER (*Co. Wellesley*). [*See* "RIVERS."]

COOMA (*Co. Beresford*), a postal town, 262 miles to the S. of Sydney, with daily mail, money-order and telegraph offices, Government savings bank, and delivery by letter-carrier. A railway station on the Cooma line, situated on the two branches of the Cooma Creek, and is a very thriving and important district. Cooma was proclaimed a municipal district in 1879, with eight aldermen and a mayor. The population is about 1,500. Courts of quarter sessions and district courts are held here periodically.

COOMA BACK CREEK (*Co. Beresford*), a tributary of Cooma Creek, rising on the W. of the Three Brothers, flowing through a pastoral country.

COOMA CREEK (*Co. Beresford*), a tributary of the Umarella River, rising in Jenny Brother, a peak of the Kiandra Range, flowing through the township of Cooma and Bunyan. It waters a good pastoral district.

COOMA HILL (*Co. Beresford*), situated about 3 miles to the S.W. of Cooma, and is a lofty peak, on the E. side of the Cooma and Gippsland and Kiandra Road.

COOMAROOY LAKES (*Co. Wakool*), a group of small lakes lying in the N. bank of the Murray, about 30 miles N.W. of the camping-place, at Swan Hill (Victoria).

COOMBING CREEK (*Co. Bathurst*), the southern tributary of the Belubula River, to the S. of Cowra, flowing across the Rockley and Cowra Road, through good agricultural land.

COOMBING MOUNT (*Co. Bathurst*), a lofty hill overlooking the Coombing Creek, and attaining an altitude of 3,500 feet above the sea level.

COOMIER CREEK (*Co. Mitchell*), a small drainage creek carrying off the overflow of the Doodle Swamp into Major's Creek.

COONABARABRAN (*Co. Leichhardt*), a pastoral township, 368 miles W. of Sydney, with a daily post; money and telegraph offices, Government savings bank, and delivery by letter-carriers. The nearest railway station is Gunnedah, 62 miles, on the western line, situated on the Namoi River, a rich pastoral district. Courts of quarter sessions and district courts are held here periodically.

COONALHUGGA ANA BRACH (*Co. Menindie*), a small creek, leading out of the Darling into some swampy country on the W. of that river.

COONAMBIDGAL CREEK (*Co. Townsend*), a small branch or tributary of the Edward River, joining it to the W. of Deniliquin.

COONAMBLE (*Co. Leichhardt*), a postal town, 375 miles W. of Sydney, with post five days a week. Money-order and telegraph offices and Government savings bank. The nearest railway station is Dubbo, 97 miles, on the western line. Situated at the junction of the Castlereagh River and the Coonamble Creek. Coonamble was proclaimed a municipal district in 1880, with five aldermen and a mayor. The population is about 850. Courts of quarter sessions and district courts are held here periodically.

COONAMBLE CREEK (*Co. Leichhardt*), an eastern tributary of the Castlereagh River, draining the flat pastoral country known as the Baronne Plains.

COONBARALBA RANGE (*Albert District*), a chain of low sandstone hills on the vast plains to the W. of the Darling River. This range is near the dividing line between South Australia and this Colony.

COONEY CREEK (*Co. Sandon*), a postal village, 369 miles S. of Sydney, with daily mail.

COONO-COONO CREEK (*Co. Pottinger*), a western tributary of the Conadilly River, to the N. of the Liverpool Range.

COONONG CREEK (*Co. Urana*), a small creek, draining the flat pastoral country to the N. of Urana.

COONONG (*Co. Urana*), a railway station, 384 miles from Sydney, on the south-western branch of the southern line, Narrandera to Jerilderie.

COOPER, a county in the Central Division of the Colony. [*See* "COUNTIES."]

COOPER (*Co. Argyle*), a proclaimed village, near the swamp of that name.

COOPER MOUNT (*Co. Wellesley*), a lofty peak, about 12 miles S. of Nimitybelle.

COOPER'S CREEK (*Co. Richmond*), a postal receiving-office, 367 miles N. of Sydney, with mail per Clarence and Richmond River steamers.

COOPER'S GULLY (*Co. Auckland*), lying to the N.W. of the town of Bega.

COOPER'S SWAMP (*Co. Argyle*), lying to the E. of Lake Bathurst, in the parish of Mullengullenga.

COOPERHANNIA CREEK GOLD-FIELDS (*Co. Georgiana*), within the Mulgunnia gold-fields, proclaimed 31st August, 1865.

COOPERNOOK (*Co. Macquarie*), a postal town, 209 miles N. of Sydney, with a daily mail, with money-order office. The nearest railway station is Hexham, 132 miles, on the northern line.

COORALDOORAN CREEK (*Co. Gough*), a small northern tributary of the Mitchell River.

COORANBONG (*Co. Newcastle*), a postal village, 123 miles N. of Sydney, with mail three days a week. Money-order and telegraph offices and Government savings bank. The nearest railway station is Morriset, 6 miles, on the northern line.

COORIDOON MOUNT (*Co. Buckland*), a peak lying to the N.E. of the township of Dungog.

COORIE MOUNT (*Co. Durham*), a high mountain, about 1 mile to the E. of the township of Dungog.

COORIMPIE (*Co. Killara*), a township on the E. bank of the Paroo River.

COOROONGOOBA CREEK (*Co. Phillip*), a small tributary of the head of the Cudgegong River, flowing through rugged, scrubby country.

COOROONGOOBA MOUNT (*Co. Phillip*), a high peak in the Blue Mountain Range, at the head of the Cudgegong River.

COORUMBUNG (*Co. Northumberland*), a village reserve, about 18 miles S. from Maitland.

COOTAMUNDRA (*Co. Harden*), a postal township, 253 miles S. of Sydney, with daily mail. Money-order and telegraph offices, Government savings bank, and delivery by letter-carriers. A railway station on the southern line. Cootamundra was proclaimed a borough in 1884, with eight aldermen and a mayor. The population is about 2,200. Courts of quarter sessions and district courts are held here periodically.

COOTAMUNDRY CREEK (*Co. Arden*), a small western tributary of the Muttama Creek, flowing on the S. side of the township of Cootamundra.

COOYAL (*Co. Wellington*), a postal village, 205 miles W. of Sydney, with mail twice a week. The nearest railway station is Mudgee, 16 miles, on the western line.

COOYAL CREEK (*Co. Phillip*), a fine stream, rising in the western slope of the Australian Alps, flowing through good agricultural land and the village of Coyal, into Wyaldra Creek.

COOYAL MOUNT (*Co. Rous*), a peak of the Macpherson Range, lying on the boundary between New South Wales and Queensland, about 16 miles W. of Point Danger.

COOYANDEROY CREEK (*Co. Narromine*), a small western tributary of the head of the Bogan River.

COP, THE (*Co. Gresham*), a high peak in the Macleay Range, lying at the head of the Henry River, and about 20 miles S.E. of Stonehenge.

COPELAND NORTH (*Co. Gloucester*), a postal village, 167 miles N. of Sydney, with daily mail; money-order and telegraph offices, and Government savings bank. The nearest railway station is Hexham, 74 miles, on the northern line.

COPE'S CREEK (*Co. Hardinge*), an eastern tributary of the Goulburn River.

COPMANHURST (*Co. Clarence*), a postal village, 384 miles N. of Sydney; mails by Clarence steamers; money-order and telegraph offices. The nearest railway station is Tenterfield, 150 miles, on the northern line. Situated on the N. bank of the Clarence River, 20 miles N.W. of Grafton.

COPPABELLA (*Co. Goulburn*), is situated about 380 miles S. of Sydney, on the Coppabella Creek, and about 30 miles S. from Albury. The district is entirely a pastoral one. The nearest railway and telegraph stations are Albury on the southern line.

COPPABELLA SWAMP (*Co. Goulburn*), a tract of marshy country lying on the Coppabella Creek.

COPPERHANNIA CREEK (*Co. Georgiana*), a creek lying N.W. of the township of Bombah, being fed by the Mulgana and Camp Creeks.

CORAKI (*Co. Richmond*), a postal village, 349 miles N. of Sydney, with mail per steamers; money-order and telegraph offices.

CORAMBA (*Co. Clarence*), a postal village, 403 miles N. of Sydney, with mail therefrom, per Grafton steamer.

CORANG (*Co. St. Vincent*), situated 212 miles S. of Sydney, about a mile N. of the Corang River, and 3 miles E. of the Shoalhaven, and about 28 miles S.W. of Braidwood, which is the nearest telegraph station. Communication with Sydney is by steamer from Nowra.

CORANG RIVER (*Co. St. Vincent*). [*See* "RIVERS."]

CORCALGONG MOUNT (*Co. Wellington*), a peak in the high tableland to the east of the Louisa Creek gold-fields, about 6 miles S.W. of the township of Cudgegong.

CORCELA CREEK (*Co. Buller*), a small stream flowing into the Clarence River, about 28 miles N.E. of Maryland.

CORCORAN'S CREEK (*Co. Carden*), a small stream rising in the flat country to the S.W. of the township of Burrowa, and flowing N.E. into the Burrowa River.

CORDEAUX RIVER (*Co. Camden*). [*See* "RIVERS."]

CORDILLERA (*Co. Bathurst*), a postal village, 210 miles S. of Sydney, with daily mail. The nearest railway station is Newbridge, 45 miles, on the southern line.

COREE (*Co. Townsend*), a postal village, 438 miles S. of Sydney, with mail three days a week. The nearest railway station is Jerilderie, 20 miles, on the Junee Junction of the south-western line.

COREEN (*Co. Hume*), a proclaimed village on Coreen Creek.

COREINBOB CREEK (*Co. Wynyard*), a small creek rising near Mount Coreinbob, and flowing N. through unsurveyed country.

CORIGUDGY MOUNT (*Co. Hunter*), lies at the head of the Cudjegong River, about 25 miles E. of Dabee, and is the highest peak in the Hunter Range, attaining an elevation of 3,000 feet above the sea level.

CORINDI (*Co. Clarence*), a postal receiving-office, 380 miles N. of Sydney. Mails by Clarence River steamers twice a week.

CORNISH SETTLEMENT (*Co. Bathurst*), a small village near the township of Guyong. It is a copper-producing district.

COROWA (*Co. Hume*), a postal town, 438 miles S. of Sydney, with mail daily; money-order and telegraph offices, and Government savings bank, with delivery by letter-carriers. The nearest railway station is Albury, 40 miles, on the southern line. Courts of quarter sessions and district courts are held here periodically.

CORPLACURRIPA (*Co. Gloucester*), a postal receiving-office, 227 miles N. of Sydney, with mail once a week.

CORRIMAL (*Co. Camden*), a postal village, 45 miles S. of Sydney, with daily mail. A railway station on the Illawarra and South Coast line.

CORRIMUL MOUNT (*Co. Camden*), a high peak in the Illawarra Range, about 4 miles N. of Wollongong, overhanging the Hamlet of Belambi.

CORROWAN (*Co. St. Vincent*), a small agricultural settlement about 4 miles to the S. of Nelligen.

CORROWONG (*Co. Wellesley*), a postal village, 382 miles S. of Sydney, with mails three days a week. The nearest railway station is Cooma, 98 miles, on the Cooma branch of the southern line.

CORUNNA (*Co. Auckland*), a post-office, 276 miles S. of Sydney, with mail twice a week. Money-order office. The nearest railway station is Tarago, 78 miles, on the Cooma line.

CORYOLA (*Co. Camden*), a village, 140 miles S. of Sydney. The nearest railway station is Moss Vale, 69 miles, on the southern line.

COSGROVE CREEK (*Co. Cumberland*), a small western tributary of the South Creek.

COSMO ISLAND (*Co. Clarence*), a small island, lying in the S. arm of the Clarence River, at the confluence of the Coldstream River.

COTTER RIVER (*Co. Cowley*). [*See* "RIVERS."]

COULSON'S CREEK (*Co. Brisbane*), a tributary of the head of the Merriwa Creek.

COUNTEGANG (*Co. Beresford*), a postal receiving-office, 291 miles S. of Sydney, with mail once a week.

# COUNTIES.

## LIST OF COUNTIES IN NEW SOUTH WALES.

| | | |
|---|---|---|
| 1. ARGYLE | 48. EWENMAR | 95. NARROMINE |
| 2. ARRAWATTA | 49. FARNELL | 96. NICHOLSON |
| 3. ASHBURNHAM | 50. FINCH | 97. NORTHUMBERLAND |
| 4. AUCKLAND | 51. FITZGERALD | 98. OXLEY |
| 5. BARADINE | 52. FITZROY | 99. PARRY |
| 6. BARRONA | 53. FLINDERS | 100. PERRY |
| 7. BATHURST | 54. FORBES | 101. PHILLIP |
| 8. BENARBA | 55. FRANKLIN | 102. POOLE |
| 9. BERESFORD | 56. GEORGIANA | 103. POTTINGER |
| 10. BLAND | 57. GIPPS | 104. RALEIGH |
| 11. BLAXLAND | 58. GLOUCESTER | 105. RANKIN |
| 12. BLIGH | 59. GORDON | 106. RICHMOND |
| 13. BOOROONDARRA | 60. GOUGH | 107. ROBINSON |
| 14. BOURKE | 61. GOULBURN | 108. ROUS |
| 15. BOYD | 62. GOWEN | 109. ROXBURGH |
| 16. BRISBANE | 63. GREGORY | 110. SANDON |
| 17. BUCCLEUCH | 64. GRESHAM | 111. SELWYN |
| 18. BUCKLAND | 65. GUNDERBOOKA | 112. STAPYLTON |
| 19. BULLER | 66. HARDEN | 113. STURT |
| 20. BURNETT | 67. HARDINGE | 114. ST. VINCENT |
| 21. CADELL | 68. HAWES | 115. TAILA |
| 22. CAIRA | 69. HUME | 116. TANDORA |
| 23. CAMDEN | 70. HUNTER | 117. TARA |
| 24. CANBELEGO | 71. INGLIS | 118. THOULCANNA |
| 25. CLARENCE | 72. IRRARA | 119. TONGOWOKO |
| 26. CLARENDON | 73. JAMISON | 120. TOWNSEND |
| 27. CLARKE | 74. KENNEDY | 121. ULABARA |
| 28. CLIVE | 75. KILFERA | 122. URANA |
| 29. CLYDE | 76. KILLARA | 123. VERNON |
| 30. COOK | 77. KING | 124. WAKOOL |
| 31. COOPER | 78. LANDSBOROUGH | 125. WALJEERS |
| 32. COURALLIE | 79. LEICHHARDT | 126. WALLACE |
| 33. COWLEY | 80. LINCOLN | 127. WARADGERY |
| 34. COWPER | 81. LIVINGSTONE | 128. WELLESLEY |
| 35. CULGOA | 82. MACQUARIE | 129. WELLINGTON |
| 36. CUMBERLAND | 83. MANARA | 130. WENTWORTH |
| 37. CUNNINGHAM | 84. MENINDIE | 131. WERUNDA |
| 38. DAMPIER | 85. MITCHELL | 132. WESTMORELAND |
| 39. DARLING | 86. MONTEAGLE | 133. WHITE |
| 40. DELALAH | 87. MOOTWINGEE | 134. WINDEYER |
| 41. DENHAM | 88. MOSSGIEL | 135. WOORE |
| 42. DENISON | 89. MOURAMBA | 136. WYNYARD |
| 43. DOWLING | 90. MURCHISON | 137. YANCOWINNA |
| 44. DRAKE | 91. MURRAY | 138. YANDA |
| 45. DUDLEY | 92. NANDEWAR | 139. YANTARA |
| 46. DURHAM | 93. NAPIER | 140. YOUNG |
| 47. EVELYN | 94. NARRAN | 141. YUNGNULGRA |

The Land Act of 1884 established three grand divisions of the Colony for Pastoral purposes, running north and south, and nearly parallel with the seaboard, as shown in the map appended.

These divisions are now known and designated by law as—

    1. The Eastern Division.
    2. The Central Division.
    3. The Western Division.

The three divisions provide for settlement upon the land of a somewhat differing character, inviting, in their climatic incidences, peoples from all parts of the civilised world as tillers of the soil. These divisions follow in detail in their numerical order.

# I.—COUNTIES IN THE EASTERN DIVISION OF THE COLONY.

## Containing an estimated area of 60,452,000 acres.

ARGYLE, a county, bounded by Westmoreland and Georgiana on the N.; Murray, S.; St. Vincent and Camden, E.; King, W.; and contains 1,249,280 acres. It is in length 60 miles, and in breadth 36 miles. The following places are within its boundaries:—

| | | |
|---|---|---|
| Billyrumbeja | Gurrunda | Oallen |
| Bangalore | Inverary | Pejah |
| Baw Baw | Jerralong | Pomeroy |
| Boro | Jerrara | Quialago |
| Bourke | Kerrawarry | Rhyana |
| Bredalbane | McAlister | Strathard |
| Bungonia | Mangamore | Tarago |
| Bunnaby | Marulan | Taralga |
| Collector | Millbany | Tarlo |
| Cookbundoon | Mullengullenga | Tirrana |
| Cooper | Mulwaree | Towrang |
| Coran | Mummel | Turnllo |
| Cululla | Murray | Upper Tarlo |
| Currawang | Mutmutbilly | Uringalla |
| Eden Forest | Nadgigomar | Wayo |
| Goulburn | Narrangarrel | Willeroo |
| Guinecor | Nattery | Wologorong |
| Gullulla | Nerrimunga | Woodhouselee |
| Gundary | Norrong | Yarralau |

The County of Argyle is one of the most important counties in New South Wales, the City of Goulburn being the central figure within it. The Great Southern railway to Melbourne and Adelaide crosses it, and the Cooma line branches off at Goulburn. It is bounded on the N. by the river Guinecor, from its junction with the Wollondilly to its source, near Burra Lagoon, on the Dividing Range; on the N. by the Dividing Range from Burra Burra by Collarin to Lake George, including the three Breadalbane Plains; on the S. by the northern margin of Lake George to Kenny's Station; from Lake George to the Alianyonyiga Mountain by a small gully descending to the lake from Alianyonyiga, by the ridge extending S.E. to the hill of Wolowolar, and from Wolowolar, by Boro Creek, to the Shoalhaven River; on the E. by the Shoalhaven River to the junction of the rivulet from Barber's to its source, across a narrow neck of land to the head of the Uringalla; by the Uringalla to its junction with the Wollondilly; and by the Wollondilly to the junction of the Guinecor above mentioned. The rivers in this county are The Shoalhaven, Wollondilly, Paddy's River, Boro, and Cockbundoon. The Shoalhaven and Wollondilly form its eastern boundary, Lake George is on its southern boundary, and Lake Bathurst is within it. The mountains are Marulan, Towrang, Macalister, Hobbes, Bilton, Wayo, and Alianyonyiga. The Great Southern Railway crosses the county, and the branch line to Cooma diverges here.

ARRAWATTA, a county (also partly in the Central Division), bounded by Gough and Clive on the E.; boundary-line of Queensland, N.; Stapylton, Burnett, and Murchison, W.; Hardinge, S.; and contains, 1,351,680 acres. The following places are within its boundaries :—

| | | |
|---|---|---|
| Adowa | Cucumber | Macintyre |
| Alpine | Dight | Mandoe |
| Anderson | Dumaresq | Merita |
| Arthur's Seat | Duncan | Myall |
| Ashby | East Yetman | N. Nullamanna |
| Ashford | Egerton | Nullamanna |
| Astley | Ellis | Pindari |
| Athol | Ena | Redbank |
| Bannockburn | Frazer | Rose |
| Barden | Goonian | Russell |
| Bebo | Gordon | St. Andrew's |
| Bengalla | Graman | Samuel |
| Biloonbah | Hallam | Severn |
| Bonshaw | Hawthorne | Swamp Oak and King's |
| Bora | Hetherington | Plains. |
| Bowman | Hogarth | Texas |
| Buckley | Hold-fast | Trigamon |
| Bukkulla | Holmes | Vivier |
| Bunal | King's Plains | Wallangra |
| Burgundy | Leslie | Wandera |
| Byron | Limestone and Macintyre | Weean |
| Campbell | Lockerby | Wyndham |
| Champagne | Lorne | Yetman |
| Chapman | Macdonald | Yetman East |
| Cox | | |

This county is the extreme northern boundary of the territory adjoining Queensland. The rivers Dumaresq, Macintyre, and Severn flow through it and the Great Falls, and Fraser's Creek with Tower Hill Mount are within ts boundaries.

ASHBURNHAM, a county (also partly in the Central Division), bounded by Hardinge and Wellington on the E.; Gordon and Kennedy, N.; Cunningham, W.; Forbes and Bathurst, S.; and contains 1,505,280 acres. The following places are within its boundaries :—

| | | |
|---|---|---|
| Barrajin | Coonambro | Molong West |
| Barton | Cudal | Moura |
| Beargamil | Cumble | Mugincoble |
| Bell | Currajong | Mumbidgle |
| Belubula | Curumbeaya | Murga |
| Bindogandra | Dowling | Nanami |
| Bocobidgle | Dulladerry | Nangar |
| Boree Cabonne | Edinburgh | Nelungalong |
| Boree Nyrang | Eugowra | Nyrang |
| Borenore | Forbes | Parkes |
| Bowan | Goimbla | Terrara |
| Brolgan | Goobang | Toogong |
| Brymedura | Goonumbla | Tragere |
| Bunberry | Gregra | Troubalgie |
| Canobolas | Gunning Bland | Wanera |
| Canomodine | Kamandra | Waugan |
| Canowindra | Mandagery | Warregal |
| Cargo | Manildra | Wise |
| Carrawabitty | Martin | Wolabla |
| Collett | Milpose | Yarragong |
| Cookamidgera | Mogong | |

The rivers in this county are the Lachlan and Belubula, and which forms its southern boundary. The Orange to Molong branch of the Great Western railway skirts it on the east.

AUCKLAND, a county bounded by Beresford and Wellesley on the W.; the dividing line of Victoria, S.; the South Pacific Ocean, E; and contains 1,167,360 acres. It is about 60 miles in length, and 40 miles in breadth. The following places are within its boundaries:—

| | | |
|---|---|---|
| Bega | Howe | Pericoe |
| Bemboka | Imlay | Puen Buen |
| Bimmil | Kameruka | Sturt |
| Bondi | Kanoonah | Tantawanglo |
| Boranda | Kiah | Tathra |
| Bowinda | Kocoboreeka | Towamba |
| Boyd | Mataganah | Victoria |
| Bredbendowra | Meringo | Waalimma |
| Brogo | Mogila | Wallagaraugh |
| Bronte | Mokoreeka | Wallagat |
| Buckle | Morkerwah | Werriberri |
| Burragate | Mumbulla | Wolumba |
| Candelo | Nalbaugh | Wolumla |
| Cobra | Narrabarba | Wonboyn |
| Colombo | Nullica | Wyndham |
| Coolangubra | Numbugga | Yambulla |
| Eden | Nungatta | Yowaka |
| Genoa | Ooranook | Yuglamah |
| Gnupa | Panbula | Yurammie |
| Gooyan | | |

This county is in the extreme S. of the territory, and adjoins that of Victoria. The rivers are the Brogo, Bemboka, Bega, Towamba, Panbula, and Genoa. The Brogo and Bemboka discharge their waters into the ocean at Tathra, and the Towamba into Twofold Bay. The mountains are Nungatta, Finlay, Mumbulla, Nimmitabil, Tennyson, Buckle, and Carlyle, and Yambulla and Wolumla Peaks.

BATHURST, a county, bounded by Georgiana on the E.; Roxburgh and Wellington N.; Ashburnham W.; Forbes and King, S. It is about 65 miles in length, and 40 miles in breadth, and contains 1,190,400 acres. The following places are within its boundaries:—

| | | |
|---|---|---|
| Aberfoil | Colville | Mount McDonald |
| Anson | Cooin | Mt. Pleasant |
| Apsley | Cowra | Napier |
| Arkell | Dunleary | Neville |
| Bangaroo | Egan | Oakley |
| Barry | Egbert | Ophir |
| Bathurst | Errol | Orange |
| Beaufort | Euroka | Osborne |
| Belubula | Frederick | Perth |
| Beneree | Freemantle | Ponsonby |
| Billimari | Galbraith | Purfleet |
| Blake | Glenlogan | Roseberg |
| Blayney | Graham | St. David |
| Bracebridge | Guyong | Shadforth |
| Bringellett | Hampton | Shaw |
| Byng | Huntley | Somers |
| Cadogan | Kenilworth | Spring Hill |
| Calvert | Lennox | Tenandra |
| Canowindra | Lewis | Three Brothers |
| Carcoar | Lindsay | Torrens |
| Carlton | Lowry | Tintern |
| Carroll | Lucan | Vittoria |
| Chambers | Lyndhurst | Waldegrave |
| Chaucer | Macquarie | Walli |
| Clarendon | Malmsbury | Waugoola |
| Clinton | Malongulli | Woodstock |
| Cole | Mandurama | Worcester |
| Coleridge | Milburn | |

This county is the central one to the Great Western interior, the main line of railway passing through it, with the Blayney and Murrumburrah branch line uniting it at the latter place with the Great Southern Line to Melbourne and Adelaide. It is bounded on the N.E. by the river Campbell, from Pepper Creek, and the river Macquarie, to the junction of Lewis Ponds; on the W. by Lewis Ponds Creek, to Blackman's Swamp, and thence by the range to Canoblas Mountains; thence by the Pannara Range and Pannara Rivulet to the Belubula stream, and by the stream to its junction with the Lachlan; on the S. by that river to the Abercrombie, and the junction of Rocky Bridge Creek, also by that creek to the river Campbell aforesaid. The rivers in this county are the Macquarie, Belubula, Campbell, Abercrombie, Coombing, and Pannara Rivulets, and the Lachlan. The Macquarie and Lachlan form its northern, eastern, and southern, and the Belubula its western, boundaries. The mountains are the Evernden, Three Brothers, Lachlan, the Canoblas, and Mount Pleasant. The Great Western Railway crosses this county, with diverging lines from Blayney to Murrumburrah connecting it with the Great Southern line at the latter place; and also a diverging line to Orange.

BERESFORD, a county, bounded by Auckland and Dampier on the E.; Murray, N.; Cowley and Wallace, W.; Wellesley, S.; and contains 901,120 acres. The following places are within its boundaries:—

| | | |
|---|---|---|
| Abercrombie | Duncan | Rivers |
| Big Badja | Flinders | Rock Flat |
| Billilingra | Gladstone | Rose Valley |
| Bidjura | Good Good | Rowland |
| Bransby | Gungoandra | Sherlock |
| Bredbo | Hill | Stannard |
| Brest | Holland | The Brothers |
| Bulgundramine | Jillamatong | Throsby |
| Bullanamong | Kybeyan | Tinderry |
| Bunyan | Kydra | Umaralla |
| Callaghan | Lucas | Undoo |
| Clifford | Micaligo | Wangrah |
| Colinton | Milford | Winifred |
| Coolringdoon | Montagu | Wise |
| Cooma | Murrumbucka | Woolumla |
| Cosgrove | Onslow | York |
| Dangelong | Palmerston | |

The rivers in this county are the Murrumbidgee, Brogo, Bemboka, Begu, Towamba, Panbula, Genoa, Bredbo, Big Badja, Umaralla, Kybegan, and the Queanbeyan. The mountains are The Brothers, Coolringdon, The Peak, One-tree Hill, Blue Peak, Cooma Hill, Big Badja Hill, and Tinderry. The Goulburn to Cooma line of railway terminates in this county.

BLAND, a county (also partly in the Central Division), bounded by Forbes and Monteagle on the E.; Gipps, N.; Bourke, W.; Clarendon and Harden, S.; and contains 1,587,200 acres. The following places are within its boundaries:—

| | | |
|---|---|---|
| Balabla | Bolungerai | Curumbi |
| Barbingal | Boonubah | Dinga Dingi |
| Barmedman | Boorangagil | Dudawman |
| Belimebung | Bribaree | Eurabba |
| Berendebba | Brymur | Euroka |
| Berrigan | Bundawarra | Garagubal |
| Berthong | Burrabijong | Geraldra |
| Bimbella | Combaning | Gidgingidginbung |
| Bimbi | Congou | Gundybindyal |
| Black Creek | Culingerai | Jingeraugle |
| Boginderra | Curraburrama | Marsden |

## BLAND—continued.

| | | |
|---|---|---|
| Maleeja | Stockinbingal | Wargin |
| Mamdamah | Temora | Warralonga |
| Marbunga | Thanowring | Warralonga |
| Marowrie | Therarbung | Weedallion |
| Memagong | Thurungly | Winga |
| Milong | Trigalong | Wyalong South |
| Mininjary | Tubbul | Wyrra |
| Moonbucca | Tumbleton | Yarran |
| Morangurel | Umaralla | Yeo Yeo |
| Mugga | Waarbilla | Yerai |
| Narraburra | Walladilly | Yiddah |
| Narragudgil | Wallundry | Yuline |

The Weddin range of mountains is on the northern boundary of this county, and the Great Southern line of railway skirts its eastern border. The Bland or Yeo Yeo Creek waters it.

BLIGH, a county, bounded by Brisbane, Phillip, and Wellington on the S. and E.; Napier and Lincoln W. It is 53 miles in length, and 41 miles in width, and contains 1,077,120 acres. The following places are within its boundaries :—

| | | |
|---|---|---|
| Bellaleppa | Dorelgunmala | Stubbo |
| Berenderry | Durridgere | Talbragar |
| Bligh | Goodiman | Tallawang |
| Bobadlen | Goolma | Terraban |
| Booyamurna | Gunna | Tomimbil |
| Borambil | Guroba | Turee |
| Bowman | Loriner | Turill |
| Bulga | Meruthera | Uarby |
| Bungaba | Moan | Ulan |
| Capillis | Mummurra | Warburton |
| Collaroy | Nagora | Wargundy |
| Collieblue | Nandoura | Warung |
| Collier | Nanima | Wellington |
| Coolah | Narragamba | Wondaby |
| Cope | Park | Worobil |
| Cunna | Puggoon | Wuuluman |
| Curryall | Rotherwood | Yarragal |
| Dalkeith | Rouse | Yarrobil |
| Denison Town | | |

The rivers in this county are the Mummurra, Krui, Goulburn, Cudgegong, Macquarie, Turee, Uarby, Cainbil, Talbragar, and Coolaburragundy. The Krui forms its eastern, the Goulburn and Wyaldra Creek its southern, and the Coolaburragundy its western, boundaries. The mountains are Macarthur or Moan, Dichard, and Wingewerra, and the Great Liverpool Range crosses the county. The Great Western railway skirts the S.W. boundary of this county.

BRISBANE, a county, bounded by Durham on the E.; Buckland, N.; Bligh, W.; Phillip and Hunter, S. It is about 90 miles long by 40 broad, and contains 1,500,160 acres. The following places are within its boundaries :—

| | | |
|---|---|---|
| Ailsa | Campbell | Denman |
| Alma | Castle Sempill | Ellerston |
| Benly | Cherson | Ellis |
| Boggibri | Clanricard | Goulson |
| Bow | Coulson | Guangua |
| Brawboy | Cranbourne | Gundy |
| Brogheda | Crawney | Gundy Gundy |
| Bunnan | Dangar | Gungal |

BRISBANE—*continued.*

| | | |
|---|---|---|
| Hall | Murrulla | Tongo |
| Halscot | Murrurundi | Tyrone |
| Haydenton | Myrabluan | Wandewoi |
| Howard | Nerobingalba | Watt |
| Isis | Oxley | Waverley |
| Killoc | Page | Webimble |
| Kynga | Park | Wentworth |
| Lincoln | Parkville | Whybong |
| Mackenzie | Scone | Wickham |
| Macqueen | Strathearn | Willis |
| Manbus | Temi | Wingen |
| Manobalai | Terell | Wollara |
| Melbourne | Tinor | Worondi |
| Merriwa | Tinagroo | Yarraman |

The rivers in this county are the Hunter, Page, Isis, Dartbrook, Goulburn, and Krui. The Hunter and Goulburn Rivers form its southern and eastern, and the Krui its western boundaries. The mountains are the Liverpool Range, Chawney Pass, Myrabluan, Temi-Tinagroo, Towari-Terell, Murulla, Wingen, and Warandi. The Great Northern railway, with branch to Narrabri, crosses this county.

BUCCLEUCH, a county, bounded by Cowley on the E.; Harden, N.; Wynyard, W.; Selwyn, S.; and contains 839,620 acres. The following places are within its boundaries:—

| | | |
|---|---|---|
| Adjungbilly | Cowrajugo | Napier |
| Baloo | Cromwell | Nimbo |
| Blowering | Darbalara | Pepercorn |
| Bogong | Garnet | Pinbeyan |
| Boraig | Gobarragandra | Talbingo |
| Bramina | Goobarralong | The Peaks |
| Brungle | Goodradigbee | Tumorrama |
| Bundarbo | Jaunama | Wagara |
| Bungonge | Jibeen | Weejasper |
| Childowla | Killimicat | Wyangle |
| Clive | Mundonga | Yarrangobilly |
| Cooleman | Nanangroe | |

The rivers in this county are the Tumut, Goodradigbee, Goubaragandra, and Murrumbidgee. The Goodradigbee forms its eastern boundary. The mountains are Talbingo, Bogong, Majongbury, and Junil.

BUCKLAND, a county (also partly in the Central Division), bounded by Parry on the E.; Darling, N.; Pottinger, W.; Bligh and Brisbane, S.; and contains 1,055,900 acres. The following places are within its boundaries:—

| | | |
|---|---|---|
| Babbinboon | Evan | Telford |
| Borambil | Ferrier | Temi |
| Breeza | Grenfell | Texas |
| Carroll | Gunnadilly | Towarri |
| Clift | Loder | Wallabadah |
| Cocridoon | Moan | Warrah |
| Cosypolly | Mooki | Werrie |
| Currabubula | Parnell | Werris Creek |
| Denver | Piallaway | Wollala |
| Dight | Quirindi | Yarrimanbah |
| Doughboy Hollow | | |

The Conadilly and Peel Rivers flow through this county, and the Conadilly forms its eastern boundary. The Great Northern railway crosses it and branches off to Narrabri. Mounts Turi, Macarthur, Parry, Moan, Terell, Towari, Tingaroo, and Temi are within its boundaries. The Australian Agricultural Company have a grant within this county.

BULLER, a county bounded by Rous on the E.; Queensland boundary line, N. and W.; Clive and Drake, S.; and contains 900,360 acres. The following places are within its boundaries:—

| | | |
|---|---|---|
| Acacia | Colongoon | Mandle |
| Antimony | Corry | Marsh |
| Beaury | Coutts | Maryland |
| Bonalbo | Cullendore | Mearimb |
| Bookookoorara | Donaldson | Peacock |
| Boomi | Ellerslie | Pocupar |
| Boonoo Boonoo | Emu | Reid |
| Boorook | Evans | Robertson |
| Buller | Gilgurry | Ruby |
| Burgees | Girard | Strathspey |
| Callanyn | Gore | Timbarra. |
| Capeen | Jenny Lind | Tooloom |
| Carroll | Kangaroo | Undercliffe |
| Cataract | Korcelah | Woodenbong |
| Clarence | Lindsay | Wylie |
| Claribell | Liston | |

The Macpherson Range is the northern boundary between this Colony and Queensland, and the Boonoo Boonoo, Tooloom, Clarence, Richmond, and Cataract Rivers flow through it. Mounts Leslie, Clunie, Bedmay, Lindsay, Wilson's Peak, North and South Obelisk, and the Chimney Pot are within its boundaries. The Great Northern railway skirts its western side on the Queensland border.

CAMDEN, a county bounded by Cumberland on the N.; Westmoreland and Argyle, W.; St. Vincent, S.; the South Pacific Ocean, E. It is about 70 miles in length and 45 in breadth, and contains 1,480,320 acres. The following places are within its boundaries:—

| | | |
|---|---|---|
| Albion Park | Colo | Murrimba |
| Bangadilly | Cooloomgatta | Nattai |
| Banksia | Cordeaux | Nundialla |
| Bargo | Couridjah | Picton |
| Belanglo | Cumbertine | Robertson |
| Berrima | Danjera | Shellharbour |
| Bong Bong | Dapto | Sutton Forest |
| Bowral | Dendbium | Terragong |
| Broughton | Dendrobium | Vanderville |
| Bugong | Ettrema | Wallandoola |
| Bulli | Fitzroy | Wallaya |
| Bulli South | Gerringong | Wanganderry |
| Bullio | Greendale | Warragamba |
| Bumballa | Illaroo | Warragamba |
| Bunberra | Jamberoo | Weromba |
| Bundanoon | Jellore | Werriberri |
| Burke | Joadja | Wilton |
| Burragorang | Kangaloon | Wingello |
| Burrawang | Kembla | Wollongong |
| Calderwood | Kiama | Wongawilli |
| Cambewarra | Killawarra | Wonona |
| Camden | Mersla | Yarrawa |
| Caoura | Mittagong | Yarrunga |
| Cawdor | Moollatto | Yerringong |
| Cobbity | Moss Vale | |

The rivers in this county are the Shoalhaven, Wingecarribee, Macquarie, Wollondilly, Nattai, Warragamba, Nepean, Bargo, Kangaroo, Cataract, Cordeaux, and Paddy's River. The Shoalhaven forms its southern, the Wollondilly its western, and the Nepean its north-eastern boundaries. Its eastern coast-line includes Wollongong, Lake Illawarra, and Kiama. The mountains are Kembla, Keira, Mittagong, Jelore, Pianang, Nundialla, Corrimal, Razorback, or Mount Hymethus. The Great Southern and the South Coast railways pass through this county.

CLARENCE, a county bounded by Richmond on the N.; Drake and Gresham, W.; Raleigh, S.; the South Pacific Ocean, E.; and contains 829,440 acres. The following places are within its boundaries:—

| | | |
|---|---|---|
| Ashby | First Falls | Red Rock |
| Banyabba | Grafton City | Richmond |
| Brushgrove | Great Marlowe | Rushforth |
| Calamia | Harwood | Southampton |
| Chapman | Iluka | South Grafton |
| Clarenza | Julmanad | Southgate |
| Clifden | Lanitza | Stuart |
| Coaldale | Lardner | Taloumbi |
| Coldstream | Lavadia | Tucabia |
| Copmanhurst | Lawrence | Tyndale |
| Cowper | Maclean | Ulmarra |
| Doubleduke | Marysale | Whiteman |
| Dundoo | Moleville | Woodford |
| Eaton | Nanegai | Woombah |
| Elland | Qwyarigo | Yamba |

The rivers in this county are the Clarence, Orara, Coldstream, Woolii Woolii, and Landon. The mountains are Whoman or Peaked Hill of Captain Cook, Elaine, Doubleduke, and Lardner.

CLARENDON, a county (also partly in the Central Division), bounded by Harden on the E.; Bland, N.; Bourke, W.; Wynyard, S.; and contains 937,100 acres. The following places are within its boundaries:—

| | | |
|---|---|---|
| Bethungra | Gwynne | North Gundagai |
| Bilda | Houlaghan | North Wagga Wagga |
| Billabunga | Hurley | Oura |
| Boree | Ironbong | Sebastopol |
| Bulgan | Ivor | South Jewnee |
| Bute | Jeralgambeth | Tenandra |
| Claris | Junee | Trevethin |
| Cooba | Kimo | Ulandra |
| Eunanoreenya | Malebo | Wallace |
| Eurongilly | Marror | Wantabadgery |
| Gobbagombalin | Merribundinah | Wanitool |
| Gundagai North | Mitta Mitta | Warre Warral |
| Gundagai South | Nangus | |

The Murrumbidgee forms the southern boundary of this county, and the Great Southern railway crosses it, and the Junee Junction to Hay diverges here.

CLARKE, a county, bounded by Fitzroy on the E.; Gresham, N.; Hardinge and Sandon, W.; Vernon, S.; and contains 942,080 acres. The following places are within its boundaries:—

| | | |
|---|---|---|
| Aberfoyle | Cunnawarra | Kangaroo |
| Allingham | Dale | Lagune |
| Avondale | Day | Look Out |
| Bagot | Doughboy | Marengo |
| Balblair | Dyke | Mitchell |
| Big Hill | Euringilly | Mount Ross |
| Blythe | Falls | Mowles |
| Brown | George | Never Never |
| Chandler | Gill | Nowland |
| Clarke | Guy Fawkes | Oban |
| Clifton | Hall | Poganbilla |
| Combalo | Howell | Rampsbeck |
| Coventry | Jeogla | Rigney |

G

## CLARKE—*continued.*

| | | |
|---|---|---|
| Rockvale | Stanton | Tubbamurra |
| Ryanda | Styx | Ward |
| Seeley | Tiara | Warner |
| Serpentine | Towagal | White |
| Snowy | | |

The rivers in this county are the Yarrow, Aberfoyle, Guy Fawkes, and Wallamumbi, and the Macleay forms its southern boundary; and Ben Lomond and the Snow Range are within it. The Great Northern railway skirts it on the W.

CLIVE, a county bounded by Drake on the E.; Buller, N.; Gough, W. and S.; and contains 993,280 acres. The following places are within its boundaries:—

| | | |
|---|---|---|
| Addison | Cranbrook | Lewis |
| Angoperran | Dickson | Limestone |
| Annandale | Donaldson | Maclean |
| Bajimba | Dumaresq | Maidenhead |
| Ballandean | Eastern Water | Mingoola |
| Barney Downs | Farnell | Moogem |
| Bates | Forest Land | Morven |
| Binghi | Frazer | Perth |
| Binny | Garrett | Purvis |
| Blain | Gibraltar | Rock Glen |
| Bloxsom | Glen Elgin | Rockvale |
| Bluff Land | Glen Lyon | Romney |
| Bolivia | Goolamanger | Silent Grove |
| Boorook | Graham | Strathearn |
| Bowman | Harden | Tarban |
| Butterleaf | Hillcrest | Tenterfield |
| Capoompeta | Irby | Timbarra |
| Cavendish | Jeffrey | Wallangarra |
| Clifton | Jennings | Woodside |
| Clive | Joudol | Wunglebong |
| Cowper | Lawson | |

This county is in the extreme N. of the territory, the Dividing Range separating it from Queensland. The Great Northern railway passes through it. The Timbarra, Rocky, and Mole Rivers flow through it. The mountains are the Doctor's Nob, High Pic, the Bluff, Cupoombeta, and Joublee.

COOK, a county bounded by Cumberland on the E.; Hunter, N.; Roxburgh, W.; Westmoreland and Camden, S. It is 60 miles in length, and 44 in breadth, and contains 1,050,160 acres. The following places are within its boundaries:—

| | | |
|---|---|---|
| Barton | Glenbrook | Magdala |
| Bilpin | Goolloovinboin | Marangaroo |
| Blackheath | Govett | Meehan |
| Bowen | Govett S. | Meroo |
| Bowenfells | Grose | Mouin |
| Brasfort | Hartley | Nepean |
| Burralow | Irvine | Rock Hill |
| Capertee | Jamieson | Rydal |
| Clwydd | Kanimbla | Strathdon |
| Colo | Katoomba | Wallangambe |
| Cooba | Kedumba | Wallangambe N. |
| Cook | Kurrajong | Wallemi |
| Coomapio | Lawson | Wallerawang |
| Coonassie | Lett | Warragamba |
| Cox | Lidsdale | Wheeny |
| Currency | Linden | Wilberforce |
| Fulnash | Lithgow | Wolgan |
| Ginduntheric | Magalong | Woodford |

The rivers in this county are the Nepean, Warragamba, Cox's, Wolgan, Capertee, Hawkesbury, Colo. The Warragamba and Nepean form its south-eastern, Colo its northern, and Cox's River its south-western boundaries. The mountains are, the Blue Mountains, Clarence. Hay, York, Walker, Kurrajong, King George's Mount, Mount Tomah, and Honeysuckle Hill. The Great Western railway passes through this country, with a branch line to Mudgee.

COWLEY, a county bounded by Beresford and Murray on the E.; Harden and King, N.; Buccleuch, W.; Beresford, S.; and contains 737,280 acres. The following places are within its boundaries:—

| | | |
|---|---|---|
| Bimberi | Currangora | Nattung |
| Boboyan | East Goodradigbee | Ororal |
| Booroomba | Fergus | Pabral |
| Bray-haw | Gibraltar | Punyibah |
| Brindibella | Greenfield | Taemas |
| Bumbalong | Gudgenby | Tharwa |
| Cavan | Long Plain | Tidbinbilla |
| Cochran | Maas | Umburra |
| Congwarra | Micalong | Urayarra |
| Cooleman | Miligan | Venterman |
| Coree | Mullion | Yaouk |
| Cotter | Murray | Yarara |
| Cuppacumbalong | Narrangullen | |

The Murrumbidgee forms its eastern, and the Goodradigbee River its western, boundaries, and the Cotter River flows through it. The Cooma railway skirts its eastern border.

CUMBERLAND, a county bounded by Northumberland on the N.; Cook, W.; Camden, S.; the South Pacific Ocean, E. It is 63 miles in length and 38 miles in breadth, and contains 914,890 acres. The following places are within its boundaries:—

| | | |
|---|---|---|
| Alexandria | Gordon | Penrith |
| Appin | Ham Common | Petersham |
| Balmain | Heathcote | Pitt Town |
| Banks Meadow | Holsworthy | Pittwater |
| Bankstown | Homebush | Prospect |
| Berowra | Hunter's Hill | Richmond |
| Botany | Liberty Plains | Rooty Hill |
| Bringelly | Liverpool | Rosehill |
| Broken Bay | Londonderry | Smithfield |
| Bulgo | Long Bay | South Colah |
| Cabramatta | Longbottom | Southend |
| Campbelltown | Luddenham | St. George |
| Castle Hill | Macdonaldtown | St. John |
| Castlereagh | Manly Cove | St. Leonards East |
| Claremont | Maroota | St. Leonards |
| Clifton | Marramarra | St. Luke |
| Cook | Melville | St. Matthew |
| Coogee | Menangle | St. Peters |
| Concord | Minto | Sutherland |
| Cornelia | Mulgoa | Sutton Forest |
| Cowan | Narellan | Sydney |
| Double Bay | Narrabeen | Wattamolla |
| Dundas | Nelson | Waverley |
| Eckersley | North Colah | Wedderburn |
| Field of Mars | North Sydney | Willoughby |
| Frederick | Parramatta | Windsor |
| Gidley | | |

The harbours in the county are, Port Jackson, Botany Bay, Broken Bay, Port Hacking, and the rivers are the Hawkesbury, Nepean, George's,

Parramatta, and South Creek. The Hawkesbury forms its north-eastern, and the Nepean its south-western, boundaries. All the railways terminate in this county at Sydney, the capital of the Colony.

DAMPIER, a county bounded by the South Pacific Ocean on the E.; the counties of Murray and St. Vincent, N.; Beresford, W.; Auckland, S.; and contains 1,024,000 acres. The following places are within its boundaries:—

| Badja | Countigany | Nerrigundah |
| Belowra | Curmulee | Noorooma |
| Bergalia | Currambene | Quaanma |
| Bermaguee | Deua | Shoalhaven |
| Big Badja | Dolondundale | Tanja |
| Boalatley | Donovon | Undoo |
| Bodalla | Guinea | Urabene |
| Brogo | Gulph | Urobodalla |
| Bumbo | Jillaga | Wadbilliga West |
| Bumbo West | Jinden | Wagonga |
| Burra | Krawarree | Wamban |
| Cadgee | Merricumbene | Wandellow |
| Cadjangarry | Moruya | Wapengo |
| Coila | Murrah | Wyanbene |
| Condella | Murrabrine | Yourie |
| Congo | Narira | |

The rivers in this county are the Shoalhaven, Tuross, Dry, Deua, Noorooma, Bermaguee, Wadbilliga, and the Moruya. The latter is the northern boundary between this county and St. Vincent. At Bodalla and Congo there are important lakes. The mountains are the Dromedary, the Big Badja, Mumbulla, and Ajimgagra.

DARLING, a county bounded by Inglis and Hardinge on the E.; Murchison, N.; Nandewar, W.; Inglis and Parry, S.; and contains 921,600 acres. The following places are within its boundaries:—

| Alfred | Fleming | Namoi |
| Baldwin | Gladstone | Nandewar |
| Barraba | Guerindie | Nangahrah |
| Barraba North | Gulligal | Newry |
| Belmore | Hall | North Barraba |
| Borah | Halloran | Rangiri |
| Borindie | Hobden | Tarpoly |
| Bundarra | Ironbark | Tiabundie |
| Darling | Keepit | Veness |
| Dinawrinda | Lowry | Warrabah |
| Dowe | Manilla | Welsh |
| Eumur | Milliwindi | Wilson |
| Fitzroy | Mundowey | Woodsreef. |

The rivers in this county are the Namoi, Horton, M'Donald, and Manilla. The mountains are the Moonbi Range on its eastern side.

DRAKE, a county bounded by Clarence and Richmond on the E.; Buller, N.; Clive, W.; Gresham, S.; and contains 911,360 acres. The following places are within its boundaries:—

| Albert | Cooraldoora | Hassan |
| Alice | Dandahra | Hongkong |
| Black Camp | Drake | Keybarbin |
| Cangi | Dunbar | Lionsville |
| Carnham | Ewingar | Malara |
| Chauvel | Fairfield | Mookima |
| Churchill | Fairfield West | Neville |
| Coombadjha | Gordon | Ogilvie |
| Coongbar | Hamilton | Picarbin |

## DRAKE—continued.

| | | |
|---|---|---|
| Pikapene | Richmond | Solferino |
| Plevna | Rodgers | Tabulam |
| Pucka | Rodham | Timbarra |
| Puhoi | Sandilands | Yarreulkiarra |
| Pulganbar | Sistova | Yulgilbar |

The rivers in this county are the Clarence, Cataract, and the Mitchell, and the latter forms its southern boundary. The mountains are Capoombeta and Jonblee.

DUDLEY, a county bounded by the South Pacific Ocean on the E.; Raleigh, N.; Sandon and Vernon, W.; Macquarie, S.; and contains 977,000 acres. The following places are within its boundaries:—

| | | |
|---|---|---|
| Bandi Bandi | Gordon | Tanban |
| Barraganyatti | Hickey | Uralgurra |
| Belgrave | Kalateenee | Vernon |
| Bellbrook | Kemp | Warbro |
| Boonanghi | Kinchela | Warne |
| Burragong | Kullatine | West Kempsey |
| Clarke | Loftus | Willawarrin |
| Cliffs | Macleay | Willi Willi |
| Clybucca | Nulla Nulla | Wittitrin |
| Coliombatti | Orcen | Wolseley |
| Comara | Panton | Yarrahapinni |
| Cooroobongatti | Parrabel | Yarranbandini |
| East Kempsey | Peedee | Yarravel |
| Frederickton | Stuart | |

The Macleay River flows through the centre of this county and enters the ocean at Trial Bay.

DURHAM, a county bounded by Gloucester on the E.; Hawes, N.; Brisbane, W.; Hunter and Northumberland, S. Is about 60 miles in length and 50 miles in breadth, and contains 1,355,200 acres. The following places are within its boundaries:—

| | | |
|---|---|---|
| Aberdeen | Fingal | Paterson |
| Albyn | Foy | Prospere |
| Allynbrook | Glendon | Ravensworth |
| Althorpe | Goonangola | Rosamonde |
| Auckland | Gotha | Rouchel |
| Avenel | Gresford | Rowan |
| Balmoral | Herschell | Russell |
| Barford | Hinton | Savoy |
| Beltrees | Holywell | Seaham |
| Biddell | Houghton | Sedgefield |
| Boonabilla | Howick | Shenston |
| Bronte | Lemington | St. Aubin's |
| Brougham | Liddell | St. Julian |
| Broughton | Liebeg | Stanhope |
| Butterwick | Lowinsbrook | Tangorin |
| Camberwell | Mamaran | Tillegra |
| Carrow | Marwood | Tudor |
| Chalmers | Merton | Tyraman |
| Clarence Town | Middlehope | Uffington |
| Colonna | Mirrannie | Underbank |
| Darlington | Moonam | Vane |
| Doon | Mount Royal | Vaux |
| Douribang | Mueclebrook | Wallarobba |
| Dungog | Oldcastle | Wolfingham |
| Dyrring | Omerdale | Wynn |

The rivers in the county are the Hunter, Paterson, Williams, and Allyn. The Hunter forms its S. and N.W., the Williams its N.E. boundaries.

The mountains are, Mount Royal, Schumlo, Hudson's Peak, Carrow, Paterson, Cabre-bald, Pyraman, Willinas, Allyn, and Arthur. The Great Northern railway crosses this county.

FITZROY, a county bounded by the South Pacific Ocean on the E.; Clarence, N.; Gresham and Clarke, W.; Raleigh, S.; and contains 839,680 acres. The following places are within its boundaries :—

| | | |
|---|---|---|
| Allan | Ernani | Orara |
| Allan's Water | Fenton | Ross |
| Bagawa | Gundar | Shannon |
| Bardool | Herborn | Shea |
| Bardsley | Hyland | Sherwood |
| Blaxland | Jardine | Stewart |
| Blicks | Koukandowie | Talawudjah |
| Bligh | Kremos | Toothill |
| Boslobrick | Leigh | Towallum |
| Brelsford | Martin | Turville |
| Chambigne | Meldrum Downs | Tyringham |
| Coff | Mongawanga | Ucombe |
| Cope | Moonee | Waihou |
| Comlaroi | Moonpar | Wilawan |
| Corindi | Nana | Wiriri |
| Duckan Duckan | Nymboida | Woogoolga |
| Ermington | | |

The rivers in this county are the Nymboi and Orara; the latter forms its N.E. boundary, and Mounts Marien and Hyland are within it.

GEORGIANA, a county, bounded by Argyle and Westmoreland on the E.; Bathurst, N.; King and Bathurst, W.; King and Argyle, S. It is 50 miles long and 40 miles broad, and contains 1,231,520 acres. The following places are within its boundaries :—

| | | |
|---|---|---|
| Abercrombie | Cullalong | Meglo |
| Arthur | Finley | Mount Costigan |
| Beemarang | Garrynian | Mount Lawson |
| Belmore | Gillendich | Mulgowrie |
| Bigga | Gilmandyke | Mulgunnia |
| Billyroo | Glengarry | Nulgumia |
| Binda | Grabine | Retreat |
| Bingham | Groveland | Rockley |
| Blackman | Gurnang | Sherwood |
| Bolong | Hillas | Stoke |
| Bombah | Isabella | Thalaba |
| Bubalahla | Jeremy | Thompson |
| Buckburridgee | Jerrong | Tuena |
| Bucumba | Julong | Tyrl Tyrl |
| Bunnaroo | Kangaloolah | Walbrook |
| Bunmango | Kempfield | Wangalo |
| Burraga | Keverstone | Werong |
| Burridgee | Kiamma | Wiarborough |
| Carrawa | Laggan | Wowagin |
| Cook's Vale | Leighwood | Wyndham |
| Copperhannia | Long Swamp | Yalbraith |
| Crabine | M'Alister | Yarraman |
| Crookwell | Markdale | Yewrangara |
| Cuddyong | | |

The rivers in this county are the Crookwell, Lachlan, Abercrombie, Campbell, Isabella, and the Retreat, or Little River The Lachlan and Crookwell Rivers form its southern and western boundaries.

GLOUCESTER, a county, bounded by Macquarie on the N.; Durham, W.; Northumberland, S.; the Pacific Ocean, E. It is 80 miles in length and 65 miles in breadth, and contains 1,894,400 acres. The following places are within its boundaries :—

| | | |
|---|---|---|
| Alfred | Fitzroy | Talawahl |
| Bachelor | Forster | Tarean |
| Barrington | Fosterton | Taree |
| Becan Becan | Gloucester | Telararee |
| Belbora | Gooloongolok | Teramby |
| Berrigo | Hewong | Thalaba |
| Beryan | Horton | Thornton |
| Bindera | Irralong | Tillegra |
| Bohnock | Karuah | Tinonee |
| Booloombayt | Knowla | Tomaree |
| Bootoowaa | Korngu | Topi Topi |
| Boranel | Kundibakh | Trevor |
| Bowman | Kyle | Tuncury |
| Bulandelah | Langworthy's | Underbank |
| Bullah Delah | Larry's Flat | Verulam |
| Copeland | Milli | Wallingat |
| Craven | Mimi | Wamboin |
| Crosbie | Myall | Wangat |
| Curecki | Nerong | Wang Wauk |
| Eldon | Port Stephens | Wawgan |
| Eurunderee | Raymond Terrace | Willabah |
| Euther | Stockton | Wilmot |
| Evans | Stowell | Wollom |
| Falkland | Stroud | Wollomba |
| Fens | Sutton | |

The rivers in this county are the Williams, Wallingal, Karuah, Maclean, Manning, Wang Wang, The Avon, Gloucester, Arundel, Barrington, Cravens, Myall, Chichester, and Crawford. The Manning forms its northern, and the Williams its south-western, boundaries. Port Hunter, Port Stephens, Myall Lake, Smith's Lake, Wallis' Lake, and Farquar Inlet are on its eastern seaboard. The Australian Agricultural Company's grant of 464,640 acres is in this county; the rivers Barrington, Avon, and Kauri, flowing across the grant; and the Manning River forms the northern boundary. The important town of Stroud is within the company's grant. The Great Northern Railway skirts its southernmost boundary.

GORDON, a county (also partly within the Central Division), bounded by Wellington on the E.; Lincoln, N.; Narromine, W.; Ashburnham, S.; and contains 931,840 acres. The following places are within its boundaries:—

| | | |
|---|---|---|
| Belmore | Dubbo | Ponto |
| Benolong | Eurimbula | Redbank |
| Benya | Ganoo | Roche |
| Bexcourt | Gil-gal | Rocky Ponds |
| Bolderogery | Greenbank | Strathorn |
| Buckinbah | Gullengambel | Terrabella |
| Burgoon | Gundy | The Gap |
| Burrawong | Hyandra | The Springs |
| Caloma | Loombah | Veech |
| Cardington | Myrangle | Wagstaff |
| Catombal | Narragal | Wandawandong |
| Cullen | Newrea | Warraberry |
| Curra | Obley | Whylandra |
| Dilga | Oxley | Yeoval |
| Draway | | |

The rivers in this county are the Macquarie, Bell, Little, and the Bogan. The Great Western railway skirts its north-eastern boundaries.

GOUGH, a county, bounded by Sandon and Clive on the E. and N.; Arrawatta, W.; Hardinge, S.; and contains 1,200,600 acres. The following places are within its boundaries:—

| | | |
|---|---|---|
| Anderson | Frazer | Parkes |
| Arvid | Glencoe | Ranger's Valley |
| Balaclava | Glen Elgin | Robertson |
| Bald Nob and Mitchell | Glen Innes | Ross |
| Ben Lomond | Gordon | Rusden |
| Blair Hill | Hamilton | Scone |
| Bloxsome | Haystack | Scott |
| Borthwick | Herbert | Severn |
| Boyd | Highland Home | Stannifer |
| Bundar | Inverell | Stonehenge |
| Campbell | Kingsgate | Strachan |
| Clifton | Land's End | Strathbogie |
| Clive | Langothlin | Strathbogie North |
| Deepwater | Louis | Swanvale |
| Dichard | Macintyre | Swanbrook |
| Ditmas | Mann | Tent Hill |
| Dumaresq | Marowan | The Brothers |
| Dundee | Mitchell | Waterloo |
| Eastern Water | Mitchell River | Wellingrove |
| Eden | Mount Mitchell | Wellington |
| Elsmore | Muir | Wellington, North |
| Emmaville | Newstead | Wellington Vale |
| Fladbury | Paradise | Yarraford |
| Flagstone | Paradise North | Yarrow |
| Fletcher | | |

The rivers in the county are the Severn, Macintyre, and Yarrow. The Great Northern railway passes through it, near Glen Innes.

GOULBURN, a county, bounded by Selwyn and Wynyard on the E.; Wynyard, N.; Hume, W.; the dividing line of Victoria, S. It contains 880,640 acres, and the following places are within its boundaries:—

| | | |
|---|---|---|
| Albury | Gerogery | Murray |
| Back Creek | Ginjellic | Nail Can Reef |
| Billabung | Hume | Narra Narra Wa |
| Bowna | Huon | Puletop |
| Carabost | Jambala | Sutton |
| Carabobala | Jergyle | Talgarna |
| Coocook | Jerra Jerra | Talmalo |
| Cookardinia | Jindera | Thurgona |
| Coppabella | Jingellic | Vautier |
| Cumbaroona | Little Billabung | Wagra |
| Curragong | May Day Reef | Woomargama |
| Dora Dora | Mitchell | Wyndham |
| Forest Creek | Mountain Creek | Yambla |
| Garryowen | Mullungandra | Yarrara |
| Germanton | Mungaburina | Yarra Yarra |

The Murray River forms the southern boundary of this county, and the Great Southern railway runs through it, joining the Melbourne line at Albury, across the Murray.

GRESHAM, a county, bounded by Fitzroy on the E.; Drake, N.; Sandon and Clark, W. and S.; and contains 768,000 acres. The following places are within its boundaries:—

| | | |
|---|---|---|
| Alder | Buccarumbi | Cunglebung |
| Barool | Camelback | Dalmorton |
| Boyd | Chaelundi | Ermington |
| Braylesford | Chandler | Glen Nevis |
| Broadmeadows | Colly | Grafton |
| Brothers | Cowan | Grange |

GRESHAM—*continued.*

| | | |
|---|---|---|
| Henry | Newbold | Stanley |
| Jackadgery | Newtown Boyd | Sturt |
| Kaloe | Nullama | Urania |
| Marara | Oakwood | Wellington |
| Marara W. | Sara | Willy |
| Marengo | Springbrook | Worra |

The rivers in this county are the Mitchell, Ann and Sara, Henry, Little Henry, Nymboi, Bogi, and Boyd. The Mitchell forms its north-western, and the Sarah Ann its south-western, boundaries. The mountains are Gunglebung, Chaelung, Barney's Hill, Shea's Knob, The Gap, Ben Lomond, and Chandler's Peak.

HARDEN, a county, bounded by Murray and King on the E.; Monteagle, N.; Bland and Clarendon, W.; Buccleuch, S.; and contains 1,010,480 acres. The following places are within its boundaries :—

| | | |
|---|---|---|
| Beggan Beggan | Cunjegong | Marribumoolo |
| Binalong | Cunningham | Mooney Mooney |
| Birrema | Cunningar | Moppity |
| Bobbara | Currawong | Murrimboola |
| Bongongalong | Deeringullen | Murrumburrah |
| Bookham | Demondrille | Muttama |
| Bowning | Douglas | Mylora |
| Burra | Eubindal | Nubba |
| Childowla | Galong | Nurung |
| Coolac | Gobarralong | Talmo |
| Cooney | Gooramina | Wallendbeen |
| Cootamundry | Harden | Wallendcon |
| Coppabella | Illalong | Wambat |
| Cowcumbala | Jindalee | Wilkie |
| Cullinga | Jugiong | Woolgarlo |
| Cumbamurra | King's Vale | |

The river Abercrombie flows through the county, and the Great Southern railway crosses it, with branch line at Murrumburrah to Blayney, connecting it with the Great Western line. The Murrumbidgee forms a part of its southern boundary. The mountains are the Condon and Barren Jack Hill.

HARDINGE, a county, bounded by Sandon and Clarke on the E.; Gough, N.; Murchison and Darling, W.; Inglis, S.; and contains 1,064,960 acres. The following places are within its boundaries :—

| | | |
|---|---|---|
| Abbington | Clerkness | Ollera |
| Aconite | Cooper | Roumalla |
| Ashton | Cope's Creek | Russell |
| Aston | Darby | Sandy Creek |
| Auburn Vale | Darbysleigh | Single |
| Baker | Drummond | Skinner |
| Balala | Elderbury | St. George |
| Baldwin | Everett | Stonybatter |
| Barlow | Honeysuckle | Swinton |
| Blake | Kimberley | Tenderden |
| Buchanan | Laura | Tienga |
| Bundarra | Mackenzie | Tingha |
| Cameron | Mayo | Torryburn |
| Chapman | Moredun | Wandsworth |
| Chigwell | Morse | Williams |
| Clare | New Valley | Yarrowick |
| Clerk | Nundle | |

The rivers in this county are the Bundarra, Rocky, and Gwydir, and the Great Northern railway skirts its eastern boundary. The Nandewar Range forms its western boundary.

HAWES, a county bounded by Macquarie on the E.; Urana, N.; Brisbane and Durham, W.; Gloucester, S.; and contains 1,024,000 acres. The following places are within its boundaries:—

| | | |
|---|---|---|
| Barnard | Hall | Rowley |
| Barry | Hawes | Rushbrook |
| Brock | Lowry | Schofield |
| Campbell | Mackay | Tobin |
| Cobb | Mernott | Togalo |
| Cooleumba | Mukki | Tomallo |
| Cooplacurripa | Mummel | Uriamukki |
| Coualtwong | Murray | Vant |
| Coudwong | Myall | Want |
| Curracabundi | Myra | Ward |
| Curricabark | Naylor | Werrikimbe |
| Devitt | Nowendoc | White |
| Garfield | Nuggetty Gully | Woko and Crosbie |
| Giro | Parkes | Yccrawun |

The rivers in this county are the Hastings, Barnard, Manning, and Wargo. The mountains are Hanging Rock, Mug, Werekimbe, Royime, Sea View, Basaltic Rock, Woolumbland, and Currukabah. The Manning and Peel Rivers form its S. and W. boundaries, and the Liverpool Range its northern.

HUNTER, a county, bounded by Northumberland on the E.; Durham and Brisbane, N.; Phillip and Roxburgh, W.; Cook, S. Its length is about 71 miles, and its breadth about 47 miles, comprising 1,315,840 acres. The following places are within its boundaries:—

| | | |
|---|---|---|
| Angorawa | Ivory | Putty |
| Arndell | Jamison | Six Brothers |
| Bacraini | Jerry's Plains | Sturt |
| Blackwater | Kekeelbon | St. Albans |
| Bulga | Kindarun | Tollagong |
| Bureen | Lemington | Tomalpin |
| Capertee | M'Lean | Tonga |
| Caroora | Macdonald | Tupa |
| Caroora | Martindale | Wambo |
| Colo | Medhurst | Wareng |
| Cook | Mediwah | Warkworth |
| Coonbaralba | Mellong | Weeney |
| Coorongooba | Milbrodale | Whilpen |
| Coorongooba | Mirrie | White |
| Coricudgy | Monundilla | Whybrow |
| Doyle | Myrtle | Windsor |
| Glen Alice | Nullo | Wirraba |
| Grono | Palomorano | Wirraba |
| Gullongulong | Parnell | Wolgan |
| Gungalwa | Parr | Wollemi |
| Hawkesbury | Parry | Wollemi |
| Hungerford | Phillip | Womerah |
| Hunter | Piribil | Wonga |
| Innes | Poppong | Yengo |

The rivers within this county are the Hunter, Goulburn, Wollombi, Capertee, Colo, Macdonald, and Hawkesbury. The Macdonald forms its eastern, the Hunter its northern, Widdin Brook its western, and Colo River its southern, boundaries. The Great Northern railway skirts its N. E. boundary.

INGLIS, a county, bounded by Vernon on the E.; Hardinge, N.; Darling, W.; Parry, S.; and contains 491,520 acres. The following places are within its boundaries:—

| | | |
|---|---|---|
| Attunga | Danglemah | Pringle |
| Bendemeer | Gill | Retreat |
| Bloomfield | Hanning | Scott |
| Bobbogullion | Kentucky | Somerton |
| Bourke | Looangra | Tamworth |
| Bourke S. | Moonbi | Tara |
| Burdekin | Mulucrindie | Winton |
| Congi | Perry | Woolmol |

The rivers in this county are the Mulucrindie, Peel, Cockburn, and Macdonald. The Cockburn forms its southern and the Moonbi Range its northern and western boundaries. The mountains are Purrenbyden, Danglemah, Gulligal, Ballemballa, and Moonboy. The Great Northern railway crosses it.

KING, a county bounded by Argyle on the E.; Georgiana and Bathurst, N.; Monteagle and Harden, W.; and Murray, S.; and contains 1,140,000 acres. The following places are within its boundaries:—

| | | |
|---|---|---|
| Alton | Grabben Gullen | Nelanglo |
| Bala | Graham | Newham |
| Bango | Gunnary | Numby |
| Barnett | Gunning | Olney |
| Biala | Hovell | Opton |
| Blakney | Jerrara | Preston |
| Branah | Jerrawa | Rabnor |
| Bunton | Kember | Romner |
| Burrowa | Kenyu | Rugby |
| Crookwell | Kildare | Taunton |
| Crosby | Lampton | Wallah |
| Cullarin | Lerida | Ware |
| Dalton | Manton | Wheeo |
| Derringallen | Merrill | Windnella |
| Dixon | Mundoonen | Wyangala |
| Garway | Narrawa | Yass North |

The rivers in this county are the Burrowa, Lachlan, Crookwell, and Yass. The Crookwell forms its north-eastern, and the Burrowa its western, boundaries. The mountains are Bowning Hill, Mundonen, Dixon's, Chaton, Cullarin, Curramumbla, and Darling. The Great Southern railway crosses the county.

MACQUARIE, a county bounded by Dudley on the N.; Hawes, W.; Gloucester, S.; the South Pacific Ocean, E. It is 60 miles in length, and 50 miles in breadth, and contains about 1,525,760 acres. The following places are within its boundaries:—

| | | |
|---|---|---|
| Albert | Cogo | Hastings |
| Arakoon | Comboyne | Innes |
| Ballengara | Coopernook | Jasper |
| Barnard | Cowangara | John's River |
| Bellangry | Cundle | Kempsey West |
| Beranghi | Dawson | Kerewong |
| Bobin | Debenham | Khatambuhl |
| Bulga | Ellenborough | Killawarra |
| Burrawan | Forbes | Kinchela |
| Cairncross | Gladstone | Kindee |
| Camden Haven | Harrington | Kippara |

## MACQUARIE—*continued*.

| | | |
|---|---|---|
| Knorrit | Marsh | Sancrox |
| Kokomerican | Moorabark | Sancrox South |
| Koree | Morton | Stewart |
| Koree | Myall | Taree |
| Lansdowne | Oxley | Tinebank |
| Lewis | Palmerston | Torrens |
| Lincoln | Pappimbarra | Vernon |
| Lorne | Prospect | Walibreesa |
| Mackay | Queen's Lake | Wingham |
| Macquarie East and West | Ralfe | Wyoming |
| Mariaville | Redbank | Yarrat. |
| Marlee | Rowley | |

The rivers in this county are the Manning, Hastings, Kindee, Nowendoc, Dawson's, Macleay, Number Two River, Stewart's, Lansdowne, Forbes, Ellenborough, and Maria's River. Crescent Head, Port Macquarie, Lake Innes, Queen's Lake, Camden Haven, Watson Taylor's Lake, and Farguhar Inlet, are on its eastern seaboard. The mountains are Kippara, Sea View, Cockamerico, Brokenbago, Cago, Tinebang, Culepatamba, Idalkangara, and Arakoon.

MONTEAGLE, a county (also partly in the Central Division), bounded by King on the E.; Forbes, N.; Bland, W.; Harden, S.; and contains 884,480 acres. The following places are within its boundaries:—

| | | |
|---|---|---|
| Baxter | Cudgymagnntry | Narralen |
| Bendick Murrell | Dananbilla | Rossi |
| Bribaree | Geegullalong | Thuddungara |
| Brundah | Grenfell | Tyagong |
| Bulla | Gungewalla | Wambanumba |
| Bumbaldry | Iandra | Weddin |
| Bungalong | Illundie | Willawong |
| Burramunda | Kikiamah | Wilton |
| Burrangong | Koorowalba | Woodonga |
| Coba | Marina | Yambira |
| Cocomiugla | Murringo | Young |
| Congera | Murringo N. | Yandoo |
| Coolegong | Murrungal | |

The rivers in this county are the Lachlan and Burrowa, and the latter forms its eastern boundary. The mountains are Widdin, Congo, Mannar, and Jimalong. The branch railway line Murrumburra to Blayney, uniting the southern and western main lines, passes through this county.

MURRAY, a county bounded by St. Vincent on the E.; Argyle and King, N.; Cowley, W.; Beresford, S. It is 78 miles in length, and 44 miles in breadth, and contains an area of 1,437,240 acres. The following places are within its boundaries:—

| | | |
|---|---|---|
| Amungula | Currandooley | Keewong |
| Ballalaba | Ellenden | Krawarree |
| Barnet | Fairy Meadow | Larbert |
| Bendullock | Gigerline | Majura |
| Boambola | Ginnindeera | Merigan |
| Bullongong | Googong | Molonglo |
| Bungendore | Goorooyaroo | Monkellan |
| Burbong | Gundaroo | Morumbateman |
| Burra | Hall | Mulloon |
| Butmaroo | Hume | Nanima |
| Bywong | Jeir | Narrabundah |
| Canberra | Jinero | Ollalulla |
| Captain's Flat | Jingera | Oronmear |
| Carwoola | Jinglemoney | Palerang |

MURRAY—*continued.*

| | | |
|---|---|---|
| Pialligo | Toual | Warri |
| Purrorumba | Tuggeranong | Warroo |
| Queanbeyan | Urialla | Weetangera |
| Sutton | Wallaroo | Werriwa |
| Talagandra | Walonglo | Yammnbeyan. |
| Tantangera | Wamboin | Yarrolumla |
| Thurralilly | Warrabundah | Yarrow |

The rivers in this county are the Shoalhaven, Queanbeyan, Yass, Murrumbidgee, Boro Creek, and Molongolo. The Murrumbidgee forms its south-western, and the Shoalhaven its eastern, boundaries, and Lake George is within it. The mountains are The Gourock Range, Bywong, Talyrang Peak, Cowangerong, Wollowolar, Eltendon, Yarrow Pic, Tinderry Mountains, or The Twins. The Goulburn and Cooma Railway crosses this county.

NORTHUMBERLAND, a county bounded by Gloucester and Durham on the N.; Hunter, W.; Cumberland, S.; the South Pacific Ocean on the E. Is 68 miles in length, and 55 in breadth, and contains 1,199,040 acres. The following places are within its boundaries:—

| | | |
|---|---|---|
| Aberglasslyn | Gosforth | Olney |
| Adamstown | Greta | Ourimbah |
| Allalong | Hamilton | Ovingham |
| Allandale | Harrowby | Patonga |
| Alnwich | Hay | Pokelbin |
| Ash Island | Heddon | Popran |
| Auburn | Hexham | Quarrybylong |
| Awaba | Kahibah | Rothbery |
| Bala | Kincumber | Rugby |
| Belford | Kooree | Singleton |
| Bishop's Bridge | Lambton | Snodgrass Valley |
| Blaxland | Lambton, New | Spencer |
| Brake | Lambton, Old | St. Albans |
| Branxton | Lochinvar | Stanford |
| Brisbane Water | Lockyer | Stockrington |
| Burragurra | Maitland, East | Stowe |
| Burton | Maitland, West | Teralba |
| Cessnock | Mandolong | Tuggerah |
| Charlestown | Mangrove | Vere |
| Congewai | Morubin | Wallambi |
| Coolamin | Melbrodali | Wallarah |
| Coonamble | Milfield | Wallsend |
| Coorabare | Minmi | Waratah |
| Coorumbung | Mornben | Warkworth |
| Cosgrove | Morrisset | Werong |
| Cowan | Mulbring | Whittingham |
| Dalton | Mummorah | Wickham |
| Dora | Narara | Wollombi |
| Eglington | Newcastle | Wyong |
| Finchley | Norah | Yango |
| Gosford | Nowan | |

The rivers in this county are The Hunter, Wollombi, Macdonald, and the Hawkesbury. The Macdonald and Hawkesbury form its S.W., and the Hunter its northern, boundaries. Broken Bay and Port Hunter, with Tuggerah Beach Lake and Lake Macquarie, are on its eastern seaboard. The mountains are Meruben, Calore, Yango, Werong, Finch, Collabeen, and Sugarloaf. The Great Northern and Homebush-Waratah Railway pass through this county, the terminus being at Newcastle.

PARRY, a county, bounded by Vernon on the E.; Inglis, N.; Buckland, W.; Brisbane, S.; and contains 784,360 acres. The following places are within its boundaries:—

| | | |
|---|---|---|
| Ainsley | Jury | Somerton |
| Anna | Loftus | Tamerang |
| Bective | Moolummoola | Turill |
| Bowling Alley Point | Moorawara | Vernon |
| Bullinbull | Mulla | Walcha |
| Callaghan | Nemingha | Winton |
| Crawney | Nundle | Wombramurra |
| Dungowan | Ogunbil | Woolomin |
| Gill | Piallamore | Yeciaria |
| Goonoo Goonoo | Royinn | Yeerowin |
| Grawney | Scott | |

The Peel and Cockburn Rivers flow through the county, and the Great Northern railway crosses it. The Moonbi Range forms its eastern, the Liverpool Range its southern, and the Peel and Cockburn its northern, boundaries. The mountains are Moorawaba, Uriari, Moolunmoola, Hanging Rock, Muc, and Royime. The Australian Agricultural Company's grant of 313,298 acres is within the county.

PHILLIP, a county, bounded by Hunter on the E.; Brisbane and Bligh, N.; Wellington, S. It is 53 miles in length, and 41 miles in breadth, and contains 1,035,520 acres. The following places are within its boundaries:—

| | | |
|---|---|---|
| Arthur | Derale | Moolarben |
| Bara | Dungeree | Murrumbo |
| Barigan | Eurundury | Never Never |
| Bayley | Fitzgerald | Nullo |
| Boogleedie | Galambine | Pomany |
| Botobolar | Growee | Price |
| Budden | Gulgong | Ruuker |
| Bumberra | Guntawang | Simpson |
| Burrumbelong | Hawkins | Tawinbang |
| Bylong | Kelgoola | Tongbong |
| Coggan | Kerrabee | Widdin |
| Comiala | Lee | Wilbertree |
| Coolealwin | Lennox | Wilpinjong |
| Cooyal | Louee | Wollar |
| Cumbo | Macdonald | Wyaldra |
| Dabee | | |

The rivers in this county are the Cudgegong and Goulburn. The mountains are Runker's Pic, Beace or Tongongwell, Cox's Crown, Willworrill, Nullo Mountains, and Pomany. The Goulburn forms its northern, Weddin Weddin Brook its eastern, and the Cudgegong its south-western, boundaries. The Great Western Branch Railway line, Wallerawang to Mudgee, skirts this county.

RALEIGH, a county, bounded by the South Pacific Ocean on the E.; Fitzroy, N.; Dudley, W. and S.; and contains 992,280 acres. The following places are within its boundaries:—

| | | |
|---|---|---|
| Allgomera | Gladstone | North Creek |
| Bellinger | Herborn | Oakes |
| Belmore | Ingalba | Raleigh |
| Bonville | Ketelghay | South Bellinger |
| Bowra | Medlow | Unkya |
| Brelsford | Merrylegai | Valley Valley |
| Buckra Bendinni | Missabotti | Vautin |
| Congarinni | Nambucera | Warrell |
| Denison | Never Never | Waverley |
| Dingle | Newry | Weekes |
| Dudley | North Bellinger | Wilson |

The rivers in this county are the Mitchell, Boyd, Clarence, Orarah, Bellinger, Colo Stream, and South Boyd; and the South Pacific Ocean forms its eastern boundary. The mountains are Comara, Camelback, and Amindrus.

RICHMOND, a county, bounded by the South Pacific Ocean on the E.; Rous, N.; Drake, W.; Clarence, S.; and contains 696,320 acres. The following places are within its boundaries:—

| | | |
|---|---|---|
| Ballina South | East Casino | Riley |
| Barrawanga | Ellangowan | Shannon |
| Bundock | Esk | South Codrington |
| Bungawalbin | Evans | South Casino |
| Busby | Gibberagee | Tabbimoble |
| Camira | Hogarth | Tatham |
| Casino | Marsh | West Coraki |
| Coombell | Mongogarie | Whiporie |
| Coraki | Myall | Woodburn |
| Darko | Myrtle | Wooroowoolgan |
| Dobie | Nandabah | Woram |
| Donaldson | Powerpa | Wyandah |
| Doubleduke | Richmond | Wyon |

The rivers in this county are the South Richmond and Richmond. The latter forms its northern, the Pacific Ocean its eastern, and the Richmond Range its southern, boundaries. The mountains are the Double Duke, Neville, and Brodie.

ROUS, a county, bounded by the South Pacific Ocean on the E.; Queensland boundary, N.; Buller and Drake, W.; Richmond, S.; and contains 1,382,400 acres. The following places are within its boundaries:—

| | | |
|---|---|---|
| Alstonville | Ettrick | Pimlico |
| Babyil | Fairy Mount | Queebun |
| Ballina | Findon | Roseberry |
| Berwick | Geneva | Runymede |
| Bexhill | Gooninbar | Sherwood |
| Billinudgel | Gundurimba E. | Stratheden |
| Blakebrook | Gundurimba S. | Terranora |
| Boombee | Hanging Rock | Teven |
| Broadwater | Jasper | Tintenbar |
| Brunswick | Jiggi | Tomki |
| Bungabbee | Kunghur | Toolond |
| Burrell | Kynnumboon | Toonumbar |
| Byangum | Kyogle | Tuckerumba |
| Byron | Langwell | Tuckombil |
| Carranba | Lismore | Tunstall |
| Chillingham | Lismore S. | Tyalgum |
| Chinderah | Lismore N. | Tyalgah |
| Clunes | Loadstone | Unumgar |
| Codrington N. | Meerschaum | Uralba |
| Condong | Mooball | Wardell |
| Cooloon | Mullum | Warrazambil |
| Coraki | Mullumbrinby | Whian Whian |
| Cougal | Murwillumbah | Winngaree |
| Cudgen | Newrybar | Wollumbin |
| Dunbible | Nimbin | Worendo |
| Dunoon | North Casino | Wyndham |
| Dyraaba | | |

The rivers in this county are the Richmond, Tweed, and Brunswick. The Macpherson Range forms its northern, the South Pacific Ocean its eastern, and the Richmond River its southern boundaries. The mountains are Worendo, Warning, Gipps, and Fairy Mount.

ROXBURGH, a county, bounded by Cook and Hunter on the E.; Phillip on the N.; Wellington and Bathurst on the W.; and Westmoreland on the S. It is 50 miles long, and 40 miles broad, and contains 972,160 acres. The following places are within its boundaries:—

| | | |
|---|---|---|
| Airly | Falnash | Rylstone |
| Bandamora | Gangguddy | Sofala |
| Ben Bullen | Goco | Solitary Creek |
| Bocoble | Goongall | Stewart |
| Brumbun | Gullen Bullen | Sunny Corner |
| Burrowandry | Hearne | Tabrabucca |
| Burrowonry | Ilford | Tayar |
| Capertee | Jedburgh | Thornshope |
| Carwell | Jesse | Turon |
| Castleton | Kelso | Umbiella |
| Churdine | Macquarie | Wallerton |
| Claudulla | Mead | Waltham |
| Coco | Meadow Lee | Warrangunia |
| Coolamigal | Melrose | Waterbeach |
| Crudine | Milla Murrah | Watton |
| Cullen Bullen | Murundarcy | Wells |
| Dullabree | Peel | Wiagdon |
| Duramana | Piper | Winburn |
| Eskdale | Raglan | Yetholme |
| Eusdale | Rydal | |

The rivers within this county are the Macquarie, Fish River, Cudgegong, and Turon. The Macquarie and Fish Rivers form its south-western boundary. The mountains are Durambang, Mount Ovens, Blackman's, Crown, Honeysuckle Hill, Marsden or Claudulla, and Tayan Pic. The Great Western railway crosses this county, and branches off to Mudgee.

SANDON, a county, bounded by Dudley on the E.; Clarke, N.; Hardinge, W.; Vernon, S.; and contains 890,880 acres. The following places are within its boundaries:—

| | | |
|---|---|---|
| Albert | Elton | Mihi |
| Arding | Enmore | Salisbury |
| Armidale | Exmouth | Saltash |
| Ben Lomond | Falconer | Sandon |
| Berryman | Ferryman | Saumarez |
| Blacknote | Gostwick | Shasta |
| Boorolong | Guyra | Sobraon |
| Butter | Harnham | Somerset |
| Clevedon | Hardinge | Springmount |
| Cooney | Hargrave | Tilbuster |
| Dangarsleigh | Hillgrove | Tiverton |
| Davidson | Kentucky | Uralla |
| Devon | Lawrence | Urota |
| Donald | Llongothlyn | Wentworth |
| Dumaresq | Merrigulah | Woolomombi |
| Duval | Metz | Yarrowich |
| Eastlake | | |

The rivers in this county are the Macleay, Wallamumba, Dyke, Apsley, Chandler, and Guyra. The mountains are Duval, Ben Lomond, Bald Nob, Chandler's Peak, Haraham Hill, Duvals, Blacknote, and Blue Mount. The Great Northern railway crosses it. The Wallamumbi River forms its eastern and the Nandewar Range its western boundaries.

SELWYN, a county, bounded by Wallace on the E.; Clarendon and Buccleuch, N.; Goulburn, W.; Victoria Boundary, S.; and contains 1,167,360 acres. The following places are within its boundaries:—

| | | |
|---|---|---|
| Beaumont | Hume | Nurenmerenmong |
| Bogandyera | Indi | Ourance |
| Brigenbong | Jagumba | Round Hill |
| Buccleuch | Jagungal | Scott |
| Buddong | Jingellic East | Selwyn |
| Burra | Khancoban | Tabletop |
| Clear Hill | King | Tooma |
| Cowra | Kosciusko | Tougaroo |
| Craven | Lea | Tumbarumba |
| Dargals | Mangar | Twynam |
| Geehi | Mannus | Victoria |
| Glenroy | Marnagle | Wallace |
| Glenken | Mate | Welaregang |
| Greg Greg | Munderoo | Welumba |
| Gungartan | Munyang | Yellowin |
| Hay | Murray | Youngal |

The rivers in this county are the Tumut and the Indi. The mountains are The Mangar, Round Mount, Kosciusko, and the Snowy Mountains, which latter forms its eastern boundary.

ST. VINCENT, a county bounded by Camden on the N.; Argyle and Murray, W.; Dampier, S.; the South Pacific Ocean, E. It is 80 miles long from N. to S., and 40 miles in width from E. to W., and contains 1,733,760 acres. The following places are within its boundaries:—

| | | |
|---|---|---|
| Albert | Currambene | Mullendaree |
| Amluen | Currock | Murrengenburg |
| Bateman | Currowan | Narriga |
| Bateman's Bay | Danjera | Nowra |
| Beecroft | Durran Durra | Numbaa |
| Benandra | East Nelligen | Quiera |
| Bendoura | Elrington | Sassafras |
| Bettowynd | Endrick | Seymour |
| Bherwerre | Ettrema | St. George |
| Bolaro | Farnham | Tallaganda |
| Boolijah | George's Basin | Tallowal |
| Borimbadill | Goba | Tamago |
| Boyne | Huskisson | Termeil |
| Braidwood | Jembaicumbene | Tianjara |
| Broulee | Jerrawangala | Tomboye |
| Buangla | Jerricknorra | Tomerong |
| Buckenbowra | Jervis Bay | Touga |
| Budawang | Kioloa | Ulladulla |
| Bulee | Little Forest | Wandrawandian |
| Burrill | Marlowe | West Nelligen |
| Clyde | Meangora | Wog Wog |
| Coghill | Milo | Wollumboola |
| Conjola | Milton | Woodburn |
| Coolumburra | Mogendoura | Yadboro |
| Corang | Mogood | Yalwal |
| Croobyar | Monga | Yatwall Creek |
| Cudmirrah | Mongarlowe | Yerriyong |

The rivers in this county are the Shoalhaven, Deua, Moruya, Clyde, Endrick, and Mongarlow. The eastern coast-line includes Jervis Bay, Bateman's Bay, and Ulladulla. The Shoalhaven forms its northern, and the Moruya its southern, boundaries. The mountains are Budawang, Currockbilly, Coyoyo, Diddel or Pigeonhouse, Jillamatong, and Nowra.

VERNON, a county, bounded by Dudley on the E.; Sandon, N.; Inglis and Parry, W.; Hawes, S.; and contains 1,054,720 acres. The following places are within its boundaries:—

| | | |
|---|---|---|
| Aberbaldie | Europambela | Norton |
| Andy | Fenwick | Oorundunby |
| Apsley | Fitzroy | Ohio |
| Benditi | Fletcher | Salway |
| Bergen-op-Zoom | Gill | Styx |
| Boulton | Glen Morison | St. Clair |
| Brassey | Halloran | St. Leonard |
| Branga | Ingleba | Tia |
| Cobrabald | Kangaroo Flat | Tiara |
| Cochrane | Kunderang | Trinidad |
| Denne | Loch | Walcha |
| Ella | Macleay | Waterloo |
| Emu | Moona | Winterbourne |
| Enfield | Mooraback | Yarrowitch |

The rivers in this county are the Macleay, Apsley, and the Tia. The mountains are Kipparah, Blue Mount, Blacknote, Ohio Peak, Bald Nob, Walcha, and Sugar Loaf. The Macleay forms its northern boundary. The Great Northern railway skirts its western boundary.

WALLACE, a county, bounded by Wellington and Beresford on the E.; Cowley, N.; Selwyn, W.; Wellesley, S.; and contains 1,361,920 acres. The following places are within its boundaries:—

| | | |
|---|---|---|
| Abington | Crackenback | Mitchell |
| Adaminiby | Dalgetty | Moyangul |
| Addicumbene | Denison | Mowamba |
| Arable | Denison W. | Munyang |
| Barkalum | Eucumbene | Murroo |
| Beurina | Gabramatta | Myack |
| Blakefield | Goandra | Myalla |
| Bobundara | Gordon | Napier |
| Bolaira | Grose | Nimmo |
| Boloka | Gungarlin | Numbla |
| Bloomfield | Guthega | Nungar |
| Bradley | Gygederick | Popong |
| Buckley's Crossing | Ingebirah | Seymour |
| Buckenderra | Ingeegoodbee | Tantaugarra |
| Bulgandara | Jimenbuen | The Gulf |
| Bullenbalong | Jinderboine | The Peak |
| Cabramurra | Kalkite | Thredbo |
| Caddigat | Kiandra | Tongaroo |
| Chippendale | Kosciusko | Townsend |
| Clapton | Lake | Wallgrove |
| Clyde | Matong | Wambrook |
| Coolamatong | Marrinumbla | Wilson |
| Coonhoonbula | Middlingbank | Wullwye |
| Cootralanta | | |

The rivers in this county are the Snowy, Crackenback, Gungarlan, Mogangul, Ingeegoodbee, Eucumbene, Mowamba, and Jacob's River. The Snowy River forms its S. and E. boundaries. The mountains are Kosciusco, 7,256 feet; The Pilot, 6,020 feet; Drest Mount, Tia Peak, The Scotchman, Mowamba, Jinderboine, Table Top, Bull's Peak, Ram's Head, Snowy, Wulwye, Jinny Brothra, Bald Hill, Gygederick, Bobundara, and Round Mountain.

WELLESLEY, a county, bounded by Auckland on the E.; Beresford, N.; Wallace, W.; boundary of Victoria, S.; and contains 942,080 acres. The following places are within its boundaries:—

| | | |
|---|---|---|
| Alexander | Delegete | Nelson |
| Ashton | Gegar | Nimmitabel |
| Bibbenluke | Glenbog | Peters |
| Biddi | Grenville | Pickering |
| Boco | Gulgin | Quidong |
| Bombala | Gunning Grach | Rodney |
| Bungarbo | Hayden | Tangaroo |
| Bungee | Ironmungy | Tarrabaudra |
| Burnima | Jettiba | Thoko |
| Burrimbucco | Lawson | Tingaringi |
| Byadbo | Maffra | Tivy |
| Cambalong | Maharatta | Tombong |
| Cathcart | Meringo | Wangellic |
| Coolumbooka | Merriangaah | Wellesley |
| Cooper | Merrumbule | Wellington |
| Creewah | Mila | Wellsmore |
| Currowang | Mount Trooper | Wollondibby |

The rivers in this county are the M'Laughlan, Little Plain, Coolumboca, Bombalo, Cambalong, Delegete, and Snowy River. The Snowy River forms its N.W. boundary. The mountains are Mounts Ringa Ringa, Cooper, One-tree Hill, The Telegraph, Bell's Peak, Bungee's Peak, Bare Hill, Coolangabra, and Trooper. The terminus of the Cooma railway is in the adjoining county, Beresford.

WELLINGTON, a county bounded by Roxburgh, and Phillip, on the E.; Bligh, N.; Gordon and Ashburnham, W.; and Bathurst, S. It is 72 miles in length and 42 miles in breadth, and contains 1,060,000 acres. The following places are within its boundaries:—

| | | |
|---|---|---|
| Avisford | Hill End | Stuart |
| Biraganbil | Ironbarks | Suttor |
| Boduldura | Kerr | Tambaroora |
| Boiga | Larras Lake | Tatuali |
| Boomey | Lewis | Three Rivers |
| Borcenor | Macquarie R. Gold-field | Towac |
| Broombee | Mannae | Toolamanang |
| Burrandong | March | Trianbil |
| Canning | Merinda | Trudgett |
| Carroll | Millenbong | Tunabidgee |
| Coolamin | Molong East | Tunnabutta |
| Cooper | Mudgee | Ulmarah |
| Copper Hill | Muckerwa | Walters |
| Cudgegong | Mulyan | Warratra |
| Cummings | Mumbil | Warburton |
| Cunningham | Nubrigyn | Warne |
| Curragurra | Omigal | Waurdong |
| Erudgere | Ophir | Wear |
| Forbes | Orange | Wellington |
| Galwadgere | Peters | Werouera |
| Gamboola | Piambong | Windeyer |
| Grattai | Rouse | Wyadere |
| Hargraves | | |

The rivers in this county are Cudgegong, Macquarie, Bell, Turon, Pyramul, and Merco. The Cudgegong forms its north-eastern and north-western boundaries. The mountains are Canoblas, Guannahill, Bocoble, and Galwadyer. The Great Western railway runs across this county.

**WESTMORELAND**, a county bounded by Camden on the E.; Cook and Roxburgh, N.; Georgiana, W.; and Argyle, S. It is 64 miles in length, and 32 miles in breadth, and contains 1,259,600 acres. The following places are within its boundaries :—

| | | |
|---|---|---|
| Abercorn | Gambenang | Mourguong |
| Adderley | Gangerang | Mozart |
| Alfred | Glenburn | Muruin |
| Antonia | Guineacor | Norway |
| Balfour | Irene | Oberon |
| Banshea | Jenolan | O'Connell Plains |
| Baring | Jocelyn | Oldbuck |
| Bimlow | Jooriland | Speedwell |
| Bindo | Kendale | St. Columba |
| Blenheim | Kenlis | Swatchfield |
| Bolton | Konangaroo | Tartarus |
| Bouverie | Kowmung | Terni |
| Bulgarres | Kowmung | The Peaks |
| Colong | Langdale | Thornshope |
| Crete | Leibnitz | Thurat |
| Cyclops | Lowther | Vulcan |
| Drogheda | Merlin | Wingecarribee |
| Duckmaloi | | |

The rivers in this county are Campbell's, Fish, Cox's, Wollondilly, and Kowmung. The Wollondilly and Cox's River, form its eastern and Campbell's River its western, and Fish River its northern, boundaries. The mountains are Murruin, Collong, Stromlo, Blaxland, Square Rock, and The Peaks. The Great Western railway skirts its northern boundary.

**WYNYARD**, a county (also partly in the Central Division), bounded by Buccleuch on the E.; Clarendon, N.; Mitchell, W.; Goulburn and Selwyn, S.; and contains 1,116,160 acres. The following places are within its boundaries :—

| | | |
|---|---|---|
| Adelong | Goldspink | Phelps |
| Bago | Gregadoo | Rowan |
| Bangus | Gumby Gumby | Selwyn |
| Batlow | Gundagai N. | Tarrabandra |
| Belmore | Gundagai S. | Tarcutta |
| Blanch | Hillas | Tumut |
| Book Book | Hindmarsh | Tywong |
| Borambula | Humula | Umbango |
| Bulagee | Keajura | Umulty |
| Cadara | Kilgowla | Umutbee |
| Calafat | Kycamba | Wagga Wagga South |
| Carrbost | Livingstone | Wallace |
| Coreinbob | Mate | Wereboldera |
| Courabyra | Minjary | Willie Ploma |
| Cunningdroo | Minyang | Wondalga |
| Dutzon | Mundarlo | Woomahrigong |
| Ellerslie | Murraguldrie | Wood |
| Euadara | Nacka Nacka | Yabtree |
| Gadara | Oberne | Yaven |
| Gilmore | | |

The rivers in this county are the Murrumbidgee and Tumut. The first-named forms its northern and the latter its eastern boundaries. The mountains are Tarcutta and the Pilot. The Great Southern railway crosses the western boundary.

## II. COUNTIES IN THE CENTRAL DIVISION OF THE COLONY.

Containing an estimated area of 55,460,000 acres.

BARADINE, a county, bounded by White on the E.; Jamison and Denham, N.; Leichhardt, W.; and Gowen, S.; and contains 1,341,440 acres. The following places are within its boundaries:—

| | | |
|---|---|---|
| Baradine | Duneverian | M'Farlane |
| Barwon | Entigal | Newman |
| Berigeric | Etoo | Orr |
| Berrybah | Evans | Parsons |
| Boorimah | Geridgeric | Pilliga |
| Bulgarie | Gidgenbar | Quegobla |
| Bulgaldie | Gince | Rundle |
| Bullerawa | Givabegan | Talluba |
| Bulliwy | Goangra | Tallama |
| Bundill | Goorianawa | Teni |
| Bungle Gully | Gora | Terembone |
| Carlo | Gulusoy | Tunis |
| Ceclong | Hall | Ukerbarley |
| Coolangoola | Janalong | Ulambie |
| Coomore South | Kenebri | Urawilkie |
| Coomore | Leslie | Walgett |
| Cooper | Mackenzie | Wambadule |
| Cox | Meit | Wangan |
| Cubbo | Merebone | Wheoh |
| Culnooy | Merimborough | White |
| Cumbil | Merritombea | Widgee |
| Cumberdoon | Midgee | Wittenbra |
| Dandry | Miller | Worigal |
| Dangar | Milchomi | Yarrigan |
| Deneroli | Minnon | Yarran |
| Doyle | Moglewit | Yearanan |
| Dubbo | Muttama | |

The Barwon and Namoi Rivers form the northern boundary of this county; and Mounts Bideaway and Barama are within it.

BENARBA, a county, bounded by Courallie and Stapylton on the E.; Queensland boundary, N.; Finch, W.; Denison and Jamison, S.; and contains 1,710,000 acres. The following places are within its boundaries:—

| | | |
|---|---|---|
| Balerang | Boroo | Carraa |
| Ballalla | Boronga | Collyie |
| Banarway | Boyanga | Colymungoul |
| Baroona | Brigalow | Cook |
| Bibble | Bucknell | Coonalgra |
| Biroo | Bunarba | Coubal |
| Boolinuckledi | Bundori | Cowmerton |
| Boomi | Bunna Bunna | Crinoline |
| Boonaldoon | Burrandoon | Cudgildool |
| Boonangar | Burragilia | Currah |
| Boonoona | Cuidmurra | Currotha |
| Boonercy | Carbeenbri | Currygundi |

BENARBA—*continued.*

| | | |
|---|---|---|
| Cooloobong | Markham | Tala |
| Dangar | Meei | Tellaraga |
| Derra | Meeroe | Tiela |
| Dindierna | Meroe | Tillaloo |
| Direlnabildi | Millebee | Turrawah |
| Doorabeeba | Mogo Mogo | Tyrell |
| Dundunga | Moorina | Tycawina |
| Galloway | Mongyer | Umbri |
| Gil Gil | Moomin | Uranba |
| Gin | Mungi | Wadden |
| Gingham | Mungindi | Wandoona |
| Gooealla | Myall | Warren |
| Gorman | Narrawall | Werrima |
| Greaves | Neargo | Whalan |
| Greenaway | Newcastle | Willalee |
| Gunalthera | Noonah | Winslow |
| Hamilton | Noora | Wirrir |
| Hill | Numby Numby | Wirrir North |
| Kamilaroi | Orcel | Wirrir South |
| Keelo | Pearse | Wolongimba |
| Krui | Pially | Yarouah |
| Kunopia | Pockataroo | Yarrol |
| Mallowra | Single | Young |

The Macintyre and Barwon Rivers form its western and northern boundaries, and The Gwydir, the Boombi, the Gill Gill, Whalon, and Moonan flow across it.

BOURKE, a county, bounded by Clarendon and Bland, on the E.; Gipps, N.; Cooper, W.; Mitchell, S.; and contains 1,218,560 acres. The following places are within its boundaries :—

| | | |
|---|---|---|
| Ardlethan | Devlin | Marror |
| Ariah | Drumston | Matong |
| Ashbridge | Dulah | Methul |
| Beaconsfield | Elliot | Minnosa |
| Berrembed | Ellon | Murrulebale |
| Berry Jerry | Fennel | Northcote |
| Boblegigbie | Ganmain | Quandary |
| Bourke | Grong Grong | Ramsay |
| Brangalan | Hooke | Robertson |
| Buddigower | Ingalba | Tara |
| Bungambil | Jillet | Tooyal |
| Clermiston | Kockibitoo | Trickett |
| Coffee | Kildary | Walleroobie |
| Coolamon | Kindra | Warren |
| Cottee | Kinilbah | Warri |
| Cowabbie | Lachlan | Willandra |
| Currawananna | Langi Kal Kal | Windeyer |
| Davidson | Lupton | Yarranjerry |
| Derry | Mandamah | Yithan |

The Murrumbidgee forms its southern boundary, and Mirrool Creek flows across it. The mountains are Algogoring, Cowabee, and Mount Arthur. The south-western railway to Hay runs across the county with a branch line to Jerilderie.

BOYD, a county, bounded by Mitchell on the E.; Cooper and Sturt, N.; Waradgery, W.; Urana, S.; and contains 942,080 acres. The following places are within its boundaries :—

| | | |
|---|---|---|
| Argoon | Boyd | Carabury |
| Banandra | Buckinery | Carrathool |
| Boona | Burt | Clifford |

BOYD—*continued*.

| | | |
|---|---|---|
| Coleambally | Kabarabejal | Tingorambah |
| Don | Kabarabarabejal | Toganmain |
| Duderbang | Mucleay | Tubbo |
| Eilginbah | Maley | Ugobit |
| Eulo | Mulberygong | Uri |
| Eunanbrennan | Mulburroga | Uroly |
| Gidgell | Mycotha | Waddi |
| Glengalla | Oolambeyan | Waddaduri |
| Gumblebogie | Ourendumbee | Wangabawgul |
| Gundadaline | Peter | Wargabaugal |
| Howell | Puckinevry | Wolseley |
| Jurumbula | | |

The Murrumbidgee River forms its northern boundary, and there are two remarkable sandhills within it. The Jerilderie railway skirts its eastern border, and the Narrandera to Hay railway its northern.

BURNETT, a county, bounded by Arrawatta on the E.; Stapylton, N.; Corallie and Stapylton, W.; Murchison, S.; and contains 1,288,000 acres. The following places are within its boundaries:—

| | | |
|---|---|---|
| Abercrombie | Glenalvon | Nunga Nunga |
| Adams | Goalonga | Oregon |
| Balfour | Goorabil | Otley |
| Baroma | Gournama | Parkhurst |
| Bledger | Gragin | Pepperbox |
| Blue Nobby | Gravesend | Rocky Hole |
| Bogamildi | Gugumburrah | Russell |
| Boobah | Gullengutta | Singapoora |
| Boyanga | Gunerai | Stack |
| Bullala | Gunnee | Stanley |
| Burnett | Hadleigh | Stevenson |
| Clave | Hollingworth | Strathmore |
| Codrington | Kiga | Stuart |
| Coolatai | Mandoe | Tackinbie |
| Cox | Mitchell | Tullin Tulla |
| Eales | Monsoon | Vicars |
| Ellis | Murgo | Warialda |
| Gill | Muscle | Yagobo |
| Gineroi | Myalla | Yallaroi |

The Gwydir River flows across this county, and the Horton River, a southern tributary. The mountains are Blue Nobby, Mount Mitchell, Mosquito, and Balfour.

CADELL, a county, bounded by Townsend on the E. and N.; Wakool, W.; boundary of Victoria, S.; and contains 563,200 acres. The following places are within its boundaries:—

| | | |
|---|---|---|
| Bama | Marah | Tataila |
| Benarca | Mathoura | Thule |
| Bunnaloo | Moama | Thyra |
| Burrumbury | Moira | Tomara |
| Caldwell | Nallam | Toorangabby |
| Caloola | Perricoota | Wirringan |
| Gotha | Porthole | Womboota |
| Gothog | Tamar | Wongal |
| Gulpa | Tantonan | Yarraman |
| Mars | | |

This county has a very long southern and eastern frontage to the Murray River, and the Deniliquin and Moama railway crosses it.

CAIRA, a county (also partly within the Western Division), bounded by Waradgery on the E.; Kilfera, N.; Taila, W.; Wakool, S.; and contains 1,582,080 acres. The following places are within its boundaries:—

| | | |
|---|---|---|
| Bahpunga | Kieeta | Roakery |
| Ballah | Kingi | Ronald |
| Balranald | Lawrence | Russell |
| Belar | Lette | St. Paul's |
| Belaimong | Lincoln | Tala |
| Benongal | Loocalle | Talpee |
| Bidura | Loorica | Tararie |
| Bluff | Macpherson | Telford |
| Boocathan | Mamangra | The Willows |
| Budgerie | Maremley | The Oaks |
| Bunumburt | Mevna | Tintin |
| Chadwick | Monkem | Toorong |
| Chillichill | Morris | Tuyerunby |
| Cooncoonburra | Muckee | Tyson |
| Crokee | Narahquong | Waldaira |
| Davy | Nap Nap | Wangorah |
| Derinun | Nicholson | Weimby |
| Fisher | Nimining | Williamson |
| Ganaway | Nullawong | Willibah |
| Geraki | Paika | Wilpee |
| Glen Emu | Parker | Windomal |
| Impimi | Penarie | Wombah |
| Jeraly | Pitarpunga | Yanga |
| Jippay | Pollen | Yarrington |
| Juanbung | Pungmallee | Yarrowal |
| Keerish | Pybolee | Yough |
| Kia | Quianderry | |

The rivers Murray and Wakool form its southern boundary. The Lachlan has its confluence with the Murrumbidgee on its eastern boundary, and the Murrumbidgee has its confluence with the Murray on the southern boundary of this county. The following lakes are within it:—Macommon, Pitarpunga, Tori, Paika, Tala, Waldaira, Canaway, and Yanga.

CANBELEGO, a county (also partly within the Western Division), bounded by Gregory on the E.; Cowper, N.; Robinson, W.; Flinders, S.; and contains 1,536,000 acres. The following places are within its boundaries:—

| | | |
|---|---|---|
| Antares | Grahweed | Orion |
| Bannan | Hall | Sturt |
| Berry | Hermitage | The Brothers |
| Boree | Kidgery | The Pines |
| Caro | King | Tootalally |
| Carnbilly | Lincoln | Tritton |
| Coolabah | Lynch | Vega |
| Coreen | Meeson | Warrego |
| Courebone | Merri | Warranbilla |
| Currawong | Monkellan | Warungo |
| Gidalambone | Muriel | Warong |
| Gillies | Neiley | Wilgabone |
| Gilgoenbon | Nirranda | Willeroon |
| Glenariff | | |

The Bogan River forms the eastern boundary of this county, and the Great Western railway crosses it with the branch line from Nyngan to Cobar. Mount Hopeless, the Alsation Hills, and Capitan Hill are within its boundaries.

COOPER, a county, bounded by Bourke on the E.; Dowling, N.; Sturt, W.; Boyd, S.; and contains 1,792,000 acres. The following places are within its boundaries:—

| | | |
|---|---|---|
| Ariah | Cudjello | Naunton |
| Barellan | Dallas | Oxley |
| Bearellan North | Dowling | Patterson |
| Berembere | Edon | Pulltop |
| Bingah | Euratha | Sandy Creek |
| Bringan | Euratha South | Sims' Gap |
| Bingan | Garoolgan | Stanley |
| Binya | Gibbs | Stanbridge |
| Bogalong | Gogeldire | Tabbita |
| Bolaro North | Golaragong | Tabbita North |
| Bolaro | Gorton | Teningeric |
| Bondi | Grong Grong | The Bluff |
| Bourke | Gurragong | The Peak |
| Brobenah | Hebden | Tuckerbill |
| Bungabil | Hulong | Waddai |
| Bungabil | Joudaryan | Wallundry |
| Bundidgery | Kolkilbertoo | Wallandry North |
| Burralong | Kolkilbertoo East | Wammera |
| Bygoo | Kolkilbertoo South | Watti |
| Camerooka | Lewes | Waugh |
| Cocoparra | Mejum | Whitton |
| Colchester | Moombooldool | Willimbong |
| Conapaira East | Moombooldool North | Wilbriggie |
| Conapara | Moura | Wyungan |
| Conapairo South | Mundaburra | Yalgogoring |
| Cuba | Narriah | Yarranjerry |
| Cudgel | Narrandera | Yenda |

The Murrumbidgee River forms the southern boundary of this county, and the south-western railway to Hay crosses it, with the branch line to Jerilderie. The mountains are The Peak, The Bluff, Cavo Hill, Round Hill, Ariah, Mailman's and Sim's Gap, and Cocaparra and M'Pherson's Ranges.

COURALLIE, a county, bounded by Murchison and Burnett on the E.; Stapylton, N.; Benarba, W.; Jamison, S.; and contains 1,267,500 acres. The following places are within its boundaries:—

| | | |
|---|---|---|
| Ardgowan | Ellis | Noona |
| Barton | Fletcher | Paramellowa |
| Berrygill | Gordon | Peacumbone |
| Biniguy | Greenbah | Pringle |
| Bogree | Gurley | Smart |
| Bombell | Gurrygedah | Talmoi |
| Boolooroo | Gyan | Terregere |
| Booboo | Harvey | Terry-hie-hie |
| Booramine | Keramingly | Tycannah |
| Bowman | King | Wallanol |
| Bullerana | Medgun | Wathagar |
| Bumble | Menadool | Weah-waa |
| Bundoowithidie | Mia-mia | Weebullabulla |
| Burranbah | Midkin | Whittaker |
| Campbell | Minna-minane | Windoondilla |
| Carore | Mooee | Wirrigurldonga |
| Combadelo | Moree | Yarraman |
| Downs | Mungie-bundie | Yatta |
| Duckhole | Nepickallina | |

The Gwydir and Moonan Rivers, and the Whea Waa flow across this county.

CUNNINGHAM, a county, bounded by Ashburnham on the E.; Kennedy, and Flinders, N.; Blaxland, W.; Dowling and Gipps, S.; and contains 1,467,520 acres. The following places are within its boundaries:—

| | | |
|---|---|---|
| Badjerribong | Geramnaran | Mowabla |
| Barratta | Gindoono | Mulguthrie |
| Berwombenia | Gillenbine | Murga |
| Bimbella | Goobang | Murrumbogie |
| Bomobbin | Greenock | Oxley South |
| Boona East | Gulgo | Oxley North |
| Boona West | Gunning | Palisthan |
| Botfields | Gunningbland | Plevna |
| Bundaburra | Jerula | Pyong |
| Burrawong | Julandery | Sebastopol |
| Carraboblin | Kalinga | Taratta |
| Cookey's Plains | Kars | Tinda |
| Condobolin | Kiargathur | Tolga |
| Corella | Manire | Tollingo |
| Corridgery | Melrose | Trundle |
| Derriwong | Micabil | Walker |
| Dulhunty | Milpose | Wicklow |
| Ellerslie | Monomie | Willama |
| Elsmore | Monwonga | Yarrabundi |
| Emu Plains | Mount Nobby | |

The Lachlan River forms the southern boundary, and the mountains are Goonumbla Hill and Mount Melville, and Tolga.

DENHAM, a county, bounded by Jamison on the E.; Benarba, N.; Finch, W.; Baradine, S.; and contains 826,840 acres. The following places are within its boundaries:—

| | | |
|---|---|---|
| Bardneal | Eton | Pagan |
| Barwan | Enrie Eurie | Pearse |
| Benn | Finley | Pian |
| Bergan | Glass | Pokataroo |
| Berryaba | Gorian | Reynolds |
| Browne | Jercel | Roberts |
| Bucklebone | Khatambone | Tareela |
| Buriembri | Long Point | Terrible |
| Cabul | Manilla | Tholoo |
| Christie | Merrywinbone | Thalaba |
| Cryon | Mungerara | Toryweewha |
| Denham | Murkadool | Walgett |
| Denuleroi | Murra Murra | Walmar |
| Dewhurst | Myall | Yarradool |
| East Lake | Myallwirrie | |

The Barwon River forms its N.W. boundary, and the Namoi its southern. Pian Creek crosses it.

DENISON, a county, bounded by Hume on the E.; Urana, N.; Townsend, W.; boundary of Victoria, S.; and contains 800,000 acres. The following towns, villages, or parishes are within its boundaries:—

| | | |
|---|---|---|
| Barooga | Cottadidda | Kilnyana |
| Berigan | Denison | Lalalty |
| Boomanoomana | Dry Forest | Langunya |
| Bull Plain | Finley | Momolong |
| Carlyle | Gereldery | Mulwalla |
| Correen West | Headford | Nungunia |

DENISON—*continued.*

| | | |
|---|---|---|
| Narrow Plains | Tongaboo | Wangamong |
| Osborne | Terramia | Warmatta |
| Sargood | Ulupna | Warragubogra |
| Savernake | Wahgunyah | Woperana |
| Tocumwal | | |

The Murray River is the southern boundary of this county, and Wore's Hill is within it.


DOWLING, a county, bounded by Gipps on the E.; Blaxland, N.; Nicholson, W.; Cooper, S.; and contains 1,335,360 acres. The following places are within its boundaries :—

| | | |
|---|---|---|
| Beaumont | Gainbil | Rutland |
| Bimbil | Garryowen | Tibeando |
| Bimbalingel | Geelooma | Tooronga |
| Blairgowrie | Guagong | Townsend |
| Boorlooree | Gumbagunda | Trigalong |
| Bootoowa | Gurrangully | Tuggerbach |
| Borapine | Jimberoo | Uabla |
| Brewer | Kikoira | Ulambong |
| Brotheroney | Killawarra | Velencia |
| Cargelligo | Lachlan | Wardry |
| Carilla | Mahetabel | Warrnal |
| Carisbrook | Merri-Merrigal | Whoyeo |
| Clowery | Mologone | Whyaddra |
| Contarlo | Moneybung | Womboyn |
| Cudgellico | Murrabung | Wondo |
| Currawong | McKellar | Yegi |
| Curriba | Narahhun | Yelkin |
| Curriba | Narden | Yarrabundry |
| Currikabakh | Narriah | Yarran |
| Davis | Regent | Yelkin Plain |
| Dowling | | |

The Lachlan River forms the north-western boundary of this county, and the mountains are Thealy, Wolia, Tockada, Monia Gap. Lake Cudgellico and Marias Lake are within it.


EWENMAR, a county, bounded by Gowen on the E.; Gregory and Leichhardt, N.; Oxley, W.; Narromine, S.; and contains, 1,208,000 acres. The following places are within its boundaries :—

| | | |
|---|---|---|
| Allamurgoola | Bungey | Eumungerie |
| Armitree | Burramilong | Eura |
| Beemunnel | Burraway | Eurombedah |
| Berida | Carrigan | Galargambone |
| Bobarah | Coboco | Gewah |
| Boebung | Collie | Healy |
| Bourbah | Collemburrawang | Kickabil |
| Breelong | Connibong | Killendoon |
| Bugabadah | Coolbaggie | Meryon |
| Bullagreen | Coradgeric | Merrygal |
| Bulladoran | Driel | Milpulling |
| Bundijoe | Drillwarina | Milda |
| Bundilla | Eimban | Moonul |
| Bundemah | Emu | Narroweena |
| Bundobering | Emogandry | Tacklebung |

### EWENMAR—continued.

| | | |
|---|---|---|
| Tenandra | Urobula | Wemabung |
| Trimbrebungie | Wirrigai | Wambianna |
| Umangla | Wonbobbie | Warrie |

The Macquarie River forms its south-western, and the Castlereagh its north-eastern, boundaries. The cataract of the Macquarie and Yalcoogran Water-holes are within it.

FLINDERS, a county, bounded by Kennedy and Oxley on the E.; Canbelego, N.; Mouramba, W.; Cunningham, S.; and contains 1,891,200 acres. The following places are within its boundaries:—

| | | |
|---|---|---|
| Babego | Grahway | Pange Creek |
| Babinda | Grayrigg | Quanda |
| Balgay | Gumbine | Quondong |
| Barrow | Hermitage Plains | Red Gilgais |
| Bebri | Hermitage | Talingaboolba |
| Belah | Honeybugle | Talgong |
| Birrigan | Howgill | The Bluff |
| Boree | Keenan | The Overflow |
| Budtha | Kinnear | Umang |
| Budgery | Lambrigg | Walton |
| Bulga | Merrilba | Walwa |
| Bulbodny | Miamley North | Walwadyn |
| Bumbaldry | Miandetta | Walker's Hill |
| Burra | Minalong | Wharfdale |
| Cameron | Mogille Plain | Wharfdale North |
| Coolibah | Mogille | Whinfell |
| Condon | Mogundale | Whitbarrow |
| Crowie | Mullah | Wicklow |
| Cumbine | Murrabudda | Wicklow |
| Currajong | Murrebonga | Widgeland |
| Delby | Murgaba | Wilmatha |
| Egeria | Myall Cowall | Yamma |
| Firebank | Nangerybone | Yarruman |
| Foster | Nardoo | Yarrow |
| Geweroo | Oberon | Yongee |
| Gilgai | Paujee | |

The Bogan River and Bulbodny and Minalong Creeks form its eastern boundary, and the Great Western Railway skirts the N.E. corner of this county at Nyngan.

FORBES, a county (also partly within the Eastern Division), bounded by Bathurst on the E.; Ashburnham, N.; Gipps, W.; Monteagle, S.; and contains 890,880 acres. The following places are within its boundaries:—

| | | |
|---|---|---|
| Bang Bang | Erasa | Neila |
| Bandon | Eualderie | Ooma |
| Binda | Gooloogong | Tallabung |
| Birangan | Goonigal | Thurungle |
| Bogalong | Jemalong | Waayonrigong |
| Boyd | Kangarooby | Walla Walla |
| Braulin | Mandry | Wangajong |
| Broula | Melyra | Warradery |
| Bundaburra | Merriganoury | Warrangong |
| Conimbla | Morongla | Warrumba |
| Cudgelong | Mulyan | Wattamondara |
| Cumbijowa | Mulyandry | Wheoga |
| Currawang | Nanima | |

The Lachlan River forms the N.E. boundary of this county, and the mountains are Mount Edwards and the Pinnacle. The Murrumburra and Blayney line, uniting the Great Western and Southern Railways, crosses it.

GIPPS, a county, bounded by Forbes on the E.; Cunningham, N.; Dowling, W.; Bourke, S.; and contains 1,573,760 acres. The following places are within its boundaries :—

| | | |
|---|---|---|
| Banar | Hiawatha | Thulloo |
| Benn | Higwath | Tirrana |
| Bibbajolee | Ilgindrie | Towyal |
| Bimbeen | Ina | Trigalana |
| Blow Clear | Jemalong West | Udah |
| Bogandillon | Kalingan | Ugalong |
| Bolagamy | Livingstone | Ungarie |
| Bygalore | Manna | Wallaroi |
| Cadalgula | Marsden | Wamboyne |
| Cadow | Merrimarotherie | Warangla |
| Caragabal | Merribooka | Waroo |
| Carawandool | Mickabil South | Wardry |
| Clear Ridge | Milbee | Woelah |
| Cookaburragong | Mildil | West Plains |
| Corringle | Moonbia | Wheoga |
| Cowal | Moora Moora | Wilbertroy |
| Crown Camp | Mulga | Wilga |
| Currah | Murreengreen | Wilga South |
| Eaton | Nerang Cowal | Woolongough |
| Euglo | Pullabooka | Wyalong |
| Euglo South | Pulligal | Yarnel |
| Gilrigal | South Borambil | Youngareen |
| Goobothery | South Condoublin | Younga Plain |
| Gorman's Hill | South Gulgo | |

The Lachlan River forms its northern, and the Weddin Range its eastern, boundaries, and Lake Cowal, with Banar and Bogan Swamps, are within it. The mountains are Wallaroy, Milbee, Bygooleer, Wamboyne, Manna, and Wheoga.

GOWEN, a county, bounded by Napier on the E.; Leichhardt, Baradine, and White, N.; Eweumar, W.; Lincoln, S.; and contains 1,118,720 acres. The following places are within its boundaries:—

| | | |
|---|---|---|
| Baby | Eringanerin | Tarambigal |
| Balumbridal | Galargambono | Terrabile |
| Bandulla | Gowang | Timor |
| Bearbung | Greenbah | Tooraweanah |
| Belar | Gumin | Tunderbrine |
| Biralbung | Gundi | Uargon |
| Bone Bone | Kirban | Ulamambri |
| Boreable | Mendooran | Urabrible |
| Boyben | Moorogan | Ulungra |
| Breelong | Mundar | Wallumburrawang |
| Burrendah | Naman | Wilber |
| Callangoan | Nandi | Windurong |
| Caigan | Nemur | Wingabutta |
| Caraghoan | Orandelbinia | Woorut |
| Cobbindil | Piangula | Yalcogrin |
| Coonabarabran | Pibbon | Yarrawin |
| Cuttabulloo | Quandong | Yarragrin |
| Deringulla | Tannabar | Youlbung |
| Dilly | | |

The rivers in this county are the Coolaburragundy and the Castlereagh. The latter forms its eastern, southern, and western boundaries. The mountains are Warrabangle Range, Moorogan, Bemgal, Bourgen, and Toondooran, or Vernon's Pic.

GREGORY, a county, bounded by Leichhardt on the E.; Finch, N.; Clyde and Canbelego, W.; Oxley and Ewenmar, S.; and contains 2,160,640 acres. The following places are within its boundaries:—

| | | |
|---|---|---|
| Bannah | Eulamoga | Morbella |
| Bebrue | Foster | Mt. Foster |
| Belar | Gandymungydel | Mumblebone |
| Belarbone | Gardiner | Narragon |
| Bena | Geerigan | Narrabone |
| Bergo | Geralgumbone | Neimby |
| Berriweba | Gerar | Ninia |
| Bibbe Jibbery | Gerwa | Noonbah |
| Billabulla | Gilgowen | Northcote |
| Blairmont | Girralong | Pentagon |
| Bokainore | Goobabone | Pullingarwarina |
| Bomagril | Goolagoola | Quabothoo |
| Bonum | Gooribun | Quambone |
| Bourbah | Graddell | Quandong |
| Buckinguy | Gradgery | Quilbone |
| Bulgala | Grahway | Sandridge |
| Bulgeraga | Gunnell | Stanhope |
| Buttabone | Haddon Rigg | Tailby |
| Canonba | Holybon | Tameribundy |
| Canonba North | Inglega | Terrigal |
| Carwell | Mara | The Mole |
| Collyburl | Marinebone | Tongamba |
| Colane | Marebone | Warrigal |
| Dryburgh | Marthaguy | Waughandry |
| Duility | Mellerstain | Weenculling |
| Dynong | Melrose | Willie |
| Dreewa | Merrimba | Wingebar |
| Embie | Merrinele | Wolagoola |
| Enaweena | Merri | Wullamgambone |
| Eula | Moballa | Wundabungay |

The Bogan River forms its western boundary, and the Macquarie River crosses it. The Great Western railway skirts its south-western corner at Nyngan.

HUME, a county (also partly within the Eastern Division), bounded by Goulburn on the E.; Urana and Mitchell, N.; Denison, W.; the boundary of Victoria, S.; and contains 952,320 acres. The following places are within its boundaries:—

| | | |
|---|---|---|
| Billabong Forest | Goombargano | Morven |
| Brocklesby | Gordon | Osborne |
| Buckargingah | Gray | Piney Ridge |
| Bungowannah | Granville | Quat Quatta |
| Bulgandry | Henley | Rand |
| Burrumbuttock | Henty | Richmond |
| Buraja | Hindmarsh | Round Hill |
| Burrangong | Horell | Ryan |
| Castlestead | Howlong | Sandy Ridges |
| Collendina | Kentucky | Sherwin |
| Comer | Lowes | Stitt |
| Coreen | Mahonga | Thugga |
| Corven | Mahonga Forest | Walbundry |
| Corowa | Moorwatha | Walla Walla |
| Creighton | Morebringer | Wilson |
| Gibson | | |

The Murray River forms the southern boundary of this county, and the Billabong Creek flows through it. The Great Southern railway runs across it near Albury.

JAMISON, a county, bounded by Murchison on the E.; Courallie and Bena rba, N.; Denham, W.; White, S.; and contains 1,377,000 acres. The following places are within its boundaries:—

| | | |
|---|---|---|
| Belar | Dangar | Merah |
| Bibil | Dealwarraldi | Merah North |
| Billaboo South | Denham | Merriah |
| Billaboo | Dewhurst | Millie |
| Bobbiwaa | Dobikin | Mindi |
| Bolcarol | Doyle | Mocma |
| Boonboaronbi | Drildool | Morgan |
| Boorah | Eckford | Myall Hollow |
| Brigalow | Edgeroi | Nowley |
| Bulyeroi | Gayalul | Orcel |
| Bunna | Galathera | Pian |
| Bunyah | Gehan | Queerbri |
| Burcarroll | Gommel | Tarlee |
| Burren | Graham | Thalaba |
| Burren East | Gundemain | Tulladunna |
| Burrendong | Helebah | Vickery |
| Clements | Jamison | Warrambool |
| Coorong | Keera | Waterloo |
| Coolga | Longpoint | Waughan |
| Courndda | Manamoi | Weeta Waa |
| Cowcinangarah | Malaraway | Woolabrar |
| Cubbaroo North | Markham | Yarranbar |
| Cubbaroo | Melburra | |

The Namoi River forms the southern boundary of this county, and the north-western railway to Narrabri terminates on its E. border—Narrabri West.

KENNEDY, a county, bounded by Gordon on the E.; Narromine, N.; Flinders, W.; Cunningham, S.; and contains 1,067,840 acres. The following places are within its boundaries:—

| | | |
|---|---|---|
| Albert | Fitzroy | Mungeric |
| Babathnil | Genanaguy | Ormonde |
| Beaconsfield | Genaren | Ossory |
| Belardery | Gillenbine | Redcliffe |
| Bengamel | Gobondery | Russell |
| Bentinck | Graddle | Salisbury |
| Boona | Hartington | Sarsfield |
| Braalghy | Hastings | Somerset |
| Bulbodney | Hawarden | Stanley |
| Burdenda | Houston | Strahorn |
| Burra | Kadina | Tabratong |
| Burrill | Limestone | Talingaboolba |
| Carolina | Merilba | Tanilogo |
| Cavendish | Meryulla | Tout |
| Cookopie | Mickibri | Weridgery |
| Coradgery | Mickimill | Wellwood |
| Coradgery West | Mingelo | Wilmatha |
| Dandaloo | Mingerong | Willanbalang |
| Davison | Minalong | Wombin |
| Derrihong | Moodana | Yralla |
| Euchabil | Moonana South | |

This county is watered by creeks, fed by the Bogan River on its north-eastern boundary. Goonimbla Hill and Warran are on its southern border.

LEICHHARDT, a county, bounded by Baradine on the E.; Finch, N.; Clyde and Gregory, W.; Gowen, S.; and contains 2,119,680 acres. The following places are within its boundaries:—

| | | |
|---|---|---|
| Aberfoyle | Gidgerygah | Sussex |
| Amos | Gilgooma | Tahrone |
| Baronne | Gilguldry | Tallegar |
| Bimble | Gilwarny | Terembone |
| Bogewang | Goorianawa | Teridgerie |
| Borgara | Gungalman | Thara |
| Brewan | Gungalman North | Tobin |
| Buchanan | Gunna | Toloora |
| Budgeon | Kendool | Toorn |
| Bulgah | Kidgar | Tooloon |
| Bulgogur | Magomoton | Triehnon |
| Bullarora | Matouree | Ularbie |
| Calgar | Mogil | Ulundry |
| Cambara | Moolambong | Urawilkie |
| Campbell | Moora | Waddiwong |
| Carrabear | Moorambilla | Waddiwong |
| Carwell | Mourabie | Walcha |
| Castlereagh | Mowlma | Walla Walla |
| Collinoule | Mundare | Wambelong |
| Colmia | Mungery | Warraba East |
| Colomy | Munna Munna | Warragan |
| Conimbla | Murraiman | Warrena |
| Coouamoona | Narratigah | Warren Downs |
| Coonamble | Nebea | Warrabah |
| Cooyeah Warrah | Nedgera | Weetaliba |
| Dahomey | Neinby | Wingadee |
| Devon | Nelgowrie | Willga |
| Dinoa | Nimbia | Winnaba |
| Edgerio | Ningear | Woolingar |
| Ellis | Noonbah | Worinjerong |
| Elongery | Nugal | Wyaberry |
| Eulah | Oural | Yarrayin |
| Euroka | Parmiduan | Yarragoora |
| Geelnoy | Pier Pier | Yoee |
| Gelambulah | Quanda Quanda | Youendah |
| Gidginbilla | Quonmoona | Yuma |

The Castlereagh River flows through this county from N. to S., and the Barwon forms its northern boundary, with numerous creeks. Mounts Bideaway are on its eastern border.

LINCOLN, a county, bounded by Bligh on the E.; Napier and Bowen, N.; Ewenmar, W.; Gordon, S.; and contains 1,370,240 acres. The following places are within its boundaries:—

| | | |
|---|---|---|
| Adelyne | Breelong | Dewar |
| Amungerie | Brocklehurst | Donelly |
| Bald Hill | Bruah | Dubbo |
| Ballimore | Bulladoran | Dunedoo |
| Barbigal | Bullinda | Elong Elong |
| Beeni | Bungielomar | Erskine |
| Bicanbeenie | Caledonia | Gamba |
| Blackheath | Cobborah | Geurie |
| Bodangora | Cobborah West | Goonoo |
| Bolaro | Cobrauraguy | Lincoln |
| Bomely | Coolbaggie | Macquarie |
| Boston | Daley | Medway |
| Breelong South | Dapper | Mendooran |

LINCOLN—continued.

| | | |
|---|---|---|
| Mickctymulga | Ponto | Tuckland |
| Mirrie | Richardson | Wallaroo |
| Mitchell | Spring Creek | Warrie |
| Murrumbidgerie | Taylor | Wooroomboonie |
| Murrungundi | Tenandra | Yanindury |
| Narran | Terramungamine | Yarrow |

This county is watered by the Castlereagh River on the N., and the Erskine River flows across it. The Great Western railway skirts its western border.

MITCHELL, a county, bounded by Wynyard, on the E.; Bourke and Cooper N.; Boyd, W.; Urana, S.; and contains 890,880 acres. The following places are within its boundaries:—

| | | |
|---|---|---|
| Arajoel | Edgehill | Mundowy |
| Ashcroft | Faithfull | Osborne |
| Berry Jerry | Gillenbah | Pearson |
| Birrego | Gobbagaula | Pulletop |
| Brewarrina | Grubben | Sandy Creek |
| Buckinbong | Hanging Rock | Tootool |
| Bulgary | Kingston | Uranquintry |
| Bullenbung | Leitch | Vincent |
| Burke | Maclean | Wauberrima |
| Burrandana | Mangoplah | Westby |
| Coffin Rock | Milbrulong | Wood |
| Corobimilla | Mimosa | Yarabee |
| Cox | Mauberrinia | Yarragundry |
| Cuddell | Mundawaddery | Yerong |

The Murrumbidgee River flows along its north-eastern boundary, and the branch line of the south-western railway to Jerilderie crosses it at Narrandera.

MURCHISON, a county, bounded by Hardinge on the E.; Burnett, N.; Courallie, W.; Darling, S.; and contains 1,208,320 acres. The following places are within its boundaries:—

| | | |
|---|---|---|
| Anderson | Dunnee | McKinnon |
| Austen | Durham | Mechi |
| Bangheet | Eulowrie | Molroy |
| Bingara | Evans | Munro |
| Boomi | Furber | Myall |
| Capel | Glass | Paleroo |
| Carodo | Gouron | Pallal |
| Cobbadah | Gun Flat | Piedmont |
| Crawley | Gundamulda | Pringle |
| Currawangandi | Hall | Rider |
| Delingera | Horton | Rusden |
| Delunga | Keera | Stag |
| Derra Derra | King | Tange |
| Digidaa | Lindesay | Terrurgee |
| Dinoga | Little Plain | Turrawarra |
| Drummond | Macintyre | Wyndham |
| Dumboy | | |

The Gwydir and Horton Rivers flow across this county, and Mounts Lindsay and Drummond are within its boundary. The Nandewar Range surrounds it on the E., S., and W., and the northern railway skirts its eastern border.

I

NANDEWAR, a county, bounded by Darling on the E.; Jamison and Murchison, N.; White, W.; Buckland, S.; and contains 829,440 acres. The following places are within its boundaries:—

| | | |
|---|---|---|
| Berrioye | Deriah | Rangira |
| Billyena | Durrisdeer | Rusden |
| Bogabri | Eulah | Therribry |
| Bolloll | Gulligal | Tippereena |
| Borobil | Gunnenbeme | Tulgumba |
| Brentry | Killarney | Vickery |
| Bullawa | Leard | Wallah |
| Burburgate | Lindesay | Wean |
| Byar | Mihi | Weetaliba |
| Carrol | Moonbil | Willuri |
| Connor | Narrabri | Yarrari |
| Coryah | Ningadheen | |

The Namoi River forms the entire south-western boundary of this county, and the north-western railway skirts its border, and terminates at Narrabri.

NAPIER, a county, bounded by Bligh and Pottinger on the E.; White, N.; Gowen, W.; Lincoln. S.; and contains 757,760 acres. The following places are within its boundaries:—

| | | |
|---|---|---|
| Alison | Dalglish | Narangarie |
| Biamble | Gundare | Neible |
| Binnaway | Lowe | Piambra |
| Binnia | Malcolm | Purlawaugh |
| Bullinda | Mendoran | Queensborough |
| Bungabah | Merrygowen | Terrawinda |
| Butheroo | Moorangourany | Toorawandi |
| Carlisle | Morven | Ulambra |
| Cookabingie | Mumbedah | Ulinda |
| Coolah | Napier | Yuggel |

The Castlereagh River forms the western, and the Coolaburragundy the south-eastern, boundaries of this county, and Pandora Pass is within it, and also Wetalabah, Oakey, and Bothero Creeks.

NARROMINE, a county, bounded by Gordon on the E.; Ewenmar, N.; Oxley, W.; Kennedy, S.; and contains 1,152,280 acres. The following places are included within its boundaries:—

| | | |
|---|---|---|
| Algalah | Enmore | Nelson |
| Backwater | Frost | Obley |
| Barton | Gilmour | Tabratong |
| Birdoo | Gin Gin | Temingley |
| Buddah | Goan | Tomoin |
| Bulgandramine | Gradell | The Oaks |
| Burrabadene | Gundong | Timbrebongie |
| Caloma | Harvey | Triangi |
| Cathundril | Meringo | Turribung |
| Cowal | Mingelo | Tyrie |
| Dandaloo | Minore | Waterloo |
| Deribong | Mono | Weemabah |
| Doonside | Mullah | Wentworth |
| Draggy | Mullah Back | Willydah |
| Dungary | Myall Camp | Wolomoon |
| Enerweena | Narromine | Yarradigerie |

The Macquarie River forms the north-eastern boundary of this county, and the Great Western railway runs across it. Raymond's, and Buller's Falls and the Boggy Cowal, are within it.

NICHOLSON, a county, bounded by Cooper and Dowling on the E.; Blaxland, N.; Franklin, W.; Boyd, S.; and contains 1,339,520 acres. The following places are within its boundaries:—

| | | |
|---|---|---|
| Amoilla | Eurella | Molesworth |
| Amoilla North | Eurugabah | Moncton |
| Beaconsfield | Fox | Moon Moon |
| Belaley | Gonowlia | Mulla Mulla |
| Bellingerambil | Goolgowie | Mullion |
| Bellingerambil East | Goolgowie South | Naradhun |
| Bellingerambil South | Goolgowie West | Neobine |
| Berangerine | Griffiths | Parker |
| Bolton | Gunbar | Redbank |
| Booligal | Honuna | Russell |
| Bootheragandra | Honuna North | South Marowie |
| Bouyaree | Hopwood | Stackpoole |
| Bowerabine | Huntawong | Synnot |
| Bulyeroi | Ivanhoe | Tambalana |
| Bunda | Lachlan | Townsend |
| Bunda East | Lake Gunbar | Wallanthery |
| Burgess | Langtree | Warrabalong |
| Caninganima | Loughnan | Weenya |
| Carilla | Mea Mia | Weepool |
| Chirnside | Mea Mia North | Weerie |
| Coowerrawine | Mea Mia South | Whealbah |
| Dandaloo | Melbergen | Yandumblin |
| East Marowie | Melbergen South | Yurdyilla |
| Elliot | | |

The Lachlan River forms its N.W. boundaries. Moon Moon and Gunbar Lakes and Sugarloaf Mount are within it.

OXLEY, a county, bounded by Ewenmar and Narromine on the E.; Gregory, N.; Flinders, W.; Kennedy, S.; and contains 761,600 acres. The following places are within its boundaries:—

| | | |
|---|---|---|
| Balcombe | Egelabra | Narromine |
| Beablebar | Elengerah | Nevertire |
| Beardina | Ganalgang | Nyngan |
| Beelban | Garfield | Ruby |
| Belingerar | Garule | Rutledge |
| Boro | Gobabla | Tabratong |
| Buddabadah | Gunningba | Terangan |
| Cajildry | Kungerbil | Terooble |
| Carval | Lawson | The Plains |
| Cookandoon | Mudall | Trangie |
| Cremorne | Mulla Mulla | Trowan |
| Curtis | Mullengudgery | Warien |
| Darouble | Mumbrabah | Warren |
| Dooran | Mungeribar | Wera |
| Eilginbah | Narrar | Woolartha |

The Bogan River forms its western, and the Macquarie River its north-eastern, boundaries; and the Great Western railway crosses it.

POTTINGER, a county, bounded by Buckland on the E.; Nandewar and White, N.; Napier and White, W.; Bligh, S.; and contains 1,658,880 acres. The following places are within its boundaries:—

| | | |
|---|---|---|
| Bando | Bommera | Calaba |
| Bann Baa | Breeza | Clarke |
| Benelarbri | Brennan | Clift |
| Bingle | Brigalow | Coogal |
| Black Jack | Brothers | Coolanbilla |
| Blackville | Brown | Coomoo Coomoo |
| Bogabri | Bulga | Curlewis |
| Bogalri | Bundulla | Denison |

## POTTINGER—*continued.*

| | | |
|---|---|---|
| Denison West | Lawson | Springfield |
| Digby | Melville | Tambar |
| Doona | Mema | Tambar Springs |
| Dubbleda | Merrigula | Tamerang |
| Emerald Hill | Millie | Tinkrameanah |
| Gill | Mooki Springs | Trinkey |
| Girrawillie | Moredevil | Tulla Mullen |
| Goally | Mucca Mucca | Urangera |
| Goolhi | Mullally | Walbollon |
| Goragilla | Nea | Walla Walla |
| Goran | Nombi | Walla Walla West |
| Gullendady | Promer | Wandoba |
| Gulligal | Pringle | Weston |
| Gunnedah | Rockgedgiel | Willala |
| Howe's Hill | Rodd | Wilson |
| Johnstone | Saltwater | Yarraman |
| Kickerbill | | |

The Namoi and the Conadilly or Moona Rivers form its entire north-eastern boundaries. The north-western railway to Narrabri runs parallel to its north-western boundary.

STAPYLTON, a county, bounded by Arrawatta on the E.; Queensland boundary, N.; Benarba, W.; Courallie and Burnett, S.; and contains 1,587,200 acres. The following places are within its boundaries:—

| | | |
|---|---|---|
| Adams | Denebry | Mungan |
| Bengerang | Douro | Mungle |
| Benson | Finley | Paine |
| Blue Nobby | Gill Gill | Paleranga |
| Boggabilla | Goorara | Stapylton |
| Boobora | Gunnyana | Tantarana |
| Boogowon | Harvey | Toongcooma |
| Boonal | Holmes | Trinkey |
| Boonanga | Illingramundi | Tubble Gap |
| Booraba | Kinnimo | Tucka Tucka |
| Browne | Lay Green | Tulloona |
| Bryannugra | Limebon | Tun Cooey |
| Canary | Mayne | Wallon |
| Careunga | Mellcallina | Warra Warrama |
| Careunga North | Merriwa | Welbon |
| Carroby | Mobbindry | Whalan |
| Cook | Moppin | Willimil |
| Coolanga | Morella | Wonga |
| Coppymurrumbill | Mount Pleasant | Yooloobill |
| Currumbah | | |

The M'Intyre River forms its northern boundary between it and Queensland, and the Whalan flows across it. The Gilgil, Bunna Bunna, and Boobora Lagoon are within it.

STURT, a county, bounded by Cooper on the E.; Nicholson, N.; Waradgery, W.; Boyd, S.; and contains 996,480 acres. The following places are within its boundaries:—

| | | |
|---|---|---|
| Alleyne | Cockburn | Hyde Park |
| Baillie | Currathool | Kooba |
| Ballingall | Currathool West | Kooroongal |
| Beabula | Denny | Learmouth |
| Bendigo | Djallah | Lethington |
| Benerambah | Downey | Livingston |
| Bringagee | Ercildoune | Mair |
| Buckley | Gallah | Maiden |
| Cajaldura | Hervey | Mills |
| Carrego | Howlong | Mirrool |

STURT—*continued.*

| | | |
|---|---|---|
| Munro | Tabbita | Warburn |
| North Bringagee | Terrapee | Wawong |
| North Uardy | Thononga | Wiveon |
| Orien | Tom's Point | Wychproof |
| Quambatook | Uardry | Yannaway |

The Murrumbidgee River forms its southern boundary, and the south-western railway to Hay crosses it. Narrabri Swamp and Mailman's Gap are within it.

TOWNSEND, a county, bounded by Denison and Urana on the E.; Boyd and Waradgery, N.; Wakool, W.; Cadell, S.; and contains 2,109,440 acres. The following places are within its boundaries :—

| | | |
|---|---|---|
| Banangalite | Dulverton | Purdanima |
| Barratta | Dunkeld | Quandong |
| Belmore | Edgar | Quiamong |
| Billabong | Euroka | Ricketson |
| Bingellibundi | Euroley | Ronald |
| Birganbigil | Finlay | Stannaforth |
| Blackwood | Gilbert | Tawarra |
| Boaroorban | Gobram | Tholobin |
| Booabula | Gonawarra | Thulabin |
| Boonoke | Gotha | Thurgoon |
| Boorga | Harold | Towool |
| Boree | Hartwood | Tumudgery |
| Bowna | Hebden | Tuppal |
| Boyeo | Jung Jung | Walla |
| Brassi | Kerranakoon | Wandook |
| Bullatella | Lamb | Wangonilla |
| Bungooka | Loch | Warbreccan |
| Campbell | Malloc | Wargam |
| Caroonboon | Monimail | Warrawool |
| Caroonboon North | Moonbria | Warristan |
| Carse | Moonbria South | Warwillah |
| Citgathen | Morago | Werai |
| Colimo | Morton | Werkenbergal |
| Coree | Moultrassie | Willeroo |
| Conargo | Mundiwa | Willurah |
| Conargo North | Nullam | Winter |
| Coolagali | Nardoo | Wollamai |
| Coolambil | Narrama | Wonnuc |
| Coronalla | Narratoola | Wononga |
| Cudoc | Nerim | Woonox |
| Currabunganung | Nyangay | Wureep |
| Currabunganung North | Officer | Yalgadoori |
| Dahwilly | Palmer | Yallakool |
| Deniliquin North | Peppin | Yallama |
| Deniliquin South | Powheep | Yaloke |
| Derrulaman | Puckaewidgee | Zara North |
| Devon | Pungulgui | Zara South |
| Drysdale | | |

The Murray River forms its southern boundary. The Edward and Wakool Rivers flow into it, and the Billabong Creek crosses it. The terminus of the Moama and Deniliquin railway is within the county.

URANA, a county, bounded by Mitchell on the E.; Boyd, N.; Townsend, W.; Denison and Hume, S.; and contains 1,761,280 acres. The following places are within its boundaries :—

| | | |
|---|---|---|
| Betts | Brookong | Cadell |
| Bingagong | Brookong North | Calkmannan |
| Bolton | Broome | Carrerney |
| Booree Gerry | Bundure | Clear Hill |
| Booroobanilly | Bundure North | Clive |
| Boree Creek | Butherwa | Clyde |

URANA—continued.

| | | |
|---|---|---|
| Cocketgedong | Howell | Stanley |
| Colombo | Jerilderie South | Summer |
| Combermere | Jerilderie North | Thurrowa |
| Coonong | Kendall | Urana |
| Coree North | Lake | Urangeline |
| Coree South | Lockhart | Wallandoon |
| Crommelin | Mairjimmy | Waloona |
| Cullivel | Morundah | Watt |
| Douglas | Morundah South | Waugh |
| Faed | Muera | Widgiewa |
| Finlay | Munoyabla | Wilson |
| Gulore | Napier | Wood |
| Goolgumbla | Nowranie | Wunnamurra |
| Gunnambill | Osborne | Yamma |
| Gunnambill North | Palmer | Yanko |
| Hardie | Piney Ridge | Yanko South |
| Hastings | Pullega | Yathong |
| Hebden | Ross | Yathony South |
| Henty | | |

Lakes Urana, Uranagong, Gullivell, and Yanko Creek are within its boundaries. The Narrandera to Jerildera railway crosses this county, and terminates there.

WAKOOL, a county, bounded by Townsend on the E.; Waradgery and Caira, N.; the boundary of Victoria, S.W.; and contains 1,832,960 acres. The following places are within its boundaries:—

| | | |
|---|---|---|
| Baldon | Gerabbit | Nyang |
| Balpool | Gnuie | Purguin |
| Barham | Gonn | Perekerten |
| Barrubu | Gwyne | Pevensey |
| Belmore | Gynong | Poon Boon |
| Benjee | Hindmarsh | Puah |
| Berambong | Jinarengle | Rabuelle |
| Beremagad | Kerkeri | Salisbury |
| Binbinette | Kirrabirri | Speewa |
| Bookit | Kyalite | Tchelery |
| Boyd | Landale | Thalaka |
| Bundynlumblah | Liewa | Tittil |
| Bungunyah | Lintot | Tooleybuck |
| Burbagodah | Lyle | Toolmah |
| Burrawang | Mallan | Toolon |
| Bymue | Mallee | Towwerruk |
| Cangan | Mein | Turora |
| Caroonboon | Mellool | Wakool |
| Chowar | Merran | Wandaragat |
| Cobwell | Merwin | Wetuppa |
| Cochran | Mia Mia | Whymoul |
| Colvin | Millen | Willakool |
| Condoulpe | Miranda | Windouran |
| Coobool | Moolpa | Winter |
| Coonamit | Moorongatta | Wood |
| Cootnite | Moulamein | Woorooma |
| Corry | Moulamein South | Worobyan |
| Cunningyeux | Murga | Yadabal |
| Curpool | Nearroongareo | Yadchow |
| Danberry | Niemur | Yanga |
| Darlot | Nunnagoyt | Yarrein |
| Firebrace | Noorong | Yellymong |
| Genoe | Nullum | |

The river Murray forms the entire S.W. frontage of this county, and the Kyolite or Edward River crosses it with innumerable creeks. Pental Island and Puggarmilly Island are situated on the Victorian side of the Murray facing this county.

WARADGERY, a county, bounded by Boyd and Sturt on the E.; Waljeers on the N.; Caira on the W.; Wakool and Townsend, S.; and contains 1,836,160 acres. The following places are within its boundaries:—

| | | |
|---|---|---|
| Abercrombie | Illiliwah | Rutherford |
| Beabula | Ina | Russell |
| Bedarbigal | Ita | Simpson |
| Benduck North | Jambuck | Sinclair |
| Benduck South | Jellalabad | Thellangering |
| Beresford | Killendoo | Thel'angering East |
| Boyong | Lang | Tindale |
| Brush | Lara | Tongul |
| Budgee | Learn | Toogimbil |
| Bulliamy | Lorraine | Toopuntul |
| Burrabogie | Magnolia | Tully |
| Chambers | Maude | Twynam |
| Cluny | Melrose | Ulonga |
| Coonoon | Midgecleugh | Wahwoon |
| Cuba | Mingah | Wallaby |
| Darcoola | Mungadal | Wandigong |
| Dowling | Narrawidgery | Waradgery |
| East Waradgery | Nerrang | Waradgery West |
| Eli Elwah | One Tree | Warrigal |
| Eurolie | Oxley | Waymca |
| Gelam | Palmer | Wilgah |
| Gilbert | Paradise | Willis |
| Godfrey | Paradise East | Wingan |
| Grant | Patterson | Wirkenbergal |
| Gre Gre | Pembelgong | Woollama |
| Hacket | Pevensey | Wooloombye |
| Hay | Pimpampa | Wooloondool |
| Hay South | Quianderry | Wyoming |
| Hiawatha | Quiandong | Yang Yang |
| Ilginbah | Rankin | Yimbaring |

The Murrumbidgee River forms its southern and the Lachlan River its northern boundaries; and the terminus of the south-western railway, at Hay, is within it. Lakes Tupuntil and Ita are within the county.

WHITE, a county, bounded by Nandewar on the E.; Jamison, N.; and Baradine, W.; Gowen, S.; and contains 1,269,760 acres. The following places are within its boundaries:—

| | | |
|---|---|---|
| Anson | Crowie | Milner |
| Arrarownie | Dampier | Mollee |
| Belmore | Dangar | Mollieroi |
| Blake | Denobollie | Narrabri West |
| Bohena | Dewhurst | Nuable |
| Borah | Galloway | Orr |
| Boral | Goona | Parkes |
| Brigalow | Gorman | Quinn |
| Bulgarra | Gurleigh | Robertson |
| Capp | Humphrey | Rocky Glen |
| Cocaboy | Iredale | Tannawanda |
| Coghill | Lloyd | Thompson |
| Cowallah | Loder | Turrawan |
| Cox | Loftus | Wee Waa |
| Cook | Mullallee | White |
| Cooma | Mullee | Yaminba |
| Coormore | Manum | Yurraman |

The Namoi River forms the northern boundary of this county, and the Narrabri terminus of the north-western railway is within it.

## III.—COUNTIES IN THE WESTERN DIVISION OF THE COLONY.

Containing an estimated area of 79,970,000 acres.

BARRONA, a county bounded by Gunderbooka on the E.; Irrara, N.; Ularara, W.; Landsborough, S.; and contains 1,361,900 acres. The following places are within its boundaries:—

|  |  |
|---|---|
| Bumburra | Goombalie |
| Coorallie | Ularara |

The Paroo forms its western, and the Warrego its eastern, boundaries. Lakes Willeroo, Chesney, and Yanderoo, with the Salt Lakes, are within its boundaries.

BLAXLAND, a county bounded by Cunningham on the E.; Mouramba, N.; Mossgiel, W.; Franklin, Nicholson, and Dowling, S.; and contains 2,567,680 acres. The following places are within its boundaries:—

| | | |
|---|---|---|
| Back Roto | Gulgunnia East | Moran Gilga |
| Back Wallandra | Gunnogie | Nombinnie |
| Back Whery | Hyandra | Oneida |
| Beauport | Hyandra North | Roto |
| Bogalo | Iathong | Salamagundia |
| Bogalo South | Illewong | Tallebung |
| Booberoi | Illewong West | Tara |
| Boorambil | Inas | Tara South |
| Boothumble | Jundrie | Tarcombe |
| Bundure | Kegiuni | Tarran |
| Bundure South | Killeen | Thule |
| Burthong | Killeen South | Thule South |
| Burthong South | Peak North | Uabba West |
| Callytria | Peak South | Ulamba |
| Cardocy | Mahurangi | Ulambong |
| Coan | Mahurangi East | Uranaway |
| Cobram | Manopa | Urambie |
| Coree | Marobee | Urambie East |
| Creamy Hills | Marobee East | Utalu |
| Cugellico | Matakana | Victor |
| Currawalla | Matakana South | Wagga |
| Daguilar | Meldior | Walla |
| Eramaran | Mellelea | Wallandra |
| Euabalong | Merrimerriwa | Warbreccan |
| Eubendery | Middle Peak | Warrabillong |
| Geragong | Moora | Whoey |
| Gondabillong | Moothumbil | Wilga |
| Gooan | Mordie | Wollong |
| Goun | Mount Allen | Yackerboon |
| Gounelgeric | Mount Hope | Yackerboon South |
| Guapa, West | Mount Solitary | Yara |
| Guapa | Mouramba | Yara East |
| Gulgunnia | Mulga | |

The Lachlan River and Willandra Billabong forms its southern boundary, and Mounts Davidson and Torrens are within the county, and the main thoroughfare to Wilcannia crosses it.

NEW SOUTH WALES. 137

BOOROONDARRA, a county bounded by Mouramba and Robinson, on the E.; Yanda, N.; Rankin and Woore, W.; Mossgiel, S.; and contains 1,456,000 acres. The following places are within its boundaries :—

| Barneto | Cowl | Paddington |
| Bulgoo | Finlay | Rankin |

Mount Balarambone and Crowl Creek are within the county.


CLYDE, a county (also partly within the Central Division) bounded by Leichhardt on the E.; Narran, N.; Cowper, W.; Gregory, S.; and contains 1,873,920 acres. The following places are within its boundaries :—

| Annan | Esperance | Richardson |
| Ballaree | Ethelberg | Ridge |
| Beemery | Galar | Stonehenge |
| Bendermere | Gangarry | Thuara |
| Billybingbone | Geera | Thudie |
| Bogalong | Ginge | Tichawanta |
| Bogan | Ginghet | Tulloch |
| Bogewong | Gobollion | Uki |
| Boree | Gongolgon | Ulowrie |
| Bouka Bouka | Grandool | Wamboin |
| Brewarrina | Grandoonbone | Wammerawa |
| Briarie | Grawlin | Wareney |
| Buckinguy | Gudgerah | Weeli |
| Carinda | Gunderwerrie | Welman |
| Cashmere | Haradon | Weribiddee |
| Charlton | Higgins | Willary |
| Clements | Langmore | Wilga |
| Coolaree | Lindsay | Willi Culling |
| Coorabur | Lynch | Willa Murra |
| Cowal | Molle | Willoi |
| Cowga | Morla | Willewa |
| Cowabee | Mundadoo | Willenbone |
| Cox | Mundawa | Wommera |
| Cuddie Springs | Navina | Yanda |
| Derriderri | Nundowah | Yarea |
| Druid | Pink Hills | Yarrawin |
| Dooral | Quabathoo | |

This county is entirely surrounded by the Darling and Bogan Rivers, except on its south-eastern side. The Macquarie River and Mara Creek, both affluents of the Darling, cross it. Mount Druitt is within it.


COWPER, a county bounded by Clyde on the E; Gunderbooka, N.; Yanda and Robinson, W.; Canbelego, S.; and contains 2,416,640 acres. The following places are within its boundaries :—

| Banga | Currawywina | Little |
| Barton | Davidson | Mackay |
| Belars | Donald | Manwanga |
| Bijoe | East Bourke | Maroona |
| Bookambone | Farnell | Miendetta |
| Borea | Finlay | Mootcha |
| Bourke | Garfield | Mooculta |
| Bye | Glengariff | Mulga |
| Byerock | Gongolgan | Nanwanga |
| Cockerminia | Hillsborough | Nidgery |
| Coolabah | Jandra | Nuruthulla |
| Coronga | Lee | Oliver |

## COWPER—continued.

| | | |
|---|---|---|
| Parailla | Ross | Wereiwa |
| Perayambone | Tarcoon | Yargunyah |
| Redbank | Tubba | Zouch |
| Robertson | | |

This county is bounded on the N.W. by the Darling, and on the N.E. by the Bogan Rivers. The mountains are Mount Oxley, Oxley's Table-land, Durban's Group, New Year's Range, and Mount Merrere. The Great Western railway runs through the centre from E. to W., and terminates at Bourke, within the county, on the E. bank of the Darling.

CULGOA, a county bounded by Narran on the E.; Queensland boundary, N.; Irrara and Gunderbooka, W. and S.; and contains 1,525,760 acres. The following places are within its boundaries:—

| | | |
|---|---|---|
| Barringun | Corella | Moulton Pins Spring |
| Belalie | Currindule | Nunty |
| Boenderra West | Diemunga | Sandy Springs |
| Brenda | Eungoniah | Shearer's Springs |
| Bunta-Worara | Goodooga | Thurmylae |
| Cawwell | Gooroomero Springs | Toolooni Springs |
| Cawwell Back | Lednapper | Wee Warra |
| Cawwell West | | |

The Culgoa River forms its eastern boundary, and the Warrego its western. There are several creeks within it.

DELALAH, a county bounded by Thouleanna, on the E.; Queensland boundary, N.; Tongowoka, W.; Yantara and Ularara, S.; and contains 1,320,960 acres. There are no recorded places ascertainable in this county. Lakes Cultamulcha and Bullwarry and Bulloo Overflow are within its boundary, and Sturt's Tree is on it, and Delalah Downs forms part of it.

EVELYN, a county bounded by Yantara, on the E.; Tongowoko and Poole, N.; South Australia boundary. W.; Farnell, S.; and contains 2,201,600 acres. The following places are within its boundaries:—

| | | |
|---|---|---|
| Milparinka | Utah | Warratta |

Lakes Gunentah, Patterson, Butlea, and Boolta are within its boundaries, also Mounts Arrowsmith and Brown and Bald Hills.

FARNELL, a county bounded by Mootwingee, on the E.; Evelyn, N.; South Australian boundary, W.; Yancowinna, S.; and contains 2,121,920 acres. The following places are within its boundaries:—

| | | |
|---|---|---|
| Alberta | Coonbaralba | Euriowie |
| Bligh | Corona | Fowler's Gap |
| Budierriyarn | Dering | Giles |
| Byjerkerno | | |

Mount Pinnacle and Coko Range form part of its eastern boundary, and there are several waterholes and creeks within it.

FINCH, a county bounded by Denham and Benarba, on the E.; Queensland boundary, N.; Narran, W.; Leichhardt, S.; and contains 2,641,920 acres. The following places are within its boundaries :—

| | | |
|---|---|---|
| Bagot | Dungalear | Moongulla |
| Baloon | Dungell | Mooni |
| Barah | Dunumbral | Mooroo |
| Barnbah | Durabeba | Moramina |
| Barrangeel | Eales | Morendah |
| Barwon | Eckford | Mullingowba |
| Bibble | Elphinstone | Mundoo |
| Bimber | Eulan | Mungeroo |
| Birben | Euminbah | Mureabun |
| Birrah | Eurawin | Narran |
| Blackwood | Finch | Nilgi |
| Bloxsome | Finley | Peelborough |
| Bogra | Gamalally | Pine |
| Bon Bon | Gingie | Pinegobla |
| Booraba | Glatherindi | Plumbolah |
| Boorooma | Gooningeri | Queega |
| Brook | Gooraway | Roberts |
| Buddah | Gordon | Rose |
| Buggee | Goric Goric | Scott |
| Bukkulla | Goundabloui | Somerville |
| Bumble | Greaves | Talawa |
| Bundabarrina | Green | Telinebone |
| Bundah | Grawin | Tomorrago |
| Bunghill | Gummanaldi | Townday |
| Burrabebe | Gunnianna | Tutawa |
| Burranbaa | Gurney | Ulah |
| Burrandown | Gurilly | Urandahly |
| Burran Burran | Hungerford | Urandool |
| Burrawandool | Imbergee | Wallah |
| Burbah | Kee Kee | Wallangulla |
| Calmuldi | Keelo | Wamnell |
| Cambo Cambo | Keilmoi | Warrambool |
| Campbell | Kenedy | Waugh |
| Carrabillina | Kigwigil | Wee Warra |
| Combadery | Kurragong | Werribilla |
| Cooeoran | Langloh | Wilby Wilby |
| Coogarah | Llanello | Wilga |
| Coolarindabri | Lolleep | Wilkie |
| Corona | Maggaric | Womborah |
| Cowelba | Manning | Wooburrabebe |
| Cumborah | Mebea | Yarraman |
| Currall | Mein | Yeranbah |
| Daraaba | Milrea | Yerangle |
| Deripas | Mogil Mogul | Yourblah |

The Barwon River forms the eastern, and the Narran River the western, boundaries of this county, and the Moonie River and the Big Warrambool cross it.

FITZGERALD, a county bounded by Killara on the E.; Clarara, N.; Yantara, W.; Yungnulgra, S.; and contains 1,566,720 acres. The following places are within its boundaries :—

| | | |
|---|---|---|
| Boolulta | Murrimbilly | Winbinyah |
| Mulkowah | Purnanga | |

The Paroo River forms the eastern boundary of this county, and lakes Yetabungee and Tongo are within it.

FRANKLIN, a county bounded by Mossgiel and Blaxland on the N.; Waljeers, W.; Nicholson, S. and E.; and contains 898,560 acres. The following places are within its boundaries:—

| | | |
|---|---|---|
| Audrey | Kirindi | Saburra |
| Baeda | Kongong | Terry |
| Bellatherie | Lallal | Thononga |
| Beremagan | Marowie | Tooloor |
| Bundunglong | Mero | Urugalah |
| Caaba | Merungle | Victa |
| Clutha | Molesworth | Waaragoodinia |
| Embagga | Moolbong | Wheelbah |
| Florabel | Mooreway | Willandra |
| Golgotherie | Myamyn | Wirringa |
| Gonowlia | Narralin | Wogonga |
| Goolagulli | Nellywanna | Wyadra |
| Hadyn | Papekurra | Wyuna |
| Ideraway | Poli | Yandombah |
| Ini | Rocta | Yaree |
| Kendal | | |

The Lachlan River forms the boundary on the S.E., and the Willandra Billabong on the N. in this county, and Mount Stewart is within it.

GUNDERBOOKA, a county bounded by Narran on the E.; Culgoa, N.; Irrara and Barrona, W.; Yanda and Cowper, S.; and contains 1,505,280 acres. The following places are within its boundaries:—

| | | |
|---|---|---|
| Corella | Gooriwarra | North Bourke |
| Currewarra | Gwyllie | Talawanta |
| Ford's Bridge | Ledknapper | Toorale |
| Goombalia | Mungunyah | Warraweena |

The Warrego River forms its eastern boundary, and the Darling its western. The Lake and Lake Sutherland are within it. The Great Western railway terminates at Bourke on the S.E. border of this county.

IRRARA, a county bounded by Gunderbooka and Culgoa, on the E.; Queensland boundary, N.; Thouleanna, W.; Barrona, S.; and contains 2,672,640 acres. The following places are within its boundaries:—

| | | |
|---|---|---|
| Berrawinia | Merita | Warpustah |
| Brindingabba | Moco-Barungha | Warroo Springs |
| Clear Water | Mungutuline | Yantabulla Springs |
| Conroy | Murroonowa | Yantabullabulla |
| Dwight | Thurnapatcha | Yernea |
| Eungonia | Wanaaring | Youngaringa Springs |
| Gibson | | |

The Warrego River forms its eastern boundary, and the Paroo its western, and the Queensland border its northern. There are many important creeks flowing within it.

KILFERA, a county bounded by Waljeers on the E.; Manara, N.; Taila, W.; Caira, S.; and contains 1,034,240 acres. The following places are within its boundaries:—

| | | |
|---|---|---|
| Bidurah | Darling | Kitcho North |
| Bomathong | Gal Gal | Magenta |
| Bomathong North | Gal Gal South | Magenta East |
| Chnowa | Glenrouth | North Turlee |
| Chnowa North | Hatfield | Oxley |
| Culpaterong | Juanbung | Sahara |
| Cuipaterong North | Kitcho | Sahara North |

## KILFERA—*continued.*

| | | |
|---|---|---|
| Sahara East | Willibah East | Yelkeer |
| Solferino | Willibah North | Yelkeer North |
| Tankie | Woolpagerie | Yhoul |
| Turlee | Woolpagerie South | Yhoul North |
| Willibah | | |

Tyson's Lake and Magenta Hill are within this county.

KILLARA, a county bounded by Rankin and Landsborough on the E. and N.; Fitzgerald, Yungnulgra, and Young, W.; Werunda, S.; and contains 1,699,840 acres. The following places are within its boundaries:—

| | | |
|---|---|---|
| Analarra | Far West | Rinpooker |
| Balara | Gigil | Tallarara |
| Ballarara | Kambula | Thoolabool |
| Barutho | Killara | Tilpa |
| Bonny | Marra | Towri |
| Bungadool | Mount Jack | Tullundra |
| Byco-Birra | Mullawoolka | Tutty |
| Callindra | Muntowa | Undelcarra |
| Calpacaira | Myali | Walker |
| Cobrilla | Myall | Warramutty |
| Coorimpo | Paroo | Watrook |
| Cultowa | Paxton | Weewaatta Springs |
| Dolora | Peri | Werunda |
| Dilkoosha | Pulcarra | Yamaranie |
| Enlo | | |

The Darling River forms its south-eastern boundary, and Lakes Coorpooka, Oleponoka, Perry, Outilla, and Gullewie are within it, with Mounts Jack, McPherson, and Thoolabool Range.

LANDSBOROUGH, a county bounded by Yanda and Gunderbooka on the E.; Barrona, N.; Killara, W.; Rankin, S.; and contains 1,187,840 acres. The following places are within its boundaries :—

| | | |
|---|---|---|
| Nalticomebe | Ouraweria | Uliara |

The Darling River forms its south-eastern boundary, and Salt Lake is within it; and it is watered by the Ana branch of the Paroo River.

LIVINGSTONE, a county bounded by Manara and Woore on the E.; Werunda and Young, N.; Tandora and Menindie, W.; Perry, S.; and contains 2,344,960 acres. The following places are within its boundaries:—

| | | |
|---|---|---|
| Albermarle | Marlborough | Steel |
| Blenheim | Menindie | Surbiton |
| Bono | Mourie | Talywalka |
| Coombilla | Mundy | Tandonnlogy |
| Foorincaca | Nartooka | Undesthi |
| Gemini | Newcombe | Wallis |
| Gulpaulin | Phelps | Wambah |
| Liddell | Pipla | Wandartillo |
| Maudy | Quandong | Yenda |
| Marle | Repton | |

The Darling River forms its N.W. boundary, and Lakes Wallace, Bullabulka, Ratcatchers, North Lake, Mosey, Teryaweyaya, Waterloo, Victoria, Brummeys, Gum, and Dry Lakes are within it. Lower Talyawalka Creek has its confluence with the Darling River.

MANARA, a county bounded by Waljeers and Mossgiel, on the E.; Woore and Livingstone, N.; Perry, W.; Kilfera, S.; and contains 2,555,520 acres. The following places are within its boundaries:—

| | | |
|---|---|---|
| Amoona | Griffin | Oberwells |
| Baymore | Gubarla | Quambic |
| Benelka | Katabutoi | Taylor |
| Billibah | Kilfera | Thoulminna |
| Bouton | Leura | Thunnula |
| Bounna | Lyons | Til Til |
| Brugarah | Mulurula | Tyson |
| Burlabah | Manara | Umalee |
| Burkett North | Mandellman | Waugh |
| Chingchanga | Manfred | Wawilly |
| Clare | Marli | Wellesley |
| Coolaminyah | Martomah | Whuminbah |
| Garathula | Matheson | Willis |
| Garperiuyah | Moomanyah | Wokobity |
| Gasey | Mulga | Woolpagerie North |
| Ghoul | Nangutwah | Yelty |
| Goondoola | Natumberah | Younga South |

The following lakes are within this county:—Pigeon-hole, Satan's Toe, Cooby's Hole, Martha's Bath, and Moornamyah; and Lignum Swamp.

MENINDIE, a county bounded by Livingstone, on the E.; Tandora and Yancowinna, N.; the South Australian boundary, W.; Windeyer, S.; and contains 1,515,520 acres. The following places are within its boundaries:—

| | | |
|---|---|---|
| Combellia | Menindie | Pinnelco |
| Coonalhugo | Naloira | Putta |
| Laidley | Paringi | West Mit'a |

The Darling River is on its eastern boundary, and Lakes Menindie, Emu, Lawnbilla, Nettlegoe, Tandon, and Kangaroo, with Peak Hill, are within the county.

MOSSGIEL, a county bounded by Blaxland on the E.; Mouramba and Woore, N.; Manara, W.; Waljeers and Franklin, S.; and contains 2,649,600 acres. The following places are within its boundaries:—

| | | |
|---|---|---|
| Ballabah | Coombie | Marowda |
| Balyah | Eildon | Marributa |
| Barrigan | Elie | Maybah |
| Bennett | Goonaburra | Minmilinji |
| Berrigembam | Gunnagia | Mipara |
| Bevan | Gunnabouna | Moolah |
| Billabah | Haines | Moongoola |
| Binda Binda | Holy Box Well | Mossgiel |
| Bolaro | Ivanhoe | Murringobuni |
| Boobooran | Katarah | Murrurah |
| Brougham | Kayuligah | Nerrada |
| Bundamutta | Keleela | Nintie |
| Burrenyinah | Kewong | Paddington |
| Burrinyanni | Kilkoobijal | Palmyra |
| Calytria | Langealeal | Papaloitoi |
| Calytria South | Largoh | Pingunnia |
| Cameron | Lowan | Plevna |
| Canoble | Malagadery | Pitterween |
| Carowra | Mallee | Scholefield |
| Carter | Manfred | St. Monans |
| Cogie | Mara | Tarraroulla |
| Cookenmabourne | Maroopna | Thatoombea |

## MOSSGIEL—continued.

| | | |
|---|---|---|
| Thara | Waiko Wanga | Wharparoo |
| Thollcolaboy | Wallangery | Whittingham |
| Thoolamagoogi | Wangaroa | Willingerie |
| Tiarra | Warbreccan | Winderima |
| Ticehurst | Warranari | Wooro |
| Tinbo | Warrenitchie | Wooroola |
| Toorak | Wee Elwah | Yalloch |
| Trewalla | Weejugalah | Yathong |
| Trida | Weenigoota | Youyang |
| Ulumbie | Weeribinyah | Yugururee |
| Umphelby | | |

The Willandra Billabong forms the southern boundary of this county.

MOOTWINGEE, a county bounded by Young and Yungnulgra on the E.; Yantara and Evelyn, N.; Farnell, W.; Yancowinna and Tandora, S.; and contains 2,191,360 acres. The following places are within its boundaries:—

| | | |
|---|---|---|
| Caloola | Gairdner's Creek | Tellawongee |
| Campbell | Moohumbulla | Tirlta |
| Donelly | Morden | Windanuka |

The lakes in this county are Windanuka, Burtopoonoo, Bencanya, and Nuncha. The Coko Range is on its western boundary.

MOURUMBA, a county bounded by Flinders on the E.; Cambelego, Robinson, and Booroondarra, N. and W.; Blaxland and Mossgiel, S.; and contains 1,509,120 acres. The following places are within its boundaries:—

| | | |
|---|---|---|
| Adams | Erimeran | Moothumbool |
| Albyn | Evans | Mossgiel |
| Barratta | Everton | Mouramba |
| Barton | Fisher | Nymagee |
| Beloura | Flinders | Pangee |
| Blaxland | Fulton | Priory Plains |
| Booroondarra | Gilgannia | Priory |
| Booth | Goold | Restdown |
| Brigstock | Gwynne | Ricketson |
| Buckambool | Hartwood | Robinson |
| Byron | Hathaway | Roset |
| Canbelego | Hume | Scott |
| Carlyle | Jamieson | Shenandoah |
| Chaucer | Johnston | The Rookery |
| Coree | Kangerong | Urolia |
| Crowl | Keira | Wallace |
| Devon | Kiamba | Werlong |
| Donaldson | Kinchelsea | Wills |
| Dowling | Kinnear | Willis |
| Dryden | Knox | Yamma |
| Dunstan | Kruge | Yanko |
| Ellis | McGregor | Youyang |
| Ellerslie | Middlesex | |

Mount Buckambool is in this county.

NARRAN, a county bounded by Finch on the E.; Queensland boundary, N.; Culgoa, W.; Clyde, S.; and contains 2,304,000 acres. The following places are within its boundaries:—

| | | |
|---|---|---|
| Angledool | Bokhara | Callawaroi |
| Ballanbillian | Boogonderra | Cato |
| Bilbil | Booroomunda | Coobeinda |
| Binndaah | Brewarrina | Cootung |
| Bogeira | Bunnawanna | Cowgi |

### NARRAN—continued.

| | | |
|---|---|---|
| Cumblegubinbah | Mildoa | Terewah |
| Curvil | Moongoonoola | Terra |
| Denman | Mogila | Teriaoola |
| Gillgi | Morella | Thulama |
| Goonoo | Muckerawea | Walka |
| Grui | Mungiladah | Wilby |
| Hammond | Narrandool | Willawillinbah |
| Hungerford | Papperton | Yamba |
| Lolah | | |

The rivers in this county are the Narran, Bokhara, Birie, Culgoa, and Darling. The Culgoa forms its western, the Darling its southern, and the Narran its eastern, boundaries. Narran Lake is within it.

PERRY, a county bounded by Manara on the E.; Livingstone, N.; Windeyer, W.; Wentworth, S.; and contains 1,822,720 acres. The following places are within its boundaries:—

| | | |
|---|---|---|
| Barritt | Peidpedidias | Tolarno |
| Barra | Pooncaira | Wentworth |
| Garpung | Tanbery | Wreford |
| Glenstal | Tareoola | Wumpa |
| Mooram | Turtna | Yenda |
| Mythe | Timpunga | |

The Darling River forms its western boundary.

POOLE, a county bounded by Tongowoko on the E.; Queensland boundary, N.; South Australian boundary, W.; Evelyn, S.; and contains 1,351,680 acres. There are no recorded places within this county. Macdonald's Peak, Pinooroo Lake, and Tilcha and Paradise Creeks are within its boundaries.

RANKIN, a county bounded by Yanda and Booroondarra on the E.; Landsborough, N.; Killara, W.; Werunda and Woore, S.; and contains 2,529,280 acres. The following places are within its boundaries:—

| | | |
|---|---|---|
| Albert | Donald | Munbunyah |
| Basin Bank | Donald's Plain | Rankin |
| Bilbo | Greenough | Tangarook |
| Booborowie | Kelor | Tilpilly |
| Budda | Killara | Woelong |
| Buckimbe | Kirkinglo | Weelongbar |
| Cameron | Mary | Wigilla |
| Campbell | Mulga | Woollandra |
| Danalage | Mullpillburry | Woore |

The Darling River forms its north-western boundary, and Lakes Naropilly and Waracoocaric, with Acres' Billabong, are within it; as also is Greenough's Group.

ROBINSON, a county bounded by Canbelego on the E.; Yanda and Cowper, N.; Booroondarra, W.; Mouramba, S.; and contains 1,948,000 acres. The following places are within its boundaries:—

| | | |
|---|---|---|
| Amphitheatre | Buckwanoon | Gidda |
| Balah | Bulgoo | Gidgie |
| Barrona | Canbelego | Goonumbertoo |
| Bee | Cobar | Grawlin |
| Billagoe | Cohn | Hillston |
| Booroondarra | Coronga | Hoskins |
| Booroomugga | Cutagulyaroo | Kaloogleguy |
| Buckambool | Davies | Kiantharellany |

ROBINSON—*continued*.

| | | |
|---|---|---|
| Lambrigo | Mulga | Tindayrey |
| Lars | Mullimut | Toy |
| Lerida | Mumbowanna | Walsho |
| Linton | Narri | Weltie |
| Louth | Nyngan | Winbar |
| Monguilamba | Priory | Yanda |
| Mopone | Tambua | |

Mounts Billagoe, See, Narri Narri, and Bobby are within this county. Cobar is the terminus of the railway from Nyngan, on the Western line.

TAILA, a county bounded by Caira and Kilfera on the E.; Perry, N.; Wentworth, W.; boundary of Victoria, S.; and contains 1,679,360 acres. The following places are within its boundaries:—

| | | |
|---|---|---|
| Bengallow | Grant | Mendook |
| Bertram | Gulthul | Merrowa |
| Bidum West | Laurie | Mundoonah |
| Boorong | Lowan | Mungo |
| Bunchie | Mallee Cliffs | Nowong |
| Burkett | Manie | Prungle |
| Coltwang | Monietta | Rainding |
| Dispersion | Marina | Spencer |
| Euston | Matalong | Taila |
| Garnett | Meilman | Zana |

The Murray River forms its southern boundary, and Lakes Benanee and Prooa, and Mount Dispersion are within it.

TANDORA, a county bounded by Livingstone and Young on the E.; Mootwinga, N.; Yancowinna, W.; Menindie, S.; and contains 1,331,200 acres. The following places are within its boundaries:—

| | | |
|---|---|---|
| Charlemont | Neila Gaari | Tandon |
| Hume | Pamamaroo | Titabaira |
| Kars | Silistria | Quondong |
| Mulveneri | | |

The Darling River forms its S.E. boundary; and Lakes Eckerboon, Silistria, Menindie, Malta, Horse, Tandare, Pamamaroo, and Speculation are within it.

TARA, a county bounded by Wentworth on the E.; Windeyer, on the N.; South Australian boundary, W.; boundary of Victoria, S.; and contains 1,505,280 acres. The following places are within its boundaries:—

| | | |
|---|---|---|
| Amoskeag | Foreaux | Ootootwa |
| Amoskeag South | Franklin | Orara |
| Balpunga | Gipps | Peekilba |
| Barry | Grose | Pelwalka |
| Belmore | Jervois | Phillip |
| Boolonkeena | Kennedy | Popiga |
| Bowen | Lila | Popiga South |
| Cal Lal | Lindsay | Robinson |
| Canterbury | Litheringee | Salt Creek |
| Crozier | Loftus | Scotia |
| Darling | Lonsdale | Scotia South |
| Denison | Marcoonia | Stephen |
| Dinwoodie | Mellee | Tara |
| Eurilla | Moorna | Utah |
| Fitzroy | Musgrave | Victoria |
| Foster | Nialia | Walkming |

K

TARA—*continued.*

| | | |
|---|---|---|
| Waltregile | Wilpatera | Woolgundah |
| Wangummah | Winda | Yantaralla |
| Wannawanna | Winda South | Yurlulla |
| Warpa | Windamingle | Yarlalla South |
| Warrawenia | Winnebaga | Young |
| Wilton | Winnebaga South | |

The Ana-branch of the Darling River forms its eastern boundary, the Murray river its southern, and the boundary of South Australia its western boundaries. The Salt Lakes and Lake Victoria or Tara are within it.

THOULCANNA, a county bounded by Irrara on the E.; Queensland boundary, N.; Delalah, W.; Ularara, S.; and contains 911,360 acres. The following places are within its boundaries:—

| | | |
|---|---|---|
| Evelyn | Thierwillar | Yeruga |
| Kelly | Westeranna | |

The Paroo River forms its eastern boundary; and the Martha Range is within it, with a portion of the Delalah Downs.

TONGOWOKO, a county bounded by Delalah on the E.; Queensland boundary, N.; Poole, W.; Evelyn and Yantara, S.; and contains 1,658,830 acres. The following places are within its boundaries:—

| | | |
|---|---|---|
| Tianjara | The Albert | Well |
| Tibooburra | Thompson's Well | |

Mount Poole and Du Faur's Peak are within this county.

ULARARA, a county bounded by Barrona on the E.; Thoulcanna and Delalah, N.; Yantara, W.; Fitzgerald, S.; and contains 1,239,040 acres. The following places are within its boundaries:—

| | |
|---|---|
| Monkilmoultha | Peke |

The Paroo River forms its eastern boundary, and the Lismore Ranges are within it.

WALJEERS, a county bounded by Nicholson and Franklin on the E.; Mossgiel, N.; Manara and Kilfera, W.; Waradgery, S.; and contains 1,272,820 acres. The following places are within its boundaries:—

| | | |
|---|---|---|
| Alma | Kingswell | Natue |
| Annan | Lagan | Nyanda |
| Arondale | Largs | Pimpara |
| Benanimie | Larnaca | Simson |
| Billabong | Lowan | Tarrawong |
| Boondara | Massie | Tartoo |
| Brassbutt | Matamong | Tinna |
| Buckonyong | Meekni | Tom's Lake |
| Bulgerbugerygam | Merrimajeel | Toopruck |
| Bungarry | Moodarnong | Touralboung |
| Corrong | Mossgiel | Trawalla |
| Culparling | Mulloga | Waljeers |
| Dimboola | Murnia | Waverley |
| Goona Warra | Murra | Yaloo |
| Gregory | Nandum | Yarto |
| Howatson | | |

The Lachlan River forms its south-eastern boundary, and Lakes Waljeers, Ryems, Bullogal, Bungarry, Tarrawong, The Dry and Tom's Lake are within it.

WENTWORTH, a county bounded by Taila on the E.; Perry and Windeyer, N.; Tara, W.; the boundary of Victoria, S.; and contains 2,232,320 acres. The following places are within its boundaries:—

| | | |
|---|---|---|
| Annan | Letheroe | Pernolingay |
| Ardmore | Lissan | Ponderry |
| Arumpo | Matong | Pulpa |
| Avoca | Merebe | Roma |
| Belar | Merno | Salt Lake |
| Bingoo | Mickengay | Scott |
| Brewang | Millie | Tapio |
| Bullonmong | Mindelwul | Tarangara |
| Bulubulla | Moangola | Thirrang |
| Bunneringee | Mono | Thitto |
| Burnguy | Moondalea | Thoomby |
| Burrie | Moorpa | Tiltao |
| Burtundyn | Mourquong | Tittal |
| Connargee | Muni | Toonton |
| Coonpa | Mundrower | Tooran |
| Copar | Murnowella | Tubrigo |
| Cowl | Nanga | Tugima |
| Curnoo | Neilpo | Uki |
| Darling | North Cowl | Ulong |
| Dean | Ogro | Wambora |
| Emu | Oporto | Wentworth |
| Gol Gol | Paara | Winnegow |
| Gulpy | Pallinjewah | Yerta |
| Ilingerry | Paringi | |

The Darling River crosses this county, and the Murray forms its southern boundary, and the Ana-branch of the Darling its western; and Lakes Milkengay and Gal Gal are within it, with Mount Look-out.

WERUNDA, a county bounded by Woore and Rankin on the E.; Killara, N.; Young, W.; Livingstone and Woore, S. The following places are within its boundaries:—

| | | |
|---|---|---|
| Catkin | Gooralga | Moira |
| Change | Greenough | Murtee |
| Coolmara | Gungulka | Onondoo |
| Cowary | Gurrangale | Poopelloe |
| Curooganu | Keilor | Talyawalka |
| Donabroe | Keiss | Werunda |
| Donala | Macpherson | Wilcannia South |
| Duroon | Manara | Wongolarroo |
| Galgoo | Merry | Woytebugga |
| Gathgeenna | Moama | Yoree |
| Goonoolgra | | |

The Darling River forms its north-western boundary, and Murty Point and Lakes Poopelloe, Gumyulka, and Pollioillaluke are within it, with part of the Greenough's Group.

WINDEYER, a county bounded by Perry on the E.; Menindie, N.; South Australian boundary, W.; Tara and Wentworth, S.; and contains 1,976,320 acres. The following places are within its boundaries:—

| | | |
|---|---|---|
| Abena | Bluebush | Ellerslie |
| Antita | Boreo | Eolia |
| Badham | Barton | Erreman |
| Barrawanna | Buckalow | Illawla |
| Barry | Conoley | Ita |
| Bingerry | Coombah | Kertue |
| Bingalong | Cuthero | Kiton |

## WINDEYER—continued.

| | | |
|---|---|---|
| Kudgee | Ootootra | Stuart |
| Leichhardt | Orara | Urutah |
| Mallara | Pearson | Wallara |
| Mallee | Polia | Wanneba |
| Manee | Polinor | Wannelia |
| Meroo | Popilta | Whurlie |
| Milang | Popio | Willotia |
| Moorley | Power | Windeyer |
| Mulga | Quamby | Wollar |
| Mullojama | Ramleh | Yallolka |
| Nadbuck | Sandridge | Yarlalla |
| Nalim | Spinnifex | Yartha |

The Darling River forms its eastern boundary, with Lakes Coomba, White, Popilta, Twins, Ratio, Nitchie, Nearie, Travellers, Yartla, Dry, Paradise, and Red Bank are within it, with Round Hill Mountain.

WOORE, a county, bounded by Mossgiel and Booroondarra on the S. and E.; Werunda, W.; Manara, S.; and contains 1,726,080 acres. No names of places are recorded in this county. The Chain of Hills Mountain is within this county.

YANCOWINNA, a county bounded by Tandora on the E.; Farnell, N.; South Australian boundary, W.; Menindie, S.; and contains 1,607,680 acres. The following places are within its boundaries:—

| | | |
|---|---|---|
| Acacia | Eurowie | Robe |
| Albert | Halliday's Dam | Sebastapol |
| Albion | Inkerman | Sentinel |
| Alma | Lewis | Silverton |
| Bolaria | Moorkaie | Soudan |
| Bomangaldy | Mount Gipps | Stephen |
| Bray | Mundi Mundi | Taltingan |
| Broken Hill | Mundybah | Tara |
| Burns | Myalla | Thackaringa |
| Cambelia | Narran | Umberumberka |
| Catcheart | Naradin | Victoria |
| Charlemont | Nevada | Wankeroo |
| Coonbaralla | Para | Willyama |
| Dhoon | Picton | Willewurrawa |
| Edgar | Pinnacles | Yancowinna |
| Enmore | Purnamoota | Yancowinna East |

The Barrier ranges and Mounts Gipps and Robe are within it, where immense deposits of silver have been developed. The railway to Adelaide, South Australia, has its terminus at Willyama in this county.

YANDA, a county, bounded by Cowper on the E.; Gunderbooka, N.; Lansborough, W.; Rankin and Robinson, S.; and contains 2,031,760 acres. The following places are within its boundaries:—

| | | |
|---|---|---|
| Cumbedore | Mitchell | Tatiara |
| Derrina | Momble | Tinderra |
| Dunlop | Mookabimbirria | Warrego |
| Gumhall | Mulga | Winba |
| Gunderbooka | Narwarree | Woodhouse |
| Kenindie | Pangunga | Woola |
| Kerie | Pulpulla | Yanda |
| Louth | Ramsey | Yandagulla |
| Merrere | Rumker | |

The Darling River forms its north-western boundary. Frazer's Lake, with Dunlop's and Rankin's Ranges, and Mounts Booroondarra, Deerina, Buckwaroon Hill, and Moolka Hill, are within it.

YANTARA, a county, bounded by Fitzgerald and Ularara on the E.; Delalah and Tongowoko, N.; Evelyn, E.; Mootwingee and Yungnulgra, S.; and contains 2,078,720 acres. The following places are within its boundaries:—

| | | |
|---|---|---|
| Mederie | Terrawinda | Yandenberry |

Lakes Altia, Yantara, Gara, Round, Cobhan, and Gurnpata, are within its boundaries.

YOUNG, a county bounded by Killara on the E.; Yungnulgra, N.; Tandara, W.; Livingstone, S.; and contains 1,761,280 acres. The following places are within its boundaries:—

| | | |
|---|---|---|
| Ardennis | Danbeny | Morriset |
| Barbiston | Dalglish | Mulga |
| Baroonrangee | Darling | Mulyoren |
| Blanche | Desailly | Murchison |
| Blumenthal | Dickens | Paradise |
| Bouley | Dry Lake | Parkes |
| Brougham | Evelyn | Peveril |
| Broughton | Garland | Robinson |
| Cameron | Greville | Sutherland |
| Campbell | Griffiths | Tallandra |
| Clayton | Jennings | Ultimo |
| Cobrilla | Kambula | Waltragalda |
| Comarto | King | Willis |
| Commerry | Loftus | Wilcannia |
| Copaka | Mackenzie | Wood |
| Correga | Mitchell | Woore |
| Culpaulin | Moorabun | Woytchugga |
| Cuthowarra | Moorguinia | Yungnulgra |

The Darling River forms its south-eastern boundary. Lakes Correga, Bunda, Woytchugga, and Copako are within it, with Mount Murchison, Comarto Hill, Torsopooroo Hill, Mount Wright, and Bondie Ranges.

YUNGNULGRA, a county bounded by Killara on the E.; Fitzgerald and Yantara, N.; Mootwingee, W.; Young, S.; and contains 1,802,240 acres. The following places are within its boundaries:—

| | | |
|---|---|---|
| Beefwood | Gnalta | Porlteo |
| Charlton | Kandie | Tarella |
| Core | Menamurtee | Ullollie |
| Danbeny | Mooney | Walla |
| Gambool | Murta | Wirra Wirra |
| Germano | Narrows | Williams |
| Goode | | |

Lake Nine-mile, Mount Danseny, Gnalta Peak, and Cootwandy Range are within this county. Bunker's Creek flows across it.

*This completes the Counties.*

COURALLIE, a county in the Central Division of the colony. [See "COUNTIES."]

COURALLIE CREEK (*Co. Courallie*), a stream rising in the Nundewar Range, flowing in a N.W. direction and discharges its waters into the Moomin Creek.

COURBIRA (*Co. Wynyard*), a village reserve lying on the Tarcutta Creek, 4 miles from Tumberumba.

COURIDJAH (*Co. Camden*), a proclaimed village to the S. of Picton.

COURINGA CREEK (*Co. Bathurst*), is a fine auriferous northern tributary of the Belubula River, rising in the Conobolas Mountains and flowing southerly through rugged country.

COUTTS' CROSSING (*Co. Clarence*), a postal village, 532 miles N. of Sydney, with mail twice a week.

COW FLAT (*Co. Wellington*), a postal village, 155 miles W. of Sydney, with daily mail, money-order office and Government savings bank. The nearest railway station is George's Plains, 3 miles, on the western line.

COWAL LAKE (*Co. Gipps*), a large swampy lagoon formed by the waters of the Yeo Yeo and Manna Creeks, about 40 miles from Condobolin on the Lachlan River.

COWAN CREEK (*Co. Cumberland*), a small stream having a wide estuary, and falling into the S. arm of Broken Bay.

COWAN'S (*Co. Harden*), a village, 260 miles S. of Sydney. The nearest railway station is Cootamundra, 15 miles, on the southern line.

COWAN'S CREEK (*Co. Gresham*), a small western tributary of the Nymboid River.

COWABEE MOUNT (*Co. Bourke*), a solitary hill lying in the vast plain between the Lachlan and Murrumbidgee Rivers.

COWARY MOUNT (*Co. Gowen*), a peak of the Warrabungle Range, lying at the head of the Bedlur Creek.

COWBED CREEK (*Co. Wellesley*), a small tributary of the Cambalong Creek.

COWBELL FALLS (*Co. Wellesley*), a waterfall on the Camalong Creek, about 16 miles N. of Bombala.

COWLONG (*Co. Rous*), a postal receiving-office, 369 miles N. of Sydney, with mail once a week.

COWLEY, a county in the Eastern Division of the County. [See "COUNTIES."]

COWPASTURES (*Cos. Cumberland and Camden*), a well-known and extensive agricultural and grazing district situated about 40 miles S. of Sydney. It is watered by a river called Cowpasture River, which, after its junction with the Warragamba, a stream issuing from the Blue Mountains, forms the Nepean. It was discovered during the government of Captain Hunter in the year 1796, and derives its name from a herd of wild cattle which were found ranging over its untraversed wilds when it was first occupied by civilised man. These cattle were the offspring of two bulls and three cows of the Cape of Good Hope, buffalo breed, which had been landed in the colony by Governor Phillip, but had strayed into the woods during the first week after the formation of Sydney, and could never afterwards be found.

COWPASTURE RIVER (*Co. Camden*), the original name of the Nepean River.

COWPER, a county in the Western Division of the Colony. [*See* "Counties."]

COWPER (*Co. Clarence*), a postal receiving-office, 340 miles N. of Sydney, with mail once a week by Grafton steamer.

COWPOLLEY CREEK (*Co. Buckland*), a northern tributary of the Quirindi Creek, lying to the N. of Quirindi, and flowing into a creek of that name.

COWRA (*Co. Bathurst*), a postal town, 203 miles W. of Sydney, with daily mail. Money-order and telegraph offices and Government savings bank, and delivery by letter-carrier. A railway station on the southern line. It was proclaimed a borough in 1888 with eight aldermen and a mayor. The population is about 1,000. Courts of quarter sessions and district courts are held here periodically. Situated on the Lachlan River, the Wangoola Creek rising in a southerly direction within a mile, and the Back Creek distant 6 miles from Cowra.

COWRA CREEK (*Co. Beresford*), a small southern tributary of the Bredbo River.

COWRA CREEK (*Co. Selwyn*), a small tributary of the Tumbarumba Creek, rising in Mane's Range, and flowing W. about 10 miles through a scrubby pastoral country.

COWRADDIE MOUNT (*Co. Jamison*), a peak of the Nundewar Range, lying at the head of the Weah Waa Creek.

COX'S CREEK (*Co. Darling*), is an agricultural and pastoral hamlet about 30 miles S.E. of the township of Narrabri.

COX'S CREEK (*Co. Darling*), a small eastern tributary of Maule's Creek, flowing through rich undulating pastoral country finely grassed.

COX'S CREEK (*Co. Phillip*), an eastern tributary of the upper part of the Cudgegong River, rising in the western slopes of the Australian Alps, and flowing into that river at the township of Dabee.

COX'S CROWN (*Co. Phillip*), a lofty detached peak lying on the W. bank of Cox's Creek, about 3 miles from the township of Dabee.

COX'S GAP (*Co. Cook*), a passage through overhanging perpendicular cliffs 676 feet high, on the old road between Sydney and Bathurst.

COX'S RIVER (*Co. Westmoreland*), a postal village, 66 miles S. of Sydney, with mail therefrom three days a week. The nearest railway station is Picton, 35 miles, on the southern line. The river is an important stream rising in the Blue Mountain Range, near Rydal, and flowing into the Wollondilly at its junction with the Warragamba, and thence into the Nepean. The course of the river is exceedingly picturesque, and one part of it is known as the Vale of Clwydd.

COX'S SIDING (*Co. Wellington*), a railway station, 163 miles W. of Sydney, on the Mudgee line.

CRACKEMBACK MOUNT (*Co. Wallace*), a high peak of the Mumorig Range. It lies in the lofty ranges near the head of the Snowy River, and attains an elevation of 4,697 feet above the sea level.

CRACKEMBACK RIVER (*Co. Wallace.*) [*See* "RIVERS."]

CRAETON (*Co. Bligh*), a village, 223 miles N. of Sydney. The nearest railway station is Muswellbrook, 120 miles, on the northern line.

CRAGIN MOUNT (*Co. Burnett*), a high solitary peak lying on the E. bank of Oxley's Creek, about 8 miles E. of Warialda.

CRAIGIE (*Co. Wellesley*), a postal village, 338 miles S. of Sydney, with mail three times a week. The nearest railway station is Cooma, 69 miles, on the southern line.

CRANBURY (*Co. Ashburnham*), a post-office, 227 miles W. of Sydney, with mail three times a week.

CRANEBROOK (*Co. Cumberland*), a postal receiving-office, 37 miles to the W. of Sydney, with daily mail.

CRAVEN CREEK (*Co. Gloucester*), a small northern tributary of Bowman's River.

CRAWFORD RIVER (*Co. Gloucester*), a western tributary of the Myall River falling into it at Bullah Dellah. [*See* "RIVERS."]

CREAM OF TARTAR CREEK (*Co. Brisbane*), a small western tributary of Harry's Creek.

CRESCENT HEAD (*Co. Macquarie*), a rocky promontory standing boldly out into the sea, between Port Macquarie and Korogoro Point.

CROCODILE ROCK (*Co. Auckland*), situated in Bass' Straits in a line midway between the W. extremity of Curtis and Rodondo Islands, nearly 9 miles from each. It is a smooth round-topped granite boulder, just protruding above the surface of the sea.

CROKI (*Manning River*), a postal town, 236 miles to the N. of Sydney, with mail daily and steamer direct. Money-order and telegraph offices.

CROMPTON ISLAND (*Co. St. Vincent*), a rocky islet, lying near the coast, about 7 miles S. of Ulladulla.

CRONULLA BEACH (*Co. Cumberland*), a sandy bight, lying on the N. of the entrance to Port Hacking, and on the S. of the South Head of Botany Bay.

CROOBYAR CREEK (*Co. St. Vincent*), a stream rising in Mount Tatalerang, and flowing into the sea a few miles N. of Ulladulla. The village reserve of Croobyar is on this creek.

CROOKED RIVER *(Co. Camden)*. [*See* "RIVERS."]

CROOKHAVEN RIVER *(Co. St. Vincent)*. [*See* "RIVERS."]

CROOKWELL *(Co. King)*, a postal town, 160 miles S. of Sydney, with a daily mail, money-order and telegraph offices, and Government savings bank. The nearest railway station is Goulburn, 20 miles, on the southern line.

CROOKWELL RIVER *(Co. King)*. [*See* "RIVERS."]

CROOME *(Co. Camden)*, a post-office, 66 miles S. of Sydney, with mail therefrom four times a week.

CROPPER CREEK *(Co. Stapylton)*, a chain of swampy water-holes to the N. of the Gilgil River, between Warialda and Whalan.

CROPPY CREEK *(Co. Bligh)*, a tributary to the Turee Creek.

CROSBIE'S CREEK *(Co. King)*, an eastern tributary of the Burrowa River rising in the Yass Plains.

CROSSING CREEK *(Co. Georgiana)*, a tributary of Clifford's Creek, rising at Carrabungle, and flowing 10 miles W. past Laggan.

CROSS ROADS *(Co. Camden)*, a postal village, 97 miles S. of Sydney, with mail therefrom four days each week. The nearest railway station is Moss Vale, 9 miles, on the southern line.

CROW MOUNTAIN DIGGINGS *(Co. Darling)*, a small alluvial gold workings, lying about 12 miles distant from the township of Barrabra.

CROWDY HEAD *(Co. Macquarie)*, a prominent headland jutting out into the bight of the Manning, from which it bears about N.E. by N. 5 miles. It affords considerable shelter to coasters from S.W. or S. winds.

CROWN RIDGE CREEK *(Co. Roxburgh)*, a small auriferous northern tributary of the head of the Turon River, rising in the southern slope of the Blackman's Crown Mountain.

CROWPAL CREEK *(Co. Bucclench)*, a southern tributary of the Murrumbidgee River, rising in the western slope of Crowpal Hill, in the N. of the county.

CROWTHER *(Co. Monteagle)*, a village, 272 miles S. of Sydney. A railway station on the Blayney branch of the southern line.

CROWTHER CREEK *(Cos. Monteagle and Forbes)*, a fine stream, rising near Marringo, to the E. of the Burrangong gold-fields, flowing into the Lachlan River, about 6 miles E. of the township of Cowra.

CROWTHER WEST BRANCH CREEK *(Co. Monteagle)*, is the western head of Crowther Creek, rising in the Burrangong gold-fields, about 4 miles S.E. of the township of Forbes.

CROYDON *(Co. Cumberland)*, an important postal suburb, 6 miles S. of the city, on the suburban main lines of railway, possessing all the conveniences attaching to the city, and no doubt named after "Croydon," in Surry, England, which is situated about 12 miles S. of London.

CRUDINE *(Co. Roxburgh)*, a postal town, 160 miles W. of Sydney, with mail four days a week. The nearest railway station is Capertee, 25 miles, on the Mudgee branch of the western line.

CUBIT PONDS *(Co. Buckland)*, a small chain of waterholes flowing from the E. into the Conadilly River, at Pullanaming Reserve.

CUDAL *(Co. Ashburnham)*, a postal village, 221 miles W. of Sydney, with mail daily. Money-order and telegraph offices and Government savings bank. The nearest railway station is Borenore, 16 miles, on the Molong branch of the western line.

CUDDELL *(Co. Mitchell)*, a proclaimed village on a branch of the Murrumbidgee River, to the S.W. of Narrandera Junction railway station.

CUDGEE *(Co. Auckland)*, a village reserve and agricultural settlement, lying 60 miles from Eden.

CUDGEBEGONG CREEK *(Co. Wellington)*, a postal town, 290 miles W. of Sydney, with mail therefrom twice a week.

CUDGEGONG *(Co. Wellington)*, a postal town, 142 miles W. of Sydney, with daily mail. Money-order office and Government savings bank. The nearest railway station is Mudgee, 22 miles, on the western line, situated on spurs of mountains 1,500 feet above the level of the sea. The district is rich in copper, iron, and coal. Cudgegong was proclaimed a municipality in 1860, with seven aldermen and a mayor. The population is about 2,500.

CUDGEGONG CREEK *(Co. Roxburgh)*, a western tributary of the Cudgegong River, lying to the N. of Keen's Swamp, and flowing into Cudgegong at the village of the same name.

CUDGEGONG RIVER *(Cos. Bligh, Roxburgh, Phillip, and Wellington)*. [*See* "RIVERS."]

CUDGEN *(Co. Rous)*, a postal receiving-office, 432 miles N. of Sydney, with mail therefrom three days each week by Brisbane steamer.

CUDGEN SCRUB *(Co. Rous)*, a postal village, 420 miles N. of Sydney, with mail therefrom three days a week by Brisbane steamer.

CUDMIRRA LAKE *(Co. St. Vincent)*, an opening into the land lying to the S. of Sussex Haven, and near the township of Farnham.

CUGABURGA CREEK *(Co. Wellington)*, an eastern tributary of the Bell River.

CUGABURGA MOUNT *(Co. Wellington)*, a high hill, lying about 13 miles S.W. of Wellington.

CULCAIRN *(Co. Goulburn)*, a postal village, 356 miles S. of Sydney, with mail daily, and money-order and telegraph offices. A railway station on the southern line.

CULGOA, a county in the Western Division of the Colony. [*See* "COUNTIES."]

CULGOA RIVER *(Co. Culgoa)*. [*See* "RIVERS."]

CULLARIN CREEK *(Co. King)*, a fine mountain stream, forming one of the heads of the Lachlan River, to the S.E. of the township of Gunning, flowing thence into the main stream of the Lachlan.

CULLARIN RANGE (*Co. King*), a portion of the great dividing chain, extending from the Blue Mountains to the northern extremity of Lake George. The average elevation of this range is about 3,000 feet above the sea level.

CULLENBONE (*Co. Wellington*), a postal town, 303 miles W. of Sydney, with mail three days a week. The nearest railway station is Mudgee, 7 miles, on the western line.

CULLEN BULLEN (*Co. Cook*), a postal village, 127 miles W. of Sydney, with mail twice a week. The nearest railway station is Portland siding, 4 miles, on the western railway. Situated within a short distance S. of the head of the Turon River.

CULLINGA (*Co. Harden*), a postal village, 248 miles S. of Sydney, with mail three times a week. The nearest railway station is Wallenbeen, 6 miles, on the Young branch of the southern line.

CULPARLING (*Co. Nicholson*), a postal receiving-office, 559 miles S. of Sydney, with mail once a week.

CULTOWA (*Co. Killara*), a township on the E. bank of the Darling River, above the township of Wilcannia.

CUMBAMURRA (*Co. Harden*), a proclaimed village on the Spring Creek.

CUMBAMURRA ROCKS (*Co. Harden*), a group of immense rocks lying on the rugged banks of the Spring Creek, about 2 miles above its junction with the Jugiong Creek.

CUMBERLAND, a county in the Eastern Division of the Colony. [*See* "COUNTIES."]

CUMBO CREEK (*Co. Bligh*), a tributary of the Wilpingong Creek, rising near Mount Morlarben.

CUMBRAE ISLE (*Co. Gloucester*), an island of the Myall Lakes. Called after the historic isles of that name in Scotland.

CUMNOCK (*Co. Wellington*), a postal office, 230 miles S. of Sydney, with mail three days a week. Telegraph and money-order offices. The nearest railway station is Molong, 13 miles, on the western line.

CUNDLETOWN (*Co. Macquarie*), a postal village, 230 miles N. of Sydney, with daily mail. Money-order and telegraph offices and Government savings bank. The nearest railway station is Hexham, 118 miles, on the northern line. Situated on the N. bank of the Manning River, within 3 miles of the township of Taree, and the head of the steam navigation of the river Ghinni-Ghinni.

CUNDLE FLAT (*Co. Macquarie*), a postal receiving-office, 259 miles N. of Sydney, with mail once a week.

CUNDONG CREEK (*Co. Narromine*), a southern tributary of the Tomingly Creek, rising in the Harvey Range W. of Obley, flowing through a pastoral country.

CUNDUMBUL (*Co. Wellington*), a postal receiving-office, 238 miles to the W. of Sydney, with mail two days a week. The nearest railway station is Molong, 22 miles, on the western line.

CUNGEGONG (*Co. Harden*), a proclaimed village on the creek of the same name.

CUNGEGONG CREEK (*Co. Harden*), a small tributary of the Muttama Creek, flowing through the village reserve of that name.

CUNGLEBUNG MOUNT (*Co. Gresham*), a lofty peak of the Macleay Range, lying on the S. bank of the Mitchell River, near the junction of the Cunglebung Creek.

CUNNINGAR (*Co. Harden*), a proclaimed township, 225 miles S. of Sydney and railway station on the southern line.

CUNNINGHAM, a county in the Central Division of the Colony. [*See* "COUNTIES."]

CUNNINGHAM (*Co. Harden*), a postal village, 225 miles S. of Sydney, with daily mail. The nearest railway station is Cunningar, 3 miles, on the southern line.

CUNNINGHAM CREEK (*Co. Harden*), a fine stream, rising in the W. of the Cunningham Plains, flowing through a pastoral and agricultural district into the creek near Boorowa.

CUNNINGHAME'S CREEK (*Co. Roxburgh*), a northern auriferous tributary of the Turon River, flowing W. and S. into the main stream about 2 miles W. of Sofala.

CUNNINGHAM'S PLAINS (*Co. Harden*). a fine tract of pasture land, lying between Jugiong and Young, near the township of Murrimboola.

CUNWENGAN (*Co. Harden*). an agricultural village, situated on the Cunningham Plains Creek, about 4 miles E. of the township of Murrumburrah.

CURBAN (*Co. Narromine*), a postal receiving-office, 336 miles W. of Sydney, with mail three times a week. The nearest railway station is Dubbo, 42 miles, on the western line.

CURIONG CREEK (*Co. Harden*), a small western tributary of the Illalong Creek, rising to the E. of the township of Binalong.

CURLEWIS (*Co. Pottinger*), a postal village, 283 miles N. of Sydney, with mail five days a week. A station on the Werris Creek branch of the north-western line.

CURL CURL LAGOON (*Co. Cumberland*), a small salt water lagoon, lying at the N. end of Cabbage-tree Bay; there is a rocky promontory standing boldly out into the ocean, about 2¼ miles N. of the N. entrance to Sydney Harbour.

CURRABUBULA (*Co. Buckland*), a postal township, 262 miles N. of Sydney, with daily mail. Money-order office. A railway station on the northern line. Situated on a creek of the same name, the nearest townships are Tamworth and Breeza, each 20 miles distant.

CURRABUBULA CREEK (*Co. Buckland*), a small water-course flowing westerly through the township of the same name into the Conadilly River.

CURRA CREEK (*Co. Wellington*), a postal receiving-office, 262 miles W. of Sydney, with mail once a week.

CURRAJONG (*Co. Forbes*), situated about 3 miles W. of the Billabong Creek. The district is a gold-mining one, principally quartz.

CURRAJONG (*Co. Cook*), a small hamlet on the Blue Mountains, lying to the W. of Richmond.

CURRAMBENE CREEK (*Co. St. Vincent*), a fine stream flowing into Jervis Bay at the township of Huskisson.

CURRIEWARRA (*Co. Gunderbooka*), a township on the Culgoa River, to the N. of Bourke.

CURRATHOOL (*Co. Sturt*), a proclaimed village, on the N. bank of the Murrumbidgee River.

CURRATHOOL WEST (*Co. Sturt*), a proclaimed village, on the opposite side of the same river.

CURRAWANG (*Co. Harden*) a postal village, 156 miles S. of Sydney, with mail three times a week, and money-order office. The nearest railway station is Goulburn, 22 miles, on the southern line. Situated on the Currawang Creek, and lies about 5 miles N.W. of the township of Murrumburrah.

CURRAWANG CREEK (*Co. Harden*), a small eastern tributary at the head of the Murrimboola Creek, draining Cunningham's Plains, flowing through some agricultural land in the parish of Currawang.

CURRAWANG CREEK (*Co. Argyle*), a small tributary of the Willero Creek, flowing into it near the village of Kenny's Point.

CURRAWANG MOUNT (*Co. Argyle*), a spur of the Australian Alps, situated 2 miles N. of Kenny's Point, on Lake George, running for some miles along the border of the lake, attaining an elevation of 1,200 feet above the bed of the lake.

CURRAWAN (*Co. St. Vincent*), a proclaimed township on the Clyde River, about 6 miles N. of Nelligen.

CURRAWANANNA (*Co. Bourke*), a proclaimed village in this county.

CURRAWEELA (*Co. Argyle*), a postal village, 175 miles S. of Sydney, with mail three times a week. The nearest railway station is Goulburn, 41 miles, on the southern line.

CURRENCY CREEK (*Co. Cook*), a small western tributary of the Hawkesbury River.

CURROCBILLY MOUNT (*Co. St. Vincent*), a lofty peak of the Budawang Range, lying between the Clyde and Shoalhaven Rivers, and about 4 miles N. of the Pigeon House.

CURROWAN CREEK (*Co. St. Vincent*), a small western tributary of the Clyde River, rising in Mount Budawang, and flowing in an easterly direction into the main stream at the township of Currowa.

CURROWANG FLAT (*Co. Argyle*), an extensive alluvial flat in the parish of Currowang, surrounded by a range of low hills which lie on the E. shore of Lake George.

CURRYGUNDI (*Co. Benarba*), a township on the confines of the N. boundary with Queensland.

CURVIL (*Co. Narran*), a township to the S.E. of the Bokahra River.

CUTACOW, on LONG SWAMP CREEK (*Co. Buccleuch*), a tributary of the Oak Creek, rising in Paddy's Rock hill, and flowing N. through swampy ground.

CUTTABRI (*Co. White*), a postal receiving-office, 432 miles N. of Sydney, with mail three times a week.

# D

DABEE (*Co. Phillip*), a small village, about 4 miles from the township of Rylstone, at the confluence of Cox's Creek and the Cudgegong River.

DAGWORTH (*Co. Northumberland*), a tract of flat and partly swampy land in the parish of Maitland, situated on Wallis' Creek.

DAHLIA CREEK (*Co. Cumberland*), a small creek near the head of George's River.

DAHWILLY (*Co. Townsend*), a proclaimed township to the N. of Deniliquin.

DALEDERRY CREEK (*Co. Ashburnham*), one of the heads of Byrnes' Creek. It is fed by Kelly's Creek.

DALEY'S CREEK (*Co. King*), a small northern tributary of Blakeney's Creek, flowing about 4 miles on the Yass Plains.

DALGETTY (*Co. Wallace*), a proclaimed township in the county to the S. of Cooma.

DALKEITH (*Co. Bligh*), a township a few miles N. of Cassilis, near the Krui River.

DALMORTON (*Co. Gresham*), a postal village, 478 miles N. of Sydney, with mail twice a week. The nearest railway station is Glen Innes, 50 miles on the northern line.

DALTON (*Co. King*), a postal town, 163 miles to the S. of Sydney, with mail daily, with money-order office. The nearest railway station is Gunning, 8 miles, on the southern line. Situated on the Oolong Creek, about 1 mile below its junction with Basin Creek, and the same distance above its junction with the Yarrawa Creek.

DAM CREEK (*Co. Murray*), a small eastern tributary of the Murrumbidgee River, flowing in the E. portion of Yass Plains.

DAMPIER, a county, in the Eastern Division of the Colony. [*See* "COUNTIES."]

DANALAGE (*Co. Rankin*), a township on the E. banks of the Darling River, between it and Acres Billabong.

DANDALOO (*Co. Nicholson*), a postal village, 362 miles W. of Sydney, with mail five times a week. Money-order and telegraph offices. The nearest railway station is Trangie, 25 miles on the western line.

DANDRY CREEK (*Co. Baradine*), an eastern tributary of the head of the Baradine Creek, rising in Mount Almambra in the Warabungle Range, near the township of Coonabarabran, flowing through rich country.

DANGAR'S FALLS (*Co. Sandon*), a waterfall on the Saumarez Creek, in the parish of Mihi. These falls are 600 feet in height, and fall over masses of hornblendic granite.

DANGAR'S LAGOON (*Co. Sandon*), a small waterhole, lying about 3 miles S.E. of the township of Uralla.

DANGER POINT (*Co. Rous*), a rocky promontory standing boldly out into the sea, and forming the coast boundary between New South Wales and Queensland.

DAPTO (*Co. Camden*), a postal village, 56 miles S. of Sydney. Money-order and telegraph offices. The Illawarra and South Coast railway passes through the district, and there is a station at Dapto. It is situated on the Mullet Creek, at the eastern foot of the Illawarra range of mountains. The district is almost exclusively an agricultural one, the principal industry being dairy farming. The surrounding country is elevated, and coal is abundant throughout the ranges, the geological formation being carboniferous, and generally ferruginous sandstone. The scenery in the neighbourhood is exceedingly beautiful, and overgrown with dense vegetation of the most luxuriant and varied kinds, and tangled creepers overhanging permanent streams of the purest and clearest water. Native game abounds in all directions, and the district is a favourite one for the sportsman.

DARBY'S FALLS (*Co. Bathurst*), a postal office, 225 miles W. of Sydney, with mail twice a week. The nearest railway station is Cowra, 15 miles, on the western line.

DARGAL MOUNTAINS (*Co. Selwyn*) is the name given to three peaks of a triple-headed mountain in the Murray and Bogong Range. They attain a very great height, and their summits are usually covered with snow for at least three-quarters of the year. The highest peak reaches an altitude of 5,490 feet above the sea level.

DARGAN CREEK (*Co. Dudley*), a small southern tributary of the head of the Nambucca River, flowing through swampy country, well timbered with cedar.

DARIGAL CREEK (*Co. Gordon*), is a southern tributary of the Buckinbar Creek.

DARKE'S FOREST (*Co. Camden*), a post-office, 33 miles S. of Sydney, with mail twice a week.

DARKWATER (*Co. Macquarie*), a township situated on the Macleay River, near the confluence of the Drinkwater Creek, about 20 miles from the mouth of the river at Trial Bay. Both streams are navigable for coasting vessels. The district is an agricultural one, and the soil very fertile. The nearest township is Kempsey, which lies 12 miles distant in a S.W. direction, where there is steam communication with Sydney by water, which is 277 miles to the S.

DARKWATER CREEK (*Co. Macquarie*), a small tributary of the Macquarie falling into it at the township of Darkwater. This creek rises in a swamp and flows N. about 16 miles. Its banks consist of fine fertile soil.

DARLING, a county in the Eastern Division of the Colony. [*See* "Counties."]

DARLING HARBOUR (*Co. Cumberland*), is a southern arm of Port Jackson, forming part of the western boundary of the city of Sydney. This bay divides the suburbs of Balmain, Pyrmont, and the Ultimo estate from Sydney, and is not second in importance to Sydney Cove. Nearly the entire steam fleet trading with the port is centered on this Bay, and the steam traffic on its waters is immense. The terminus of our entire railway lines, for heavy goods, is concentrated to this point in the harbour of Port Jackson.

DARLINGHURST (*Co. Cumberland*), forms a portion of the eastern side of the city of Sydney where the gaol is situated. Contiguous thereto the assizes and Central Criminal Courts are held.

DARLING MOUNT (*Co. King*), a detached mountain on the road from Cowra to Weeho, and between the Lachlan River and Hovell's Creek.

DARLING POINT (*Co. Cumberland*), is a rocky promontory on the S. side of Port Jackson, lying between Double and Rushcutters' Bays. The Darling Point Road extends about 1 mile to the South Head Road. Many very fine villa residences are situated on this point. The Darling Point Road is a beautiful drive or ride.

DARLINGTON (*Co. Cumberland*), postal suburb, 8 miles W. of Sydney, with mail therefrom twice a day. Money-order, Government savings bank, and telegraph offices. Delivery by letter-carriers. Situated between the Glebe and Redfern. It was proclaimed a borough in 1864, with eight aldermen and a mayor.

DARLINGTON (*Co. Durham*), a township, 147 miles N. of Sydney, adjoining Singleton, on the Newcastle, Maitland, and Singleton line. Situated in the parish of Auckland, on the Hunter River, and is a fertile agricultural district, with excellent pastoral country adjoining.

DARLINGTON POINT (*Co. Sturt*), a postal village, 388 miles S. of Sydney, with daily mail, telegraph and money-order offices. The nearest railway station is Darlington, 8 miles, on the south-western line. Situated on the Murrumbidgee River near the confluence of the Mirool Creek.

DARLINGTON RAILWAY STATION (*Co. Sturt*), situated on the south-western line, 385 miles S.W. of Sydney, with mail therefrom five times a week, and telegraph office.

DARLOW'S CREEK (*Co. Wynyard*), an eastern tributary of the Yaven-Yaven Creek, rising in the Adelong gold-field.

DARNANGRY CREEK (*Co. Bligh*), a small tributary at the lower end of the Wialdra Creek.

DART BROOK (*Co. Brisbane*), a tributary of the Hunter River, rising by two heads in the S. part of the Liverpool Range, known as Kingdon Ponds and Dart Brook. The tributaries are the Petwynne Valley, Middle, and Sharke's Creek.

DAUBENEY MOUNTAIN (*Co. Yungnulgra*), a lofty mount to the S. of Gnalta Peak and the W. of the Darling River, and is an E. spur of the Stanley Range.

DAVIDSON'S MOUNTAIN (*Co. Blaxland*), a lofty mount to the N. of the Lachlan River and the S.W. line of railway.

DAVIES CREEK (*Co. Brisbane*), a post-office, 209 miles N. of Sydney, with mail twice a week. The nearest railway station is Aberdeen, 28 miles, on the northern line.

DAVIS CREEK (*Co. Georgiana*), a small southern tributary of the Abercrombie River, rising to the N. of the village of Bigga.

DAVIS TOWN (*Co. Northumberland*), a postal village, 61 miles N. of Sydney, with daily mail.

DAVIS TOWN (*Co. Buckland*), a village, 242 miles N. of Sydney. The nearest railway station is Quirindi, on the northern line.

DAVY'S CREEK (*Co. Bathurst*), a western tributary of the Campbell River, fed by the Foster's Valley Creek.

DAVY'S CREEK (*Co. Westmoreland*). [*See* "STONY CREEK."]

DAWES' POINT (*Co. Cumberland*), on the S. side of Port Jackson, at the northern end of George-street, within the city of Sydney, and from the western head of Sydney Cove. The artillery barracks are located here, and the Corporation baths.

DAWSON'S RIVER (*Co. Macquarie*). [*See* "RIVERS."]

DAY DREAM (*Co. Waradgery*), is a post-office, 834 miles S. of Sydney, with mail twice a week. The nearest railway station is Hay, 420 miles, on the south-western line.

DAYSDALE (*Co. Goulburn*), a post-office 413 miles S. of Sydney, with mail twice a week. The nearest railway station is Jerilderie, 50 miles, on the southern line.

DEADHORSE CREEK (*Co. Goulburn*), a small tributary of the upper part of the Bowna Creek. Schistose, with granite cropping out at the tops of the mountains.

DEADMAN'S CREEK (*Co. Cumberland*), a small tributary of George's River, joining it near its fall into Botany Bay.

DEADMAN'S CREEK (*Co. Northumberland*), a small eastern tributary of Black Creek.

L

DEADMAN'S CREEK (*Co. Roxburgh*), a small northern tributary of the Solitary Creek, flowing S. through good pastoral land, in the parish of Thornhope.

DEAN'S (or FOUR-MILE) CREEK (*Co. Goulburn*), a small tributary at the head of the Billabong Creek, passing through rugged country.

DEEP CREEK (*Co. Gloucester*), a post-office, 356 miles N. of Sydney, with mail three times a week. The nearest railway station is Hexham, 241 miles, on the northern line.

DEEP CREEK (*Co. Durham*), a small creek at the head of the Karaula River.

DEEP CREEK (*Co. Georgiana*), a small eastern tributary of the Burangylong Creek, draining scrubby country to the N. of the Tuena goldfield.

DEEP CREEK (*Co. King*), a small western tributary of the Hovell Creek, draining through the Burrowa Plains.

DEEP CREEK (*Co. Monteagle*), a small western tributary of the lower part of the Cookoomingala Creek.

DEEP CREEK (*Co. Richmond*), a small southern tributary of the Richmond River.

DEEP FALL (*Co. Sandon*), is a waterfall on the Mihi Creek, in the parish of Eastlake.

DEEPWATER (*Co. Clive*), a postal village, 421 miles N. of Sydney, with daily mail, money-order and telegraph offices. A railway station on the northern line.

DEEPWATER CREEK (*Co. Clive*), a southern tributary of the head of the Mole River, rising in the western slope of the Australian Alps, under Mount Capoompeta.

DEERINA MOUNTAIN (*Co. Yanda*), a solitary high hill to the W. of the Darling River.

DEER PARK (*Co. Phillip*) is the name of a tract of good pastoral country, to the E. of Dabee.

DEERUBBUN RIVER, the native name of the Hawkesbury River.

DELALAH, a county in the Western Division of the Colony. [See "COUNTIES."]

DELEGETE (*Co. Wellesley*), a postal village, 314 miles S. of Sydney, with mail three times a week. Money-order and telegraph offices. The nearest railway station is Cooma, 73 miles, on the Cooma line. It is an elevated mountainous district, rising 2,000 feet above the sea-level.

DELEGETE PLAIN (*Co. Wellesley*), a tract of bold and undulating country, lying to the S. of the county, and adjoining the dividing line between New South Wales and Victoria.

DELEGETE RIVER (*Co. Wellesley*). [See "RIVERS."]

DEMON CREEK (*Co. Clive*), a western tributary of the Timbarra Rivulet, rising in Mount Gerard, flowing S.

DEMONDRILLE (*Co. Harden*), a postal village, 236 miles S. of Sydney, with mail three times a week. Money-order and telegraph offices. A railway station on the Young and Cowra line.

DEMONDRILLE CREEK (*Co. Harden*), a western auriferous tributary of the Cunningham Creek, flowing through the Burrangong gold-fields, and is fed by the Back and Wombat Creeks.

DEMPSEY ISLAND (*Co. Northumberland*), a small island in Port Hunter, situated between Ash Island and Mosquito Island.

DENHAM, a county in the Central Division of the Colony. [*See* "COUNTIES."]

DENHAM COURT (*Co. Cumberland*), situated on the Anvil Creek, midway between Liverpool and Campbelltown. The Great Southern Railway passes through it where there is siding. It is distant from Sydney 26½ miles. The district is very picturesque.

DENHAM LAKE (*Co. Irrara*), a large lake to the N.W. of the Warrego River.

DENILIQUIN (originally WOOLSHED), (*Co. Townsend*), a postal town, 480 miles S.W. of Sydney, with daily mail. Money-order and telegraph offices, and Government savings bank, with delivery by letter-carrier. Deniliquin is the terminus of the railway from Moama, and the latter place meets the main Victorian line at Echuca, on the opposite side of the Murray, where it has an easy access for all its produce to Melbourne, the capital of Victoria. The nearest railway to reach Sydney is Jerilderie, 50 miles, a branch of the south-western line. Deniliquin is situated on the banks of the Edward River, and holds a most important position as a commercial centre, surrounded as it is by rich pastoral possessions. Deniliquin was proclaimed a municipal district in 1868, with eight aldermen and a mayor. The population is about 2,500. Sittings of the supreme court, courts of quarter sessions and district courts are held at Deniliquin periodically.

DENISON, a county in the Central Division of the Colony. [*See* "COUNTIES."]

DENISON (*Co. Wallace*), a proclaimed township, 240 miles S. of Sydney, in the county of Wallace.

DENISON FORT (or PINCHGUT ISLAND) (*Co. Cumberland*), is a well-known rock in Port Jackson, opposite the mouth of Woolloomooloo Bay. It takes its present name from a stone fort (constructed during the Governorship of Sir William Denison) which is built upon it, and which consists of a main building and a Martello tower at the N.E. end.

DENISON TOWN (*Co. Bligh*), a postal village, 299 miles N. of Sydney, with mail three times a week. The nearest railway station is Mudgee, 50 miles, on the Mudgee line, situated on the right bank of the Talbragar River, near the junction of the Coolahbaragundi River. The district is very fertile, and agriculture is carried on with great success.

DENMAN (*Co. Brisbane*), a postal town, 195 miles N. of Sydney, with daily mail. Money-order, telegraph office, and Government savings bank. The nearest railway station is Musclebrook, 16 miles, on the northern line, situated about 2 miles above the junction of the Goulburn and Hunter Rivers. The district is a rich, pastoral, and agricultural one.

DENNIS DOG KENNEL (*Co. Northumberland*), situate 78 miles to the N. of Sydney, a camping ground with good grass and plenty of water.

DENNIS ISLAND (*Co. Bathurst*), situate on the Queen Charlotte Vale Creek; is an agricultural settlement, lying about 12 miles to the W. of Bathurst.

DERABUNG MOUNT (*Co. Bland*), a solitary hill lying in the vast plains between the Lachlan and Murrumbidgee Rivers.

DERALE MOUNT (*Co. Phillip*), a lofty peak, lying on the N. bank of the Cudgegong River, about 10 miles E. of the township of Mudgee.

DERING MOUNTAIN (*Co. Farnell*), a lofty solitary mount near the South Australian boundary.

DERRIBONG (*Co. Kennedy*), a township on Bulboding Creek; a tributary of the Bogan River.

DERRINGELLAN CREEK (*Co. Harden*), a northern tributary of the Yass River, crossing the Yass and Gundagai road, about 5 miles E. of Bowning.

DERUBBA (*Co. Richmond*), a small western tributary of the Richmond River.

DERUEN CREEK (*Co. Phillip*), a tributary of the head of Barigan Creek.

DEUA RIVER (*Co. Dampier*), a considerable stream flowing past Moruya, having its embochure at Toregy Point, on the E. seaboard.

DEVIL'S BOTTOM (*Co. Camden*), a deep valley situate on the road leading from the Great South Road to the Wollondilly and Goulburn Plains, about 90 miles from Sydney.

DEVIL'S HOLE CREEK (*Co. Wellington*), a small auriferous tributary of the Kingarragan Creek, rising in the N.E. of the upper Waurdury Range.

DEVIL'S PASS (*Co. Harden*), a rugged pass over the S. end of the Black Ranges, about 6 miles S.W. of the township of Yass.

DEVIL'S PINCH (*Co. Sandon*), a steep incline on the main northern road, about 12 miles N. of the township of Armidale.

DEVIL'S PINCH (*Co. Wellington*), a steep hill on the road from Sofala to Tambaroora, about 8 miles N.N.W. of Sofala.

DEVLIN'S SIDING (*Co. Bourke*), a post-office, 228 miles S. of Sydney, with daily mail therefrom.

DEWINBUNG MOUNT (*Co. Gordon*), a lofty hill, lying between the Curra Creek and the Little River, about 8 miles S. of Wellington.

DIAMOND BAY (*Co. Cumberland*), a small opening in the perpendicular cliffs of the coast, about 2 miles to the S. of the entrance of Port Jackson. There are several curious caves in the rocks lying near to the S. of this Bay.

DIAMOND CREEK (*Co. Georgiana*), a small southern tributary of the Wagaloola Creek, draining the country E. of the township of Binda.

DIAMOND CREEK (*Co. King*), a fine mountain stream, rising in the western slopes of the Australian Alps, flowing through part of the Yass Plains into the Cullarin Creek.

DIAMOND CREEK (*Co. Roxburgh*), a small tributary of the Cheshire Creek, rising in the Limestone Creek.

DIAMOND SWAMP CREEK (*Co. Roxburgh*), a northern tributary of the Fish River, rising to the S.E. of the Kirkconnell gold-fields, and fed by the Meadow Flat Creek.

DICKENSON'S CREEK (*Co. Macquarie*), a small northern tributary of the Manning River, falling into it E. of Cundletown.

DICKSON'S CREEK (*Co. King*), a small eastern tributary of the Cullarin Creek, to the N.E. of Yass Plains.

DIDDEL MOUNT (*Co. St. Vincent*). [*See* "PIGEON HOUSE."]

DIEGGA FLAT (*Co. Northumberland*), a tract of flat country lying on the N.W. of Lake Macquarie and on the banks of Cockle Creek.

DIEHARD CREEK (*Co. Gough*), a small northern tributary of the Mitchell River.

DIEHARD MOUNT (*Co. Bligh*), a high solitary peak lying on the N. bank of the Macquarie River, near Wellington.

DIEMUNGA (*Co. Narran*), a postal receiving-office, 595 miles W. of Sydney, with mail once a week.

DIGHT'S FOREST (*Co. Goulburn*), a village, 370 miles S. of Sydney. The nearest railway station is Gerogery, 8 miles, on the southern line.

DIGIDAA MOUNT (*Co. Courallie*), a lofty peak of the Nundawar Range, lying about 36 miles to the S.E. of the township of Narrabri.

DIGNAM'S CREEK (*Co. Auckland*), a postal village, 289 miles S. of Sydney, with daily mail.

DINDIERNA (*Co. Finch*), a township on the Narran River, and the Queensland boundary-line.

DINGO CREEK (*Co. Macquarie*), a postal village, 257 miles N. of Sydney, with mail three times a week. The nearest railway station is Hexham, 127 miles, on the northern line. An agricultural district, and lies about 12 miles to the E. of Wingham.

DINGY CREEK (*Co. Rous*), a small creek rising in Mount Congal, and falling into the Tweed River.

DINNEY CREEK (*Co. Bligh*), a small northern tributary of the Cudgegong River, falling into it near the Merinda gold-fields.

DIRTHOLE CREEK (*Co. Wellington*), a small tributary at the lower end of the Piambong Creek. Also an auriferous tributary of the Green Valley Creek.

DIRTY BUTTER CREEK (*Co. St. Vincent*), a small auriferous creek falling into the Araluen Creek, and forming part of the gold workings there.

DIRTY CREEK (*Co. Fitzroy*), a small tributary of the Fitzroy River.

DISASTER BAY (*Co. Auckland*), on the E. seaboard, to the S. of Green Cape.

DIXON MOUNT (*Co. King*), a lofty peak of the Cullarin Ranges, about 8 miles S. of Gunning, attaining an elevation of about 3,000 feet above the sea-level.

DIXSON'S CREEK (*Co. Roxburgh*), a small drainage creek flowing through the parish of Ensdale, into the Fish River, near Kenlis.

DJALLAH (*Co. Sturt*), a township, to the S. of the S.W. Railway and the Murrumbidgee River.

DOBIE MOUNT (*Co. Richmond*), a high hill, about 8 miles N.W. of the township of Gordon, and on the E. side of the road from Grafton to Tabulam.

DOBROYD HILL (*Co. Cumberland*), a hill in the parish of Manly, between North and Middle Harbours, facing the opening of Port Jackson, and about 908 feet above the sea-level.

DOBROYD POINT (*Co. Cumberland*), a rocky promontory on the N. side of Port Jackson, forming the western head of North Harbour.

DOCTOR'S NOSE (*Co. Clive*), a lofty mountain lying about 4 miles W. of Tenterfield.

DOGGREL CREEK (*Co. Gloucester*), a small eastern tributary of the Williams River.

DOG PLAIN (*Co. Beresford*), an extensive flat on the E. bank of the Murrumbidgee River, and N. of the Goorudee Rivulet and swamp, surrounded by high ranges of hills.

DOG TRAP CREEK (*Co. Wellington*), a small tributary of the head of the Piambong Creek, rising in the ranges to the W. of Mudgee.

DOG TRAP FLAT (*Co. Wynyard*), a tract of flat swampy land, lying on the Macka-Macka Creek, about 6 miles to the S.W. of the town of Adelong.

DOG TRAP ROAD (*Co. Cumberland*), the main road between Parramatta and Liverpool.

DON DORRIGO RIVER (*Co. Fitzroy*), the name given to the head waters of the Nymboi River, fed by the Wild Cattle, Allan's, Little, and Murray Creeks.

DONGDINGALONG (*Co. Dudley*), an agricultural hamlet, a few miles from Kempsey, on the Macleay River.

DOODLE SWAMP (*Co. Urana*), an important lagoon to the N. of Morven.

DOONSIDE (*Co. Cumberland*), a railway station, 24 miles W. of Sydney, on the western line.

DORA (*Co. Goulburn*), a small agricultural village on the Murray River, lying to the E. of Albury.

DORA CREEK (*Co. Northumberland*), a post-office, 81 miles N. of Sydney, with mail therefrom twice a week. A railway station on the Newcastle line.

DORA CREEK (*Co. Goulburn*), a small tributary of the Murray, and falling into it at Dora.

DOREE (*Co. Northumberland*), a post-office, 126 N. of Sydney, with mail therefrom three times a week.

DOUBLE BAY (*Co. Cumberland*), a postal suburb of the City of Sydney, situated about 3 miles distant from the General Post Office, in the parish of Alexandria, the Municipality of Woollahra, and the Police District of Sydney. It lies between the New South Head Road on the S. and E., the waters of the bay on the N., and the ridge along which the Darling Point Road runs upon the W., and forms a portion of the Piper Estate.

DOUBLE CHANNEL FALLS (*Co. Clarence*). [*See* "ROCKY FALLS."]

DOUBLEDUKE MOUNT (*Cos. Clarence & Richmond*), a lofty isolated mountain of considerable elevation, being remarkable at a considerable distance out at sea.

DOUGHBOY CREEK (*Co. Gresham*), a small eastern tributary of the Nymboi River.

DOUGHBOY HOLLOW (*Co. Buckland*), a postal village 201 miles S. of Sydney, with mail daily; a railway station on the Wallangarra and Brisbane line. Situated in the Liverpool Range about 5 miles from Murrurundi.

DOUGHBOY HOLLOW CREEK (*Co. Buckland*), a small tributary of Chilcott's Creek, rising in the Australian Alps and flowing through the village of Doughboy Hollow.

DOUGHBOY SWAMP (*Co. Dudley*), lying at the head of the Clybucca River, a tributary of the Macleay River, near its mouth.

DOUGLAS (*Co. Cumberland*), a railway station, 25 miles from Sydney, on the Windsor and Richmond line.

DOUGLAS CREEK (*Co. Harden*), a tributary of the head of the Spring Creek, in the parish of Nurring.

DOUGLAS GAP (*Co. Conteagle*) a post-office, 262 miles S. of Sydney, with mail once a week.

DOUGLAS PARK (*Co. Camden*), a post-office, 45 miles S. of Sydney, with mail twice a day, and telegraph office. A railway station on the southern line.

DOULAYUNALLA (*Co. Bligh*), a village reserve on the Talbragar River, about 3 miles N.W. of Cassilis.

DOURIBANG (*Co. Durham*), a proclaimed village in this County.

DOVEDALE (*Co. Raleigh*), situated 250 miles S. of Sydney, on the Bellinger River, a cedar-cutting district, about 55 miles N. of Fredrickton, and 70 miles S. of Grafton.

DOWLING, a county in the Central Division of the Colony. [*See* "COUNTIES."]

DOWLING RANGE (*Co. Northumberland*), a part of the Hunter Range, lying between Snodgrass Valley on the S., and M'Donald's Flat on the N.

DOWNSIDE (*Co. Clarendon*), a postal receiving-office, 323 miles S. of Sydney, with mail once a week.

DOYLE'S CREEK (*Co. Hunter*), a postal receiving-office, 178 miles N. of Sydney, with mail once a week. The nearest railway station is Singleton, 28 miles on the northern line. The creek is a western tributary of the Hunter River.

DRAGON'S INN SWAMP (*Co. Wellesley*), a marshy flat lying to the N. of the township of Cathcart, and draining into Badgory Swamp.

DRAKE (*Co. Drake*), a postal village, 507 miles N. of Sydney, with mail daily. Money-order and telegraph offices and Government savings bank, Tenterfield, 32 miles, is the nearest railway station on the northern line.

DRAWAY CREEK (*Co. Gordon*), a tributary of the Little River flowing into it, 1 mile N. of the village of Obley.

DROMEDARY MOUNT (*Co. Dampier*).—The name conferred upon it by Captain Cook. It lies midway between Bega and Moruya, about 4 miles inland, and is a prominent land-mark both for the surrounding country and also for vessels at sea, being known by its shape resembling that of the back of a dromedary.

DRUITT TOWN (*Co. Cumberland*), a postal village, 9 miles S. of Sydney, with mail twice a day. It is 3 miles from Burwood railway station on the suburban line.

DRUMMOND MOUNT (*Co. Hardinge*), a lofty solitary peak lying on the N. side of the road from Armidale to Cobbadale.

DRUMMOYNE (*Co. Cumberland*), a postal suburb, about 6 miles S. of Sydney, with mail twice each day; with delivery by letter-carrier. Telegraph and money-order offices, Government savings bank. It was proclaimed a municipal district in 1890, and divided into three wards, viz., Birkenhead ward, Bourke ward, and Drummoyne ward, with eight aldermen and a mayor.

DRY CREEK (*Co. King*), a small watercourse leading into Blakeney's Creek from the S.

DRY LAGOON (*Co. Argyle*), a small lagoon lying to the S. of the third Breadalbane plains.

DRY LAKE (*Co. Franklin*), a post-office, 437 miles S. of Sydney, with mail once a week.

DRY PLAIN (*Co. Wallace*), a post-office, 273 miles S. of Sydney, with mail once a week. The nearest railway station is Cooma, 20 miles, on the Goulburn and Cooma line.

DRY RIVER (*Co. Dampier*), a postal receiving-office, 302 miles S. of Sydney, with mail daily. The nearest railway station is Cooma, 30 miles, on the Goalburn and Cooma line.

DUBBO (*Co. Lincoln*), a postal town, 281 miles W. of Sydney, with daily mail. Money-order and telegraph offices, and Government savings bank, with delivery by letter-carriers. A railway station on the Bathurst to Bourke line. Dubbo was proclaimed a municipal district in 1872, with eight aldermen and a mayor to form the Council. The population is about 4,000. Sittings of the supreme court, courts of quarter sessions, and district courts are held at Dubbo periodically.

DUCK CREEK (*Co. Cumberland*), a southern tributary of the Parramatta River, falling into it between Homebush and Parramatta.

DUCK CREEK (*Co. Grego*), an eastern tributary of the Bogan River. The township of Canonbar is situated on its banks.

DUCK CREEK (*Co. Rous*), a small northern tributary of the estuary of the Richmond River, falling into it a few miles from its mouth.

DUCK FLAT (*Co. Argyle*), a postal receiving-office, 162 miles S. of Sydney, with mail twice a week.

DUCKINALOO (*Co. Cook*), a post-office, 144 miles W. of Sydney, with mail three times a week. The nearest railway station is Tarana, 24 miles, on the Bathurst and Bourke line.

DUDAUMAN (*Co. Harden*), a postal receiving-office, 263 miles S. of Sydney, with daily mail.

DUDLEY, a county in the Eastern Division of the Colony. [*See* "COUNTIES."]

DUFF'S PASS (*Co. Hunter*), a crossing-place over Doyle's Creek, from Singleton to the neighbourhood of Dabee.

DUGLE-BEAGLE CREEK (*Co. Wellington*), an auriferous tributary of the Cudgegong Creek, falling into it below Burrendong.

DUGUID'S HILL (*Co. Northumberland*), a hill on the northern railway line, about 2 miles S.W. of Lochinvar.

DULGIGIN CREEK (*Co. Richmond*), a small eastern tributary at the head of the Clarence River.

DULHUNTY'S CREEK (*Co. Roxburgh*), a small tributary of the Williwa Creek, flowing through Cullen Bullen into Williwa Creek.

DULWICH HILL (*Co. Cumberland*), a postal suburb, 4 miles from Sydney, with mail twice daily. Money order and telegraph offices.

DUMARESQ (*Co. Sandon*), a postal town, 364 N. of Sydney, with daily mail therefrom; a railway station on the northern line.

DUMARESQ CREEK (*Co. Sandon*), a western tributary of the Tilbuster Ponds, flowing S.E. through the town of Armidale into the main stream.

DUMARESQ RIVER (*Cos. Arrawatta and Clive*). [*See* "RIVERS."]

DUMMY'S CREEK (*Co. Bathurst*), a small tributary of Coombing Creek, draining Bryem's Swamp, in the parish of the Three Brothers.

DUNBAR'S CREEK (*Co. Durham*), a post-office, 188 miles N. of Sydney, with mail twice a week. It is 12 miles distant from Muswellbrook, the nearest station on the northern line.

DUNDEE (*Co. Gough*), a postal village, 410 miles N. of Sydney, with mail twice daily. Telegraph and money-order offices. A railway station on the northern line.

DUNDELLO CREEK (*Co. Pottinger*), an eastern tributary of the Turrabeile Creek, watering the rich pastoral country known as Bowen Plain.

DUNDERLAGO CREEK (*Co. Harden*), a stream at the head of the Illalong Creek, rising in Murray's Big Hill.

DUNDOO CREEK (*Co. Clarence*), a small tributary at the head of the Orara River, fed by the Halfway Creek.

DUN-DUN CREEK (*Co. Wellington*), a small tributary of the Waurdong Creek, in the Louisa Creek Gold-field.

DUNEDOO (*Co. Lincoln*), a township on the Erskine River, to the N.E. of Dubbo.

DUNGARABBEE CREEK (*Co. Rous*), a northern tributary of the lower end of the Richmond River, falling into it 6 miles to the W. of Wardell.

DUNGAREE (*Co. Phillip*), a postal village, 172 miles W. of Sydney, with daily mail. The nearest railway station is Lue, 1 mile, on the western line.

DUNGAREE CREEK (*Co. Phillip*), a southern tributary of Lawson's Creek, flowing into it at Dungaree.

DUNGEON CREEK (*Co. Bathurst*), a small northern tributary of the Princess Charlotte Vale Creek, flowing in the parish of Cole.

DUNGLEMAH MOUNT (*Co. Inglis*), a double-peaked hill, lying on the east side of the road from Tamworth to Bendemeer. The name of the smaller peak is Bullimballa.

DUNDAS (*Co. Cumberland*), a postal village, 18 miles W. of Sydney, with daily mail. It was proclaimed a municipal district in 1889, with eight aldermen and a mayor.

DUNMORE (*Co. Camden*), a post-office, 68 miles S. of Sydney, with mail therefrom daily. Situate near the south coast railway at Shellharbour.

DUNGOG (*Co. Durham*), a postal town, 156 miles N. of Sydney, with daily mail. Money-order and telegraph offices, and Government savings bank, with delivery by letter-carrier. The nearest railway station is Morpeth, 36 miles, on the northern line. Situated on the W. bank of the Williams River. It is a fertile agricultural district, producing cereals and hay in great abundance for the Sydney and other markets.

DUNGOWAN (*Co. Parry*), a postal town, 305 miles N. of Sydney, with mail five times a week. It is 16 miles from Tamworth, the nearest railway station on the northern line.

DUNKELD (*Co. Bathurst*), a postal village, 152 miles W. of Sydney, with mail five times a week. It is 7 miles from Bathurst, the nearest railway station on the western line.

DUNLOP (*Co. Yanda*), a township on the W. bank of the Darling River to the S. of Dunlop's Range.

DUNLOP'S RANGE (*Co. Yanda*), a group of hills on the E. bank of the Darling River, about 60 miles S.W. of Bourke.

DUNOON (*Co. Rous*), a post-office, 365 miles W. of Sydney, with mail per steamers.

DURAL (*Co. Cumberland*), a postal village, 29 miles W. of Sydney, with daily mail. It is 14 miles from Parramatta, the nearest railway station on the suburban line. The district is very fertile, and large orchards abound, supplying fruit of all kinds for the Sydney market.

DURAMANA CREEK (*Co. Roxburgh*), a western tributary of the Winburndale Rivulet, flowing through good agricultural land lying to the N.W. of the township of Peel.

DURAMANA (*Co. Roxburgh*), a postal village, 155 miles W. of Sydney, with mail four days a week. The nearest railway station is Bathurst, 10 miles, on the western line.

DURAMBANG MOUNT (*Co. Phillip*), a high peak of the Blue Mountain Range, lying in the S.E. corner of the county, and at the head of the Gungudby Creek.

DURBAN'S GROUP (*Co. Cowper*), a range of hills on the E. bank of the river Darling, about 20 miles S. of Fort Bourke.

DURHAM, a county in the Eastern Division of the Colony. [*See* "COUNTIES."]

DURI (*Co. Parry*), a postal receiving-office, 270 miles N. of Sydney, with daily mail. A railway station on the northern line.

DURIDGEREE (*Co. Phillip*), a village reserve on the Goulburn River, 14 miles S. of Cassilis.

DUROBY CREEK (*Co. Rous*), a small drainage creek flowing into lake Newraugy, on the W. side.

DURRAN DURRA CREEK (*Co. St. Vincent*), an eastern tributary of the Shoalhaven River, rising to the N. of Braidwood, flowing into the main stream near Larbert.

DUVAL (*Co. Sandon*), a railway station, 371 miles from Sydney, on the northern line.

DUVAL'S MOUNTAIN (*Co. Sandon*), a lofty peak in the main dividing range, about 8 miles to the N. of the township of Armidale. It attains an altitude of 4,174 feet above sea-level.

DYKE RIVER (*Co. Dudley*), a northern tributary of the Macleay River. [*See* "RIVERS."]

DYRING (*Co. Durham*), a peak of the Mount Royal Range on the E. bank of the Falbrook, and about 12 miles S.W. of Lostock. 3,000 feet above sea-level.

# E

**EAGLETON** (*Co. Durham*), an agricultural settlement lying near the township of Raymond Terrace.

**EAST BLUFF** (*Co. Buckland*), a sharp Peak of the Liverpool Range, lying to the W. of Mount Mooan.

**EAST BRANCH RIVER** (*Co. Selwyn.*)  [*See* "RIVERS."]

**EAST BROOK** (*Co. Bligh*), a tributary of the head of the Munmurrah Creek.

**EAST CREEK** (*Co. Drake*), an eastern tributary of the Timbarra Rivulet.

**EASTERN CREEK** (*Co. Cumberland*), a post office, 24 miles W. of Sydney, with mail daily. It is 2 miles from Rooty Hill, the nearest railway station, on the western line. The creek is a fine stream, rising near Smithfield, and flowing N.W. through Blacktown and Rooty Hill into the South Creek, near Windsor.

**EAST KANGALOON** (*Co. Camden*), a postal village, 106 miles S. of Sydney, with mail twice a day. It is 13 miles from Bowral, the nearest station on the southern line. [*See also* "KANGALOON."]

**EAST KEMPSEY** (*Co. Dudley*), a postal town, 295 miles N. of Sydney, with daily mail. Money-order office. The nearest railway station is Hexham, 195 miles, on the northern line. [*See also* "KEMPSEY."]

**EAST RALEIGH** (*Co. Raleigh*), a post-office, 379 miles N. of Sydney, with mail twice a week, and per steamer.

**EAST WARDELL** (*Co. Richmond*), a post-office, 352 miles N. of Sydney, with mail per steamers therefrom.

**EASTWOOD** (*Co. Cumberland*), a postal village, 13 miles W. of Sydney, with daily mail. A railway station on the Ryde and Hawkesbury River line.

**EATONSVILLE** (*Co. Richmond*), a postal receiving-office, 360 miles N. of Sydney, with mail per steamer.

**EBENEZER** (*Co. Cumberland*), a postal village, 41 miles W. of Sydney, with mail three times a week. The nearest railway station is Windsor, 8 miles, on the Richmond line.

**ECCLESTON** (*Co. Durham*), a postal village, 166 miles N. of Sydney, with mail three times a week. The nearest railway station is East Maitland, 25 miles, on the northern line.

**ECLIPSE BLUFF** (*Co. Cumberland*), a bold headland on the rocky and precipitous coast, lying about 4 miles S. of the entrance to Port Jackson.

**EDEN** (*Co. Auckland*), a postal town, 350 miles S. of Sydney, with mail three times a week, and by every steamer. Telegraph and money-order offices, and Government savings bank. The nearest railway station is Cooma, 90 miles, on the Goulburn and Cooma line. Eden is situated on the N.

shore of Twofold Bay, and is the port for the whole of the S.E. districts of New South Wales. The Kiah and Nalligah Rivers flow into the bay, and Mount Imlay lies about 20 miles to the S.W. The district is an agricultural and pastoral one. Courts of quarter sessions and district courts are held at Eden periodically.

EDEN CREEK (*Co. Richmond*), a small western tributary of the Richmond River.

EDEN FOREST (*Co. Argyle*), a tract of rich agricultural and grazing land, lying on the Wollondilly River, and on the road from Berrima to Tarlo.

EDENGLASSIE (*Co. Cook*), a tract of agricultural land lying about 5 miles south-west of the township of Penrith; occupied by small farmers.

EDGECLIFFE (*Co. Cumberland*), a postal suburb of Sydney, with mail twice daily. Telegraph and money-order offices and Government savings bank.

EDITH (*Co. Westmoreland*), a postal receiving-office, 141 miles W. of Sydney, with mail three times a week.

EDITH BREAKER (*Co. Gloucester*), is a rocky islet, awash, lying directly on the line of coasters' track when passing between the Seal Rocks and the mainland. It has 25 feet on it at low water, with from 18 to 20 fathoms immediately around, and, with any swell, forms a dangerous breaker.

EDWARD RIVER (*Cos. Wakool and Townsend.*) [*See* "RIVERS."]

EGAN (*Co. Bathurst*), a township to the S. of Newbridge, on the Great Western railway.

EGANTON (*Co. Bathurst*), a postal receiving-office, 195 miles W. of Sydney, with mail twice a week.

EGLINTON (*Co. Bathurst*), a postal town, 148 miles W. of Sydney, with daily mail therefrom.

EIGHT-MILE CREEK (*Co. Goulburn*), a tributary of the head of Thurgonia Creek, watering good agricultural land.

EINERGUENDI MOUNT, situated in the district of Liverpool Plains, near the Namoi River.

ELAINE MOUNT (*Co. Clarence*), a detached mountain lying at the head of the Glen Ugie Creek, about 12 miles S.E. from the township of Grafton.

ELDERSLIE (*Co. Durham*), a postal village, 133 miles N. of Sydney, with mail twice a week. The nearest railway station is Branxton, 4 miles, on the northern line.

ELIZABETH BAY (*Co. Cumberland*), a postal suburb of the city of Sydney, on the western shore of Rushcutter Bay, and lying to the S.E. of Potts' Point. The curious rock, known as the Horse's Head, or the Kangaroo, forms a fancied resemblance to one or the other of those objects, and lies on its S.E. side.

ELIZABETH ISLAND (*Co. Clarence*), a small island in the Clarence River, to the N.E. of Grafton.

ELIZABETH POINT (*Co. Gloucester*), a rocky promontory projecting boldly out into the sea between the Sugarloaf Point on the S. and Cape Hawke on the N.

ELIZABETH ROCKS (*Co. Gloucester*).—Three small rocky islets, lying to the S. of Elizabeth Point, and half-way between that and Sugarloaf Point.

ELLALONG (*Co. Northumberland*). a postal village, 138 miles N. of Sydney, with mail three times a week. The nearest railway station is Farley, 27 miles, on the northern line.

ELLALONG CREEK (*Co. Northumberland*), a small eastern tributary of the Wollombi Brook.

ELLALONG LAGOON (*Co. Northumberland*), a small swampy lake in the parish of Ellalong, into which the Quarrybylong Creek drains.

ELLENBOROUGH (*Co. Macquarie*), a postal village, 306 miles N. of Sydney, with mail three times a week. It is situated on the Ellenborough River, near its confluence with the Hastings River, and about 10 miles W. of the Thoul River. The nearest railway station is Hexham, 184 miles, on the northern line.

ELLENBOROUGH RIVER (*Co. Macquarie*). [*See* " RIVERS."]

ELLERSLIE (*Co. Cumberland*), an agricultural village, in the parish of Narellan, near Camden.

ELLREMA CREEK (*Co. St. Vincent*), a fine tributary of the Yalwal Creek, rising by several heads, and flowing N.E., through rugged pastoral country.

ELRINGTON (*Co. St. Vincent*), is the Government name of a township on the Major's Creek gold-field. [*See* " MAJOR'S CREEK."]

ELRINGTON MOUNT (*Co. St. Vincent*), a high hill, overlooking the township of Elrington, on the Major's Creek gold-field.

ELSMORE (*Co. Gough*), a postal village. 440 miles N. of Sydney, with mail five times a week. The nearest railway station is Glen Innes, 30 miles, on the northern line.

EMERALD HILL (*Co. Pottinger*). a postal receiving-office, 304 miles N. of Sydney, with daily mail. A railway station on the north-western line.

EMIGRANT CREEK (*Co. Rous*), a postal receiving-office, 367 miles N. of Sydney, with mail per steamer to Richmond River. The creek is a small tributary of the estuary of the Richmond River, falling into it a few miles from its mouth.

EMMAVILLE (*Co. Gough*), a postal town, 463 miles N. of Sydney, with daily mail. Telegraph and money-order offices and Government savings bank. The nearest railway station is Deepwater, 18 miles, on the northern line. Courts of quarter sessions and district courts are held here periodically.

EMU (*Co. Cook*), a postal town, 37 miles W. of Sydney, with mail twice daily. With money-order office. The nearest railway station is Emu Plains, 2 miles, on the western line. Situated on the Nepean River, Glenhope Creek being in the neighbourhood. The district is agricultural and pastoral, the land consisting of rich alluvial soil.

EMU CREEK (*Co. Buller*), a western tributary of the head of the Clarence River, flowing through scrubby pastoral country.

EMU CREEK (*Co. Forbes*), a northern tributary of the Burrangong Creek.

EMU CREEK (*Co. Phillip*), a small stream flowing from the W. into the Widdin Brook.

EMU CREEK (*Co. Vernon*), a small northern tributary of the Apsley River, joining it about 8 miles E. of Walcha.

EMU FERRY (*Co. Cook*), is a suburb of Emu, situated at the old crossing-place of the Nepean River, and 4 miles W. of South Creek.

EMU FLAT (*Co. Clarence*), a small flat, with a good waterhole, on the track from the Orara River Heads to the Clarence River Heads, about 10 miles E. of Grafton.

EMU PLAINS (*Co. Cook*), a postal village, 36 miles W. of Sydney, with mail three times daily. Money-order and telegraph offices. A railway station on the western line. Emu Plains is a tract of fine fertile undulating country, suitable for agricultural and grazing farms. The towns of Emu and Penrith are both in the neighbourhood.

EMU SWAMP CREEK (*Co. Bathurst*), an auriferous stream rising in the parish of Anson, and flowing N. into the Frederick's Valley Creek at the township of Ophir; running through good agricultural land to the W. of the village of Byng.

ENA CREEK (*Co. Gwydir*), a western tributary of the Macintyre River, flowing through scrubby pastoral country.

ENDRICK RIVER (*Co. St. Vincent*). [*See* "RIVERS."]

ENFIELD (*Co. Cumberland*), a postal suburb of the city, 8 miles S. of Sydney, with mail twice daily, and delivery by letter-carrier. Situated in the parish of Concord, about 2 miles S. of Cook's River, and 7 miles N.W. of Saltpan Creek. Enfield was proclaimed a borough in 1889, with eight aldermen and a mayor.

ENFIELD (*Co. Cook*), a postal village, 41 miles W. of Sydney, with daily mail and telegraph office. The nearest railway station is Richmond, 3 miles, on the Windsor line. The Hawkesbury River flows within a mile of the village.

ENMORE (*Co. Cumberland*), is a suburb of Newtown, lying on the S. side of the main suburban railway, in the angle formed by the railway and the Cook's River Road, which it crosses at that place.

ENNGONIA. (*Co. Culgoa*), a postal town, 563 miles W. of Sydney, with mail twice a week. Telegraph and money-order offices. The nearest railway station is Bourke, 67 miles, on the western line.

ENNIS (*Co. Macquarie*), a postal village, 290 miles N. of Sydney, with mail three times a week. The nearest railway station is Hexham, 139 miles, on the northern line.

EOLIA (*Co. Windeyer*), a township on the W. bank of the Darling River, to the N. of Pooncarie.

ERANGEROO (*Co. Parry*), a high peak of the Peel Range, lying about 5 miles E. of the township of Carroll.

ERAGEBRA CREEK (*Co. Hardinge*), a small auriferous tributary of the upper end of George's Creek, fed by Sandy Creek.

ERINA (*Co. Cumberland*), a post-office, 54 miles N. of Sydney, with mail three times a week. The nearest railway station is Gosford, 2 miles, on the Sydney and Newcastle line.

ERINGANERIN (*Co. Gowen*), a township on the N. bank of the Castlereagh River, near Breelong.

ERITH (*Co. Cook*), a township, 1 mile from Bundanoon, the nearest railway station on the southern line.

ERMINGTON (*Co. Cumberland*), a postal village, 20 miles W. of Sydney, with daily mail. The nearest railway station, Ryde, 1 mile, on the Hawkesbury River line.

ERRARING BAY (*Co. Northumberland*), a small bay on the W. shore of Lake Macquarie.

ERRINGANERIN (*Co. Gowen*), a proclaimed township on the N. bank of the Castlereagh River in this county.

ERROWINGBANG CREEK (*Co. Bathurst*), a northern tributary of the Belubula Creek, rising on the S.E. of the Canoblas cluster of hills.

ERSKINE FLAT (*Co. Wellington*), on the Turon diggings, about 1 mile E. from the township of Sofala.

ERSKINE POINT (*Co. Roxburgh*), a well-known point on the Turon River, lying about 1 mile E. of Sofala.

ERSKINE RIVER (*Cos. Lincoln and Bligh.*) [*See* "RIVERS."]

ERSKINEVILLE (*Co. Cumberland*), a suburb of Sydney, and a railway station, 2 miles S., on the Hurstville and Waterfall line.

ESK RIVER (*Co. Clarence.*) [*See* "RIVERS."]

ESKBANK (*Co. Cook*), a railway station, 95 miles W. of Sydney, on the western line.

ESKDALE (*Co. Durham*), a postal town, 133 miles N. of Sydney, with mail three times a week.

ESROM (*Co. Bathurst*), a postal village, 146 miles W. of Sydney, with daily mail. The nearest railway station is Bathurst, 3 miles, on the western line.

ESSINGTON (*Co. Westmoreland*), a postal village, 153 miles W. of Sydney, with mail three times a week. The nearest railway station is Brewongle, 43 miles, on the western line.

ETTAMOGAH, (*Co. Goulburn*), a railway station, 381 miles S. of Sydney, on the southern line.

ETTY MOUNT (*Co. Wellington*), is the northern extremity of the Stony Ridge Range, lying on the S. side of the road from Wellington to Burrendong.

EUABALONG (*Co. Blaxland*), a postal town, 369 miles W. of Sydney, with mail four times a week. Telegraph and money-order offices and Government savings bank. The nearest railway station is Borenore, 176 miles, on the western line.

EUABALONG (*Co. Blaxland*), a township on the banks of the Lachlan River, to the N. of Lake Cargellico.

EUCUMBENE RIVER (*Co. Wallace*). [*See* "RIVERS."]

EUGLO (*Co. Gipps*), a township on Euglo Creek, to the S. of Lachlan River.

EUGOWRA (*Co. Ashburnham*), a postal town, 240 miles W. of Sydney, with daily mail. Money-order and telegraph offices and Government savings bank. The nearest railway station is Orange, 19 miles, on the western line.

EUGOWRA (*Co. Ashburnham*), a roadside village, 196 miles to the W. of Sydney, situate on the Eugowra Creek, on the main road from Forbes to Orange. This village attained an unenviable notoriety in 1861, as being the place where Gardiner's gang stuck up and robbed the gold escort.

EULA CREEK (*Co. Jamison*), a small tributary of the mouth of the Ballewa Creek.

EULOURIE (*Co. Darling*), a postal village, 357 miles N. of Sydney, with mail twice a week. The nearest railway station is Tamworth, 102 miles, on the northern line.

EUMERALLA (*Co. Beresford*). [*See* "NUMERELLA."]

EUMUR CREEK (*Co. Darling*), a small auriferous eastern tributary of the Manilla River.

EUREKA (*Co. Rous*), a postal village, 374 miles to the N. of Sydney, with mails per Clarence and Richmond River steamers.

EUREKA ISLAND (*Co. Clarence*). [*See* "HARWOOD ISLAND."]

EURIOWIE (*Co. Farnell*), a postal town, 986 miles S. of Sydney, with mail four times a week, *via* Adelaide, and telegraph office.

EUROBODALLA (*Co. Wallace*), a postal village, 264 miles S. of Sydney, with daily mail. Money-order and telegraph offices. The nearest railway station is Tarago, 61 miles, on the Cooma line.

EUROKA (*Co. Dudley*), a small agricultural hamlet, near the township of Kempsey, on the Macleay River.

EUROKA (*Co. Bathurst*), a proclaimed village in this county.

EUROKA VALLEY (*Co. Cook*), a deep valley on the Nepean River, lying 4 miles S.W. of Penrith.

EURONGILLY (*Co. Wynyard*), a postal village, 272 miles S. of Sydney, with mail twice a week. The nearest railway station is Illabo, 11 miles, on the southern line.

EURUNDEREE (*Co. Phillip*), a postal village, 194 miles W. of Sydney, with daily mail. The nearest railway station is Mudgee, 3 miles, on the western line.

EURUNGERE CREEK (*Co. Wellington*), a western tributary of the Cudgegong River, rising to the W. of Mudgee, and flowing into the main stream at the crossing of the main road from Mudgee to Wellington.

EURYUNDURRY CREEK (*Co. Phillip*), a small northern tributary of the Cudgegong River, flowing into the main stream at Wilberforce.

EUSDALE CREEK (*Co. Roxburgh*). [*See* "DIXON'S CREEK."]

EUSTON (*Co. Taila*), a postal town, 640 miles S. of Sydney, with mail three times a week. Telegraph and money-order offices and Government savings bank. The nearest railway station is Hay, 180 miles, on the south-western line. Situated on the Murray River, 9 miles S.W. from Benanee Lake, and is a purely pastoral district.

EVANS' CREEK (*Co. Richmond*), a small stream, flowing into the Oran, at Evan's Lead, between the Clarence and Richmond Rivers.

EVANS' CROWN (*Co. Westmoreland*), a lofty peak, of the Blue Mountain Range, on the main western road between Hartley and O'Connell. This mountain is both singular and beautiful in its formation, and, being at an elevation of 3,200 ft. above sea level, it attracts attention from a great distance. Mr. Evans, the first European discoverer, gave its name, and from its summit he first saw the Bathurst Plains.

EVAN'S HEAD (*Co. Richmond*), on the E. seaboard, to the S. of Woodburn.

EVANS' PLAINS (*Co. Bathurst*), a tract of fine land, near the township of Mount Pleasant. It is watered by the Princess Charlotte Vale Creek, and the road from Bathurst to Orange passes through it.

EVANS' PLAINS (*Co. Bathurst*), a postal village. 194 miles W. of Sydney, with mail three times a week. The nearest railway station George's Plains, 4 miles, on the western line. Situated on the Princess Charlotte Vale Creek, at the junction of the Spring Creek. Cherrytree Hill and Mount Apsley gold-fields are each about 1 mile distant E., and 4 miles W. from the City of Bathurst.

EVELEIGH (*Co. Cumberland*), a suburb of Sydney, about a mile from the Sydney station, where large operations for railways are established.

EVELYN, a county in the Western Division of the Colony. [*See* "COUNTIES."]

EVELYN CREEK (*Co. Evelyn*), a stream rising near Mount Browne and flowing into Evelyn Plains.

EVELYN PLAINS (*Co. Evelyn*), is a large tract of flat country lying to the S.E. of the Grey range of mountains.

EVERENDEN MOUNT (*Co. Bathurst*), a lofty mountain standing on the E. bank of the Princess Charlotte's Vale Creek, about 6 miles S. of Bathurst.

EVERLASTING SWAMP (*Co. Clarence*), a long tract of boggy country, lying to the S. of the township of Lawrence and on the E. bank of the Clarence River.

EWENMAR, a county in the Central Division of the Colony. [*See* "COUNTIES."]

EWINGAR CREEK (*Co. Drake*), a small western tributary of the Clarence River.

EXCELSIOR SIDING (*Co. Cook*), a railway station, 133 miles W. of Sydney, on the western line.

EXMOUTH MOUNT (*Co. Leichhardt*), the highest peak in the Warrabungle Range. It attains the elevation of 3,000 feet above the sea level, and its peak consists of a perpendicular cliff of 1,000 feet in height.

EZROM (*Co. Bathurst*), an agricultural village lying to the W. of Bathurst, distant about 2 miles, and forming a suburb of that township.

# F

FAILFORD (*Co. Gloucester*), a postal town, 219 miles N. of Sydney, with mail three times a week.

FAIRFIELD (*Co. Drake*). [*See* "TIMBURRA."]

FAIRFIELD (*Co. Cumberland*), a postal suburb, 18 miles S. of Sydney, with mail twice daily and telegraph office. A railway station on the southern line.

FAIRFIELD (*Co. Argyle*), a town 66 miles from Tarago, the nearest railway station on the Goulburn and Cooma line.

FAIRVIEW (*Co. Buckland*), a postal village, 256 miles N. of Sydney, with mail twice a week. The nearest railway station, Quirindi, 13 miles, on the northern line.

FAIRY MEADOW (*Co. Murray*), a railway station, 166 miles S. of Sydney, on the Goulburn and Cooma line.

FAIRY MEADOW (*Co. Camden*), a postal village, 64 miles S. of Sydney, with mail daily. Situated between Bulli and Wollongong.

FAIRY MOUNT (*Co. Rous*), a high hill, situated on the E. bank of the upper part of the Richmond River, about 20 miles N. of Casino.

FALBROOK (*Co. Durham*), a small northern tributary of the Hunter River. It flows past the township of Camberwell, and is fed by the Carron and Goorangoola Creeks, and the Foybrook.

FALCONBRIDGE (*Co. Cook*), a postal receiving-office, 49 miles W. of Sydney, with daily mail. A railway station on the western line.

**FALCONER** (*Co. Sandon*), a village, 390 miles N. of Sydney, situated on the Guyra River, Ben Lomond mountain being 12 miles distant N. A large lagoon known as "The Mother of Ducks" 4 miles S., and the Ben Lomond Lagoon or Lake 10 miles N. The district is agricultural, pastoral, and mining, the latter being known as the Oban diggings. The agricultural portion of the country is splendid and eminently adapted to the growth of cereals. The nearest places are Armidale, 26 miles S., and Glen Innes, 33 miles N.

**FALCONER'S** (*Co. Sandon*), a township 36 miles from Mudgee, the nearest railway station on the western line.

**FALLS CREEK** (*Co. St. Vincent*), a postal town, 103 miles S. of Sydney, with daily mail.

**FARLEY** (*Co. Northumberland*), a post-office, 120 miles N. of Sydney, with daily mail. It is a railway station on the northern line.

**FARM COVE** (*Co. Cumberland*), on the S. side of Port Jackson, between Mrs. Macquarie's Chair and Battery Point. The head of the Cove is the site of the Botanical Gardens, and the eastern shore forms part of the Domain, and the western shore that of Government House and grounds. The name Farm Cove was given to it on account of a farm of nine acres having been cleared in 1788, on the side of the Cove near the town, and sown with corn of different kinds which had been brought from Brazil and the Cape, and which was found to thrive well.

**FARM CREEK** (*Co. Gloucester*), a small northern tributary of the Carowery Creek.

**FARMERS CREEK** (*Co. Cook*), a stream flowing about 14 miles from Mount Victoria. It is a tributary of the upper part of Cox's River, just under Mount Walker.

**FARNELL**, a county in the Western Division of the Colony. [*See* "COUNTIES."]

**FARNHAM** (*Co. St. Vincent*), an agricultural settlement on the road from Jervis Bay to Ulladulla, and on the Wandrawandian Creek.

**FARRINGDON** (*Co. St. Vincent*), a postal receiving-office, 190 miles S. of Sydney, with mail once a week.

**FASSIFERN** (*Co. Northumberland*), a postal village, 87 miles N. of Sydney, with daily mail. Telegraph office. A railway station on the Sydney and Newcastle line.

**FAVORA** (*Co. Wakool*), a small hamlet lying on the Wakool River, about 20 miles S. of Balranald.

**FAWCETT** (*Co. Rous*), a small agricultural hamlet on the Richmond River, lying 20 miles above the township of Cassilis.

**FERGUSON MOUNT** (*Co. Wellington*), a high hill lying on the east bank of the Bell River, about 4 miles S.E. of Wellington.

**FERNMOUNT** (*Co. Raleigh*), a postal village, 371 miles N. of Sydney, with mail three times a week. Telegraph and money-order offices, and Government savings bank.

FERRIERS (*Co. Mitchell*), A postal town, 317 miles S. of Sydney, with mail three times a week.

FIELD OF MARS (*Co. Cumberland*), a postal village, 13 miles W. of Sydney, with daily mail. The nearest railway station is Carlingford, on the Ryde and Hawkesbury River line. Situate on the western side of Lane Cove, and on the northern side of the Parramatta River.

FIELD PLAINS, tract of flat land lying on the Lachlan River at its lower end, and liable to be inundated in time of flood.

FIG TREE (*Co. Camden*), a post-office 49 miles S. of Sydney, with daily mail. It is about three miles from Wollongong, the nearest railway station on the Illawarra and South Coast line.

FIG TREE BAY (*Co. Cumberland*), a small bend on the south side of the Parramatta River, lying between Five Dock Bay and the old Bedlam Ferry.

FIG TREE POINT (*Co. Cumberland*) is the northern head of Long Bay, and a rocky promontory of the west side of Middle Harbour.

FINCH, a county in the Central Division of the Colony. [*See* "COUNTIES."]

FINCH MOUNT (*Co. Northumberland*), a peak in the Hunter range, lying about 6 miles south-east of Wollombi.

FINGAL BAY (*Co. Durham*), a small indentation in the land, lying to the S. of the south head of Port Stephen.

FINGAL POINT (*Co. Rous*), a rocky promontory, lying to the S. of Point Danger.

FIREFLY CREEK (*Co. Gloucester*), a settlement. 261 miles N. of Sydney. The creek is a tributary of the head of the Burril Creek. The nearest railway station is Hexham, 66 miles, on the northern line.

FIRST FALLS (*Co. Clarence*), a proclaimed village on the Clarence River.

FISH RIVER (*Co. Westmoreland*), a railway station 161 miles S. of Sydney, on the southern line.

FISH RIVER CAVES (*Co. Westmoreland*), a series of caverns lying in the valley of the Fish River.

FISH RIVER CREEK (*Co. Westmoreland*), a post-office, 139 miles W. of Sydney, with mail three times a week. It is 20 miles from Tarana. The nearest railway station is Tarana, 20 miles, on the western line. The creek is a stream rising at the western foot of the Australian Alps, east of Swatchfield, and flowing into the Fish River.

FISHERMAN'S POINT (*Co. Cumberland*). [*See* "BROKEN BAY."]

FISHERY CREEK (*Co. Northumberland*), a small western tributary of the lower end of Wallis' Creek.

FITTON MOUNT (*Co. Murray*), a peak of the Collarin range, attaining a height of about 3,000 feet above sea-level.

FITZGERALD, a county in the Western Division of the Colony. [*See* "Counties."]

FITZGERALD VALLEY (*Co. Bathurst*), a postal village, 162 miles W. of Sydney, with mail three times a week. The nearest railway station is George's Plains, 6 miles on the western line.

FITZGERALD VALLEY CREEK (*Co. Bathurst*), a small tributary or head of the Princess Charlotte's Vale Creek, rising in the Three Brothers mountains.

FITZROY, a county in the Eastern Division of the Colony. [*See* "Counties."]

FITZROY (*Co. Camden*), a proclaimed village near Berrima, on the southern railway.

FITZROY IRON MINES (*Co. Camden*). [*See* "Nattai."]

FIVE DOCK (*Co. Cumberland*), a postal suburb 6 miles W. of Sydney, with mail twice daily, and delivery by letter-carrier, and telegraph office. The nearest railway station is Ashfield, on the suburban line. It was proclaimed a municipal district in 1871 under the Municipalities Act, with five aldermen and a mayor.

FIVE DOCK BAY (*Co. Cumberland*), a bay on the S. side of the Parramatta River, lying between Five Dock Point on the east, and Blackwall point on the west. It lies about 4 miles in a straight line west of Sydney.

FIVE ISLANDS (*Co. Bathurst*), a small agricultural hamlet lying about 8 miles from Carcoar, in a southerly direction.

FIVE ISLANDS (*Co. Camden*), a group of five rocky islets lying off the coast to the south-east of Wollongong.

FIVE ISLANDS (*Co. Cumberland*), a cluster of five small sandbanks, above high-water-mark, at the mouth of Cockle Creek, in the northern part of Lake Macquarie.

FIVE-MILE CREEK (*Co. Harden*), a post-office, 213 miles S. of Sydney, with mail twice a week.

FIVE-MILE CREEK (*Co. Hardinge*), a small northern tributary of the Gwydir River.

FIVE-MILE CREEK (*Co. King*), a small northern tributary of the Yass River, rising to the west of Mount Chaton, in the S.W. of the Bredalbane Plains.

FLAGGY CREEK (*Co. Cumberland*), a small creek flowing in the neighbourhood of Newcastle.

FLAGSTONE CREEK (*Co. Richmond*), a small eastern tributary of the head of the Clarence River, flowing through scrubby pastoral country.

FLAKENEY'S RANGE (*Co. Wynyard*), a group of scrubby mountains lying in the western part of the county, near O'Brien's Creek, and to the E. of the road from Wagga Wagga to Albury.

FLAT ROCK CREEK (*Co. Cumberland*), a small stream flowing into the head of Long Bay, a branch of the Middle Harbour.

FLAT ROCK ISLAND (*Co. Northumberland*), a small rock above high-water-mark in Broken Bay, opposite Porto Bay.

FLEA CREEK (*Co. Cowley*), a small eastern tributary of the Goodradigbee Creek, rising in Mount Parnel.

FLEMINGTON (*Co. Cumberland*), a railway station, 9 miles from Sydney, on the suburban line.

FLETCHER'S NOB (*Co. Gough*), a high hill on the road from Glen Innes to Inverell, about 10 miles W. of the former place.

FLINDERS, a county in the Central Division of the Colony. [*See* "COUNTIES."]

FLINT MOUNT (*Co. Wynyard*), a peak of the Comatawa Range, lying on the E. bank of the Kiamba Creek, and to the N. of the township reserve of Kiamba.

FLINTER'S GAP (*Co. Harden*) is a passage over the N. shoulder of the Black Range, on the main road from Yass to Gundagai, about 7 miles W. of Bowring.

FLINTY CREEK (*Co. Cowley*), a small tributary of Mountain Creek, in the Yass Plains.

FLINTY POINT CREEK (*Co. Goulburn*), a small northern tributary of the Billabung Creek, falling into it near the township of Billabung.

FLINTY POINT GULLY (*Co. Goulburn*), a rugged gully lying between the two spurs of a range of high schistose hills, in the northern part of the county, and near the Billabung village reserve.

FLOOD CREEK (*Co. Farnell*) is a stream rising in the Barrier Range and flowing in a N.W. direction.

FLY ROAD (*Co. Gloucester*), between Stephens' Point and Toomeree Heads, offers a good protection to coasting vessels during heavy weather from the W., particularly in the winter season. Small vessels may anchor near Narrowgut, as there is plenty of water within less than a quarter of a mile of the beach.

FLYER'S (*Co. Bathurst*), a small gold-working on the Flyer's Creek, forming part of the Bathurst gold-field.

FLYER'S CREEK (*Co. Bathurst*). [*See* "ERROWINBANG CREEK."]

FOLEY'S FOLLY (*Co. Parry*), is a quartz-mining village situated about 3 miles from the township of Hanging Rock.

FORBES, a county in both the Central and Eastern Divisions of the Colony. [*See* "COUNTIES."]

**FORBES** (*Co. Ashburnham*), a postal town, 276 miles W. of Sydney, with daily mail. Telegraph and money-order offices, Government savings bank, and delivery by letter-carrier. Courts of quarter sessions and district courts are held here periodically. The nearest railway station is Cowra, 60 miles, on the Murrumburra and Blayney line. It is situated on the N. bank of the Lachlan River, on the road from Canowindra to Wagga Wagga and Booligal, and is the chief town on the Lachlan gold-fields. Forbes was proclaimed a municipal district in 1870, and is governed by eight aldermen and a mayor. The population is about 3,200.

**FORBES RIVER** (*Co. Macquarie*), a northern tributary of the upper part of the Hastings River.

**FORDWICK** (*Co. Northumberland*.) [*See* "BROKE."]

**FOREST CREEK** (*Co. King*), a small drainage creek of the Burrowa Plains, flowing N. about 8 miles.

**FOREST CREEK** (*Co. Murray*), a small tributary of the Brassil Creek, flowing through the south part of Yass Plains.

**FOREST HILL** (*Co. Wallace*), a lofty peak of the Warragong chain of the Australian Alps. It forms the point where the dividing line between Victoria and this colony is drawn in a south-east direction to the sea at Cape Howe.

**FOREST REEFS** (*Co. Bathurst*), a post-office, 186 miles W. of Sydney, with mail three times a week. Money-order office. The nearest railway station is Milthorpe, 6 miles, on the western line.

**FOREST ROAD** (*Co. Cumberland*), a post-office, 11 miles S. of Sydney, with daily mail therefrom. Telegraph office.

**FORSTER** (*Co. Gloucester*), a postal town, 227 miles N. of Sydney, with mail three times a week. Telegraph and money-order offices and Government savings bank. The nearest railway station is Hexham, 112 miles, on the northern line.

**FORT BOURKE** (*Co. Cowper*), near the junction of the Darling and Bogan Rivers, about 8 miles S.W. of the township of Bourke.

**FORT DENISON** (*Co. Cumberland*). [*See* "DENISON FORT."]

**FORTIS CREEK** (*Co. Clarence*), a small eastern tributary of White-man's Creek.

**FOSTER MOUNT** (*Co. Gregory*) is a granite hill lying in the midst of a vast marshy flat plain, on the west bank of the Macquarie River, about 40 miles N. of Warren.

**FOSTER'S VALLEY** (*Co. Bathurst*), a small tract of low-lying land at the head of Davy's Creek, to the N. of Rockley.

**FOSTER'S VALLEY CREEK** (*Co. Bathurst*), a small tributary of Davy's Creek, in the parish of Oakley.

**FOSTERTON** (*Co. Gloucester*), an agricultural hamlet on the Chichester River, lying about 10 miles N. of Dungog.

FOUR-MILE CREEK (*Co. Bligh*), a tributary of the Munmurra Creek.

FOUR-MILE CREEK (*Co. Roxburgh*), an eastern tributary of Cunningham's Creek, flowing to the N. of Sofala.

FOUR-MILE CREEK (*Co. Goulburn*), a small tributary to the Ten-mile Creek, rising near Woomargama Village. Also a small tributary of the Upper Bowna Creek.

FOUR-MILE CREEK (*Co. Northumberland*), a small southern tributary of the Hunter River, flowing through the agricultural settlement of Miller's Forest.

FOUR-MILE CREEK (*Co. Wellington*), a small western tributary of the Cudgegong River, rising in Mount Bocoble, and flowing into the main stream about 4 miles S. of Cudgegong.

FOWLER'S SWAMP (*Co. Goulburn*), a tract of flat grassy land, lying to the S.W. of Mount Jergyle Range.

FOWLER'S SWAMP CREEK (*Co. Goulburn*), a small tributary of the Murray River, falling into the main stream about 10 miles E. of Albury.

FOX GROUND (*Co. Camden*), an agricultural settlement to the S.W. of Gerringong, from which place it is distant about 7 miles.

FOXGROUND (*Co. Camden*), a postal town, 146 miles S. of Sydney, with daily mail.

FOXLOW (*Co. Murray*), a township, 180 miles S. of Sydney and 18 miles from Bungendore, the nearest railway station on the Goulburn and Cooma line.

FOY BROOK (*Co. Durham*), a small northern tributary of the Hunter River, flowing into the main stream near Camberwell.

FRAMPTON (*Co. Harden*), a railway station, 261 miles from Sydney, on the southern line.

FRANKLIN, a county in the Western Division of the Colony. [*See* "Counties."]

FRAZER'S CREEK (*Co. Gough*), a fine stream rising to the S.W. of the township of Wellingrove, flowing through the township of Ashford into the Severn River.

FREDERICK (*Co. Bathurst*), a proclaimed township to the S. of Orange.

FREDERICK POINT (*Co. Northumberland*) is a tongue of land jutting out into Brisbane Water Harbour, and forming part of the township of Gosford.

FREDERICK'S VALLEY (*Co. Bathurst*), a small agricultural village lying near the creek of the same name, and on the road from Orange to Bathurst, between the former place and the township of Gregory.

FREDERICK'S VALLEY CREEK (*Co. Bathurst*) is an auriferous stream rising to the south-east of Pretty Plains, in the parish of Shadforth, and flowing in a northerly direction into Lewis' Ponds Creek, at the township of Ophir.

FREDERICKTON (*Co. Macquarie*), a postal town, 366 miles N. of Sydney, with mail three times a week. Telegraph and money-order offices. Situated on the Macleay River, in the parish of Cooroobingatta. The nearest places are Kempsey, 4 miles S., and Darkwater 7 miles E.

FREEMAN'S BEACH (*Co. Cumberland*), a postal village, 36 miles W. of Sydney, with daily mail. The nearest railway station is Windsor, 4 miles, on the Richmond line.

FREEMANTLE (*Co. Roxburgh*), a post-office, 168 miles W. of Sydney, with mail once a week. The nearest railway station is Bathurst, 20 miles, on the western line.

FRENCH PARK (*Co. Mitchell*), a postal receiving-office, 337 miles S. of Sydney, with mail once a week. The nearest railway station is The Rock, 4 miles, on the southern line.

FROG'S HOLE CREEK (*Co. Beresford*), a small creek draining some good pastoral country. It flows northerly into the Bredbo River.

FROG'S HOLLOW (*Co. Auckland*). [*See* "KAMERUKA."]

FROGMORE (*Co. King*), a postal village, 246 miles S. of Sydney, with mail twice a week. Money-order office. The nearest railway station is Binalong, 23 miles, on the southern line.

FROME MOUNT (*Co. Phillip*), a peak lying on the N. bank of the Cudgegong River, about 4 miles E. of the township of Mudgee.

FRYINGPAN (*Co. Roxburgh*) is situated 106 miles to the W. of Sydney, on the Fryingpan Creek, near the Fish River, and is in an agricultural district, the nearest places being Bathurst, 15 miles W., and Meadow Flat, 7 miles N.

FRYINGPAN CREEK (*Co. Roxburgh*), a northern tributary of the Fish River, rising in the Kirconnell gold-fields, near Yetholme, and flowing into the main stream near the township of Kenlis.

FRYINGPAN CREEK (*Co. Wallace*), a small eastern tributary of the Eucumbene River, flowing into it past the town of Seymour.

FULLERTON (*Co. Georgiana*), a postal village, 171 miles S. of Sydney, with mail twice a week. The nearest railway station is Goulburn, 40 miles, on the southern line.

FULLERTON COVE (*Co. Gloucester*), a large lagoon on the N. shore of the Hunter River, opposite Newcastle. It is almost dry at low water. A large sandy island, called Wallis' Island, lies on its western side, and a small sandbank at its entrance.

FURRUCABAD CREEK (*Co. Gough*), a small tributary of the Rocky Ponds Creek, flowing near the township of Glen Innes, through good agricultural land.

# G

GADARA CREEK (*Co. Wynyard*), a small tributary of the Gilmore Creek, flowing from the E. of the Adelong gold-fields.

GAIRDNER CREEK (*Co. Farnell*), a stream rising in the Barrier Range, and flowing in an easterly direction.

GALLAH (*Co. Sturt*), a township to the N. of Thononga on the S.W. railway.

GALLAGAMBROON CREEK (*Co. Gowen*), an eastern tributary of the Castlereagh River, rising in Mount Nemur, and flowing through the village of Mogomodine into the main stream at the village of Gallagambroon.

GALLARGAMBONE (*Co. Gowen*), a township on the bank of the Castlereagh River.

GALLEY SWAMP (*Co. Bathurst*), a postal receiving-office, 194 miles W. of Sydney, with mail twice a week.

GALLIMBINE MOUNT (*Co. Phillip*), a high peak lying on the N. bank of the Cudgegong River, about 8 miles N.W. of the town of Mudgee.

GALMERANG MOUNT (*Co. Wellesley*). [See "COOPER MOUNT."]

GALONG (*Co. King*), a postal village, 216 miles S. of Sydney, with daily mail. A railway station on the southern line.

GALORE MOUNT (*Co. Mitchell*), a lofty hill at the head of the Bronong Creek, and on the road from Urana to Wagga Wagga.

GALSTON (*Co. Cumberland*), a postal receiving-office, 32 miles W. of Sydney, with daily mail.

GALWADGERE MOUNT (*Co. Wellington*), a high peak on the south bank of the Macquarie River, about 3 miles W. of Burrendong.

GAMBENANY CREEK (*Co. Cook*), a small tributary of Cox's River, which it joins about 10 miles S. of Little Hartley. There are vast deposits of alum and salt found in the part of the Blue Mountains where this creek has its source.

GAMMON PLAINS (*Co. Brisbane*), a tract of good agricultural land lying round the township of Merriwa.

GANBENANY CREEK (*Co. Westmoreland*), a tributary of the Cox's River.

GANGAN BRANCH (*Co. Courallie*), a watercourse conveying the overflow of the Gwydir River in a north-easterly direction into the Goonal Swamp.

GANGANGAR CREEK (*Co. Wallace*), a small southern tributary of the upper part of the Murrumbidgee River, rising at Mount Tantangara.

GANNON'S FOREST (*Co. Cumberland*), situate about 11 miles S. of Sydney, in the parish of St. George and police district of Parramatta, lying between Cook's and George's Rivers.

GAP (*Co. Buckland*), a railway station, 257 miles N. of Sydney, on the north-western line to Narrabri.

GAP, THE (*Co. Cumberland*), a favourite place of resort of the citizens of Sydney by steamer to Watson's Bay. The Gap displays a grandeur of the open ocean not obtainable elsewhere along the eastern seaboard of the South Pacific. It is an opening in the perpendicular rocky cliffs, about a mile S.S.E. of the inner South Head, in the village of Watson's Bay. It is a short distance to the northward of the spot where the ill-fated ship "Dunbar" was driven on shore on the night of the 20th August, 1857, and all hands lost save one—a seaman named Johnson, who was thrown upon a ledge of the rock, and remained there a long time before he was discovered.

GAP, THE (*Co. Phillip*), a passage over the Blue Mountains, on the road from Sofala to Merriwa and Cassilis, about 10 miles N. of Dabee.

GAP CREEK (*Co. Cowley*), a western tributary of the Upper Murrumbidgee River, rising in Mount Clear, and flowing through the Boboyon Flats.

GAP HILL (*Co. Wellesley*), a small peak lying in the Gap Creek, about 4 miles N. of the dividing line between New South Wales and Victoria.

GAP RANGE (*Co. King*), is 169 miles to the S. of Sydney. It is situated on the Jerrawa Creek, 1 mile from the Chain of Ponds, and 10 miles N. from the Yass River, between Gunning and Yass. The district is agricultural and pastoral.

GARAH (*Co. Jamison*), a village 105 miles from Narrabri, the nearest railway station on the north-western line.

GARDEN ISLAND (*Co. Cumberland*), a well known island in Port Jackson, opposite Woolloomooloo Bay. This island is now used entirely as a marine depôt for the use of the men-of-war in port.

GARDS (*Co. Wellington*) is a gold working, forming part of the Turon diggings, and lying about 7 miles from the township of Sofala.

GARLAND (*Co. Bathurst*), a postal receiving-office, 195 miles W. of Sydney, with daily mail.

GARLAND'S HILL (*Co. Wellesley*), a lofty eminence, lying about 10 miles S.W. of the township of Nimmitibel.

GARRA (*Co. Wellington*), a postal village, 222 miles W. of Sydney, with daily mail. The nearest railway station is Molong, 8 miles, on the Orange and Molong line.

GARRA CREEK (*Co. Argyle*), a small tributary of the Nadgigoman Creek.

GARRANAGNY (*Co. Kennedy*), a township near the Back Creek, and to the N.E. of that creek.

GARRYOWEN (*Co. Wynyard*), a village, 62 miles from Wagga Wagga, the nearest railway station on the southern line.

GECAR or COW'S FLAT (*Co. Wellesley*), is a piece of good alluvial land, lying at the confluence of the Bombala River and Aston's Creek.

GEDDAI (*Co. Bathurst*), a small township reserve and agricultural settlement, lying about 159 miles W. of Sydney.

GEERA (*Co. Clyde*), a township on the S. bank of the Barwon River.

GEERINGREEMAH or PHIL'S CREEK (*Co. King*), a branch of Hovell Creek, rising in the Burrowa Plains and flowing N. about 18 miles.

GEGALLALONG CREEK (*Co. Monteagle*), a small tributary to the Burrowa River, to the N.W. of the township of Burrowa.

GEGEDZERIC (*Co. Beresford*), a village, 20 miles from Cooma, the nearest railway station on the Goulburn and Cooma line.

GENANGIE (*Co. Ashburnham*), a postal receiving-office, 306 miles W. of Sydney, with mail twice a week.

GENERAL STEWART'S GAP (*Co. Monteagle*), a passage through the scrubby ranges on the road from Murringo to Cowra.

GENOA RIVER (*Co. Auckland*), a river rising in the southern part of the South Coast Range, flowing in a S.E. direction over the Victorian border into the Maliacoota inlet.

GENOE LAKE (*Co. Wakool*). [*See* "COOMAROOY LAKES."]

GENTLEMAN'S HALT (*Co. Cumberland*), a postal office, 88 miles W. of Sydney, with mail twice a week. Situated on the Hawkesbury River.

GEORGE CAPE (*Co. St. Vincent*). [*See* "ST. GEORGE CAPE."]

GEORGE LAKE (*Cos. Argyle and Murray*), is the largest and most important of the inland lakes of New South Wales. It lies about 25 miles S.W. from the city of Goulburn to the S. of the Breadalbane and the W. of the Goulburn Plains. The village of Kenny's Point lies on the E. shore, and Point Oudajong a little further N. Lake Bathurst, a smaller lake, lies 10 miles E., and Lakes Tarago and Wolojorong about 7 and 10 miles respectively. George Lake is 21 miles in length, with an average width of 7 or 8 miles. It is situate on the top of the table-land of the dividing range, 2,129 feet above sea level.

GEORGE LAKE RANGES (*Co. Argyle*), a spur of the dividing range which divides the E. and W. sides of Lake George. The highest peak is Mount Alianoyonyiga, which attains an elevation of 3,500 feet above the level.

GEORGE'S (*Co. Dudley*), a small northern tributary of the Macleay River.

GEORGE'S CREEK (*Co. Hardinge*), an eastern auriferous tributary of the Gwydir River, rising near Falconer township. It is fed by the Erragerra Creek at its upper end.

GEORGE'S HEAD (*Co. Cumberland*), a bold rocky promontory on the N. shore, facing the entrance to Port Jackson.

GEORGE'S PLAINS (*Co. Bathurst*), a postal village, 152 miles W. of Sydney, with daily mail and telegraph office. A railway station on the western line.

GEORGE'S RIVER (*Co. Cumberland*). [See "RIVERS."]

GEORGE TOWN (*Co. Cumberland*), a village in the parish of Bankstown, is situated on the N. bank of George's River.

GEORGIANA, a county in the Eastern Division of the Colony. [See "COUNTIES."]

GERAPMA CREEK (*Co. Cadell*), a tributary of the Edward River, falling into it at Deniliquin.

GERARD MOUNT (*Co. Clive*), a lofty peak lying on the S. bank of Gerard's Creek, about 4 miles W. of the township of Drake.

GERMAN CREEK (*Co. Rous*), a postal town, 360 miles N. of Sydney, with daily mail therefrom.

GERMAN'S HILL (*Co. Bathurst*), a postal town, 198 miles W. of Sydney, with mails three times a week.

GERMANTON (*Co. Goulburn*), a postal town, 373 miles S. of Sydney, with daily mail, telegraph and money-order offices, and Government savings bank. The nearest railway station is Culcairn, 18 miles on the southern line. Situated in the parish of Germanton, on the Ten-mile Creek, the Billabong Creek being distant 6 miles W., and Coocook Hill lying 3 miles E. The cultivation of the vine is carried on here successfully.

GEROGERY (*Co. Goulburn*), a postal town, 368 miles S. of Sydney, with daily mail, telegraph, and money-order offices, and Government savings bank. A railway station on the southern line.

GEROGERY CREEK (*Co. Goulburn*), a northern tributary of the Bowna Creek, rising near and flowing through the village of the same name.

GEROGERY RANGE (*Cos. Goulburn and Hume*), a range of rugged schistose and granite hills—the source of the Gerogery and Dead Horse Creeks.

GERRINGONG (*Co. Camden*), a postal village, 78 miles S. of Sydney, with daily mail. The nearest railway station is Kiama, 10 miles on the Illawarra and South Coast line, situated in the parish of Gerringong. The district is agricultural and pastoral, the soil is rich and well cultivated. It was proclaimed a municipal district in 1871, and is governed by eight aldermen and a mayor.

GERRYMBERRYN (*Co. Clarence*), a postal village, 357 miles N. of Sydney, with mail per Clarence River steamers.

GEURIE (*Co. Lincoln*), a postal town, 261 miles W. of Sydney, with daily mail. A railway station on the western line.

GHEAN CREEK (*Co. Jamison*), a southern tributary of the Moornia Creek, rising near the village of Malaraway, on the Narrabri and Moree road, and flowing through good country.

GHINI-GHINI (*Co. Macquarie*), a postal village, 235 miles N. of Sydney, with daily mail. The nearest railway is Hexham, 123 miles on the northern line. Situated on the N. bank of the Manning River, 3 miles E. of Cundletown and 6 miles E. of Taree.

GIANDERRA or KIANDRA RANGE (*Co. Wallace*), an eastern spur of the northern part of the Muniong or Snowy Mountains, covered with snow in winter. The highest peak is called Mount Tantangara.

GIANT'S CREEK (*Co. Brisbane*), a postal receiving-office, 206 miles N. of Sydney, with daily mail. The creek is a northern tributary of the Goulburn River.

GIBRALTAR CREEK (*Co. Cowley*), is a tributary of the Tidbimbilla Creek, flowing in a northerly direction and fed by Paddy's Creek.

GIBRALTAR HILL (*Co. Cook*), a lofty mountain on the Blue Mountain Range, lying about 18 miles S. from Little Hartley. Vast quantities of alum and salt of good quality are embedded in this hill.

GIBRALTAR HILL (*Co. Cowley*), a high peak lying about 14 miles N.W. of Tharwa, and on the W. of the Murrumbidgee River.

GILGAI (*Co. Hardinge*), a postal village, 423 miles N. of Sydney, with mail three times a week. The nearest railway station is Uralla, 57 miles on the northern line.

GILGANDRA (*Co. Narramine*), a postal village, 292 miles W. of Sydney, with mail three times a week. Telegraph office. The nearest railway station is Dubbo, 32 miles, on the western line.

GIL-GIL RIVER (*Co. Stapylton*). [*See* "RIVERS."]

GILGUNNIA (*Co. Oxley*), a postal village, 490 miles N. of Sydney, with mail once a week. The nearest railway station is Nyngan, 99 miles, on the western line.

GILL MOUNT (*Co. Forbes*), a lofty peak, lying to the S. of the Lachlan River, and near the head of Kangarooby Creek.

GILLENBAH or YANKO (*Co. Mitchell*), a postal receiving-office, 349 miles S. of Sydney, with mail twice a week. Situated on the Murrumbidgee River, close to the township of Narrandera.

GILLIMATONG CREEK (*Co. St. Vincent*), a small auriferous stream, from near Braidwood into the Shoalhaven River.

GILMANDYKE CREEK (*Co. Georgiana*), a western tributary of the Campbell River, rising in the Long Swamp. It is crossed by the road from Reckley to Bolong.

GILMORE (*Co. Wynyard*), a postal village, 318 miles S. of Sydney, with daily mail. The nearest railway station is Gundagai, 30 miles, on the Cootamundra and Gundagai line.

GILMORE CREEK (*Co. Wynyard*), an important auriferous stream, rising in the northern slope of Mane's Range, and flowing through the upper Adelong gold-fields into the Tumut River, at the township of Tumut. In November, 1850, the late James Macarthur, Esq., discovered two hot springs at Mount Hugel.

GILMORE GOLD FIELD (*Co. Wynyard*), comprises the Betlow and Long-flat diggings, about 12 miles S.E. of the township of Adelong.

GINALLIGULLA (*Co. Cumberland*), a hill in the parish of Alexandria, and suburban municipality of Woollahra, between the heads of Rose and Double Bays.

GINGEDLICK DIGGINGS (*Co. Selwyn*). [*See* "TUMBERUMBA."]

GINGERBEER CREEK (*Co. Harden*), a small western tributary of the Muttama Creek, rising and flowing into the parish of Coolac.

GINGERRA STATION (*Co. Murray*), a postal receiving-office, 324 miles S. of Sydney, with mail twice a week.

GINGHAM GAP (*Co. Gordon*), a pass through the Hervey Range of mountains, on the road from Obley to Condobolin.

GININGININDERY CREEK (*Co. Murray*), an eastern tributary of the Murrumbidgee River, crossing the road from Queanbeyan to Yass. It is fed by the Gooroman Chain of Ponds.

GINGKIN (*Co. Cook*), a postal village, 148 miles W. of Sydney, with mail three times a week. The nearest railway station is Tarana, 30 miles, on the western line.

GINNINDERRA (*Co. Murray*), a postal village, 230 miles S. of Sydney, with daily mail. Telegraph and money-order offices and Government savings bank. The nearest railway station is Queanbeyan, 16 miles, on the Goulburn and Cooma line.

GIPPS, a county in the Central Division of the Colony. [*See* "COUNTIES."]

GIPPS TOWN (*Co. Cumberland*), is a small village on the Five Dock Estate, in the parish of Concord, about 8 miles from Sydney, and 2 miles from Ashfield, the nearest railway station on the suburban line.

GIRILAMBONE (*Co. Canbelego*), a postal village, 405 miles W. of Sydney, with daily mail. Telegraph and money-order offices and Government savings bank. A railway station on the western line.

GIRO (*Co. Hawes*), a proclaimed township on the Barnard River.

GIRVAN (*Co. Gloucester*), a postal village, 155 miles N. of Sydney, with mail therefrom three days a week.

GLADESVILLE (*Co. Cumberland*), a postal suburb, 7 miles W. of Sydney, with mail twice daily. Telegraph and money-order offices, Government savings bank, and delivery by letter-carrier. The nearest railway station is Ryde, 3 miles, on the Ryde and Hawkesbury River line, and in the parish of Hunter's Hill. It is situated on the S. bank of the Parramatta River, where steam communication to and from Sydney and Parramatta is supplied to the residents, as well as to pleasure seekers on this lovely branch river of the Harbour of Port Jackson.

GLADSTONE (*Co. Macquarie*), a postal town, 326 miles N. of Sydney, with mail three times a week. Telegraph and money-order offices and Government savings bank. The nearest railway station is Hexham, 208 miles, on the northern line.

GLANMIRE (*Co. Roxburgh*), a postal village, 143 miles W. of Sydney, with daily mail. The nearest railway station is Raglan, 4½ miles, on the western line. Situated on St. Anthony's Creek, in the parish of Peel.

GLEBE (*Co. Cumberland*), an important postal suburb of the City of Sydney, with mail twice daily. Telegraph and money-order offices, and Government savings bank, and delivery by letter-carriers. It lies to the N.W. of Sydney, and is reached either by tram or omnibus every five minutes. It was proclaimed a borough in 1859, and is governed by eleven aldermen and a mayor. The population is about 20,000.

GLEBE ISLAND (*Co. Cumberland*), is now joined to the mainland of Balmain by an embankment, and is situated in Johnstone's Bay, in the parish of Petersham, between White and Rozella Bays. The Corporation abattoirs are built thereon, and is the principal slaughtering place for the city and suburbs of Sydney.

GLEBELAND (*Co. Northumberland*), a village, 2 miles from Adamstown. The nearest railway station is Newcastle, 3 miles, on the northern line.

GLEN ALICE (*Co. Cook*), a postal village, 157 miles W. of Sydney, with mail four times a week. The nearest railway station is Capertee, 26 miles, on the western line.

GLENARIFF (*Co. Cowper*), a railway station, 442 miles from Sydney, on the western line.

GLENBOWER (*Co. King*), a post-office, 204 miles S. of Sydney, with mail once a week. The nearest railway station is Yass, 14 miles, on the southern line.

GLENBROOK (*Co. Cook*), a postal village, 40 miles W. of Sydney, with daily mail. A railway station on the western line. The brook is a small tributary of the Nepean River, flowing near the township of Emu.

GLENBURN (*Co. Westmoreland*), a proclaimed village in this county.

GLENCOE (*Co. Gough*), a postal village, 408 miles N. of Sydney, with daily mail. A railway station on the northern line.

GLENDARNEL (*Co. Camden*), an agricultural settlement lying near the village of the Oaks.

GLENDON BROOK (*Co. Durham*), a postal village, 159 miles N. of Sydney, with mail twice a week. A railway station on the western line. The Brook is a fine stream rising in the Mount Royal Ranges, flowing into the Hunter River between Maitland and Singleton.

GLENDHU (*Co. Arrawatta*), a post-office, 567 miles N. of Sydney, with mail therefrom once a week.

GLEN ELGIN (*Co. Gough*), a small gold-field, lying within 20 miles E. of the township of Glen Innes.

GLENFIELD (*Co. Cumberland*), a postal receiving-office, 25 miles S. of Sydney, with daily mail. A railway station on the southern line.

GLEN FINLAS (*Co. Wellington*), an agricultural settlement, lying on the Molle River, about 20 miles W. of the township of Wellington.

N

GLENGARRY CREEK (*Co. Georgiana*), a branch or mouth of the Mulgowrie Creek, falling into the Lachlan River.

GLEN INNES (*Co. Gough*), a postal town, 423 miles N. of Sydney, with mail daily. Telegraph and money-order offices, and Government savings bank, and delivery by letter-carriers. A railway station on the northern line. Situated on the Rocky Ponds, the Furrucabad Creek and Beardy Creek being contiguous thereto. Ben Lomond, a remarkable mountain, and the highest part of New England stands about 20 miles S. near the Oban diggings. A gold-field, known as Glen Elgin, is within 20 miles E. of the town. Glen Innes has a court-house, where the district court and petty sessions are held. It was proclaimed a municipal district in 1872, and is governed by eleven aldermen and a mayor. The population is about 3,500. Courts of quarter sessions and district courts are held here periodically.

GLEN LOGAN (*Co. Bathurst*), a small agricultural settlement, lying about 10 miles W. of the town of Cowra.

GLENMORE (*Co. Cumberland*), a deep picturesque gully, lying between Paddington and the New South Head Road, on the E. side of the City of Sydney.

GLENMORE CREEK (*Co. Cumberland*), a small tributary of the Rushcutters' Creek, rising in Upper Paddington, and flowing N.W.

GLEN MORRISON (*Co. Parry*), a post-office, 345 miles N. of Sydney, with mail twice a week. The nearest railway station is Walcha, 25 miles, on the western line.

GLENNIE'S CREEK (*Co. Durham*), a postal town, 156 miles N. of Sydney, with daily mail. A railway station on the northern line.

GLENOAK (*Co. Northumberland*), a postal village, 135 miles N. of Sydney, with daily mail. The nearest railway station is Morpeth, 9 miles, on the East Maitland and Morpeth line.

GLENQUARRY (*Co. Camden*), a postal village, 89 miles S. of Sydney, with daily mail therefrom.

GLENROCK CREEK (*Co. Argyle*), a fine stream flowing near the township of Marulan.

GLENROUTH (*Co. Mitchell*), a proclaimed village within this county.

GLENROY (*Co. Westmoreland*), an agricultural settlement, lying on the road between Hartley and Bundo Flat.

GLENTHORNE (*Co. Macquarie*), a postal village, 226 miles N. of Sydney, with mail three times a week.

GLEN UGIE CREEK (*Co. Clarence*), a small western tributary of the Coldstream River.

GLEN WILLIAM (*Co. Durham*), a postal village, 145 miles N. of Sydney, with mail three times a week. The nearest railway station is Morpeth, 25 miles, on the East Maitland and Morpeth line. It is an agricultural settlement, lying on the Williams River, about 5 miles from Clarence-town.

GLOUCESTER, a county in the Eastern Division of the Colony. [See "COUNTIES."]

GLOUCESTER (*Co. Gloucester*), a postal town, 176 miles N. of Sydney, with daily mail. The nearest railway station is Hexham, 65 miles, on the northern line. Situated on the Gloucester River, about 2 miles above the junction of the Barrington River and Avon Creek, and 20 miles above the Manning River.

GLOUCESTER RIVER (*Co. Gloucester*). [See "RIVERS."]

GLUPTON (*Co. Brisbane*), a township, 232 miles N. of Sydney, on the northern line.

GNALL (*Co. Young*), a village, 450 miles from Hay, the nearest railway station on the south-western line.

GOANGRA (*Co. Denham*), a proclaimed township, on the N. bank of the Namoi River.

GOAT ISLAND (native name, MEMEL), (*Co. Cumberland*), an island in Port Jackson, lying between Balmain and North Sydney, at the mouth of the Parramatta River.

GOBA CREEK (*Co. Monteagle*), a small western tributary of the Burrowa River.

GOCUP (*Co. Buccleuch*), a postal village, 305 miles S. of Sydney, with daily mail. The nearest railway station is Gundagai, 10 miles, on the Cootamundra and Gundagai line. It is an agricultural settlement lying near Tumut.

GODFREY'S CREEK (*Co. Monteagle*), a stream rising in the hills E. of the township of Wambanumba, which, with the Mountain Hut, forms the Cookoomingala Creek.

GOLDEN GULLY (*Co. Wellington*), an auriferous gully on the Tambaroora diggings, situated at the head of the Tambaroora and Bald Hills Creeks, about 20 miles N.E. of Sofala, and the same distance N.E. of Ophir.

GOLDEN POINT (*Co. Roxburgh*), a spot on the Turon River, lying about 1 mile E. of Sofala.

GOL GOL (*Co. Wentworth*), a proclaimed township, on the N. bank of the Murray River.

GOL GOL CREEK (*Co. Taila*), a water-course from Mount Golgol, in a S.W. direction, into the Murray River, near the village of Colwang.

GOL GOL LAKE (*Co. Wentworth*), a large lake of fresh water to the N. of the Murray River.

GOLGOL MOUNT (*Co. Wentworth*), a range of low hills, lying to the N. of the dense mallee scrub country N. of Euston.

GOLSPIE (*Co. Argyle*), a postal village, 178 miles S. of Sydney, with mail three times a week. The nearest railway station is Goulburn, 44 miles, on the southern line.

GONGOLGON (*Co. Cowper*), a postal village, 466 miles W. of Sydney, with mail twice a week. Telegraph and money-order offices, and Government savings bank. The nearest railway station is Nyngan, 88 miles, on the western line.

GONOWLIA CREEK (*Co. Franklin*), is a tributary of the Lachlan River, flowing from the W. of the lower part of that stream.

GOOANDRA CREEK (*Co. Wallace*), a tributary of the Gangangar Creek, flowing to the N. of Kiandra.

GOOBANG (*Co. Ashburnham*), a township, on the Dalladerry Creek, near the town of Parkes.

GOOBANG (*Co. Ashburnham*), a proclaimed village, on the creek of the same name.

GOOBANG CREEK (*Co. Ashburnham*), a fine northern tributary of the Lachlan River, rising in Mount Warrobil, and flowing to the N. of the Lachlan gold-fields, across the Brolgon Plains, into the main stream at Condobolin.

GOOBURRAGANDRA CREEK (*Co. Buccleuch*)), a fine stream, rising in Peppercorn Hill, and flowing N.W. into the Tumut River, about 4 miles S. of Tumut.

GOOD DOG OR CUMBEWARRA (*Co. Camden*), is the name of the private township of the late Messrs. Berry.

GOOD DOG MOUNT (*Co. Camden*), a peak of the Cambewarra Range, overhanging the township of Cambewarra. It contains two seams of coal, very hard, probably anthracite, and difficult to work.

GOOD GOOD RIVER (*Monaro District*), a fine stream flowing in the rugged country, in the southern part of this district.

GOODOOGA (*Co. Culgoa*), a postal village, 562 miles N. of Sydney, with mail three times a week. The nearest railway station is Byrock, 141 miles, on the western line.

GOOD HOPE (*Co. King*), a postal receiving-office, 203 miles S. of Sydney, with mail twice a week. The nearest railway station is Yass, 15 miles, on the Albury and Melbourne line.

GOODRADIGBEE (*Co. Cowley*), a proclaimed village, on the river of the same name in the north part of the county.

GOODRADIGBEE RIVER (*Cos. Culgoa and Buccleuch*). [*See* "RIVERS."]

GOODRICH (*Co. Ashburnham*), a town, 40 miles from Molong, the nearest railway station on the Blayney-Murrumburrah line.

GOODWOOD ISLAND (*Co. Clarence*). [*See* "HARWOOD ISLAND."]

GOOLAGONG (*Co. Forbes*), a postal village, 242 miles W. of Sydney, with mail twice a week. The nearest railway station is Cowra, 25 miles, on the Blayney-Murrumburrah line.

GOOLMA (*Co. Bligh*), a postal village, 282 miles W. of Sydney, with mail four times a week. The nearest railway station is Wellington, 27 miles, on the western line.

GOOLMA CREEK (*Co. Bligh*), a northern tributary of the Cudgegong River, flowing into that river at the crossing of the Mudgee and Wellington road.

GOOLMANGAR (*Co. Rous*), a post-office, 372 miles north of Sydney, with mail once a week.

GOOLMUNGAR CREEK (*Co. Rous*), a small tributary of the N. arm of the Richmond River, flowing into it 9 miles N.W. of Lismore.

GOOLTIA (*Co. Pottinger*), a township to the S.W. of Gunnedah, in the same county.

GOOMBALIA (*Co. Gunderbooka*), a proclaimed village on the E. bank of the Warrego River, in 31° S. lat.

GOOMBARGONA (*Co. Goulburn*), a post-office, 426 miles S. of Sydney, with mail twice a week. The nearest railway station is Gerogery, 24 miles, on the southern line.

GOOMOORAH (*Co. Gough*), a post-office, 488 miles N. of Sydney, with mail twice a week.

GOONA (*Co. White*), a township to the W. of Baan Baa, on the N.W. railway.

GOONAMBIL (*Co. Urana*), a township, on the Billabong Creek, S. of Urana.

GOONIMUR LAKE (*Co. Wakool*). [See "COOMAROOY LAKES."]

GOONOO-GOONOO (*Co. Parry*), a postal village, 277 miles N. of Sydney, with mail twice a week. Money-order office and Government savings bank. The nearest railway station is Duri, 8 miles, on the northern line. Situated on the Goonoo-Goonoo Creek, near the Peel River, being a gold-mining district on that river. It is elevated about 1,450 feet above sea level.

GOONOO-GOONOO CREEK (*Co. Parry*), a southern tributary of the Peel River, rising near the township of Goonoo-Goonoo, and flowing into the Peel at Tamworth.

GOONUL BRANCH (*Co. Courallie*), a watercourse flowing into the Goonul Swamp.

GOONUL SWAMP (*Co. Courallie*), a large tract of swampy country, formed by the expansion of the Gunal and Gangan branches of the Gwydir River.

GOONUMBLA (*Co. Narromine*), a high detached mountain, lying at the head of the Cookopie Ponds.

GOORANGOOLA (*Co. Durham*), a postal village, 173 miles N. of Sydney, with mail twice a week. The nearest railway station is Glennie's Creek, 18 miles, on the northern line.

GOORANGOOLA CREEK (*Co. Durham*), a small tributary of the Falbrook, fed by the Campbell's Creek.

GOORANGOOR CREEK (*Co. Wellington*), a northern auriferous tributary of the Meroo Creek, rising in Mount Muggerbil, and flowing through the Meroo gold-fields.

GOORANGOOREE MOUNT (*Co. Wellington*), a peak in the Stony Creek Range, on the E. bank of the Bell River, lying about 3 miles W. of the Ironbark diggings.

GOOROMON PONDS (*Co. Murray*), a series of waterholes supplying the pastoral country between Queanbeyan and Yass.

GOOROOMER SPRING (*Co. Culgoa*), one of a series of springs on the border of Queensland in this county.

GOORUDEE RIVULET (*Co. Wallace*), a small southern tributary of the Murrumbidgee River, rising to the N.E. of the township of Denison, and flowing through rugged country.

GOORUDEE RIVULET (*Co. Wallace*), a small eastern tributary of the Eucumbene River rising in a swampy flat near Bolaira.

GORAN LAKE (*Co. Buckland*), a postal town, 296 miles N. of Sydney, with mail twice a week.

GORDON, a county partly in the Eastern and Central Division of the Colony. [*See* "COUNTIES."]

GORDON (*Co. Cumberland*), a postal village, 9 miles N. of Sydney, with mail daily and money-order office. A railway station on the Hornsby branch of northern line.

GORDON (*Co. Drake*), a proclaimed village on Gordon Brook, a tributary of the Clarence River.

GORDON'S BAY (*Co. Cumberland*), a small indentation in the cliffs on the coast, lying about 6 miles S. of the entrance of Port Jackson.

GORDON'S CREEK (*Co. Richmond*), a small eastern tributary of the Clarence River. It is fed by Hassan's Creek.

GORE COVE (*Co. Cumberland*), a small bay, forming the western part of Ball's Head Bay, on the N. side of the harbour. The township of Greenwich lies on the W. side of the bay.

GORE HILL (*Co. Cumberland*), a postal town, 4 miles N. of Sydney, with daily mail.

GORE'S CREEK (*Co. Jamison*). [*See* "BULLEWA CREEK."]

GOREE CREEK (*Co. Cowley*). [*See* "PABRAL CREEK."]

GORRIE'S FLAT (*Co. Wellington*), a small gold workings, forming part of the Meroo gold-field, and lying to the S. of the township of Avisford.

GORUNGUWA MOUNT (*Co. Bligh*), a peak lying to the N.W. of the confluence of the Macquarie and Cudgegong Rivers.

GOSFORD (*Co. Northumberland*), a postal town, 50 miles N. of Sydney, with daily mail. Telegraph and money-order offices, and Government savings bank. A railway station on the Sydney and Newcastle line. Gosford is situated on a magnificent and exceedingly romantic inlet of the sea from Broken Bay, called the Broadwater. Tuggerah Lake lies about 9 miles in a northerly direction. It was proclaimed a borough in 1886, with five aldermen and a mayor.

GOSFORTH (*Co. Northumberland*), an agricultural settlement, lying on the N. road, 10 miles distant from Maitland.

GOSLING CREEK (*Co. Bathurst*), a western tributary of the Frederick's Valley Creek, rising on the eastern slopes of the Canobolas Mountains, and flowing into the main stream near the crossing of the Bathurst and Orange Road.

GOUGH, a county in the Eastern Division of the Colony. [*See* "COUNTIES."]

GOULBURN, a county in the Eastern Division of the Colony. [*See* "COUNTIES."]

GOULBURN (34° 45′ S. lat., 149° 44′ 48″ E. long.) (*Co. Argyle*), parish of Goulburn, 134 miles S. of Sydney, with daily mail therefrom. Telegraph and money-order offices, and Government savings bank. The Great Southern Railway passes through the city, and is on the through line to Sydney and Brisbane on the N. and Melbourne to Adelaide on the S. The branch line to Cooma converges at this point. It is situated near an angle formed by the junction of the Mulwarree chain of ponds and the Wollondilly River, Lakes George and Bathurst lying respectively about 25 miles distant. Goulburn is an assize town, and has long been incorporated under the Municipalities Act, and is governed by eleven aldermen and a mayor. The buildings are of a substantial character, and the commercial importance is much enhanced by the railway facilities it commands. The district is elevated, being 2,129 feet above sea level. The area of the city and suburban lands comprise about 1,730 acres. Sittings of the supreme court, courts of quarter sessions, and district courts are held here periodically. The population is about 11,000.

GOULBURN PLAINS (*Co. Argyle*), a large tract of flat tableland lying S. of Goulburn, and between that place and Lake Bathurst. These plains lie at an elevation of 2,000 feet above the level of the sea.

GOULBURN RIVER (*Cos. Hunter, Brisbane, Bligh, and Phillip*). [*See* "RIVERS."]

GOULDSVILLE (*Co. Northumberland*), a postal village, 320 miles N. of Sydney, with mail therefrom three days a week.

GOUROCK RANGE (*Co. Murray*), a range of lofty mountains forming part of the Great Dividing Range, attaining an elevation of about 4,300 feet above sea level, and running from the northern part of Lake George to the sources of the most eastern tributaries of the Murrumbidgee River.

GOVERNOR'S HILL (*Co. Murray*), a peak of the western spur of the Australian Alps, situated about 6 miles S. of Kenny's Point, from which place it has the appearance of an immense cone; also a hill lying to the E. of the township of Goulburn.

GOVETT'S LEAP (*Co. Cook*), a fine cataract on a small tributary creek of the head of the Grose River, situated about 3 miles N. of Blackheath, and 70 miles W. of Sydney.

GOWADTH MOUNT (*Co. Wellington*). [*See* "CANOBOLAS."]

GOWDAWADA CREEK (*Co. Wellington*), an auriferous tributary of the Waramagallon Creek, flowing through the western part of the Louisa Creek gold-fields.

GOWEN, a county in the Central Division of the Colony. [*See* "COUNTIES."]

GOWRIE (*Co. Parry*), a postal receiving-office, 282 miles N. of Sydney, with mail once a week.

GRABBEN GULLEN (*Co. King*), a proclaimed township and a postal receiving-office, 161 miles S. of Sydney, with mail therefrom three times a week.

GRABBEN GULLEN CREEK (*Co. King*), a fine stream rising in the western slopes of the Australian Alps, and flowing into the upper part of the Lachlan River.

GRAFTON (*Co. Clarence*), 29° 40' S. lat., 152° 53' E. long., in the parish of Great Marlow, 528 miles N. of Sydney, with mails therefrom by Clarence River steamers, and by railway via Glen Innes. Telegraph and money-order offices, and Government savings bank. It lies 55 miles W. from the sea, situated on the left bank of the Clarence River, and is a seaport accessible for ships drawing 10 feet of water. The streets are laid out on the model plan, by being very wide and having trees planted along their main thoroughfares, and the cross streets are at right angles with them, after the design of the city of Melbourne. The district is a most productive one in maize and other agricultural requirements, and the sugar-cane is cultivated very successfully on the rich alluvial flats of the Clarence. There is no railway communication nearer than Glen Innes on the Great Northern line, and the commerce of the city is principally carried on by water traffic. The area of the city and suburban lands comprise about 1,730 acres. Grafton was proclaimed a municipality in 1859, with a governing body of ten aldermen and a mayor. The population is about 5,200. Sittings of the supreme court, courts of quarter sessions, and district courts are held here periodically.

GRAFTON (SOUTH) (*Co. Clarence*), in the parish of Southampton, 528 miles N. of Sydney, with mail therefrom by Clarence River steamers and by railway via Glen Innes on the Great Northern line. Telegraph and money-order offices, and Government savings bank. Situated on the right bank of the Clarence River, and partaking of the characteristics of the sister city on the opposite side of the river, except that the heavy traffic has to be conveyed across the Clarence by steam-punts to Grafton, but the ocean steamers call at the wharf for cargo and passengers for transit to Sydney or elsewhere on every trip. South Grafton is incorporated under the Municipalities Act. The area of the city and suburban lands of South Grafton is about 870 acres.

GRAHAM (*Co. Bathurst*), a township, 30 miles from Cowra. The nearest railway station on the Blayney-Murrumburrah line.

GRAHAM'S CREEK (*Co. King*), a small western tributary of the Lachlan River, rising in the southern slope of Mount Darling, on the road from Cowra to Weeks.

GRAHAM'S VALLEY (*Co. Gough*), a post-office, 418 miles N. of Sydney, with mail once a week. The nearest railway station is Glencoe, 7 miles, on the northern line.

GRAHAMSTOWN (*Co. Buccleuch*), a postal village, 304 miles S. of Sydney, with daily mail. The nearest railway station is Gundagai, 16 miles, on the Cootamundra and Gundagai line.

GRAMAN (*Co. Burnett*), a post-office, 503 miles N. of Sydney, with mail twice a week.

GRAMAN CREEK (*Co. Burnett*), a small western tributary of the Macintyre River.

GRANNY'S FLAT CREEK (*Co. Beresford*), a small tributary of the Umaralla River, flowing into it about 4 miles N. of Nimmitabel.

GRANT'S CREEK (*Co. Westmoreland*), a tributary of Cox's River.

GRANT'S HEAD (*Co. Macquarie*), a rocky promontory lying a few miles to the N. of the entrance to Camden Haven.

GRANVILLE (*Co. Cumberland*), a postal suburb, 13 miles W. of Sydney, with daily mail. Telegraph and money-order offices, Government savings bank, and delivery by letter-carriers. A railway station on the suburban line. Granville is situated at the junction of the Great Western and Southern Railway lines, near Parramatta. It was proclaimed a borough in 1885, and is governed by eight aldermen and a mayor.

GRASSHOPPER ISLAND (*Co. St. Vincent*), a small rocky islet, lying off the coast 8 miles N. of Bateman's Bay.

GRASSTREE (*Co. Durham*), a railway station, 173 miles from Sydney, on the northern line.

GRATTAI (*Co. Wellington*), a small mining village on the Grattai Creek, about 6 miles N. of the township of Avisford, and forms part of the Meroo gold-fields.

GRAWAY (*Co. Flinders*), a township on Graway or Punjee Creek flowing in the county.

GREAT DIVIDING RANGE, is a chain of rugged and bold precipitous mountains, running N. and S., and nearly parallel to the sea-coast. This chain forms a portion of an immense cordillera, stretching without interruption through the whole length of the E. and S.E. coasts of Australia, and forming, through its whole extent, the main watershed of the country. The average elevation is about 3,500 feet, though some peaks are much higher. The Great Dividing Range is subdivided into :—1, New England Range ; 2, Liverpool Range ; 3, Blue Mountain Range ; 4, Cullarin Range ; 5, Gourock Range ; 6, Manaroo Range ; and 7, the Munion Range. In general, the middle or Blue Mountain part is a conglomerate of freestone, the S. of limestone, and the N. of trap formation.

GREAT FALLS (*Co. Sandon*), a waterfall on the Gyra Creek, about 5 miles to the E. of Armidale, also to three waterfalls on the Rocky River, near the town of Uralla.

GREAT SOUTHERN COLLIERY (*Co. Camden*), a postal receiving-office, 84 miles S. of Sydney, with mail three times a week.

GREENBACK BRANCH (*Co. Courallie*), a small watercourse connecting the Gwydir River and the Ana branch, near the township of Moree.

GREENDALE (*Co. Cumberland*), a postal village, 46 miles S. of Sydney. The nearest railway station is Penrith, 13 miles, on the southern line.

GREENFIELD FARM (*Co. Cumberland*), a postal village, 201 miles S. of Sydney, with mail twice a week. The nearest railway station is Yass, 17 miles, on the southern line.

GREENHILLS (*Co. Cumberland*), the first name given to the township of Morpeth.

GREENHILLS (*Co. Forbes*), a postal village, 314 miles N. of Sydney, with mail three times a week. Money-order office. The nearest railway station is Hexham, 187 miles, on the northern line.

GREENHILLS (*Co. Cumberland*), one of the original districts of New South Wales, bounded by the Richmond district and the Hawkesbury River.

GREEN ISLAND (*Co. St. Vincent*), a small rocky islet, lying off the entrance to the Conjurong Lake or Creek.

GREEN CAPE (*Co. Auckland*), a promontory standing boldly out into the ocean, about N.E. 15 miles from Cape Howe.

GREENMANTLE (*Co. Bathurst*), a post-office, 207 miles W. of Sydney, with mail once a week. The nearest railway station is Lyndhurst, 20 miles, on the Blayney-Murrumburrah line.

GREENOUGH'S GROUP (*Co. Livingstone*), a range of sandstone hills, lying in the vast flat between the Bogan and Darling Rivers.

GREENPOINT (*Co. Cumberland*), situated just inside of the inner S. head of Port Jackson.

GREENRIDGE (*Co. Richmond*), a postal receiving-office, 396 miles W. of Sydney, with mail per steamers.

GREEN SWAMP (*Co. Roxburgh*), a tract of marshy land in the parishes of Eskdale and Melrose, lying to the E. of Glenmire diggings.

GREEN VALLEY (*Co. Inglis*), a post-office, 318 miles N. of Sydney, with mail once a week.

GREEN VALLEY CREEK (*Co. Wellington*), a southern auriferous tributary of the Pyramul Creek, flowing on the eastern side of the Tambaroora gold-field. It rises in the Kangaroo Flat.

GREEN WATTLE CREEK (*Co. Wellington*), an auriferous tributary of the Tunnabidgee Creek, in the eastern part of the Tambaroora gold-fields.

GREEN WATTLE SWAMP (*Co. Wellington*), an auriferous flat, contiguous to the township of Windeyer. It is situated on the S. bank of the Tuunabidgee Creek.

GREENWELL POINT (*Co. St. Vincent*), a postal village, 132 miles S. of Sydney, with daily mail. Telegraph and money-order offices, and Government savings bank. The nearest railway station is Kiama, 34 miles, on the Illawarra and South Coast line. Situated on the Crookhaven, on the S. bank of the Shoalhaven River.

GREENWICH (*Co. Cumberland*), a postal suburb, 12½ miles W. of Sydney, with mail twice daily. It is an arm of the harbour on the N. side of the Parramatta River, in the parish of Willoughby, at the mouth of Lane Cove.

GREENWICH PARK (*Co. Cumberland*), a postal receiving-office, 126 miles S. of Sydney, with mail three times a week. The nearest railway station is Marulan, 14 miles, on the southern line.

GREGAAP CREEK (*Co. Wynyard*), a western tributary of O'Brien's Creek, to the S. of Wagga Wagga.

GREG GREG (*Co. Selwyn*), a township to the N. of Howlong, in same county.

GREGHAMSTOWN (*Co. Bathurst*), a postal receiving-office, 178 miles W. of Sydney, with mail twice a week.

GREGORY, a county in the Central Division of the Colony. [*See* "COUNTIES."]

GREGRA (*Co. Wellington*), a postal receiving-office, 233 miles W. of Sydney, with mail twice a week.

GREIG'S FLAT (*Co. Auckland*), a postal town, 343 miles S. of Sydney, with mail therefrom three days a week.

GRENFELL (*Co. Monteagle*), a postal town, 287 miles W. of Sydney, with daily mail. Telegraph and money-order offices, and Government savings bank, with delivery by letter-carriers. The nearest railway station is Cowra, 24 miles, on the Blayney-Murrumburrah line. Grenfell was incorporated a municipal district in 1883, and is governed by five aldermen and a mayor. The population is about 700. Courts of quarter sessions and district courts are held here periodically.

GRESFORD (*Co. Durham*), a postal village, 121 miles N. of Sydney, with daily mail. Telegraph and money-order offices, and Government savings bank. The nearest railway station is East Maitland, 28 miles, on the northern line. Situated on the Paterson River, about 1½ mile W. from the Allyn River. The district is an agricultural one, tobacco and corn being grown in large quantities. The vine is also extensively cultivated.

GRESHAM, a county in the Eastern Division of the Colony. [*See* "COUNTIES."]

GRETA (*Co. Northumberland*), a postal village, 130 miles N. of Sydney, with daily mail. Telegraph and money-order offices, Government savings bank, and delivery by letter-carriers. A railway station on the northern line. Situated on the Hunter River, about 11 miles W. of Maitland. It was incorporated a municipal district in 1890, and the population about 1,800.

GREY'S CREEK (*Co. Hunter*), a southern tributary of the river Hunter.

GREY RANGE (*Co. Tongowoko*), a chain of flat-topped hills to the W. of the Darling, attaining an elevation of 2,000 feet above sea-level. This range lies near the line dividing this Colony from South Australia.

GROGAN (*Co. Beresford*), a postal receiving-office, 274 miles S. of Sydney, with mail twice a week.

GROGAN'S CREEK (*Co. Beresford*,) a tributary of the Granny's Flat Creek, joining it about 4 miles on the road from Nimmitabel to Umaralla.

GRONG GRONG (*Co. Bourke*), a postal village, 334 miles S. of Sydney, with a daily mail. A railway station on the south-western line.

GROONGAL (*Co. Sturt*), a railway station 411 miles from Sydney, on the south-western line.

GROSE CREEK (*Co. Vernon*), a small eastern tributary of the head of the Ohio Creek.

GROSE FARM (*Co. Cumberland*), lying within the municipality of Newtown, and upon which the University of Sydney and the affiliated colleges are built.

GROSE'S PLAINS (*Co. Wallace*), lying to the S. of the Moamba River, and crossed by the road from Cooma to Gippsland via Jindabyne.

GROSE RIVER (*Co. Cook*). [*See* " RIVERS."]

GROSE VALE (*Co. Cook*), a postal village, 48 miles W. of Sydney, with daily mail.

GROSE VALLEY (*Co. Cook*), a stupendous ravine on the Blue Mountains, being a precipitous rocky chasm between Mount Hay on the S., and Mount Tomah and King George on the N. At the bottom of this chasm, the Grose, at a depth of 3,000 feet from the summit of the mountain, meanders.

GROTTO POINT (*Co. Cumberland*), a bold rocky point, being the northern head of Middle Harbour, on the N. shore of Port Jackson.

GROWEE SWAMP (*Co. Phillip*), a swampy county lying on the E. of the road from Dabee to Merriwa.

GRUBBENBUN CREEK (*Co. Bathurst*), a southern tributary of the Belubula River, to the S. of Lyndhurst.

GUANGUA CREEK (*Co. Brisbane*), an eastern tributary of Wybong Creek.

GUDGENBY HILL (*Co. Cowley*), a lofty peak in the southern part of the Murrumbidgee range of mountains, lying on the road from Queanbeyan to Kiandra.

GUDGENBY RIVER (*Co. Cowley*). [*See* " RIVERS."]

GUILDFORD (*Co. Cumberland*), a postal suburb, 17 miles S. of Sydney, with daily mail. It is a railway station on the southern line.

GUINECOR CREEK (*Co. Argyle*), a fine stream rising near Teralga, flowing eastward into the Wollondilly River.

GUISE'S CREEK (*Co. Murray*), a small stream rising in the eastern bank of the Upper Murrumbidgee River, between Queanbeyan and Jingery.

GULARGAMBONE (*Co. Lincoln*), a postal village, 352 miles W. of Sydney, with mail three times a week. Telegraph and money-order offices. The nearest railway station is Dubbo, 17 miles, on the western line.

GULF, THE (*Co. Phillip*), a passage over the Blue Mountains, on the road from Dabee to Merriwa.

GULF CREEK (*Co. Cowley*), a small mountain tributary to the Murrumbidgee River near its source, rising in Mount Murray, and flowing through the Gulf diggings.

GULF CREEK (*Co. Ashburnham*), a small northern tributary of the head of the Billabong Creek.

GULF FORD (*Cos. Wallace and Wellesley*), the crossing place over the Snowy River, of the old track into Gippsland, near Mount Jewrena.

GULF GOLD-FIELD (*Co. Dampier*), a gold-field lying on the N. side of the Tuross River.

GULGAMREE (*Co. Roxburgh*), a postal receiving-office, 154 miles W. of Sydney, with mail twice a week.

GULGIN MOUNT (*Co. Wellesley*), a peak in a range lying on the S. bank of the Maharatta Creek, S. of Bombala.

GULGONG (*Co. Phillip*), a postal town, 202 miles W. of Sydney, with daily mail. Telegraph and money-order offices, and Government savings bank. The nearest railway station is Mudgee, 20 miles, on the western line. It was incorporated a municipal district in 1876, and is governed by eight aldermen and a mayor.

GULLEN (*Co. King*), a postal village, 155 miles S. of Sydney, with mail three times a week. The nearest railway station is Goulburn, 16 miles, on the southern line.

GULLENDADDY (*Co. Pottinger*), a township to the W. of Gunnedah, on the N.E. railway.

GULLENGALONG MOUNT (*Co. Hunter*), a peak of the Hunter Range, lying near the bed of the Tupa Creek.

GULLIGAL (*Co. Pottinger*), a township, 276 miles N. of Sydney, situated on the Gulligal or Sparke's Lagoon, about 1¼ mile S. of the Namoi River, and 20 miles S. of the Dividing Range, between the Liverpool Plains and the Gwydir district. The nearest township is Gunnedah, 16 miles E.

GULLIGAL MOUNT (*Co. Inglis*), a high solitary peak lying on the western side of the Mulucrindie Creek, near the township of Bendemeer.

GULONG MOUNT (*Co. Northumberland*), a high peak in the Hunter Range, in the parish of Blaxland, and to the S.W. of Wollombi township.

GULPA CREEK (*Co. Townsend*), lying between Deniliquin and the Tuppal Creek, and the upper portion of the Edward River.

GULPH CREEK (*Co. Dampier*), a small creek flowing into the Tuross River, through the Gulph or Gulf gold-fields.

GUM CREEK (*Co. Ashburnham*), a small stream flowing into the Belubula River, below Canowindra.

GUM FLAT (*Co. Murchison*), a postal town, 426 miles N. of Sydney, with mail daily.

GUNBAR (*Co. Nicholson*), a postal town, 506 miles S. of Sydney, with mail three times a week. Money-order office. The nearest railway station is Carrathool, 35 miles, on the south-western line.

GUNDABLUI (*Co. Finch*), a proclaimed township on the Moorne River, on the Queensland border.

GUNDAGAI (*Co. Clarendon*), a postal town, 287 miles S. of Sydney, with daily mail. Telegraph and money-order offices, Government savings bank, and delivery by letter-carrier. A railway station on the Cootamundra and Gundagai line. Situated on the Murrumbidgee River, in the police district of Gundagai. The river is navigable up to this place. The district is an agricultural, pastoral, and mining one. There is a court-house where the quarter and petty sessions and the district court are held. It was incorporated a municipal district in 1889, and is governed by eight aldermen and a mayor.

GUNDAGAI SOUTH (*Co. Buccleuch*), a postal town, 289 miles S. of Sydney, with daily mail. The nearest railway station is Gundagai, 7 miles, on the Cootamundra and Gundagai line. Situated on the S. bank of the Murrumbidgee River, opposite to the township of Gundagai proper, and near the Stony, Big Ben, and Adelong Creeks, and in the Police District of Gundagai. A bridge across the river connects South Gundagai with the township proper. Gundagai was proclaimed a municipality in December, 1871, with a governing body of eight aldermen and a mayor, with a population of about 4,700. Courts of quarter sessions and district courts are held at Gundagai periodically.

GUNDAROO (*Co. Murray*), a town, 175 miles to the S. of Sydney. It is situated on the Yass River, and 8 miles N. of Lake George. The nearest railway station is Gunning, 20 miles, on the Albury and Melbourne line.

GUNDAMULDA CREEK (*Co. Murchison*), a southern tributary of Middle Creek, forming portion of the Bingara Gold-fields.

GUNDARIMA (*Co. Richmond*), a small cedar cutting and farming settlement, in the police district of Richmond, situated on the N. arm of the Richmond River, 4 miles from Lismore.

GUNDAROO CREEK (*Co. King*), a tributary of the Yass River, rising to the E. of Mount Chaton, falling into the Yass River at the township of Gundaroo.

GUNDERBOOKA, a county in the Western Division of the Colony. [*See* "COUNTIES."]

GUNDERMAN CREEK (*Co. Northumberland*), a small northern tributary of the lower end of the Hawkesbury River, falling into it near Wiseman's Ferry.

GUNDURIMBAH (*Co. Rous*), a postal town, 363 miles N. of Sydney, with mails per steamers ; telegraph office.

GUNDY (*Co. Brisbane*), a postal village, 200 miles N. of Sydney, with mail twice a week. The nearest railway station is Scone, 10 miles, on the northern line.

GUNERAI (*Co. Burnett*), a township, on the Horton River, a tributary of the Gwydir River.

GUNGAL (*Co. Brisbane*), a postal village, 212 miles N. of Sydney, with daily mail. The nearest railway station is Musclebrook, 34 miles, on the northern line.

GUNGAL CREEK (*Co. Brisbane*), a northern tributary of the Goulburn River.

GUNGARLIN MOUNT (*Co. Wallace*), a lofty peak in the Munioug Range attaining an elevation of 5,337 ft. above the sea-level.

GUNGARLIN RIVER (*Co. Wallace*), a mountain stream, near the head of the Snowy River, rising in the Munion Range. [*See* "RIVERS."]

GUNGUDDY CREEK (*Co. Phillip*), a small tributary at the head of the Cudgegong River, rising in Mount Darambang.

GUNGULWA CREEK (*Co. Hunter*), a western tributary of Guy's Creek.

GUNIPERMUEKO MOUNT (*Albert District*), a flat topped hill, lying on W. bank of the Darling River.

GUNNEDAH (*Co. Pottinger*), a postal town, 295 miles N. of Sydney, with daily mail, telegraph and money-order offices. Government savings bank, and delivery by letter-carrier. A railway station on the north-western line. The district is an agricultural and pastoral one. Gunnedah was incorporated a municipal district in 1885, and is governed by eight aldermen and a mayor, with a population of about 1,100. Courts of quarter sessions and district courts are held at Gunnedah periodically.

GUNNEL CREEK (*Co. Wellington*), a small tributary of the Gudgegong River, flowing into it to the S.W. of the Louisa Creek Gold-fields.

GUNNING (*Co. King*), a postal village, 164 miles S. of Sydney, with daily mail, telegraph, money-order offices, and Government savings bank. A railway station on the southern line. Situated on Meadow Creek, in the parish of Gunning, the Lachlan River being 3 miles N.E., and the Jerrawa Creek 8 miles S.W.

GUNNING CREEK (*Co. Gregory*), an eastern tributary of the Bogan River, rising on the W. bank of the Macquarie River, in the county of Oxley. It is fed by the Beleringa Creek.

GUNNING REACH (*Co. Wellesley*), a lofty peak in the bold ranges on the Cambalong Creek, about 16 miles S.W. of Bombala.

**GUNTAWANG** (*Co. Phillip*), a postal village, 193 miles W. of Sydney, with mail four times a week. The nearest railway station is Mudgee, 16 miles, on the western line. Situated on the E. bank of the Cudgegong Creek, in the parish of Guntawang.

**GUOGONG MOUNT** (*Co. Westmoreland*), a hill on the S. bank of Cox's River, near the confluence of Konangoola Creek.

**GURRAVEMBI CREEK** (*Co. Dudley*), a fine mountain stream, rising on Mount Yarrahapini, and flowing into the ocean, about 10 miles N. of Trial Bay.

**GURRUNDAH** (*Co. Argyle*), a postal receiving-office, 156 miles S. of Sydney, with mail once a week. The nearest railway station is Bredalbane, 11 miles, on the southern line.

**GUY FAWKES RIVER** (*Co. Clarke*). [See "RIVERS."]

**GUY'S RANGE** (*Co. Wallace*), a range of rocky mountains, on the road from Cooma to Gippsland, via Buckley's crossing-place.

**GUYONG** (*Co. Bathurst*), a postal village, 184 miles W. of Sydney, with mail three times a week and money-order office. The nearest railway station is Milthorpe, 6 miles, on the western line. Situated in the source of the Lewis Ponds Creek, in the parish of Colville, police district of Orange, about 16 miles S. of the Ophir diggings, and the confluence of the Summerhill Creek. The district is well adapted for agricultural and pastoral purposes. It also abounds in gold, copper, lead, black sand, and sulphur.

**GUYRA** (*Co. Clarke*), a postal village, 385 miles N. of Sydney, with daily mail, telegraph and money-order office and Government savings bank; a railway station on the western line.

**GWILLIE** (*Co. Gunderbooka*), a township on the banks of the Warrego River, to the N. of its confluence with the Darling.

**GWYDIR RIVER** (*Cos. of Benarba and Courallie*). [See "RIVERS."]

**GYRA RIVER** (*Co. Sandon*). [See "RIVERS."]

**GYRO** (*Co. Macquarie*), a small agricultural village, situated on the Barnard River.

# H

**HACKING CREEK** (*Co. Cumberland*), a small creek flowing into the head of Port Hacking from a southerly direction.

**HACKING (PORT)** (*Co. Cumberland*), a fine harbour situated about 18 miles S. of Port Jackson. The Cronulla Beach lies at its N. entrance. Port Hacking is only available for small craft.

**HALF-MOON BAY** (*Co. Cumberland*), a small bight in the western shore of Long Cove.

**HALF-WAY CREEK** (*Co. Clarence*), a postal receiving-office, 518 miles N. of Sydney, with mail therefrom once a week.

HALF-WAY CREEK (*Co. Clarence*), a small tributary at the head of the Dundoo Creek.

HALL (*Co. Murray*), a postal village, 192 miles S. of Sydney, with mail daily.

HALL'S CREEK (*Co. Darling*), a southern tributary of the Mulueriudie, rising in the western slope of Mount Gulligal, and flowing into the main stream N.E. of Manilla.

HALL'S LAGOON (*Co. Courallie*), a small creek or series of water-holes flowing into the Gwydir River, near Moree.

HALLIDAY'S POINT (*Co. Gloucester*), a sandy beach, lying about half-way between Cape Hawke on the S. and Farquhar inlet on the N.

HALTON (*Co. Durham*), a postal receiving-office, 160 miles N. of Sydney, with mail three times a week. The nearest railway station is East Maitland, 24 miles, on the East Maitland and Morpeth line.

HAMBURG (*Co. Northumberland*), an agricultural settlement, situated near Waratah, about 8 miles W. of Newcastle.

HAMILTON (*Co. Northumberland*), a postal township, 100 miles S. of Sydney, with mail twice daily; telegraph and money-order offices, Government savings bank, and delivery by letter-carrier. A railway station on the Newcastle and Lake Macquarie line. It was proclaimed a municipal district in 1871, with eight aldermen and a mayor. Population, 4,700.

HAMILTON PLAINS (*Co. Mitchell*), a tract of fine agricultural land, lying on the Murrumbidgee River, 20 miles S. of Narrandera.

HAMMILL'S CREEK (*Co. Bathurst*), a small creek at the head of the Waugoola Creek.

HANGING ROCK (*Co. Parry*), a postal village, 327 miles N. of Sydney, with mail three times a week. The nearest railway station is Tamworth, 46 miles, on the northern line. Situated on the Oakenville Creek; the rivers Peel, Barnet, and Manning taking their rise in the surrounding mountains. The district is principally a mining one, both alluvial and quartz.

HANGING ROCK (*Co. Northumberland*), a remarkable block of red sandstone on the bank of the Wollombi Brook, N. of Mount Colabeen.

HANGING ROCK (*Co. Goulburn*), a town, 2 miles from The Rock station on the Albury and Melbourne line.

HANGING ROCK (*Co. Parry*), a lofty peak of the Liverpool Range, attaining an altitude of 3,413 feet above sea-level.

HANGING ROCK CREEK (*Co. Parry*), a small auriferous eastern tributary of the upper end of the Peel River, rising in the western slope of the Australian Alps, and flowing into the main stream between Nundle and Dungowany.

HAPPY VALLEY (*Co. Parry*), an auriferous gully, lying between Wallabadah and Hanging Rock.

o

HARDEN, a county, in the Eastern Division of the Colony. [See "COUNTIES."]

HARDEN (*Co. Harden*), a postal village, 228 miles S. of Sydney, with daily mail. Telegraph and money-order offices, and Government savings bank. A railway station on the Blayney-Murrumburrah line.

HARDINGE, a county, in the Eastern Division of the Colony. [See "COUNTIES."]

HARDINGE (*Co. Cumberland*), is a hundred which comprises the parishes of Maroota, Cornelia, and Frederick.

HARDWICK RANGE (*Liverpool Plains*). [See "NUNDEWAR RANGE."]

HAREFIELD (*Co. Clarendon*), a postal village, 294 miles S. of Sydney, with daily mail. A railway station on the southern line.

HARGRAVE (*Co. Wellington*). [See "LOUISA CREEK."]

HARGRAVES (*Co. Wellington*), a postal town, 190 miles W. of Sydney, with mail four times a week. Telegraph and money-order offices. The nearest railway station is Mudgee on the Wallerawang and Mudgee line.

HARNHAM HILL (*Co. Sandon*), a spur of the main Dividing Range, lying 6 miles S. of the township of Uralla, in the parish of Harnham. It attains an elevation of 3,681 feet above sea-level.

HARRINGTON (*Co. Macquarie*), a postal village, 250 miles N. of Sydney with mail twice a week, and telegraph office.

HARRINGTON INLET (*Co. Macquarie*), is the entrance to the Manning River, the N. head of which is known as Crowdy Head.

HARRIS CREEK (*Co. Monteagle*), a small western tributary of the Cookoomingala Creek, falling into it near its junction with the Burrowa River.

HARRIS' LAGOON (*Co. Harden*), a waterhole on the Burrowa River, in the parish of Eubindai, to the W. of the village reserve of Kangiaroo.

HARRIS MOUNT (*Co. Gregory*), a barren granite rock, on the Macquarie River, about 40 miles N. of Warren.

HARRIS PARK (*Co. Cumberland*), a railway station, 14 miles from Sydney, on the suburban line.

HARRISON MOUNT (*Co. Leichhardt*). [See "MOUNT BOOLEMDILE."]

HARRY'S, OR MIDDLE CREEK (*Co. Brisbane*), a western tributary of the head of the Merriwa Creek.

HARTLEY (*Co. Westmoreland*), a postal town, 83 miles W. of Sydney, with daily mail and money-order office. The nearest railway station is Mount Victoria, 7 miles, on the western line. Situated on the river Lett, in the parish of Hartley. The rivers Cox and Warragamba flow within a short distance; Mount York lies 3 miles E.; Mount Clarence 3 miles, Hassan's Wells 3 miles, and Mount Blaxland 5 miles. The district abounds in coal and kerosene shale.

HARTLEY LITTLE (*Co. Westmoreland*), a hamlet, contiguous to the township of Hartley on the river Lett, in the S.E. corner of the Vale of Clwydd. [*See "* SLATTERY."]

HARTLEY VALE (*Co. Westmoreland*), a postal village, 81 miles W. of Sydney, with daily mail. It is a railway station on the western line.

HARWOOD ISLAND (*Co. Clarence*) a postal village, 320 miles N. of Sydney, with mail per steamers to the Clarence. Telegraph and money-order offices and Government savings bank.

HARWOOD ISLANDS (*Co. Clarence*), a group of low islands formed by the various channels of the estuary of the Clarence River. Very fertile and mostly occupied by small settlers.

HASLEM'S CREEK (*Co. Cumberland*), about 11 miles W. of Sydney, on the suburban line of railway. The Necropolis is situated here.

HASSAN'S CREEK (*Co. Clarence*), a small tributary of Gordon's Creek.

HASSAN'S WALLS (*Co. Westmoreland*), a steep chain of sandstone hills overlooking the Vale of Hartley, and being part of the Blue Mountain Range.

HASTINGS POINT (*Co. Rous*), a small sandy point, forming the S. head of a lagoon on the coast between Cape Byron and Point Danger.

HASTINGS RANGE (*Co. Hawes*), a branch of the New England Range, and forms the water-shed between the Macleay and Hastings Rivers. It is very lofty, attaining an elevation of 6,000 feet above the sea-level.

HASTINGS RIVER (*Co. Macquarie*). [*See* "RIVERS."]

HAT HILL (*Co. Northumberland*). [*See* "MOUNT WARRAWOLONG."]

HATFIELD (*Co. Kilfera*), a post-office, 655 miles S. of Sydney, with mail twice a week.

HAVILAH (*Co. Wellington*), a railway station, 177 miles W. from Sydney, on the western line.

HAWDON PLAIN (*Cos. Tara and Windeyer*), bounded on the S. by the Murray, and on the E. by the Darling River, lying in the S.W. corner of the colony.

HAWES, a county in the Eastern Division of the Colony. [*See* "COUNTIES."]

HAWKE CAPE (*Co. Gloucester*), a rocky promontory, standing boldly out into the ocean. It is situated 16 miles to the N. of Sugarloaf Point. From Cape Hawke to Manning River the land is generally low and unbroken.

HAWKE CAPE (*Co. Gloucester*) lies on the Maclean and Wollombi Rivers, on Lake Wallis, and on the sea-coast. It is a small agricultural and timber-cutting settlement.

HAWKE'S NEST (*Co. Durham*), a postal village, 148 miles N. of Sydney, with mail three times a week. Money-order office and Government savings bank. The nearest railway station is Hexham, 40 miles, on the northern line.

HAWKESBURY RAILWAY STATION (*Co. Northumberland*), a station 36 miles from Sydney, on the Ryde and Hawkesbury River line.

HAWKESBURY RIVER (*Cos. Northumberland, Cumberland, Cook, and Camden*). [*See* "RIVERS."]

HAWKIN'S CREEK (*Co. Darling*), a small southern tributary of the Manilla River.

HAWKIN'S CREEK (*Co. Phillip*), a tributary of Lawson's Creek, rising in the western slope of the Australian Alps, and flowing into that creek near Dungaree.

HAY (*Co. Waradgery*), a postal town, 454 miles S. of Sydney, with mail five times a week. Telegraph and money-order offices, Government savings bank, and delivery by letter-carrier. Situated in the parish of Hay, and a railway station on the south-western line. When the river is navigable, steamers ply between this township and Adelaide, Goolwa, and Echuca. The township is prettily situated in a bend of the Murrumbidgee River. It was proclaimed a municipal district in 1872, with eight aldermen and a mayor. The population is about 2,700. Sittings of the supreme court, courts of quarter sessions, and district courts are held at Hay periodically.

HAY MOUNT (*Co. Cook*), a lofty peak of the Blue Mountains, lying on the S. bank of the Grose River, and forming one of the precipitous sides of the tremendous ravine known as the Grose Valley.

HAY SOUTH (*Co. Waradgery*), a proclaimed township on the S. side of the Murrumbidgee River, opposite Hay.

HAYCOCK PEAK (*Co. Wellesley*), is the highest elevation of a western spur of the South Coast Range, in the parish of Coolanbooka, two miles E. of the township of Bombala.

HAYCOCK REACH (*Co. Northumberland*) is a part of the Hawkesbury River, lying above Mangrove Creek.

HAYDONTON (*Co. Brisbane*), a postal township, 217 miles N. of Sydney, with mail twice daily. The nearest railway station is Murrurundi, 1 mile, on the northern line.

HAYSTACK MOUNT (*Co. Roxburgh*), a lofty hill lying at the head of Carwell Creek, about 6 miles S. of Rylstone.

HAYSTACKS (*Co. Nandewar*), two picturesque peaks of the Nandewar Range, lying about 12 miles E. of the township of Narrabri.

HAZLEBROOK (*Co. Cook*), a railway station, 56 miles from Sydney, on the southern line.

HAZLEGROVE (*Co. Westmoreland*), a postal town, 132 miles W. of Sydney, with daily mail.

HEATHCOTE (*Co. Cumberland*), a postal village, 20 miles S. of Sydney, with daily mail. A railway station on the Hurstville and Waterfall line.

HEBERSHAM CREEK (*Co. Cumberland*) is in the parish of Rooty Hill, 24 miles to the W. of Sydney. The nearest railway station is Blacktown, 3 miles, on the western line. Situated on the Eastern Creek, which flows through the lower part of the township.

HEDGERS, a town, 87 miles from Mudgee, the nearest railway station on the Wallerawang and Mudgee line.

HEFFRON'S GULLY (*Co. Phillip*), situated on the N.E. side of the Blue Mountains, near the Gap between Dabee and Merriwa.

HELENSBURGH (*Co. Cumberland*), a postal village, 27 miles S. of Sydney, with mail twice daily. A railway station on the Illawarra and South Coast line.

HELL'S HOLE CREEK (*Co. Roxburgh*), a tributary of the Jabuck-Jabuck Creek, flowing in the parish of Watton.

HEN AND CHICKEN BAY (*Co. Cumberland*), on the S. side of the Parramatta River, about 5 miles W. of Sydney, and opposite the village of Ryde.

HENRY RIVER (*Co. Gough*), a small stream rising near Mount Mitchell, flowing E. into the Boyd River, near Barney's Hill. [*See* "RIVERS."]

HENTY (*Co. Hume*), a postal village, 316 miles S. of Sydney, with daily mail.

HERMITAGE PLAINS (*Co. Flinders*), a postal village, 407 miles W. of Sydney, with mail three times a week. The nearest railway station is Nyngan, 46 miles, on the western line.

HERVEY'S RANGE (*Co. Gordon*), a chain of low hills with occasional high peaks, which lies to the S.W. of Wellington, and divides the waters of the Bogan from those of the Macquarie River.

HERVEY'S RANGE CREEK (*Co. Gordon*), a western tributary of the Little River, joining it near the township of Obley.

HEXHAM (*Co. Cumberland*), a postal village, 108 miles N. of Sydney, with daily mail, telegraph, and money-order office, and Government savings bank. A railway station on the northern line. Situated in the parish of Hexham, lying on the S. bank of the Hunter River, between Newcastle and East Maitland.

HEXHAM SWAMPS (*Co. Northumberland*), a large tract of marshy land, in the parish of Hexham, between that township and Minmi. The greater portion of the swamps are submerged by the overflow of the Hunter River during rainy seasons.

HIAWATHA (*Co. Gipps*), a township near Englo Creek.

HICKEY'S CREEK (*Co. Dudley*), a postal village, 320 miles N. of Sydney, with mail twice a week. The nearest railway station is Hexham, 208 miles, on the northern line. The creek is a small northern tributary of the Macleay River.

HIDE'S CREEK (*Co. Parry*), a small auriferous tributary of the Peel River, joining it at Bowling Alley Point diggings.

HIGH PEAK (*Co. Clive*), a peak on the mountain known as the Doctor's Nose, near Tenterfield.

HIGH-STREET STATION (*Co. Northumberland*), a railway station on the northern line, 19 miles N. of Newcastle.

HIGHAM ROAD (*Co. Northumberland*), a township, 4 miles from Waratah, the nearest railway station on the northern line.

HIGHEST PEAK (*Co. Buccleuch*). [*See* "BLOWERING MOUNTAINS."]

HIGHLANDS (*Co. Cook*), a tract of fine agricultural country, on the south bank of the Hawkesbury River, near the township of Richmond.

HILL END (*Co. Wellington*), a postal village, 205 miles W. of Sydney, with mail three times a week. Telegraph and money-order offices, Government savings bank, and delivery by letter-carriers. The nearest railway station is Bathurst, 60 miles, on the western line. It was proclaimed a borough in 1873, with eight aldermen and a mayor. The population is about 500.

HILLAS CREEK (*Co. Wynyard*). [*See* "YAVEN-YAVEN CREEK."]

HILLAS CREEK (*Co. Wynyard*), a postal village. 311 miles S. of Sydney, with mail three times a week. The nearest railway station is Gundagai, 25 miles, on the Cootamundra and Gundagai line.

HILLGROVE (*Co. Sandon*), a postal village, 381 miles N. of Sydney, with daily mail, telegraph and money-order offices, and Government savings bank. The nearest railway station is Armidale, 22 miles, on the northern line.

HILLSTON NORTH (*Co. Nicholson*), a proclaimed township, on the N. bank of the Lachlan River, opposite to Hillstone.

HILLSTON (*Co. Nicholson*), a postal town, 435 miles S. of Sydney, with mail four times a week, telegraph and money-order offices, and Government savings bank. The nearest railway station is Carathool, 70 miles, on the south-western line. It was proclaimed a municipal district in 1888, with five aldermen and a mayor. Courts of quarter sessions and district courts are held here periodically.

HILLTOP (*Co. Cook*), a postal village, 69 miles S. of Sydney, with daily mail. A railway station on the southern line.

HINDMARSH (*Co. Richmond*). [*See* "TRAVELLER'S REST."]

HINDMARSH CREEK (*Co. Wynyard*), a small auriferous tributary of the Adelong Creek, on the Adelong gold-fields.

HINTON (*Co. Durham*), a postal town, 122 miles N. of Sydney, with daily mail. The nearest railway station is Morpeth, 2 miles, on the East Maitland and Morpeth line. Situated in the parish of Hinton, at the junction of the Paterson and Hunter Rivers, and to the S. of the Mount Royal ranges. The district is an agricultural one.

HOBBES' MOUNT (*Co. Argyle*). [*See* "SUGARLOAF."]

HOBBY'S YARD (*Co. Bathurst*), a postal village, 172 miles W. of Sydney, with daily mail. The nearest railway station is Newbridge, 9 miles, on the western line.

HOGAN'S CREEK (*Co. Gough*), a small tributary of the upper end of the Severn River, flowing into it at the village of Severn or Dundee.

HOLDSWORTHY (*Co. Cumberland*), one of the original districts of the country, bounded by George's River on one side and Bunbury Curren Creek on the other.

HOLDSWORTHY DOWNS (*Co. Brisbane*), an elevated flat, situated above the confluence of the Dartbrook with the Kingdon Ponds, 178 miles to the N. of Sydney, about a mile to the W. of Scone.

HOLT'S FLAT (*Co. Beresford*), a postal village, 292 miles S. of Sydney, with mail four times a week. The nearest railway station is Cooma, 22 miles, on the Goulburn and Cooma line.

HOLMWOOD (*Co. Bathurst*), a railway station, 209 miles W. of Sydney, on the Murrumburrah and Blayney line.

HOMEBUSH (*Co. Cumberland*), a postal suburb, 8 miles S. of Sydney, with mail three times daily. Money-order office and Government savings bank, and delivery by letter-carriers. A railway station on the suburban line, situated in the parish of Concord.

HOME RULE (*Co. Phillip*), a postal village, 195 miles W. of Sydney, with daily mail, money-order office, and Government savings bank. The nearest railway station is Mudgee, 14 miles, on the western line.

HONEY'S CREEK (*Co. Hardinge*), a small western auriferous tributary of the Kentucky Ponds, forming part of the Rocky River diggings.

HONEYSUCKLE (*Co. Auckland*), an agricultural village, lying about 12 miles W. of Pambula.

HONEYSUCKLE CREEK (*Co. Goulburn*), a small tributary of the Murray River, falling into the main stream near Dora.

HONEYSUCKLE CREEK (*Co. Hardinge*), is one of the heads of the Gwydir River, and is an auriferous creek in the Rocky River or Uralla gold-fields.

HONEYSUCKLE HILL (*Co. Cook*), a lofty peak of the Blue Mountain Range, attaining an elevation of about 4,000 feet.

HONEYSUCKLE HILL (*Co. Roxburgh*), a lofty peak in the Blue Mountain Range, attaining an aititude height of 4,000 feet above sea level, lying in the parish of Falnash, and on the W. of the township of Rydal.

HONEYSUCKLE POINT (*Co. Northumberland*), a railway station on the Newcastle and Lake Macquarie line.

HONEYSUCKLE RANGES (*Co. Buccleuch*), a range of hills, lying on the E. of the Tumut River, and about 10 miles from the township of Gundagai.

HOPEFIELD (*Co. Hume*), a postal receiving-office, 434 miles S. of Sydney, with mail once a week.

HOPELESS MOUNT (*Co. Clyde*), a lofty hill, on the W. bank of the Bogan River, about 36 miles N.W. of Canonbar.

HORE'S SWAMP (*Co. Goulburn*), situate about 8 miles S.W. of the village of Dora, on the Murray River and Hore's Creek.

HORE'S SWAMP CREEK (*Co. Goulburn*), a northern tributary of the Murray River, and flowing into the main stream at Wagra.

HORNING CREEK (*Co. Northumberland*), a small tributary of the estuary of the Mangrove Creek.

HORNSBY JUNCTION (*Co. Cumberland*), a postal village, 21 miles N. of Sydney, with daily mail. A railway station at the Hornsby junction, on the Sydney and Newcastle line. Situate in the parish of Colah. The district is an agricultural one, and large quantities of oranges and other fruits are grown here to supply the Sydney market.

HORSHAM CREEK (*Co. Murchison*), a small western tributary of Maule's Creek.

HORTON RIVER (*Co. Murchison*). [*See* "RIVERS."]

HOSKINGTOWN (*Co. Murray*), a postal village, 221 miles S. of Sydney, with mail three times a week. Money-order office. The nearest railway station is Bungendore, 12 miles on the Goulburn and Cooma line.

HOSKINSON'S CREEK (*Co. Darling*), a small western tributary of the Manilla River.

HOULAHAN'S CREEK (*Co. Clarendon*), a northern tributary of the Murrumbidgee River, flowing to the N. of Wagga Wagga into the main stream about 3 miles W. of that township.

HOUSE CREEK (*Co. Selwyn*), a tributary of the Murray River, flowing into it, E. of Jingelloc.

HOUSEFLAT CREEK (*Co. Goulburn*), a small creek, rising in Mount Jergyle, and flowing S. into the Dora Creek.

HOVELL CREEK (*Co. King*), a southern tributary of the Lachlan River, flowing past Mount Darling through Burrowa Plains.

HOWE CAPE (*Co. Auckland*), a rocky promontory, about 240 miles S. from Sydney, at the dividing point on the coast between Victoria and New South Wales.

HOWE'S VALLEY (*Co. Durham*), a postal village, 188 miles N. of Sydney, with daily mail. The nearest railway station is Singleton, 45 miles, on the northern line.

HOWLONG (*Co. Hume*), a postal town, 405 miles S. of Sydney, with mail twice a week, telegraph and money-order offices, and Government savings bank. The nearest railway station is Gerogery, 15 miles on the southern line. Situated in the parish of Hume, on the river Murray, and is a border township. The grape-vine and tobacco are successfully cultivated here.

HOXTON PARK (*Co. Cumberland*), a post office, 26 miles S. of Sydney, with mail twice a week.

HUGEL MOUNT (*Co. Wynyard*), a high peak, lying on the E. bank of Darlow's Creek, about 9 miles from Adelong.

HULK BAY (*Co. Cumberland*). [*See* "LAVENDER BAY."]

HUME, a county, partly in the Central and Eastern Divisions of the Colony. [*See* "COUNTIES."]

HUMULA (*Co. Wynyard*), a postal village, 479 miles S. of Sydney, with mail three times a week.

HUNGERFORD (*Co. Urana*), a postal village, 643 miles W. of Sydney, with mail once a week. The nearest railway station is Bourke, 140 miles, on the western line.

HUNGRY FLAT (*Co. Northumberland*), a flat, on the Great North Road from Sydney to Maitland, lying near the Darling Range of mountains.

HUNGRY HILL (*Co. Clarke*), a high hill, lying about 6 miles N. of Giro, on the New England route.

HUNTER, a county in the Eastern Division of the County. [*See* "COUNTIES."]

HUNTER PORT (*Co. Northumberland*). [*See* "NEWCASTLE."]

HUNTER RANGE (*Cos. Hunter and Durham*), a branch of the Blue Mountain Range, separating the tributaries of the Hawkesbury from those of the Hunter. The principal summit is Coricudgy.

HUNTER RIVER (*Cos. Northumberland, Durham, and Hunter*.) [*See* "RIVERS."]

HUNTER'S BAY AND BEACH (*Co. Cumberland*), a beautiful sandy beach, at the S. side of the entrance to Middle Harbour from Port Jackson. Balmoral is situated on the opposite side of the Bay.

HUNTER'S HILL (*Co. Cumberland*), a postal suburb, 4 miles W. from Sydney, with mail twice a day. Telegraph and money-order offices, Government savings bank, and delivery by letter-carriers. The nearest railway station is Ryde, 4 miles on the Ryde and Hawkesbury River line. Situated in the parish of Hunter's Hill, on the Parramatta and Lane Cove Rivers. The district is a favourite one, and numerous villa residences are scattered over it. The Parramatta steamers ply constantly to and from Sydney. It was proclaimed a municipality in 1861, with eight aldermen and a mayor. Population, 3,500.

HUNT'S LOOK OUT (*Co. Harden*), a lofty eminence on the W. bank of Barber's Creek, above Bojolara Waterfalls and S.W. of Bookham.

HUNTINGDON (*Co. Macquarie*), a postal village, 290 miles N. of Sydney, with mail three times a week. The nearest railway station is Hexham, 164 miles, on the northern line. Situated in the parish of Huntingdon, on the S. bank of the river Hastings, about 20 miles from its mouth.

HUNTLEY (*Co. Bathurst*), a railway station, 186 miles from Sydney, on the western line.

HUON (*Co. Goulburn*), a proclaimed village in the county.

HURDLE CREEK (*Co. Cowley*), a small western tributary of the Tidbinbilla Creek to the N. of Mount Tidbinbilla.

HURSLEY *(Co. Macquarie)*, a township, 256 miles N. of Sydney, in the parish of Hursley, on a navigable branch of the Hastings River, Morton Creek, also navigable, being about 4 miles distant, and Rawdon Island lying directly opposite.

HURSTVILLE *(Co. Cumberland)*, a postal suburb, 9 miles S. of Sydney, with mail twice a day. Telegraph and money-order offices and delivery by letter-carriers. A railway station on the Hurstville and Waterfall line. It was proclaimed a municipal district in 1887, with eight aldermen and a mayor.

HUSKISSON *(Co. St. Vincent)*, a postal town, 145 miles S. of Sydney, with mail twice a week. The nearest railway station is Kiama, 47 miles, on the Illawarra and South Coast line. Situated on the W. bank of Jervis Bay, at the point where the Currambene Creek falls into it.

HYANDRA CREEK *(Co. Gordon)*, a western tributary of the Wylandra Creek.

HYALITE RIVER *(Co. Wakool)*. [*See* "EDWARD RIVER."]

HYNMAN'S CREEK *(Co. Macquarie)*, a small creek, flowing into the Hastings River, W. of Huntingdon.

HYTHE *(Co. Cumberland)*, situated on the N.E. of Five Dock Bay, near the old punt, over the Parramatta River.

# I

ICELY *(Co. Bathurst)*, a township 190 miles W. of Sydney. The nearest railway station is Millthorpe, 11 miles, on the western line.

ICELY MOUNT *(Co. Bathurst)*, a lofty mountain, on the E. bank of the Limestone Creek.

IDAVILLE *(Co. Brisbane)*, a postal town, 260 miles N. of Sydney, with mail therefrom once a week.

ILFORD *(Co. Roxburgh)*, a postal village, 138 miles W. of Sydney, with mail daily, and money-order office. A railway station on the western line.

ILLABO *(Co. Clarendon)*, a postal village, 276 miles S. of Sydney, with daily mail. Money-order office. A railway station on the southern line.

ILLABONG CREEK *(Co. Harden)*, a small creek, rising in the S. of Burrowa Plains, and flowing into the Jugiong Creek, near Binalong.

ILLALONG SWAMP *(Co. Northumberland)*, a swamp, lying to the E. of the township of Morpeth.

ILLAROO *(Co. Camden)*, an agricultural village, lying on the N. bank of the Shoalhaven River, 8 miles from Numba.

ILLAWARRA *(Co. Camden)*. The Illawarra district consists of a belt of land enclosed between the mountain and the ocean of exuberant fertility. It is truly called the garden of New South Wales. It is situated about 50 miles S. of Sydney, and the Illawarra and South Coast line of railway runs through the district. The coal-seams crop out on the face of the escarpment of the mountain which is quite perpendicular, attaining a height of 1,500 feet above the sea level. Bituminous and anthracite coal-beds abound with kerosene shale. Central Illawarra was proclaimed a municipal district in 1859, with a council of eight aldermen and a mayor. The population is about 2,000.

ILLAWARRA LAKE (*Co. Camden*), a fine inlet or wide arm of the sea, lying to the S.E. of Dapto, about 60 miles S. of Sydney.

ILLAWARRA NORTH (*Co. Camden*), in the parishes of Wonona and Wollongong, was proclaimed a municipality in December, 1868, with a governing body of eight aldermen and a mayor. It adjoins the district of Central Illawarra.

ILLAWARRA RANGE (*Co. Camden*), a lofty and precipitous range of mountains, forming the eastern edge of the south table-land, which encloses the fertile Illawarra valley.

ILUKA (*Co. Richmond*), a postal town, 308 miles to the N. of Sydney, with mail per steamers. A small village on the north head of the entrance to the Clarence River.

IMBANA (*Co. Drake*), a small agricultural settlement, about 18 miles S. of Tenterfield.

IMLAY MOUNT (*Co. Auckland*), a lofty and remarkable detached peak, about 9 miles S.W. of Twofold Bay. It is a prominent land-mark for vessels making the bay. It attains an elevation of 2,900 feet above the level of the sea.

INACCESSIBLE MOUNT (*Co. Roxburgh*), a high peak on the Blue Mountain Range, about 12 miles S. of Rylstone.

INDI RIVER (*Co. Selwyn*). [*See* "RIVERS."]

INDIAN HEAD (*Co. Macquarie*), a rocky promontory, situated between the entrance to the Manning River and Camden Haven.

INGALARA CREEK (*Co. Beresford*), a small eastern tributary of the Murrumbidgee River, flowing into it to the N. of the township of Clinton.

INGEBIRAH (*Co. Wallace*), a high peak on the road from Cooma to Gippsland, S. of Grose's Plains.

INGEEGOODBEE WATERFALL (*Co. Wallace*), a cataract in the river of that name, near its source.

INGLEBA CREEK (*Co. Vernon*), a small S.E. tributary of the head of Mulcrindi River.

INGLEBAR (*Co. Vernon*), a small township in the police district of Armidale, and about 30 miles N.E. of Hanging Rock.

INGLEBURN (*Co. Cumberland*), a postal village 28 miles S. of Sydney, with daily mail therefrom. A railway station on the southern line.

INGLEDON (*Co. Murray*), a postal receiving-office, 186 miles S. of Sydney, with mail therefrom three times a week.

INGLEWOOD *(Co. Bligh)*, a postal receiving-office, 242 miles W. of Sydney, with mail therefrom twice a week.

INGLIS, a county in the Eastern Division of the Colony. [*See* "COUNTIES."]

INGLISTON *(Co. Northumberland)*, a township 120 miles N. of Sydney. Hexham is the nearest railway station on the northern line.

INVERARY *(Co. Argyle)*, an agricultural settlement lying to the S. of the township of Bungonia and to the W. of the Shoalhaven River.

INVERELL *(Co. Gough)*, a postal town, 468 miles N. of Sydney, with daily mail therefrom. Telegraph and money-order offices, Government savings bank, and delivery by letter-carriers. The nearest railway station is Glen Innes, 40 miles, on the northern line. Situated on the Macintyre River, and in the police district of Wellingrove. The district is an agricultural and grazing one. It was proclaimed a municipal district in 1872, with a council of eight aldermen and a mayor. The population is about 3,000. Courts of quarter sessions and district courts are held periodically at Inverell.

INVERGOWRIE *(Co. Sandon)*, a postal receiving-office, 369 miles N. of Sydney, with mail twice a week.

INVERLOCHY *(Co. Argyle)*, a postal receiving-office, 146 miles S. of Sydney, with daily mail.

IONA *(Co. Durham)*, a small settlement near Largs.

IRISH CREEK *(Co. Buccleuch)*, a small tributary of the Adjungbilli Creek, rising in the eastern slope of Mount Tumorrama.

IRISH JACK'S CREEK *(Co. Harden)*, a small eastern tributary of the Currawong Creek.

IRISHTOWN *(Co. Cumberland)*, a small village in the parish of Liberty Plains, on the Liverpool Road, 14 miles from Sydney.

IRISHTOWN *(Co. Georgiana)*, a small hamlet, situated on the Reedy Creek, a few miles from the township of Laggan.

IRONBARK CREEK *(Co. Darling)*. [*See* "TIANDUNDIE CREEK."]

IRONBARK CREEK *(Co. Northumberland)*, a small southern tributary of the Hunter River, falling into it below Hexham. Also, a small tributary of the Mangrove Creek.

IRONBARKS *(Co. Cumberland)*, a small agricultural settlement on the Southern Road, about 7 miles from Sydney.

IRONBARKS *(Co. Wellington)*. [*See* "STUART TOWN."]

IRONBONG *(Co. Clarendon)*, a postal receiving-office, 278 miles S. of Sydney, with mail once a week.

IRONCOVE *(Co. Cumberland)*, a small bight at the head of Lane Cove, formed by a ledge of sandstone rock running out from the main land, about 5 miles to the W. of Sydney.

IRONCOVE BRIDGE *(Co. Cumberland)*, a postal suburb of Sydney 7 miles W. thereof, with mail twice a day. The nearest railway station is Ashfield, 1 mile, on the suburban railway line.

IRONDALE (*Co. Roxbourgh*), a railway station 109 miles from Sydney on the western line.

IRRARA, a county in the Western Division of the Colony. [*See* "Counties."]

IRRARA CREEK (*Co. Irrara*), a creek of good water, taking its rise on the Queensland border, flowing into the Warrego River, about 50 miles S. of the dividing line.

IRVINGTON (*Co. Clarence*), a postal receiving-office, 387 miles N. of Sydney, with mail per Clarence River steamers.

ISABELLA CREEK (*Co. Georgiana*), a fine stream, rising to the N.E. of the Tuena gold-fields, and flowing S. into the Abercrombie River at the village of Bingham.

ISABELLA RIVER (*Co. Georgiana*). [*See* "Rivers."]

ISIS RIVER (*Co. Brisbane*), a fine stream rising in the Liverpool Range, near Downey's Pass, and flowing into the Page River, near Gundy-Gundy. [*See* "Rivers."]

IVANHOE (*Co. Cumberland*), a suburb of Sydney, situated in the parish of Alexandria, between Waverley and Bondi Bay.

IVANHOE (*Co. Mossgiel*), a postal village, 374 miles S. of Sydney, with mail three times a week. Telegraph and money-order office and Government savings' bank. The nearest railway station is Hay, 132 miles, on the south-western line.

# J

JABUSH-JABUCK CREEK (*Co. Roxburgh*), a small eastern tributary of the Macquarie River, flowing in the parish of Watton.

JACK'S CREEK (*Co. Buckland*), a southern tributary of the Borambil Creek. It is fed by the Little Jack's, Onus, and Macdonald's Creeks.

JACK'S CREEK (*Co. Cook*), a tributary of Cox's River.

JACK HALL'S CREEK (*Co. Roxburgh*), an eastern tributary of the Round Swamp Creek.

JACK SMITH'S GAP (*Co. Buccleuch*), an opening between the peaks of the Honeysuckle Ranges, through which there is a track from Adjungbilly to Gundagai.

JACKSON, PORT (*Co. Cumberland*), is the principal harbour in the South Pacific Ocean. Its opening is between two rocky promontories known as the North and South Heads. There are two lighthouses, one at an elevation of 344 feet above sea-level, and the other near the southern head of the entrance, 60 feet high. On entering the harbour a floating light is shown, known as the Sow and Pigs; and on Fort Denison, nearer the city, a red harbour light is exhibited. [*See* "Ports and Harbours."]

JACKSON WATERHOLES (*Co. Mitchell*), a postal receiving-office, 357 miles S. of Sydney, with mail twice a week.

JACOB AND JOSEPH CREEK (*Co. Buckland*), a small drainage creek rising in the western slope of the Australian Alps, and flowing into the Quirindi Creek at Quirindi.

JACOB'S LADDER (*Co. Cumberland*), a well-known descent on the eastern face of the cliff overlooking the ocean, between the Gap and the outer South Head of Port Jackson.

JACOB'S POINT (*Co. Wallace*), is the crossing place of the Snowy River, on the track into Gippsland from Cooma *via* Buckley's crossing-place.

JACOB'S RIVER (*Co. Wallace*). [See "RIVERS."]

JAGUNGAL MOUNT (*Co. Selwyn*), a lofty peak in the Murray Range, attaining an altitude of 6,763 feet above sea-level.

JAMBEROO (*Co. Camden*), a postal village, 86 miles S. of Sydney, with mail twice a day. Telegraph and money-order offices and Government savings bank. The nearest railway station is Kiama, 6 miles, on the Illawarra and South Coast line. Situated in the parish of Jamberoo, on the Minnamurra Creek, Illawarra Lake being 5 miles N.E., and Mount Terry 4 miles N. Coal exists in abundance in the ranges.

JAMBEROO MOUNTAIN (*Co. Camden*), a postal receiving-office, 112 miles S. of Sydney, with daily mail.

JAMES'S CREEK (*Co. Hunter*). [See "BARRAMI CREEK."]

JAMISON, a county in the Central Division of the Colony. [See "COUNTIES."]

JAMISON TOWN (*Co. Cook*), a postal town, 38 miles W. of Sydney, with daily mail therefrom.

JAMISON'S VALLEY (*Co. Cook*), a valley, situated on the Great Western Road, 59 miles W. from Sydney. A small creek flows through the valley into Cox's River.

JASPER BRUSH (*Co. Camden*), a postal receiving office, 89 miles S. of Sydney, with daily mail.

JASPER MOUNT (*Co. Macquarie*), a lofty mountain lying at the head of the Hastings River, near Mount Seaview.

JEIR (*Co. Murray*), a postal town, 120 miles S. of Sydney, with mail therefrom daily. The nearest railway station is Yass, 18 miles, on the southern line.

JEJEDZERICK HILL (*Co. Wallace*), a lofty peak, lying on the E. bank of the Wullwye Creek.

JELLA-JELLEL (*Co. Auckland*), a small southern tributary of the lower portion of the Bega River.

JELLORE CREEK (*Co. Camden*), a small tributary of the head of the Nattai River, rising near Berrima, and flowing to the E. of Jellore Mountain.

JELLORE MOUNT (*Co. Camden*), an isolated mountain, near the Mittagong Range of hills, and near the source of the Nattai River. It is conical in shape, and is plainly visible at Sydney, a distance of 70 miles.

JEMBAICUMBENE (*Co. St. Vincent*), a postal village, 193 miles S. of Sydney, with mail daily. The nearest railway station is Tarago, 39 miles, on the Goulburn and Cooma line. Situated on the banks of the Jembaicumbene Creek, and is a gold-bearing district, 3 miles from Major's Creek and 7 miles from Braidwood.

JEMBAICUMBENE CREEK (*Co. St. Vincent*), an eastern tributary of the Shoalhaven River, rising to the W. of Monga.

JENNINGS (*Co. Clive*), a proclaimed township in the county.

JENNY'S CREEK (*Co. Parry*), a small auriferous tributary of the Peel River, joining it at Bowling Alley Point Diggings.

JENOLA MOUNT (*Co. Westmoreland*), is a hill on the S. bank of Cox's River, near the confluence of the Konangoola Creek.

JENOLAN CAVES (*Co. Westmoreland*), a postal village, 193 miles W. of Sydney, with mail three times a week, and telegraph office. The nearest railway station is Tarana, 28 miles, on the western line. These wonderful limestone caves occur in a deep valley, on the eastern watershed of the Great Dividing Range, which contributes its waters to the Cox River, an affluent of the Nepean and Hawkesbury Rivers, which reaches the coast at Broken Bay. The caves are 2,400 feet above sea-level. The following extract, from "Geological Observations on the Jenolan Caves," by C. S. Wilkinson, Esq., F.G.S., will be read with interest:—

"It is not uninteresting to reflect that this limestone, now a compact grey marble, was once a mass of living corals, 'stone lilies,' and molluscs, revealing the former existence, in the Siluro-Devonian epoch, of conditions of marine life somewhat resembling those which support the beautiful living forms which build up the reefs in the coral seas of the present day; and it is significant of the vast changes that this part of the surface of the earth has undergone, when we see fresh-water streams, at an elevation of several thousand feet above the sea, now flowing through rocks that were originally formed beneath the waves of the ocean, at a very remote period of the earth's history. First, the decaying vegetation of some ancient forest is invisibly distilling the gas known as carbonic acid; then a storm of rain falls, clearing the air of the noxious gas, and distributing a thousand streamlets of acid water over the surrounding country, which, as it drains off, not only wears the rocks it passes over but dissolves them in minute quantities, especially such as contain much lime; and then, laden with its various compounds, flows off to the distant sea, where reef corals, lying in fringing banks round the coast, are slowly absorbing the lime from the water around them and building the fragile coatings that protect them during life. Slowly as the land sinks the coral bank increases in height, for reef corals can only live near the surface of the water, and soon a considerable thickness has been obtained; while below the upper zone of live corals lies a vast charnel-house of dead coral coverings. Then comes a change; suitable temperature or some other essential condition fails, killing out all the corals, and through long ages other deposits accumulate over them, gradually crushing and consolidating the coral bank into a firm rock. At last a convulsion of the earth's crust brings it up from the buried depth in which it lies, leaving it tilted on its edge, but still, perhaps, below the surface of the ground. Rain, frost, and snow slowly remove what covers it, until it lies exposed again to the sunlight, but so changed that only for the silent but irresistible testimony of the fossil forms of which it is composed, it were hard to believe that this narrow band of hard grey rock was once the huge but fragile coral bank glistening in the bright waters with a thousand hues. And now the process is repeated; the decaying vegetation of the surrounding forest produces the carbonic acid, the rains spread it over the ground, which is now the most favourable for being dissolved, and the consequence is that the acid water saturates itself with the limestone rock, and, whenever the least evaporation takes place, has to deposit some of its dissolved carbonate of lime in one of the many stalactitic forms before it can flow off to the sea and distribute its remaining contents to fresh coral banks. Thus the old coral reef melts away far inland, and the lime that formed the coatings of its corals is again utilised for the same purpose. What a simple succession of causes and effects! and yet, before the circle is completed, long ages of time have come and gone. And what a fine example of the balance between the waste and reproduction that take place in nature!"

**JERABORUBERA CREEK** (*Co. Murray*), a southern tributary of the Molonglo River, rising to the S. of Queanbeyan, and flowing into the Molonglo, near the last-named township.

**JERANGLE** (*Co. Murray*), a postal receiving-office, 212 miles S. of Sydney, with mail once a week.

**JEREMIAH CREEK** (*Co. Buccleuch*), a southern tributary of the Murrumbidgee River. It is fed by Pepper Creek.

**JERGYLE MOUNTAIN** (*Co. Goulburn*), a lofty peak lying in the middle of the county, standing high above the surrounding ranges.

**JERILDERIE** (*Co. Urana*), a postal village, 412 miles S. of Sydney, with mail four times a week. Telegraph and money-order offices and Government savings bank. A railway station on Junee and Jerilderie line. The district is an agricultural and pastoral one. It was proclaimed a municipal district in 1890, with a council of eight aldermen and a mayor. The population is about 500.

**JERIMBUL** (*Co. Dampier*), a small agricultural settlement, lying 18 miles N. of Bega.

**JERRA-JERRA CREEK** (*Co. Goulburn*), a small northern tributary of the Billybung Creek.

**JERRABALGULLA CREEK** (*Co. Murray*), is the name of the western head of the Shoalhaven River, rising in the Gowrock range.

**JERRARA CREEK** (*Co. Argyle*), a western tributary of the Shoalhaven River, flowing into it to the N.W. of Bungonia. It is fed by the Bungonia Creek.

**JERRAWA** (*Co. King*), a postal village, 175 miles S. of Sydney, with daily mail. A railway station, on the southern line.

**JERRAWA CREEK** (*Co. King*), is one of the heads of the Lachlan River, rising in Mount Mandonen, and flowing across the Yass Plains to its junction with the Oolong and Cullarin Creeks, which form the Lachlan River.

**JERRICKNORRA CREEK** (*Co. St. Vincent*), a small tributary of the Corang River, rising in the Pigeon House Mountain.

**JERRONG** (*Co. Argyle*), a postal village, 186 miles S. of Sydney, with mail once a week. The nearest railway station is Goulburn, 45 miles, on the southern line.

**JERRY'S PLAINS** (*Co. Hunter*), a postal town, 169 miles N. of Sydney, with mail three times a week. Telegraph and money-order offices and Government savings bank. The nearest railway station is Singleton, 18 miles, on the northern line. Situated on the Hunter River. The plain is surrounded by high ridges, known as the Bulga Mountains. The district is exceedingly fertile.

**JERSEYVILLE** (*Co. Rous*), a postal village, 328 miles N. of Sydney, with mail three times a week.

JERVIS BAY (*Co. St. Vincent*), a capacious bay and harbour 80 miles to the S. of Sydney. The entrance is 2 miles wide, and is a safe port for ships of the largest tonnage.

JESSE CREEK (*Co. Roxburgh*), a northern auriferous tributary of the head of the Cheshire Creek rising in the Limekiln Range.

JETTING CREEK (*Co. Wynyard*), a southern tributary of the Murrumbidgee River.

JEW'S FLAT (*Co. Beresford*), a small plain on which the township of Bunyan is situated.

JEWINE MOUNT (*Co. Wellesley*), a high peak lying about 6 miles N. of Bombala.

JEWEENA MOUNT (*Co. Wallace*), a high peak near the fall of Reedy Creek into the Snowy River, about 4 miles N. of Guildford.

JIGGI (*Co. Rous*), a postal town, 376 miles N. of Sydney, with weekly mail therefrom.

JILLAMATONG (*Co. Wallace*), a solitary hill, one of the Mowamba Group, lying on the S. bank of the Mowamba River.

JILLIBY-JILLIBY CREEK (*Co. Northumberland*), a fine northern tributary of the Wyong Creek, fed by the Nellering Creek.

JIMEMBUAN (*Co. Beresford*), a postal village, 376 miles S. of Sydney, with weekly mail. The nearest railway station is Cooma, 48 miles, on the Goulburn and Cooma line.

JINCUNBILLY (*Co. Wellesley*), a peak, standing between Bombala and Nimmitibel.

JINDABYNE (*Co. Wallace*), a postal village, 292 miles S. of Sydney, with mail twice a week. The nearest railway station is Cooma, 30 miles, on the Goulburn and Cooma line. Situated in the parish of Jindabyne, on the Snowy River.

JINDALEE (*Co. Harden*), a postal village, 246 miles S. of Sydney, with daily mail.

JINDERA (*Co. Goulburn*), a postal village, 396 miles S. of Sydney with mail three times a week. Telegraph and money-order offices and Government savings bank. The nearest railway station is Albury, 10 miles, on the southern line.

JINDULIAN MOUNT (*Co. Murray*), is the highest peak of the Gourock Range, attaining an elevation of 4,300 feet above the sea level.

JINEROO MOUNT (*Co. St. Vincent*), a branch of the Gourock Range, lying near the west bank of the Shoalhaven River. It contains lodes of lead and argentiferous galena.

JINGELLEE (*Cos. Goulburn and Selwyn*), is a small village on the Murray River, lying between the two counties, and on the Jingellic Creek.

JINGELLEE MOUNT (*Co. Goulburn*), an auriferous creek, rising in Mount Aitken, and flowing into the river Murray at Jingellee.

P

JINGELLEE MOUNTAINS (*Co. Goulburn*), a range of high peaks, lying in the S.E. portion of the county, and almost parallel to the banks of the Murray River.

JINGELLIC (*Co. Selwyn*), a postal receiving-office, 93 miles S. of Sydney, with mail twice a week.

JINGERY MOUNTAINS (*Co. Murray*), a mountain spur, in the Gourock Range, lying on the east bank of the Queanbeyan River, on the road to Monga, and attains an elevation of 2,500 feet above sea level.

JINGO CREEK (*Co. Auckland*), a northern tributary of the Towamba River, falling into it at the township of Sturt.

JINNYBRUTHERA (*Co. Wallace*), a high peak on the Monaro Range, about 10 miles W. of Nimmitibel.

JOADJA CREEK (*Co. Camden*), a postal village, 93 miles S. of Sydney, with daily mail. Money-order office, and Government savings bank. The nearest railway station is Mittagong, 18 miles, on the southern line.

JOCK'S (*Co. Westmoreland*), a bridge over a mountain stream, running into Cox's River, and is 3,000 feet above sea level.

JOHN MOUNT (*Co. Sandon*), a detached peak, in the parish of Arding, about 5 miles N. of Uralla.

JOHN'S RIVER (*Co. Macquarie*), a postal receiving-office, 220 miles N. of Sydney, with daily mail. A small rivulet flowing into Watson Taylor's Lake.

JOHN'S RIVER (*Co. Macquarie*). [*See* "RIVERS."]

JOHNSON'S CREEK (*Co. Cumberland*), a small watercourse, rising in the estate of Mr. R. Johnson, and flowing N. about 3 miles into Port Jackson, at the head of Rozelle Bay.

JOHNSTON'S CREEK (*Co. Camden*), a small tributary of the Macquarie Rivulet.

JOHNSTONE'S BAY (*Co. Cumberland*), a western arm of Darling Harbour, lying between the suburbs of Balmain and Pyrmont.

JOHNSTONE'S CREEK (*Co. Cumberland*), a small creek, rising in the suburban municipality of Newtown. It is fed by the Orphan School Creek, and crosses the Parramatta Road at Camperdown.

JONATHAN'S FLAT (*Co. Wellington*), an auriferous flat, lying at the head of Pyramid Creek, to the S.W. of Cudgegong township.

JONBLEE (*Co. Clive*), a small roadside village, lying 99 miles N. of Armidale.

JONES' BAY (*Co. Cumberland*), lying at the south head of Johnstone's Bay, in the suburb of Pyrmont, to the W. of Sydney.

JONES' ISLAND (*Co. Macquarie*), situated about 202 miles to the N. of Sydney, in the Manning River, and 8 miles from the bar. The soil is rich alluvial.

JONNAMA CREEK (*Co. Bucclench*), a small stream rising in the S. of the Bogan Range, flowing W. into the Tumut River, at the village of Talbingo.

JOORTLAND CREEK (*Co. Westmoreland*), a western tributary creek of the Wollondilly River, rising near Mount Colong.

JUAN AND JULIA ISLANDS (*Co. Rous*), lying to the S.E. of the entrance of the Brunswick River, in the bight between Cape Byron and Sutherland Point.

JUDD'S CREEK (*Co. Georgiana*), a postal town, 178 miles W. of Sydney, with mail three times a week.

JUDGE DOWLING (*Co. Northumberland*), a range of mountains situated 65 miles W. of Sydney, formerly known as the Devil's Backbone.

JUG HILL (*Co. Harden*), a lofty hill, lying to the E. of the town of Jugiong.

JUGIONG (*Co. Harden*), a postal town, 292 miles S. of Sydney, with mail three times a week. Telegraph and money-order offices. The nearest railway station is Coolac, 14 miles, on the Cootamundra and Gundagai line. It is situated on the Murrumbidgee River, in the parish of Jugiong and police district of Gundagai. The district is an agricultural and pastoral one.

JUGIONG CREEK (*Co. Harden*), a large and important northern tributary of the Murrumbidgee River, rising near Bogolong and falling into the main stream at the township of Jugiong, on the road from Yass to Gundagai.

JULADERIN (*Co. Cunningham*), a township on the bank of the Lachlan River.

JUMPING SAND HILL (*Co. Waljeers*), an immense land deposit in the middle of the county, on Umbrella Creek.

JUMP-UP (*Co. Clive*).—A postal receiving-office, 478 miles N. of Sydney, with daily mail.

JUMP-UP CREEK (*Co. Northumberland*), a small southern tributary of the Hunter River, flowing through the township of Belford.

JUNCTION, THE (*Co. Northumberland*), a postal town, 77 miles N. of Sydney, with daily mail, and delivery by letter-carrier. It is within the City of Newcastle, and lies about half-a-mile from the Harbour, and is rich in coal deposits.

JUNCTION (*Co. Wellesley*), a small gold diggings to the N. of the Delegete Plains, on the Delegete River.

JUNCTION DIGGINGS (*Co. Wellington*), a small gold working, forming part of the Muckerwa Gold-field.

JUNCTION GOLD-MINE (*Co. Bathurst*), a village, 6 miles from Lyndhurst. The nearest railway station on the Murrumburrah and Blayney line.

JUNCTION POINT (*Co. Bathurst*), a postal village, 286 miles S. of Sydney, with daily mail. The nearest railway station is Newbridge, on the western line.

JUNEE JUNCTION (*Co. Clarendon*), a postal village, 287 miles S. of Sydney with daily mail. Telegraph and money-order offices, and Government savings bank, and delivery by letter-carrier. A railway station on the southern line. It was proclaimed a borough in 1886, with a council of eight aldermen and a mayor. The population is about 2,600.

JUNEE ROAD (*Co. Clarendon*), a village, 290 miles S. of Sydney. The nearest railway station is Old Junee, on the southern line.

JURI (*Co. Parry*), a township on the northern railway, to the S. of Tamworth.

# K

KADINA (*Co. Ashburnham*), a postal receiving-office, 296 miles W. of Sydney, with mail twice a week.

KAHIBAH POINT (*Co. Northumberland*), a proclaimed village at the entrance to Port Macquarie.

KAISER (*Co. Wellington*), a village, 12 miles from Wellington, the nearest station on the western line.

KALINGALUNGAGAY CREEK (*Co. Cunningham*), a small northern tributary of the point of the Lachlan River.

KALLOBUNGUNG CREEK (*Co. Macquarie*), a small eastern tributary of the Ellenborough River.

KALUBRUTHA SWAMP (*Co. Monara*), a large swamp, to the S.E. of Moonanya Lake.

KAMANDRA (*Co. Ashburnham*), a postal receiving-office, 292 miles W. of Sydney, with daily mail therefrom.

KAMERUKA (*Co. Auckland*), a village, 61 miles from Cooma, the nearest railway station on the Goulburn and Cooma line.

KANCOBYN CREEK (*Co. Selwyn*), a small tributary of the eastern branch of the Murray River, rising N. of Mount Kosciusko.

KANGALOOLA (*Co. Georgiana*), a small village in the police district of Carcoar, situated on the Kangaloola Creek, near Binda.

KANGALOOLA CREEK (*Co. Georgiana*), a fine stream, flowing S.W. into the Crookwell River, W. of Binda township.

KANGALOOLA ARM CREEK (*Co. Georgiana*), an eastern branch of the head of the Tuena Creek.

KANGALOON (*Co. Camden*), a postal village, 88 miles S. of Sydney, with mail twice daily, and money-order office. The nearest railway station is Bowral, 19 miles, on the southern line. Situated on the Double Folly Creek, in the parish of Kangaloon. The district is an agricultural one, with exceedingly fertile soil.

KANGARATHA POINT (*Co. Auckland*), a headland lying a few miles to the S. of Tathra.

KANGAROO CAMP (*Co. Sandon*), a postal receiving office, 413 miles N. of Sydney, with mail three times a week. The nearest railway station is Guyra, 30 miles, on the northern line.

KANGAROO CREEK (*Co. Georgiana*), a tributary of the upper part of the Menunday Creek.

KANGAROO CREEK (*Co. Sandon*), a postal village, 363 miles to the N. of Sydney, with mail per Grafton steamers.

KANGAROO FLAT (*Co. Wellington*), an auriferous flat, forming part of the Tuena gold-fields.

KANGAROO FLAT CREEK (*Co. Wellington*), a small southern auriferous tributary of the Green Valley Creek.

KANGAROO GROUND (*Co. Camden*), a remarkable and extensive tract of country, and is supposed to be the bed of a former lake, being rich with vegetable mould of considerable depth. It is watered by the Kangaroo River.

KANGAROO MOUNTAIN (*Co. Buccleuch*), a peak of the Honeysuckle Ranges, lying on the E. bank of the Tumut River.

KANGAROO POINT (*Co. Cumberland*). [*See* "MOONEY MOONEY POINT."]

KANGAROO RIVER (*Co. Camden*). [*See* "RIVERS."]

KANGAROO VALLEY (*Co. Camden*), a postal village, 109 miles S. of Sydney, with daily mail. The nearest railway station is Moss Vale, 22 miles, on the southern line.

KANGAROOBIE (*Co. Wellington*), a postal receiving-office, 204 miles W. of Sydney, with mail three times a week.

KANGAROOBY CREEK (*Co. Forbes*), a small southern tributary of the Lachlan River, rising in the N. of the county, and flowing into the main stream, near its confluence with the Belubula River.

KANGRA CREEK (*Co. Northumberland*), a small tributary of the Mangrove Creek.

KANUMBLE CREEK (*Co. Westmoreland*), a tributary of Cox's River, rising on the northern slopes of Pulpit Hill.

KARABAR (*Co. Cook*), a railway station, 45 miles W. of Sydney, on the western line.

KARAGHINE CREEK (*Co. Macquarie*), a small tributary of the head of the Ellenborough River.

KAR'S SPRINGS (*Co. Gloucester*), a postal village, 22 miles N. of Sydney, with mail twice a week.

KARRAGANBAL POINT (*Co. Northumberland*). [See "TUGGERAH BEACH LAKES."]

KARUAH RIVER (*Cos. Durham and Gloucester*). [See "RIVERS."]

KARULA RIVER (*New England*). [See "RIVERS."]

KATOOMBA (*Co. Cook*), a postal village, 66 miles, W. of Sydney, with mail daily. Telegraph and money-order offices, Government savings bank, and delivery by letter-carriers. A railway station on the western line. It is situated on the Blue Mountains, and is a favorite place of resort in the summer months. It was incorporated a Municipal District in 1889, and is governed by a Council of five aldermen and a mayor.

KAYUGA (*Co. Durham,*) a postal village, 182 miles N. of Sydney, with mail three times a week. The nearest railway station is Musclebrook, 4 miles on the northern line.

KEAJURA CREEK (*Co. Wynyard*), a watercourse rising in the W. of Kilgowla Hills, flowing N. through a gap in Comalawa Range.

KEELO (*Co. Benarba,*) a township, on the E. bank of the Barwon River.

KEENE'S SWAMP (*Co. Roxburgh*), a village, 125 miles W. of Sydney, situated in the parish of Warrengunyah, about 14 miles from Cudgegong, on the main road to Mudgee.

KEEPIT (*Co. Parry*), a postal village, 313 miles N. of Sydney, with mail twice a week. The nearest railway station is Tamworth, 34 miles, on the northern line.

KEERA CREEK (*Co. Murchison*), a southern tributary of the Gwydir River, falling into it near the township of Bingara.

KEERABEE CREEK (*Co. Phillip*), is a southern tributary of the Goulburn River.

KEGINNIE (*Co. Blaxland*), a chain of mountains on W. side of the county.

KEIRA MOUNT (*Co. Cumberland*), a well-known mount on the South Coast, about 64 miles to the S. of Sydney, attaining an elevation of 1,500 feet above the sea level, and is almost perpendicular and overhangs the lovely and fertile valley of Illawarra. The foot of the mountain is clothed with semi-tropical vegetation, the various tree ferns, indigenous to the district, being most luxuriant. On the face of the escarpment there are seams of coal cropping out at various altitudes.

KEIRAVILLE (*Co. Camden*), a post-office, 50 miles S. of Sydney, with daily mail, near Wollongong.

KEKEELAH HILL (*Co. Hunter*), a spur of the Dividing Range.

KELGOOLA MOUNT (*Co. Phillip*), a peak in the Blue Mountain Range, near the head of the Cudgegong River.

KELLY'S HUT CREEK (*Co. Gough*), is a small creek at the head of the Yarrow River.

KELLY'S PLAINS (*Co. Sandon*), a postal village, 330 miles N. of Sydney, with daily mail. A railway station on the northern line.

KELLYVILLE (*Co. Cumberland*), a postal village, 32 miles W. of Sydney, with daily mail.

KELSO (*Co. Bathurst*), a postal village, 143 miles W. of Sydney, with daily mail. Telegraph and money-order offices. It is a railway station on the western line, situated on the Macquarie River, about a mile distant from the last-named place. The district is chiefly an agricultural one, and is very fertile.

KEMBLA MOUNT (*Co. Camden*), a lofty peak in the Illawarra Range, overhanging the villages of Kembla and Dubbo, on the road between Wollongong and Kiama. The mountain presents a very conspicuous object from the ocean.

KEMPSEY (*Co. Dudley*), a postal town, 311 miles N. of Sydney, with daily mail. Telegraph and money-order offices, Government savings bank, and delivery by letter-carrier. The nearest railway station is Hexham, 196 miles on the northern line. Situated in the parish of Yarreval, on the Macleay River, which divides it into East and West Kempsey. The river is navigable and steamers ply to and from Sydney regularly, besides sailing craft. The district is principally an agricultural one, and the soil very fertile. It was incorporated a Borough in 1886, with a council of eight aldermen and a mayor. The population is about 3,000. Courts of quarter sessions and district courts are held here periodically.

KENLIS (*Co. Westmoreland*), a small village lying on the Fish River, 5 miles E. of O'Connell.

KENMARE (*Co. Murray*), is a small village in the vicinity of Gundaroo.

KENNEDY. A county in the Central Division of the Colony. [*See* "COUNTIES."]

KENNEDY'S CREEK (*Co. Sandon*), a small tributary of the Rocky River, forming part of the Uralla or Rocky River diggings.

KENNY'S CREEK (*Co. Cumberland*), a small eastern tributary of the South Creek.

KENNY'S POINT (*Co. Argyle*), a village, 155 miles W. of Sydney, situated about 10 miles N.W. of Collector, and 16 miles S. of Bungendore and the Currawang Copper mines, 4 miles due north.

KENTHURST (*Co. Cumberland*), a postal village, 29 miles W. of Sydney, with mail three times a week.

KENTUCKY (*Co. Sandon*), a postal town, 334 miles N. of Sydney, with daily mail. A railway station on the northern line.

KENTUCKY PONDS (*Co's. Sandon and Hardinge*), a southern auriferous tributary of the Rocky River, rising in the western slopes of the Australian Range, and flowing through the village of Kentucky.

KERAMINGLY (*Co. Courallie*), a proclaimed village in the county.

KEREWALLY CREEK (*Co. White*), a small western tributary of the Tarrebeile Creek, flowing through the Melville Plains.

KERR'S CREEK (*Co. Wellington*), a postal receiving-office, 210 miles W. from Sydney, with daily mail. A railway station on the western line.

KERRABEE (*Co. Durham*), a postal village, 224 miles N. of Sydney, with mail three times a week. The nearest railway station is Musclebrook, 35 miles, on the northern line.

KERRAWANG CREEK (*Co. Georgiana*), a small western tributary of the Cookbundoon River.

KHANCOBAN (*Co. Selwyn*), a postal village, 424 miles S. of Sydney, with mail once a week. The nearest railway station is Gundagai, 50 miles, on the southern line.

KHANGAT MOUNT (*Co. Gloucester*), a lofty peak lying on the S. bank of the Manning River, about 16 miles W. of Wingham.

KHAPPINGAL CREEK (*Co. Gloucester*), a small southern tributary of the Kooraingal Creek.

KHATAMBUHL CREEK (*Co. Macquarie*), a small northern tributary of the Manning River.

KIAH (*Co. Auckland*), a postal receiving-office, 291 miles S. of Sydney, with mail per steamer to Eden.

KIAH RIVER (*Co. Auckland*). [See "TOWAMBA RIVER."]

KIALA (*Co. St. Vincent*), a postal village, 175 miles S. of Sydney, with mail three times a week.

KIAMA (*Co. Camden*), a postal town, 71 miles S. of Sydney, with mail twice daily. Telegraph and money-order offices, Government savings bank and delivery by letter-carriers. A railway station on the Illawarra and South Coast lines. The Illawarra Lake lies about 4 miles N.W. It was proclaimed a municipality in 1859, with a council of eight aldermen and a mayor.

KIAMA (*Co. Georgiana*), a small agricultural village lying on the Crookwell River, near the township of Laggan.

KIAMBLA CREEK (*Co. Wynyard*), a southern tributary of the Murrumbidgee River, rising to the N. of the township of Billabong.

KIANDRA (*Co. Cowley*), a postal town, 313 miles S. of Sydney, with mail three times a week. The nearest railway station is Cooma, 30 miles, on the Goulburn and Cooma line. Situated in the parish of Gianderra, on the Eucumbene River, Bullock-Head Creek, being 1 mile, and Charcoal Creek 3 miles distant. The district is an alluvial-mining one, and the surrounding country is mountainous.

KIANDRA PLAINS (*Co. Wallace*), a flat lying to the N.W. of the town of Kiandra, amidst the Gianderra or Kiandra range of mountains.

KIANDRA RANGE (*Co. Wallace*). [See "GIANDERRA RANGE."]

KILDARE CREEK (*Co. King*), a small western tributary of the Upper Lachlan River, flowing into Yass Plains.

KILDARY (*Co. Bourke*), a postal receiving-office, 371 miles S. of Sydney, with mail once a week.

KILEY'S HILL (*Co. Buccleuch*), is the S. peak of the Honeysuckle Ranges, on the E. bank of the Tumut River.

KILFERA, a county in the Western Division of the Colony. [*See* "COUNTIES."]

KILGIN (*Co. Clarence*), a postal receiving-office, 312 miles N. of Sydney, with mail per Clarence River steamers.

KILLARA, a county in the Western Division of the Colony. [*See* "COUNTIES."]

KILLARA (*Co. Rankin*), a township on the W. bank of the Darling River, to the S. of Rankin's Range.

KILLAWARRA (*Co. Macquarie*), a postal village, 238 miles N. of Sydney, with mail three times a week.

KILLIMICAT CREEK (*Co. Buccleuch*), a small eastern tributary of the Tumut River, rising in the Wyangle Hill.

KILLIMICAT HILL (*Co. Buccleuch*), a lofty detached hill in the parish of Killimicat, near the town of Tumut.

KILLOONG MOUNT (*Co. Bland*), a solitary hill lying in the vast plains between the Lachlan and Murrumbidgee Rivers.

KILRUSH (*Co. Harden*), a postal receiving-office, 263 miles S. of Sydney, with mail once a week.

KIMBERLEY (*Co. Hardinge*), a proclaimed township on Copes' Creek in the county.

KIMBRIKI (*Co. Gloucester*), a postal town, 220 miles N. of Sydney, with mail twice a week. The nearest railway station is Hexham, 90 miles, on the northern line.

KIMBRIKI (*Co. Gloucester*), a postal village, 220 miles N. of Sydney, with mail once a week. The nearest railway station is Hexham, 90 miles, on the northern line.

KIMDIBAKH (*Co. Gloucester*), a postal village, 211 miles N. of Sydney, with daily mail.

KIMO DIGGINGS (*Co. Harden*), an alluvial quartz diggings in the Kimo Ranges, within 3 miles of the township of Gundagai.

KINCHELA (*Co. Dudley*), a small agricultural hamlet in the parish of the Hastings, near Kempsey, on the Macleay River.

KINCHELA CREEK (*Co. Dudley*), a postal village, 335 miles N. of Sydney, with mail three times a week, and by the Macleay River steamers.

KINCUMBER (*Co. Northumberland*), a postal village, 57 miles N. of Sydney, with mail five times a week. The nearest railway station is Gosford, 10 miles, on the Newcastle line

KINDAROON MOUNT (*Co. Hunter*), a peak of the Hunter Range, lying near the head of the Tuppa Creek.

KINDEE BROOK (*Co. Macquarie*), a small northern tributary of the Hastings River.

KING, a county in the Eastern Division of the Colony. [*See* "COUNTIES."]

KING MOUNT (*Co. Tongowoko*), a peak of the Grey Range.

KING GEORGE MOUNT (*Co. Cook*), a lofty peak of the Blue Mountains, 3,620 feet above the sea-level, and known as the Saddle-backed hill, seen from Sydney.

KING JOHN'S CREEK (*Co. Hardinge*), a western tributary of the upper part of the Gwydir River.

KING WILLIAM MOUNT (*Co. Clarence*), a hill lying to the N.E. of Copmanhurst, on the N. bank of the Clarence River.

KING'S CREEK (*Co. Macquarie*). [*See* "NARRAN CREEK."]

KING'S PLAINS (*Co. Bathurst*), a postal receiving-office, 176 miles W. of Sydney, with mail twice a week. The nearest railway station is Blayney, 8 miles, on the Blayney and Murrumburrah line.

KING'S PLAINS (*Co. Argyle*), a piece of fine country to the N.W. of the township of Goulburn, in the parish of Narrangarril.

KING'S PLAINS (*Co. Bathurst*), a tract of auriferous county to the N. of Blayney and S. of Guyong, and watered by the Belubula River.

KING'S PLAINS (*Co. Gough*), a tract of good pastoral land lying to the W. of the township of Wellingrove.

KING'S TABLE-LAND (*Co. Cook*), an elevated tract of country situated on the Great Western Road, and being 2,727 feet above the level of the sea. The ascent of the Blue Mountains is gorgeously grand. The Prince Regent's Glen, and the valleys adjacent to the Weatherboard and Blackheath, imparts to the scenery a wild grandeur of a very uncommon character.

KINGARRAGAN CREEK (*Co. Wellington*), an auriferous tributary of the Burraba Creek, flowing to the E. of the Louisa Creek gold-fields.

KINGDON PONDS (*Co. Brisbane*), a small agricultural village on the creek of the same name, about 6 miles N. of Scone.

KINGDON PONDS (*Co. Brisbane*), is a tributary stream at the head of the Dartbrook rising in Mount Murulla.

KINGSGATE (*Co. Gough*), a proclaimed village in the county.

KINGSGROVE (*Co. Cumberland*), a village to the W. of Sydney. The nearest railway station is Ashfield, 5 miles, on the suburban line.

KINGSTON (*Co. Mitchell*), a proclaimed village, 320 miles S. of Sydney, near the southern railway line.

KINGSTOWN (*Co. Inglis*), a post-office, 374 miles N. of Sydney, with mail twice a week. The nearest railway station is Uralla, 35 miles, on the northern line.

KINGSVALE (*Co. Harden*), a postal receiving-office, 238 miles S. of Sydney, with daily mail. A railway station on the Blayney-Murrumburrah line.

KINGSWOOD (*Co. Cumberland*), a postal receiving-office, 33 miles W. of Sydney, with daily mail. A railway station on the western line.

KIORA (*Co. Dampier*), a postal village. 244 miles S. of Sydney, with mail three times a week. The nearest railway station is Tarago, 46 miles, on the Goulburn and Cooma line. Situated in the parish of Kiora, on the Moruya River. The Sugarloaf Mountain lies 9 miles S.

KIPPARA MOUNT (*Co. Macquarie*), a high, solitary peak, at the head of Wilson's River, near Kempsey.

KIPPIELAW (*Co. Argyle*), a small settlement near Goulburn.

KIRCONNEL (*Co. Roxburgh*), situated on the Kirconnel Creek, near Meadow Flat, in the parishes of Castleton and Yetholme.

KIRCONNELL CREEK (*Co. Roxburgh*). a small tributary of the head of the Winburndale Rivulet, flowing into the Kirconnell gold-fields.

KIRCONNELL GOLD-FIELDS (*Co. Roxburgh*), a gold-field lying to the S. of the Turon River gold-fields.

KIRRIBILLI POINT (*Co. Cumberland*). one of the forts in Port Jackson in St. Leonard's, opposite to Farm Cove.

KITO RIVER (*Co. Narran*), a mouth of the Bokhara River, flowing into the Barwon or Upper Darling Rivers.

KITTICARRARA (*Co. Harden*), a northern tributary of the Murrumbidgee River, rising in the eastern part of the Muttama gold-field.

KITTY'S CREEK (*Co. Gresham*), a small western tributary of the Guy Fawkes River, flowing into the Sara River.

KNOCKFEN (*Co. Northumberland*), a rural hamlet adjacent to the postal village of Lochinvar.

KNORRIT FLAT (*Co. Macquarie*), a post-office, 250 miles N. of Sydney, with mail once a week. The nearest railway station is Hexham, 147 miles, on the northern line.

KOGARAH (*Co. Cumberland*), a suburban postal town, 8 miles S. of Sydney, with mail three times a day. Telegraph and money-order offices, Government savings bank, and delivery by letter-carriers. A railway station on the Hurstville and Waterfall line. Situate in the parish of St. George, on the Kogarah Creek and George's River. It was proclaimed a municipal district in 1885, with a council of eight aldermen and a mayor.

KOOKABOOKARA (*Co. Gresham*), a township 40 miles from Guyra, the nearest railway station on the northern line.

**KOORAINGEL CREEK** (*Co. Gloucester*), a small stream rising to the S. of Tiuonee, flowing into the ocean at Halliday's Point.

**KOORANGAL** (*Co. Sturt*), a proclaimed village on the N. bank of the Murrumbidgee River, and to the S. of the south-western railway, near Hay.

**KOORAWATHA** (*Co. Forbes*), a postal village, 277 miles S. of Sydney, with daily mail. It is a railway station on the Blayney-Murrumburrah line.

**KOORE CREEK** (*Co. Northumberland*), a small tributary of the Mangrove Creek.

**KOOROWATHA** (*Co. Monteagle*), a proclaimed township in the police district of Binalong, situated on the Crowther and Bang Bang Creeks.

**KOROGORO POINT** (*Co. Macquarie*), a rocky promontory standing boldly out into the sea S. of Smoky Cape.

**KORRIBAKLE CREEK** (*Co. Gloucester*), a small creek draining Larry's Flat, and flowing into Burril Creek.

**KOSCIUSKO MOUNT** (*Cos. Wallace and Selwyn*), is a part of the Muniong range of mountains, attaining an elevation of 7,308 feet above sea level, and covered with snow most of the year. It was ascended by Count Strzelacki and Messrs. M'Arthur and Riley, on February 15th, 1840. The view from the summit takes in the whole area all round to the horizon, and is a perfect panorama.

**KOWNUNG CREEK** (*Co. Westmoreland*), is a tributary of Cox's River.

**KRAMBACH** (*Co. Gloucester*), a postal village, 218 miles N. of Sydney, with daily mail, and money-order office.

**KRAWAREE** (*Co. Wallace*), a postal village, 226 miles S. of Sydney, with mail three times a week. The nearest railway station is Tarago, 69 miles, on the Goulburn and Cooma line.

**KREMNOS MOUNT** (*Co. Clarence*), a high hill on the N. bank of the Orara River, and about 20 miles S. of Grafton.

**KRUI RIVER** (*Co. Bligh*). [See "RIVERS."]

**KUMBALINE RIVER** (*Co. Macquarie*), a tributary of Wilson's River, rising in Mount Kippora. [See "RIVERS."]

**KUNDABAKL CREEK** (*Co. Gloucester*), a small tributary of Burril Creek, draining Larry's Flat.

**KUNDERANG CREEK** (*Co. Dudley*), a small southern tributary of the Macleay River.

**KUNOPIA** (*Co. Benarba*), a postal village, 478 miles N. of Sydney, with mail twice a week. The nearest railway station is Narrabri, 140 miles, on the north-western line. Situated on the Boomi River, on the road from Walgett to Queensland.

KURRABA (*Co. Cumberland*), a precipitous rocky point, standing out boldly from the N. shore of Port Jackson, opposite Woolloomooloo Bay.

KURRAGONG (*Co. Cumberland*), a postal village, 45 miles W. of Sydney, with daily mail. Telegraph and money-order offices. The nearest railway station is Richmond, 7 miles, on the Windsor and Richmond line.

KURRAJONG HEIGHTS (*Co. Cumberland*), a postal village, 51 miles W. of Sydney, with daily mail. The nearest railway station is Richmond, 12 miles, on the Windsor line.

KUTENBRUN MOUNT (*Co. Northumberland*), a peak in the Hunter Range, lying about 5 miles S.E. of Wollumbi.

KYAMBA (*Co. Clarendon*), a postal receiving-office, 346 miles S. of Sydney, with mail three times a week. The nearest railway station is Wagga Wagga, 26 miles, on the southern line.

KYBEAN PEAK (*Co. Beresford*), a lofty peak in the Dividing Range, lying at the head of the Kybean River, near Nimmitabel, attaining an altitude of 4,010 feet above sea level.

KYBEYAN RIVER (*Co. Beresford*). [*See* "RIVERS."]

KYLE (*Co. Gloucester*), a postal village, 261 miles N. of Sydney, with mail three times a week. The nearest railway station is Hexham, 66 miles, on the northern line.

KYNGE (*Co. Durham*), a township, situated on the W. bank of the Hunter River, at its confluence with Dartbrook, near the township of Aberdeen.

# L

LACHLAN (OR FORBES) GOLD FIELD (*Co. Ashburnham*), an alluvial diggings on the N. bank of the Lachlan River, near the township of Forbes.

LACHLAN RIVER (*Lachlan and Wellington District*). [*See* "RIVERS."]

LACHLAN SWAMPS (*Co. Cumberland*), situated in the parish of Alexandria, and to the S.E. of the city of Sydney. The supply of water to the city and suburbs was obtained from these swamps until the Nepean water supply was completed.

LACMALAC (*Co. Buccleuch*), a postal receiving-office, 261 miles S. of Sydney, with mail twice a week.

LACROZA VALE (*Co. Cumberland*), a deep hollow, lying on the E. side of the city of Sydney, between Darlinghurst and Paddington.

LADY BAY (*Co. Cumberland*), a rocky bight, on the side of the inner S. head of Port Jackson, just round the point at the back of the Hornby Lighthouse.

LAGGAN (*Co. Georgiana*), a postal village, 155 miles S. of Sydney, with mail three times a week. The nearest railway station is Goulburn, 24 miles, on the southern line. Situated on the Reedy Creek, and on the W. side of the main dividing range, 4 miles W. of the head of the Wollondilly River.

LAGOON GULLY (*Co. Sandon*), a valley in the course of the Saumarez Ponds.

LAGOONS (*Co. Bathurst*), a village, 132 miles W. of Sydney, and 10 miles S. of that township. The nearest railway station is Perth, 6 miles, on the western line.

LAGUNA (*Co. Northumberland*), a postal village, 161 miles N. of Sydney, with mail three times a week. The nearest railway station is Farley, 38 miles, on the northern line. Situated on the Laguna Creek, and 6 miles from the latter township.

LAHEY'S CREEK (*Co. Wellington*), a postal receiving-office, 219 miles W. of Sydney, with mail twice a week. The nearest railway station is Mudgee, 48 miles, on the north-western line.

LAIDLEY'S PONDS (*Co. Menindie*), a chain of water-holes, flowing into the Darling River, at Perry.

LAIDLEY'S PONDS CREEK (*Co. Menindie*), a creek conveying the overflow of the Darling River into the Cawadella Lake, which it joins near the township of Menindie.

LAKE ALBERT (*Co. Wynyard*), a postal village, 315 miles S. of Sydney, with mail three times a week.

LAKE BATHURST (*Co. Argyle*), a postal town, 153 miles S. of Sydney, with daily mail. A railway station on the Goulburn and Cooma line.

LAKE CUDGELLICO (*Co. Dowling*), a postal town, 465 miles W. of Sydney, with mail twice a week. Telegraph and money-order office, and Government savings bank. The nearest railway station is Whitton, 108 miles, on the south-western line.

LAKE MACQUARIE ROAD (*Co. Northumberland*) is a suburb of the city of Newcastle, in the parish of St. John, situated on the road leading to Lake Macquarie.

LAKE MILKENGAY (*Co. Wentworth*), a large fresh-water lake, an affluent of the Cura branch of the Darling River.

LAKE'S PADDOCK (*Co. Wellington*), a small alluvial diggings on the Burrendong gold-fields.

LALLAROOK (*Co. Camden*), a postal receiving-office, 51 miles S. of Sydney, with mail three times a week.

LAMB'S CREEK (*Co. Durham*), a postal receiving-office, 136 miles N. of Sydney, with mail twice a week. The nearest railway station is West Maitland, 17 miles, on the northern line.

LAMB'S VALLEY CREEK (*Co. Durham*), a small northern tributary of the Hunter River.

LAMBING GULLY CREEK (*Co. Sandon*), a small southern tributary of the Saumarez Creek.

LAMBTON (*Co. Northumberland*), a postal town, 103 miles N. of Sydney, with daily mail. Telegraph and money-order offices, Government savings bank, and delivery by letter-carriers. The nearest railway station is Broadmeadow, 2 miles, on the Newcastle and Lake Macquarie line. The Lambton coal-mines adjoin the township. It was proclaimed a municipal district in 1871, with a council of eight aldermen and a mayor. The population is about 4,500.

LAMBTON CREEK (*Co. King*), a small creek flowing from the E. into the upper part of the Lachlan River.

LANDSBOROUGH, a county, in the Western Division of the Colony. [*See* "COUNTIES."]

LANDSDOWN (*Co. Macquarie*), a postal town, 239 miles N. of Sydney, with mail twice a week. The nearest railway station is Hexham, 94 miles, on the northern line.

LANE COVE (*Co. Cumberland*) is 9 miles N. of Sydney, in the parish of Gordon. Situated on the Lane Cove River, and on the main road between Sydney and Gosford. The district is an agricultural one, the soil being admirably adapted for the growth of fruit and vegetables, and it is especially celebrated for its beautiful orangeries. The village of Hornsby is a few miles to the N.

LANE COVE RIVER (*Co. Cumberland*). [*See* "RIVERS."]

LANGWORTHY (*Co. Gloucester*), a postal village, 155 miles N. of Sydney, with daily mail, situated in the parish of Stroud. On the E. bank of the Karuah River, and about 3 miles W. of Johnson's Creek. The nearest railway station is Hexham, 45 miles, on the northern line.

LANKEY'S CREEK (*Co. Goulburn*), a stream of fine water, rising to the E. of Coocook Range, and flowing S.E. into the Coppabella Creek.

LANSDOWN RIVER (*Co. Macquarie*). [*See* "RIVERS."]

LANYON (*Co. Murray*), a town, situated near the township of Queanbeyan. The nearest railway station is Queanbeyan, 16 miles, on the Goulburn and Cooma line.

LA PEROUSE (*Co. Cumberland*), a postal town, 11 miles S. of Sydney, with daily mail, and telegraph office.

LARBERT (*Co. St. Vincent*), a postal receiving-office, 193 miles S. of Sydney, with mail twice a week. Situated at the junction of the Durran-Durran Creek with the Shoalhaven River.

LARDNER MOUNT (*Co. Clarence*), a peak on a low range of hills, lying in the N.W. corner of the coast.

LARGE CREEK (*Co. Wynyard*), a small western tributary of the Kiambla Creek, flowing N.E. through good pastoral country.

LARGS (*Co. Durham*), a postal village, 119 miles N. of Sydney, with daily mail, and telegraph office. The nearest railway station is East Maitland, 3 miles, on the East Maitland and Morpeth line.

LARRY'S FLAT (*Co. Gloucester*), lying to the S. of the Manning River, a few miles to the S.W. of Tinonee.

LARRAS LAKE (*Co. Wellington*) is an eastern tributary of the Bell River.

LAURA CREEK (*Co. Hardinge*) is a small tributary of Smashern's Creek.

LAUREL HILL (*Co. Wynyard*), a postal receiving-office, 344 miles S. of Sydney, with mail once a week.

LAURISTON (*Co. Macquarie*), a postal town, 271 miles N. of Sydney, with mail four times a week. Telegraph and money-order offices, and Government savings bank. The nearest railway station is Hexham, 129 miles, on the Newcastle, Maitland, and Singleton line.

LAVENDER BAY (*Co. Cumberland*), a beautiful bay, on the N. shore of Port Jackson, lying in St. Leonards, opposite Dawes' Point. The North Shore Steam Ferry Company have a landing here for passengers, and the Hornsby branch of the Sydney and Newcastle railway has its terminus at the S.E. head of the Bay.

LAVENSTRUTH (*Co. Fitzroy*), an agricultural settlement, on the Urara River, 10 miles from Grafton.

LAWLER CREEK (*Co. Gloucester*), a small rivulet, at the head of Karuah River.

LAWLER'S SPRINGS (*Co. Buccleuch*), small tributaries of the upper end of the Adjungbilli Creek.

LAWRENCE (*Co. Clarence*), a postal town, 330 miles N. of Sydney, with mails per steamers. Telegraph and money-order offices, Government savings bank, and delivery by letter-carrier. It is situated on the Clarence River, in the parish of Lawrence, at a distance of 25 miles from the sea. The district is rich in agricultural produce.

LAWSON (*Co. Cook*), a postal village, 58 miles W. of Sydney, with mail twice daily. Telegraph and money-order offices, and Government savings bank. A railway station on the western line.

LAWSON'S CREEK (*Co. Phillip*), a good stream, rising in Rumker's Peak, near the Trugbong Gap, and flowing into the Cudgegong River, near the township of Mudgee.

LEAMINGTON (*Co. Hunter*), an agricultural village, on Jerry's Plains, near the Hunter River, 16 miles W. of Singleton.

LEATHER JACKET CREEK (*Co. Selwyn*), a small tributary creek of the Upper Murray, rising in Mount Koscinsko.

LEDKNAPPER (*Co. Culgoa*), a township to the S. of Shearers' Springs.

LEET'S VALE (*Co. Cumberland*), a postal office, 68 miles W. of Sydney, with mail twice a week.

LEICHHARDT, a county in the Central Division of the Colony. [*See* "COUNTIES."]

LEICHHARDT *(Co. Cumberland)*, an important postal suburb, 4 miles W. of the city, with mail twice daily. Telegraph and money-order offices, Government savings bank, and delivery by letter-carrier. The nearest railway station is Petersham, 1 mile, on the suburban line. It is situated in the parish of Petersham, on the W. side of White's Creek. It was incorporated a municipal district in 1871, with a council of eleven aldermen and a mayor. The population is about 14,300.

LEIGHWOOD *(Co. Argyle)*, a postal village, 170 miles S. of Sydney, with mail three times a week.

LEMINGTON *(Co. Hunter)*, a proclaimed village, on the banks of the Hunter River, to the S. of Jerry's Plains.

LENNOX HEAD *(Co. Rous)*, a promontory, about 4 miles N. of Ballina, the mouth of the Richmond River.

LERIDA CREEK *(Co. King)*, a fine mountain stream, rising in the Cullarin Range, flowing N. into the Cullarin Creek.

LESLIE MOUNT *(Co. Buller)*, a prominent peak of the Macpherson Range, lying at the head of Acacia Creek, and on the boundary-line between New South Wales and Queensland.

LEUMEAH *(Co. Cumberland)*, a railway station, 33 miles from Sydney, on the Liverpool and Campbelltown line.

LEWIN'S BROOK *(Co. Durham)*, an eastern tributary of the Allyn River, falling into it about 4 miles E. of Gresford.

LEWIS' MOUNT *(Co. Bathurst)*, a hill, lying near the confluence of the Lachlan and Belubula Rivers, about 3 miles S.W. of Canowindra.

LEWIS' PONDS *(Co. Bathurst)*, a postal village, 208 miles W. of Sydney, with daily mail, and money-order office. The nearest railway station is Orange, 16 miles, on the Orange and Molong line.

LEWIS PONDS CREEK *(Co. Bathurst)*, a rich auriferous stream, rising in the mountainous country near Guyong, flowing into the Macquarie River, S. of Tambaroora. The townships of Guyong, Byng, and Ophir are situated on this stream.

LEWINSBROOK *(Co. Durham)*, a village in the parish of St. Mary's, situated on the Allyn River, the Pinnacle Mountains lying 7 miles distant. The district is an agricultural one.

LEWISHAM *(Co. Cumberland)*, a railway station, 4 miles from Sydney, on the suburban line.

LEYCESTER'S CREEK *(Co. Rous)*, a fine stream, and a tributary to the Richmond River, falling into its head on the western side.

LIBERTY PLAINS *(Co. Cumberland)*, one of the original districts of the county, surrounded by the Sydney Road to Parramatta, and the Liverpool Road and Cook's River to Johnstone's Farm and Iron Cove Creek.

LICKINGHOLE CREEK *(Co. Bathurst)*, a small eastern tributary of the Liscombe Pools Creek, in the parish of Malongulli.

LIDDELL (*Co. Durham*), an agricultural settlement, lying on the Saltwater River, 13 miles N.W. of Singleton.

LIDDELL (*Co. Durham*), a postal village, 164 miles N. of Sydney, with daily mail therefrom. A railway station on the northern line.

LIDSDALE (*Co. Cook*), a postal village, 106 miles W. of Sydney, with daily mail. Money-order office and Government savings bank. The nearest railway station is Wallerawang, 2 miles, on the Mudgee line.

LIGHTHOUSE, SYDNEY (*Co. Cumberland*). is situate in the parish of Alexandria, on the southern head of Port Jackson. A revolving light, and stands 353 feet above sea level.

LILLYDALE (*Co. Cumberland*), a railway station, 29 miles S. of Sydney, on the Illawarra and South Coast line.

LILYFIELD (*Co. Cumberland*), a postal suburb, 4 miles from Sydney, with mail twice daily.

LIMEBURNERS' CREEK (*Co. Gloucester*), a postal village, 126 miles N. of Sydney, with daily mail. The nearest railway station is Hexham, 18 miles, on the northern line. Situated on the creek whence it derives its name, 16 miles N. of Raymond Terrace.

LIMEBURNERS' CREEK (*Co. Durham*), a small creek flowing into the estuary of the Karuah River.

LIMEBURNERS' CREEK (*Co. Macquarie*), a small drainage creek falling into the mouth of the Hastings River by a side estuary.

LIMEKILNS (*Co. Roxburgh*), a postal village, 157 miles W. of Sydney, with mail twice a week. The nearest railway station is Bathurst, 18 miles, on the Bathurst to Bourke line. Situated in the parish of Jesse, on the Jesse Creek.

LIMESTONE CREEK (*Co. Bathurst*). a southern tributary of the Belubula Creek, flowing N. through good agricultural land.

LIMESTONE CREEK (*Co. Buccleuch*), a western tributary of the Goodradigbee River, flowing N.E. about 8 miles.

LIMESTONE CREEK (*Co. Harden*), a small western tributary of the Derringellan Creek, flowing S.E. about 4 miles, also a small northern tributary of the Murrumbidgee River, flowing to the S. of Bogolong.

LIMESTONE CREEK (*Co. Hardinge*), the southern head of Clarke's Creek.

LIMESTONE PLAINS (*Co. Murray*). on the Molonglo and Queanbeyan Rivers, the township of Queanbeyan being situated upon it.

LIMESTONE GULLIES AND RANGES (*Co. St. Vincent*), the name given to the rocky cliffs overhanging the Shoalhaven River, and the deep gullies spurring off at right angles from its course.

LIMESTONE ROCKS (*Co. Buccleuch*), lying on the W. bank of the Goodradigbee River, S. of the Gooradigbee Reserve.

LIMESTONE VALLEY CREEK (*Co. Ashburnham*), a small northern tributary of the Belubula River.

LINBURN (*Co. Wellington*), a postal village, 199 miles W. of Sydney, with mail twice a week. The nearest railway station is Mudgee, 9 miles, on the Mudgee line.

LINCOLN, a county in the Central Division of the Colony. [*See* "COUNTIES."]

LINCOLN (*Co. Lincoln*), a postal village, 260 miles W. of Sydney, with mail four times a week. The nearest railway station is Wellington, 10 miles, on the western line.

LINDEN (*Co. Cook*), a postal village, 52 miles W. of Sydney, with daily mail. A railway station on the western line.

LINDSAY MOUNT (*Co. Courallie*), is the highest peak of the Nundawar Range. It attains an elevation of 3,000 feet above the sea level.

LINDSAY MOUNT (*Co. Rous*), is the highest peak in the Macpherson Range. It lies on the boundary-line between New South Wales and Queensland, attaining an altitude of 3,000 feet above the sea level.

LIONSVILLE (*Co. Drake*), a postal village, 420 miles N. of Sydney, with mail per Clarence River steamers.

LISCOMBE POOLS CREEK (*Co. Bathurst*), a small stream flowing into the Belubula River, rising near the Carcoar and Canowindra Roads.

LISCOMBE'S CREEK (*Co. Bathurst*), a small stream flowing into the head of the Princess Charlotte Vale Creek.

LISMORE (*Co. Rous*), a postal town, 357 miles N. of Sydney, with mail per Clarence and Richmond River steamers. Telegraph and money-order office, Government savings bank, and delivery by letter-carriers. It is situated on the N. arm of the Richmond River, at the junction of the Leycester and Wilson's Creeks with that river, in the parish of Lismore, and police district of Lismore. The district is an agricultural and pastoral one, and very fertile. It was proclaimed a municipal district in 1879, with a council of seven aldermen and a mayor. Courts of quarter sessions and district courts are held here periodically.

LISTON (*Co. Buller*), a township on the Queensland border, near Stanthorpe.

LITHERINGEE (*Co. Tara*), a township on the South Australian border.

LITHGOW (*Co. Cook*), a postal village, 96 miles W. of Sydney, with mail twice daily. Telegraph and money-order offices, Government savings bank, and delivery by letter-carriers. A railway station on the western line. It was proclaimed a municipal district in 1889, with a council of eight aldermen and a mayor. The population is about 3,000. Courts of quarter sessions and district courts are held here periodically.

LITTLE BALD HILL CREEK (*Co. Bathurst*), a small auriferous eastern tributary of the lower part of the Lewis Ponds Creek.

LITTLE BILLABONG (*Co. Goulburn*), a postal village, 360 miles S. of Sydney, with mail three times a week. The nearest railway station is Culcairn, 38 miles, on the southern line.

LITTLE BILLABONG CREEK (*Co. Goulburn*), a small tributary at the head of the Billabong Creek, rising in Main's Range.

LITTLE BOMBAY (*Co. Murray*), a postal receiving-office, 195 miles S. of Sydney, with mail once a week. The nearest railway station is Tarago, 38 miles, on the Goulburn and Cooma line.

LITTLE BUMBLE CREEK (*Co. Jamison*), a small tributary of the Ghean Creek.

LITTLE CREEK (*Co. Fitzroy*), a small eastern tributary of the Don Dorrigo River.

LITTLE DORA (*Co. Clarence*), a postal receiving-office, 506 miles N. of Sydney, with mail once a week.

LITTLE HARTLEY (*Co. Cook*), a postal town, 80 miles W. of Sydney, with daily mail, and money-order office. The nearest railway station is Mount Victoria, 47 miles, on the western line.

LITTLE JACK'S CREEK (*Co. Buckland*), a small tributary of Jack's Creek, rising to the W. of Mount Towarri.

LITTLE LAGOON (*Co. Sandon*), a small sheet of water, about 10 miles S. of the township of Falconer, in the parish of Exmouth.

LITTLE MANLY (*Co. Cumberland*). [*See* "SPRING COVE."]

LITTLE OAKEY (*Co. Roxburgh*), a small auriferous stream, rising in the Wattle Flat gold-field, flowing into the Turon River, E. of the township of Sofala.

LITTLE PITTWATER (*Co. Cumberland*), a small indentation into the land, on the S. side of Broken Bay.

LITTLE PLAIN (*Co. Wellesley*), a tract of bold undulating country, lying about 12 miles S.S.W. of Bombala, and 1 mile from the village of Delegate.

LITTLE PLAIN (*Co. Wellesley*), a postal receiving-office, 366 miles S. of Sydney, with mail twice a week. The nearest railway station is Cooma, 47 miles, on the Goulburn and Cooma line.

LITTLE PLAIN (*Co. Murchison*), a postal receiving-office, 479 miles N. of Sydney, with daily mail.

LITTLE PLAIN (*Co. Wynyard*), a tract of flat auriferous country, forming part of the Adelong gold-fields, about 6 miles to the W. of the township of Adelong.

LITTLE PLAIN RIVER (*Co. Wellesley*). [*See* "RIVERS."]

LITTLE RIVER (*Co. Gordon*). [*See* "RIVERS."]

LITTLE SPRING CREEK (*Co. Monteagle*), a small auriferous tributary of the head of the Burragong Creek, falling into it at the township of Young.

LITTLETON (*Co. Roxburgh*), a village, 112 miles W. of Sydney. It is situated on the Antonio Creek, in the police district of Bathurst, a few miles from the Winburndale Rivulet.

LITTLE WALLABY (*Co. Wellington*), a village, lying within 3 miles of township of Sofala, and forming part of the Turon diggings.

LIVERPOOL (*Co. Cumberland*), a postal town, 22 miles S. of Sydney, with mail twice daily. Telegraph and money-order offices, Government savings bank, and delivery by letter-carriers. A railway station on the Liverpool and Campbelltown line. Situated on the George's River. There are extensive wool-washing establishments and a paper-mill carried on here, successfully employing many hands. Liverpool was proclaimed a municipal district in 1872, with a council of eight aldermen and a mayor. The population is about 4,000.

LIVERPOOL PLAINS, a well-known pastoral district, in the N.E. part of the colony. The Australian Agricultural Company possess in fee simple 562,898 acres of land here. The district is famous for its cereals. The chief towns are Murrurundi, Narrabri, Nundle, Tamworth, Wee Waa, Breeza, Gulligal, Walgett, and Bendemeer.

LIVERPOOL RANGE, a portion of the main dividing range, and was named after Lord Liverpool by Mr. Oxley. It commences at the termination of the New England Range, and runs in a general western course for about 150 miles, separating the valley of the Hunter from the Liverpool Plains and connecting the two table-lands. The highest point in the range is Mount Mooan or Arthur, 5,000 feet above sea-level.

LIVINGSTONE, a county in the Western Division of the Colony. [*See* "COUNTIES."]

LIVINGSTONE (*Co. Camden*), a small village at Little Forest, situated at the junction of the Berrima and Mittagong roads.

LLANDELO (*Co. Cumberland*), a town 4 miles from St. Mary's. It is a railway station 29 miles from Sydney, on the Bathurst and Bourke line.

LLANGOTHLEN (*Co. Sandon*), a post-office, 303 miles N. of Sydney, with mail three times a week. It is a railway station on the northern line.

LLANGOTHLEN MOUNT (*Co. Sandon*), is a small peak in the main dividing range, lying between Falconer and Stonehenge.

LOB'S HOLE (*Co. Buccleuch*), a deep valley, about 16 miles N.W. of Kiandra, on the road to Tumberumba, over the Tumut River.

LOCHINVAR (*Co. Northumberland*), a postal village, 125 miles N. of Sydney, with daily mail. Telegraph and money-order offices and Government savings bank. A railway station on the northern line. Situated on the Hunter River, in the parish of Gosford. The locality is noted for its fine vineyards, and the district is both agricultural and pastoral.

LOCKSLEY (*Co. Roxburgh*), a postal village, 130 miles W. of Sydney, with daily mail. A railway station on the western line.

LOCKYER MOUNT (*Co. Northumberland*), a high peak in the parish of Lockyer, about 16 miles S. of Wollombi, at a place called Simpson's Pass. The mountain is known as Dowling's Range.

**LOFTUS JUNCTION** *(Co. Cumberland)*, a railway station, 16 miles S. of Sydney, on the Hurstville and Waterfall line.

**LOFTY MOUNT** *(Co. Fitzroy)*, a high peak of the Macleay Range, lying on the S. bank of the Nymboi River, and to the W. of Nymboida.

**LOG BRIDGE CREEK** *(Co. Buccleuch)*, a small eastern tributary of the Tumut River, rising in Mount Blowering.

**LONDON BRIDGE** *(Co. Murray)*, a small agricultural hamlet, situated about 23 miles from Queanbeyan.

**LONG BAY** *(Co. Cumberland)*, a western arm of Middle Harbour. At the head of this bay is the well-known cataract, the Willoughby waterfall.

Also an opening in the cliffs on the coast N. of the north head of Botany Bay.

**LONGBOTTOM** *(Co. Cumberland)*, a small village in the parish of Concord, and adjoining Burwood, 6 miles S.E. of Sydney.

**LONG BUNBERI** *(Co. Cowley)*, a lofty peak in the Murrumbidgee Range, between the Cotter and Goodradigbee Rivers.

**LONG COVE** *(Co. Cumberland)*, a southern arm of the Parramatta River, receiving the waters of the Iron and Long Cove Creeks. It has several small bays, the principal being Sisters and Half Moon bays, and Iron Cove. This cove lies between Balmain and Five Dock.

**LONG COVE CREEK** *(Co. Cumberland)*, a small stream rising near the village of Canterbury, flowing N. into the head of Long Cove.

**LONG CREEK** *(Co. Phillip)*, a postal village, 183 miles W. of Sydney, with mail three times a week. Situated on the Long Creek and near the Meroo River, in the Louisa Creek gold-field.

**LONG FLAT** *(Co. Wynyard)*, a tract of fine country on the banks of the Gilmore Creek, and forming part of the Gilmore gold-field.

**LONG ISLAND** *(Co. Westmoreland)*, a sandy island at the mouth of the Hawkesbury River.

**LONG NOSE CREEK** *(Co. Georgiana)*, a small stream rising near Tuena and flowing N.E. into Phil's River.

**LONG NOSE POINT** *(Co. Cumberland)*, a well-known point on the Parramatta River to the W. of Snail's Bay in Balmain, on the S. side of Port Jackson, about 2 miles N.W. of Sydney.

**LONG PLAIN** *(Co. Buccleuch)*, a swampy flat on the W. bank of the head of the Murrumbidgee River.

**LONG REACH** *(Co. Argyle)*, a postal village, 140 miles S. of Sydney, with mail three times a week. The nearest railway station is Marulan, 6 miles on the southern line. Situated on the S. side of Wollondilly River, the Gibraltar Mountain lying 3 miles to the N.W.

**LONG REEF** *(Co. Cumberland)*, a dangerous and well-known reef of rocks running out from the coast at Long Point, 5 miles N. of the entrance to Port Jackson.

LONG SWAMP CREEK (*Co. Westmoreland*), a tributary of Cox's River.

LONG SWAMP (*Co. Georgiana*), a postal receiving-office 189 miles W. of Sydney, with mail once a week. The nearest railway station is Newbridge, 14 miles, on the western line. Situated in the parish of Corowa, on the Groove Creek, about 20 miles from Carcoar.

LORD'S HILL (*Co. Wellesley*), a peak of a northern spur of the South Coast Range, about 4 miles S.W. of the township of Bombala.

LORIMER CREEK (*Co. Bligh*), a small tributary of the head of the Krui River, rising in the Liverpool Range.

LOST RIVER (*Co. King.*) [*See* " RIVERS."]

LOSTOCK (*Co. Durham*), a postal village, 154 miles N. of Sydney, with mail three times a week. The nearest railway station is East Maitland, 43 miles on the East Maitland and Morpeth line. Situated on the Paterson River, about 9 miles from Gresford, in an agricultural, dairy, and pastoral district. Along the banks of the creeks are fine alluvial flats.

LOUISA CREEK (*Co. Wellington*), an auriferous creek rising in the N.W. of the Upper Waurdong Range, and flowing through the Louisa Creek diggings into the Meroo Creek, near Maitland Bar.

LOUISA CREEK GOLD-FIELDS (*Co. Wellington*), an extensive tract of auriferous country lying on the Louisa Creek and its tributaries. The chief town is Hargraves.

LOUTH (*Co. Yanda*), a postal village, 573 miles W. of Sydney, with mail twice a week. Telegraph and money-order offices and Government savings bank. The nearest railway station is Bourke, 73 miles on the western line.

LOVE'S CREEK (*Co. Selwyn*), a tributary of the Tumbarumba Creek, and flowing into the main stream at the crossing-place of the Albury and Snowy River road.

LOW'S SWAMP (*Co. Westmoreland*), a broad and treacherous morass, 102 miles from Sydney, called Sidmouth Valley.

LOWER BOTANY (*Co. Cumberland*), a postal suburb 6 miles S. of Sydney, with mail twice daily. Telegraph and money-order offices, Government savings bank, and delivery by letter-carrier.

LOWER BOTOBOLAR (*Co. Wellington*), a postal receiving-office, 201 miles W. of Sydney, with mail twice a week.

LOWER BELFORD (*Co. Northumberland*), a postal receiving-office, 140 miles N. of Sydney, with mail three times a week.

LOWER COROWA (*Co. Hume*), a postal receiving-office, 440 miles S. of Sydney, with mail daily.

LOWER GUNDAROO (*Co. King*), a postal village, 184 miles S. of Sydney, with mail twice daily. Telegraph and money-order offices and Government savings bank. The nearest railway station is Gunning, 23 miles on the southern line.

LOWER HAWKESBURY (*Co. Cumberland*), a post-office, 74 miles W. of Sydney, with mail twice a week. The nearest railway station is Hawkesbury, on the Ryde and Hawkesbury line.

LOWER MANGROVE (*Co. Northumberland*), a post-office, 62 miles W. of Sydney, with mail therefrom twice a week.

LOWER MOOKERAWA (*Co. Wellington*), a postal receiving-office, 250 miles W. of Sydney, with mail three times a week.

LOWER PORTLAND (*Co. Cumberland*), a postal town, 53 miles W. of Sydney, with mail three times a week, and money-order office. The nearest railway station is Windsor (21 miles) on the Richmond line.

LOWER TALYAWALKA CREEK (*Co. Livingstone*), an important tributary of the Darling River.

LOWER TARCUTTA (*Co. Wynyard*), a postal receiving-office, 317 miles S. of Sydney, with mail three times a week.

LOWER TURON (*Co. Roxburgh*), a town 31 miles from Bathurst, the nearest railway station on the Bathurst and Bourke line.

LOWER YAMMATREE (*Co. Clarendon*), a postal town, 286 miles S. of Sydney, with mail twice a week.

LOWESDALE (*Co. Urana*), a postal village, 421 miles S. of Sydney, with mail twice a week. The nearest railway station is Jerilderie, 6 miles on the Junee and Jerilderie line.

LOWRY MOUNT (*Co. Darling*), a lofty hill on the W. side of the road from Bendemeer to Inverell.

LOWTHER (*Co. Westmoreland*), a postal village, 88 miles W. of Sydney, with mail twice a week. The nearest railway station is Lithgow, on the western line.

LOWTHER CREEK (*Co. Westmoreland*), a tributary of Cox's River.

LUCASVILLE (*Co. Cumberland*), a railway station, 172 miles W. of Sydney, on the western line.

LUCKNOW (*Co. Bathurst*), a postal village, 198 miles W. of Sydney, with daily mail. Telegraph and money-order offices. The nearest railway station is Spring Hill, 4 miles, on the western line.

LUCKY SWAMP (*Co. Roxburgh*), a tract of marshy land on the Kirkconnell Creek, in the parish of Castleton.

LUDDENHAM (*Co. Cumberland*), a postal town, 49 miles W. of Sydney, with daily mail and money-order office. The nearest railway station is Penrith, 12 miles, on the western line.

LUE (*Co. Phillip*), a proclaimed village and a railway station, 172 miles W. of Sydney, on the Wallerawang and Mudgee line.

LUE SIDING (*Co. Bathurst*), a village 1 mile from Blayney. The nearest railway station on Blayney-Murrumburrah line.

LUMLEY (*Co. Argyle*), a small agricultural settlement, lying about 5 miles distant from Bungonia.

LUNTSVALE (*Co. Wynyard*), a postal receiving-office, 349 miles S. of Sydney, with mail three times a week. The nearest railway station is Wagga Wagga, 48 miles, on the southern line.

LUPTON'S INN (*Co. Camden*), a well-known inn, about 8 miles S. of Camden. It lies at an elevation of 1,200 feet above the sea-level.

LUSKINTYRE (*Co. Northumberland*), a small agricultural hamlet, on the Hunter River, adjacent to the village of Lochinvar.

LYELL, MOUNT (*Co. Yancowinna*), the highest peak in the Stanley or Barrier Range. It attains an elevation of 2,000 feet above sea-level.

LYNDHURST (*Co. Bathurst*), a postal village, 191 miles W. of Sydney, with daily mail and telegraph office. A railway station on the Murrumburrah and Blayney line.

LYTTLETON (*Co. Clarendon*), a postal village, 312 miles S. of Sydney, with mail four times a week. A telegraph and money-order office. The nearest railway station is Cooma, 50 miles, on the Goulburn and Cooma line.

# M

MACARTHUR'S POINT (*Co. Cumberland*), is the northern point of the south head of Johnstone's Bay, in the suburb of Pyrmont.

MACARTHUR RIVER (*Co. Gloucester*). [*See* "RIVERS."]

MACDONALD RIVER (*Cos. Northumberland and Cook*). [*See* "RIVERS."]

MACDONALD RIVER (*Cos. Hunter and Northumberland*). [*See* "RIVERS."]

MACDONALD RIVER (*Co. Vernon*), a postal receiving-office, 316 miles N. of Sydney, with daily mail. A railway station on the western line.

MACDONALD TOWN (*Co. Cumberland*), a postal suburb, 4 miles S. of Sydney, with mail twice daily. Telegraph and money-order offices, Government savings bank, and delivery by letter-carriers. A railway station on the suburban line. It was incorporated a municipal district in 1872, with a council of eight aldermen and a mayor. The population is about 5,200.

MACDONALD'S CREEK (*Co. Bathurst*), a southern tributary of Jack's Creek, flowing through the Australian Agricultural Company's grant of 249,600 acres.

MACGUIRE'S CREEK (*Co. Rous*), a small northern tributary of the estuary of the Richmond River, falling into it near its mouth.

MACHINY CREEK (*Co. Cumberland*), a southern tributary of the Parramatta River, falling into it near Homebush.

MACINTYRE CREEK (*Co. Murchison*), a southern tributary of the Keera Creek, lying to the N. of the Ironbark gold-field.

MACINTYRE RIVER (*Co. Benarba*). [*See* "RIVERS."]

MACKSVILLE (*Co. Macquarie*), a postal town, 346 miles N. of Sydney, with mail three times a week. Telegraph and money-order offices, and Government savings bank.

MACLEAN (*Co. Clarence*), a postal town, 323 miles N. of Sydney, with mail twice a week, and per steamer. Telegraph and money-order offices, Government savings bank, and delivery by letter-carriers. Situated at Rocky Mouth, on the Clarence River. It was incorporated a municipal district in 1887, with a council of five aldermen and a mayor. The population is about 1,500. It has a court of quarter sessions and district court, which are held here periodically.

MACLEAN RIVER (*Co. Gloucester*). [*See* "RIVERS."]

MACLEAY RIVER (*Cos. Dudley and Macquarie*). [*See* "RIVERS."]

MACLEAY RANGE (*Cos. Gresham and Fitzroy*), a branch of the New England Range, and separates the basin of the Clarence and Macleay. It branches from New England Range, near Chandler's Creek, and terminates near the coast.

MACOMMON LAKE (*Co. Caira*), one of a series of lakes in this county, on the Murrumbidgee River.

MACPHERSON SWAMP CREEK (*Co. Buccleuch*), a southern tributary of the Murrumbidgee River, rising to the W. of the Goodradigbee River.

MACPHERSON'S RANGE (*Cos. Buller and Rous*), a branch of the New England Range, and lies between the basins of the Logan (Queensland) on the N. and the Clarence and Richmond on the S. The highest point is Mount Lindsay, which attains an altitude of 5,700 feet above sea-level.

MACQUARIE, a county in the Eastern Division of the Colony. [*See* "COUNTIES."]

MACQUARIE, EAST (*Co. Macquarie*), a proclaimed township in this county.

MACQUARIE, WEST (*Co. Macquarie*), a proclaimed township in this county.

MACQUARIE CATARACT (*Co. Ewenmar*), a fall on the Macquarie River. It lies 680 feet above sea-level.

MACQUARIE FIELDS (*Co. Cumberland*), a railway station, 27 miles from Sydney, on the southern line.

MACQUARIE LAKE (*Co. Northumberland*), a large inlet of the sea, forming a lake or lagoon, connected with the Pacific Ocean by a narrow passage called Reid's Mistake. The village of Kahiba is situated at the entrance to the lake. It is about 20 miles in length, and averages about 3 miles in width. The opening to this lake lies about 12 miles S. of Newcastle. Easy access is afforded to the lake by the Newcastle and Sydney railway. There is an abundance of coal in the vicinity. The entrance to the lake is about 50 miles N. from the N. head of Port Jackson, and 5 miles from Red Head. Its waters abound in fish, and flocks of wild fowl give ample sport for the gun.

MACQUARIE MARSHES (*Co. Clyde*), is the name given to an expansion of the Macquarie River.

MACQUARIE PLAINS (*Co. Roxburgh*), a village, 3 miles from Brewongle, the nearest railway station on the western line.

MACQUARIE RANGE (*Cos. Wellington and Bathurst*).—This range is one of the western spurs of the Blue Mountain Range, and divides the waters of the Macquarie from those of the Lachlan. One of the peaks on this range, Mount Canobolas, rises to an elevation of 4,610 feet above the sea-level.

MACQUARIE RIVER (*Cos. Bathurst, Roxburgh, Wellington, Lincoln, Gordon, and Bligh*). [*See* "RIVERS."]

MACQUARIE RIVULET (*Co. Camden*). [*See* "RIVERS."]

MACQUARIE TOWER (*Co. Cumberland*), situated on Cape Banks, in the parish of Botany. It was built by Governor Macquarie.

MACQUARIE'S (MRS.) CHAIR (*Co. Cumberland*), a beautiful part of the Government Domain, on the southern side of Port Jackson, being the western head of Woolloomooloo Bay. Mrs. Macquarie, the wife of Governor Macquarie, in dedicating this lovely spot for the use of the citizens of Sydney and the public generally, had inscribed on the rock overhanging the seat, the following words : " Be it thus recorded that the road round the inside of the Government Domain, called Mrs. Macquarie's Road, is named by the Governor on account of her having originally planned it, measuring 3 miles 377 yards ; was finally completed on the 13th day of June, 1816."

MACQUEEN (*Co. Brisbane*), a township on the Goulburn River, to the S. of Moonan Brook.

M‘ALISTER (*Co. Argyle*), a proclaimed village in this county.

M‘CANN, MOUNT (*Co. Bathurst*), a peak on the N. side of the road from Bathurst to Ophir, in the parish of Byng.

M‘CARTHY'S MOUNT (*Co. Gough*), a peaked hill lying about 5 miles E. of the township of Inverell.

M‘CULLOCH'S RANGE (*Co. Livingstone*), a range of sandstone hills, lying between the Bogan and Darling Rivers.

M‘DONALD'S FLAT (*Co. Northumberland*), lying about 8 miles S. of the Wollombi township, on the Wollombi Brook.

M‘DONALD'S PEAK (*Co. Tongowoko*), a peak of the Grey Range.

M‘EWEN'S CAVE (*Co. Westmoreland*), is the name of one of the Fish River caves, on the Ducanalong Creek.

M‘LAUGHLAN'S CREEK (*Co. Murray*), a tributary creek of the head of the Yass River, forming one of its sources. It rises in Mount Ainslie, N. of Queanbeyan, and joins the Yass River, near the foot of Mount Bywong.

M'LAUGLIN RIVER (*Co. Wallace*). [See "RIVERS."]

M'PHERSON MOUNT (*Co. Landsborough*), a flat-topped hill, lying on the W. bank of the Darling River, about 130 miles S.W. of Bourke.

M'QUOID MOUNT (*Co. Northumberland*), is a high hill in the Dowling Range, about 9 miles S. of Wollombi township.

MADGORA CREEK (*Co. Leichhardt*), a western tributary of the Castlereagh River, rising to the W. of Coonamble.

MAESTER'S SWAMP (*Co. Sandon*), a swamp on the Kentucky Ponds, in the parish of Kentucky.

MAGINCOBLE CREEK (*Co. Ashburnham*), a southern tributary of the Goobang Creek, flowing to the N. of the Lachlan gold-fields.

MAHARATTA CREEK (*Co. Wellesley*), a tributary of the Bombala River, rising on the western side of Mount Coolangubra.

MAHONGA (*Co. Urana*), a postal town, 434 miles S. of Sydney, with mail three times a week.

MAIN CREEK DIGGINGS (*Co. Murchison*), an alluvial diggings on Bingara gold-field, about 12 miles S. of the township of Bingara.

MAITLAND EAST (*Co. Northumberland*), a postal town, 93 miles N. of Sydney, with mail twice daily. Telegraph and money-order offices, Government savings bank, and delivery by letter-carrier. It is a railway station on the Newcastle, Maitland, and Singleton line, and is situated on Wallis' Creek, which divides it on its western side from West Maitland, and on the Hunter River which flows on its northern side, in the parish and police district of Maitland. East Maitland is the assize town of the district, and the law Courts and the gaol, both spacious and convenient edifices, are built here. The thriving township of West Maitland is about 1 mile to the N.W. The district is an agricultural and pastoral one. There are coal-mines within 2 miles of the E. end of the township, and the horse and cattle market and sale-yards are the largest and best in the district. It was proclaimed a borough in 1862, with a council of eight aldermen and a mayor. Population is about 3,000. Sittings of the supreme court, courts of quarter sessions, and district courts are held here periodically.

MAITLAND WEST (*Co. Northumberland*), a postal town, 95 miles N. of Sydney, with mail twice daily. Telegraph and money-order offices, Government savings bank, and delivery by letter-carriers. It is a railway station on the Newcastle, Maitland, and Singleton line, in the parish and police district of Maitland, on the S. side of the Hunter River, being separated from East Maitland (the Government township) by a tributary of that river known as Wallis' Creek. The Hunter River lies on the N. of the township, and Wallis' Creek on the E. and S.E. The district is wholly agricultural, the soil being well adapted for the growth of all kinds of grain, fruits, and vegetables. Lucerne is extensively grown here. Coal is also abundant. It was proclaimed a borough in 1863, with a council of eleven aldermen and a mayor.

MAITLAND BAR (*Co. Wellington*), a quartz and alluvial gold working, forming part of the Meroo gold-field, situated about 2 miles W. of the township of Avisford.

MAITLAND POINT (*Co. Sandon*), a small village reserve, situated near the township of Armidale.

MAJOR'S CREEK (*Co. Hume*), a small northern tributary of the Billabung Creek, rising to the N. of the township of Morven.

MAJOR'S CREEK (*Co. St. Vincent*), a postal village, 198 miles S. of Sydney, with mail three times a week. Telegraph and money-order offices, and Government savings bank. The nearest railway station is Tarago, 45 miles, on the Goulburn and Cooma line. Situated in the parish of Elrington, on Major's Creek, about 10 miles S. from Braidwood. The district is an alluvial mining one. The Shoalhaven River flows past the township, within 6 miles W.

MALADY'S PEAK (*Co. Wallace*).—This peak attains an elevation of 3,880 feet above sea-level, situate about 10 miles W. of Nimitybelle.

MALEBO (*Co. Wynyard*), a postal village, 314 miles S. of Sydney, with mail three times a week.

MALLOWA BRANCH (*Co. Courallie*), a southern outlet of the Gwydir River, flowing into the Moonin Brook.

MALONGULLI (*Co. Bathurst*), a proclaimed village in this county.

MANAR (*Co. St. Vincent*), a postal receiving-office, 179 miles S. of Sydney, with daily mail. The nearest railway station is Tarago, 22 miles, on the Goulburn and Cooma line.

MANARA, a county in the Western Division of the Colony. [*See* "COUNTIES."]

MANDALONG (*Co. Northumberland*), a postal village, 85 miles N. of Sydney, with mail three times a week.

MANDAMA (*Co. Bourke*), a proclaimed village in this county.

MANDURAMA (*Co. Bathurst*), a postal village, 188 miles W. of Sydney, with daily mail and telegraph office. A railway station on the Murrumburrah and Blayney line.

MANDURAMA PONDS CREEK (*Co. Bathurst*), a chain of ponds lying between the townships of Lyndhurst and Somers, flowing through the latter into the Grubbenbun Creek.

MANGAROO CREEK (*Co. Cook*), a tributary of the Cox's River.

MANGOPLA (*Co. Mitchell*), a village, 306 miles S. of Sydney. The nearest railway station is Wagga Wagga, 25 miles, on the southern line.

MANGROVE CREEK (*Co. Clarence*), a northern tributary of the Clarence River, joining it to the N.E. of Ashby.

MANGROVE CREEK (*Co. Northumberland*), a post-office, 68 miles N. of Sydney, with mail twice a week. The nearest railway station is Hawkesbury, 12 miles, on the Ryde and Hawkesbury line. It lies on a creek flowing into the N. bank of the Hawkesbury River.

MANGROVE ISLAND (*Co. Northumberland*), a small island in the Broadwater, Brisbane Water.

MANILDRA CREEK (*Co. Ashburnham*), a proclaimed village; one of the heads of Byrne's Creek, near Orange.

MANILLA (*Co. Darling*), a postal town, 309 miles N. of Sydney, with daily mail. Telegraph and money-order offices, and Government savings bank. The nearest railway station is Tamworth, 30 miles, on the northern line. Situated on the Namoi River, near the junction of the Manilla River, and in the police district of Tamworth. The district is a pastoral and quartz-mining one.

MANILLA RIVER (*Co. Darling*). [*See* "RIVERS."]

MANLY (*Co. Cumberland*), a postal suburb, 9 miles E. from Sydney, with mail four times daily. Telegraph and money-order offices, Government savings bank, and delivery by letter-carriers. It was proclaimed a municipal district in 1878, with a council of eight aldermen and a mayor. Population, about 2,500.

MANLY BEACH (*Co. Cumberland*), a sandy beach at the head of Manly Cove in Port Jackson; a favourite place of resort for invalids and pleasure-seekers, and is now called "the Brighton of the Southern Hemisphere." The steamboat accommodation between it and Sydney is luxurious. The sea-beach on the eastern side of the cove is a charming resort; at all seasons of the year it is enjoyable, and the citizens avail themselves of the charms which the broad expanse of ocean inspires and the sea-breeze invigorates. Manly was named by Governor Phillip on the 28th January, 1788.

MANNA CREEK (*Co. Gipps*), a name given to the lower part of the Yeo-Yeo Creek, where it drains the overflow of Lake Cowal into the Bogandillan Lagoon.

MANNA FIELD (*Co. Argyle*), a village, 124 miles S. of Sydney, and the nearest railway station is Towrang, 1 mile, on the southern line.

MANNA MOUNT (*Co. Gipps*), a solitary hill lying between the Lachlan and Murrumbidgee Rivers, S. of Condobolin.

MANNERING CREEK (*Co. Northumberland*), a fine stream rising in Mount Warrawolong, and flowing into Lake Macquarie.

MANNING MOUNT (*Co. Northumberland*), a high peak in the parish of Lockyer, on the W. side of the road from Maitland to Sydney *via* Wollombi.

MANNING RIVER (*Cos. Gloucester and Macquarie*). [*See* "RIVERS."]

MANOBALAR MOUNT (*Co. Brisbane*), a high hill lying a few miles N.E. of Wickham.

MANTON'S CREEK (*Co. King*), a northern tributary of the Yass River, rising in Mount Mandomen, and falling into the main stream near the township of Yass.

MARABA CREEK (*Co. Leichhardt*), an eastern tributary of the Castlereagh River, lying to the S.W. of Barrabool Plains.

MARACKET (*Co. Goulburn*), a postal receiving-office, 465 miles S. of Sydney, with mail twice a week. The nearest railway station is Albury, 79 miles, on the southern line.

MARACKET MOUNT (*Co. Goulburn*), a high peak of the Jingellec mountains, overhanging the Murray River, near the village of Talmalino.

MARA-MARA CREEK (*Co. Cumberland*), a small creek, falling into the head of Broken Bay, on its S. side.

MARAGLE CREEK (*Co. Selwyn*), a tributary of the Tumberumba Creek, rising in the S.E. end of Mane's Range, and flowing W. past the S. of Maraglc Hill.

MARAGLE BACK CREEK (*Co. Selwyn*), a small tributary of Maraglo Creek.

MARAGLE FIELD (*Co. Selwyn*), an undulating grassy plain, lying between Maragle and Cowra Creek, to the W. of Mane's Range.

MARAH (*Co. Bathurst*), a postal village, 198 miles W. of Sydney, with mail twice a week. The nearest railway station is Orange, 6 miles, on the western line.

MARANGAROO (*Co. Roxburgh*), a railway station, 101 miles W. of Sydney, on the western line.

MARANGULLA CREEK (*Co. Bathurst*), a small tributary of the Belubula River, flowing N. through the township of Euro.

MARARA CREEK (*Co. Goulburn*), a small western tributary of the Coppabella Creek, rising in Mane's Range.

MARE'S WATER-HOLE (*Co. Ashburnham*), a postal receiving-office, 271 miles W. of Sydney, with mail once a week.

MARENGO (*Co. Monteagle*), a postal village, 241 miles S. of Sydney, with daily mail. Telegraph and money-order offices, and Government savings bank. The nearest railway station is Young, 12 miles, on the Murrumburrah and Blayney line. Situated on the Marengo Creek, in the parish of Marengo. The district is an agricultural and pastoral one. The nearest gold-field is Young, 14 miles W.

MARIA'S RIVER (*Co. Macquarie*). [*See* "RIVERS."]

MARIAVILLE (*Co. Macquarie*), a small agricultural settlement, situate on Maria's River, 8 miles S. of Kempsey.

MARKDALE (*Co. Georgiana*), a postal receiving-office, 178 miles S. of Sydney, with mail three times a week.

MARLEE (*Co. Gloucester*), a postal village, 245 miles N. of Sydney, with mail three times a week. The nearest railway station is Morpeth, 125 miles, on the Maitland and Morpeth line.

MARLOW (*Co. St. Vincent*), a small agricultural village, lying on the E. side of the Shoalhaven River, about 16 miles N. of Braidwood.

MAROOMBILI CREEK (*Co. Wellington*), a tributary of the Louisa Creek, flowing from the table-lands of the Louisa Creek diggings.

MAROUBRA BAY (*Co. Cumberland*), a rocky bight in the coast, lying between Port Jackson and Botany, about 8 miles S. of the entrance to Port Jackson.

MARRA CREEK (*Co. Clyde*), a southern tributary of the Barwon River.

MARRANA CREEK (*Co. Durham*), a postal receiving-office, 169 miles N. of Sydney, with mail twice a week.

MARRAR (*Co. Clarendon*), a postal receiving-office, 301 miles S. of Sydney, with daily mail. A railway station on the south-western line.

MARRICKVILLE (*Co. Cumberland*), a postal suburb, 4 miles S.W. of Sydney, with mail twice daily. Telegraph and money-order office, Government savings bank, and delivery by letter-carrier; also a railway station on the Illawarra and South Coast line. It is a municipal village; in the parish of Petersham, with a council of eleven aldermen and a mayor. Situated about 1 mile S.W. of Newtown. The soil is very fertile. Population, about 2,500.

MARSDEN (*Co. Gipps*), a postal village, 318 miles W. of Sydney, with mails three times a week. Telegraph and money-order offices, and Government savings bank. The nearest railway station is Young, 75 miles, on the Murrumburrah and Blayney line.

MARSDEN PARK (*Co. Cumberland*), a postal village, 29 miles W. of Sydney, with daily mail. The nearest railway station is Riverstone, 16 miles, on the Windsor and Richmond line.

MARSDEN'S CREEK (*Co. Cumberland*), a small creek flowing near the village of Dural, on the N. road from Parramatta to Wiseman's Ferry.

MARSHALL MOUNT (*Co. Camden*), a postal village, 78 miles S. of Sydney, with mail three times a week. The nearest railway station is Dapto, 4 miles, on the Illawarra and South Coast line. It is a small agricultural village, on the eastern slope of the Illawarra Range.

MARSHAL M'MAHON REEF (*Co. Roxburgh*), a postal village, 237 miles S. of Sydney, with mail twice a week, and money-order office.

MARTAGUY CREEK (*Co. Ewenmar*), an eastern tributary of the lower end of the Macquarie River, rising near the township of Mendooran, and falling into the Barwon.

MARTIN (*Co. Ashburnham*), a proclaimed village in this county.

MARULAN (*Co. Argyle*), a postal village, 114 miles S. of Sydney, with mail twice daily. Telegraph and money-order offices, and Government savings bank; also a railway station on the southern line. Situated on the Marulan Creek, near its junction with the Shoalhaven River, and within 6 miles S.W. of the Wollondilly River.

MARY VALE (*Co. Lincoln*), a postal village, 254 miles W. of Sydney, with daily mail. Telegraph and money-order offices, and Government savings bank; also a railway station on the western line.

MARYBUNG (*Co. Waradgery*), a village, 454 miles S.W. of Sydney. The nearest railway station is Hay, on the south-western line.

MARYLAND (*Co. Buller*), a postal village, 499 miles N. of Sydney, with daily mail. The nearest railway station is Tenterfield, 44 miles, on the northern line. Situated on a creek flowing into the Clarence.

MATAGANA CREEK (*Co. Auckland*), a northern tributary of the upper part of the Towamba River.

MATCHEM'S CREEK (*Co. Buccleuch*), a small southern tributary of the Murrumbidgee River.

MATE'S GULLY (*Co. Wynyard*), a small creek flowing from Mount Bijengun.

MATHESON (*Co. Gough*), a postal receiving-office, 429 miles N. of Sydney, with daily mail.

MATHOURA (*Co. Cadell*), a postal town, 556 miles S. of Sydney, with daily mail. Telegraph and money-order offices. The nearest railway station is Hay, 105 miles, on the south-western line.

MATONG PEAK (*Co. Wallace*), a solitary hill to the S. of Buckley's Crossing-place.

MATTA MOUNT (*Lachlan District*).—This mountain is situated in the centre of the Lachlan District, to the N. of Jones' Hill.

MAUDE (*Co. Waradgery*), a postal village, 490 miles S. of Sydney, with mail three times a week. The nearest railway station is Hay, 33 miles, on the south-western line. Situated on the N. bank of the Murrumbidgee River, and the district is purely a pastoral one.

MAULE'S CREEK (*Co. Nandewar*), a village, 318 miles N.E. of Sydney. The nearest railway station is Boggabri, 28 miles, on the north-eastern line. The creek is a northern tributary of the Namoi River, rising in the S.E. spur of the Nundawar Range.

MAY'S HILL (*Co. Cumberland*), a postal village, 16 miles W. of Sydney, with daily mail. The nearest railway station is Parramatta, 1 mile, on the suburban line.

MAYBOLE (*Co. Sandon*), a postal receiving-office, 409 miles N. of Sydney, with mail once a week.

MAYFIELD (*Co. Murray*), a postal village, 174 miles S. of Sydney, with mail twice a week. The nearest railway station is Tarago, 20 miles, on the Goulburn and Cooma line.

MAYO'S HILL (*Co. Harden*), a lofty hill, lying on the E. bank of the Demondrille Creek, and part of the Wombat diggings.

MEADOW BANK (*Co. Cumberland*), a railway station, 11 miles W. of Sydney, on the Ryde and Hawkesbury line.

MEADOW FLAT (*Co. Roxburgh*), a postal village, 120 miles W. of Sydney, with daily mail. The nearest railway station is Rydal, 9 miles, on the western line. Situated on the Meadow Flat, or Scott's Creek, 3½ miles from Mount Lambie, in the parish of Falnash. The district produces nearly every fruit in the highest perfection.

R

MEADOW FLAT CREEK (*Co. Roxburgh*), an eastern tributary of the Diamond Swamp Creek, rising in the western slopes of the Blue Mountain Range, and flowing S.W. through the village of Meadow Flat.

MEADOW LEA (*Co. Roxburgh*), a proclaimed township, 126 miles W. of Sydney, near the Great Northern railway and Tarana.

MEADOW PLAINS (*Co. Jamison*), a tract of fine land, lying on Burran Creek, 25 miles N. of Narrabri.

MEADOW PONDS (*Co. Jamison*), a chain of waterholes, flowing into the Welcome Ponds, near Narrabri.

MEADOWS, (*Co. Wellington*), is situated 160 miles W. of Sydney, on the Molong Rivulet, 4 miles E. of Orange, and 5 miles N. of the Canobolas. The district is purely agricultural, and much cultivated. The nearest railway station is Orange, 4 miles, on the western line.

MEADOW'S CREEK (*Co. Gordon*).—A small creek at the head of Wylandra Creek.

MEDLOW (*Co. Cook*), a railway station, 70 miles W. of Sydney, on the western line.

MEEKHAM (*Co. Cook*), one of the original districts of the county, bounded by the Phillip District and the Hawkesbury River.

MEERMAUL (*Co. Pottinger*), a postal receiving-office, 301 miles N. of Sydney, with mail twice a week.

MEGALONG CREEK (*Co. Westmoreland*), a tributary of Cox's River.

MEHI (*Co. Narran*), a postal village, 556 miles N. of Sydney, with mail twice a week. Telegraph station.

MELVILLE (*Co. Cumberland*), one of the original districts of the county, bounded by Cabramatta and the southern and eastern creeks.

MELVILLE PLAINS (*Co. Pottinger*), a tract of pastoral country in the district of Liverpool Plains to the W. of Gulligal and Gunnedah.

MELROSE (*Co. Sandon*), a postal village, 343 miles N. of Sydney, with mail therefrom twice a week. The nearest railway station is Uralla, 30 miles, on the northern line.

MENANGLE (*Co. Camden*), a postal village, 40 miles S. of Sydney, with mail twice daily, and telegraph office ; also a railway station on the southern line. Situated on the Nepean River, in the parish of Menangle. The district is very rich and fertile.

MENINDIE, a county in the Western Division of the Colony. [*See* "COUNTIES."]

MENINDIE (*Co. Menindie*), a postal town, 880 miles S. of Sydney, with mail three times a week. The nearest railway station is Hay, 360 miles, on the south-western line. Situated on the W. bank of the Darling River. The district is wholly a pastoral anc.

MENUNDA CREEK (*Co. Georgiana*), a small drainage creek, flowing into Malgowrie Creek, which is fed by the Kangaroo Creek.

MERANBURN (*Co. Wellington*), a postal village, 237 miles W. of Sydney, with daily mail. Telegraph and money-order offices, and Government savings bank. The nearest railway station is Molong, 15 miles, on the Orange and Molong line.

MEREDITH FOREST (*Co. Camden*), a tract of fine agricultural land, about 10 miles W. of Berrima.

MEREWETHER (*Co. Northumberland*), a postal village, 76 miles N. of Sydney, with daily mail. Telegraph and money-order offices. It was incorporated a municipal district in 1885, with a council of eight aldermen and a mayor.

MERIMBULA (*Co. Auckland*), a postal town, 272 miles S. of Sydney, with mail per steamer. Telegraph and money-order offices and Government savings bank. The nearest railway station is Cooma, 114 miles, on the Goulburn and Cooma line. Situated on a lake of the same name, lying 10 miles N. of Eden and 16 miles S. of Bega, in the parish of Panbula. The village is a seaport for the shipment of produce from the Monaro District. It is a very flourishing and productive district.

MERINDA (*Co. Wellington*), a proclaimed village on the creek of the same name.

MERINDA CREEK (*Co. Wellington*), a fine stream rising to the W. of Mudgee, and flowing through the Merinda gold-field into the Meroo Creek.

MERINGLO (*Co. Auckland*), a postal receiving-office, 268 miles S. of Sydney, with mail once a week.

MERINGO MOUNT (*Co. Wellesley*), a small hill on the Delegate River, lying near the Quedong Copper Mines.

MERINO MOUNT (*Co. Rous*), a peak of the Macpherson Range, lying about 25 miles W. of Point Danger.

MERMAID REEF (*Co. Macquarie*).—This reef, on which the sea constantly breaks, lies 2¼ miles from the shore, nearly opposite Camden Haven.

MEROE (*Co. Courallie*), a postal town, 497 miles N. of Sydney, with mail twice a week. The nearest railway station is Narrabri, 72 miles, on the north-western line.

MEROO (*Co. Wellington*), a village, 168 miles W. of Sydney, situated on the river Hargraves. The nearest railway station is Mudgee, 6 miles, on the western line.

MEROO CREEK (*Co. Wellington*), a fine auriferous stream, rising near Mount Bocoble and flowing through the townships of Windeyer and Avisford into the Cudgegong River on the Merinda gold-field.

MEROOL CREEK (*Co. Bland*), a postal village, 396 miles S. of Sydney, with mail twice a week.

MERRANG (*Co. Wakool*), a tributary of the Wakool River, draining the pastoral country lying between the Murray River and the township of Jegar.

MERRENDEE (*Co. Wellington*), a postal village, 245 miles W. of Sydney, with mail three times a week. The nearest railway station is Mudgee, 20 miles, on the western line.

MERRI MERRI CREEK (*Cos. Ewenmar and Gregory*), a tributary of the Macquarie River, flowing past the village of Merri Merri or Quambone.

MERRIANGLEDRE (*Co. Wellington*), a western tributary of the Maroombili Creek, flowing in the table-land of Louisa Creek diggings.

MERRIBUL CREEK (*Co. Wakool*), a branch of the Wakool River at its upper end, flowing through flat pastoral country.

MERRIBUNG (*Co. Nicholson*), a village, 377 miles, W. from Sydney. The nearest railway station is Nyngan on the Bathurst and Bourke line.

MERRIGAL (*Co. Ewenmar*), a postal receiving-office, 357 miles W. of Sydney, with mail twice a week.

MERRILLA (*Co. Goulburn*), a postal village, 155 miles S. of Sydney, with mail three times a week. The nearest railway station is Breadalbane, 7 miles, on the southern line.

MERRINGAAH MOUNT (*Co. Wellesley*), a peak in the Broken Range of the Snowy and MacLaughlin Rivers.

MERRIWA (*Co. Brisbane*), a postal village, 228 miles N. of Sydney, with mail daily. Telegraph and money-order office, and Government savings bank. The nearest railway station is Muswellbrook, 30 miles, on the northern line. Situated on the Merriwa Creek. The district is chiefly a pastoral one, being well watered and the soil good.

MERRIWA CREEK (*Co. Brisbane*), a small northern tributary of the Goulburn River, flowing past the township of Merriwa.

MERRYGOEN (*Co. Napier*), a postal village, 250 miles W. of Sydney, with mail twice a week. The nearest railway station is Wellington, 65 miles, on the western line.

MERRYGOEN CREEK (*Co. Napier*), a tributary of the Castlereagh River, rising to the E. of the village of Bullinda and flowing into the main stream at the township of Mendooran.

MERYLA (*Co. Camden*), a railway station, 89 miles S. of Sydney, on the southern line.

MERYLA CREEK (*Co. Camden*), a small tributary of the Kangaroo River, falling into the Shoalhaven River.

MERRYLANDS (*Co. Cumberland*), a postal village, 15 miles S. of Sydney, with mail twice daily. A railway station on the Liverpool and Campbelltown line.

MEWSTONE ISLAND (*Co. Auckland*) is a rock a-wash in the entrance to Twofold Bay.

MIAH-MIAH CREEK (*Co. Courallie*), a small southern tributary of the Gwydir River. It is crossed at its mouth by the road from Bingera to Moree.

MIANGAR CREEK (*Co. Georgiana*), a small tributary of Clifford's Creek falling into it N. of Laggan.

MICALAGO (*Co. Murray*), a postal village, 224 miles S. of Sydney, with daily mail therefrom. A railway station on the Goulburn and Cooma line. Situated on the Micalago Creek, in the parish of that name. The district is both pastoral and agricultural.

MICALAGO CREEK (*Cos. Beresford and Murray*), a small eastern tributary of the Upper Murray River, rising in Tinderry Creek, N. of the Monaro Plains, known as the Furies, flowing into the main stream at the village of Micalago.

MICALONG CREEK (*Co. Beresford*), a western tributary of the Gooradigbee River, rising at Mount Tumarama, flowing past Weejasper Hill, crossing the road from Yass to Kiandra.

MIDDLE ADELONG (*Co. Wynyard*), a postal receiving-office, 320 miles S. of Sydney, with mail twice a week.

MIDDLE ARM (*Co. Argyle*), a postal village, 152 miles S. of Sydney, with mail three times a week. The nearest railway station is Goulburn, 18 miles, on the southern line.

MIDDLE CREEK (*Co. Brisbane*), a western tributary of Dartbrooke.

MIDDLE CREEK (*Co. Gough*), a fine creek flowing through the township of Inverell into the Macintyre River, near Byron.

MIDDLE CREEK (*Co. King*), a small northern tributary of Blakeney's Creek, flowing in the Yass Plains.

MIDDLE CREEK (*Co. Murchison*), a southern tributary of Reedy Creek, fed by the Gundamunda Creek, on the Bingara gold-workings.

MIDDLE HARBOUR (*Co. Cumberland*), a beautiful northern arm of Port Jackson, about 2 miles W. of the N. head of the port. The opening of the harbour is marked by two bold headlands, known as Middle Head on the S. and Grotto Point on the N. side. It is crossed at the Spit by a ferry on the road from Sydney to Pittwater and Manly, and the various indentations or bays are the favourite resort of pleasure-seekers. The scenery is of the most romantic and beautiful character.

MIDDLE HEAD (*Co. Cumberland*), a bold rocky promontory on the N. shore of Port Jackson, opposite its entrance, and forming the S. head of Middle Harbour.

MIDDLEDALE (*Co. Hume*), a post-office, 430 miles S. of Sydney, with mail once a week,

MIDERULA MOUNT (*Co. Phillip*), a peak in the Blue Mountain Range, near the head of the Cudgegong River.

MIDWAY RIVULET (*Co. Camden*), a small stream, forming the S. head of Wingecarribee River, flowing through Sutton Forest.

MIHI CREEK (*Co. Sandon*), a tributary of the upper part of the Macleay River, rising in Bald Nob.

MIHI FALLS (*Co. Sandon*), a waterfall on the Mihi Creek, above Dangar's Falls.

MILBAI CREEK (*Co. Gloucester*), a small tributary of the Manning River, falling into it at Tinonee.

MILBEE MOUNT (*Co. Dowling*), a solitary hill lying between the Lachlan and Murrumbidgee Rivers, S. of Condobolin.

MILBRODALE (*Co. Northumberland*), an agricultural village on the Wollombi Brook, 10 miles S.W. of Singleton.

MILBURN CREEK (*Co. Bathurst*), a postal receiving-office, 215 miles W. of Sydney, with daily mail. The nearest railway station is Woodstock, 11 miles, on the Murrumburrah and Blayney line. The creek is a northern tributary of the Lachlan River, to the S. of Lyndhurst.

MILK BEACH (*Co. Cumberland*), a sandy beach on the rocky E. shore of Rose Bay, Port Jackson.

MILL BROOK (*Co. Gloucester*), a small tributary of the Belbora Creek.

MILLAMURRAH (*Co. Roxburgh*), a postal village, 160 miles W. of Sydney, with mail once a week. The nearest railway station is Bathurst, 17 miles, on the western line. Situated on the Millamurrah Creek. The district is a good wheat-growing one.

MILLAMBURRAH CREEK (*Co. Roxburgh*), a northern tributary of the Winburndale Rivulet.

MILLENBONG MOUNT (*Co. Wellington*), a peak on the Louisa Creek Diggings, about 7 miles W. of Avisford.

MILLER'S CREEK (*Co. Buckland*), a small western tributary of the head of the Onus' Creek.

MILLER'S FOREST (*Co. Durham*), a postal town, 97 miles N. of Sydney, with daily mail, telegraph, and money-order offices. The nearest railway station is Morpeth, 9 miles, on the East Maitland and Morpeth line. Situated on the Hunter River, in the parish of Alnwick. The district is very fertile.

MILLEWA DIGGINGS (*Co. Roxburgh*), a gold-workings, forming part of the Bathurst gold-field.

MILLFIELD (*Co. Northumberland*), a postal village, 143 miles N. of Sydney, with mail three times a week. The nearest railway station is Farley, 25 miles, on the northern line. Situated on the Wollombi Brook in an agricultural district.

MILLIE (*Co. Nandewar*), a postal village, 301 miles N. of Sydney, with daily mail, telegraph, and money-order offices. The nearest railway station is Narrabri, 40 miles, on the north-western line. It is an agricultural district, lying near the township of Narrabri.

MILLINGANDI (*Co. Auckland*), a postal village, 272 miles S. of Sydney, with mail three times a week.

MILLIWINDI (*Co. Darling*), a proclaimed village, on the Namoi River.

MILPARINKA (*Co. Evelyn*), a postal town, 862 miles S. of Sydney, with mail twice a week, and money-order office. The nearest railway station is Hay, 350 miles, on the south-western line.

MILSON'S POINT (*Co. Cumberland*), a rocky projection from the N. shore of Port Jackson, at East St. Leonard's, opposite the Circular Quay, whence steam ferry boats ply at short intervals to and from Sydney.

MILTHORPE (*Co. Bathurst*), a postal village, 179 miles W. of Sydney, with daily mail, telegraph, and money-order offices, and Government savings bank. A railway station on the western line.

MILTON (*Co. St. Vincent*), a postal town, 160 miles S. of Sydney, with daily mail, telegraph and money-order offices, and Government savings bank. The nearest railway station is Kiama, 62 miles, on the Illawarra and South Coast line. Situated about 3 miles N.W. from Lake Curril, an arm of the sea, and 12 miles E. of the Pigeon House Mountain. Courts of quarter sessions and district courts are held here periodically.

MIMOSA, EAST (*Co. Goulburn*), a postal receiving-office, 320 miles S. of Sydney, with mail twice a week.

MINANDICHI LAKE (*Co. Menindie*), a small lake or lagoon, separated from Lake Cawndilla by a sandbank. It lies about 36 miles S.W. of Menindie.

MINGAR MOUNT (*Co. Selwyn*), a lofty peak in the Murray Range of mountains, lying near the junction of the N. and S. heads of Tooma River.

MINGUTTA MOUNT (*Co. Auckland*), a hill on the Mingutta Creek, on the road from Gippsland, *via* Genoa River.

MINJARY (*Co. Wynyard*), a proclaimed village, to the S. of Gundagai.

MINJARY MOUNTAIN (*Co. Wynyard*), a group of high peaks on the N.E. part of the Adelong gold-fields, and on the W. bank of the Tumut River.

MINMI (*Co. Northumberland*), a postal town, 111 miles N. of Sydney, with daily mail. Telegraph and money-order offices, and Government savings bank, with delivery by letter-carriers. The nearest railway station is Hexham, 6 miles, on the northern line. Situated in the parish of Hexham, about 6 miles distant from the Hunter River. The district is a coal-mining one, and the population principally employed in coal-mining pursuits.

MINTO (*Co. Cumberland*), a postal village, 31 miles S. of Sydney, with mail twice daily, a railway station on the southern line. It is one of the original districts of the county.

MINUMURRA CREEK (*Co. Camden*), a creek rising on the Coast Range, flowing through the township of Jamberoo, entering the ocean between Kiama and Shellharbour.

MIRRICALDRIE CREEK (*Co. Wynyard*), a swampy creek, flowing S.E. into the Nunbaroo Creek.

MIRROOL CREEK (*Co. Cooper*), a water-course rising in the Derabong Hills, flowing into the Murrumbidgee River, near the village of Liorongai.

MISERABLE FLAT (*Co. Bligh*), a village, 248 miles W. of Sydney, and 7 miles from Wellington, which is the nearest railway station on the western line.

MITCHANGULLIMA CREEK (*Co. Bathurst*), a small tributary of the Pannara Rivulet.

MITCHELL.—A county in the Central Division of the Colony. [*See* "COUNTIES."]

MITCHELL (*Co. Gough*), a proclaimed township on the Mitchell River, a western tributary of the Nymboi River.

MITCHELL, SUNNY CORNER (*Co. Cook*), a village, 111 miles W. of Sydney, and 15 miles from Rydal, the nearest railway station on the western line.

MITCHELL MOUNT (*Co. Gresham*), a high peak of the Macleay Range, lying at the head of the Sara River.

MITCHELL RIVER (*Co. Gough*). [*See* "RIVERS."]

MITCHELL'S CREEK (*Co. Cunningham*) is a small arm of the Lachlan River, flowing to the east of Condobolin.

MITCHELL'S CREEK (*Co. Lincoln*), a village, 261 miles W. of Sydney, and 6 miles from Geurie, the nearest railway station on the Bathurst and Bourke line. The creek is a southern tributary of the Erskine River.

MITCHELL'S CREEK (*Co. Roxburgh*), a village, 112 miles to the W. of Sydney. It is an agricultural and mining district in the parish of Castleton, 5½ miles from the township of Meadow Flat.

MITCHELL'S CREEK (*Co. Roxburgh*), a small auriferous creek, rising to the N. of Kirkconnell gold-fields, and flowing into the Winburndale Rivulet.

MITCHELL'S ISLAND (*Co. Gloucester*), a postal town, 242 miles N. of Sydney, with mail twice weekly. Situated on the Manning River.

MITOOKISBA CREEK (*Co. Argyle*), a small creek, rising to the E. of Kenny's punt, flowing into the Willeroo Creek.

MITTA MITTA (*Co. Clarendon*), a postal village, 280 miles S. of Sydney, with mail twice a week. The nearest railway station is Bethungra, 10 miles, on the southern line.

MITTA MITTA CREEK (*Co. Clarendon*), a small eastern tributary of the Billabong Creek, flowing W. about 10 miles.

MITTAGONG (*Co. Camden*), a postal town, 77 miles S. of Sydney, with mail twice daily. Telegraph and money-order offices, Government savings bank, and delivery by letter-carrier. The district is an elevated one, and a favourite resort for invalids. A railway station on the southern line. It was proclaimed a municipal district in 1859, with a council of three aldermen and a mayor.

MITTAGONG RANGE (*Co. Camden*) is an eastern spur of the Blue Mountains, the highest point attaining an elevation of 2,454 feet above the sea-level. This range divides the waters of the Nepean and Wingecarribee Rivers. The scenery is highly romantic, and joins the coast mountains overlooking the Illawarra district.

MOAMA (*Co. Cadell*), a postal town, 578 miles S. of Sydney, with mail twice daily. Telegraph and money-order offices, Government savings bank, and delivery by letter-carrier. The nearest railway station is Hay, 128 miles, on the south-western line. Moama is situated on the N. bank of the Murray River, opposite Echuca, and is a calling place for the river steamers. The district is chiefly a pastoral one.

MOAN MOUNT (*Co. Brisbane*), is the highest peak of the Liverpool Range, attaining an elevation of 4,200 feet above sea-level. It is situated towards the W. end of the range.

MOATEFIELD (*Co. Clarendon*), a postal village, 261 miles S. of Sydney, with daily mail.

MOGENDORA CREEK (*Co. St. Vincent*), a small tributary of the Moruya River, falling into it about 10 miles from its mouth.

MOGIL MOGIL (*Co. Finch*), a postal village, 490 miles N. of Sydney, with mail twice a week. Telegraph and money-order offices, and Government savings bank. The nearest railway station is Narrabri, 110 miles, on the north-western line.

MOGILA CREEK (*Co. Narran*), a small tributary of the Birie River, flowing into it near the boundary between New South Wales and Queensland.

MOGILLA (*Co. Beresford*), a postal village, 267 miles S. of Sydney, with mail twice a week. The nearest railway station is Cooma, 55 miles, on the Goulburn and Cooma line.

MOGO (*Co. St. Vincent*), a postal town, 205 miles S. of Sydney, with mail three times a week. Telegraph and money-order offices. The nearest railway station is Tarago, 48 miles, on the Goulburn and Cooma line. It lies about 8 miles from the township of Bateman's Bay.

MOGONG (*Co. Ashburnham*), a small agricultural village, lying about 8 miles N. of Canowindra.

MOGRAM CREEK (*Co. Gloucester*), a small eastern tributary of the Gloucester River.

MOGUL (*Co. Finch*), a proclaimed township, on the Barwon River, near the Queensland border.

MOHONGA (*Co. Hume*), a village, 368 miles S. of Sydney. The nearest railway station is Gerogery, 48 miles, on the southern line.

MOIKA (*Co. Pottinger*), a Government village, lying 20 miles N.W. of the township of Quirindi.

MOIRA (*Co. Cadell*), a postal village, 559 miles S. of Sydney, with mail four times a week. The nearest railway station is Albury, 120 miles, on the southern line.

MOIRA LAKES (*Co. Cadell*), a series of lagoons on the N. bank of the Murray River, on the road from Moama to Deniliquin.

MOJOREKA POINT (*Co. Dampier*), is the name of the N. head of the entrance of the Bega River, about 2 miles N. of Tathra.

MOLE RIVER (*Co. Clive.*) [*See* "RIVERS."]

MOLEVILLE (*Co. Clarence*), a township in this county.

MOLONG (*Co. Wellington*), a postal town, 216 miles W. of Sydney, with daily mail. Telegraph and money-order offices, Government savings bank, and delivery by letter-carrier. A railway station on the Orange and Molong line. Situated in the parish of Molong, on the Molong Rivulet, about 7 miles S. of the junction with the Bell River. It is an agricultural and pastoral district, abounding in minerals, principally copper. It was incorporated a municipal district in 1878, with a council of five aldermen and a mayor. Population, about 1,000. Courts of quarter sessions and district courts are held here periodically during each year.

MOLONG CREEK (*Co. Wallace*), a small stream, rising near the Scotchman's Hill, and flowing S. into the Snowy River.

MOLONG RIVER (*Co. Wellington*), an auriferous tributary of the Bell River. The country abounding in copper ore. [*See* "RIVERS."]

MOLONGLO (*Co. Murray*), a postal village, 188 miles S. of Sydney with daily mail. Telegraph and money-order offices, and Government savings bank. A railway station on the Goulburn and Cooma line. Situated on the Molonglo River. The district is an agricultural and pastoral one.

MOLONGLO PLAINS (*Co. Murray*), is a fine tract of undulating grazing country, lying on the upper part of the Molonglo River, and to the S. of Lake George. The townships of Molonglo and Bungendore are situated on these plains and afford fine grazing for cattle.

MOLONGLO RIVER (*Co. Murray*). [*See* "RIVERS."]

MOLOWRAN MOUNT (*Co. Wellington*), a peak of the Stony Creek Range, on the east bank of the Bell River.

MOMUNDILLA MOUNT (*Co. Hunter*), an elevated peak of the Hunter Range, its summit being 2,500 feet above sea-level, and lies to the W. of Patrick's Plains.

MONARA is the name of a pastoral district (now included in the Eastern Pastoral Division of the Colony) lying to the N. of the Victorian boundary. The principal towns are Bega, Cooma, Bombala, Moruya, Nerrijunda, Nimmitabel, Adaminaby, Crown Flat, Delegate, and Araluen. The district abounds in vast stores of mineral wealth, and grain of all kinds flourish to perfection, and very productive.

MONARO PLAINS (*Co. Beresford*), a large tract of fine undulating pastoral country, lying between the Murrumbidgee River on the W. and the coast range on the E. These plains form a plateau of 2,000 feet above sea-level, and remarkably well-watered. The townships of Cooma, Bunyan, and Colinton are situated on these plains, of which the first named is the principal one.

MONARO RANGE (*Co. Beresford*).—This range encloses the most extensive elevated tract of country in the Colony, and forms the watershed between the streams flowing W. and N. to the Murrumbidgee, E. to the coast, and S. to the Snowy River. The summits of some of the ridges rise to an elevation of from 3,000 to 4,000 feet above the sea-level.

MONGARLOW GOLD-FIELDS (*Co. St. Vincent*), a tract of auriferous country, lying on the Mongarlow River, to the E. of the township of Marlow, and N. of Braidwood. Monga is the principal town.

MONGARLOW RIVER (*Co. St. Vincent*). [*See* "RIVERS."]

MONKERAI (*Co. Gloucester*), a postal village, 163 miles N. of Sydney, with mail twice a week. The nearest railway station is Morpeth, 42 miles, on the East Maitland and Morpeth line. Situated on the Karuah River. The district is agricultural and pastoral, but is mountainous and thickly covered with gigantic timber.

MONOLON RANGE (*Co. Tandora*), a chain of low sandstone hills lying on the W. side of the Darling River, about 160 miles N. of Menindie.

MONTAGUE ISLAND (*Co. Dampier*), a rocky islet, lying about 3 miles from the land, and N.E. of Mount Dromedary. It attains an elevation of 210 feet above sea-level, and is nearly 2 miles in length.

MONTEAGLE, a county in the Central and Eastern Divisions of the Colony. [*See* "COUNTIES."]

MONTEAGLE (*Co. Monteagle*), a postal village, 261 miles S. of Sydney, with daily mail. A railway station on the Murrumburrah and Blayney line.

MONTEFIORES (*Co. Bligh*), a postal village, 249 miles W. of Sydney, with daily mail. The nearest railway station is Wellington, on the western line. Situated in the parish of Wellington, on the Bell and Macquarie Rivers, which separates it from the township of Wellington. It is an agricultural and pastoral district, with gold workings on Mitchell's Creek, about 9 miles distant.

MONWONGA (*Co. Cunningham*), a village, W. of Sydney, in this county.

MOOCULTA *(Co. Cowper)*, a railway station, 483 miles W. of Sydney, on the south-western line.

MOODONG CREEK *(Co. St. Vincent)*, a western tributary of the Deua River, or upper part of the Moruya River.

MOOKI RIVER *(Cos. Buckland and Pottinger)*. [*See* "RIVERS."]

MOOKI SPRINGS *(Co. Pottinger)*, lying to the N. of Kickerbell and W. of the Mooki River.

MOOLUMOOLA MOUNT *(Co. Buckland)*, a peak in a range of low granite hills, lying to the E. of Carroll.

MOOMIN RIVER *(Co. Benarba)*. [*See* "RIVERS."]

MOOMUNNUR MOUNT *(Co. Buller)*. [*See* "WILSON'S PEAK."]

MOON ISLAND *(Co. Northumberland)*, a small rocky islet lying at the entrance of Lake Macquarie, or Reid's Mistake.

MOONA MOONA CREEK *(Co. St. Vincent)*, a small creek at the N. end of the St. George's basin.

MOONAN BROOK *(Co. Brisbane)*, a postal village, 224 miles N. of Sydney, with mail twice a week, and money-order office. The nearest railway station is Scone, 35 miles, on the northern line. Situated on the Moonan Brook, or Bell's Creek, an affluent of the Hunter River, which is distant about 4 miles W., in the parish of Moonan. The district is a pastoral, agricultural, and mining one.

MOONBAH *(Co. Wallace)*, a postal receiving-office, 303 miles S. of Sydney, with mail therefrom once a week.

MOONBI *(Co. Inglis)*, a postal town, 294 miles N. of Sydney, with daily mail. Telegraph and money-order offices, and Government savings bank. A railway station on the northern line. Situated on the Moonbi Creek, at the foot of the Great Moonbi range of mountains, and to the N. of the Cockburn River. The district is a pastoral one, and very fertile. Distant from Tamworth and Bendemeer about 12 miles.

MOONBI CREEK *(Co. Inglis)*, a small western tributary of the Cockburn River, rising in Mount Bullimbala, and flowing S. through the township of Moonbi.

MOONBI RANGE *(Co. Parry)*, a spur of the New England range of mountains, separating the waters of the Mulucrindie from those of the Peel River, at an altitude of 3,593 feet above sea-level.

MOONDALE *(Co. Wentworth)*, a township on the E. bank of the Darling River, above Wentworth.

MOONEE CREEK *(Co. Clarence)*, a postal receiving-office, 401 miles N. of Sydney, with mail by Grafton steamers.

MOONEY-MOONEY CREEK (*Co. Northumberland*), a small stream flowing into the N. of Broken Bay by a wide estuary.

MOONEY-MOONEY POINT (*Co. Northumberland*), a tongue of land forming the N. head of the confluence of Mooney-Mooney Creek with Broken Bay.

MOONIE CREEK (*Co. Raleigh*), a small drainage creek falling into the ocean about 2 miles N. of the Bellinger River.

MOOR CREEK (*Co. Inglis*), a postal village, 287 miles N. of Sydney, with mail twice a week. The nearest railway station is Tamworth, 5 miles, on the northern line.

MOORARA (*Co. Perry*), a township, on the E. bank of the Darling River.

MOORAWBA (*Co. Parry*), a peak of the Peel Range, lying on the N.E. of the township of Carroll.

MOORE CREEK (*Co. Inglis*), a small northern tributary of the Peel River, rising in Mount Purrenbyden, N.W. of Moonbi, and flowing into the Peel River, at Attunga.

MOORE'S LAGOON (*Co. Northumberland*). [*See* "BULBARNING LAKE."]

MOOREBANK (*Co. Cumberland*), a postal receiving-office, 23 miles S. of Sydney, with daily mail therefrom.

MOOREWAY (*Co. Franklin*), a township in this county.

MOORLAND (*Co. Wallace*), a postal village, 249 miles N. of Sydney, with daily mail.

MOORLARBEN CREEK (*Co. Bligh*) is one of the heads of the Goulburn River, rising in Mount Betealween.

MOORILDA (*Co. Bathurst*), a postal village, 169 miles W. of Sydney, with daily mail. The nearest railway station is Newbridge, 3 miles, on the western line.

MOORILLA CREEK (*Co. Buckland*). [*See* "PHILLIP'S CREEK."]

MOORNA (*Co. Wentworth*), a small village, on the river Murray, lying about 20 miles W. of Wentworth. It has a steamer wharf.

MOORNA (*Co. Tara*), a proclaimed village, on the N. bank of the Murray River, above Wentworth.

MOOROGAN MOUNT (*Co. Gowen*), a peak of the Warrabungle range of mountains, lying at the head of the Caronne River.

MOORWATHA (*Co. Hume*), a postal village, 414 miles S. of Sydney, with mail twice a week. The nearest railway station is Gerogery, 16 miles, on the southern line.

MOOTWINGEE, a county in the Western Division of the Colony. [See "Counties."]

MOPPITY GAP (*Cos. Harden and Monteagle*), a passage over the ranges lying to the S.E. of the township of Young, on the road from Murrimboola to Murringo.

MORAGO (*Co. Townsend*), a postal receiving-office, 494 miles S. of Sydney, with mail twice a week. The nearest railway station is Hay, 97 miles, on the south-western line.

MORANGARELL (*Co. Monteagle*), a postal town, 286 miles S. of Sydney, with mail twice a week, and telegraph office. The nearest railway station is Young, 46 miles, on the Murrumburrah and Blayney line.

MORBURY CREEK (*Co. Murray*), a stream rising in the Gourock Range, near Talerang Pic, flowing into the Shoalhaven River, near Larbert township.

MOREDUN CREEK (*Co. Hardinge*), a small eastern tributary of the head of the Bundarra River, rising in the county of Hardinge, flowing W. into the main stream.

MOREE (*Co. Courallie*), a postal village, 421 miles N. of Sydney, with daily mail. Telegraph and money-order offices, Government savings bank, and delivery by letter-carriers. The nearest railway station is Narrabri, 75 miles, on the north-western line. Situated 2 miles S. of the Gwydir or Big River. The district is a rich pastoral one, and all kinds of grain and fruit flourish. Courts of quarter sessions and district courts are held here periodically during each year.

MORGAN'S GULLY CREEK (*Co. Wellington*), a small western tributary of the Frederick's Valley Creek.

MORNA POINT AND BAY (*Co. Durham*), a rocky promontory and sandy bight, to the N. of it, lying a few miles S. of Port Stephens.

MORONGLO CREEK (*Co. Bathurst*), a postal receiving-office, 262 miles S. of Sydney, with mail twice a week.

MOROOWIN BROOK (*Co. Macquarie*), a small tributary of the head of the Wilson's River.

MORPETH (*Co. Northumberland*), a postal town, 120 miles N. of Sydney, with mail twice daily. Telegraph and money-order offices, and Government savings bank, with delivery by letter-carrier. A railway station on the Maitland and Morpeth line. Situated on the south bank of the Hunter River, in the parishes of Alnwick and Morpeth, at the head of the navigation of the Hunter River. The district is an agricultural and mining one. The communication with Sydney is both by water and railway. It is the seat of the Bishop of Newcastle (Church of England). Lucerne and maize are extensively grown. Morpeth was proclaimed a borough in 1865, with a council of eight aldermen and a mayor. Population, about 900.

MORPHETT CREEK (*Co. Farnell*), a stream rising in the Barrier Range, flowing in a westerly direction.

MORRIS' LAGOON (*Co. Gipps*), a small swampy lagoon of the Yeylo Creek, between the Lachlan and Murrumbidgee Rivers.

MORRISSET (*Co. Northumberland*), a proclaimed township, and a postal receiving-office, 76 miles N. of Sydney, with daily mail therefrom. A railway station on the Newcastle line.

MORRISSET'S CHAIN OF PONDS (*Co. Ewenmar*), a series of waterholes, lying between the Macquarie and Castlereagh Rivers.

MORTLAKE (*Co. Cumberland*), a postal village, 7 miles W. of Sydney, with mail twice daily. It is an island in the Parramatta River, where the gasworks are situated.

MORTON'S CREEK (*Co. Northumberland*), a village near Hexham, 85 miles N. of Sydney. The nearest railway station is Hexham, on the northern line.

MORTON'S CREEK (*Co. Macquarie*), a small creek, flowing into the Hastings River, about 4 miles from Huntingdon.

MORUBEN MOUNT (*Co. Northumberland*), a peak on the Hunter range of mountains, on the E. bank of the Macdonald River.

MORUMBATEMAN CREEK (*Co. Murray*), a southern tributary of the Yass River, flowing in the eastern part of the Yass Plains.

MORUMDURY MOUNT (*Co. Roxburgh*), a lofty peak on the Blue Mountain Range, lying on the S. bank of the Capertee River.

MORUNDAH (*Co. Mitchell*), a railway station, 367 miles S. of Sydney, on the Junee and Jerilderie line.

MORUYA (*Co. St. Vincent*), a postal village, 196 miles S. of Sydney, with mail twice a week, with money-order office. The nearest railway station is Tarago, 36 miles, on the Goulburn and Cooma line. The district is an agricultural and mining one, and from its elevation is cool, and suitable for the growth of European fruits of all kinds.

MORUYA (*Co. Dampier*), a postal town, 242 miles to the S. of Sydney, with mail daily, telegraph and money-order offices, and Government savings bank. The nearest railway station is Tarago, 78 miles on the Goulburn line. It is situated on the S. bank of the Moruya River, about 4 miles from its mouth. There is communication with Sydney by steamer, via Bateman's Bay, distant about 20 miles. The district is an agricultural and mining one. Courts of quarter sessions and district courts are held here periodically.

MORUYA RIVER (*Co. Dampier*). [See "RIVERS."]

MORVEN (*Co. Hume*), a postal town, 360 miles S. of Sydney, with daily mail. The nearest railway station is Culcairn, 9 miles, on the southern line.

MOSQUITO ISLAND (*Co. Northumberland*), a large island in the Hunter River, about 5 miles W. of Newcastle, and separated from Ash Island by a narrow channel.

MOSSGIEL, a county, in the Western Division of the Colony. [*See* "COUNTIES."]

MOSSGIEL (*Co. Waljeers*), a postal town, 545 miles S. of Sydney, with mail three times a week, telegraph and money-order offices, and Government savings bank. The nearest railway station is Hay, 100 miles, on the south-western line.

MOSSMAN'S BAY (*Co. Cumberland*) is a beautiful inlet, to the E. of Bradley's Head, in the harbour of Port Jackson. This bay is one of great beauty, and is a favourite place of resort for all pleasure-seekers. Steamers ply regularly to and fro from the Circular Quay.

MOSS VALE (*Co. Camden*), a postal village, 86 miles S. of Sydney, with mail twice daily. Telegraph and money-order offices and Government savings bank. It is a railway station on the southern line. It was proclaimed a municipal district in 1888, with a council of eight aldermen and a mayor. Population, 800. Courts of quarter sessions and district courts are held here periodically.

MOTHER OF DUCKS' LAGOON (*Co. Sandon*), a large waterhole, about 10 miles in circumference, distant about 4 miles from the township of Falconer.

MOUKILMONTHA (*Co. Ularara*), a township, on the W. bank of the Paroo River.

MOULAMEIN (*Co. Wakool*), a postal town, 541 miles S. of Sydney, with mail twice a week. Telegraph and money-order offices. The nearest railway station is Hay, 160 miles, on the south-western line. Situated in the parish of Moulamein, at the junction of the Billabong Creek and the Hyalite or Edward River. The district is exclusively a pastoral one.

MOUMIN CREEK (*Co. Courallie*), a series of water-holes, flowing from the Weah Waa Creek to the Gwydir River, near its mouth.

MOUNT ADRAH (*Co. Buccleuch*), a postal town, 323 miles S. of Sydney, with mail once a week. The nearest railway station is Gundagai, 36 miles, on the Cootamundra and Gundagai line.

MOUNT ALLEN (*Co. Beresford*), a postal receiving-office, 227 miles, S. of Sydney, with mail therefrom once a week.

MOUNT AUBREY (*Co. Bligh*), a postal receiving-office, 292 miles W. of Sydney, with mail twice a week. The nearest railway station is Wellington, 35 miles, on the western line.

MOUNT BROWNE (*Co. Evelyn*), a postal receiving office S. of Sydney, with mail once a week. The nearest railway station is Hay, 350 miles, on the south-western line.

MOUNT COSTIGAN (*Co. Bathurst*), a postal village, 204 miles S. of Sydney, with daily mail. The nearest railway station is Newbridge, 39 miles, on the western line.

MOUNT DRUITT (*Co. Cumberland*), a postal receiving-office, 27 miles W. of Sydney, with daily mail. A railway station on the southern line.

MOUNT ELLIOTT ISLAND (*Co. Northumberland*), an island in Broken Bay, opposite the entrance to the Broadwater (Brisbane Water).

MOUNT GIPPS (*Co. Yancowinna*), a postal village, 953 miles W. of Sydney, with mail three times a week, and money-order office. The nearest railway station is Hay, 280 miles, on the south-western line.

MOUNT HARRIS (*Co. Oxley*), a postal village, 398 miles W. of Sydney, with mail twice a week. The nearest railway station is Nevertire, 57 miles, on the western line.

MOUNT HOPE (*Co. Blaxland*), a postal village, 517 miles W. of Sydney, with mail three times a week. Telegraph and money-order offices and Government savings bank. The nearest railway station is Nyngan, 70 miles, on the western line.

MOUNT HUNTER (*Co. Camden*), a postal town, 44 miles S. of Sydney, with mail three times a week.

MOUNT HUNTER RIVULET (*Co. Camden*), a small tributary of the Nepean River.

MOUNT IDA (*Co. Sturt*), a postal receiving-office, 410 miles S. of Sydney, with mail twice a week.

MOUNT KEIRA (*Co. Camden*), a postal village, 51 miles S. of Sydney, with daily mail. The nearest railway station is Wollongong, 3 miles, on the Illawarra and South Coast line.

MOUNT KEMBLA (*Co. Camden*), a postal village, 54 miles S. of Sydney, with daily mail. The nearest railway station is Wollongong, 4 miles, on the Illawarra and South Coast line.

MOUNT LOWRY CREEK (*Co. Darling*), a northern tributary of the Muluerindi River, rising in Mount Lowry.

MOUNT MACQUARIE (*Co. Bathurst*), a postal village, 189 miles W. of Sydney, with mail three times a week. The nearest railway station is Blayney, 17 miles, on the Murrumburrah and Blayney line.

MOUNT M'DONALD (*Co. Monteagle*), a postal town, 218 miles W. of Sydney, with daily mail. Telegraph and money-order offices, and Government savings bank. The nearest railway station is Woodstock, 13 miles, on the Murrumburrah and Blayney line.

MOUNT MITCHELL (*Co. Clarke*), a postal town, 395 miles N. of Sydney, with mail once a week.

MOUNT PLEASANT (*Co. Inglis*), a postal receiving-office, 325 miles N. of Sydney, with mail three times a week. The nearest railway station is Tamworth, 43 miles, on the northern line.

MOUNT PLEASANT (*Co. Cumberland*), a village, 34 miles W. of Sydney. The nearest railway station is Penrith, 3½ miles, on the Bathurst and Bourke line.

MOUNT POOLE (*Co. Tongowoko*), a village, 454 miles W. of Sydney. The nearest railway station is Hay, on the south-western line.

MOUNT ROYAL RANGE (*Co. Durham*), a branch of the Liverpool Range, commencing near the Hanging Rock. The northern portion separates the streams flowing into the Manning River from the tributaries of the Hunter. The highest point is 3,000 feet above the sea-level.

MOUNT TENNANT CREEK (*Co. Raleigh*), a small western tributary of the Gudgenby River, rising in Mount Tennant, near the township of Thaywa.

MOUNT, THE (*Co. Bathurst*), a hill on the southern part of the county, in the parish of Coota, about 3 miles E. of the township of Cowra.

MOUNT THORPE (*Co. Canbelego*). a village, 377 miles W. of Sydney. The nearest railway station is Nyngan, 154 miles, on the western line.

MOUNT VICTORIA (*Co. Cook*), a postal village, 77 miles W. of Sydney, with mail twice daily. Telegraph and money-order offices and Government savings bank. A railway station on the western line.

MOUNT VINCENT (*Co. Northumberland*), a postal village, 109 miles N. of Sydney, with mail three times a week, and money-order office. The nearest railway station is East Maitland, 18 miles, on the East Maitland and Morpeth line.

MOUNT WILSON (*Co. Cook*), a postal receiving-office, 93 miles W. of Sydney, with daily mail.

MOUNT WOODS CREEK (*Co. Wellington*), a small western tributary of the Macquarie River, rising on the Mullions Range.

MOUNTAIN CREEK (*Co. Cowley*), a fine stream, rising in the northern slope of Mount Pabral, and flowing into the Murrumbidgee River, crossing the Yass and Kiandra roads.

MOUNTAIN CREEK (*Co. Goulburn*). [*See* "WOOMARAGARMA CREEK."]

MOUNTAIN SLUT CREEK (*Co. Monteagle*), a small tributary of the head of the Cookoomingala Creek, rising to the E. of the township of Wambanumba.

# MOUNTAIN RANGES IN THE COLONY.

BARRIER RANGE, 32° S. lat. 141 E. long., situated in the extreme W. of the Colony, beyond the Darling River, in the counties of Yancowinna and Farnell, nearly on the dividing line between this Colony and South Australia. The silver-mines at Broken Hill, Silverton, and Thackaringa have been opened and developed in this range. Enormous lodes of silver and lead ores exist here, and are being successfully worked. The highest peaks in the range are:—

|  | feet. |
|---|---|
| Mount Lyell | 2,000 |
| Mount Robe | not ascertained |
| Mount Gipps | ,, |

There is a line of railway from Adelaide, *via* Petersburgh, to the mines in these ranges.

BLUE MOUNTAIN RANGE, stretching from the Liverpool Range to Lake Burrah Burrah, S. of the 34th parallel, in the counties of Roxburgh, Cook, and Westmoreland. The principal elevations are:—

|  | feet. |  | feet. |
|---|---|---|---|
| Beemerang | 4,100 | King George Mount | 3,620 |
| Blaxland Mount | 3,256 | Marsden Mount, | not ascertained |
| Clarence Mount | 3,900 | Tayan Pic | 4,000 |
| Dunambang | not ascertained | Tomah Mount | 3,240 |
| Evan's Crown | 3,200 | Victoria Mount | 3,700 |
| Hay Mount | not ascertained | York Mount | 3,440 |
| Honeysuckle Hill | 4,000 |  |  |

CULLARIN RANGE, in the county of King and Argyle, extending to the N. extremity of Lake George, in the county of Murray. The principal elevations in this range are:—

|  | feet. |  | feet. |
|---|---|---|---|
| Carrangil | 3,100 | Dixon Mount | 3,000 |
| Chatou Mount | 3,000 | Pitton Mount | 3,300 |
| Cullarin | 3,000 | Therlonong | 3,100 |

CURROCKBILLY OR BUDAWANG, situate about the 35th to about the 36th parallel, in the county of St. Vincent. The principal elevations in this range are:—

|  | feet. |
|---|---|
| Budawang | 3,800 |
| Currockbilly | not ascertained |
| Pigeon-house | 2,340 |
| Talaterang | not ascertained |
| Wombullaway | ,, |

The Pigeon-house was named by Captn. Cook, on account of its resemblance to a dove-cot, with a dome at its top. From the sea it forms a prominent landmark.

GOUROCK RANGE is in about the 35th and 36th S. lat., county of Murray. It forms part of the Great Dividing Range. The principal elevations are:—

|  | feet. |
|---|---|
| Jindalian ... | 4,300 |
| Talerang ... | not ascertained |
| Tumanwong | ,, |
| Urunbeen ... | 3,800 |

GREY RANGE, in the 29th and 30th S. lat., 141st and 142nd E. long., counties of Poole and Evelyn, on the dividing line between this Colony and South Australia. The principal elevations are :—

|  | feet. |
|---|---|
| Mount Arrowsmith | 2,000 |
| Mount Brown ... | not ascertained |
| Mount Poole ... | ,, |

HASTINGS RANGE forms the N.W. boundary of the county of Hawes, and is a branch of the New England Range. The principal elevation is:—

|  | feet. |
|---|---|
| Mount Sea View ... | 6,000 |
| Kippara Mount ... | not ascertained |

HUNTER RANGE is in 30° S. lat., in the counties of Hunter and Durham. The principal elevations are:—

|  | feet. |  | feet. |
|---|---|---|---|
| Coricudgy... | 3,000 | Poppong ... | 2,500 |
| Gullongalong | not ascertained | Warrawolong | 2,500 |
| Momundilla | 2,500 | Werong ... | 2,500 |
| Nullo ... | 2,500 |  |  |

ILLAWARRA RANGE is the coast range commencing at Bulli, in the county of Camden, extending S. to the county of St. Vincent, where it is known as the Cambewarra Range. The principal elevations are :—

|  | feet. |
|---|---|
| Corrimal Mount | not ascertained |
| Mount Keira ... | 1,500 |
| Mount Kembla ... | 2,000 |

LIVERPOOL RANGE is a continuation of the New England Range, in the counties of Phillip, Brisbane, and Bligh. The principal elevations are :—

|  | feet. |  | feet. |
|---|---|---|---|
| Hanging Rock ... | 3,413 | Oxley's Peak | 4,000 |
| Moan or Mount M'Arthur | 4,200 | Pandora's Pass | 3,872 |
| Mount Parry | not ascertained | Terell ... | 4,000 |
| Mount Temi ... | 4,000 | Tinagroo ... | 4,000 |
| Murrulla ... | 3,710 | Towarri ... | 4,000 |

MACPHERSON RANGE forms a portion of the N. boundary between this colony and Queensland, in the counties of Rous and Buller. The principal elevations are :—

|  | feet. |  | feet. |
|---|---|---|---|
| Ballow Mount... | not ascertained. | Mount Gipps | 5,000 |
| Boololagung Mount | ,, | Mount Merino | not ascertained |
| Congal Mount ... | ,, | Mount Lindsay ... | 5,700 |
| Mount Barney ... | 5,000 | Wilson's Peak | not ascertained |

MACQUARIE RANGE is a spur of the Blue Mountain Range, about the 34th parallel of S. lat., in the counties of Wellington and Bathurst. The principal elevations are:—

|  | feet. |
|---|---|
| Mount Canoblas | 4,610 |
| Coombing | 3,500 |

MITTAGONG RANGE is an E. spur of the Blue Mountain Range, in the county of Camden. The principal elevation is known as—

|  | feet. |
|---|---|
| Highest Point | 2,500 |

MONARO RANGE is a continuation of the Gourock Range, in the county of Beresford. The principal elevations are:—

|  | feet. |  | feet. |
|---|---|---|---|
| Bobundura Hill | not ascertained | Jennibruthera | not ascertained |
| Brothers | ” | Jejedzerick Hill | ” |
| Coobringdon | ” | Mulay's Peak | 3,880 |
| Cooma Hill | ” | Nimmitabel Hill | 3,500 |
| Head of Kybean River | 4,000 | Tantangara | not ascertained |
| Head of Winifred's Peak | 3,700 |  |  |

MOONBI RANGE is a branch of the New England Range of Mountains, in the county of Parry. The highest elevation is—

|  | feet. |
|---|---|
| The Summit | 3,600 |

MOUNT ROYAL RANGE is a branch of the Liverpool Range, in the county of Durham. This range and its branches close in the E. side of the Hunter River valley. The principal elevations are:—

|  | feet. |
|---|---|
| Carrow | not ascertained |
| Cobra Bald | 3,000 |
| Dyring | 3,000 |
| Mount Royal | not ascertained |
| Wollen | 3,000 |

MUNDOONAN RANGE is a spur of the Cullarin Range, in the counties of King and Murray. The only elevation is:—

| Mundoonan | not ascertained |
|---|---|

MUNIONG RANGE forms the highest land in the colony, in the counties of Selwyn, Wallace, and Buccleuch. The principal elevations are:—

|  | feet. |  | feet. |
|---|---|---|---|
| Crackenback | 4,700 | Rain's Head | 6,838 |
| Gungarling | 5,337 | Jagungal | 6,763 |
| Mount Kosciusko | 7,171 | The Pilot | not ascertained |
| Mount Townsend | 7,256 |  |  |

MURRAY RANGE is a spur of the Muniong Range, in the county of Selwyn, to the N. of Mount Kosciusko. The principal elevations are:—

|  | feet. |
|---|---|
| Mount Dugal | 5,490 |
| Nackie Nackie | 2,242 |
| Tumburumba | not ascertained |

MURRUMBIDGEE RANGE is a spur from the Muniong Range, in the county of Cowley, and for some distance running parallel to the Murrumbidgee River. The principal elevations are:—

|  | feet. |  | feet. |
|---|---|---|---|
| Jallula | 6,934 | Mount Tennant | not ascertained. |
| Murragural | 6,987 | Sentry Box | ,, |
| Mount Clear | ...not ascertained |  |  |

NANDEWAR RANGE is a branch of the New England Range, in the counties of Hardinge and Inglis. The principal elevations are:—

|  |  | feet. |
|---|---|---|
| Boodnboaronbi | | not ascertained |
| Mount Lindsay | | 3,000 |

NEW ENGLAND RANGE commences at the N. extremity of the colony, in the 28th parallel S. lat., and the chain of mountains reaches to nearly the 32nd parallel, in the 151° and 152° E. long. The principal elevations are:—

|  | feet. |  | feet. |
|---|---|---|---|
| Apsley Range | 3,800 | Chimney Pot | not ascertained |
| Ben Lomond | 5,000 | Clark's Lookout | 3,435 |
| Black Nob | not ascertained | Harnumhill | 3,681 |
| Blue Mountain | 4,126 | Joconda | 4,927 |
| Boulgering Peak | 4,754 | Mount Duval | 4,174 |
| Capoompeta | 4,730 | Ohio Hill | 3,579 |
| Chandler's Peak | 4,501 | Rumbee | 4,947 |

NORTH COAST RANGE.—This chain of mountains extends from the Clarence to the Hastings Rivers, nearly parallel with the coast, and at a distance from it of about 35 miles. The principal elevations are:—

|  | feet. |
|---|---|
| Mount Cung'ebung | 3,000 |
| Mount Hyland | 3,000 |

PEEL RANGE is a spur from the Liverpool Range, in the counties of Buckland and Parry. The principal elevations are:—

|  | feet. |
|---|---|
| Turi | 2,952 |
| Moolummoola | not ascertained |

SOUTH COAST RANGE is a spur from the Monaro Range, in the counties of Auckland, Beresford, and Wellesley. The principal elevation is:—

|  | feet. |
|---|---|
| Coolungubbera | 3,712 |

TUMUT RANGE is a spur from the Murnong Range, in the county of Buccleuch. The principal elevation is:—

| Talbingo | Height not ascertained |
|---|---|

WARROMBUNGLE RANGE is a W. prolongation of the Liverpool Range, in the county of Leichhardt. The principal elevations are—

|  | feet. |  | feet. |
|---|---|---|---|
| Barama | Not ascertained | Mount Harrison | not ascertained |
| Boreable | ,, | Vernon's Peak | ,, |
| Exmouth | 3,000 |  |  |

MOURA CREEK (*Co. Ashburnham*), a small western tributary of the Byrnes Creek, flowing to the N.E. of the Lachlan gold-fields.

MOURQUONG (*Co. Wentworth*), a township on the N. bank of the Murray, E. of the township of Wentworth.

MOWAMBA MOUNT (*Co. Wallace*), a detached mountain on the S. bank of the Mowamba River, and to the N. of Grose's Plains.

MOWARRY HEAD (*Co. Auckland*), a rocky headland projecting into the sea, about 24 miles S. of the head of Twofold Bay.

MOWBRAY POINT or SAILOR'S BAY (*Co. Cumberland*), a well-known bay on the W. side of Middle Harbour, about 2 miles N.W. of the entrance.

MOWLMA CREEK (*Co. Leichhardt*), a western branch of the Castlereagh River, flowing into it to the N. of Coonamble.

MOWRAMBA, a county in the Western Division of the Colony. [*See* "COUNTIES."]

MOWRAMBA RIVER (*Co. Wallace*). [*See* "RIVERS."]

MUAMMBA (*Co. Northumberland*), a small agricultural village situate at Patrick's Plains.

MUCK MOUNT (*Co. Parry*), a lofty peak in the Liverpool Range, attaining an altitude of 3,872 feet above the sea-level.

MUCKERWA CREEK (*Co. Wellington*), a western auriferous tributary of the Macquarie River, rising to the N. of Mount Aquila, and draining the Muckerwa gold-fields.

MUCKERWA DIGGINGS (*Co. Wellington*), a small gold-fields, lying on the Muckerwa Creek, about 5 miles N.E. of Ironbarks.

MUD ISLAND (*Co. Northumberland*), a small island in the estuary of the Hawkesbury River, Broken Bay, between the Berowra and Mooney-Mooney Creeks.

MUDALL (*Co. Oxley*), a township on the E. bank of the Bogan River.

MUDBANK (*Co. Cumberland*), a small settlement in the parish of Botany, lying on the N. shore of Botany Bay.

MUDGEE (*Co. Phillip*), a postal town, 190 miles W. of Sydney, with daily mail. Telegraph and money-order offices, and Government savings bank, with delivery by letter-carrier. A railway station on the western line. Situated on the Cudgegong River, in the parish of Mudgee. The district is agricultural, pastoral, and mining, and is noted for the excellent breeding of its sheep. It is rich in mineral deposits, and the soil is very productive. Mudgee is a large flourishing town, and the resources of the country around almost unlimited. Mudgee was proclaimed a borough in 1860, with a council of eight aldermen and a mayor. Population, about 3,000. Sittings of the supreme court, court of quarter sessions, and district courts are held here periodically.

MUGGERBIL MOUNT (*Co. Wellington*), a solitary peak, on the E. bank of the Grattai Creek and 10 miles S. of Mudgee.

MULBRING (*Co. Northumberland*), a proclaimed village, and a postal receiving-office, with daily mail from Sydney, 109 miles to the N. thereof.

MULBRING CREEK (*Co. Northumberland*), a small western tributary of the head of Wallis' Creek.

MULGANA CREEK (*Co. Georgiana*), an eastern tributary of the Copperhannia Creek, rising in the Long Swamp.

MULGOA (*Co. Cumberland*), a postal village, 40 miles W. of Sydney, with daily mail. The nearest railway station is Penrith, 8 miles, on the western line. Situated on the Nepean.

MULGOWRIE CREEK (*Co. Georgiana*), a stream rising to the N. of Binda, flowing W. into the Lachlan River. It is fed by the Mennenday and Breakfast Creeks.

MULGRAVE (*Co. Cumberland*), a postal village, 33 miles W. of Sydney, with mail twice daily. A railway station on the Windsor and Richmond line.

MULGUTHERIE (*Co. Ashburnham*), a postal receiving-office, 311 miles W. of Sydney, with mail twice a week.

MULLALEY (*Co. Pottinger*), a postal village, 317 miles N. of Sydney, with mail three times a week.

MULLAMUDDY CREEK (*Co. Wellington*), a small tributary of the Cudgegong River, flowing into the river at Mullamuddy.

MULLANJANDRA CREEK (*Co. Goulburn*), a small northern tributary of the Bowna Creek, flowing into it at the township of Bowna.

MULLENDERIE (*Co. Dampier*), a postal village, 234 miles S. of Sydney, with mail three times a week. The nearest railway station is Tarago, 77 miles, on the Goulburn and Cooma line. Situated in the parish of Kiora, and on the N. bank of the Moruya River.

MULLENGANDRA (*Co. Goulburn*), a postal town, 398 miles S. of Sydney, with daily mail. The nearest railway station is Albury, 20 miles on the southern line.

MULLENGUDGERY (*Co. Oxley*), a postal town, 361 miles W. of Sydney, with daily mail. A railway station on the western line.

MULLET CREEK (*Co. Camden*), a small creek flowing through the village of Dapto.

MULLET CREEK (*Co. Northumberland*), a railway station, 40 miles N. of Sydney, on the Sydney and Newcastle line. The creek flows into the northern part of Broken Bay.

MULLET ISLAND (*Co. Northumberland*), a small island in Broken Bay, opposite the confluence of Broken Bay.

MULLINBURRA POINT (*Co. Dampier*), a rocky headland, standing boldly out into the ocean, half-way between the entrances of the Tuross and Moruya Rivers.

MULLINBURRAN CREEK (*Co. Bligh*), a small northern tributary, Cudgegong River falling into it near the Merinda gold-fields.

MULLION CREEK (*Co. Wellington*), a postal village, 203 miles W. of Sydney, with daily mail. A railway station on the western line. The creek is a western tributary of the Frederick's Valley Creek.

MULLION'S, THE (*Co. Wellington*), a range of high scrubby hills to the S.E. of Stoney Creek gold-fields, and giving rise to numerous tributaries of the Bell and Macquarie Rivers.

MULLOON (*Co. Murray*), a postal village, 165 miles S. of Sydney, with mail three times a week. The nearest railway station is Tarago, 18 miles, on the Goulburn and Cooma line.

MULLOON CREEK (*Co. Murray*), a tributary of the Reedy Creek, rising near Balallaba, flowing to the W. of the Shoalhaven River.

MULLUBA PLAINS (*Co. Darling*), a tract of flat land in the valley between the rivers Manle and Mulucrindic.

MULLUMBIMBY (*Co. Rous*), a proclaimed village and a postal receiving-office, 409 miles N. of Sydney, with mail per steamers to Lismore.

MULWALLA (*Co. Denison*), a postal town, 427 miles S. of Sydney, with daily mail. Telegraph and money-order offices. The nearest railway station is Albury, 70 miles, on the southern line. Situated on the Murray River, about 36 miles W. of Howlong.

MULWAREE (*Co. Argyle*), a proclaimed village and the native name of the Goulburn Plains.

MULWAREE PONDS (*Co. Argyle*), a tributary of the head of the Wollondilly River, flowing through the Goulburn Plains and fed by the Bonguralaby and Bungalore Creeks.

MULYEO MOUNT (*Co. Yanda*), a large flat-topped hill lying on the W. bank of the Darling River, about 90 miles S.W. of Bourke.

MUMBAR (*Co. Gunderbooka*), a township on the E. bank of the Warrego River to the W. of Bourke.

MUMBIL (*Co. Wellington*), a postal town, 232 miles W. of Sydney, with daily mail. A railway station on the western line.

MUMBLA PEAK (*Co. Wallace*), a peak in the Rocky Mountain Ranges, at the head of the Matong Creek.

MUMBULLA MOUNT (*Co. Dampier*), a lofty solitary mountain, lying to the N. of the Brogo River, about 8 miles to the N. of Moruya.

MUMMEL (*Co. Argyle*), a postal village, 140 miles S. of Sydney, with mail three times a week. The nearest railway station is Goulburn, 72 miles, on the southern line. Situated in the parish of Mummel, on Dixon's Creek, about 3 miles from the Wollondilly River.

MUMMEL RIVER (*Co. Macquarie*). [*See* "RIVERS."]

MUNDARLO (*Co. Wynyard*), a township on the S. bank of the Murrumbidgee River.

MUNDARNGONG MOUNT (*Co. Wellesley*), a hill on the Bombala River, lying about 10 miles W. of Bombala.

MUNDAWADDERA (*Co. Mitchell*) a postal receiving-office, 346 miles S. of Sydney, with mail three times a week.

MUNDAY POINT (*Co. Roxburgh*), a point on the Turon River, about 1½ miles S. of Sofala.

MUNDOE CREEK (*Co. Benarba*), a small eastern tributary of the Macintyre River.

MUNDOONEN RANGE (*Cos. King and Murray*), one of the spurs of the Cullarin Range, dividing the waters of the Murrumbidgee from those of the Lachlan. It attains an elevation of 3,000 feet above sea-level.

MUNDOORAN (*Co. Gowen*), a postal village, 256 miles W. of Sydney, with mail twice a week. Telegraph and money-order offices, and Government savings bank. The nearest railway station is Dubbo, 50 miles, on the western line.

MUNDY CREEK (*Co. Landsborough*), a stream rising in the N. of the Grey Range, and flowing in a N.E. direction.

MUNGA CREEK (*Co. Dudley*), a small northern tributary of the Macleay River.

MUNGI (*Co. Benarba*), a township on the Gilgil, a tributary to the Barwon River.

MUNGINDI (*Co. Benarba*), a postal village, 501 miles N. of Sydney, with mail twice a week. Telegraph and money-order offices. The nearest railway station is Narrabri, 120 miles, on the north-western line.

MUNGUNYAH (*Co. Gunderbooka*), a postal village, 553 miles W. of Sydney, with mail twice a week. The nearest railway station is Bourke, 52 miles, on the western line.

MUNGUTULINE (*Co. Irrara*), a township on the Paroo River and the Queensland boundary.

MUNION RANGE (*Cos. Selwyn, Wallace, and Buccleuch*), in the northern portion of the Great Warragong Chain (Australian Alps), and forms the highest land in the Colony, 6,000 to 7,000 feet above the sea-level, its culminating point being Mount Kosciusko.

MUNMURRA (*Co. Bligh*), a postal receiving-office, 267 miles N. of Sydney, with mail once a week.

MUNMURRA BROOK (*Co. Bligh*), a northern tributary of the Goulburn River, flowing through the township of Cassilis.

MUNNIMBAH CREEK (*Co. Northumberland*), a small southern tributary of the Hunter River, rising near the township of Broke.

MUNRO'S CREEK (*Co. Parry*), a small auriferous tributary of the Peel River, joining in at Bowling-alley Point diggings.

MUNYABLA (*Co. Mitchell*), a postal receiving-office, 350 miles S. of Sydney, with mail once a week.

MURCHISON, a county partly in the Central and Eastern Division of the Colony. [*See* "Counties."]

MURCHISON, MOUNT (*Co. Young*), lying on the W. side of the Darling River, about 100 miles N.E. of Menindie.

MURGA (*Co. Ashburnham*), a postal village, 233 miles W. of Sydney, with daily mail. The nearest railway station is Borenore, 31 miles, on the Orange and Molong lines. Situated on the Murga Creek, near its junction with Eugowra Creek.

MURGABA (*Co. Flinders*), a township on the W. bank of the Bogan River.

MURINGO (*Co. Monteagle*), a township to the E. of the town of Young.

MURRABINE RIVER (*Co. Dampier*). [*See* "Rivers."]

MURRAGANG (*Co. Clarence*), a postal receiving-office, 370 miles N. of Sydney, with mail per Clarence River steamers.

MURRAGULDRIE (*Co. Wynyard*), a village, 309 miles S. of Sydney. The nearest railway station is Wagga Wagga, 80 miles, on the southern line.

MURRANG CREEK (*Co. Georgiana*), a small tributary of the Cookbundoon River, rising near Chatsbury.

MURRAY, a county in the Eastern Division of the Colony. [*See* "Counties."]

MURRAY CREEK (*Co. Fitzroy*), a small eastern tributary of the Don Dorrigo River.

MURRAY FLAT (*Co. Urana*), a postal village, 432 miles S. of Sydney, with mail three times a week. The nearest railway station is Jerilderie, 25 miles, on the Junee and Jerilderie line.

MURRAY MOUNT (*Co. Cowley*), a prominent peak of the Murrumbidgee Range, attaining an elevation of 6,987 feet above the sea-level.

MURRAY RANGE (*Co. Selwyn*), a spur of the Munion Range, commencing at the N. of Mount Kosciusko, separating the tributaries of the Murray and Tumut as far as the Murrumbidgee. Its highest peak is Mount Dargal, which is 5,490 feet above sea-level.

MURRAY RIVER. [*See* "Rivers."]

MURRAY'S BIG HILL (*Co. Harden*), a lofty hill at the head of the Dunderaligo Creek, about 5 miles N.W. of Browning.

MURRAY'S FLAT (*Co. Argyle*), a proclaimed village and small agricultural settlement, lying about 5 miles from Goulburn.

MURRAYGURAL MOUNT (*Co. Cowley*) is the most elevated point in the Murrumbidgee Range, attaining a height of 7,000 feet above the sea-level.

MURREBONGA (*Co. Flinders*), a township on the W. branch of the Bogan River.

MURRIMBA *(Co. Camden)*, a proclaimed township to the N. of Marulan, on the southern railway.

MURRIMBILLY *(Co. Fitzgerald)*, a township on the Paroo River.

MURRIMBOOLA *(Co. Harden)*, a village on the creek of the same name.

MURRIMBOOLA CREEK *(Co. Harden)*, a creek at the head of the Cunningham Creek, falling into it at Murrimboola.

MURRIMBOOLA HILL *(Co. Harden)*, a high mountain, lying to the N.N.W. of Murrimboola.

MURRIMBULA LAKE *(Co. Auckland)*, a large saline lagoon on the E. coast, on the border of which the village of Murrimbula is built. The township of Panbula lies about 2 miles S.

MURRINGO *(Co. Monteagle)*, a proclaimed village to the E. of the town of Young.

MURROMBO MOUNT *(Co. Goulburn)*, a peak in the ranges to the S. of the Goulburn River, opposite the confluence of the Merriwa rivulet.

MURROONOWA *(Co. Irrara)*, a township on Cuttaburra Creek and Queensland boundary.

MURRUIN CREEK *(Co. Westmoreland)*, a western tributary of the Wollondilly River, rising near Mount Werong.

MURRUMA *(Co. Dampier)*, a small inlet of the sea, lying about 30 miles N.W. of Moruya.

MURRUMBAH *(Co. Camden)*, a village 102 miles S. of Sydney, situated on Paddy's River. The Wollondilly River flows 4 miles N.W. Is an agricultural and pastoral district.

MURRUMBATEMAN *(Co. Murray)*, a postal village, 203 miles S. of Sydney, with daily mail. The nearest railway station is Yass, 17 miles, on the southern line.

MURRUMBIDGEE RANGE *(Co. Cowley)*, a spur of the Munion Range. Its highest peak (Murragural) attains an elevation of 6,987 feet above the level of the sea.

MURRUMBIDGEE RIVER. [*See* "Rivers."]

MURRUMBIDGERIE *(Co. Gordon)*, a postal village, 267 miles W. of Sydney, with daily mail therefrom. It is a railway station on the western line.

MURRUMBULA CREEK *(Co. Wellesley)*, a small tributary of the Snowy River.

MURRUMBURRAH *(Co. Harden)*, a postal village, 229 S. of Sydney, with daily mail. Telegraph and money-order offices and Government savings bank. A railway station on the Murrumburrah-Blayney line. Situated on the Murrumboola Creek. The district is an agricultural, pastoral, and mining one. It was incorporated a municipal district in 1890.

MURRUNA INLET (*Co. Dampier*), a small arm of the sea, and the estuary of the Murabine Creek, lying to the S.E. of Mount Dromedary.

MURRUNGUNDY (*Co. Wellington*), a postal village, 276 miles W. of Sydney, with mail twice a week.

MURRURUNDI (*Co. Brisbane*), a postal village, 218 miles N. of Sydney, with mail twice daily. Telegraph and money-order offices and Government savings bank. A railway station on the northern line. Situated on the Page River. It was proclaimed a municipal district in March, 1890. The population is about 1,500. Courts of quarter sessions and district courts are held here periodically.

MURUNDAI (*Co. Cooper*), a postal village, 367 miles N. of Sydney, with mail four times a week.

MURULLA MOUNT (*Co. Brisbane*), a high peak of the Liverpool Range, about 4 miles S. of the town of Murrurundi. The highest peak is 4,000 feet above the sea-level.

MURULLA (*Co. Brisbane*), a village on the bank of the river Page, opposite Blandford, in the Upper Hunter District.

MURWILLUMBAH (*Co. Richmond*), a postal village, 407 miles N. of Sydney, with daily mail. Telegraph and money-order offices, and Government savings bank. It is situated on the extreme northern boundary of the Colony, adjoining Queensland, and on the Tweed River. Courts of quarter sessions and district courts are held here periodically.

MURWIN MOUNT (*Co. Northumberland*), a high peak in the Hunter Range, lying in the parish of Werong, and near the head of the Werong Creek.

MUSCLE BROOK (*Co. Durham*), a small eastern tributary of the Hunter River, falling into it at the township of the same name.

MUSK VALLEY CREEK (*Co. Clarence*), a small tributary of the Clarence River, flowing into the main stream at South Grafton.

MUSWELLBROOK (*Co. Durham*), a postal town, 178 miles N. of Sydney, with mail twice daily. Telegraph and money-order offices, Government savings bank, and delivery by letter-carriers. A railway station on the northern line. Situated in the parish of Rowan. The Hunter River skirts the township on its western side. The district is agricultural and pastoral. It was proclaimed a municipal district in 1870, with a council of seven aldermen and a mayor. Population, about 1,000. Courts of quarter sessions and district courts are held at Muswellbrook periodically.

MUSQUITO CREEK (*Co. Burnett*), a small northern tributary of the Gwydir River, rising in Mount Musquito.

MUSQUITO MOUNT (*Co. Burnett*), a high solitary peak, near the Gilgil River, about 12 miles N.W. of Warialda.

MUSQUITO TOWN (*Co. Northumberland*), a village, 55 miles N. of Sydney, in the parish of Kincumber. Situated about 10 miles E. of Gosford, and is an agricultural district.

MUTTAMA (*Co. Harden*), a postal village, 269 miles S. of Sydney, with daily mail. A railway station on the Cootamundra and Gundagai line.

MUTTAMA CREEK (*Cos. Harden and Clarendon*), an important auriferous creek, to the S. of the Burrangong gold-fields, flowing through the township of Cootamundra.

MUTTON FALLS (*Co. Westmoreland*), a village, 120 miles W. of Sydney. Situated on the Fish River, near its junction with the Macquarie River. The nearest railway station is Tarana, 3 miles, on the western line.

MYALL CREEK (*Co. Denham*), a small western tributary of the Williams River, flowing into the main stream at Dungog.

MYALL CREEK (*Co. Murchison*), an auriferous tributary of the Gwydir River, rising to the W. of Inverell, and flowing about 5 miles N.W. of Bingara.

MYALL CREEK (*Co. Clive*), a small eastern tributary of the Severn River, falling into it below its confluence with Frazer's Creek.

MYALL LAKE (*Co. Gloucester*), a large salt-water lake formed by an expansion of the Myall River in its course to Port Stephens. It is about 17 miles long and 6 miles wide.

MYALL PLAINS (*Co. Ewenmar*), a postal receiving-office, 362 miles S. of Sydney, with mail twice a week.

MYALL RIVER (*Co. Gloucester*.) [*See* "RIVERS."]

MYALLA (*Co. Bathurst*), a postal receiving-office, 280 miles W. of Sydney, with mail therefrom once a week. A railway station on the Murrumburrah and Blayney line.

MYALLA CREEK (*Co. Beresford*), a small creek flowing near Cooma.

MYLADY CREEK (*Co. Vernon*), a small northern tributary of the Apsley River, joining it about 4 miles E. of Walcha.

MYRANGLE (*Co. Gordon*), a proclaimed village on the creek of the same name.

MYRANGLE CREEK (*Co. Gordon*), a southern tributary of the Buckinbar Creek.

MYRTLE CREEK (*Co. Camden*), a small tributary of the Nepean River.

MYRTLE CREEK (*Co. Northumberland*), a small northern tributary of the lower end of the Hawkesbury River, falling into it near Wiseman's ferry.

MYRTLE CREEK (*Co. Richmond*), a postal receiving-office to the N. of Sydney, with mail per steamer. It is the name given to the south arm of the Richmond River.

MYRTLEVILLE (*Co. Argyle*), a postal village, 154 miles S. of Sydney, with daily mail. The nearest railway station is Goulburn, on the southern line. Situated in the parish of Taralla, on the Myrtle Creek, 12 miles from Tarlo River.

NAAS VALLEY (*Co. Cowley*), a deep and fertile valley, running in a line with the W. bank of the Murrumbidgee River.

NAAS VALLEY CREEK (*Co. Cowley*), a fine stream of water, rising on the eastern slope of Gudgenby Hill, flowing through the fertile Naas Valley, falling into the Gudgenby River, about 6 miles S. of Tharwa.

NACKA NACKA CREEK (*Co. Wynyard*), a southern auriferous tributary of the Murrumbidgee River, rising in the middle of Adelong gold-fields.

NACKA-NACKA MOUNT (*Co. Wynyard*), a lofty peak in the Murray Ranges, attaining an elevation of 2,242 feet above sea-level, and near the township of Adelong.

NADJIGOMAR CREEK (*Co. Argyle*), a small tributary of the Budjong Creek.

NAGHA LAKE (*Co. Auckland*), a small lagoon, lying about 3 miles N. of Cape Howe. The entrance is a shifting sand, sometimes open, and often closed.

NAIL-CAN DIGGINGS (*Co. Goulburn*), a small quartz and alluvial diggings, about 3 miles to the N. of Albury, under the Black Range of Mountains.

NALBAUGH HILL (*Co. Auckland*), an elevation on the Wog-Wog River, on the road from Twofold Bay to Bombala.

NALOWA (*Co. Menindie*), a township on the W. bank of the Darling River, to the S. of Menindie.

NALTICOMEBE (*Co. Landsborough*), a township on the E. bank of the Darling River, opposite Dunlop's Range.

NAMBUCCA HEADS (*Co. Raleigh*), a postal village, 356 miles N. of Sydney, with mail three times a week. Telegraph and money-order offices, and Government savings bank. The nearest railway station Hexham, 342 miles, on the Newcastle, Maitland, and Singleton line. It is the northern head of the Nambucca River, lying about 12 miles N. of Trial Bay.

NAMBUCCA RIVER (*Co. Raleigh.*) [*See* "RIVERS."]

NAMOI RIVER (*Cos. Baradine, Denham, and Jamison.*) [*See* "RIVERS."]

NANA (*Co. Fitzroy*), a proclaimed village in this county.

NANAMA (*Co. King*), a postal receiving-office, 206 miles S. of Sydney, with mail twice a week.

**NANDEWAR**, a county in the Central Division of the Colony. [*See* "COUNTIES."]

**NANDI CREEK** (*Co. Leichhardt*), a small water-course, rising in the hill of the same name, and falling into the Castlereagh River, near the township of Coonabarabran.

**NANDI MOUNT** (*Co. Leichhardt*), a small conical-shaped hill, near the head of the Castlereagh River, at the township of Coonabarabran.

**NANDILLION PONDS** (*Co. Wellington*), a chain of waterholes connected by a running stream, and flowing into Larras Lake Creek.

**NANGAHRA CREEK** (*Co. Darling*), an auriferous stream, rising to W. of Mount Lowry, and flowing through the Ironbark gold-field.

**NANGAR** (*Co. Ashburnham*), a postal receiving-office, 240 miles S. of Sydney, with mail twice a week.

**NANGERYBONE** (*Co. Flinders*), a township on the W. side of the county.

**NANGUS** (*Co. Clarendon*), a postal receiving-office, 298 miles S. of Sydney, with mail twice a week. The nearest railway station is Illabo, 18 miles, on the southern line.

**NANNIS POINT** (*Co. Cumberland*), a rocky promontory on the N. side of Port Jackson, opposite Long Nose Point. The township of Greenwich stands on this point.

**NANY MOUNT** (*Co. Buckland*), a peak of the Liverpool Range, attaining an altitude of 3,000 feet above sea-level, and lying at the head of Taylor's Creek.

**NAPIER**, a county in the Central Division of the Colony. [*See* "COUNTIES."]

**NARANGULLEN MOUNT** (*Co. Cowley*), a lofty hill, lying on the E. bank of the Goodradigbee River, near the head of the Sugar-loaf Creek.

**NARARA** (*Co. Cumberland*), a postal village, 52 miles N. of Sydney, with daily mail. It is a railway station on the Sydney and Newcastle line.

**NARELLAN** (*Co. Cumberland*), a postal village, 38 miles S. of Sydney, with mail twice daily. Situated in the parish of Narellan. The tramway from Campbelltown to Camden passes through the village, where there is a station.

**NARELLAN CREEK** (*Co. Monteagle*), a fine western tributary of the Burrowa River, rising to the E. of Murringo.

**NARGUS CREEK** (*Co. Clarendon*), a small northern tributary of the Murrumbidgee River, flowing S.W. about 8 miles.

**NAROOMA** (*Co. Dampier*), a postal village, 268 miles S. of Sydney, with mail twice a week.

NARRA-NARRA-WA MOUNT (*Co. Goulburn*), a lofty peak of the broken mountainous country in the middle of the county.

NARRABEEN (*Co. Cumberland*), a postal receiving-office, 17 miles N. of Sydney, with daily mail. Situated on the sea-coast, to the N. of Manly.

NARRABEEN LAGOON (*Co. Cumberland*) is a shoal inlet from the sea, lying on the coast half-way between the North Head of Port Jackson and Broken Bay.

NARRABRI (*Co. Nandewar*), a postal town, 351 miles N. of Sydney, with daily mail. Telegraph and money-order offices, Government savings bank, and delivery by letter-carrier. A railway station on the north-western line. Situated on the Narrabri Creek, an Ana-branch of the Namoi River, and about a mile distant E. of that river. The district is a pastoral one. The Namoi joins the Barwon at Walgett. It was proclaimed a borough in 1883, with a council of eight aldermen and a mayor. Population, about 1,825. Courts of quarter sessions and district courts are held here periodically.

NARRABURRA (*Co. Bland*), a postal receiving-office, 288 miles S. of Sydney, with mail twice a week.

NARRABURRA CREEK (*Co. Bland*), a southern tributary of the upper part of the Yeo-Yeo Creek.

NARRAN, a county in the Western Division of the Colony. [*See* "COUNTIES."]

NARRAN CREEK (*Co. Macquarie*), a small southern tributary of the Hastings River.

NARRANDERA (*Co. Cooper*), a postal town, 347 miles S. of Sydney, with daily mail. Telegraph and money-order offices, Government savings bank, and delivery by letter-carrier. A railway station on the south-western line. Situated in the parish of Narrandera, on the Murrumbidgee River. The district is almost exclusively pastoral. It was proclaimed a borough in 1885, with a council of eight aldermen and a mayor. The population is about 1,500. Courts of quarter sessions and district courts are held at Narrandera periodically during each year.

NARRAN RIVER (*Cos. Finch and Narran*). [*See* "RIVERS."]

NARRAN SWAMP (*Co. Clyde*), a large marshy lagoon, into which the Narran River empties itself, and in wet seasons overflows into the Barwon River.

NARRAWA (*Co. Argyle*), a postal town, 175 miles S. of Sydney, with mail twice a week. The nearest railway station is Goulburn, 41 miles, on the southern line.

NARRIGA (*Co. St. Vincent*), a township to the E. of the Shoalhaven River.

NARIGAN CREEK (*Co. Argyle*), a small drainage creek from the Dividing Range, flowing N.E. into Lake Bathurst through the town of Boro.

NARROMINE, a county in the Central Division of the Colony. [*See* "COUNTIES."]

NARROMINE (*Co. Narromine*), a postal village, 300 miles W. of Sydney, with daily mail. Money-order office. A railway station on the western line.

NARROWGUT (*Co. Northumberland*), situated on the S. bank of the Hunter River, about 1 mile N.W. of Morpeth. The district is highly cultivated, the soil being very rich.

NATIONAL PARK (*Co. Cumberland*), a public recreation ground, 18 miles S. of Sydney. The nearest railway station is Loftus, on the Illawarra and South Coast line. The National Park is fast becoming one of the favourite resorts for public enjoyment.

NATIVE DOG CREEK (*Co. Buccleuch*), a small western tributary of the Goodradigbee Creek, flowing through the Yass Plains.

NATIVE DOG CREEK (*Co. Clarendon*), a small northern tributary of the Murrumbidgee River.

NATIVE DOG CREEK (*Co. Gordon*) is a western tributary of the Bell River.

NATIVE DOG CREEK (*Co. Goulburn*), a small eastern tributary of the Woomargarma Creek, rising near the village of that name.

NATIVE DOG CREEK (*Co. Wellesley*), a small tributary of the upper part of the Cambelong Creek.

NATIVE DOG CREEK (*Co. Westmoreland*), a small eastern tributary of the Stony Creek.

NATIVE DOG FLAT (*Co. Wellesley*), a piece of bold undulating land, near the head of the Native Dog Creek, and to the S. of the Undore heights, to the N. of Bombala.

NATTAI OR MITTAGONG (*Co. Camden*), a township, 74 miles S. of Sydney, in the parishes of Mittagong, Narellan, and Picton. It is situated on the Nattai Creek, at an elevation of about 2,500 feet above the level of the sea, and is a railway station on the Albury and Melbourne line. The district is an agricultural, pastoral, and mining one, the minerals worked being coal and iron, of both of which there are large deposits. The former is good in quality, and found in tolerably thick seams, and is used principally in the production of iron, of which there are large and rich deposits. The celebrated Fitzroy iron-works are in the township. One of the largest railway tunnels in the colony is cut through the Gibraltar Hill, at a distance of about 1 mile from the town.

NATTAI RIVER (*Co. Camden*). [*See* "RIVERS."]

NEALE'S WATERHOLES (*Co. Bathurst*), a series of lagoons, flowing from near the township of Vittoria into the head of the Belubula River.

NEEDLE CREEK (*Co. Wellesley*), a small western tributary of the Cambalong Creek.

NEEDLES (*Co. Wellesley*), a range of peaks on the W. bank of the Comalong Creek, about 10 miles from Bombala.

NEIMUR CREEK (*Co. Wakool*), a large tributary stream of the Wakool River, and joins it near its fall into the Edward River.

NELBOTHERY (*Co. Wellesley*), a small diggings, lying on the Delegate River, to the N. of the Delegate Plains, about 14 miles from Bombala.

NELLIGEN (*Co. St. Vincent*), a postal town, 183 miles S. of Sydney, with mail three times a week. Telegraph and money-order offices, and Government savings bank. The nearest railway station is Tarago, 65 miles, on the Goulburn and Cooma line. It is a seaport township, lying on the S. bank of the estuary of the Clyde River.

NELLIGEN CREEK (*Co. St. Vincent*), a small creek, rising near Monga, flowing W. into the Clyde River, at Nelligen.

NELSON AND UPPER NELSON (*Co. Cumberland*), two original districts of the county, bounded by the Hawkesbury River and South Creek, Cattai, and the Windsor Road.

NELSON'S BAY (*Co. Gloucester*), a postal village, 178 miles N. of Sydney, with mail three times a week, and telegraph office. The bay is an anchorage of Port Stephens, convenient for vessels when wind and weather bound.

NELSON'S PLAINS (*Co. Durham*), a postal village, 116 miles N. of Sydney, with daily mail. The nearest railway station is Hexham, 8 miles, on the northern line. It is an agricultural settlement at the confluence of the Hunter and Williams Rivers, near Raymond Terrace.

NELSONGLADE CREEK (*Co. King*), a small tributary of the Yass River, rising in the S.W. slopes of Mount Chaton.

NEMINGHA (*Co. Parry*), a postal receiving-office, 287 miles N. of Sydney, with mail four times a week.

NEMUR CREEK (*Co. Gowen*), is the northern tributary or head of Gallagambroon Creek.

NEMUR, MOUNT (*Co. Gowen*), a peak of the Warrabungle Range, lying at the head of the Wallamburrawang Creek.

NEPEAN RIVER (*Co. Camden*). [*See* "RIVERS."]

NERAMBELLA PLAINS (*Co. Bathurst*), a tract of good pastoral land, lying about 2 miles W. of Rockley, on the Pepper Creek.

NEROBINGABLA CREEK (*Co. Brisbane*), is the western head of the Guangua Creek.

NERRIGA (*Co. St. Vincent*), a postal village, 231 miles S. of Sydney with mail twice a week. The nearest railway station is Tarago, 49 miles, on the Goulburn and Cooma line. Situated in the parish of the same name. The water communication to Sydney is from Nowra, distant 45 miles by land.

NERRIGUNDAH (*Co. Dampier*), a postal village, 273 miles S. of Sydney, with daily mail. Money-order office. The nearest railway station is Tarago, 110 miles, on the Goulburn and Cooma line. Situated on the Gulf Creek, a tributary of the Tuross River. The district is a good bearing one, and agricultural pursuits are carried on successfully. The communication with Sydney by water is from Woyonga, on Clyde River, distant 16 miles.

NERRIMUNGO CREEK *(Co. Argyle)*, a western tributary of the Shoalhaven River, formed by the confluence of the Yarralow and Windellama Creeks.

NETTERING CREEK *(Co. Northumberland)*, a small watercourse, falling into the Jillaby-Jillaby Creek on its W. bank.

NETTLE CREEK *(Co. Richmond)*, a small northern tributary of the Clarence River, flowing through good country.

NEUREA *(Co. Wellington)*, a postal village, 244 miles W. of Sydney, with daily mail. The nearest railway station is Springs, 3 miles, on the western line.

NEUTRAL BAY *(Co. Cumberland)*, an important bay on the N. side of Port Jackson, to the E. of Kirribilli Point.

NEUTRAL BAY *(Co. Cumberland)*, a postal suburb of Sydney, with mail twice daily. Telegraph office and Government savings bank, with delivery by letter-carrier.

NEVADA *(Co. Yancowinna)*, a proclaimed village, to the N.E. of Silverton.

NEVER NEVER *(Co. Rous)*, a postal village, 386 miles N. of Sydney, with mail once a week, and *per* Fernmount steamer.

NEVERTIRE *(Co. Oxley)*, a postal village, 341 miles W. of Sydney, with daily mail. Telegraph and money-order office, and Government savings bank. A railway station on the western line.

NEVILLE, MOUNT *(Co. Richmond)*, a high hill, about 8 miles N.W. of the township of Gordon.

NEWBRIDGE *(Co. Bathurst)*, a postal village, 164 miles W. of Sydney, with daily mail. Telegraph and money-order office. A railway station on the western line.

NEWCASTLE *(Co. Northumberland)*, 32° 57′ S. lat., 151° 47′ E. long., in the parish of Newcastle, 102 miles N. of Sydney, with mail therefrom twice daily. Telegraph and money-order offices, and Government savings bank. It is the second seaport in the Colony, situated on the right or S. bank of the Hunter River, at its outlet into the sea, and has a tidal rise and fall of about 5 feet at the wharf. Newcastle was formerly called Kingstown, and the river Hunter, known as the Coal River, by which name it is called in all old records of the Colony. Newcastle is the seat of the coal-mining enterprise, which gives it a pre-eminence over all the colonies in the South Pacific. Every modern facility is in existence for the easy and expeditious shipment of coal, to enable the shipping trade to carry off the supply which is in daily want. The export of coal for the last year amounted to 2,553,512 tons. The port has monopolised the whole of the trade of the Hunter district, as well as that of the pastoral country beyond, and the Great Northern railway has tended to consolidate and confirm that supremacy. The signalling and appliances for protecting the mariner and the large and increasing shipping trade of the port are of the most complete character. The city cannot be cited as a model one in the formation of its streets or buildings; it is, however, an incorporated municipality under the Act, with a council of eleven aldermen and a mayor, and has much improved of late. The communication with Sydney is by first-class sea-going steamers, as well as by direct railway transit. The area of the city proper is about 870 acres, but the incorporated district of Newcastle comprises 112,028 acres. Courts of quarter sessions and district courts are held at Newcastle periodically during each year. Population, about 27,700.

NEW CRYAN (*Co. Nandewar*), a postal receiving-office, 454 miles N. of Sydney, with mail twice a week.

NEW ENGLAND RANGE, a portion of the main dividing chain, commencing at the northern boundary of the Colony, and extending as far south as the 32nd parallel. Its character and elevation vary in different parts, but its average height is about 3,500 feet. Its highest point is Ben Lomond, which is 5,000 feet above the sea-level.

NEW FREUGH (*Co. Durham*), a village reserve, lying on the Northern Road, 7 miles from Singleton.

NEWINGTON (*Co. Cumberland*), a suburb of the city, about 6 miles W. of Sydney, and on the S. side of the Parramatta River. The Wesleyan Collegiate Institution is situated here.

NEW ITALY (*Co. Clarence*), a postal receiving-office, 338 miles N. of Sydney, with mail per steamers.

NEW LAMBTON (*Co. Northumberland*), a township, 2 miles from Waratah, the nearest railway station on the northern line. It was proclaimed a borough in 1889, with a council of eight aldermen and a mayor.

NEWLANDS (*Co. Cunningham*), a postal receiving-office, 191 miles W. of Sydney, with mail twice a week.

NEW ORIEL (*Co. Nandewar*), a village, 350 miles N.W. of Sydney. The nearest railway station is Narrabri, 84 miles, on the north-western line.

NEWPARK (*Co. Durham*), a postal town, 150 miles N. of Sydney, with mail three times a week. The nearest railway station is Morpeth, 32 miles, on the East Maitland and Morpeth line.

NEW PIPECLAY (*Co. Wellington*), a village, 190 miles W. of Sydney. The nearest railway station is Mudgee, 5 miles, on the western line.

NEWPORT (*Co. Cumberland*), a postal receiving-office, 23 miles N. of Sydney, with daily mail. A beautiful spot on the sea-coast.

NEWREA (*Co. Gordon*), a small Government village, in the parish of the same name, and police district of Wellington. It is situated on the Bell River, on the Molong Road.

NEWREA CREEK (*Co. Gordon*), a western tributary of the Bell River.

NEW SOUTH WALES is the parent Colony in the Australasian group of Colonies. Sydney, the capital of New South Wales, being the spot chosen by Governor Arthur Phillip, on the 26th of January, 1788, whereon to found the first settlement in New South Wales. It is bounded on the east by the South Pacific Ocean, with a coast-line of 680 miles, extending from Point Danger on the north to Cape Howe on the south; on the north by the Queensland boundary-line; on the west by the South Australian boundary; and on the south by the boundary of Victoria; and comprises an estimated area of 198,848,000 acres, or 310,700 square miles. By the Land Act of 1884 the Colony was divided into three grand divisions: 1. The Eastern; 2. The Central; 3. The Western. The map appended illustrates the geographical lines of the divisions as proclaimed under the Act.

**NEWSTEAD CREEK** (*New England*), a small northern tributary of the upper part of the Macintyre River, which it joins at the village of Newstead.

**NEWTON BOYD** (*Co. Gresham*), a proclaimed township, on the Mitchell River.

**NEWTOWN** (*Co. Cumberland*), a branch office of the General Post Office, Sydney, with all the accommodation pertaining thereto. It is situated on the main trunk line of railway, 2 miles from Sydney, in the parish of Petersham, and forms the continuation of the western portion of the city. It was proclaimed a borough in 1862, with a council of eleven aldermen and a mayor. Population, about 17,500.

**NICHOLAS LAGOON** (*Co. Buckland*), a waterhole, on the junction of the Cooepolly and Quirindi Creeks, N.W. of the township of Quirindi.

**NICHOLSON**, a county, in the Central Division of the Colony. [*See* "COUNTIES."]

**NICHOLSON'S** (*Co. Wellesley*), a postal receiving-office, 328 miles S. of Sydney, with mail three times a week.

**NIMBIN** (*Co. Rous*), a postal village, 381 miles N. of Sydney, with mail therefrom once a week, *via* Lismore.

**NIMMITIBEL MOUNTAIN** (*Co. Auckland*), a mountain range, lying on the road from Nimitibel to Bega and Panbula. It is situated about 3 miles from the N. bank of the Bemboka River, and attains an elevation of 3,465 feet above the sea-level.

**NIMMITIBEL** (*Co. Wellesley*), a postal town, 282 miles S. of Sydney, with daily mail. Telegraph and money-order offices, and Government savings bank. The nearest railway station is Cooma, 23 miles, on the Goulburn and Cooma line. Situated at the head of Babundarah Creek. The district is an agricultural and pastoral one.

**NINE-MILE** (*Co. Gough*), a postal receiving-office, 430 miles N. of Sydney, with mail twice a week.

**NINE-MILE PINCH** (*Co. Wallace*), a steep ascent of 4 miles in length, on the road from Cooma to Gippsland and the Ovens, *via* Forest Hill, after crossing the Snowy River.

**NINGADOON, MOUNT** (*Co. Nandewar*), a peak of the Nandewar Range, about 12 miles inland, E. of the township of Narrabri.

**NINGEE NAMBLA CREEK** (*Co. St. Vincent*), a small creek, on the E. side of the Shoalhaven River, rising on the N.E. of Marlow, and flowing into that river.

**NOB'S REEF** (*Co. King*), a quartz and alluvial diggings, on the Nob's Creek, about 20 miles from the township of Laggan.

NOBBY'S (*Co. Northumberland*), a remarkable island, lying at the S. side of the entrance to the Hunter River, at Newcastle. It is 92 feet in height, and about 90 yards in diameter at the top, and is now connected with the mainland by a breakwater half a mile in length, constructed to protect the shipping in Port Hunter from the sea. A lighthouse is erected on its top, showing a fixed white light, at an elevation of 115 feet above the sea-level.

NODGUNGULLA CREEK (*Co. St. Vincent*), a small tributary of the lower end of the Corang River.

NODRIGAR CREEK (*Co. Drake*), a small western tributary of the Clarence River.

NOLAN CREEK (*Co. Gloucester*), a small eastern tributary of the Williams River.

NOMBINNIE (*Co. Blaxland*), a proclaimed township, W. of Mount Hope.

NONAN POINT (*Co. Northumberland*). [See "BRISBANE RIVER."]

NOOCERA CREEK (*Co. Murchison*), a southern tributary of the Horton River, flowing into it at Eulowrie.

NOORONG (*Co. Townsend*), a postal receiving-office, 546 miles S. of Sydney, with mail once a week. The nearest railway station is Hay, 150 miles, on the south-western line.

NOOROOMA (*Co. Dampier*), a proclaimed village, in this county.

NORAH (*Co. Northumberland*), a proclaimed village, at Norah Lead.

NORAH LEAD (*Co. Northumberland*), a headland, on the peninsular which separates the northern part of Tuggerah Lake from the sea, about 5 miles N. of the entrance.

NORIE'S LEAD (*Co. Rous*) is a small promontory lying about 2 miles N. of Hastings Point.

NORTH BERRY JERRY (*Co. Bourke*), a postal village, 321 miles S. of Sydney, with mail three times a week. The nearest railway station is Coolamon, 12 miles, on the south-western line.

NORTH BOURKE (*Co. Gunderbooka*), a postal receiving-office, 509 miles W. of Sydney, with mail three times a week.

NORTH FORSTER (*Co. Gloucester*), a postal receiving-office, 199 miles N. of Sydney, with mail three times a week.

NORTH GOBBARRALONG (*Co. Harden*), a postal village, 353 miles S. of Sydney, with mail twice a week. The nearest railway station is Coolac, 15 miles, on the southern line.

NORTH HARBOUR (*Co. Cumberland*), a wide open roadstead, lying on the N. of Port Jackson, and to the W. of the North Head.

NORTH HEAD, INNER (*Co. Cumberland*), a lofty perpendicular rocky cliff, on the S.E. of the promontory known as the North Head, and is the inner North Head of Port Jackson, and has an elevation of about 260 feet above sea-level. The quarantine ground is situate on this point.

NORTH HEAD, OUTER (*Co. Cumberland*) is a lofty, perpendicular rocky peninsular, which stands at the N. entrance to Port Jackson, lying between the ocean on the E. and North Harbour on the W., and connected with the mainland by a narrow, low neck of sandy beach, on which the village of Manly (or Brighton) is built. This vast mass of sandy rock towers majestically out of the water to a height of 264 feet, attaining at its highest point an altitude of 358 feet above sea-level.

NORTH KIAMA (*Co. Camden*), a railway station, 70 miles S. of Sydney, on the Illawarra and South Coast line.

NORTH MENANGLE (*Co. Camden*), a railway station, 40 miles S. of Sydney, on the southern line.

NORTH PARRAMATTA (*Co. Cumberland*), a suburb of Parramatta proper, 16 miles W. of Sydney, with mail therefrom twice daily, and telegraph office.

NORTH PIMLICO (*Co. Clarence*), a postal receiving-office, 360 miles N. of Sydney, with mails by Clarence and Richmond steamers.

NORTH POINT (*Co. Cumberland*) is the N.E. point of the N. head of Port Jackson.

NORTH RICHMOND (*Co. Cumberland*), a postal village, 42 miles W. of Sydney, with daily mail. The nearest railway station is Richmond, 3 miles, on the Windsor line.

NORTH RYDE (*Co. Cumberland*), a suburb of Ryde proper, 11 miles W. of Sydney, with daily mail.

NORTH SIDING (*Co. Cook*), a village, 66 miles W. of Sydney, about 1 mile from Katoomba station, on the western line.

NORTH SPRINGWOOD (*Co. Cook*), a post-office, 51 miles W. of Sydney, with mail three times a week.

NORTH SYDNEY (*Co. Cumberland*), a postal suburb of the city of Sydney, is situated in the parish of Willoughby, county of Cumberland, on the N. shore of Port Jackson, opposite the city, and is only divided from it, at the nearest points, by 712 yards of water. It is a municipal borough, proclaimed on the 29th July, 1890, with an estimated population of 17,500, having thirty-three aldermen as a governing body, with a mayor chosen from and by the aldermen. It has a water frontage to the harbour of Port Jackson and Middle Harbour, extending around 30 miles of coast-line. The communication with the city of Sydney is by well-arranged ferry-boats, running every fifteen minutes. These boats ply to and from Milson's Point, M'Mahon's Point, and Lavender Bay, to the N. and W.; and to Neutral Bay and Mossman's Bay to the E. There is a wire tram-line from Milson's Point to the public reserve, and thence to Lane Cove Road, where its joins the Hawkesbury and Newcastle line. The tram and ferry-boats run in union with one another to secure speedy transit across the harbour. The branch railway from Milson's Point to Hornsby, a distance of 11 miles, now all but completed, will here join the Hawkesbury and Newcastle line, giving easy access to the northern districts, and through Queensland to the city of Brisbane, the capital of that Colony. As a suburb of Sydney the district possesses natural advantages not obtainable in any other suburb of the city. The gradual rise in the land affords splendid building sites and charming landscape scenery. From the water's edge at Milson's Point to the Hornsby Junction the elevation of 592 feet above the sea-level, passing the highest suburb, and at Wahroogah 632 feet, is attained. The drive along the ridge, called the Military Road, to the fortifications at Middle Head is almost without a parallel in any part of the world. At this point the view of the opening of the heads of Port Jackson to the South Pacific Ocean is truly sublime, and Byron's grand apostrophe to the ocean could not be found a more fitting spot to be repeated:

"Roll on thou dark blue ocean, roll,"

\* \* \* \* \* \*

A company has been formed, called the Sydney Investment and Tramway Company, and the work commenced for opening up most enchanting country for suburban residences. Its operations commence in Miller-street, and is a continuation of the Government wire tram-line. The company's line will cross Long Bay, a branch of the Middle Harbour, with a suspension bridge, which will be the largest on the Southern Continent, and fourth only to the structures of a like character in the old world. The particulars of its design and dimension are given in the following particulars by J. E. F. Coyle, Esq., C.E.:—
"This bridge is constructed on the stiffened suspension principle, and has one central span of 500 feet, and two end spans of 150 feet each. The masonry consists of two piers of Gothic design, each formed of two embattled towers connected by double arches similarly decorated. The abutments are of the same order of architecture, all being in massive ashlar work. The superstructure passes over the lower arch, and is suspended from six cables arranged three over each pair of towers. The cables are composed of forty-two ropes, each 4¼ inches in circumference, of plough steel, having an ultimate resistance of 8,700 tons, and are said to be the highest class cables yet manufactured. The chambers in which the cables are secured are placed 75 feet below the surface, in the solid rock, the tunnels leading thereto being filled in with concrete. The superstructure is composed of Siemens-Martin steel, and consists of two main longitudinal stiffening lattice girders, hinged in the middle of the central span and at the towers, and is braced against wind pressure by four sets of triangulation in the planes of the upper and lower booms between each pair of cross-girders. There are sixty-two plate cross-girders placed 12 feet 6 inches apart to centres, and suspended directly from the cables, and upon these girders the whole of the superstructure rests. The roadway is 28 feet wide between the parapets, and provides for a raised passenger footpath, tramline, and carriage-way. The parapet is composed of wrought and cast iron, and has two three-branch lamps in the centre of the main span, and two at the towers. The summit of the tower battlements is 258 feet, and the level of the roadway 187 feet above the level of the water. The bridge presents a very striking appearance, and is of the highest class of construction."

NORTH TUMBULGUM (*Co. Rous*), a postal village, 432 miles N. of Sydney, with daily mail.

NORTH WILLOUGHBY (*Co. Cumberland*), a postal village, 5 miles N. of Sydney, with mail twice daily. Money-order office and Government savings bank.

NORTH YANCO (*Co. Mitchell*), a postal village, 361 miles S. of Sydney, with mail five times a week.

NORTHERN COAST RANGE (*Macleay District*).—This range lies between the Clarence and Manning Rivers, at a distance of about 35 miles from the sea-coast and nearly parallel with it. Its average elevation is about 3,000 feet above sea-level.

NORTHUMBERLAND, a county in the Eastern Division of the Colony. [*See* "COUNTIES."]

NORTON (*Co. Bathurst*), a postal receiving-office, 176 miles W. of Sydney, with mail three times a week. The nearest railway station is Blayney, 4 miles, on the western line.

NORWOOD (*Co. Cumberland*), is a residential suburb lying on the Parramatta Road, between Camperdown and Petersham.

NOTT MOUNT (*Co. Forbes*), a lofty peak, lying to the S. of the Lachlan River, about 20 miles S.E. of Forbes.

NOWENDOC (*Co. Macquarie*), a postal village, 226 miles N. of Sydney, with mail once a week. The nearest railway station is Hexham 115 miles, on the northern line.

NOWENDOC RIVER (*Co. Macquarie*). [*See* "RIVERS."]

NOWLANDS CREEK (*Co. Gresham*), a small southern tributary of the Sara River.

NOWRA (*Co. St. Vincent*), a postal town, 124 miles S. of Sydney, with mail twice daily. Telegraph and money-order offices, Government savings bank, and delivery by letter-carrier. The nearest railway station is Kiama, 26 miles, on the Illawarra and South Coast line. Situated on the Shoalhaven River, in the parish of Nowra. The district is both agricultural and pastoral, and is very productive. It was proclaimed a municipal district in 1871, with a council of eight aldermen and a mayor. The courts of quarter sessions and district courts are held here periodically.

NOWRA CREEK (*Co. St. Vincent*), a small tributary of the lower part of the Shoalhaven River, flowing through the township of Nowra.

NUBBA (*Co. Harden*), a postal town, 237 miles S. of Sydney, with daily mail. A railway station on the southern line.

NUBRIGYU CREEK (*Co. Wellington*), a southern tributary of the Stony Creek.

NUGAL (*Co. Leichhardt*), a township on the Castlereagh River.

NUGGETTY GULLY (*Co. Wellington*), a small diggings on the Louisa Creek gold-field, about 4 miles E. of the township of Windeyer.

NUGGETTY GULLY CREEK (*Co. Wellington*), an auriferous tributary of the Barraba Creek, to the E. of the Louisa Creek gold-field.

NULLA-NULLA CREEK (*Co. Dudley*), a small northern tributary of the Macleay River.

NULLAMANNA (*Co. Gough*), a postal village, 453 miles N. of Sydney, with mail four times a week. The nearest railway station is Glen Innes, 40 miles, on the northern line.

NULLING MOUNT (*Co. Wellington*), a peak to the S.E. of Mudgee, about 5 miles from it, and at the head of Grattai Creek.

NULLO MOUNT (*Co. Phillip*), a high peak of the Hunter Range, lying on the E. bank of the Widdin Brook, about 25 miles N.W. of Dabee. It is 2,500 feet above sea-level.

NUMANTIA (*Co. Cumberland*), a railway station, 52 miles to the W. of Sydney, on the western line.

NUMBA (*Co. St. Vincent*), a postal village, 128 miles S. of Sydney, with daily mail. Money-order office and Government savings bank. The nearest railway station is Kiama, 27 miles, on the Illawarra and South Coast line. Situated on the S. bank of the Shoalhaven River, in the parish of Numba. Steam communication with Sydney from Greenwell Point, on the Crookhaven River, about 7 miles distant. It was proclaimed a municipal district in 1868, with a council of five aldermen and a mayor.

NUMBUGGA (*Co. Auckland*), a postal village, 324 miles S. of Sydney, with mail three times a week. Telegraph and money-order offices, and Government savings bank. The nearest railway station is Cooma, 66 miles, on the Goulburn and Cooma line.

NUMERALLA (*Co. Beresford*), a postal village, 279 miles S. of Sydney, with mail twice a week. Situated in the parish of Numeralla, at the junction of the Bigbadja and Numeralla Rivers. The district is a pastoral one.

NUNDAWAR RANGE (*Liverpool Plains*), is a branch of the New England Range, commencing near its southern extremity, and extending for a considerable distance in a N.W. direction. The highest point, Mount Lindsay, is about 3,000 feet above sea-level.

NUNDLE (*Co. Parry*), a postal town, 321 miles N. of Sydney, with mail four times a week. Telegraph and money-order offices, and Government savings bank. The nearest railway station is Tamworth, 40 miles, on the Wallangarra and Brisbane line. Situated on the confluence of the Nundle Creek and the Peel River, in the parish of Nundle. Gold-bearing district.

NUNDLE CREEK (*Co. Parry*), a small auriferous eastern tributary of the head of the Peel River, rising in the N.E. slope of the Hanging Rock.

NUNDLE CREEK (*Co. Hardinge*), a western auriferous tributary of the Gwydir River, rising near the road from Bendemeer to Inverell.

NURANGY LAKE (*Co. Rous*), a small saltwater lagoon, formed by a N. expansion of the estuary of the Tweed River.

NURSERY CREEK (*Co. Cowley*), a small tributary of the Gugenby River, rising between the Murrumbidgee River and Bimberi Range.

NURUNG GAP (*Co. Harden*), a pass over some high rugged country, in the parish of Nurung.

NYMAGEE (*Co. Mouramba*), a postal village, 441 miles W. of Sydney, with mail three times a week. Telegraph and money-order offices, and Government savings bank. The nearest railway station is Nyngan, 68 miles, on the western line.

NYMBOI RIVER (*Cos. Drake, Gresham, and Fitzroy*). [*See* "RIVERS."]

NYMBOIDA (*Co. Fitzroy*), a small hamlet on the Nymboi River, about 24 miles S.W. of Grafton.

NYNGAN (*Co. Oxley*), a postal village, 377 miles W. of Sydney, with daily mail. Telegraph and money-order offices and Government savings bank, and delivery by letter-carrier. A railway station on the western line, where the branch line to Cobar diverges.

NYRANG CREEK (*Co. Ashburnham*), a small northern tributary of the Belubula River, falling into it below Canowindra.

# O

OAKS THE (*Co. Camden*), a postal village, 50 miles S. of Sydney, with daily mail, and money-order office. The nearest railway station is Picton, 10 miles, on the southern line. Situated on the Werriberry Creek, a tributary of the Warragamba River, in the parish of Werombi.

OAK CREEK (*Co. Buccleuch*), a southern tributary of the Murrumbidgee River, rising in Paddy's Rock Hill.

OAK CREEK (*Co. Harden*), a northern tributary of the Murrumbidgee River, flowing into the plain near Bogolong.

OAKS CREEK (*Co. Buccleuch*), a small eastern tributary of the Adjungbilli Creek, running in a portion of the Yass Plains.

OAKEY CREEK (*Co. Napier*), a village, 241 miles to the W. of Sydney, situated on the Oakey Creek. The nearest town is Coola, 17 miles S.

OAKEY CREEK (*Co. Roxburgh*), a small auriferous stream flowing into the Turon River, close to the township of Sofala.

OAKEY CREEK (*Co. Wellington*), a small western tributary of Lewis Ponds Creek, rising in the Mullion Range.

OAKEY CREEK (*Co. Ashburnham*), a small southern tributary of the Bowrimbla Creek.

OAKEY CREEK (*Co. Bathurst*), a northern tributary of the Lachlan River, rising near the mouth of the Abercrombie River.

OAKEY CREEK (*Co. Darling*), a small eastern tributary of Maule's Creek. Also a small tributary of Tarporley Creek, flowing S.W. of Barraba.

OAKEY CREEK (*Co. Dudley*), one of the heads of the Styx River.

OAKEY CREEK (*Co. King*), a small eastern tributary of the Hovell Creek, rising in Mount Darling.

OAKEY CREEK (*Co. Murray*), an eastern tributary of the Murrumbidgee River, having two heads.

OAKEY CREEK (*Co. Napier*), a northern tributary of the Weetalaba Creek, rising in the Boogamurra Plains.

OAKLANDS (*Co. Urana*), a postal receiving-office, 428 miles S. of Sydney, with mail twice a week.

OAKVALE (*Co. Northumberland*), an agricultural district, lying on the road from Maitland to Mount Vincent.

OAKWOOD (*Co. Gough*), a postal-village, 483 miles N. of Sydney, with mail twice a week. The nearest railway station is Glen Innes, 55 miles, on the northern line.

OATGRASS CREEK (*Co. Ashburnham*), a small northern tributary of the Billabong Creek.

OATLEY'S (*Co. Cumberland*), a railway station, 11 miles S. of Sydney, on the Illawarra and South Coast line.

OBAN (*Co. Sandon*), a postal village, 405 miles N. of Sydney, with mail once a week. The nearest railway station is Guyra, 20 miles, on the northern line.

OBELISK BAY (*Co. Cumberland*), a small rocky bay, with a sand-patch on its head, lying on the N. shore of Port Jackson, between Middle and George's Heads.

OBELISK MOUNTAINS NORTH AND SOUTH (*Cos. Rous and Buller*), the name given to two lofty peaks of the Macpherson Range, on the W. bank of the Tooloom River, near Colt's station.

OBERN HILL (*Co. Wynyard*), is a peak lying between the Nakie-Nakie and Tarcutta Creeks.

OBERON (*Co. Westmoreland*), a postal village, 136 miles W. of Sydney, with daily mail. Telegraph and money-order offices, and Government savings bank. The nearest railway station is Tarana, 18 miles, on the western line. Situated in the parish of Oberon, on the Fish River Creek, the Duemoloi Racecourse, King's and Wiseman's Creeks flowing in the neighbourhood.

OBLEY (*Co. Gordon*), a postal village, 253 miles W. of Sydney, with mail four times a week. The nearest railway station is Molong, 247 miles on the Orange and Molong line. Situated in the parish of Obley, on the Mary or Little River.

O'BRIEN'S CREEK (*Co. Wynyard*), a western tributary of the Kiambla Creek, flowing N.E. to the S. of the Murrumbidgee.

O'CONNELL (*Co. Westmoreland*), a postal village, 139 miles W. of Sydney, with daily mail, and money-order office. The nearest railway station is Brewongle, 5 miles, on the western line. Situated on the Fish River.

O'CONNELL CRESCENT (*Co. Cumberland*), a small agricultural settlement in the parish of Petersham, being a part of Camperdown, on the Cook's River Road, about 3 miles S. of Sydney.

O'CONNELL TOWN (*Co. Cumberland*), situated on the Cook's River Road, about 3 miles S. of Sydney, and in the parish of Petersham.

OGUNBIL CREEK (*Co. Parry*), an eastern auriferous tributary of the Peel River, rising on the western slopes of the Australian Alps.

OHIO CREEK (*Co. Vernon*), a northern tributary of the Apsley River, flowing on the E. of the township of Walcha.

OHIO HILL (*Co. Inglis*), a lofty peak of the New England Range, lying about 8 miles N. of Walcha. It attains an altitude of 3,579 feet above sea-level.

OLDBURY (*Co. Camden*), a small agricultural hamlet, situated about 3 miles from Sutton Forest.

OLD GOREE (*Co. Urana*), a postal receiving-office, 384 miles S. of Sydney, with mail twice a week.

OLD JUGIONG HILL (*Co. Harden*), a high hill on the N. bank of the Murrumbidgee River, within the town boundary of Jugiong.

OLD JUNEE (*Co. Clarendon*), a postal village, 291 miles S. of Sydney, with daily mail. Money-order office and Government savings bank. A railway station on the south-western line.

OLD MAN'S CREEK (*Co. King*), a drainage creek to the N. of the Yass Plains, flowing through the upper part of the Lachlan River.

OLD SNOWY CREEK (*Co. Buccleuch*), is one of the heads of the Bumbolee Creek, rising to the S. of Red Hill.

OLLERA (*Co. Hardinge*), a village, 385 miles to the N. of Sydney. The nearest railway station is Guyra, 13 miles, on the northern line.

OMADALE CREEK (*Co. Gloucester*), an eastern tributary of the head of the Hunter River, flowing past the S. side of Omadale Hill.

OMALEAH CREEK (*Cos. Buckland and Pottinger*), a western tributary of the Conadilly River, rising to the W. of Mount Parry.

OMIGAL (*Co. Wellington*), a proclaimed township, to the S. of Wellington.

ONAL CREEK (*Co. Gloucester*), a small drainage creek, flowing into Port Stephens on its N. shore.

ONANNA HILL (*Co. Wellington*), a lofty hill, lying on the W. side of the road from Orange to Molong.

ONDYONG POINT (*Co. Argyle*), situate in the parish of Collector, projecting into Lake George on the eastern shore, about 5 miles to the N. of Kenny's Point.

ONE TREE (*Co. Waradgery*), a proclaimed village, to the S.W. of the Lachlan River.

ONE TREE HILL (*Co. Beresford*), a high mountain, situated about 4 miles N.W. of Nimittibel, on the road to Cooma.

ONE TREE HILL (*Co. Cook*), an agricultural settlement, situated about 6 miles from the township of Hartley.

ONE TREE HILL (*Co. Wellesley*), is a peak of the Sherwin Range, lying on the Bungee Creek.

ONE TREE REACH (*Cos. Cumberland and Northumberland*), a part of the Hawkesbury River, below Wiseman's Ferry.

ONION POINT (*Co. Cumberland*), is the western head of the Lane Cove River, lying on the N. side of the Parramatta River, nearly N. of Cockatoo Island.

ONUS CREEK (*Co. Buckland*), a small southern tributary of Jack's Creek, flowing through the Australian Agricultural Co.'s grant of 249,000 acres.

OOLONG CREEK (*Co. King*), a small stream, forming one of the heads of the Lachlan River, flowing into the Jerrawa Creek, through the township of Dalton.

OOMA CREEK (*Co. Forbes*), a southern tributary of the Lachlan River, flowing through the Lachlan gold-fields into the main stream, W. of the township of Forbes.

OPEN SWAMP (*Co. Wellesley*). a tract of swampy country on the eastern road to Gippsland, under the Bare Hill, and receives the overflow of the Maharatta Creek.

OPHIR (*Co. Wellington*), a postal village, 216 miles W. of Sydney, with mail twice a week. The nearest railway station is Orange, 16 miles, on the Orange and Molong line. Situated near the Summer Hill Creek. Ophir is the oldest gold-field in the Colony. The district is rich in minerals of all kinds.

ORABAH (*Co. Hardinge*), a postal receiving-office, 350 miles N. of Sydney, with mail once a week.

ORANGE (*Co. Wellington*), a postal town, 192 miles W. of Sydney, with daily mail. Telegraph and money-order offices, Government savings bank, and delivery by letter-carrier. A railway station on the Orange and Molong line. Situated on the Blackman's Swamp Creek. Gold and copper are found in the district, the Ophir and Wentworth workings being the principal diggings, and the neighbourhood of Orange is as rich in mineral wealth as any part of the Colony. It was proclaimed a municipality in 1860, with a council of eight aldermen and a mayor. Courts of quarter sessions and district courts are held at Orange periodically.

ORANMEIR (*Co. Murray*), a small auriferous creek, flowing to the S. of Ballabla into the Shoalhaven River.

ORANMEIR CREEK (*Co. St. Vincent*), a village, 200 miles S. of Sydney. Situated on the Shoalhaven River, and is an agricultural, pastoral, and alluvial mining district.

ORARA RIVER (*Cos. Clarence and Fitzroy*). [*See* "RIVERS."]

OREEN BROOK (*Co. Dudley*), a small southern tributary of the Macleay River.

OREGON CREEK (*Co. Clarence*), a small western tributary of the Coldstream River, flowing through good agricultural land.

ORPHAN SCHOOL CREEK (*Co. Cumberland*), a small tributary of Johnstone's Creek, flowing through the Sydney University grounds and Camperdown.

ORRORAL RIVER (*Co. Cowley*.) [See "RIVERS."]

ORTON PARK (*Co. Bathurst*), a railway station, 147 miles W. of Sydney, on the western line.

ORUNDUMBI (*Co. Vernon*), a postal receiving-office, 356 miles N. of Sydney, with mail once a week.

OSWALD (*Co. Northumberland*), a small rural hamlet, lying about 1 mile from Lochinvar.

OTFORD (*Co. Cumberland*), a postal village, 30 miles S. of Sydney, with daily mail. A railway station on the Illawarra and South Coast line.

OTLEY (*Co. Burnett*), a small agricultural settlement, lying 30 miles N. of Warialda.

OURA (*Co. Clarendon*), a proclaimed village within this county.

OURAWERIA (*Co. Landsborough*), a township on the E. bank of the Darling River, above Louth.

OURIMBAH (*Co. Northumberland*), a postal village, 67 miles N. of Sydney, with daily mail and telegraph office. A railway station on the Sydney and Newcastle line.

OURIMBA CREEK (*Co. Northumberland*), a fine stream with two branches, one flowing into the Tuggerah Beach Lake, and the other into Brisbane Water.

OURNANE CREEK (*Co. Goulburn*), a tributary of the Murray River, rising to the W. of Mount Atkins.

OURNIE (*Co. Hume*), a postal receiving-office, 463 miles S. of Sydney, with mail twice a week. The nearest railway station is Albury, 72 miles, on the southern line.

OVERTON (*Co. Urana*), a postal town, 399 miles S. of Sydney, with mail twice a week.

OXLEY, a county in the Central Division of the Colony. [*See* "COUNTIES."]

OXLEY (*Co. Cumberland*), one of the original districts of the county, bounded by the Field of Mars, Lane Cove River, the S.W. arm of Broken Bay, and the W. by the Castle Hill district.

OXLEY (*Co. Waljeers*), a postal town, 605 miles S. of Sydney, with mail three times a week. The nearest railway station is Hay, 60 miles, on the south-western line.

OXLEY CREEK (*Co. Burnett*), a fine stream rising to the N.E. of the township of Warialda, and flowing through good country to the S. of Bengalla.

OXLEY ISLAND (*Co. Macquarie*), a postal village, 239 miles N. of Sydney, with mail therefrom twice a week. The nearest railway station is Hexham, 90 miles, on the northern line.

OXLEY PIC (*Co. Bligh*), a sharp peak of the Liverpool Range, attaining an altitude of 4,000 feet above sea-level.

OXLEY'S TABLE-LAND (*Co. Clyde*), consists of two almost perpendicular hills, the one named Mount Oxley is steep on all sides, but the other gradually declines from the S. Distant about 20 miles E. of Bourke.

# P

PAARA (*Co. Wentworth*), a township on the W. bank of the Darling River. Situated to the N. of the township of Wentworth.

PABRAL CREEK (*Co. Cowley*), a tributary of the Cotter River, rising in Mount Pabral, the northern extremity of the Bimberi Range.

PABRAL MOUNT (*Co. Cowley*), the northern point of the Murrumbidgee Range of mountains, and is a lofty peak lying between the Murrumbidgee and Goodradigbee Rivers.

PACK-SADDLE (*Co. Mootwingee*), a high mountain, near Pack-saddle Creek.

PACKENHAM (*Co. Cumberland*), a hundred, comprising the parishes of Broken Bay, Gordon, Narrabeen, Manly Cove, and Willoughby, and the islands within those parishes.

PADDINGTON (*Co. Cumberland*), a postal suburb of Sydney, with mail twice daily. Telegraph and money-order offices, and Government savings bank, with delivery by letter-carriers. Situated on the high land to the E. of the city, and on the Old South Head Road. The military barracks lie in this suburb, and the high-level water reservoir is situated here. It is a favourite place of residence for persons having business in Sydney. Paddington was proclaimed a municipality in 1860, with a council of eleven aldermen and a mayor.

PADDY'S CREEK (*Co. Cowley*), a small tributary of Gibraltar Creek, rising in the N. slope of Mount Tennant.

PADDY'S RIVER (*Co. Camden*). [*See* "RIVERS."]

PADDY'S RIVER (*Co. Gordon*). [*See* "RIVERS."]

PADDY'S ROCK (*Co. Buccleuch*), a granite rocky hill, lying at the head of Oak Creek, and to the N. of Adjungbilly Creek.

PADDY'S ROCK CREEK (*Co. Buccleuch*), a small tributary of the Adjungbilly Creek, rising in the Paddy's Rock Hill.

PADDY'S ROCK HILL (*Co. Buccleuch*), a rugged peak in the scrubby ranges on the Adjungbilly Creek, about 20 miles E. of Gundagai.

PAGAN'S CREEK (*Co. Durham*), a branch of the Barwon River, flowing into that river at the confluence of Thalaba Creek, about 5 miles N. of Walgett.

PAGE RIVER (*Co. Brisbane.*) [*See* "RIVERS."]

PAGE'S CREEK (*Co. Brisbane*), a western tributary of the head of the Hunter River.

PAHPOO CREEK (*Co. Macquarie*), a small northern tributary of the Manning River.

PAIKA LAKE (*Co. Caira*), a small lagoon, on the W. bank of the Murrumbidgee River, about 16 miles N. of Balranald.

PALLAMALLAWA (*Co. Jamison*), a postal village, 441 miles N. of Sydney, with mail twice a week. The nearest railway station is Narrabri, 90 miles, on the north-western line.

PALMER MOUNT (*Co. Buckland*), a sharp peak of the Liverpool Range, lying at the head of the Yarrimanbah Creek.

PALMER'S ISLAND (*Co. Clarence*), a postal village, 316 miles N. of Sydney, with mails by steamers. Telegraph and money-order offices, and Government savings bank. Situated on the lower end of the Clarence River, in the parish of Toolomba. This island is very productive, being flat, alluvial, and fluviatile deposit.

PALMER'S OAKEY (*Co. Roxburgh*), a postal village, 149 miles W. of Sydney, with mails twice a week. The nearest railway station is Rydal, 25 miles, on the western line. It forms part of the Turon diggings, lying within 8 miles E. of the township of Sofala.

PAMMUMAROO CREEK (*Co. Tandora*), a small western tributary of the Darling River, flowing into the main stream about 12 miles N. of Menindie.

PANBULA (*Co. Auckland*), a postal town, 339 miles S. of Sydney, with mail four times a week. Telegraph and money-order offices, and Government savings bank. The nearest railway station is Cooma, 100 miles on the Goulburn and Cooma line. Situated on the Panbula River, in the parish of Towacka. There is water communication with Sydney by steamer, *via* Murrimbula, calling at Eden.

PANBULA RIVER (*Co. Auckland*). [*See* "RIVERS."]

PANDORA'S PASS (*Co. Bligh*), a pass over the Liverpool Range, discovered by Cunningham in 1824. It lies 24 miles from Cassilis.

PANNARA RIVULET (*Co. Bathurst and Ashburnham*), a northern tributary of the Belubula River, rising on the S. of the Canobolas cluster of peaks. It divides the county of Bathurst from that of Ashburnham.

PAPRAN CREEK (*Co. Northumberland*), a small tributary of the estuary of the Mangrove Creek.

PARA CREEK (*Co. Camden*), a small creek flowing from Mount Keira into the sea, to the N. of Wollongong.

PARABEL CREEK (*Co. Dudley*), a small tributary of the Macleay River.

PARADING GROUND (*Co. Gloucester*), a settlement on the sea-coast, about 12 miles N.E. of Raymond Terrace.

PARADISE (*Co. Sandon*), a township, 385 miles to the N. of Sydney. The nearest railway station is Guyra, on the Wallangarra and Brisbane line.

PARADISE CREEK (*Co. Arrawatta*), a small northern tributary of the Upper Macintyre River, crossing the road from Stonehenge to Inverell.

PARA MEADOW (*Co. Camden*), a postal village, 46 miles S. of Sydney, with daily mail. A railway station on the Illawarra and South Coast line.

PARAMEDOWA (*Co. Burnett*), a small settlement on the Gwydir, lying between Warialda and Moree.

PARAMELLOWA (*Co. Courallie*), a, township on the Gwydir River.

PARATER CREEK (*Co. St. Vincent*), a small tributary of the upper part of the Currambene Creek.

PARK (*Co. Brisbane*), a proclaimed village in this county.

PARKES (*Co. Ashburnham*), a postal town, 296 miles W. of Sydney, with daily mail. Telegraph and money-order offices, Government savings bank, and delivery by letter-carriers. The nearest railway station is Molong 54 miles, on the Orange and Molong line. It was proclaimed a municipal district in 1883, with a council of eight aldermen and a mayor.

PARKES (*Co. Cumberland*), a railway station, 30 miles W. of Sydney, on the western line.

PARKESBOURNE (*Co. Bathurst*), a postal receiving-office, 149 miles S. of Sydney, with mail three times a week. The nearest railway station is Breadalbane, 4 miles, on the southern line.

PARKVILLE (*Co. Buckland*), a postal town, 199 miles N. of Sydney, with daily mail. A railway station on the northern line.

PAROO RIVER (*Cos. Barrona and Irraba*). [*See* "RIVERS."]

PARRAMATTA (*Co. Cumberland*), a postal town, 15 miles W. of Sydney, with mail five times daily. Telegraph and money-order offices, Government savings bank, and delivery by letter-carriers. It is a railway station on the suburban line, and is situated on both sides of the Parramatta River, in the parishes of St. John and Field of Mars. The first railway in the Colony was made from Sydney to Parramatta by a private company in the year 1853, and afterwards taken over by the Government, before the introduction of Responsible Government. Parramatta was established in November, 1788, by Governor Phillip, who made it his residence, but from the close of Governor Sir Charles Fitzroy, 1853, it has been abandoned as a vice-regal residence. The district is highly productive in fruits of all kinds, but more especially for orange culture. Parramatta was proclaimed a municipality in 1861, with a council of eleven aldermen and a mayor. Courts of quarter sessions and district courts are held here periodically. Population, about 12,000.

PARRAMATTA RIVER *(Co. Cumberland)*, a continuation of Port Jackson to the W. for about 18 miles, and is the head of the navigation of this port. Steamboats ply constantly to and from Sydney, and the trip is celebrated for its beauty of scenery. The banks are studded with residences of a first-class character, and many villages and townships are in proximity to the river. [*See* "RIVERS."]

PARRAMELLOWA *(Co. Courallie)*, a proclaimed village on the N. bank of the Gwydir River.

PARRY, a county in the Central Division of the Colony. [*See* "COUNTIES."]

PARRY MOUNT *(Co. Buckland)*, a detached peak, lying to the N. of the East Bluff and Mount Moam, on the Liverpool Range.

PARSON, THE *(Co. Buccleuch)*, a lofty peak, standing at the head of Matchem's Creek, and on the S. bank of the Murrumbidgee River.

PARSON'S CREEK *(Co. Hunter)*, is a western tributary of the Wollombi Brook.

PARSON'S HILL *(Co. Buckland)*, a ridge of hills, spurring from the Liverpool Range, N. of Mount Nany.

PARSON'S HILL *(Co. Northumberland)*, a hill on the road from West Maitland to Wollombi, and about 3 miles W. of the former place.

PASS, THE *(Co. Northumberland)*, a gap in the Sugar-loaf Range of hills, in the parish of Mulbring, on the road from Maitland to Sydney, *via* Lake Macquarie.

PATERSON *(Co. Durham)*, a postal town, 105 miles N. of Sydney, with daily mail. Telegraph and money-order offices, and Government savings bank. The nearest railway station is East Maitland, 12 miles, on the East Maitland and Morpeth line. Situated on the Paterson River, in the parish of Houghton. The district is essentially an agricultural one; the soil being rich and well cultivated, all kinds of fruit and cereals are produced in abundance.

PATERSON MOUNT *(Co. Durham)*, a high peak of the Mount Royal Range, situate at the head of the Paterson River. It attains an altitude of about 3,000 feet above sea-level.

PATERSON POINT *(Co. Wellington)*, a gold workings on the Turon diggings, about 2 miles from the township of Sofala.

PATERSON RIVER *(Co. Durham)*. [*See* "RIVERS."]

PATMORE CREEK *(Co. Roxburgh)*, an auriferous southern tributary of the Turon River.

PATONGA CREEK *(Co. Northumberland)*, a small creek flowing into Broken Bay on its N. side.

PATRICK'S PLAINS (*Cos. Hunter and Durham*) is a large tract of fine pastoral and agricultural country, lying on both sides of the Hunter River, near Singleton. The district is celebrated for its dairy produce, and for its fattening capability for cattle.

PEACOCK CREEK (*Co. Rous*), a small eastern tributary of the head of the Clarence River.

PEACOCK POINT (*Co. Cumberland*), the most eastern point of the suburb of Balmain, opposite the Flagstaff Hill, Sydney, and on the western head of Darling Harbour.

PEAK HILL (*Co. Lincoln*), a postal town, 272 miles W. of Sydney, with daily mail therefrom.

PEAKHURST (*Co. Cumberland*), a postal village, 13 miles S. of Sydney, with daily mail. The nearest railway station is Hurstville, 3 miles, on the Illawarra and South Coast line.

PEAKS, THE (*Co. Westmoreland*), a remarkable triple-peaked mountain, on the W. side of the Wollondilly River, about 9 miles S.W. of Burragorang.

PEAKVIEW (*Co. Beresford*), a postal receiving-office, 353 miles S. of Sydney, with mail once a week.

PEARCE'S CREEK (*Co. Clarence*), a postal town, 374 miles N. of Sydney, with mails per Clarence River steamers.

PEARL BAY (*Co. Cumberland*), a small bight on the W. side of Middle Harbour, to the W. of the Spit.

PEAT'S FERRY (*Co. Northumberland*), is the ferry over the Hawkesbury River, on the road from Sydney to Gosford. A well known crossing place on the old Northern road.

PEDDAI MOUNT (*Co. Phillip*), a lofty peak on the S. of the Goulburn River, opposite the confluence of the Merriwa Rivulet.

PEEDEE CREEK (*Co. Dudley*), a small northern tributary of the Macleay River.

PEEL (*Co. Roxburgh*), a postal village, 150 miles W. of Sydney, with daily mail. The nearest railway station is Bathurst, 9 miles, on the western line. Situated on the Clear Creek, in the parish of Peel. The district is a pastoral, agricultural, and mining one, the latter both alluvial and quartz, and the diggings surrounding the township on every side.

PEEL RANGE (*Co. Bland*), a branch of the Liverpool Range, separating the basin of the Peel from that of the Conadilly.

PEEL RIVER (*Cos. Brisbane and Parry*). [*See* "RIVERS."]

PEELWOOD (*Co. Georgiana*), a postal village, 181 miles S. of Sydney, with mail three times a week. The nearest railway station is Goulburn, 60 miles, on the southern line.

PEIDPEDIDIA (*Co. Perry*), a township on the N.E. bank of the Darling River.

PEJAR *(Co. Argyle)*, a postal village, 151 miles S. of Sydney, with mail twice a week. The nearest railway station is Goulburn, 37 miles, on the southern line. Situated at the junction of Pejar Creek and the Wollondilly River, about 3 miles S.W. of the village of Woodhouselee.

PEJAR CREEK *(Co. Argyle)*, a northern tributary of the Wollondilly River, flowing into the main stream at Baw Baw.

PEKE *(Co. Ularara)*, a township on the W. bank of the Paroo River.

PELICAN CREEK *(Co. Rous)*, a western tributary of the North Richmond River.

PELICAN FLAT *(Co. Northumberland)*, a village, 91 miles N. of Sydney. The nearest railway station is Cockle Creek, 17 miles, on the Sydney and Newcastle line.

PENDER'S CREEK *(Co. Roxburgh)*, a small tributary of the head of the Cheshire Creek, rising in the Limekiln Range.

PENNANT HILL *(Co. Cumberland)*, a postal village, 25 miles W. of Sydney, with daily mail. A railway station on the Ryde and Hawkesbury River line. Situated on the N. of the Parramatta River, in the parish of Castlehill.

PENNYWEIGHT FLAT *(Co. Wellington)*, a gold workings on the Turon diggings, lying 3 miles from the township of Sofala.

PENRITH *(Co. Cumberland)*, a postal village, 34 miles W. of Sydney, with mail three times daily. Telegraph and money-order offices, and Government savings bank, with delivery by letter-carriers. A railway station on the western line and is situated on the Nepean River, in the parishes of Castlereagh and Mulgoa. The district is an agricultural one, comprising a number of cultivation and grazing farms. Penrith was proclaimed a municipal district in 1871, with a council of eight aldermen and a mayor. Courts of quarter sessions and district courts are held here periodically.

PENSHURST *(Co. Cumberland)*, a railway station, 10 miles from Sydney, on the Illawarra and South Coast line.

PEPPER CREEK *(Cos. Bathurst and Georgiana)*, a western tributary of the Campbell River, flowing through the township of Rockley.

PEPPER CREEK *(Co. Buccleuch)*, a small drainage creek from swampy flats, and flowing W. into Jeremiah Creek.

PEPPER'S CREEK *(Co. Beresford)*, a small tributary of the Big Badja River, rising in a western spur of the Australian Alps.

PEPPERCORN CREEK *(Co. Buccleuch)*, a western tributary of the head of the Goodradigbee River, rising in the northern slope of Peppercorn Hill.

PEPPERCORN HILL *(Co. Buccleuch)*, a lofty peak, lying on the E. side of the road from Kiandra to Yass, and 16 miles N. of the village of Yarrangobilly.

PERICA CREEK (*Co. Auckland*), a small tributary of the Mowamba River, falling into it near the township of Sturt.

PERICOE (*Co. Auckland*). a postal town, 301 miles S. of Sydney, with mail therefrom twice a week.

PERICOOTA (*Co. Cadell*), a postal village, 591 miles S. of Sydney, with mail four times a week. The nearest railway station is Hay, 130 miles, on the south-western line.

PERPENDICULAR POINT (*Co. St. Vincent*), a rocky promontory, forming the N. head of Jervis Bay. It stands boldly out on the peninsular to the N. of the bay, and in a perfectly vertical position, 275 feet above the sea-level.

PERRIER'S CREEK (*Co. Bathurst*), a small eastern tributary of Lewis Ponds, rising in Mount M'Cann.

PERRY, a county in the Western Division of the Colony. [*See* "COUNTIES."]

PERRY (*Co. Menindie*). [*See* "MENINDIE."]

PERTH (*Co. Bathurst*), a postal village, 150 miles W. of Sydney, with daily mail. A railway station on the western line.

PETERBOROUGH HILL (*Co. Camden*), a small agricultural settlement, 3 miles distant from the township of Shellharbour.

PETER MOUNT (*Co. Wynyard and Mitchell*), a peak in a range which forms the division of the two counties.

PETER'S CREEK (*Co. Bligh*), a small eastern tributary of the head of the Four-mile Creek.

PETER'S CREEK (*Co. Vernon*), a small southern tributary of the Apsley River.

PETER'S CREEK (*Co. Wellington*), a small auriferous northern tributary of the Green Valley Creek, flowing near Sparrow Hill.

PETER'S LAGOON (*Co. Wellesley*), a small waterhole in the plains lying between the M'Laughlin and Snowy Rivers, to the W. of the Pipeclay Range.

PETERSHAM (*Co. Cumberland*), a postal suburb, 3 miles W. of Sydney, with mail three times daily. Telegraph and money-order offices, Government savings bank, and delivery by letter-carriers. A railway station on the suburban line, and is situated in the parish of Petersham, on the Long Cove Creek. The surrounding neighbourhood is studded with pretty villa residences. Petersham was proclaimed a municipality in 1871, with a council of eleven aldermen and a mayor.

PETROLIA VALE (*Co. Cook*), a small valley, lying 4 miles N.E. of Hartley. Kerosene shale abounds in the district, and mines have been opened.

PETWYNN VALLEY CREEK (*Co. Brisbane*), a tributary of the Kingdon Ponds. It rises in Mount Tinagroo, and flows into the main stream at the village of Wingen.

PHEASANT GROUND (*Co. Camden*), a postal receiving-office, 108 miles S. of Sydney, with mail therefrom three times a week.

PHELP'S MOUNT (*Co. Selwyn*), a lofty peak on the Adelong goldfields, and about 12 miles S.W. of the township of Adelong.

PHIL'S RIVER (*Co. Georgiana*), a western tributary of the Bolong River, rising to the N.E. of Bindi.

PHILLIP, a county in the Eastern Division of the Colony. [*See* "COUNTIES."]

PHILLIP'S CREEK (*Co. Buckland*), a name given to the eastern head of the Conadilly River, rising near Mount Parry.

PHILLIP'S MOUNT (*Co. Cowley*), a peak in the ranges, lying to the N. of Bolairo, and near the head of Alum Creek.

PHŒNIX PARK (*Co. Durham*), is the name of an estate opposite to the town of Morpeth. It is formed by the Paterson and Hunter Rivers; they enclose between their deep channels this peninsula, of about 1,200 acres.

PIALLAMORE (*Co. Parry*), a proclaimed village on the Peel River.

PIAMBONG CREEK (*Co. Wellington*), a southern tributary of the Cudgegong River, rising in the ranges to the W. of Mudgee, flowing into the main stream near Wyadere.

PIAMBRA CREEK (*Co. Napier*), a small eastern tributary of the upper part of the Castlereagh River.

PIAN CREEK (*Co. Denham*), a drainage creek of the Namoi River, rising to the N. of Barrabool Plains, and flowing into the main stream at Walgett.

PIANENG MOUNT (*Co. Camden*), a conical peak of the Mittagong Range, lying on the S. bank of Wingecarribee River, about 16 miles W. of Berrima.

PICKERING'S PEAK (*Co. Wellesley*), a lofty hill in a range between Undowah and Camalong Rivers, about 10 miles N. of Bombala.

PICTON (*Co. Camden*), a postal town, 54 miles S. of Sydney, with mail three times daily. Telegraph and money-order offices and Government savings bank. A railway-station on the southern line, and is situated on the Stonequarry Creek. The district is an agricultural one.

PICTON LAKES (*Co. Camden*), a railway station, 59 miles S. of Sydney, on the southern line.

PIER CREEK (*Co. Bligh*), a small eastern tributary of the Slapdash Creek.

PIER HEAD (*Co. Northumberland*), a rocky promontory, to the N. of Cabbage-tree Head, and about 12 miles N. of the entrance to the Tuggerah Lake.

PIGEON CREEK (*Co. Roxburgh*), a small auriferous northern tributary of the Cheshire Creek.

PIGEON-HOUSE (*Co. St. Vincent*), a remarkable peaked hill of the Budawang Range, 12 miles W. from the coast at Ulladulla. From the sea it forms a remarkable land-mark, and received its name from Captain Cook on account of its resemblance to a dove-house with a dome at its top. It is 2,340 feet above the level of the sea.

PILLAGA (*Co. Baradine*), a postal village, 412 miles N. of Sydney, with mail three times a week. Telegraph and money-order offices, and Government savings bank. The nearest railway station is Narrabri, 60 miles, on the north-western line.

PILAGALALA CREEK (*Co. Wynyard*), a small tributary of the Pulletop Creek, rising in the Sugar-loaf Hill.

PILCHER'S MOUNT (*Co. Durham*), a lofty peak of the Mount Royal Ranges, lying about 6 miles W. of the township of Dungog, and is somewhat celebrated for the numerous caverns and fissures which are found in it.

PILLAN RANGE (*Co. Clarence*), a range of hills lying about 10 miles E. of the township of Grafton.

PILLAR VALLEY (*Co. Clarence*), a grassy valley or gully on the N.E. of the Pillar range of hills, about 10 miles E. of Grafton.

PILOT, THE (*Co. Selwyn*), a very remarkable mountain formed of coarse granite rock, lying to the S. of the Munion Range, near the head of the Murray River.

PILOT, THE (*Co. Wynyard*), a high peak, lying to the N. of the Dago Reserve, and at the head of Darlow's Creek.

PILOT HILL CREEK (*Co. Selwyn*), a small tributary of the Upper Murray, rising in the Pilot Peak of the Great Dividing Range.

PINCH RIVER (*Co. Wallace*). [*See* "RIVERS."]

PINEBRUSH CREEK (*Co. Raleigh*), a small drainage creek, falling into the sea about 8 miles N. of the Bellinger River.

PINEGOBLAR (*Co. Finch*), a township to the E. of the Big Warrambool.

PINE MOUNTAIN (*Co. Buccleuch*), a peak in a group of hills, lying in the parish of Killimicat, about 7 miles N. of the town of Tumut.

PINE RIDGE (*Co. Buckland*), a postal village, 262 miles N. of Sydney, with mail twice a week. The nearest railway station is Quirindi, 16 miles, on the northern line.

PINEY RANGE (*Co. Goulburn*), a postal receiving-office. 297 miles S. of Sydney, with mail twice a week. It is a small agricultural and pastoral village situate about 32 miles N.W. of the village of Germanton.

PINEY RANGE (*Co. Hume*), a chain of low hills, lying on the S. bank of the Billabong Creek, to the N.W. of Albury.

PINEY RANGE CREEK (*Co. Hume*), a small southern tributary of the Billabong Creek, rising in the western extremity of Mane's Range.

PINK HILLS (*Co. Clyde*), a group of low sandstone hills, on the W. bank of the Bogan River, about 32 miles S.E. of Bourke.

PINNACLE CREEK (*Co. Murchison*), a small western tributary of Maule's Creek, flowing through rich pastoral country.

PINNACLE CREEK (*Co. Phillip*), a small creek draining the Pinnacle Swamp, in the parish of Tongbong, into the Cudgegong Creek.

PINNACLE MOUNT (*Co. Ashburnham*), a peak, lying near the Widdin Mountains to the N.E. of Forbes.

PINNACLE SWAMP (*Co. Phillip*), a tract of alluvial ground on the N. bank of the Cudgegong River, in the parish of Tongbong, about 4 miles N.W. of the town of Rylstone.

PINNACLES (*Co. Yancowinna*), a postal village, 989 miles S. of Sydney, with mail five times a week, and money-order office.

PIPECLAY CREEK (*Co. Durham*), a small stream flowing into the estuary of the Karuah River.

PIPECLAY RANGE (*Co. Wellesley*), a ridge of hills in the bold undulating pastoral country to the S.W. of Nimmitibel.

PIPER POINT (*Co. Cumberland*), a rocky promontory, on the S. side of Port Jackson, forming the western head of Rose Bay, and about 2½ miles S.W. of the inner South Head.

PIPER'S CREEK (*Co. Macquarie*), a western tributary of Maria's River, crossing the road from Port Macquarie to Kempsey.

PIPER'S FLAT (*Co. Roxburgh*), a postal village, 110 miles W., with daily mail. It is a railway station on the western line.

PIPER'S FLAT (*Co. Roxburgh*), an auriferous flat at the head of Little Oakey Creek, and forming part of the Wattle Flat gold-field.

PIPER'S TOWN (*Co. Cumberland*), a village, situate in the parish of Petersham, and in the hundred of Sydney, on the Parramatta Road, about 3 miles from Sydney.

PITNACREE (*Co. Northumberland*), an agricultural district on the banks of the Hunter River, within the municipal boundary of East Maitland.

PITT TOWN (*Co. Cumberland*), a postal village, 38 miles W. of Sydney, with daily mail. The nearest railway station is Windsor, 4 miles, on the Richmond line. Situated three quarters of a mile from the Hawkesbury River, in the parish of Pitt Town.

PITT WATER (*Co. Cumberland*) is a fine harbour, running in a southerly direction from near the entrance of that bay about 8 miles, and separated from the sea by a narrow tongue of land, consisting of rocky cliffs called Barrenjoey. Pittwater has deep water for the largest ships, and good and secure anchorage. The locality is greatly celebrated for the beauty of its scenery, and is a favourite trip by water for excursion parties.

PLAINS CREEK (*Co. Harden*), a small drainage creek, on the Cunningham Plains, flowing W. about 4 miles into Cunningham Creek, at Murrimboola.

PLAINS CREEK (*Co. Lincoln*), a small southern tributary of the Erskine River.

PLATTSBURG (*Co. Northumberland*), in the parishes of Hexham and Kahibah, proclaimed a borough under the Municipalities Act in 1867, with a council of eight aldermen and a mayor. It is a suburb of Newcastle, and adjoins Wallsend. The population is engaged in coal-mining.

PLEASANT MOUNT (*Co. Bathurst*), a high hill, overhanging the township of the same name, on the N. side. It lies on Evans Plains, and on the S. bank of the Macquarie River. Also a small hamlet, at the foot of the same hill, 4 miles N.W. of Bathurst.

PLOMER PORT (*Co. Macquarie*), a bold promontory, standing out from the land, about 8 miles N. of Port Macquarie entrance.

PLOUGHED GROUND (*Co. Camden*), a tract of country lying on the road from the Wollondilly to Berrima. This place is distinguished by the name of the Ploughed Ground from a remarkable resemblance the ground bears to land which has been tilled.

PLOVER ISLAND (*Co. Clarence*), a small rocky islet, lying close to the coast, about 20 miles S. to the entrance of the Clarence River.

PLUMBAGO CREEK (*Cos. Buller and Clive*), a fine stream, rising in the ranges to the W. of Barney Downs, and flowing into the Clarence River, near Tabulam. The township of Drake is situated on the lower part of the creek.

PLUM PUDDING HILL (*Co. Mitchell*), a peak lying on the E. of the road from Wagga Wagga to Albury, about 10 miles S. of the former place.

PLUMPTON (*Co. Cumberland*), a postal village, 27 miles W. of Sydney, with mail twice daily. Money-order office and Government savings bank.

POCKATOROO (*Co. Benarba*), a township on the E. bank of the Barwon River.

POCUPAP MOUNT (*Co. Rous*), a detached peak, lying between the Tooloom and Clarence Rivers.

POINCAIN (*Co. Wynyard*), a small hamlet on the Darling River, about 80 miles from Wentworth.

POKOLBIN (*Co. Northumberland*), a postal village, 146 miles N. of Sydney, with mail three times a week. The nearest railway station is Branxton, 12 miles on the northern line.

POLEBANGI CREEK (*Co. Baradine*), a small eastern tributary of the Baradine Creek.

POMANY MOUNT (*Co. Phillip*), a lofty peak, lying between the Weddin Brook and the Emu Creek, about 36 miles N.E. of Dabee.

POMNAIRO CREEK (*Co. Wellington*), a small tributary of the Green Valley Creek, draining the country to the E. of the Tambaroora goldfield.

PONDS CREEK (*Co. Wellington*), a small tributary of the head of the Goondawada Creek, flowing on the Louisa gold-field.

PONTEBADGERY PLAINS (*Co. Waradgery*), situated on the Murrumbidgee River. The river running E. and W. forms its southern boundary. It is about 2 miles in breadth by about 4 miles in width, and the soil is of the richest description.

PONTO (*Co. Gordon*), a postal village, 258 miles W. of Sydney, with mail four times a week. The nearest railway station is Geurie, 6 miles, on the western line.

PONTO HILL (*Co. Gordon*), an elevation on the W. bank of the Macquarie River, about 10 miles N.W. of Wellington.

POOLE, a county in the Western Division of the Colony. [*See* "COUNTIES."]

POONCARIE (*Co. Perry*), a postal village, 800 miles S. of Sydney, with mail three times a week. Telegraph and money-order offices. The nearest railway station is Hay, 306 miles, on the south-western line.

POPONG CREEK (*Co. Wallace*), a small tributary of the Snowy River.

POPPET CREEK (*Co. Buccleuch*), an eastern tributary of Jeremiah Creek, rising in Macpherson's Swamp.

POPPINBARRA CREEK (*Co. Macquarie*), a small northern tributary of the Hastings River.

POPPONG (*Co. Hunter*), a high mountain of the Hunter Range, attaining an altitude of 2,500 feet above sea-level, and lies to the west of the township of Broke.

PORT HACKING (*Co. Cumberland*), a postal receiving-office, 21 miles S. of Sydney, with daily mail therefrom.

PORT MACQUARIE (*Co. Macquarie*), a postal-village, 275 miles N. of Sydney, with daily mail. Telegraph and money-order offices, and Government savings bank. The nearest railway station is Hexham, 164 miles, on the northern line. Situated on the sea-coast, at the entrance of the Hastings River. The district is an agricultural and mining one. Vessels of small tonnage trade directly between Port Macquarie and Sydney, carrying passengers and cargo. It was proclaimed a municipality in 1887, with a council of five aldermen and a mayor. Population, about 800. Courts of quarter sessions and district courts are held here periodically.

PORT STEPHENS (*Co. Gloucester*), is the estuary of the Myall River, and a beautiful harbour, the entrance points being named Yacoba and Tomaree. The estuary is about 15 miles in length. It forms a harbour little inferior to Port Jackson. The tidal rise is 6 feet. The lighthouse is a circular white tower, 126 feet above the sea-level, and the flash, white and red, can be seen a distance of 17 miles at sea.

# PORTS, HARBOURS, LIGHTHOUSES, AND RIVERS ON THE SEABOARD,

Commencing on the extreme North and travelling South.

[*Vide* Diagram facing Title-page.]

TWEED RIVER, 28° 13′ S. lat., 153° 32′ E. long., and 372 miles N. of Port Jackson, in the county of Rous. The N. bank of the Tweed is on the dividing line between Queensland and New South Wales, at Point Danger. Coolougatta is the village at its mouth, where there are two hotels, one of which is claimed by Queensland and the other by this Colony. Owing to the uncertainty of the bar navigation the development of the rich agricultural lands of the district has been tardy. The Colonial Sugar Company have works up the river, and the chief town of the district, Murwillumbah, is fast rising into importance. The contemplated improvement of the river and the approved railway project will, in the near future, render the Tweed a place of more than ordinary importance. Steamers drawing 6 feet of water can trade to this river, and a tug is stationed at the bar. On Fingal Head, near the Tweed, there is a fixed dioptric white light, visible 8 miles.

BRUNSWICK RIVER.—This small river is situated a few miles N. of Cape Byron. The entrance is not good, and small craft only can enter. It is not likely that money will be expended upon improving the entrance in the view of a coast railway to the Tweed.

CAPE BYRON (*Byron Bay*), 28° 38′ S. lat., 153° 38′ E. long., 345 miles N. of Port Jackson. Hitherto the bay has afforded shelter for small vessels only from S. and S.E. gales, there being about 4 to 5 fathoms of water, but there is a heavy swell with southerly winds, and vessels are often driven on the beach, but the suggested breakwater would render the port safe and enhance the value of the fine jetty recently erected. The railway from Lismore to the Tweed will touch Byron Bay, and the port will be alike valuable for commerce and as a harbour of refuge should the breakwater be constructed.

RICHMOND RIVER.—The embrouchure of this river is at the port of Ballina, distant 325 miles N. of Sydney, in lat. 28° 55′ S., long. 153° 30′ E., and available for steamers of about 8 feet draft. Extensive improvements are being initiated for rendering the entrance reliable. Breakwaters and training-walls are to be constructed, and it is anticipated that in a few years Ballina as a port will be worthy of the magnificent district watered by the Richmond. Between Ballina and Lismore the road passes through splendid table-land of exceptional fertility known as the Big Scrub. Here, as well as on the low lands, the sugar-cane is extensively grown; this, with wool, tallow, maize, and timber, gives an importance to the Richmond River not surpassed by any district in the Colony. The river has three branches, and is navigable on the main arm as far as Casino, 62 miles, and on Wilson's Creek to Lismore, 60 miles, from the sea. A powerful steam-tug is stationed at Ballina, and from the North Head, 2 fixed white lights, fourth order dioptric, are visible at a distance of 10 miles.

**CLARENCE RIVER.**—The Clarence Heads are in lat. 29° 30′ S., long. 153° 19′ E., and distant from Sydney 294 miles. The steamers entering the port are from 300 to 700 tons burthen, and of draft 11 feet downwards. Nothing has been done towards improving the entrance during the past few years, but extensive works will shortly be undertaken commensurate with the importance of the Clarence, which drains an area larger than the watershed of any river of the eastern seaboard. From its rise in the Main Dividing Range this river pursues a course of 240 miles, and empties itself into the ocean at Shoal Bay, where the anchorage is safe and commodious. The Lower Clarence is a fine stream, and is navigable for 70 miles, as far as Copmanhurst. Ocean-going steamers of large tonnage reach Grafton, a distance of 42 miles from the ocean. A fourth order dioptric fixed white light can be seen 10 miles from the south head of the Clarence.

**SOLITARY ISLANDS,** 30° 12′ S. lat., 153° 20′ E. long. Upon the South Solitary there is a first order dioptric white light visible 18 miles.

**BELLINGER RIVER,** 30° 32′ S. lat., 152° 5′ E. long. The entrance to this river is 228 miles N. of Sydney, and 9 miles N. of Nambucca. The Bellinger is a stream navigable only for small craft. Steamers of 7 feet draft ply fairly regular from Sydney. Raleigh, Fernmount, and Boat Harbour are towns on the banks of the river. Most of the best land fringing the river banks is under cultivation. River-deepening operations are being carried on, but at present the ocean steamers load at the heads, where a steam-tug can always be relied upon.

**NAMBUCCA RIVER,** 30° 45′ S. lat., 153° 1′ E. long., is distant 219 miles N. of Port Jackson. Steamers and sailing vessels drawing 7 feet trade to Sydney. The exports are chiefly maize and timber. The area available for agricultural settlement on Worrel Creek and Taylor's Arm, tributaries of the Nambucca, is very considerable. Active steps are being taken to improve the river navigation, in order to develop the resources of this district. The Nambucca is navigable to Bowra, 30 miles from its entrance, and some distance further. Ocean steamers load at the heads, where a steam-tug is always available.

**MACLEAY RIVER,** 30° 52′ S. lat., 153° 0′ E. long., 212 miles N. of Sydney. The Macleay has long had the reputation of being the chief maize-producing district of this Colony. The river, which is navigable for 36 miles to Greenfield's, a few miles above Kempsey, falls into the sea at Yarrahappin, about 5 miles N. of Smoky Cape. The bar and river will admit of steamers of 7 feet draft, and except in unfavourable seasons, the trade with the metropolis finds employment for two steamers and many sailing vessels. The exports from the river are maize, timber, and live stock. River steamers ply daily from Kempsey towards the heads. The Macleay takes its rise near Ben Lomond, and is fed by the Gyra and Apsley Rivers, and pursues a course of 200 miles from its source to its embouchure.

**TRIAL BAY,** 30° 53′ S. lat., 153° 3′ E. long., 207 miles N. of Sydney. It is situated N.W. of Smoky Cape, and affords good shelter for vessels seeking it with wind from W. to S.E., but it is not safe for shipping with an easterly gale. The long stretch of coast-line from Port Stephens to Cape Moreton, 420 miles, with no shelter from easterly or N.E. gales, rendered it imperative that a harbour of refuge should be formed, and Trial Bay being already partially one, it was decided to construct, with prison labour, a port that could be availed of by all kinds of vessels. Rapid progress is being made with the necessary breakwaters, and in a few years this harbour of refuge will be available. The finest light along the coast is here located, at an elevation of 450 feet. It is visible at a distance of 27 miles, and is triple flashing white. There is also a red subsidiary light on Fish Rock, S. of Smoky Cape.

HASTINGS RIVER (*Tacking Point*), 31° 29' lat., 152° 49' E. long., 172 miles N. of Sydney. It is a small river fed by the Wilson and Maria, and empties itself into the sea at Port Macquarie.

PORT MACQUARIE, 31° 29' S. lat., 152° 47' E. long., is the embouchure of the Hastings River and its tributaries, the Wilson and Maria Rivers. Fifty years ago it was a place of importance as a penal settlement, but it is now a watering-place for the adjacent inland towns, and has a high sanitary reputation. Steamers of 7 feet draft ply to Sydney, and considerable quantities of maize, timber, live-stock, and wine are exported. Settlement has been tardy, considering the time that has elapsed since the district was opened up. A subsidised tug is stationed at Port Macquarie, and a fourth order dioptric fixed white light is visible 12 miles from Tacking Point, S. of the entrance.

CROWDY HEAD, 31° 33' S. lat., 152° 45' E. long. Here there is a fourth order dioptric fixed white light, showing red over Mermaid Reef.

CAMDEN HAVEN, 31° 43' S. lat., 150° 46' E. long. This small port is about 15 miles S. of Port Macquarie. Light draft sailing vessels ply to Sydney and Newcastle, chiefly laden with timber from Watson-Taylor and Queen's Lakes, which connect with the sea at Camden Haven, near Camden Head. Laurieton is the chief town of the district. A steam-tug is stationed at this port.

MANNING RIVER, 31° 57' S. lat., 152° 14' E. long., distant 141 miles N. of Port Jackson. The Manning River, flowing through a rich agricultural district, has two ports of discharge at the sea, viz., Farquhar's Inlet and Harrington. The former has not been used by steamers for many years, Harrington Inlet being the safest port. Steamers and sailing vessels of 7 feet draft trade to Sydney. The river is navigable to Wingham, about 30 miles. The chief towns are Taree, Wingham, and Cundletown. The exports are maize, timber, and live stock. A subsidised steam-tug is always to be found at Harrington, just inside the heads. The Manning rises in the Main Dividing Range, and its tributaries are the Barrington, Barnard, Dawson, and Lansdown Rivers, with other small streams.

CAPE HAWKE (*Forster*), 52° 17' S. lat., 152° 32' E. long., is the port of the Wollumba River, leading to a chain of lakes. There are many saw-mills in the district, and the navigation of the river is being gradually improved by dredging. Forster is the principal town, but the district is rather sparsely populated. A steam-tug is in attendance at the bar, which is only available for vessels of light draft.

SEAL ROCKS (*Sugar Loaf*), 32° 28' S. lat., 152° 32' E. long., 100 miles N. of Sydney. Upon Sugarloaf Point (Seal Rocks) there is a first order dioptric revolving white light, visible 22 miles, with subsidiary green light over the Seal Rocks.

PORT STEPHENS, 32° 44′ S. lat., 152° 12′ E. long., distant 81 miles N. of Sydney. Although a very good port, formed by nature, and often availed of as a harbour of refuge, it has but little importance from a commercial standpoint, comparatively little settlement having gone forward during the last sixty years. The chief trade of the district is in timber from the Myall Lakes and River which flow into Nelson's Bay. The Australian Agricultural Company has large possessions here. Upon Port Stephens Point there is a catoptric revolving red and white light, visible 17 miles, and in Nelson Bay a fixed white catoptric white light.

PORT HUNTER (*Nobby's*), 32° 52′ S. lat., 151° 46′ E. long., distant 62 miles N. of Port Jackson, is the chief coal-shipping port of Australasia, and furnishes a remarkable example of what can be effected by judicious engineering skill. Less than twenty years ago it was a port shunned by foreign-going ships as dangerous to enter, and without accommodation when entered; it is now second only to Port Jackson in all its nautical requirements. Vessels laden with 4,000 tons of coal, at a draft of 28 feet, can safely cross the bar, and the facilities for coal shipment are such that 3,000,000 tons of coal can be shipped annually. Direct shipments of wool are now made to England, and merchandise is directly shipped in return. Steamers of over 1,000 tons burthen ply from Sydney to Morpeth, the head of navigation, 30 miles from Newcastle, conveying to the metropolis agricultural produce from districts which have been fittingly called the "Garden of the Colony." The towns of East and West Maitland, situated on the Hunter River, are amongst the most thriving in the Colony, and are now connected with Sydney by rail. The port of Newcastle has a length of wharfage frontage exceeding 2 miles. Upon Nobby's, the south head of the port, there is a catoptric fixed white light, visible 18 miles; red and green lights are placed on the breakwater.

THE HUNTER RIVER has its embouchure at Port Hunter, on the shores of which is situated the city of Newcastle. This river pursues a course of over 200 miles from its rise in the Liverpool Range, and receives numerous tributaries before it reaches the ocean, the chief of which are the Wollombi, the Paterson, and the Williams, in addition to the Goulburn. The Hunter is navigable for sea-going steamers to Morpeth, a distance of 30 miles, whilst the Paterson and the Williams are navigable for a distance of 18 and 20 miles each respectively, and it drains an area of over 11,000 square miles, including the most important coal-field of Australia, whose emporium is Newcastle, the second city in the Colony.

LAKE MACQUARIE, 33° 5′ S. lat., 151° 35′ E. long. This picturesque lake is situated about 12 miles S. of Newcastle, and is the watering-place for that city and adjacent towns. The entrance from the sea to the lake is being rapidly improved by breakwaters and dredging; and it is expected that as a coal-shipping port it will soon be a rival of Newcastle, there being sufficient deep water in the lake to accommodate the combined navies of the world, and inexhaustible coal-fields are worked within a short distance of the shores of the lake.

BROKEN BAY (*Barrenjuey*), 33° 33′ S. lat., 151° 15′ E. long., 30 miles N. of Port Jackson. Into the middle of Broken Bay the river Hawkesbury discharges its mountain-gathered waters, while on its northern shores the quiet arm known as Brisbane Water has its embouchure. The village of Gosford, one of the oldest in the Colony, is situated on Brisbane Water, but it has never risen to importance. At the southern part of the bay is Pittwater. Broken Bay and the adjacent districts are interesting to the tourist and pleasure-seekers rather than to the commercial man at present, but the recent discovery of coal in the district may change its now quiet aspect. The Broadwater near Gosford is the centre of an extensive ship-building district. Upon Barrenjuey, in Broken Bay, there is a second order dioptric fixed red light, visible 15 miles.

THE HAWKESBURY RIVER takes its rise not many miles from Goulburn, and receives the waters of Cox's River, which originates in the Blue Mountains, and is known as the Warragamba. Before entering the ocean at Broken Bay the Hawkesbury receives the tributaries of the Cataract and Cordeaux, from which Sydney now obtains its water supply, the Nepean, the Grose, the Colo, and the Macdonald Rivers. It pursues a tortuous course of over 300 miles, and its drainage area covers 8,000 square miles. Navigation extends as far as Windsor, 70 miles from the sea at Broken Bay. The Hawkesbury is crossed by a magnificent railway bridge on the Sydney to Newcastle line.

PORT JACKSON, 33° 52' S lat., 151° 16' E. long. The entrance to Port Jackson is grand and imposing in the extreme, its perpendicular cliffs rising to several hundred feet high. Its natural shipping facilities and the most perfect security from all weathers gives it a foremost place among all the harbours of the world. It embraces 15 square miles of water-surface, and 165 miles of shore-line in the harbour proper of the port. The heaviest draft ships built can enter Sydney harbour with safety by keeping the eastern channel, which has been deepened to 27 feet at low water. The western channel, divided from the eastern by the Sow and Pigs reef, carries 20 feet at low water, and for moderate-sized vessels is most frequently used. After Bradley's Head is passed, the harbour draft of water is practically unlimited, the largest ships being discharged while moored close to the abrupt rocky frontages from Dawes' Point to Darling Harbour. There are two lighthouses on the South Head, the Hornby, a fixed white catoptric light, 50 feet high, and visible 15 miles; and the Macquarie South Head Sydney Lighthouse, of the first order dioptric white electric and revolving, 356 feet high, and visible 21 miles. The following are the

## DOCKS, SLIPS, AND ENGINEERING ESTABLISHMENTS OF THE PORT.

### Fitzroy Dock.

FITZROY DOCK, one of the Government Docking Establishments of the port, situated at Cockatoo Island, Parramatta River, is distant about 3½ miles from the General Post Office.

The dock was principally constructed by prison labour, Cockatoo having been a penal station. In 1870, however, this was broken up, and after a short interregnum the dock was placed under the control of the Engineer-in-Chief for Harbours and Rivers. It was then about 300 feet long, since which time it has been twice lengthened by means of free labour, and is now capable of taking in a ship of 475 feet in length, a dimension considerably in excess of that of the s.s. "Orient."

Some large ships-of-war and other first-class vessels have been taken in the dock. Amongst the former may be mentioned H.M.S. "Galatea," commanded at the time by H.R.H. the Duke of Edinburgh, and the French ironclad "Atalanta"; and amongst the latter the steamships "Whampoa" and "Chimborazo."

The dock is in almost constant occupation, H.M. war-ships, foreign men-of-war, and the mail-ships of the P.M.S. Company being regularly accommodated there, together with the numerous fleet of tugs, dredges, &c., belonging to the Colonial Government. Dredges, tugs, and punts for the dredge service are built at the island, a large staff of mechanics

X

being constantly employed by the Harbours and Rivers Department for this purpose, and for keeping in repair the large fleet of dredges, tugs, &c., belonging to the department. Its dimensions are as follows:—

| | |
|---|---|
| Length on keel floor | 475 feet. |
| Width between coping at entrance | 50 ,, |
| Depth of water on sills at high-water spring tides | 20½ ,, |
| And at high-water neaps | 18½ ,, |

### THE SUTHERLAND DOCK.

In 1880 Parliament determined on the construction of a first-class graving dock, capable of meeting the requirements of the largest class of vessels, including ironclads. The sum of £150,000 was accordingly voted for the work, and the first contract for the excavation of the work was commenced in October, 1882, and completed in December, 1884. The second contract was commenced in March, 1883, and completed in 1887. Cockatoo Island, the location of the Sutherland Dock, is situate in a well sheltered part of the harbour, where there is good anchorage and ample depth of water at all states of the tide for ships of the heaviest draught.

The entrance to the new dock is on the western side of the island (that of the existing Fitzroy Dock being on the eastern side); the heads of the two docks approach within 250 feet of each other, and their longitudinal axes form so obtuse an angle between them as to allow of utilizing this intervening space for the construction of a graving dock for dredges and small craft, having either of the large docks as a medium for entrance or departure.

The extreme length of the new dock at coping level is 635 feet, the length of the keel floor 580 feet, the width between copings at caisson stop of entrance is 84 feet, and the batter of the walls 1 in 24. The width inside the dock is 108 feet between copings, diminishing by a series of altars to an average width of 43 feet 6 inches at the level of floor, a broad altar about midway between coping and floor running the whole length of the dock on both sides. The dock is divided longitudinally into four bays by three vertical piers on either side, 30 feet in width, having flights of steps on one side of them, these arrangements giving ample facilities for shoring vessels and easy access to the workmen employed. The depth of water on the sill at high-water ordinary spring tides is 32 feet, and high-water ordinary neap tides 29 feet 6 inches.

The opening and closing of the dock is effected by a wrought iron sliding or rolling caisson, having a camber formed in the side wall for its reception when the dock is open. It is provided with an air chamber, so as to be used if necessary as a floating caisson.

The dock is the largest single graving dock yet constructed, and is capable of receiving the largest vessel afloat. The steamers "Kaiser Wilhelm," "Australien," and H.M.S. "Orlando" have been docked in it. It is provided with all the appliances adopted in modern graving docks, including the electric light, so that the dock is available both night and day.

---

*Rountree's Floating Dock, Waterview Bay.*—Length of dock, 164 feet; breadth, 42 feet; depth of water for vessels using dock, 12 feet. Vessels of 600 tons can be docked. Sawmill, blacksmith's shop, and all materials are on the premises for building and repairing ships.

*Mort's Dock and Engineering Company, Mort's Bay, Balmain.*—The works of this company are situated at the head of Mort's Bay, one of the numerous arms of Port Jackson (for which the harbour is so widely celebrated), and which has a sufficient depth of water for the largest vessels right up to the company's wharfs. These latter occupy an irregular piece of ground of about 15 acres in extent, running round the head of the bay, and having a frontage to the water of 600 feet on the north, 602 feet on the north-west, and 286 feet on the south-west side, making a total wharfage of about 1,488 feet. The graving dock has its entrance in the western corner of the bay, and has a depth of water on the sill of 20 feet 9 inches at spring tides. It is 410 feet long, with a length of 390 feet of patent keel blocks; width of caisson, 68 feet. The floor of the dock is 2 feet below the sill, so that a vessel drawing about 20 feet may be taken in, and a clear space of 2 feet left underneath for workmen to effect repairs. There are three patent slips in connection with the work. No. 1 has a length of carriage of 250 feet, and will take up vessels up to 1,500 tons dead weight. No. 2 has a length of carriage of 200 feet, and will accommodate vessels up to 1,000 tons burthen. No. 3 is suitable for small steamers up to 40 tons. Both large slips are worked by hydraulic machinery, and there is sufficient length of shipway for a large vessel to be taken off the cradle for repairs or lengthening and for another to be hauled up behind for cleaning and painting. The principal workshops consist of iron and brass foundries; engineers' fitting, turning, and machine shops; boiler-makers', blacksmiths', erecting, coppersmiths', and pattern shops; saw-mill and boat-sheds—covering a space of about 3 acres. The machine shops contain a large number of lathes (one of which has a 16-foot face plate), planing, slotting, and shaping machines, radial and vertical drills, nut-shaping, screwing, nibbling, and ferrule machines. The boiler-shop has plate and angle furnaces, punching and shearing machines, plate rollers, steam riveter, plate planing machines, countersink drills, tube cutters, &c., &c. The smithy has six steam hammers from 10 tons downwards, the largest being about 120 tons weight, and striking a blow equal to 80 tons, bolt-making machines, rivet-making machines, saw for hot iron, and about twenty forges. The foundry is 150 feet long, has three stoves, six cranes, and one of Scott's wheel-moulding machines, the cupola being outside the building. The erecting shop is 140 feet by 40 feet and 30 feet high to the beam. It is fitted with two 20-ton travellers of 40-foot span. In the saw-mill, joiners', and pattern shops there are circular, vertical, and band saws, lathes, planing, mortising, tenoning, and treenail-making machines. The shipwrights' department is found in the usual metal punching machines, steaming kilns, and other appliances for stripping and recoppering vessels, or building new ones. There is, in connection with the works, a set of patent iron steam tripod sheer-legs, capable of lifting boilers and other heavy weights up to 60 tons; also a number of cranes on the wharfs for discharging and loading. In addition to ship, engine, and boiler building, they manufacture locomotives, quartz-crushing machinery, iron bridges, girders, columns, flour-mill, gas, sugar, distilling, pumping, winding, mining, sheep-washing, saw-mill, brick-making, wool-pressing, hydraulic, and all kinds of machinery.

*Atlas Foundry and Engineering Company.*—The Atlas Engineering Company's works are situated on the Parramatta River, just opposite the Fitzroy Dock, Cockatoo Island. Extensive workshops are erected and specially laid out to meet the growing requirements of the mercantile marine frequenting the port. The foundry and appliances are the largest and most complete in the colonies, and castings of 20 tons can be turned out and handled with perfect ease by means of a large overhead steam travelling crane, and the machinery in the engineers' department can finish the same, there being upwards of fifty machines. The largest lathe can take a casting of 16 feet diameter. The boiler-shop is fitted with every appliance for making and repairing the heaviest class of boiler and ship work. The smiths' shop is well fitted up with steam hammers (two), converting furnace, hot saws, and lifting apparatus for all classes of smiths' work. The ship-building yard is of sufficient area to lay down four 1,000-ton vessels at one time. The company are constructing a set of floating sheer-legs to lift up to 50 tons, and are importing a floating dock upon the pontoon grid principle, calculated to lift vessels of 2,000 tons. The dock enables the company to raise and repair ships of 2,000 tons with quicker despatch than any other appliances in the colonies. The works have a deep water frontage of about 500 yards, where vessels of the largest class can be berthed with safety. All the different shops are connected by tramways and cranes to the wharfs, and all the most modern and labour-saving appliances have been adopted.

*Mr. Grant's Boilermaking Establishment, Pyrmont*, has a wharf frontage of 160 feet with a depth of 17 feet of water at low tide. The sheer-legs will lift 30 tons, and the works have all appliances for executing every kind of boiler-work. Mr. Grant has likewise boiler works at the foot of Erskine-street.

*The Balmain Engineering Company's Works* are situated at the foot of Adolphus-street, Balmain, and have wharf frontage to Johnstone's Bay.

*Messrs. Foster and Minty* have works near Peacock's Point, Balmain, at which they have built small iron coasting steamers and lighters. *Messrs. Chapman and Co.'s* engine and boiler works, Druitt-street, are referred to in the description of wharfs, &c., and *Messrs. Halliday and Co.*, largely engaged in building engines and boilers for harbour steamers, &c., have their works at the foot of Erskine-street, adjacent to the Illawarra Company's wharf.

*Brown's Iron Works.*—For some time past iron of excellent quality has been manufactured at these works, which have a considerable water frontage to Johnstone's Bay, near the eastern approach to Glebe Island Bridge.

*Saunders' Wharf.*—Between Messrs. Brown's ironworks and the Colonial Sugar Company's establishment Mr. Saunders has erected a fine wharf for general use, but chiefly in connection with the Pyrmont building-stone trade.

## SHIPPING TRADE.

856 steamers and sailing vessels, representing 102,047 tons net, are registered in the books of the Custom-house, as belonging to the port of Sydney.

## WHARFAGE ACCOMMODATION.

The Government wharfs and jetties, available for the largest class of vessels, are situated at Circular Quay, Woolloomooloo Bay, and Darling Harbour.

The wharfage at Circular Quay affords, on the eastern shore of the cove, sufficient deep water and shed accommodation for the steamers of the P. and O., Messageries, Orient, Gulf, and other lines; while on the western side, besides sailing ships and British steamers, the various German companies trading to Europe and to the islands of the Eastern seas find ample wharf and storage accommodation.

For some years past the railway has been connected with Government wharfs at the head of Darling Harbour, where a considerable timber and shale trade has developed. Owing to the increase in the export of Metropolitan coal, two long jetties have recently been erected in Darling Harbour, north of Pyrmont Bridge. Here powerful steam-cranes ship coal into the largest ships trading to the port, and Sydney now promises to largely share with Newcastle the profits of Australian coal shipment.

Round the southern shore of Darling Harbour, and extending some distance along the Pyrmont frontage, a continuous line of iron wharfage has been erected, and here ships and steamers, drawing from 13 to 20 feet of water, discharge and receive cargo from trucks running on the Southern and Western Railways.

The frontage of 1,260 feet is divided into nine berths, comprising five jetties of 60 feet each in width, and four berths of 240 feet in length, vessels berthing at the latter overlapping those moored at the former.

An overhead steam travelling crane used for lifting weights of 8 tons is available at the eastern jetty, and at two of the others 10-ton travelling cranes and coal shoots are erected. In addition there are two powerful derrick cranes erected on the wharf.

## PRIVATE WHARFAGE ACCOMMODATION.

*Fresh Food and Ice Company's Wharf.*—One jetty; can berth a vessel of 200 tons.

*Byrnes' Coal Wharf.*—One jetty; can berth three vessels of from 200 to 500 tons; there is 10 feet at low water alongside; wharf used for discharging coal and timber.

*Byrnes' Coal Wharf.*—One jetty; can accommodate three vessels of small class, say 60 tons.

*Barker's Wharf*, 63 feet of frontage, at which a vessel of about 100 tons can discharge.

*Russell's Wharf (now Taylor's).*—Sufficient accommodation for three or four vessels.

*Wearne's Wharf*, 160 feet frontage, with 15 feet draught and storage accommodation for 1,000 tons goods.

*Seamer's Wharf and a side Wharf.*—160 feet of frontage, with a depth of 17 feet; two vessels of 500 tons can discharge; storage for 4,000,000 feet of timber. Seamer's steam saw-mill and joinery works are here.

*Pacific Wharf and Chapman & Co.'s Engineering Works.*—220 feet of wharfage; draught, 16 feet. Union Company of New Zealand have here two fine long jetties with deep water.

*Allen and Walker's Wharf (Wentworth's)* can accommodate two vessels of 100 and one of 150 tons.

*McIlwraith's Wharfs*, comprising two fine jetties with deep water, suited for the largest ships frequenting the port.

*Albion Wharf (John See & Co. and Hinton).*—This wharf can berth three vessels of 200 tons and one smaller one; used for timber trade.

*Baltic Wharf (Burns, lessee).*—Two jetties, at which two vessels of 500 tons, or three of 100 tons, can be placed. Mr. Burns' principal saw-mill establishment is at Balmain, where there is 320 feet of wharf frontage.

*Corporation Ballast Wharf.*—Jetty, 130 ft. x 30 ft.; used solely for Corporation work.

*Market Wharf (Kethel, lessee).*—This wharf comprises three jetties, each of 160 feet in length, at which six vessels of 800 tons and 15-foot draught can be berthed. There is covered storage on the premises for 5,000 tons of goods. Here the North Coast Company's steamers trading to the northern rivers, are accommodated, and here also Messrs. John Booth & Co. have their Sydney stores and jetty.

*Newcastle and Hunter River Steam Company's Wharf.*—There is here 166 feet frontage to Darling Harbour; the land extends back from stone wall; frontage, about 250 feet eastward. A pier built on piles extends westward from the water frontage to Darling Harbour.

*Messrs. W. Howard Smith and Sons' Wharf (late Struth's).*—The wharfage accommodation here consists of two jetties, one 155 and one 165 feet in length, in addition to which there is a wharf abutting on King-street 155 ft. x 35 ft.

*Corporation Wharf, foot of King-street.*—One short jetty, used for small steamers plying on the Parramatta River.

*Caledonia Wharf.*—One jetty, 140 feet long, with 13 feet of water.

*W. Howard Smith and Sons' New Jetty.*—This jetty, erected on the site of the old Patent Slip, is 235 feet in length by 24 feet wide, and has 23 feet of water on the north with 15 feet on the south side.

*Patent Slip Wharf (Seamer or Langley's).*—This wharf will accommodate from four to five vessels of 200 to 300 tons.

*Newcastle Steamship Company's Wharf.*—Here there are two jetties of 220 feet by 30 feet wide.

At the foot of Erskine-street are Byrnes' and Joubert's jetties for steamers plying to Pyrmont and Lane Cove, Spiers' coal wharf, and, further north, the terminus of the ferry steamers plying to Balmain and Mort's Dock, Waterview Bay.

*Illawarra Steam Navigation Company's Wharf.*—This wharf has an available water frontage of 640 feet. There is accommodation for 800 tons of cargo. The steamers owned by the company ply from this wharf to southern ports.

*Preddy's Wharf.*—This wharf can accommodate vessels of 300 tons.

*Taylor's Timber Wharf.*—Here there is one jetty 100 feet long, capable of berthing one vessel of 300 tons and one of 100 tons.

*Huddart, Parker & Co.'s (Russell's) Wharf.*—One jetty, 165 ft. x 25 ft., at which two ships can be berthed, one of upwards of 2,000 tons on one side, and a smaller one of about 400 tons on the other.

*Union Steamship Co. of New Zealand.*—One long jetty, with 21 feet of water alongside, at which two of the largest ships can be discharged.

*Union Steam Co.'s Wharf (late Tasmanian Co.'s).*—There is one jetty here of 270 feet in length, at which two ships each of 2,000 tons burthen and drawing 20 feet can be berthed.

*North Coast S. N. Co's. Wharf.*—Here there are two large jetties, at which large ships are berthed.

*Frazer & Company (late Grafton Wharf), leased to the A.U.S.N. Co.*—The premises known in Sydney as the Grafton Wharf comprise about 3½ acres, and are situated in Darling Harbour, which is the centre of the great shipping trade of the port. Grafton Wharf is also amongst the oldest in Sydney, and was for many years selected for the principal intercolonial trade. Its position in the harbour, and the facility of communication with the heart of the commerce of the town, give it without question very great advantages over any other. These advantages have induced the proprietors (Messrs. John Frazer & Co.) to carry out a complete work of reconstruction; and, after sweeping away the whole of the former jetties and wharf, they have constructed a new wharf, with piers of the most substantial character, and capable of receiving and shipping cargo of any character and weight. The wharf has a frontage to Darling Harbour of about 430 feet; and there are three piers, two each 250 feet long, and one 310 feet long from the face of the wharf, and of the respective widths of 40, 50, and 54 feet. All the piers are covered by sheds to the extent of about 140 feet from the wharf, for the purpose of receiving cargo of a perishable nature, which may then be taken from the hold of the ship and lodged in a dry and protected place until removed to the adjacent stores. The depth of water available at the wharf and jetties is 23 feet at low tide. The storage accommodation is the largest on any one estate, public or private, in the Australian colonies. There are fourteen warehouses, affording storage for over 44,500 tons measurement of cargo. In two of the warehouses wool-pressing machinery has been provided, by which 16,000 bales can be dumped daily. There are three spacious enclosed sheds close to the wharf frontage and parallel to it, capable of containing 2,300 tons of goods. Spacious offices and captains' rooms are provided. The Tasmanian S.S. Company lease part of Frazer & Co.'s northern jetty, and berth their vessels trading to Tasmania and Eden.

*Gas Company's Wharf.*—This wharf has a frontage of 730 feet, at which two steamers of 400 tons can berth.

*Dibbs' Wharf (now Gibbs, Bright, & Co.).*—Here seven vessels, each of 400 tons, can be berthed. Alongside the jetties there is a depth varying from 20 to 25 feet at low water; and upon the premises which cover an area of 5½ acres 10,000 tons of goods can be stored.

*Smith's Wharfs.*—Seven ships of 4,000 tons can be discharged here. There is storage on the property for 12,000 tons of goods, and at the wharfs there is a depth of from 19 to 22 feet of water; the premises extend over 4½ acres of land.

*Moore's Wharf (Sydney Stevedoring Co.)*—This wharf had originally a water-frontage of 442-ft. 6-in., which has since been extended by the erection of three jetties on the échelon principle of respective lengths—No. 1, 183-ft. 6-in.; No. 2, 332-ft. 6-in.; and No. 3, 180-ft. Some of the largest cargo-carrying steamers and sailing ships up to 3,100 tons have been berthed at this wharf, the depth of water being from 19 to 31 feet. Exclusive of the jetties, the area of the ground is 1 acre 2 roods 23 perches. Bonded and free stores are erected upon it, capable of containing 5,500 tons of goods, also sheds for protecting a considerable quantity of goods from the weather.

*Towns' Wharf (Dalgety's), west of Kent-street.*—The wharfs here are so designed that 453 feet collectively of berthing room is obtained. There is large storage accommodation on the property.

*Dalgety's (late Parbury's) Wharf.*—This wharf has a water frontage of 140 feet, and has a jetty running out 340-ft. x 48-ft. wide, capable of berthing the largest steamer coming to the port, also a ship of 2,000 tons at the same time. There is a large store built of brick (capable of storing 12,000 tons of goods), supplied with the most improved hydraulic lifts and wool shoots. A large covered shed on the wharf is capable of storing an additional 3,000 tons of goods. Wool-pressing is carried to the extent of 2,000 bales per diem. Telephonic communication is established to Exchange and town office of the proprietors.

*Central (late Alfred Lamb's) Wharf.*—Most extensive improvements have been effected on this property. Two jetties, each 360 feet long by 50 feet wide, with a depth of 26 feet alongside, extend outwards from the stores, in which 15,000 bales of wool can be placed. Wool-pressing to the extent of 2,000 bales per diem is carried on within the premises, and telephonic communication is established to the Exchange and the town offices of the proprietors, Messrs. A. Lamb & Co.

*Dalton's Wharf.*—This wharf is owned by Dalton Brothers, of Pitt-street, and is approached from Windmill-street. There is a water frontage of 252 feet, partly covered by an iron roofed shed. There are two tapering jetties, each 262 feet long, with an average width of 45 feet. These can berth three steamers of 3,000 tons each. In the rear of the wharf are seven warehouses, two of which are bonded stores, and all are supplied with the most improved hydraulic hoisting apparatus. One of the lifts is capable of lifting 15 tons, and hoists up, as required, a loaded waggon with horses and men complete, a distance in height of 35 feet to Lower Fort-street. The amount of wharfage business transacted may be judged from the fact that last year fifty-three vessels, each of a mean tonnage of 2,500 tons, were unloaded—or more than a ship per week. The stores aggregate a storage capacity of 35,000 tons. On the jetties are hydraulic cranes for discharging vessels.

*Alger's Wharf (S. Hoffnung & Co.)*—Here three vessels of 1,500 tons each can be berthed. There is 22 feet of water alongside the wharf and jetty, and storage for 8,000 tons of merchandise. The premises cover an acre of ground.

*Parbury's Wharf.*—Here is a water-frontage of 264 feet, at which the Orient steamers have been berthed. Besides an open shed on the wharf, there is storage accommodation for 9,000 tons of goods.

*Walker's Wharf (Dalgety & Co.)*—A 3,500-ton ship, drawing 22 feet of water, can be berthed here. There is storage accommodation in Alger's No. 2 warehouses for 7,000 tons goods upon the premises, which stand upon half-an-acre of ground.

*Government Wharf—Australasian Steam Navigation Company's (late Campbell's Wharf).*—Vessels of 3,200 tons, drawing 24 feet of water, can be berthed at this property.

*Jetties and Waiting Rooms.*—Round the crown or southern boundary of Sydney Cove, jetties and waiting rooms have been erected by the Government at great cost to meet the constantly-increasing harbour and ferry traffic.

*Eastern Wharfs, Circular Quay.*—On the eastern shore of Sydney Cove a wharf-frontage of 1,340 feet has recently been built by the Government for the accommodation of the largest steamers and ships trading to Sydney.

In the centre of the line of wharfage there is a projection of 320 feet, with an available depth of water of 28 feet at low tide. Here the Orient steamers are berthed and the cargoes received in a well-arranged store, 200 ft. by 40 ft. The Messageries Co. steamers berth at the north-eastern end of the wharf, where there is a frontage of 488 feet and a similar good-shed to the one built at the Orient wharf. At the southern division there is an available frontage of 535 feet, and here the largest class of wool ships and British cargo steamers are berthed. There is a goods store 178 ft. x 35 ft. on the wharf. Between the Messageries Co's. wharf and Fort Macquarie the P. & O. Co.'s steamers are berthed, and further north is the horse ferry approach for the North Shore.

*Cowper Wharf, Woolloomooloo.*—This is a public wharf, 945 feet in length, constructed of wood, and used hitherto chiefly for foreign-going timber-laden ships, and for steamers employed in bringing blue metal from Melbourne and Kiama. There is an 8-ton crane on the wharf, and an available depth of water alongside of 20 feet, but this is sometimes lessened by the sewage deposits from the large sewers which discharge here. Adjoining the wharf, at its western end, is one 344 feet in length, erected for the Imperial Government. It is intended to deepen the frontage of this wharf to 30 feet and to erect a 20-ton crane upon it. A jetty 260 feet long by 25 feet wide has recently been built for the accommodation of the passenger steamers plying to the watering-places down the harbour; but it is at present used for berthing large ships from Britain.

*Goodlet and Smith's Wharf, Pyrmont.*—This wharf has a water-frontage of 475 feet, formed into wharfs (on the échelon principle), at which three vessels of from 150 to 600 tons and two vessels of 2,000 tons can be berthed. The wharf has timber storage for 8,000,000 feet, and on the ground adjoining is erected saw-mills and joinery works fitted with the newest and most approved machinery, also a six-storied store capable of holding 10,000 tons of merchandise. The wharf and stores are worked by hydraulic cranes and lifts.

*The Colonial Sugar Co.,* at their extensive works in Johnstone's Bay, have well-arranged wharfs and jetties; two of the jetties are respectively 216 and 153 feet in length. There is available deep water for large ships and excellent facilities for discharging coal for the Company's use. Three of Sir William Armstrong's hydraulic lifts, equal to a ton each, are made use of.

BOTANY BAY. 34° S. lat., 151° 16′ E. long. Nine miles S. of the South Head of Port Jackson is the entrance to Botany Bay, and is half a mile in width. Cape Banks forms the north head, and Cape Solander the south head. There is a good navigable channel, with not less than 12 feet of water to the Government pier, near the water-works, and to the wharf at Lady Robinson's Beach, but the bay generally is shallow. George's River finds its outlet in Botany Bay, and Cook's River also discharges its waters in the northern part of the bay. These two small rivers have their sources on the eastern slopes of the ranges in which the Nepean, Cordeaux, and Cataract rise, and after rapid courses, fall into the bay. Extensive improvements are being made to the banks of Cook's River, and a canal is in course of construction towards Sydney.

PORT HACKING. 34° 3′ S. lat., 151° 10′ E. long., 22 miles S. of Sydney. This small port is chiefly interesting as being the seaport of the National Park. The entrance between Hacking Head and Glaiser's Point is about half-a-mile in width, and at a distance of about a mile inside there is a bar with 6 feet of water on it, beyond which there is an inlet with shallow water. This little port is susceptible of considerable improvement, and attention will doubtless ere long be directed to it, so that the public may have the full advantage of the splendid grounds which, thanks to the foresight of the late Sir John Robertson, have been secured to them.

COAL CLIFF COMPANY'S JETTY.—Not working.

**NORTH ILLAWARRA COAL COMPANY'S JETTY.**—Not working.

**BULLI JETTY.**—This jetty has been erected by the Bulli Coal Company for the shipment of coal from their mines. The output for the past year was 49,512 tons.

**WOONONA JETTY.**—This jetty has been erected by the Woonona or Bulli Company for the shipment of coal from their mines. The output for the past year was 97,073 tons.

**SOUTH BULLI JETTY.**—This jetty has been erected by the company for the shipment of coal from their mine. The output for the past year amounted to 112,860 tons.

**SOUTHERN COAL COMPANY'S JETTY.**—This jetty has been erected by the Southern Coal Company for shipping coal from their mine. The output for the past year amounted to 54,702 tons.

**KEMBLA JETTY.**—This jetty has been erected by the Kembla Coal Company for shipping coal from the Kembla mine. The output for the past year amounted to 141,558 tons.

**WOLLONGONG**, 34° 22′ S. lat., 150° 58′ E. long., 41 miles S. of Sydney. For fifty years and upwards steamers have been plying from Sydney to Wollongong; but it is only since the development of the southern coal industry that it has risen to importance as a seaport. It is now managed by a harbour trust, and it is proposed to entirely reorganise the shipping appliances, which at present consist of three coal-staiths and two steam-cranes. The excavation of the present "Belmore Basin" was a difficult task, owing to the material (rock) dealt with. There is a depth of 17 feet at the eastern side of the basin, and colliers have been loaded in the harbour. There is a lighthouse erected, with a white light visible 10 miles.

**LAKE ILLAWARRA**, 34° 24′ S. lat., 150° 58′ E. long., is situated 60 miles S. of Sydney. The area of the lake or inlet is 9,000 acres. The scenery of this lake is most picturesque. The eastern shores are densely timbered, and of sufficient height to shelter the waters of the lake from easterly gales, while the lofty range of the Illawarra Mountains, 5 miles to the westward, afford protection from westerly winds. To the N. and S. there is hilly country running from 100 to 300 feet in height, so that the lake may be said to be completely sheltered. The western shores are indented by large bays, notably, Yalla and Connawarry Bays. To the N. of the latter Mullet Creek extends from the lake to the main road, a distance of about 5 miles. There are few stretches of water in Australia to compare with this creek for beauty of surroundings and facilities for boating. The creek is about 75 yards in width, with reaches up to half a mile in length. The banks of the creek are well timbered, and the water communicating with that of the lake preserves a uniform level. Within the waters of the lake are three islands of considerable area, formed of volcanic rock, and the rich soil resulting from its decomposition. The semi-tropical vegetation of these islands imparts to them a great charm, and has caused them to become famous as a resort for pic-nic and pleasure parties. The lake is about to be converted into a commodious harbour by the Illawarra Harbour and Land Corporation, who, in December, 1890, obtained an Act of Parliament authorising them to carry out the harbour works and a railway service in connection therewith. The intended operations of this Company are of such a magnitude, and if carried out to a successful issue will be of such great importance, not only to the district but to the whole of Australia, that the following particulars, derived from evidence taken before the Select Committees on the Company's Bill will be of interest to our readers :—The depth of water in the lake at present is 12 to 14 feet. The bottom of the lake has been proved by systematic borings to consist of stiff mud to a great depth. At the sea entrance, at a distance of about 200 yards, is a small island (Windang), 1,000 feet in length and about 150 feet in height. The Company intend to connect this island with the southern bank of the entrance by a massive masonry mole, and to run out breakwaters from the island, and also from the northern bank of the entrance. By this means complete shelter will be afforded to incoming vessels, and the shifting sands which at present block the channel will be trapped. A channel will then be dredged through the mud bottom of the lake, a distance of $3\frac{1}{2}$ miles, to the Company's properties on the western shores of the lake, where extensive wharfage accommodation will be provided for the simultaneous loading with coals of twelve of the largest vessels afloat. The Company own 2,920 acres of land, having $4\frac{1}{2}$ miles frontage to the lake. The wharfs will be connected by railway with the Government main line, and also with ten large coal-mines in the range immediately to the W. of the lake. Facilities will thus be given for the direct shipment of the coal, which is found in inexhaustible quantities for 20 miles N. and S. of the lake. There being no harbour worthy of the name between Port Jackson and Jervis Bay, the coal trade of the south has hitherto been carried on in a desultory fashion ; but with the harbour accommodation to be provided by the Company, the export of this coal, of excellent quality and unsurpassed for cheapness of production, should attain great dimensions, and Lake Illawarra become one of the busiest harbours in the world. Vast stores of mineral wealth, both coal and iron, are proved to be in the Illawarra Mountain, and the time must come when this wealth will be utilised to its fullest extent. The day is probably not far distant when the rich agricultural lands bordering the lake will support a large population busily engaged in the most important manufactures.

SHELLHARBOUR, 34° 27′ S. lat., 150° 27′ E. long. Between Wollongong and Kiama is the small harbour known as Shellharbour, with but a limited trade chiefly carried on by a small steamer, which conveys dairy and other produce. The celebrated Lake Illawarra is near Shellharbour.

KIAMA, 34° 38′ S. lat., 150° 27′ E. long. Fifteen miles S. of Wollongong, and 56 miles from Sydney, is the port of Kiama. Here a very fine basin, named after the late Sir John Robertson, has been excavated. There are about 1,100 feet of available wharfage, and an average width of 400 feet, with 18 feet depth of water. The trade to the port is chiefly in blue metal, very large supplies being sent to Sydney. The town of Kiama is perhaps the most charmingly picturesque of all the towns on the coast. The celebrated Blow-hole, near the harbour, imparts additional interest to the district. The shipping trade both here and at Wollongong has been considerably affected since the railway passed through the district. There is a light-house with a fixed green light here visible from 8 to 12 miles, also a red danger-light, and a green light at breakwater.

GERRINGONG, 34° 14′ S. lat , 150° 14′ E. long. This is a small open roadstead, at which moorings have been laid down for small steamers and trading vessels. It is situated between Kiama and Shoalhaven, about 12 miles from the former place.

SHOALHAVEN AND CROOKHAVEN, 34° 47' S. lat., 150° 47' E. long. These two ports within a few miles of each other, situated between Black and Beecroft Points, are both embouchures of the Shoalhaven River. Crookhaven the most southerly, is almost wholly used. There is a bar at the entrance, with about 7 feet at low water. The large Sydney steamers ply to Greenwell Point, and the smaller ones to the towns of Berry and Nowra. The district is a rich agricultural dairy one, and has some historical interest as being the original estate of the late Alexander Berry, whose homestead, Coolangatta, is prettily situated near the coast. The Shoalhaven River traverses a course of about 250 miles, but is only navigable for a few miles. There is a fixed red light, visible 8 miles, at the Pilot station, at the Crookhaven entrance.

JERVIS BAY (*Cape St. George*), 35° 3' S. lat., 150° 80' E. long., 82 miles S. of Sydney. The entrance to this bay is about 2 miles in width, and there is safe anchorage within it. It has often been asked why this fine harbour, second only to Port Jackson, has been so little used, the answer being the character of the surrounding district in its unsuitableness for settlement. The extension of railway communication, and the opening up of rich coal-mines, will doubtless soon create a very considerable trade with Victoria and other southern colonies. The vessels at present visiting the bay are chiefly whalers, for wood and water, and war-ships for target practice. Three miles S. of the entrance is the lighthouse, with a revolving white, red, and green light. The white light is visible 18 miles, and the red and green, 14 miles.

ULLADULLA COVE, 35° 18' S. lat., 150° 30' E. long. This pretty embayment is situate 20 miles S. of Jervis Bay, and 102 miles from Sydney. Excellent shelter for moderate-sized vessels can be relied upon in all weathers inside pier, which is about 200 feet in length, and upon the end of which is a fixed white light, visible 16 miles. Ulladulla is the port for "Milton," a rising town, distant 3 miles from the sea. The ground is classic, being the birthplace of Australia's sweetest singer, Henry Kendall.

CLYDE RIVER, 35° 37' S. lat., 150° 8' E. long. An important river flowing into Bateman's Bay, taking its rise in the mountain known as the Pigeon-house. It is navigable for small craft, and the townships of Currowan and Nelligen are situated upon it.

BATEMAN'S BAY, 35° 39' S. lat., 150° 12' E. long. Is an inlet of some importance situate 123 miles S. of Sydney. The river Clyde falls into the sea at Bateman's Bay. The bay is from 4 to 5 miles wide at the entrance, and tapers towards the river mouth, where there is a shallow bar, crossable only at high water. Ocean steamers ply to Nelligen some distance up the river. Twenty-five years ago a large trade was carried on, the river being the outlet for the business of the celebrated Braidwood gold-diggings.

MORUYA, 35° 52' S. lat., 150° 2' E. long. Is 139 miles S. of Sydney. The Moruya River, which flows past the Duke of Edinburgh range of mountains, winds to the sea through the picturesque valley of Araluen, and has its embouchure 4 miles S. of Broulee. Extensive improvements are being carried on at the mouth of the river where there is already a breakwater. At present the trade is limited to steamers of 6 feet draft. The district is rich and the climate salubrious. It is the shipping port for Bodalla, of cheese-making fame, the river Tuross, 12 miles S., upon which Mr. T. S. Mort founded his model estate, not being available for large sea-going vessels. N. of Moruya is Tomakin, a small port availed of for shipping timber.

BEGA RIVER, 36° 38′ S. lat., 149° 50′ E. long. Is 180 miles S. of Sydney. It takes its rise near Mount Nimmitibel, and after a course of about 60 miles has its embouchure at Tathra. The town of Bega is situated on this river, which is generally called the Bega below, and the Bemboka above, the township.

MONTAGUE ISLAND, is noteworthy in connection with the ports as having placed upon it a first order dioptric, fixed and flashing white light, 262 feet high, and visible 21 miles. Its position is 36° 15′ 20″ S. lat., 150° 14′ 30″ E. long. The island is 155 miles S. of Sydney, and is about 3½ miles from the coast, and 50 miles from Twofold Bay.

BERMAGUY is situated a few miles S. of Montague Island; shelter is found for coasters when the wind is at S. There is a limited trade for timber at Bermaguy.

TATHRA BIGHT, 36° 41′ S. lat., 150° E. long. Here moorings have been laid down, and are availed of by steamers using the pier and conveying produce for Bega, which is distant 7 miles. Tathra is about 23 miles N. of Twofold Bay.

MERIMBULA BAY, 36° 49′ S. lat., 149° 56′ E. long. Situated between Merimbula Point and Ioala Point, which are distant from each other 2½ miles. The bay is nearly 2 miles in length, with good water. The river Pambula discharges into the S.W. corner of the bay, and Merimbula Creek into the N.W. corner. At high water the creek is available for steamers trading to the town.

TWOFOLD BAY, 37° 3′ S. lat., 149° 55′ E. long. Distant 208 miles S. of Sydney. The most southern and one of the best of the eastern seaboard ports; had formerly a considerable repute as a whaling station; the late Benjamin Boyd was largely engaged therein, East Boyd Bay being named after him. Eden is the principal town, but the produce from the back country is chiefly sent to Merimbula. Steamers from Tasmania call at Twofold Bay, and it is the limit of the Illawarra Steam Company's trade. There is a red light at Point Lookout, visible only a few miles away. The Watkin River and Myrual Creek flow into the bay.

GREEN CAPE, 37° 15′ S. lat., 150° 2′ E. long., 217 miles S. of Sydney. N. of Disaster Bay is Green Cape, the scene of the loss of the "Ly-ee-Moon," and distant 16 miles from Cape Howe. Bellangabee Cove is about 3 miles N. of the Cape, and some small vessels trade thereto. The Green Cape light is one of the first order dioptric; it is a revolving white and shows a flash every minute, and is visible 19 miles.

TOWAMBA RIVER, 35° 7′ S. lat., 149° 36′ E. long. It is at the extreme S. of the Colony, and empties itself into the Pacific, at Twofold Bay. The Towamba is an important stream, and is fed by the Perica, Woy Woy, Jingo, and Matagana Creeks, and takes its rise on the eastern slope of the South Coast Range, opposite Catchcart, and has a tortuous course of about 40 miles through fine pastoral and agricultural country.

GABO ISLAND, 37° 34′ 15″ S. lat., 149° 55′ 10″ E. long. The lighthouse on Gabo Island is first order catoptric, fixed white light, and visible 17 miles, and distant from Sydney 277 miles.

*This concludes the Eastern Seaboard of the Colony.*

PORTER'S RETREAT (*Co. King*), a postal receiving-office, 167 miles W. of Sydney, with mail twice a week.

PORTLAND SIDING (*Co. Cook*), a railway station, 112 miles from Sydney, on the western line.

PORTO BAY (*Co. Cumberland*), a small bay on the S. side of Broken Bay, lying about 7 miles from the entrance.

POTTEN CREEK (*Co. King*), a small southern tributary of the Crookwell River, flowing into it about 6 miles W. of the township of Binda.

POTTINGER, a county in the Central Division of the Colony. [See "Counties."]

POTTS' HILL (*Co. Cumberland*), a postal-village, 12 miles W. of Sydney, with daily mail.

POTTS' POINT (*Co. Cumberland*), a rocky promontory on the S. shore of Port Jackson, lying between Rushcutters' Bay on the E., and Woolloomooloo Bay on the W. It is a favourite place for suburban residences on both sides of Macleay-street (the main street leading from Darlinghurst to the Point).

POUNI MOUNT (*Co. Murray*), a bold and lofty hill, lying on the N.W. of Yass Plains, and forming a land-mark for the surrounding country.

PRESLEY'S CREEK (*Co. Bathurst*), a small western tributary of the Rocky Bridge Creek.

PRESTON (*Co. Cumberland*), a postal receiving-office, 26 miles S. of Sydney, with daily mail.

PRETTY GULLY (*Co. Clive*), a postal receiving-office, 533 miles N. of Sydney, with daily mail. The nearest railway station is Tenterfield, 65 miles, on the northern line.

PRETTY PLAINS (*Co. Bathurst*), a tract of fine agricultural land in the parish of Shadforth, near the head of Frederick's Valley Creek, on the road from Bathurst to Orange.

PRIMROSE VALLEY CREEK (*Co. Murray*), a southern tributary of the Molonglo River, watering the Molonglo Plains.

PRINCESS CHARLOTTE VALE CREEK (*Co. Bathurst*) is a western tributary of the Macquarie River, rising in the Three Brothers' Range, flowing past the township of Mount Pleasant and Evans' Plains.

PROOA LAKE (*Co. Taila*), one of a series of lagoons which lie on the N. bank of the river Murray, about 10 miles E. of Euston.

PROSPECT (*Co. Cumberland*), a postal village, 22 miles W. of Sydney, with daily mail therefrom. The nearest railway station is Fairfield, 5 miles, on the southern line, situated in the parish of Prospect. It was proclaimed a municipal district in 1872, with a council of eight aldermen and a mayor.

PROSPECT CREEK (*Co. Cumberland*), a small tributary of George's River, falling into it at its lower end.

PROSPECT RESERVOIR (*Co. Cumberland*), a postal village, 27 miles W. of Sydney, with daily mail, telegraph and money-order offices, and Government savings bank.

PUA (*Co. Wakool*), a proclaimed village in this county.

# PUBLIC SCHOOLS IN THE COLONY.

### Under 43 Vic. No. 23.

These Schools came into operation in the year 1881, and the first report for the year 1882 there were 146,106 pupils enrolled, and in 1891 they increased to 195,241. The total expenditure of the year has been £704,259.

## SCHOOLS IN THE EASTERN DIVISION.

| School | No. on roll | School | No. on roll | School | No. on roll |
|---|---|---|---|---|---|
| **Argyle, County of.** | | Parkesbourne | 26 | Cave Creek | 13 |
| Argyle | 16 | Pejar | 25 | Cranbury | 15 |
| ,, East | 18 | Pomeroy | 24 | Cudal | 131 |
| Bangalore | 19 | Rhyanna | 24 | Cumnock | 80 |
| Bannaby | 24 | Run of Water | 25 | Deep Lead | 26 |
| Baw Baw | 31 | Sherwin's Flats | 50 | Eugowra | 52 |
| Bell's Creek | 30 | Spring Valley | 27 | Fair Hill | 29 |
| Boro | 12 | Taradale | 22 | Flagstone Creek | 25 |
| Breadalbane | 50 | Tarago | 32 | Forbes | 425 |
| Broken Bridge | 18 | Taralga | 76 | Galway Creek | 19 |
| Buckhobble | 29 | Tarlo Gap | 20 | Geranagny | 13 |
| Bungonia | 23 | Third Creek | 29 | Goobang | 40 |
| Burra | 16 | Thornford | 33 | Green Grove | 15 |
| Carrick | 16 | Towrang | 36 | Gregray | 24 |
| Collector | 51 | Windellama East | 7 | Grove, The | 18 |
| Curra Creek | 9 | ,, West | 17 | Gunning | 122 |
| Currawang | 58 | Woodhouselee | 17 | Kadina | 12 |
| Currawecla | 34 | | | Limestone | 17 |
| East Grove | 186 | **Arrawatta, County of.** | | Mandagery Creek | 9 |
| Goulburn | 629 | Arthur's Seat | 16 | Manildra | 39 |
| ,, North | 437 | Ashford | 23 | Meranburn | 50 |
| ,, South | 237 | Byron Creek | 20 | Mickie's Plains | 15 |
| Golspie | 22 | Coolootai | 19 | Mogong | 13 |
| Grace Mount | 15 | Dumaresq | 30 | Murga | 16 |
| Gullen | 47 | ,, Island | 17 | Nangar | 23 |
| Gullen Flat | 28 | Glen | 71 | Nyrang Creek | 24 |
| ,, West | 33 | Graman | 26 | Parkes | 208 |
| Gurrunda | 23 | King's Plains | 51 | Parkesborough | 28 |
| Hoskintown | 24 | Nullamanna | 29 | Reedy Creek | 29 |
| Inverary Park | 10 | Redbank | 44 | Soldier's Flat | 26 |
| Jacqua | 30 | Swamp Oak | 24 | Ten-mile Ridges | 14 |
| Jerralong | 15 | Wyndam | 59 | Terrara | 76 |
| Kingsdale | 38 | Yetman | 24 | Toogong | 33 |
| Lerida | 25 | | | Trajere | 22 |
| Long Reach | 40 | **Ashburnham, County of.** | | Trelswarren | 32 |
| Mangamore | 29 | Bindogundra | 26 | Watergumben | 33 |
| Mannafield | 49 | Black Monut | 21 | | |
| Manar | 23 | Boree | 24 | **Auckland, County of.** | |
| Marulan | 69 | Boree Cabonne | 12 | Angledale | 40 |
| Merrigan Creek | 19 | Borenore | 57 | Bega | 313 |
| Merilla | 36 | Bowman's Creek | 10 | Bournda South | 11 |
| Merry Vale | 11 | Brolgan | 66 | ,, North | 23 |
| Mummell | 29 | Bumbury | 32 | Brogo | 20 |
| Myrtleville | 32 | Canoblas | 54 | Candelo | 82 |
| New County Flat | 12 | Cargo | 50 | Cobargo | 95 |
| Norwood | 29 | Carrawabilly | 11 | Cobbora | 17 |

334                GEOGRAPHICAL ENCYCLOPÆDIA,

| | No. on roll. | | No. on roll. | | No. on roll. |
|---|---|---|---|---|---|
| Digman's Creek | 23 | Greghamstown | 30 | Michelaga | 40 |
| Eden | 77 | Haddonville | 13 | Mowenbar Lower | 22 |
| Eden Valley | 46 | Hampton | 26 | Norongo | 18 |
| Gourlay | 22 | Hobby's Yard | 37 | Rock Flat | 19 |
| Greig's Flat | 24 | Ingliswold | 22 | Rose Valley | 25 |
| Howe's Valley | 31 | Lewis Ponds | 97 | Rose Vale | 29 |
| Jellat Jellat | 40 | Long Swamp | 27 | Tallbar Creek | 21 |
| Kameruka | 21 | Lucknow | 88 | Tuulergal Lake | 27 |
| Lochiel | 24 | Lyndhurst | 44 | Timberry Range | 30 |
| Merimbula | 29 | Murangulla | 32 | Townsend | 26 |
| Meringlo | 39 | Milburn Creek | 30 | Umaralla | 29 |
| Millengandie | 30 | Millthorpe | 131 | Umaralla Siding | 41 |
| Nethercote | 22 | Milltown | 351 | White's Point | 13 |
| Panbula | 68 | Mount Macquarie | 67 | | |
| Perico | 11 | ,, M'Donald | 44 | **Bland, County of.** | |
| Rocky Hall | 36 | ,, Tamar | 31 | Bagdad | 26 |
| Spring Vale | 30 | ,, Tarana | 71 | Balubla | 26 |
| Tantawanglo | 37 | Moorilda | 57 | Barmedman | 54 |
| Tarragandah | 25 | Moronglo Creek | 49 | Boginderra | 11 |
| Three-mile Waterhole | 75 | Mountain Home | 12 | Dinga Dingi | 19 |
| Toothdale | 31 | Myalla | 20 | Dudanman | 20 |
| Towamba | 29 | Newbridge | 82 | Euroka | 85 |
| Wallagcot | 24 | Perth | 53 | Marowie South | 13 |
| Wolumla South | 44 | Pine Ridge | 22 | Marsden | 49 |
| ,, North | 30 | Porter's Mount | 20 | Milong | 22 |
| Wyndham | 59 | Shadforth | 34 | Temora | 152 |
| Yarramine | 30 | Shaw | 32 | Thanowring | 25 |
| | | Shaw's Creek | 20 | Tubbul | 23 |
| | | Shooters Hill | 22 | Yeo Yeo | 35 |
| | | Slippery Creek | 12 | | |
| **Bathurst, County of.** | | Springhill | 98 | **Bligh, County of.** | |
| Aberfoil | 25 | Springside | 58 | Ben Buckley | 12 |
| Anson | 24 | Swallow Creek | 18 | Bimbijong | 10 |
| Bathurst | 918 | Swallows' Nest | 16 | Borambil | 24 |
| Benerce | 72 | Thommoud | 15 | Bulga | 39 |
| Black Springs | 19 | Trunkey | 59 | Cambill Creek | 29 |
| Blayney | 188 | Waldegrave | 31 | Cassilis | 44 |
| Blossom Vale | 13 | Walli | 41 | Cattle Creek | 18 |
| Broula | 23 | Waugoola | 73 | Cooba Bulga | 19 |
| Brownlea | 30 | Wattle Grove | 17 | Coolah | 70 |
| Brown's Creek | 64 | Wattleville | 33 | Coolah Bridge | 24 |
| Burkville | 40 | Yarra | 33 | Cudgebegong | 16 |
| Burnt Yards | 25 | | | Denison Town | 26 |
| Byng | 38 | **Beresford, County of.** | | Goolma | 18 |
| Cadia | 31 | Anembo | 7 | Lambing Hill | 30 |
| Caloola | 20 | Berridale | 37 | Munoeurra | 11 |
| Campfield | 7 | Bubundara | 17 | Muumurra Lower | 21 |
| Canowindra | 96 | ,, North | 15 | Narrangerie | 21 |
| Carcoar | 97 | Boggy Plain | 13 | Oxley's Peak | 21 |
| Carrol Gap | 25 | Bredbo | 29 | Rosedale | 15 |
| Chaucer | 24 | Brown Mountain | 63 | Rous | 58 |
| Clarendon | 29 | Burragundra | 19 | Stubbo | 28 |
| Coota | 54 | Canimbla | 27 | Tallawang Lower | 22 |
| Cow Flat | 27 | Colinton | 29 | ,, Upper | 42 |
| Cowra | 239 | Cooma | 267 | Turill | 29 |
| Darby Falls | 26 | Counteganey | 20 | Uarbry | 11 |
| Essington | 18 | Coobringdoon | 11 | Ulan | 24 |
| Evan's Plains | 32 | Dairyman's Plains | 20 | Wagorbill | 20 |
| Fitzgerald's Valley | 22 | Good Good | 19 | Wellington | 220 |
| Galley Swamp | 53 | Jillimatong | 17 | | |
| George's Plains | 30 | Jingera | 14 | **Brisbane, County of.** | |
| Glenlogan | 30 | Kybean | 15 | Alma | 190 |
| Goolagong | 58 | Kydra | 17 | Blandford | 31 |
| Gosling Creek | 36 | | | | |
| Guyong | 43 | | | | |

| Name | No. on roll. | Name | No. on roll. | Name | No. on roll. |
|---|---|---|---|---|---|
| Boggabri | 136 | Gaspard | 21 | Cordeaux River | 20 |
| Bow Ridge | 10 | Jacob and Joseph Creek | 30 | Dapto | 50 |
| Bunnan | 13 | M'Donald's Creek | 34 | ,, West | 48 |
| Bylong | 14 | Mount Parnell | 27 | Elmwood | 38 |
| Collaroy | 12 | Narraburra | 22 | Five Islands | 24 |
| Cox's Gap | 15 | Quipolly | 26 | Fountaindale | 26 |
| Cuan | 15 | ,, Creek | 43 | Fox Ground | 40 |
| Denman | 83 | Quirindi | 180 | Gerringong | 96 |
| Donald's Creek | 20 | Spring Ridge | 19 | Glen Hill | 18 |
| Ellerston | 21 | Tamarang | 34 | Gondarin Creek | 24 |
| Glen Dhu | 17 | Wallabadah | 54 | Greendale | 32 |
| Gundy | 21 | Warrah | 25 | Harley Hill | 51 |
| Harben Vale | 30 | Werris Creek | 52 | Helensburgh | 133 |
| Harparary | 24 | Willow Tree | 51 | High Range | 11 |
| Isis River | 17 | | | Hill Top | 26 |
| Kellick | 20 | **Buller, County of.** | | Illaroo | 23 |
| Merriwa | 44 | Acacia Creek | 33 | Innescliff | 19 |
| Moonan Brook | 40 | ,, Dam | 63 | Jamberoo | 130 |
| ,, Flat | 21 | Boonoo Boonoo | 24 | Jellore | 24 |
| Murrurundi | 166 | Maryland | 28 | Jerrunga | 39 |
| Middle Creek | 26 | Murragang | 14 | Joadja | 116 |
| Mount Mooby | 42 | Tabulam | 25 | Jooriland | 10 |
| Nandowra | 20 | Tooloom | 24 | Kangaloon East | 42 |
| Owen's Gap | 22 | Warwick | 9 | ,, West | 49 |
| Oxley | 47 | | | Kangaroo River | 14 |
| Page's Creek | 12 | **Camden, County of.** | | ,, Valley | 69 |
| ,, River | 18 | Albion Park | 49 | Kiama | 292 |
| Parkville | 33 | Balmoral | 33 | Killawarra | 55 |
| Redwell | 18 | Barber's Creek | 21 | Lakelands | 18 |
| Rosemount | 9 | Burgo | 28 | Malundi | 12 |
| Scone | 138 | Barrengarry | 55 | Manchester Square | 22 |
| St. Helena | 19 | Balgownie | 171 | Mandemar | 18 |
| Timor | 15 | Belanglo | 28 | Marshall Mount | 58 |
| Turonville | 16 | Berrima | 93 | Meryla | 20 |
| Wentworth | 203 | ,, Colliery | 24 | Milton | 149 |
| Wingen | 18 | Bolong | 19 | Minnamurra | 59 |
| Wollar | 27 | Bembalaway | 28 | Mittagong | 265 |
| Wybong Creek | 20 | Bellawangarah | 33 | ,, Lower | 23 |
| ,, Upper | 11 | Bendella | 19 | ,, Upper | 34 |
| | | Berkeley | 26 | ,, Cottage Homes | 74 |
| **Buccleuch, County of.** | | Bomaderry | 31 | Moss Vale | 127 |
| Blowering | 43 | Bowral | 325 | Mount Hunter | 60 |
| Bowbowlee | 24 | Brookfield | 39 | ,, Keira | 254 |
| Gocup | 40 | Broughton Vale | 25 | ,, Kembla | 166 |
| Goobarralong | 39 | ,, Village | 23 | ,, Murray | 23 |
| Kimo | 19 | Budjong | 21 | Mullet Creek | 16 |
| Lacmalac | 32 | ,, Vale | 27 | Oakdale | 31 |
| Mount Adrah | 15 | Bulli | 205 | Omega Retreat | 51 |
| Mundong | 51 | Bulli Mountain | 28 | Picton | 178 |
| Pine Mount | 18 | ,, North | 84 | Razorback | 19 |
| Shepherdston | 91 | Bundanoon | 71 | Ringwood | 23 |
| | | Burragorang | 24 | Robertson | 87 |
| **Buckland, County of.** | | Burrawang | 97 | Robbinsville | 154 |
| Blackville | 44 | Burrier | 26 | Shellharbour | 90 |
| Breeza | 49 | Cambewarra | 100 | Spaniard's Hill | 42 |
| Bundella | 22 | Cambewarra West | 41 | Springborough | 29 |
| Castle Mountain | 37 | Camden | 188 | St. Joseph's | 23 |
| Chilcot Plains | 7 | Caoura | 8 | Stockyard Mountain | 27 |
| Colly Blue | 35 | Cawdor | 45 | Sutton Forest | 70 |
| Currabubula | 77 | Chalkerville | 20 | Thirlmere | 47 |
| Doughboy Hollow | 45 | Clifton Hill | 16 | Tongarra | 23 |
| Duri | 14 | Cobbitty | 20 | Toolejoon | 36 |
| Fairview | 36 | Comarong | 28 | Tullinbar | 60 |

## GEOGRAPHICAL ENCYCLOPÆDIA,

| | No. on roll. | | No. on roll. | | No. on roll. |
|---|---|---|---|---|---|
| Unanderra | 103 | Toothill | 18 | Clive | 18 |
| Walangur | | Towallum | 19 | Cowper | 91 |
| Wattamolla | 25 | Tyndale | 43 | Cranebrook | 71 |
| Wild's Meadow | 40 | Ulmarra | 135 | Goolmanger | 18 |
| Williamswood | 17 | „ Lower | 28 | Graham | 18 |
| Wilton | 53 | Urara | 17 | Groombridge Swamp | 42 |
| Werombi | 25 | Whiteman's Creek | 37 | Hill Crest | 30 |
| Werriberri | 29 | Winegrove | 23 | Lawson | 35 |
| Wollongong | 549 | Woolgoolgah | 23 | Leech's Gully | 46 |
| Woodhill | 48 | Yamba | 43 | Perth | 53 |
| Woonoona | 326 | | | Sandy Hill | 18 |
| Wingello | 19 | **Clarendon, County of.** | | Steinbrook | 40 |
| Yarrawah | 24 | Bethungra | 25 | Sunnyside | 47 |
| Yarrunga | 62 | Bloomfield | 9 | Tarrington | 50 |
| | | Blowclear | 16 | The Gulf | 15 |
| **Clarence, County of.** | | Boree | 24 | | |
| | | Brucedale | 19 | **Cook, County of.** | |
| Alum Creek | 21 | Bulga Hut | 18 | Anarel | 31 |
| Bucca Creek | 14 | Burnthut Creek | 18 | Black Heath | 85 |
| Buccurumbi | 19 | Bute | 34 | Bowenfells | 61 |
| Burragan | 47 | Burra | 16 | Brewongle | 56 |
| Caunk's Creek | 13 | Collengullia | 19 | Capertee | 9 |
| Carr's Creek | 71 | Cooba Creek | 18 | Cheetham Flats | 21 |
| Chatswood Island | 135 | Currawurra | 30 | Colo Central, No. 1 | 11 |
| Coaldale | 17 | Edwardstown | 54 | „ No. 2 | 12 |
| Coldstream Lower | 26 | Elong Elong | 17 | Cooerwull | 77 |
| „ Upper | 42 | Gundagai | 133 | Duddawarra | 23 |
| Copmanhurst | 82 | „ South | 98 | Emu | 118 |
| Corindi | 18 | Gwynne | 23 | Eskbank | 697 |
| Cowling | 30 | Harefield | 31 | Good Forest | 16 |
| Cowper | 91 | Illabo | 26 | Hartley | 32 |
| Dondymun | 48 | Ivor | 24 | „ Vale | 118 |
| Dorroughby Grass | 24 | Junee | 35 | Katoomba | 145 |
| Eatonville | 37 | „ Junction | 282 | Kurrajong North | 50 |
| Fern Glen | 22 | „ Reefs | 15 | „ South | 46 |
| Grafton | 717 | Kyamba | 15 | Kierson | 25 |
| „ South | 211 | Mitta Mitta | 33 | Lawson | 35 |
| Harwood Island | 120 | Nangus Creek | 18 | „ Creek | 30 |
| Iluka | 45 | Sam's Corner | 18 | Lowther | 18 |
| Lavadia | 25 | Sebastopol | 23 | Marangaroo | 39 |
| Lawrence | 121 | Wagga Wagga | 581 | Meroo | 49 |
| „ Lower | 44 | „ North | 109 | Mount Victoria | 72 |
| Maclean | 184 | Wagragobilly | 23 | Off Flat | 24 |
| Maryvale | 65 | Yathella | 23 | Piper's Flat | 43 |
| Micalo Island | 18 | | | Rydal | 51 |
| Morora | 38 | **Clarke, County of.** | | Springwood | 72 |
| Myrtle Creek | 24 | Avondale | 41 | Thorpe's Pinch | 45 |
| O.B.X. Creek | 21 | Big Hill | 20 | Wallerawang | 164 |
| Pimlico North | 43 | Chandler's Peak | 17 | Wentworth Falls | 25 |
| Pulginbar Creek | 17 | Everett | 25 | Woodford Dale | 52 |
| Ramornie | 54 | Falls The | 25 | „ Leigh | 62 |
| Red Rock | 22 | Kyanda | 27 | | |
| Rushford | 26 | Marengo | 52 | **Cowley, County of.** | |
| Seelands | 40 | Mitchell | 223 | Cavan | 20 |
| Small's Forest | 28 | | | Kiandra | 19 |
| South Arm | 59 | **Clive, County of.** | | Mullion Creek | 25 |
| Southgate | 82 | Amosfield | 41 | | |
| „ Lower | 28 | Ballandean | 15 | **Cumberland, County of.** | |
| Stiark Creek | 22 | Black Swamp | 27 | *Schools within the City of Sydney.* | |
| Stockyard Creek | 32 | Bolivia | 23 | | |
| Strontian Park | 33 | Border Sawmills | 20 | Albion-street | 478 |
| Stuart Town | 79 | Bryan's Gap | 60 | Blackfriars | 1219 |
| Tatham | 32 | Bluff River | 18 | | |
| Taloumbi | 58 | | | | |

## NEW SOUTH WALES.

| | No. on roll. | | No. on roll. | | No on Roll. |
|---|---|---|---|---|---|
| Castlereagh-street | 322 | Darlington | 896 | Marsden Park | 48 |
| Cleveland-street | 1390 | Darling Road | 1238 | Menangle | 30 |
| Crown-street | 1563 | Double Bay | 96 | Minto | 54 |
| Darlinghurst | 612 | Douglas | 25 | Mona Vale | 21 |
| Fort-street | 1441 | Druitt Town | 172 | Mortdale | 67 |
| Macquarie-street, South | 506 | Drummoyne | 160 | Mortlake | 105 |
|    ,,    Lower | 371 | Dulwich | 289 | Moorfield | 74 |
| Plunkett-street | 317 | Dural | 59 | Mossman's Bay | 112 |
| Pyrmont | 650 | Dural, Upper | 27 | Mulgoa | 51 |
| Surry Hills, South | 1280 | Eastwood | 52 | ,, Forest | 27 |
| Sussex-street | 373 | Ebenezer | 33 | ,, Mountain | 21 |
| Sydney Grammar School | 526 | Enmore | 714 | Narrabeen | 27 |
| Ultimo | 672 | Erina | 32 | Narellan | 85 |
| William-street | 832 | Erskine Park | 37 | Narembern | 200 |
| Riley-street | 250 | Exeter Farm | 22 | Nelson | 42 |
| | | Fairfield | 137 | Neutral Bay | 235 |
| | | Five Dock | 101 | Newport | 45 |
| *Beyond the City boundaries.* | | Forest Lodge | 763 | Newtown | 1244 |
| | | Freeman's Reach | 78 | ,, North | 518 |
| Annandale | 810 | Galston | 54 | Nicholson-st., Balmain | 300 |
| Appin | 60 | Gardener's Road | 242 | North Rocks | 26 |
| Arncliffe | 223 | Gentleman's Halt | 27 | Paddington | 1252 |
| Ashfield | 744 | Gladesville | 126 | Parramatta, North | 875 |
| Australia-st., Newtown | 158 | Glebe | 1217 | ,, South | 734 |
| Avoca Vale | 33 | Gledswood | 21 | Pennant Hills | 109 |
| Balgowlah | 41 | Glenfield | 46 | Penrith | 585 |
| Balmain | 1066 | Glenmore | 35 | Petersham | 906 |
| Baulkham Hills | 41 | ,, Road | 384 | Peakhurst | 87 |
| Banks Meadow | 108 | Gordon | 64 | Pitrow | 234 |
| Bankstown | 130 | Goughtown | 49 | Pitt Town | 108 |
| Barrenjoey | 26 | Granville | 400 | Pittwater | 47 |
| Beaconsfield | 19 | ,, North | 400 | Portland, Lower | 39 |
| Belmore | 47 | ,, South | 369 | Prospect | 123 |
| Bexley | 177 | Green Valley | 39 | Randwick | 330 |
| Birchgrove | 811 | Greenwich | 67 | Redfern | 1316 |
| Blacktown | 84 | ,, Park | 21 | ,, West | 486 |
| Blakehurst | 54 | Guildford | 32 | Regentville | 41 |
| Botany | 241 | Hawkesbury, Lower | 14 | Richmond | 280 |
| ,, Heads | 13 | Heathcote | 52 | ,, North | 66 |
| Bondi | 221 | Holdsworthy | 35 | Richmond Vale | 31 |
| Bringelly | 28 | Hoxton Park | 51 | Riverstone | 145 |
| Brooklyn | 42 | Homebush | 151 | Rockdale | 520 |
| Brookvale | 27 | Hornsby | 66 | Rookwood | 233 |
| Bulgo | 35 | Hornsby Junction | 95 | Rose Hill | 42 |
| Burwood | 887 | Hurlstone | 170 | Rooty Hill | 57 |
| Buttsworth Swamp | 18 | Hunter's Hill | 91 | Rouse Hill | 52 |
| Camdenville | 566 | Ing'eburn | 55 | Ryde | 325 |
| Campbelltown | 162 | Ingliswald | 22 | ,, North | 60 |
| Camperdown | 720 | Johnson's Creek | 21 | Sackville Reach | 40 |
| Canley Vale | 65 | Kegworth | 436 | Sandhurst | 32 |
| Canterbury | 325 | Kellyville | 41 | Sandringham | 77 |
| Carlingford | 189 | Kenthurst | 41 | Seven Hills | 97 |
| Castle Hill | 89 | Kogarah | 355 | Skinner's Creek | 21 |
| Castlereagh, Upper | 47 | Laughtendale | 41 | Smith-street, Balmain | 640 |
| Charleville | 27 | Leichhardt | 972 | Smithfield | 187 |
| Chatswood | 94 | ,, West | 344 | Stanmore | 761 |
| Claremont | 23 | Liverpool | 426 | St. Ives | 61 |
| Clifton | 131 | Longueville | 38 | St. Leonards | 1004 |
| Colinton | 20 | Luddenham | 58 | ,, East | 359 |
| Concord | 125 | Macdonaldtown | 1234 | ,, North | 179 |
| Coogee | 89 | Manly | 274 | St. Mary's | 258 |
| Cornwallis | 20 | Marota | 34 | St. Peter's | 654 |
| Croydon | 427 | Marrickville | 640 | Summer Hill | 481 |
| Croydon Park | 283 | ,, West | 448 | Sutherland | 74 |

Y

338  GEOGRAPHICAL ENCYCLOPÆDIA,

| Place | No. on roll. | Place | No. on roll. | Place | No. on roll. |
|---|---|---|---|---|---|
| Sutton Forest | 70 | Dongdingalong | 26 | Pipeclay Creek | 38 |
| Sydney, North | 127 | Frederickton | 153 | Putty | 25 |
| Tempe | 384 | George's Creek | 28 | Quaroobolong | 22 |
| Theresa Park | 41 | Gladstone | 118 | Ravensworth | 42 |
| Toongabbie | 59 | Kempsey East | 129 | " North | 25 |
| Vineyard | 32 | " West | 243 | Rix's Creek | 43 |
| Waterloo | 695 | Seven Oaks | 130 | Rouchel | 35 |
| Watson's Bay | 100 | Toorooka | 26 | " Vale | 17 |
| Waverley | 790 | Turner's Flat | 40 | Seaham | 58 |
| Wilberforce | 78 | Warne | 35 | Sedgefield | 22 |
| Windsor | 396 | Yarrahapinni | 25 | Stanhope | 38 |
| Woollahra | 899 | | | Stewart's Brook | 8 |
| Yarramundi | 61 | **Durham, County of.** | | Sugarloaf Creek | 42 |
| | | Aberdeen | 39 | Vacy | 48 |
| **Dampier, County of.** | | Avenal | 29 | Wallalong | 92 |
| | | Atherton | 2 | William Town | 73 |
| Belowra | 37 | Bandon Grove | 41 | Worrowolong | 15 |
| Bermagui | 46 | Belltrees | 33 | Wortwell | 17 |
| Bodalla | 45 | Belmont | 49 | | |
| Coolagolite | 14 | Benbolba | 53 | **Fitzroy, County of.** | |
| Curin Creek | 11 | Big Creek | 12 | | |
| Eurobodalla | 30 | Bowman's Creek | 10 | Beresford | 29 |
| Moggendoura | 17 | Brushy Hill | 24 | Comleroy Road | 77 |
| Moruya | 145 | Campsie | 24 | Coramba | 19 |
| Mumbulla | 28 | Carrabolla | 15 | Ermington | 69 |
| Nerrigundah | 36 | Carroll | 38 | Gunbar | 48 |
| Noorooma | 33 | Carrow Brook | 19 | Nymboida | 32 |
| Quaama | 38 | Clairwood | 19 | Shannon Vale | 31 |
| Snaphook | 20 | Clarence Town | 153 | Sherwood | 66 |
| Tanja | 31 | Colstown | 20 | | |
| Tilba Tilba | 40 | Croome | 53 | **Georgiana, County of.** | |
| Wagonga | 6 | " Park | 12 | | |
| Walluga Lake | 21 | Cross Creek | 10 | Aliwal | 31 |
| Wapengo | 15 | Darlington Point | 21 | Apsley Grange | 14 |
| | | Davis' Creek | 20 | Bigga | 14 |
| **Darling, County of.** | | Dungog | 182 | Binda | 30 |
| | | Dunmore | 107 | Boolong | 30 |
| Barraba | 71 | Dunsadie | 26 | Bundarigo | 25 |
| Bell's Mountain | 22 | Eagleton | 36 | Burrago Bow | 69 |
| Cluri | 21 | Eccleston | 23 | Chain of Ponds | 26 |
| Colouna | 25 | Falbrook | 25 | Cordillera | 112 |
| Hall's Creek | 41 | Falbrook Middle | 31 | Crookwell | 136 |
| Hawarden | 23 | Glendon Brook | 47 | " River | 24 |
| Keepit | 8 | Glen William | 53 | Curran's Creek | 14 |
| Manilla | 94 | Gourangoola | 23 | Diamond | 8 |
| " Upper | 42 | Gresford | 83 | " Swamp | 22 |
| Ukolan | 24 | Hinton | 133 | Eagle Vale | 20 |
| Wilson | 15 | Iona | 78 | Irishtown | 36 |
| Wongan Creek | 20 | Kayuga | 34 | Julong | 13 |
| | | Karrabee | 27 | Laggan | 37 |
| **Drake, County o.** | | Kimbriki | 29 | Leighwood | 16 |
| | | Kirkton | 57 | Memundie | 23 |
| Drake | 145 | Lostock | 50 | Mount Costigan | 71 |
| Dunbar's Creek | 24 | Miller's Forest | 71 | Mount Lawson | 29 |
| Gerrymberryn | 52 | Mount Rivers | 34 | Myanga Creek | 11 |
| Glenreagh | 35 | Mount Thorley | 24 | Peelwood | 33 |
| Kangaroo Creek | 11 | Munni | 28 | Redground | 17 |
| Pretty Gully | 14 | Muscle Creek | 13 | Rockley | 90 |
| Solferino | 23 | Musclebrook | 194 | Streamville | 16 |
| | | Nelson's Plains | 55 | Thalaba | 67 |
| **Dudley, County of.** | | Oakendale | 39 | Tuena | 52 |
| | | Oak Park | 17 | Victoria Flat | 25 |
| Aldavilla | 43 | Paterson | 105 | Wallbrook | 18 |
| Clybucca | 17 | | | Wowagin | 17 |

| | No. on roll. | | No. on roll. | | No. on roll. |
|---|---|---|---|---|---|
| **Gloucester, County of.** | | Suntop | 24 | Sutton | 31 |
| Aliceton | 8 | Terra Belle | 36 | Talmalmo | 28 |
| Barrington | 47 | Warraderry | 21 | Thurgoona | 73 |
| Bo Bo Creek | 20 | Yeoval | 31 | Wagra | 33 |
| Boolambayte | 12 | Yullundry | 19 | Woomargama | 32 |
| Booral | 47 | | | Yambla | 25 |
| Bulladelah | 68 | **Gough, County of.** | | | |
| Bungwall Flat | 36 | Airlie Brake | 11 | **Gresham, County of.** | |
| Burraduc | 40 | Beardy | 33 | Ermington | 69 |
| Chichester | 34 | „ Bridge | 20 | Guy Fawkes | 15 |
| Clareval | 21 | Beaufort | 39 | Marenga | 52 |
| Clarkson's Crossing | 54 | Ben Lomond | 16 | Oakwood | 42 |
| Coolongolook | 45 | Big Plains | 17 | | |
| Copeland North | 54 | Brodie's Plains | 50 | **Harden, County of.** | |
| Crawford River | 26 | Brookside | 25 | Barwang | 21 |
| Cucumbark | 31 | Clairvaulx | 20 | Beggan Beggan | 21 |
| Darawank | 28 | Clear Bank | 17 | Berremangra | 21 |
| Eurunderee | 33 | Deepwater | 75 | Binalong | 37 |
| Forster | 57 | Dundee | 42 | Bongongo | 17 |
| „ North | 38 | Emmaville | 232 | Bongongalony | 20 |
| Fullerton Cove | 52 | Fernhill | 41 | Bookham | 20 |
| Girvan | 19 | Fladbury | 20 | Bowning | 71 |
| Glenora | 21 | Glencoe | 28 | Burra Creek | 13 |
| Gloucester | 21 | Glen Innes | 335 | Burrowa Flats | 21 |
| Hannah Bay | 23 | Goonoowigal | 64 | Caulderwood | 20 |
| Koribahk | 30 | Gough Town | 49 | Chidowla | 17 |
| Larry's Flat | 52 | Graham's Valley | 21 | Congera | 19 |
| Limeburner's Creek | 17 | Inverell | 352 | Cooney | 18 |
| Malvern | 20 | Mitchell | 223 | Cootamundra | 220 |
| Mondrook | 27 | Mount Mitchell | 30 | Coolac | 49 |
| Monkerai | 35 | Mount Russell | 20 | Cungegong | 30 |
| Myall Upper | 19 | Newstead | 29 | „ North | 12 |
| Raymond Terrace | 163 | Nine Mile | 37 | Cunningar | 34 |
| Rosenthal | 36 | Paradise | 25 | Demondrille | 42 |
| Seal Rocks | 12 | Pond's Creek | 32 | Derringullen | 30 |
| Stockton | 446 | Red Range | 61 | Good Hope | 23 |
| Sutton | 31 | Round Mount | 21 | Jindalee | 36 |
| Nelson's Bay | 15 | Sapphire | 17 | „ West | 34 |
| Nerong | 15 | Scone | 138 | Jugiong | 49 |
| Stroud | 89 | Stannifer | 63 | Khahangan | 21 |
| Tea Gardens | 24 | Staggy Creek | 22 | King Vale | 28 |
| Thalabah | 67 | Stonehenge | 61 | Lang's Creek | 19 |
| Tinonee | 33 | Swanbrook | 20 | Mooney Mooney | 21 |
| Valla | 15 | Swanvale | 30 | Moppity | 16 |
| Wallamba Lower | 38 | Wandera | 15 | Murrumboola | 25 |
| Ward's River | 21 | Wellingrove | 18 | Murrumburrah | 164 |
| | | Willow Grove | 24 | Muttama | 37 |
| | | Yarraford | 27 | Nimby | 14 |
| **Gordon, County of.** | | | | Nubba | 71 |
| Arthurville | 21 | | | Nurung | 20 |
| Baker's Swamp | 37 | **Goulburn, County of.** | | Pudman Creek | 42 |
| Belmore | 47 | Albury | 616 | Tanginangaroo | 39 |
| Burrawong Station | 9 | Bell's Lagoon | 21 | Wallendbeen | 37 |
| Cullen | 36 | Black Range | 34 | Watson's Reef | 55 |
| Curra Creek | 24 | Bowna | 50 | | |
| Dubbo | 351 | Burrumbuttock | 43 | **Hardinge, County of.** | |
| Greenbank | 14 | Clear Hill | 22 | Bell Brook | 8 |
| Gundy | 21 | Daisydale | 11 | Buchanan | 50 |
| Killeigh | 24 | Germanton | 79 | Bundarra | 75 |
| Little River | 59 | Gerogery | 19 | Cameron's Creek | 22 |
| Newrea | 24 | „ railway st'n. | 25 | Demondrille Junction | 44 |
| Obley | 17 | Huon | 26 | Digby | 20 |
| Oxley | 47 | Jindera | 40 | Haystack | 27 |
| Ponto | 17 | Khancoban | 10 | Honeysuckle Springs | 22 |
| Rocky Ponds | 27 | Mullungandra | 23 | | |

| Name | No. on roll | Name | No. on roll | Name | No. on roll |
|---|---|---|---|---|---|
| Kilrush | 32 | Grabben Gullen | 33 | Mount George | 24 |
| Loch End | 72 | Gunnary | 17 | Narani | 33 |
| Mount Drummond | 19 | ,, Creek | 18 | Oxley Island | 67 |
| New Valley | 29 | Gunning | 122 | Port Macquarie | 169 |
| Ollera | 25 | Hovell | 36 | Rawdon Island | 64 |
| Pee Dee | 23 | Jeir | 29 | Rolland's Plains | 24 |
| Sandy Creek | 23 | Jerrara | 42 | Stewart's River | 11 |
| Springs | 22 | Kentgrove | 41 | Summer Island | 91 |
| Stanborough | 19 | Last River | 25 | Taree | 174 |
| Stonybatter | 22 | Manton | 25 | Telegraph Point | 15 |
| Tenterden | 31 | Merrill Creek | 20 | Wingham | 143 |
| Tingha | 172 | Mugwill | 36 | | |
| Wandsworth | 26 | Mullengrove | 22 | **Monteagle, County of.** | |
| Woolshed | 19 | Mundoonen | 21 | | |
| Yarrowick | 35 | Nanama | 23 | Amaroo | 37 |
| | | Narrawa | 25 | Aramagong | 20 |
| **Hawes, County of.** | | Nelanglo | 29 | Barbagal | 27 |
| | | Rye Park | 59 | Barbingal | 17 |
| Mummell | 29 | Smelley's Lagoon | 19 | Bendick Murrell | 24 |
| Myalla | 20 | Taylor's Flat | 20 | Bimbi | 16 |
| | | Toual | 14 | Bullock Creek | 33 |
| **Hunter, County of.** | | Waggallalah | 31 | Burrangong | 51 |
| | | Wargela | 27 | ,, Heights | 50 |
| Doyle's Creek | 4 | Winduella | 31 | Calabash | 19 |
| Jerry's Plains | 75 | Yamburra West | 27 | Cocomingla | 19 |
| Neilson's Creek | 17 | Yass | 159 | Cudgell Creek | 27 |
| Warkworth | 54 | | | Geegullalong | 23 |
| | | | | Grenfell | 240 |
| **Inglis, County of.** | | **Macquarie, County of.** | | Koorawatha | 52 |
| | | Arakoon | 28 | Marina | 24 |
| Attunga | 36 | Ashlea | 33 | M'Henry's Creek | 52 |
| ,, Springs | 38 | Ballengarra | 36 | Memagong | 20 |
| Bell's Swamp | 29 | Beechwood | 33 | Mitten's Creek | 35 |
| Bendemeer | 61 | Blackman's Point | 57 | Monteagle | 42 |
| Bonavista | 21 | Brombin | 42 | Rossi | 21 |
| Cockburn River | 40 | Bulga | 39 | Thuddungra | 26 |
| Kentucky | 33 | Callaghan's Creek | 25 | Wambanumba | 34 |
| Maluerindi | 31 | Camden Haven | 44 | Warrangong | 25 |
| Moonbi | 19 | ,, ,, Crossing | 14 | Warronui | 20 |
| Somarton | 15 | Cattai Creek | 30 | Wanchope | 78 |
| Tara | 17 | Cedar Party Creek | 31 | Weddin | 26 |
| Tintinhull | 44 | Cogo | 32 | Wombat | 60 |
| | | Coopernook | 78 | Woodonga | 27 |
| **King, County of.** | | Croki | 70 | Young | 508 |
| | | Cundletown | 96 | | |
| Bango | 14 | Dingo Creek | 42 | **Murray, County of.** | |
| Bendenine | 58 | Ellenborough | 10 | | |
| Berebangelo | 29 | Forbes River | 10 | Brook's Creek | 28 |
| Brewer's Flat | 19 | Ghinni Ghinni | 33 | Bungendore | 94 |
| Broughtonsworth | 18 | Glenthorne | 25 | Canberra | 23 |
| Burrowa | 78 | Green Hills | 22 | Captain's Flat | 134 |
| Blakney Creek | 21 | Hanging Rock | 45 | Carwoola | 21 |
| Boambola | 22 | Harrington | 15 | Eualdrie | 13 |
| Clonalton | 18 | Hastings, Upper | 18 | Fairy Meadow | 102 |
| Cottawalla | 34 | Jasper's Brush | 87 | Foxton | 17 |
| Crookwell | 136 | John's River | 26 | Gibraltar | 26 |
| Cullarin | 27 | Kikiamah | 21 | Gidleigh | 14 |
| Digger's Flat | 13 | Killobahk | 23 | Ginnindera | 30 |
| Drofwall | 31 | Koppin Yarratt | 39 | Glenwood | 29 |
| Elizabethfield | 19 | Landsdowne | 22 | Googong | 21 |
| Euralie | 24 | Laurieton | 46 | Gundaroo | 31 |
| Felled-timber Creek | 23 | Lonely Point | 8 | Gungahleen | 29 |
| Ferncliffe | 22 | Marlee | 29 | Inglewood Forest | 22 |
| Flowerburn | 24 | Mitchell's Flat | 50 | Jerrabutgulla | 22 |
| Frogmore | 67 | ,, Island | 57 | Keewong | 20 |
| Gooda Creek | 27 | | | | |

NEW SOUTH WALES.                                              341

| | No. on roll. | | No. on roll. | | No. on roll. |
|---|---|---|---|---|---|
| Kowen | 21 | Halton | 28 | Wickham | 970 |
| Mayfield | 30 | Hamilton | 673 | Wiseman's Ferry | 47 |
| Molonglo | 22 | Hanbury | 321 | Wyong | 75 |
| Murrumbateman | 38 | Hay | 323 | ,, Creek | 25 |
| New Line East | 12 | Hexham | 91 | Yango | 24 |
| Notherwono Lagoon | 13 | Horseshoe Bend | 133 | Yarramalong | 43 |
| Primrose Valley | 5 | Islington | 178 | | |
| Queanbeyan | 185 | Jilliby Jilliby | 25 | **Parry, County of.** | |
| Reidsdale | 23 | Jesmond | 215 | Bowling Alley Point | 66 |
| Rob Roy | 30 | Kangyangy | 33 | Duncan's Creek | 11 |
| Sawpit Gully | 18 | Kincumber | 41 | Dungowan Lower | 51 |
| South Lead | 40 | Laguna | 47 | ,, Upper | 16 |
| Stony Creek | 21 | Lambton | 571 | Goonoo Goonoo | 29 |
| ,, Lower | 21 | ,, New | 427 | Gowrie | 32 |
| Stony Pinch | 32 | Lochinvar | 54 | Grabham's Vineyard | 13 |
| Tallagandra | 19 | Mangrove Creek | 22 | Moor Creek | 42 |
| Tuggeranong | 39 | ,, Upper | 25 | Hanging Rock | 45 |
| Turlinjah | 21 | Maitland East | 386 | Nemingah | 49 |
| Urila | 18 | ,, West | 880 | Nundle | 95 |
| Wallaroo | 27 | Mandalong | 19 | Tamworth | 533 |
| Waterholes | 13 | M'Donald Central | 30 | ,, West | 255 |
| Weetangerra | 23 | ,, Lower | 17 | Turill | 29 |
| Werriwa | 11 | ,, Upper | 39 | Walcha | 162 |
| Williamsdale | 16 | Merannie | 39 | ,, Road | 26 |
| Woodfield | 22 | Millfield | 36 | Walhollow Forest | 20 |
| Yarmlumla | 25 | Minmi | 553 | Wombramurra | 24 |
| | | Morpeth | 168 | Wooloombin | 15 |
| | | Mosquito Island | 61 | Woolomol | 39 |
| **Northumberland, County of.** | | Mount Finch | 11 | Wooloban | 32 |
| Aberglasslyn | 66 | ,, View | 44 | | |
| Adamstown | 615 | Mulbring | 61 | **Phillip, County of.** | |
| Allandale | 30 | Narara | 41 | | |
| Ash Island | 62 | Newcastle | 752 | Bara Creek | 19 |
| Auburn | 445 | ,, East | 333 | Batobolar | 56 |
| Awaba | 15 | ,, South | 972 | Bayly | 25 |
| Bar Point | 18 | Northumberland | | Beryl | 25 |
| Belford | 32 | Colliery | 36 | Burrundulla | 46 |
| Bishop's Bridge | 56 | Oakhampton | 43 | Coggan | 13 |
| Black Hill | 29 | Ourimbah | 55 | Cooyal | 67 |
| Branxton | 77 | Pelican Island | 79 | Dabee | 15 |
| Broke | 35 | Plattsburgh | 729 | Dungaree | 44 |
| Brokenback | 68 | Pokolbin | 56 | Frome's Creek | 20 |
| Brownmuir | 19 | Rothbury | 46 | Gulf, The | 15 |
| Carrington | 289 | Roughit | 73 | Gulgong | 178 |
| Cessnock | 39 | St. Alban's | 55 | Guntawang | 55 |
| Charlestown | 192 | St. Ethel's | 221 | Hawkin's Creek | 51 |
| Cockle Creek | 21 | Simpson's Ridge | 36 | Honeysuckle Springs | 22 |
| Cook's Hill | 744 | Singleton | 532 | Mehah | 21 |
| Cooranbong | 22 | Swansea | 73 | Millsville | 26 |
| Dairy Arm | 16 | Sweetman's Creek | 23 | Mudgee | 600 |
| Dalton | 73 | Tarro | 20 | ,, South | 49 |
| Dora Creek | 42 | Tea Tree | 19 | Murragamba | 14 |
| Dunolly | 46 | Telegharry | 34 | Pyangle | 25 |
| Eglinford | 26 | Toralba | 60 | Tunnabutta | 29 |
| Eglington | 64 | Tighe's Hill | 352 | Warburton | 11 |
| Elderslei | 40 | Vere | 29 | Wiadra | 8 |
| Ellalong | 52 | Wallambine Creek | 22 | Wilbertree | 32 |
| Fassifern | 24 | Wallsend | 817 | Wilpinijong | 20 |
| Fishery Creek | 55 | Wallsend West | 86 | Wollar | 27 |
| Four-mile Creek | 28 | Wamberall | 22 | Wyaldra | 30 |
| Glassville | 28 | Waratah | 139 | | |
| Glen Mitchell | 193 | Warkworth | 54 | **Raleigh, County of.** | |
| Gosford | 136 | Wattagon | 24 | Argent's Hill | 20 |
| Gosforth | 45 | Welshman's Creek | 36 | Bellinger | 64 |
| Greta | 357 | Whittingham | 30 | | |

| | No. on roll | | No. on roll | | No. on roll |
|---|---|---|---|---|---|
| Bellinger South | 12 | Murwillumbah | 28 | Walang | 32 |
| ,, Heads | 33 | Never Never | 24 | Warrangunyah | 22 |
| Bonville | 10 | Pelican Creek | 19 | Wattle Flat | 91 |
| Bowra | 63 | Pimlico | 54 | Wheatfield | 13 |
| Buccrabandini | 27 | Point Danger | 29 | White Rock | 43 |
| Coff's Harbour | 13 | Runnymede | 22 | Wyagdon | 16 |
| Fernmount | 63 | Teven Creek | 20 | | |
| ,, South | 32 | Tintenbar | 44 | **Sandon, County of.** | |
| Nambucca | 52 | Tirranneah Creek | 54 | | |
| ,, Heads | 83 | Tomki | 43 | Armidale | 555 |
| ,, Lower | 21 | Tuckombil | 23 | Bell Flat | 7 |
| Oakes | 47 | Tumbulgum | 42 | Ben Lomond | 16 |
| Rainbow Reach | 29 | Wardell | 110 | Big Ridge | 31 |
| Raleigh | 59 | Whian Whian | 25 | Black Mountain | 70 |
| Taylor's Arm | 25 | Woodlawn | 20 | Blaxland's Flat | 14 |
| Warrell Creek | 19 | Wyrallah | 89 | Boorolong | 82 |
| | | | | Castle Doyle | 35 |
| **Richmond, County of.** | | **Roxburgh, County of.** | | Chandler | 12 |
| Ballina | 229 | | | Dangar's Lagoon | 22 |
| Brooklet | 25 | Arkstone | 11 | Dirrenanurra | 17 |
| Bungawalbiju | 36 | Ben Bullen | 31 | Donald | 26 |
| Casino | 192 | Bloomhill | 41 | Duval View | 35 |
| ,, South | 55 | Bradshaw's Flat | 22 | Eversleigh | 31 |
| Cumbalum | 26 | Brookstead | 25 | Everton Vale | 21 |
| Dungarubba | 33 | Camboon | 36 | Gainsborough | 11 |
| Irvington | 65 | Capertree | 9 | Gollorowong | 18 |
| Myrtle Creek | 24 | Carwell | 22 | Gostwych | 24 |
| New Italy | 40 | Clandulla | 21 | Hill Grove | 250 |
| North Creek | 31 | Coomber | 26 | Hill View | 26 |
| Oaklands | 39 | Crudine | 28 | Kelly's Plains | 41 |
| Palmer's Island | 72 | Cullen | 36 | Manuka | 26 |
| ,, ,, Lower | 37 | Dullaberry | 12 | May Vale | 28 |
| Pearce's Creek | 17 | Duramana | 50 | Mount Butler | 22 |
| Richmond | 280 | Fell Timber | 15 | Oban | 22 |
| Swan Creek | 54 | Flatlands | 10 | Pinch Flat | 28 |
| ,, Bay | 27 | Forest The | 33 | Puddledock | 12 |
| Tucki Tucki | 22 | German's Hill | 22 | Riley's Flat | 12 |
| Wooroowoolgan | 23 | Glanmire | 33 | Rocky River | 76 |
| | | Glen Alice | 23 | Salisbury | 30 |
| **Rous, County of.** | | Hollybrook | 20 | ,, Plains | 30 |
| | | Ilford | 37 | Salt Ash | 31 |
| Alstonville | 55 | Kelso | 66 | Saumerez | 68 |
| Bexhill | 36 | Kirkconnell | 40 | Sidebrook | 24 |
| Boggumbil | 36 | Limekilns | 27 | Sobraon | 16 |
| Broadwater | 117 | March | 32 | Spring Mount | 27 |
| Brook Park | 15 | M'Donald's Hole | 13 | Tilbuster | 22 |
| Brunswick River | 16 | Meadow Flat | 48 | Tipperary Gully | 43 |
| Bungabee | 14 | Narrango | 19 | Tiverton | 28 |
| Byangum | 17 | Neila Creek | 16 | Tullich | 11 |
| Byron Creek | 38 | O'Connell | 39 | Turkey Creek | 30 |
| Clunes | 40 | Paling Yards | 7 | Uralla | 128 |
| Codrington | 28 | Palmer's Oakey | 22 | Wallun | 23 |
| ,, North | 24 | Peel | 38 | Wirrialpa | 14 |
| Condong | 20 | Piper's Flat | 43 | Wollomambi | 15 |
| Cooper's Creek | 28 | Porters Retreat | 10 | Woodford | 12 |
| Coraki | 97 | Raglan | 40 | | |
| Cudgen | 42 | Rawdon | 16 | **Selwyn, County of.** | |
| Dunoon | 35 | Round Swamp | 26 | | |
| Goomellebah | 65 | Rylstone | 169 | Beaumont | 22 |
| Gordonville | 17 | Sally's Flat | 13 | Burra Lake | 33 |
| Gundurimba | 62 | Sofala | 56 | Cowra | 230 |
| Lismore | 338 | Tabrabucca East | 12 | Glenroy | 27 |
| M'Lean's Ridges | 54 | Tong Bong | 25 | Hay | 323 |
| Meerschaum Vale | 38 | Turon Upper | 13 | Jingellic East | 22 |
| Mullumbimby | 28 | Vincent's Hole | 22 | Ournic | 14 |

## NEW SOUTH WALES. 343

| | No. on roll. |
|---|---|
| Round Hill | 93 |
| Spring Flat | 22 |
| Tongaree | |
| Tooma | 19 |
| Tumberumba | 81 |

### St. Vincent, County of.

| | No. on roll. |
|---|---|
| Araluen | 65 |
| Araluen West | 49 |
| Back Creek | 14 |
| Ballalaba | 16 |
| Bamarang | 16 |
| Bateman's Bay | 70 |
| Benandarah | 26 |
| Berlang | 15 |
| Bergalia | 54 |
| Bettowynd | 10 |
| Bombay | 12 |
| Braidwood | 191 |
| Broonan | 25 |
| Buckendoon | 44 |
| Burrill | 38 |
| Burry | 17 |
| Cararawell | 12 |
| Charleyong | 29 |
| Clydesdale | 10 |
| Conjola | 34 |
| Coolangatta | 71 |
| Corang River | 14 |
| Corindah | 23 |
| Croobyar | 54 |
| Cullendulla | 21 |
| Currowan | 14 |
| ,, Creek | 11 |
| Deua River | 9 |
| Durran Durrah | 17 |
| Durras | 18 |
| East Lynne | 7 |
| Falls, The | 25 |
| Farnham | 31 |
| Farringdon | 24 |
| Greenwell Point | 41 |
| Harold's Cross | 12 |
| Huskisson, North | 22 |
| Januang | 13 |
| Janugarrah | 10 |
| Jembaicumbene | 47 |
| Jinglemoney | 14 |
| Kiola | 25 |
| Larbert | 11 |
| Limekilns | 27 |
| Major's Creek | 100 |
| Meangora | 16 |
| Mogo | 57 |
| Monga | 24 |
| Mudbury Creek | 22 |
| Mudmelong | 0 |
| Nelligen | 58 |
| Nerriga | 32 |
| New Bristol | 8 |
| Nowra | 228 |
| Numba | 38 |
| Packwood | 27 |
| Reedy Creek | 29 |

| | No. on roll. |
|---|---|
| Riley | 12 |
| Pyree | 83 |
| Sassafrass | 25 |
| Shallow Crossing | 15 |
| Six-mile Flat | 17 |
| Tallagandra | 27 |
| Termeil | 23 |
| Tomaga | 31 |
| Tomerong | 49 |
| Ulladulla | 79 |
| Woodburn | 107 |
| Woola Woola | 23 |
| Worragee | 42 |
| Yalwal | 28 |
| Yatteyattah | 48 |
| Yerriyong | 51 |

### Vernon, County of.

| | No. on roll. |
|---|---|
| Branga | 36 |
| Cockatoo Flat | 29 |
| Emu | 118 |
| Glen Arm | 12 |
| Glen Morrison | 45 |
| Hartford | 23 |
| Manie's Creek | 36 |
| Moona | 30 |
| Norton | 29 |
| Orundumbi | 23 |
| Tia | 33 |
| Ugly Range | 19 |
| Walcha | 162 |
| Walcha Road | 26 |
| Yarrowitch | 35 |

### Wallace, County of.

| | No. on roll. |
|---|---|
| Adaminiby | 91 |
| Alumn Creek | 49 |
| Arable | 33 |
| Bolairo | 14 |
| Buckley's Crossing | 16 |
| Bulgundra | 15 |
| Caddigat | 22 |
| Cootralanta | 27 |
| Dalgetty | 37 |
| Eaglehawk | 37 |
| Forest Hill | 30 |
| Gordon | 64 |
| Gundillon | 12 |
| Hemsby | 9 |
| Ingebyra | 13 |
| Jimenbuan | 16 |
| Jindabine | 28 |
| Jinden | 11 |
| Kiandra | 43 |
| Longfield | 28 |
| Middlingbank | 33 |
| Mitchell | 223 |
| Moonbah | 23 |
| Murroo | 36 |
| Myalla | 20 |
| Numbla | 14 |
| Oak Vale | 16 |
| Paupong | 22 |

| | No. on roll. |
|---|---|
| Rock Villa | 29 |
| Rocky Hall | 36 |
| ,, Plain | 29 |
| Square Range | 25 |
| Wallgrove | 49 |
| Wilson | 15 |

### Wellesley, County of.

| | No. on roll. |
|---|---|
| Bibbenluke | 40 |
| Bombala | 152 |
| Brown's Camp | 26 |
| Burrembooka | 27 |
| Catheart | 59 |
| Craigie | 44 |
| Currowang | 58 |
| Delegate | 34 |
| Glenbog | 38 |
| Glenroy | 27 |
| Gulargambone | 35 |
| Jettiba | 25 |
| Killarney Swamp | 28 |
| Lawson | 35 |
| Lord's Hill | 33 |
| Maharatta | 34 |
| Mila | 22 |
| Nelbothery | 23 |
| Nelson | 42 |
| Nimitabel | 56 |
| Pipeclay Spring | 26 |
| Saucy Creek | 25 |
| Tarrabandra | 19 |
| Tombong | 17 |
| Wallendibby | 10 |
| Wellesley | 22 |

### Wellington, County of.

| | No. on roll. |
|---|---|
| Avisford | 15 |
| Ballimore | 11 |
| Belgravia | 32 |
| Beri | 21 |
| Bocoble | 17 |
| Boomey | 16 |
| Boorenore | 57 |
| Box Ridge | 27 |
| Bridgewater | 22 |
| Brokenshaft Creek | 22 |
| Bulbudgerie | 30 |
| Burrendong | 12 |
| Campbell's Creek | 10 |
| ,, ,, Upper | 25 |
| Carroll | 38 |
| Catombel | 13 |
| Charleville | 14 |
| Coffey Hill | 26 |
| Collingwood | 14 |
| Combo | 8 |
| Comobella | 9 |
| Coolaman | 41 |
| Cudgegong | 55 |
| Cullenbone | 37 |
| Cundumbul | 39 |
| Dun Dun | 10 |
| Forbes | 425 |
| Galwadgere | 28 |

|  | No. on roll. |  | No. on roll. |  | No. on roll. |
|---|---|---|---|---|---|
| Garra | 53 | Pyramul Lower | 8 | Alfred Town | 27 |
| Gowing Run | 12 | Spicer's Creek | 22 | Bago | 19 |
| Grattai | 21 | Store Creek | 15 | Batlow | 44 |
| Gulgamree | 40 | Tambaroora | 69 | Belmore River | 21 |
| Gulgowra | 18 | Towac | 17 | ,, ,, Upper | 27 |
| Hargraves | 45 | Wellington | 226 | Clearmont | 30 |
| Havilah | 14 | Windeyer | 54 | Courabyra | 27 |
| Hill End | 198 | Windora | 16 | Currawananna | 30 |
| Kangaroo Flat | 17 | World's End | 20 | Downside | 34 |
| Kerr's Creek | 25 |  |  | Ferndale | 35 |
| Leaning Oak | 21 | **Westmoreland, County of.** |  | Gadara | 18 |
| Linburn | 64 |  |  | Greenwood | 33 |
| Lincoln | 15 | Bimlow | 20 | Gregadoo | 28 |
| Loombah | 13 | Blackgolar | 23 | Gundagai | 124 |
| March | 32 | Bolton Vale | 19 | ,, South | 103 |
| Meroo Flat | 12 | Brisbane Valley | 22 | Humula South | 11 |
| ,, Upper | 10 | Chatham Valley | 13 | ,, | 32 |
| Merrendee | 25 | Duckmaloi | 24 | Jellingrove | 16 |
| Molong | 188 | Edith | 30 | Kalafat | 20 |
| Mookerawa | 16 | Fish River Creek | 32 | Kenjure Creek | 23 |
| ,, Lower | 19 | Ganbenang | 19 | Kildary | 16 |
| Morangulan | 18 | Glenburn | 20 | Lake Albert | 62 |
| Mudgee | 600 | Kendale | 29 | Manus | 16 |
| ,, South | 47 | Mount Stromboli | 17 | Moorong | 26 |
| Mullamuddy | 22 | Norway | 19 | Mount Blanc | 17 |
| Mulyan | 30 | Oberon | 81 | Oberne | 24 |
| Mumbil | 44 | Reinville | 13 | Tarcutta | 48 |
| Munghorn | 29 | Swatchfield | 33 | ,, Lower | 28 |
| Nora Creek | 28 | Tanner's Mount | 20 | Tumut | 278 |
| Nubrygyn | 11 | Vulcan | 9 | ,, Plains | 58 |
| Oak Creek | 25 |  |  | Tumberumba, Upper | 26 |
| Ophir | 25 |  |  | Umbango | 19 |
| Orange | 722 | **Wynyard, County of.** |  | Uplands | 14 |
| Peabody | 29 | Adelong | 226 | Wagga Wagga | 581 |
| Piambong | 16 | ,, Grove | 17 | ,, North | 109 |
| ,, Lower | 8 | ,, Upper | 30 | Windowie | 33 |
| Pyramul | 40 | ,, Crossing | 58 | Wondalga | 14 |

## SCHOOLS IN THE CENTRAL DIVISION.

| **Baradine, County of.** |  | **Boyd, County of.** |  | Cummeragunja | 48 |
|---|---|---|---|---|---|
|  |  |  |  | Mathoura | 50 |
| Baradine | 49 | Carathool | 38 | Moama | 160 |
| Goorianawa | 6 | Toganmain | 7 | Moira | 23 |
| Kienbri | 10 |  |  | Tamar | 13 |
| Pilliga | 23 |  |  | Tataila | 44 |
| Walgett | 149 | **Burnett, County of.** |  | Tori | 10 |
|  |  | Binneguy | 23 | Wamboota | 20 |
| **Benarba, County of.** |  | Cradock | 15 | Yellow Waterholes | 13 |
| Warren | 96 | Eulowrie | 10 |  |  |
|  |  | Kulki | 18 | **Caira, County of.** |  |
| **Bourke, County of.** |  | Oakey Creek | 24 |  |  |
|  |  | Pallamallawa | 39 | Balranald | 92 |
| Berry Jerry | 20 | Rockwell | 15 | Paika | 18 |
| ,, ,, North | 19 | Stonefield | 20 | Wombah | 54 |
| Gobbagumblin | 20 | Warialda | 134 |  |  |
| Methul | 17 | Yallaroi | 25 |  |  |
| Murrill Creek | 19 |  |  | **Canbelago, County of.** |  |
| Murrubale | 31 |  |  |  |  |
| Trickett | 22 | **Cadell, County of.** |  | Berry | 180 |
| Willandra | 33 | Altcar | 1 | Coolabah | 20 |
| Winchendon Vale | 21 | Bunaloo | 24 | Girilambone | 45 |

NEW SOUTH WALES. 345

### Cooper, County of.

| | No. on roll. |
|---|---|
| Bogolong | 30 |
| Grong Grong | 33 |
| Narrandera | 273 |
| Whitton | 79 |
| Warangesda | 34 |

### Courallie, County of.

| | |
|---|---|
| Boonaldoon | 17 |
| Moree | 172 |
| Terry-hie-hie | 20 |
| Wee Waa | 52 |

### Cunningham, County of.

| | |
|---|---|
| Condobolin | 79 |
| Derriwang | 23 |
| Elsmore | 57 |
| Wardry | 16 |

### Denham, County of.

| | |
|---|---|
| Thalaba | 67 |

### Denison, County of.

| | |
|---|---|
| Leniston | 17 |
| Mulwala | 53 |
| Nangunia | 25 |
| Osborne | 31 |
| Tocumwall | 48 |

### Dowling, County of.

| | |
|---|---|
| Lake Angelico | 84 |

### Ewenmar, County of.

| | |
|---|---|
| Bundemar | 21 |
| Bungay | 23 |
| Collie | 20 |
| Wougy | 12 |

### Flinders, County of.

| | |
|---|---|
| Gilgai | 61 |
| Mogille | 33 |
| Quandong | 46 |
| Yamma | 62 |

### Forbes, County of.

| | |
|---|---|
| Bangaroo North | 20 |
| Braulin | 29 |
| Budgerabong | 12 |
| Bundaburra Gap | 27 |
| Bungerellingong | 14 |
| Kangarooby | 11 |
| Tomanbil | 34 |
| Trundle | 22 |
| Walla Walla | 47 |
| Warroo | 18 |
| Wattamandaa | 35 |

### Gipps, County of.

| | No. on roll. |
|---|---|
| Borambil South | |
| Tirrana | 35 |

### Gowen, County of.

| | |
|---|---|
| Appletree | 24 |
| Belar Creek | 23 |
| Bogaldie | 14 |
| Gilgandra | 41 |
| Kerbin | 24 |
| Mundooran | 41 |
| Orandelbinnia | 24 |
| Toorawcenah | 19 |

### Gregory, County of.

| | |
|---|---|
| Eulamogo | 16 |
| Moballa | 66 |

### Hume, County of.

| | |
|---|---|
| Brocklesby West | 21 |
| Bulgandra | 14 |
| Bull Plain | 12 |
| Bungowannah | 24 |
| Cookardinia | 27 |
| Collendina | 15 |
| Coreen | 27 |
| Corowa | 131 |
| Hopefield | 33 |
| Howlong | 77 |
| Jubilee Downs | 14 |
| Martindale | 25 |
| Moorwatha | 33 |
| Morebringer | 25 |
| Quat Quatta North | 1 |
| Walbundrie | 19 |

### Jamison, County of.

| | |
|---|---|
| Weeta Waa | 16 |

### Kennedy, County of.

| | |
|---|---|
| Coradgerie | 22 |

### Leichhardt, County of.

| | |
|---|---|
| Billeroy | 17 |
| Bone Bone | 18 |
| Brightling Park | 21 |
| Castlereagh | 47 |
| Coonabarabran | 104 |
| Coonamble | 181 |
| Noonbar Creek | 20 |
| Nullabong | 24 |
| Riverside | 20 |
| Ulamambri | 20 |
| Yalcogrin | 13 |

### Lincoln, County of.

| | |
|---|---|
| Armatree | 21 |
| Ballarah | 43 |
| Belarbigill | 20 |
| Beni | 23 |

| | No. on roll. |
|---|---|
| Briggil | 22 |
| Brocklehurst | 39 |
| Bunglegumbie | 27 |
| Bunninyong | 21 |
| Cobborah | 25 |
| Coolbaggie | 12 |
| Curban | 29 |
| Dapper | 20 |
| Dark Corner | 15 |
| Eschol | 35 |
| Geurrie | 31 |
| Manoa | 18 |
| Medway | 21 |
| Murrumbidgerie | 41 |
| Plain Creek | 21 |

### Mitchell, County of.

| | |
|---|---|
| Abercrombie | 23 |
| Cuddell Sidings | 25 |
| Culcairn | 32 |
| Mimosa Dell | 24 |
| ,, East | 16 |
| ,, Park | 18 |
| Mundewaddera | 12 |
| Osborne Hill | 30 |
| Rawsonville | 9 |
| Tootal | 19 |
| Uranquintry | 27 |
| Yarragundry | 20 |
| Yerong Creek | 30 |

### Murchison, County of.

| | |
|---|---|
| Bingara | 167 |
| Bobby Whitlow's Creek | 18 |
| Coorangoora | 22 |
| Gum Flat | 47 |
| Horton River, Upper | 21 |
| Little Plain | 37 |
| Molroy | 17 |
| Saddler's Flat | 17 |

### Nandewar, County of.

| | |
|---|---|
| Appletree Clump | 10 |
| Berrigal Creek | 11 |
| Come-by-Chance | 21 |
| Edgeroi | 15 |
| Eulah Creek | 44 |
| Galathara Road | 31 |
| Gunnenbeme | 23 |
| Narrabri | 398 |
| ,, Railway Station | 102 |
| Rock, The | 40 |
| Nowley | 22 |
| Sparke's Creek | 27 |
| Tippereenah | 32 |
| Weetalaba | 15 |

### Napier, County of.

| | |
|---|---|
| Binnaway | 40 |
| Bramble | 16 |
| Warkton | 19 |

### Narromine, County of.
| | No. on roll. |
|---|---|
| Dandeloo | 14 |
| Dappo Springs | 22 |
| Minore | 23 |
| Narromine | 43 |
| Pandora's Pass | 13 |
| Tomingly | 53 |
| Tranjie | 72 |
| Tumbrebongie | |

### Nicholson, County of.
| | |
|---|---|
| Booligal | 35 |
| Hillston | 79 |

### Oxley, County of.
| | |
|---|---|
| Belairingah | 21 |
| Boundary Gate | 20 |
| Canonbar | 17 |
| Garfield | 37 |
| Mayview | 20 |
| Nevertire | 42 |
| Nyngan | 205 |
| Triangle Flat | 28 |
| Wilga | 19 |

### Pottinger, County of.
| | No. on roll. |
|---|---|
| Bando | 20 |
| Bollol Creek | 6 |
| Curlewis | 29 |
| Emerald Hill | 15 |
| Gunnedah | 238 |
| Mullaly | 12 |
| Springfield | 19 |
| Tambar Springs | 31 |
| Willowdale | 8 |

### Stapylton, County of.
| | |
|---|---|
| Boggabilla | 39 |
| Mount Pleasant | 42 |

### Townsend, County of.
| | |
|---|---|
| Booroorban | 10 |
| Bowan | 46 |
| Conargo | 19 |
| Deniliquin | 281 |
| Dunkeld | 52 |
| Mia Mia | 7 |
| Pretty Pine | 18 |

### Wandrook, North ... 12
### Wanganilla ... 10

### Urana, County of.
| | No. on roll. |
|---|---|
| Colombo Creek | 16 |
| Jerilderie | 68 |
| Lowesdale | 28 |
| Overton | 17 |
| Urana | 95 |

### Wakool, County of.
| | |
|---|---|
| Moulamein | 26 |

### Waradgery, County of.
| | |
|---|---|
| Illilliwa | 38 |
| Maude | 15 |
| Tongul | 16 |

### White, County of.
| | |
|---|---|
| Baan Baa | 40 |
| Rocky Glen | 12 |

## SCHOOLS IN THE WESTERN DIVISION.

### Blaxland, County of.
| | |
|---|---|
| Euabalong | 31 |
| Great Central | 55 |
| Mount Hope | 58 |
| Murrin | 19 |

### Cowper, County of.
| | |
|---|---|
| Bourke | 383 |
| Bourke North | 29 |
| Byerock | 64 |

### Clyde, County of.
| | |
|---|---|
| Brewarrina | 83 |
| Brewarrina Mission | 24 |
| Gongolgan | 19 |
| Mundawa | 44 |

### Culgoa, County of.
| | |
|---|---|
| Barringun | 58 |
| Goodroga | 55 |

### Evelyn, County of.
| | |
|---|---|
| Milparinka | 23 |
| Mount Brown | 20 |

### Finch, County of.
| | |
|---|---|
| Collarendebri | 29 |

### Irrara, County of.
| | |
|---|---|
| Wanaaring | 51 |

### Kilfera.
| | |
|---|---|
| Hatfield | 11 |

### Menindie, County of.
| | |
|---|---|
| Menindie | 85 |

### Mossgiel, County of.
| | |
|---|---|
| Ivanhoe | 25 |

### Mourambah, County of.
| | |
|---|---|
| Nymagee | 145 |

### Narran, County of.
| | |
|---|---|
| Angledool | 30 |

### Perry, County of.
| | |
|---|---|
| Cuthero | 31 |

### Robinson, County of.
| | |
|---|---|
| Cobar | 180 |

### Taila, County of.
| | |
|---|---|
| Euston | 26 |

### Tara, County of.
| | |
|---|---|
| Tara | 16 |

### Tongowoko.
| | |
|---|---|
| Tibooburra | 54 |

### Waljeers, County of.
| | |
|---|---|
| Mossgiel | 26 |

### Wentworth, County of.
| | |
|---|---|
| Avoca | 27 |
| Cal Lal | 20 |
| Pooncarie | 13 |
| Wilpataria | 16 |

### Yancowinna, County of.
| | |
|---|---|
| Pinnacle | 28 |
| Purnamoota | 40 |
| Silverton | 195 |
| Thackaringa | 50 |
| Umberumberke | 63 |

### Yanda, County of.
| | |
|---|---|
| Louth | 26 |

### Young, County of.
| | |
|---|---|
| Wilcannia | 199 |

*This concludes the Public Schools in the Colony.*

PUDDLEDOCK (*Co. Sandon*), a postal receiving-office, 377 miles N. of Sydney, with mail once a week. The nearest railway station is Black Mountain, 16 miles, on the northern line.

PUDDLEDOCK CREEK (*Co. Sandon*), a stream rising near the Devil's Pinch, flowing S. into the Tilbuster Ponds, about 6 miles N.E. of Armidale.

PUDGEWOY HILL (*Co. Northumberland*), a hill lying to the N.W. of Tuggerah Beach Lake, in the parish of Wallarah.

PUDMAN CREEK (*Co. King*), a fine stream rising and flowing in the Yass Plains, into the Burrowa River, about 2 miles N. of the township of Burrowa.

PUGGOON CREEK (*Co. Bligh*), a northern tributary of the Cudgegong Creek, rising near the Mudgee and Cobborah Road.

PULBAH ISLAND (*Co. Northumberland*), a small sandy island situate in Lake Macquarie.

PULPIT HILL (*Co. Cook*), a postal receiving-office, 70 miles W. of Sydney, with daily mail therefrom.

PULLETOP CREEK (*Co. Mitchell*), a tributary of the Billabong Creek, rising in Mount Yerong. It is fed by the Pilagalala Creek.

PULLIN'S CREEK (*Co. Bathurst*), a small auriferous tributary of the Lewis' Ponds Creek, falling into it near Pullin's Ponds.

PULLIN'S PASS (*Co. Bathurst*), a pass through the ranges at the lower end of the Lewis' Ponds Creek, on the road from Ophir to Tambaroora.

PULPIT HILL (*Co. Cook*), a lofty peak of the Blue Mountains between the Weatherboard and Blackheath, about 70 miles W. of Sydney.

PULPIT POINT (*Co. Cumberland*), a rocky promontory, on the N. side of the Parramatta River, to the N. of Spectacle Island.

PUMBY CREEK (*Co. Durham*), a small western tributary of the Paterson River, flowing into it about 12 miles N. of Hinton.

PUMPKIN POINT (*Co. Gloucester*), a bend in the Karuah River, noted for its rich alluvial soil.

PUNKALLA (*Co. Dampier*), a postal village, 275 miles S. of Sydney, with daily mail therefrom.

PUNT, THE (*Co. Wellesley*), a crossing-place over the Snowy River, on the road from Gippsland to Eden, between the Scotchman's and Bobundera Creeks.

PURFLEET (*Co. Macquarie*) is an agricultural settlement, lying on the Manning River, near Taree.

PURGATORY CREEK (*Co. Gresham*), a small southern tributary of the Clarence River, flowing through pastoral country.

PURNAMOOTA *(Co. Yancowinna)*, a postal village, 840 miles S. of Sydney, with mail twice a week. The nearest railway station is Hay, 415 miles, on the south-western line.

PURRIMBYDEN MOUNT *(Co. Inglis)*, a high peaked hill, lying about 2 miles from the township of Moonbi.

PUTTY *(Co. Cook)*, a postal village, 124 miles W. of Sydney, with mail once a week. The nearest railway station is Richmond, 65 miles, on the Windsor line.

PYE'S CREEK *(Co. Clive)*, a village, 459 miles N. of Sydney. The nearest railway station is Bolivia, 8 miles, on the northern line.

PYMBLE *(Co. Cumberland)*, a post-office and railway station, 25 miles N. of Sydney, with daily mail. Situate at the Hornsby Junction, on the Newcastle line.

PYRAMBANGO MOUNT *(Co. Parry)*, a peak of the Peel Range, lying on the S. bank of the Namoi River, and about 4 miles from the township of Carroll.

PYRAMID CREEK *(Co. Wellington)*, a tributary of the Macquarie River.

PYRAMUL *(Co. Wellington)*, a village, 127 miles to the W. of Sydney. Situated on the Pyramul Creek, forming part of the Louisa Creek gold-field. The nearest railway station is Capertee, 35 miles, on the western line.

PYRAMUL CREEK *(Co. Wellington)*, a fine auriferous stream rising in Mount Carcalgong, and flowing W. between the Louisa Creek and Tambaroora gold-fields into the Macquarie River.

PYREE *(Co. St. Vincent)*, a postal village, 130 miles S. of Sydney, with daily mail. The nearest railway station is Kiama, 32 miles, on the Illawarra and South Coast line. It is situated on the S. bank of the Shoalhaven River, near the town of Numba.

PYRMONT *(Co. Cumberland)*, a suburb of Sydney, with mail therefrom four times daily. Telegraph and money-order offices and Government savings bank, with delivery by letter-carriers. It lies in the parish of St. Andrew, on a tongue of land which divides the Blackwattle Cove from Darling Harbour. The goods traffic of the railways has its terminus in Pyrmont.

PYRMONT BAY *(Co. Cumberland)*, an indentation on the W. side of Darling Harbour, opposite the Phœnix Wharf.

# Q

QUAKER'S HAT *(Co. Cumberland)*, a rocky point of peculiar form on the W. side of Middle Harbour, and forming the S. head of Long Bay.

QUAAMAA *(Co. Dampier)*, a proclaimed township in this county.

QUABOOTHO *(Co. Clyde)*, a township to the S. of Bogolong.

QUAMBONE *(Co. Gregory)*, a postal village, 382 miles W. of Sydney, with mail three times a week. The nearest railway station is Dubbo, 59 miles, on the western line.

QUAQUINGAME LAKE (*Co. Waradgery*), a swampy lake, near the confluence of the Murrumbidgee and Lachlan Rivers, and about 10 miles N.W. of Maude.

QUARANTINE COVE (*Co. Cumberland*), a small bay in Spring Cove, on the W. side of the North Head and the E. side of the North Harbour of Port Jackson.

QUART-POT CREEK (*Co. St. Vincent*), a small tributary creek of the Buckenbowra Creek.

QUARTZ RIDGE (*Co. Wellington*), a township 145 miles W. of Sydney. Situated in the parish of Sofala, about 1 mile from the Turon River, on the road from Bathurst to Tambaroora. The district is partly a pastoral and partly a mining one. The nearest railway station is Bathurst, 35 miles, on the western line.

QUEANBEYAN (*Co. Murray*), a postal town, 194 miles S. of Sydney, with daily mail. Telegraph and money-order offices and delivery by letter-carrier. A railway station on the Goulburn and Cooma line. Queanbeyan is pleasantly situated on the river of that name. The district is pastoral and agricultural. It was proclaimed a borough in 1885, with a council of eight aldermen and a mayor. Population, about 1,000. Courts of quarter sessions and district courts are held here periodically during each year.

QUEANBEYAN RIVER (*Co. Murray*). [*See* "RIVERS."]

QUEDONG MOUNT (*Co. Wellesley*), a hill on the Delegate River, to the W. of Bombala. There are extensive lead and copper mines at Quedong.

QUEEN CHARLOTTE'S VALE (*Co. Bathurst*), a township 149 miles W. of Sydney. The nearest railway station is Perth, 6 miles, on the western line.

QUEEN CHARLOTTE VALE CREEK (*Co. Bathurst*) is a fine stream rising by three heads, and flowing N.E. into the Macquarie River, at the town of Bathurst. Its tributaries, or rather heads, are Bath's, Brown's, and Caloola Creek.

QUERRA CREEK (*Co. Arrawatta*), a small northern tributary of the upper part of the Macintyre River, crossing the road from Stonehenge to Inverell.

QUIPOLLY CREEK (*Co. Inglis*), a postal village, 245 miles N. of Sydney, with daily mail. A railway station on the northern line.

QUIRINDI (*Co. Buckland*), a postal town, 243 miles N. of Sydney, with mail twice daily. Telegraph and money-order offices, Government savings bank, and a railway station on the northern line. Situated on the Quipolly and Jacob and Joseph Creeks. The district is an agricultural one, the soil being admirably adapted for the growth of all kinds of cereals.

QUIRINDI CREEK (*Co. Buckland*), a fine stream rising in the western slope of the Australian Alps, a few miles N. of Mount Temi, and flowing through the townships of Wallabada and Quirindi into the Conadilly River.

QUOROBOLONG (*Co. Durham*), a small agricultural village, lying about 6 miles from Millfield.

QUOTABRA (*Co. White*), a township on the S. bank of the Namoi River.

# R

## RAILWAYS, TRAMWAYS, AND TELEGRAPH LINES.

The question of Railway construction in New South Wales first began seriously to occupy the attention of the colonists towards the end of 1845. The survey of the line from Sydney to Parramatta was completed in December, 1849. The first turf of the first railway in the Australian Colonies was turned by the Hon. Mrs. Keith Stewart on the 3rd July, 1850, and on the 26th September, 1855, the first section of the line, Sydney to Parramatta, 14 miles in length, was opened for traffic.

On the 30th June, 1891, 2,182 miles were open for traffic, the total amount spent in construction and equipment being £31,768,617.

During the year ending the 30th June, 1891, the gross earnings were £2,974,421, the working expenses £1,831,371, and the net earnings £1,143,050. 19,037,760 passengers were carried during that period, and the goods tonnage amounted to 3,686,998, and the live stock tonnage to 115,851, while the train mileage reached 8,410,421 miles.

The railways at present are divided into three divisions, viz., 'the Southern, the Western, and the Northern, Sydney being the starting point of each.

### I.—SOUTHERN LINE AND BRANCHES.

The Southern main line from Sydney to Albury is 386 miles in length, and forms a portion of the intercolonial system, uniting the capitals of Queensland, New South Wales, Victoria, and South Australia in one unbroken line of railway communication. The distance from Brisbane to Adelaide is 1,781 miles.

The first divergence from the main line is at Strathfield, 7 miles from the Sydney station, to Hamilton station, a running distance of 100 miles, where it joins the Great Northern line to Brisbane, in the colony of Queensland.

Campbelltown, 34 miles from Sydney, forms the junction for the steam tramway, connecting with Camden, the distance between the two places being about 7½ miles.

Passing Goulburn, distant 134 miles from Sydney, the line branches off in a southerly direction at Joppa Junction, and passes through Bungendore and Queanbeyan, to Cooma, the terminus, 264 miles from Sydney.

At Yass station, 187 miles from Sydney, a steam tramway branches off to the township of Yass, distant 2 miles.

Harden, 228 miles from Sydney, forms the junction station for the branch line to Blayney, on the Western line, thus uniting the two systems. The length of this connecting line is 113 miles.

At Cootamundra, 253 miles from Sydney, the line branches off to Gundagai with a running distance of 34 miles, 287 miles from Sydney.

At Junee Junction, 287 miles from Sydney, the South-Western line branches off, via Narrandera to Hay, a running distance of 167 miles from Junee Junction and 454 miles from Sydney. Narrandera, 347 miles from Sydney, forms the junction station for the branch line to Jerilderie, 64 miles distant.

A branch line, 47½ miles in length from Culcairn, 356 miles from Sydney, is in course of construction to Corowa, and will be opened for traffic at an early date.

A private line, 45 miles in length, connects Deniliquin with Moama, on the Victorian border, and facilitates the traffic to Melbourne by means of the Echuca-Melbourne railway.

## II.—THE ILLAWARRA OR SOUTH COAST LINE.

Shortly after passing Eveleigh, 1 mile from Sydney, this line branches off to the south and runs almost parallel with the coast, passes through the National Park, Bulli, Wollongong, to its present terminus, Kiama, 70 miles from Sydney. An extension of this line to Nowra, 22½ miles in length, is nearing completion.

At Rockdale, 6 miles from Sydney, a private tram, 1½ miles long, branches off to Lady Robinson's Beach, Botany Bay; and from Kogarah, 7 miles from Sydney, a steam tramway runs in connection with railway to George's River.

From Loftus Junction, 16 miles from Sydney, a branch railway nearly 2 miles in length runs across Loftus Heights to National Park.

## III.—WESTERN LINE AND BRANCHES.

The Western line extends from Sydney to Bourke, the distance being 503 miles. It branches off the Main Southern Line at Granville, 13 miles from Sydney, and crosses the Blue Mountains during its course.

Blacktown, 22 miles from Sydney, is the junction station for the Windsor and Richmond line, 16 miles in length.

At Wallerawang, 105 miles from Sydney, a branch line turns off in a northerly direction to Mudgee, 85 miles distant, and 190 miles from Sydney.

Blayney, 172 miles from Sydney, is the junction for the branch line, connecting the Southern and Western Railway systems, thus avoiding the transit through Sydney, of passengers and goods, between distant Western stations and Melbourne, and stations on the Southern line. This is the Blayney-Murrumburrah line.

At Orange, 192 miles from Sydney, a line branches off to Molong, distant 24 miles. An extension from Molong to Parkes, 73 miles, is now in course of construction.

From Nyngan, 377 miles from Sydney, a branch line to Cobar is completed; this line is 81½ miles in length, and 458½ miles from Sydney.

## IV.—THE GREAT NORTHERN LINE AND BRANCHES.

The Northern line extends from Sydney to Wallangarra, a distance of 490 miles, where it unites with the Queensland Railway to Brisbane. Originally Newcastle formed the Southern terminus, but since the completion of the line between Strathfield (9 miles from Sydney) and Hamilton junction, the starting point has been transferred to Sydney. This portion of the line, which in its course crosses the Hawkesbury River, is also known as the North-coast line.

At Pearce's Corner, about 22 miles from Sydney, a line, 10 miles in length, branches off to North Sydney. This line is now being extended to the deep waters of Port Jackson (Milson's Point), a distance of 2¾ miles.

At Fassifern, 87 miles from Sydney, a private tram, 2 miles in length, branches off to Toronto, on Lake Macquarie.

Waratah, 4 miles from Newcastle, and 102 miles from Sydney, is the junction of a short line, 4 miles in length, to Wallsend.

The branch line to Morpeth, 3 miles in length, turns off at East Maitland, 116 miles from Sydney.

At Werris Creek 254 miles from Sydney, the North-western line branches off to Narrabri, distant 350 miles from Sydney. The line is 96 miles in length, and passes through Gunnedah and Boggabri.

The distance by rail from Sydney to Brisbane is     722 miles.
,,     ,,     ,,     Melbourne     576½ ,,
,,     ,,     ,,     Adelaide     1,059 ,,

Government railways open for traffic, 30th June, 1891, 2,182 miles.
* Private, Deniliquin to Moama ... ... 45 miles.
   ,,    Silverton to Broken Hill ... 35¾ ,,

*This does not include lines used only for the conveyance of coal and other minerals.

### LINES UNDER CONSTRUCTION.

| | | |
|---|---|---|
| Culcairn to Corowa ... .. | 47 miles | 39 chains. |
| Lismore to the Tweed... ... | 39 ,, | 24 ,, |
| St. Leonards to Milson's Point | 2 ,, | 65 ,, |
| Kiama to Nowra ... ... | 22 ,, | 33 ,, |
| Molong to Parkes ... ... | 72 ,, | 66 ,, |

### V.—GOVERNMENT TRAMWAYS.

On the 30th June, 1891, there were 42½ miles open for traffic, viz. :—

| | |
|---|---|
| City and Suburban ... ... ... ... | 33½ miles. |
| North Shore Cable Line ... ... ... | 1¾ ,, |
| Newcastle to Plattsburg ... ... ... | 7½ ,, |

The cost of lines open for traffic was £1,004,212; the total earnings were £292,850; and the net earnings £53,171.

The following extensions have been opened since the above date:—

| | | |
|---|---|---|
| Castlereagh-street to Randwick Road | ... 1 mile | 6 chains. |
| Ashfield to Enfield ... ... ... | ... 1 ,, | 74 ,, |
| Newtown Bridge to St. Peter's ... | ... 0 ,, | 56 ,, |
| Forest Lodge to Balmain ... ... | ... 1 ,, | 58 ,, |

### TELEGRAPH LINES.

There are 11,697 miles of line open, covering 24,780 miles of wire, communicating with all parts of the Globe, open to the Telegraph wire.

*This concludes the Railways, Tramways, and Telegraph Lines.*

RAGLAN (*Co. Roxburgh*), a postal village, 140 miles W. of Sydney, with daily mail. A railway station on the western line. A small agricultural village lying about 3 miles E. of Kelso and Bathurst.

RAINBOW BEACH (*Co. Macquarie*), a postal village, 330 miles N. of Sydney, with mail twice a week. The nearest railway station is Hexham, 207 miles, on the northern line.

RALEIGH, a county in the Eastern Division of the Colony. [*See* "COUNTIES."]

RALEIGH (*Co. Raleigh*), a proclaimed village to the S. of the Bellinger.

RAM'S HEAD (*Co. Wallace*), a lofty peak on the Bald Mountains, Munnion Range, lying near the head of the Crackenback River, and about 6 miles S. of Kosciusko. It is one of the loftiest peaks in the range, and attains a height of 6,838 feet above sea-level; covered with snow most of the year round.

RAMORNIE (*Co. Clarence*), a postal receiving-office, 362 miles N. of Sydney, with mails per Clarence River steamers.

RAMSGATE ROAD (*Co. Cumberland*), a station, 2 miles S. of Sydney, on the Sans-Souci tramway line.

RANDWICK (*Co. Cumberland*), a suburb, 4 miles S. of Sydney, with mail therefrom three times daily. Telegraph and money-order offices, and Government savings bank, and delivery by letter-carriers. A tram station on the Sydney and Coogee line. The Destitute Children's Asylum is here built, and the Randwick race-course is within the district. The Bishop of Sydney's palatial residence stands on a high commanding position overlooking the ocean and the beautiful bay of Coogee. Randwick was proclaimed a municipality in 1859, with a council of eight aldermen and a mayor.

RANGER'S VALLEY (*Co. Gough*), the name given to a depression in the course of the Beardy Waters, about 8 miles W. of Severn or Dundee.

RANKIN, a county in the Western Division of the Colony. [*See* "COUNTIES."]

RANKIN, MOUNT (*Co. Roxburgh*), a lofty hill in the parish of Jedburgh, about 4 miles N.W. of Bathurst, and near the N. bank of the Macquarie River.

RANKIN'S RANGE (*Co. Cowper*), a group of three hills lying on the E. bank of the Darling River, about 100 miles S.W. of Bourke.

RANKIN'S SPRINGS (*Co. Cooper*), a postal village, 453 miles S. of Sydney, with mail twice a week. The nearest railway station is Whitton, 60 miles, on the south-western line.

RANTER'S CREEK (*Co. Lincoln*), a tributary of the Castlereagh River.

RAVENSWORTH (*Co. Durham*), a postal village, 160 miles N. of Sydney, with daily mail. A railway station on the northern line.

RAWDON CREEK (*Co. Macquarie*) is a small northern tributary of the Hastings River.

RAWDON ISLAND (*Co. Macquarie*), a postal town, 287 miles N. of Sydney, with mail therefrom three times a week. It is an island lying in the Hastings River, about 4 miles long and 1 mile wide, directly opposite the village of Horsley.

RAWDON STREAM (*Co. Gloucester*), the name of the S. head of the Barrington River.

RAWDON VALE (*Co. Macquarie*), a postal village, 204 miles N. of Sydney, with mail twice a week. The nearest railway station is Hexham, 91 miles, on the northern line.

RAWORTH (*Co. Northumberland*), a railway station on the East Maitland and Morpeth line.

RAYMOND TERRACE (*Co. Gloucester*), a postal village, 144 miles N. of Sydney, with daily mail. Telegraph and money-order offices, Government savings bank, and delivery by letter-carrier. The nearest railway station is Hexham, 6 miles, on the northern line. Situated on the E. bank of the Hunter River, in the parish of Eldon. It has steam communication by water, as well as by rail to and from Sydney. The district is an agricultural one, and highly productive. The grape vine flourishes to perfection, and the wine is of the highest quality. It was proclaimed a municipal district in 1884, with a council of five aldermen and a mayor.

RAZORBACK CREEK (*Co. Gresham*), a small tributary of the Boyd River, flowing into it at Broadmeadows.

REDBANK (*Co. Macquarie*), a postal village, 233 miles N. of Sydney, with mail three times a week. The nearest railway station is Hexham, 121 miles, on the northern line. Situated on the Manning River. The district is entirely an agricultural one, and very productive. There is communication with Sydney by steamer *via* Cundletown, distant 7 miles.

REDBANK CREEK (*Co. Benarba*), a small western tributary of the Macintyre River, flowing into it about 2 miles S. of the township of Ashford.

REDBANK, NORTH (*Co. Macquarie*), a village, 121 miles from Hexham, the nearest railway station on the northern line.

REDBANK RIVER (*Co. Fitzroy*). [*See* "RIVERS."]

REDBANK, SOUTH (*Co. Camden*), a village 57 miles S. of Sydney. The nearest railway station is Thirlmere, 2 miles on the southern line.

REDFERN (*C. Cumberland*), a suburb of Sydney, with mail therefrom twice daily. Telegraph and money-order offices, Government savings bank, with delivery by letter-carriers. Situated in the parish of Alexandria, and adjoins the city boundary; the suburb of Waterloo lying on the E. and S., and the railway terminus adjoins it on the N. It was proclaimed a municipality in 1859, with a council of eleven aldermen and a mayor.

REDHEAD (*Co. Northumberland*), a rocky promontory of red sandstone, standing boldly out into the sea, about 6 miles S. of the entrance to Port Hunter.

REDHEAD (*Co. St. Vincent*), a rocky promontory on the coast, forming the S. head of the Sussex Haven.

RED HILL (*Co. Tongowoko*), a peak of the Grey Range.

RED HILL (*Co. Wellington*), a village, 241 miles W. of Sydney. The nearest railway station is Springs, 4 miles, on the western line.

RED HILL (*Co. Bathurst*), a low, scrubby hill, in the parish of Cole, and on the road from Bathurst to Blayney.

RED HILL (*Co. Buccleuch*), a high peak lying to the N.E. of the township of Tumut, and on the N.E. boundary of the parish of Wyangle.

RED HILL (*Co. Goulburn*), a detached group of hills in the parish of Jindera, about 10 miles N. of the town of Albury.

RED POINT (*Co. Auckland*) is a rocky promontory, near the entrance to Twofold Bay.

RED POINT ISLAND (*Co. Camden*), a small island lying off the coast, near Wollongong.

RED RANGE (*Co. Gough*), a postal village, 435 miles N. of Sydney, with mail twice a week. The nearest railway station is Glen Innes, 14 miles, on the northern line.

RED ROCK (*Co. Clarence*), a postal village, 528 miles N. of Sydney, with mail three times a week.

RED ROCK (*Co. Clarence*), a small rocky islet, lying near the coast, about 20 miles N. of the Solitary Islands.

REEDY CREEK (*Co. Ashburnham*), a postal receiving-office, 489 miles N. of Sydney, with mail twice a week.

REEDY CREEK (*Co. Ashburnham*), a western tributary of the Burnes Creek, flowing to the N.E. of the Lachlan gold-fields.

REEDY CREEK (*Co. Durham*) is a small tributary of the Glendon Brook.

REEDY CREEK (*Co. Georgiana*), a small creek flowing through the township of Laggan into the Bolong River, about 16 miles N. of Laggan.

REEDY CREEK (*Co. Murchison*), a southern, auriferous tributary of the Keera Creek, rising in the northern slope of Mount Drummond.

REEDY CREEK (*Co. Murray*), a tributary of the Modbury Creek, rising in the Main Dividing Range, to the S. of Lake Bathurst, being fed by the Mulloon Creek.

REEDY CREEK (*Co. Phillip*), a small tributary of the Hawkins Creek.

REEDY CREEK (*Co. Wellington*), a small, auriferous, western tributary of the Molong River.

REEDY FLAT (*Co. Wynyard*), a village, 287 miles S. of Sydney. The nearest railway station is Gundagai, 53 miles, on the Cootamundra and Gundagai line.

REGENT'S LAKE (*Co. Ashburnham*), a lake or lagoon lying near the Lachlan River, with a low sandy beach on the N., and a bold shore, with red cliffs, on the S. side.

REGENTVILLE (*Co. Cumberland*), an agricultural village in the parish of Mulgoa, situated on the banks of the Nepean River, about 3 miles from the township of Penrith.

REIDSDALE (*Co. Murray*), a postal village, 185 miles S. of Sydney, with mail twice a week. The nearest railway station is Tarago, 40 miles, on the Goulburn and Cooma line.

REID'S FLAT (*Co. King*), a postal village, 237 miles S. of Sydney, with mail three times a week. The nearest railway station is Binalong, 58 miles, on the southern line, situated on the Lachlan River. The district is chiefly agricultural.

REID'S MISTAKE (*Co. Northumberland*), the name of the entrance to Lake Macquarie, about 12 miles S. of Newcastle.

REKEELBON MOUNT (*Co. Hunter*), a peak of the Hunter Range, lying at the head of the Blackwater Creek, about 25 miles E. of Dabee.

RENDEZVOUS CREEK (*Co. Cowley*), a small tributary of the Gudgenby River, rising between the Murrumbidgee River and the Bimberi Ranges.

RETREAT RIVER (*Co. Georgiana*), a stream rising in the western slope of the Australian Alps, and N. of Mount Werong.

RHODES (*Co. Cumberland*), a railway station, 10 miles W. of Sydney, on the Ryde and Hawkesbury River line.

RICHARDS' SIDING (*Co. Cumberland*), a railway station, 28 miles W. of Sydney, on the Windsor and Richmond line.

RICHLEATH HILL (*Co. Sandon*), a peak spurring from the Dividing Range, about 8 miles S.W. of the town of Armidale, in the parish of Elton.

RICHMOND, a county in the Eastern Division of the Colony. [*See* "COUNTIES."]

RICHMOND (*Co. Cumberland*), a postal town, 38 miles W. of Sydney, with mail twice daily. Telegraph and money-order offices, Government savings bank, with delivery by letter-carriers, and is the terminal station on the Windsor and Richmond line. Situated about 2 miles from the S. bank of the Hawkesbury River, in the parish of Ham Common. The district is an agricultural one, the soil being of the richest description, and the produce therefrom most abundant. On the opposite side of the river is the far-famed Kurrajong, with its scenery of unsurpassing beauty and loveliness. It was proclaimed a borough in 1872, with a council of seven aldermen and a mayor.

RICHMOND RIVER (*Co. Richmond*). [*See* "RIVERS."]

RICHMOND RIVER HEADS (*Co. Richmond*) forms the entrance to the Richmond River, and its latitude is 28° 52' S., and longitude 153° 32' E. It is a bar entrance, and a pilot's boat and crew are stationed near the north head for the protection of vessels entering.

RICHMOND TERRACE (*Co. Cumberland*), situated and lying on the W. of Richmond. It is an elevated table-land of about 3 miles in extent.

RICKABY'S CREEK (*Co. Cumberland*), a small eastern tributary of the Hawkesbury River, falling into it a little distance above Windsor.

RINNAKUNYARRA WATERHOLE (*Co. Evelyn*), on the South Australian boundary.

# RIVERS IN THE COLONY—THEIR SOURCES AND COURSES.

ABERCROMBIE RIVER. This river takes its rise in the county of Georgiana, in Mount Werong, and, after a course of nearly 100 miles, joins the Lachlan, of which it is one of its tributaries, near Cowra. The districts are fairly good through which it flows, and forms fine pastoral country. The Abercrombie is fed by Copperhania, Cook's Vale, Blackman's, Burra Burra, Davis', Isabella, Rocky Bridge, Tuena, Thompson's, and Picsley's Creeks, and flows through the villages of Bunmango, Bingham, Cullalong, and Crabine, and the township of Bombah and the Tuena gold-fields. It is an important auriferous stream, with generally a stony bottom and clear water.

ABERFOYLE RIVER takes its rise in Chandler's Peak, in the county of Gresham, and flows through well-timbered pastoral country, where cedar and other valuable trees abound. It is a tributary of the Guy Fawkes River, which flows into the Clarence, and is fed by the Boundary and Bullock Creeks.

ALLYN RIVER rises in the Mount Royal Range, in the county of Durham, flowing through the village of Ecclestone into the Paterson River, which is one of the tributaries of the Hunter. The Allyn is fed by Lewin's Brook, and the soil is rich and productive through which it flows.

ANN RIVER is an auriferous stream, a tributary of the Sara River flowing through the Oban diggings, in the county of Gresham, and finally enters the Macleay River.

APSLEY RIVER is a fine stream rising near the Basaltic Column, in the New England Range, in the county of Vernon. It pursues a course of nearly 50 miles, and flows through the township of Walcha, after which it enters the Tia River, and thence to the Macleay. The course of the Apsley is through deep ravines and stupendous chasms, where there are several fine waterfalls. Oxley, on his second journey, in 1818, thus describes one of the deep defiles in this river:—" This tremendous ravine runs nearly N. and S.; its breadth at the bottom does not apparently exceed 100 or 200 feet, whilst the separation of the outer edges is from 2 to 3 miles. In perpendicular depth it exceeds 3,000 feet. The slopes from the edges were so steep and covered with loose stones that any attempt to descend them, even on foot, was impracticable." The Apsley is fed by the Yarrowitch, Peter's, Trinidad, Wilson's, Tiarra, Stony, Emu, My Lady, Ohio, and Swampy creeks. The district is thickly timbered with gigantic trees and shrubs and creeping vines.

AVON RIVER is a fine S. tributary of the Gloucester River, taking its rise in the county of that name, flowing through rough agricultural and pastoral land into the main stream at the township of Gloucester.

BANNOO RIVER takes its rise in Mount Bolumboin, in the county of Macquarie, to the S. of the Hastings River, flowing into the Ellenborough River, on its E. side, and with it becomes a tributary of the Hastings.

BARGO RIVER is a small tributary of the Nepean River, having its confluence with that river on its W. bank, a few miles to the S. of Picton, in the county of Camden. It takes its rise near Mittagong, and flows in a N. direction through Bargo Brush, where it joins the main stream.

BARNARD RIVER takes its rise in the New England Range, near Hanging Rock, in the county of Hawes, and flows through the counties of Gloucester and Macquarie, where it enters the Manning River, of which it is an important tributary, at the junction of the roads from Wingham to Nowendoc and Gloucester, and to the W. of the township of Giro.

BARWON RIVER is the eastern continuation of the Darling, and is sometimes called the Upper Darling. It flows past the counties of Benarba, Denham, Baradine, Leichhardt, Finch, Clyde, and Narran, and is fed by the Mooni, Gwydir, Namoi, Castlereagh, Macquarie, Narran, and Bokhara Rivers. The tributary creeks are Thalaba, Pagan, Wanouri, Ana, and Marra. The Barwon is a fine river, flowing about 150 miles through the township of Walgett, at the junction of the Namoi River, to the confluence of the Culgoa and the Bogan, the three forming the Darling River. It is formed by the junction of the Macintyre, Bombi, Whalan, and Gilgil Rivers. Narrabri is the nearest railway station to Walgett, on the Barwon River, 125 miles. The Barwon has a course of about 510 miles.

BEGA RIVER takes its rise in the South Coast Range, near Mount Nimmitabel, and flows through the counties of Dampier and Auckland for a distance of about 60 miles, and empties itself into the ocean at Tathra. It is an important stream, but its estuary is navigable only for small craft. The country, however, through which it flows is highly productive, and the flourishing town of Bega is situated on the banks of the river. It is fed by the Brogo River, and the Colombo, Black's Flat, Butler's, Candelo, Tandawangalo, Wolumla, Sandy, Sheep Station, and Jella-Jellel Creeks.

BELL RIVER rises to the N.W. of Orange, in the counties of Wellington and Gordon, flowing into the main stream at Wellington. It is a fine tributary of the Macquarie River, and is fed by numerous tributaries, many of which are auriferous. The principal are the Boldadura, Calombal, Cugaburga, Newrea, Two-mile, Native Dog, Molong, Larcas Lake, and Weandre Creeks.

BELLINGER RIVER takes its course from the mountain range forming the N. boundary of the county of Raleigh, known as Barren Range, and flows through a flat country, where the cedar-tree flourishes. It is a small stream, with a shifting channel at its mouth, which lies about 24 miles N. of Trial Bay. The Bellinger is only frequented by small vessels trading in cedar and other timbers.

BELUBULA RIVER is an important tributary of the Lachlan River, in the county of Bathurst, rising in the hilly country in the Main Dividing Range bordering the King's Plains gold-fields, and joining the Lachlan at Bangaroo. Its course is about 90 miles through fairly good pastoral and agricultural land, watering the townships of Blayney, Carcoar, and Canowindra. The principal tributaries of the Belubula are Cargo, Carrangle, Cadiangalong, Cowriga, Neale's Waterholes, Mandurama, Errowinbang, Grubbenbun, Marangula, Limestone, Davy, Liscombe Pool, Pannara, Nyrang, and Gum Creeks. The rich black soil on the banks of this river is highly productive in herbage.

BEMBOKA RIVER is a continuation of the Bega, before described. The Bemboka is so called above the township of Bega, and below it is called the Bega.

BIGBADJA RIVER takes its rise in the E. slope of Bigbadja Mount in the Australian Alps, in the county of Beresford, and is the N. tributary of the Umarella River. Its course is about 16 miles S.W. through excellent pastoral country, extending over part of the Monaro Plains. The Bigbadja is fed at its upper end by Pepper's Creek.

BIRIE RIVER is a tributary of the Culgoa River, which takes its rise in Queensland. In New South Wales the Birie joins the Culgoa to the N. of its confluence with the Barwon, in the county of Narran. It is fed by the Bubbermore Creek, and although the banks of the river are well timbered the country through which it passes is of an indifferent character.

BLAKE'S RIVER is a small W. tributary of the head of the Nymboi River, taking its rise in the mountain range in the county of Fitzroy, and is an affluent of the Clarence River.

BOGAN RIVER.—This important river takes its rise in Goonambla Hill, a mountain range in the county of Kennedy, and pursues a course of 450 miles to its confluence with the Darling, about 36 miles N.E. of Fort Bourke. It flows through the counties of Narromine, Kennedy, Flinders, Oxley, Gregory, and Clyde; and is fed by Cookopie Ponds, Cargi Ponds, Ten-mile, Tomingley, Bullock, Gunningba, and Duck Creeks, and has no tributaries for the last 100 miles of its course. It was on this river that Cunningham, the botanist and explorer, was murdered by the blacks in April, 1835.

BOKHARA RIVER enters New South Wales from Queensland, where it takes its rise in the county of Narran, and becomes an important tributary of the Barwon, above the confluence of that river with the Darling. The Bokhara flows from N. to S. through the county named, and there are two tributary creeks within it—the Hospital and the Cato Creeks.

BOLONG RIVER takes its rise in the W. slope of the Australian Alps, in the county of Georgiana, and is a fine stream flowing through scrubby country for about 40 miles, into the Abercrombie River, and, as an affluent of the lastnamed, becomes a tributary of the Lachlan. Its course is through the township of Bolong, where it receives the waters of Phil's River.

BOMBALA RIVER takes its rise in the W. slope of the S. coast range, and pursues a course of about 50 miles through good country and across the S. portion of Monaro Plains. It is fed by the Undowah, Coolumbooka, Brugolong, Cambalong, Maharatta, and Slaughter-house Creeks, and the Delegate River. Bombala River is an important tributary of the Snowy River. The township of Bombala lies at the junction of the river and the Coolumbooka Creek.

BOOMBI RIVER is a branch of the Macintyre River, flowing out of it at Borongo, in the county of Stapylton, and, after a course of about 70 miles, joining it again near its fall into the Barwon River, in the county of Benarba, to the N. of Caidmurra. It flows through sterile and mostly unoccupied country.

BOONOO BOONOO RIVER is a small auriferous stream rising in the E. slope of the Great Dividing Range, in the county of Buller, on the Queensland border, and is a tributary of the Clarence River. The district is exceedingly mountainous, abounding in lucid streams flowing into the Clarence.

BOWMAN'S RIVER is a small stream rising in the W. of the county of Gloucester, and flowing W. about 20 miles into the main stream, through the township of Bowman, being fed by the Craven Creek. There are agricultural settlers along the banks of the river and surrounding country.

BOYD RIVER is a tributary of the Nymboi River, taking its rise in the mountainous districts of the county of Gresham. The Ann and Sara Rivers, and Chandler's and Boyd's Creeks, are tributary streams of the Boyd, which latter flows past Barney's Hill into the Nymboi before entering the Clarence River.

BREDBO RIVER takes its rise in the W. slope or the Australian Alps, near Bigbadja Hill, in the county of Beresford, and is an E. tributary of the Murrumbidgee River, and is fed by the Tinderry, Cowra, and Froghole Creeks. The Bredbo flows through well-timbered and fertile country about 25 miles in a W. direction, and is crossed by the Cooma railway to the N. of Colinton.

BROGO RIVER is a fine stream rising in the S. coast range to the N.E. of Mount Nimmitabel, in the county of Auckland, which it crosses from W. to E. It flows in a S.E. direction about 30 miles, and enters the Bega River at the township of Bega. The Brogo passes through fine pastoral country, and well suited for agricultural purposes.

BRUNSWICK RIVER is a small stream entering the South Pacific Ocean in the extreme N. of the Colony, in the county of Rous. It has a shifting sandy bar, and is only navigable for small craft. The district of the Brunswick is very rich and productive, and the vegetation of a semi-tropical order.

BUNDARRA RIVER is a small affluent of the upper part of the Gwydir River, flowing in the counties of Murchison and Hardinge, where it takes its rise, flowing N. before joining the main stream.

BURROWA RIVER is a tributary of the Lachlan River, and takes its rise in the Main Dividing Range, in the counties of Monteagle, Harden, and King, to the S. of Burrowa Plains, and joins the dividing lines between the counties of Monteagle and Harden on the W. and King on the E. It is a fine affluent of the Lachlan, and has a course of about 65 miles N. through good undulating pastoral country, and is fed by Crosbie's, Corcoran's, Geegullalong, Pudman, Gaba, Stoney, Narellan, and Cookoomingala Creeks; and flows through the township of Burrowa, at which place it is crossed by the road from Binalong to Binda.

CAMPBELL'S RIVER takes its rise in the W. slope of the Australian Alps, near Swatchfield, in the counties of Bathurst and Westmoreland, and forms the W. head of the Macquarie River. It flows in a N. direction past the W. part of Bushrangers' Hill, and the E. foot of Mount Evernden to its confluence with the Fish River, the two forming the Macquarie River. It is fed by the Gilmandyke, Pepper, Davy's, and Stony Creeks. The course of the Campbell is through very good country, and the soil on both sides of the river is rich, and the grass luxuriant, and much of the land is taken up for agricultural purposes.

CAPERTEE RIVER takes its rise in the mountain range on the E. side of the county of Roxburgh, and its course separates the counties of Hunter and Cook, where it joins the Colo River, and enters the Hawkesbury at Broken Bay. Its tributaries are the Wolgan River and Tapa Creek.

CASTLEREAGH RIVER takes its rise in the Warrabungle Range, in the county of Bligh, and, after a tortuous course of upwards of 360 miles, enters the Barwon, in the county of Leichhardt, and of which river it is an important tributary. The Castlereagh surrounds the county of Gowen on all sides except its N. boundary, and flows through the counties of Napier, Ewenmar, and Leichhardt, and past the townships of Coonabarabran, Mendooran, Eringanerin, Terabile, and Coonamble, and is fed by the Ulimambra, Belar, Weetalaba, Piambra, Butheroo, Merrygoen, Bandalla, Wallamburrawong, Terabile, Gallagambroon, Baronne, Coonamble, Maraba, and Madgora Creeks. This noble river—the Castlereagh—was discovered by Oxley, in his second expedition, in 1818. The diversity of the character of the country through which it flows is very great and various, and floods and droughts alternate, which renders the occupation of the surface of the soil somewhat difficult and troublesome.

CATARACT RIVER (*Cos. Camden and Cumberland*) takes its rise in the W. slope of the coast range, in the counties of Cumberland and Camden, and is an important tributary to the Sydney water supply. Its course is through very deep and rocky chasms—the retreat of the lyre bird and the platypus—before its confluence with the Nepean River. The Cataract flows N.W., and passes the villages of Appin and Wilton.

CATARACT RIVER (*Co. Buller*) is a fine auriferous stream, rising in the ranges E. of Tenterfield, in the county of Buller, in the extreme N. of the Colony, and flows in a N.E. course through rugged pastoral country. It is a tributary of the Upper Clarence River.

CHANDLER RIVER takes its rise in the mountain ranges in the county of Sandon, and, with the Wallamumbi River, becomes a considerable stream, and has its embouchure in the Macleay River.

CHICHESTER RIVER takes its rise in the county of Gloucester, and is a fine stream, forming the E. head of the Williams River, flowing into the main stream at Forsterton. The country through which it flows is somewhat of a barren character.

CLARENCE RIVER is the largest river on the E. seaboard of the Colony, and takes its rise in the Main Dividing Range, near the Obelisk Mountains, flowing, with its tributaries, through the counties of Rous, Buller, Drake, Richmond, and Clarence, and pursues a course of over 240 miles before emptying itself in the South Pacific Ocean at Trial Bay. It is fed by the Cataract, Nymboi, Timbarra, Orara, Coldstream, Mitchell, and Esk Rivers; the Tooloon, Timbarra, and Tabulam Rivulets; and the Emu, Peacock, Bottle, Plumbago, Flagstone, Alice, Dulgigin, Ewingar, Nogrigar, Washpool, Gordon's, Bunginbar, Nettle, Purgatory, Whiteman's, Musk Valley, Allpon, Alum, Swan, Shark, Sportsman's, Rocky Mouth, and Mangrove Creeks. The Clarence is navigable for large steamers and vessels a distance of about 80 miles from the entrance, or 20 miles above Grafton, the chief town of the district. Above the township of Copmanhurst there are several extensive and picturesque waterfalls, known as the Rocky, Smith's, Tindall's, Bullock, and Double Channel Falls. The Lower Clarence is a magnificent stream, averaging half a mile in width from its mouth upwards for nearly 50 miles; and the rich alluvial plains through which this noble river flows is well known by the valuable and varied produce which the district is enabled to supply to other parts of the colony less favourably endowed.

CLYDE RIVER is an important one, and takes its rise in the Pigeon-house Mountain, in the county of St. Vincent, and, after a course of about 70 miles, enters the ocean at Bateman's Bay, and is fed by the Cockwhy, Currowan, and Nelligen Creeks. This river is navigable for small vessels only, and the townships of Currowan and Nelligen are situated upon it. The Clyde passes through rich, undulating, agricultural country, and drains an area of about 450 square miles.

COCKBURN RIVER.—This river forms the boundary-line between the counties of Parry and Inglis, and is an auriferous tributary of the Peel River, and takes its rise in the W. slope of the Moonbi Range. It is fed by the Moonbi Creek, and waters the fine but rugged pastoral country lying between Tamworth, Moonbi, and Walcha.

COLO RIVER.—This river is a continuation of the Capertee, and separates the counties of Hunter and Cook, flowing into the Hawkesbury at its confluence with the Macdonald, of which it is an important tributary. It takes its rise near the Tayan Pic, and is fed by the Coco, Bowen's, Wallemi, and Wollangambe Creeks, and the Wolgan River. The course of the Colo is through somewhat rugged country, with some good patches of land suitable for agricultural and pastoral pursuits.

CONADILLY (or MOOKI) RIVER takes its rise in the N. slope of the Australian Alps, near the E. bluff, in the counties of Buckland and Pottinger. It flows N. through the townships of Breeza and Gunnedah into the Namoi at the latter place, and separates the counties of Buckland and Pottinger. It is fed by the Yarrimambah, Omateah, Barambil, Quirindi, Cubit Ponds, and Carroll Creeks, and flows through good pastoral and agricultural land, with considerable cultivation on its banks.

COOK'S RIVER falls into the head of Botany Bay, and although named after Captain Cook, the great discoverer, the course of this river is not sufficiently significant even to have its course traced on the maps of the Colony. The river has a watershed of considerable area, and the land along its banks is under cultivation by market gardeners. There is a good tidal dam across its mouth, and the South Coast railway runs over it not far from the dam.

COOKBUNDOON RIVER takes its rise near Mount Hobbes, in the county of Georgiana, and is fed by the Murrang and Kerrawang Creeks. It flows through scrubby and broken country, past the township of Tarlo into the Wollondilly River, near Mundalla.

COOLABURRAGUNDY RIVER is a small stream taking its rise on a spur of the Liverpool Range, near Pandora's Pass, in the counties of Napier and Bligh, flowing through rugged country into the Erskine River at Dunedoo, in the county of Lincoln, and thence into the Macquarie River at Brocklehurst.

COOLUMBOOKA RIVER takes its rise in the rugged country to the N.E. of Cathcart, in the parish of Wellesley. It is an important affluent of the upper part of the Bombala River, flowing through the township of Cathcart, with the main stream at Bombala. The course of this river is through good pastoral and agricultural country.

CORANG RIVER takes its rise in the W. slopes of the Pigeon-house Mountain, in the county of St. Vincent, and is fed by the Jerricknorra and Nodgungulla Creeks. The course of this stream is through good pastoral country for about 20 miles, and is an affluent of the Shoalhaven River.

CORDEAUX RIVER rises on the W. slope of Mount Keira, in the county of Camden, near Wollongong, flowing through rugged and picturesque country into the Nepean, near East Bargo. The Cataract and Cordeaux Rivers form the source of the waterworks from which Sydney now draws its supply, before these streams enter the Nepean River. The well-known Pheasant's Nest, the seat of the late Sir Thomas Mitchell, once Surveyor-General of the Colony, is surrounded by the Cataract and Cordeaux Rivers.

COTTER RIVER takes its rise in the mountain ranges in the centre of the county of Cowley, flowing about 35 miles through rugged country into the Murrumbidgee River, about 8 miles of its junction with the Molonglo. The Cotter is fed by the Pabral, or Goree, and the Tidbinbilla Creeks.

COX RIVER.—This important river takes its rise in the Blue Mountain Range, in the county of Westmoreland, in the neighbourhood of Rydal, flowing through wild gorges, wherein may be found some of the most magnificent scenery in Australia, into the Nepean River; one of the most beautiful of the chasms is known as the Vale of Clwydd. It is fed by numerous tributary mountain streams, among which are Mangaroo, Farmer's, Jack's, Lowther, Grant's, Blackheath, Kanumbla, Ganbenang, Long Swamp, Megelory, Cedar, Kownung, and Butcher's Creeks. The course of the Cox River is inaccessible for about 4 miles, where it is united with the Werriberri, and in other parts it is very rugged.

CRACKEMBACK RIVER takes its rise in the Mumorig Range, near Mount Crackemback, a high peak near the head of the Snowy River, in the county of Wallace. Its course is about 20 miles, through some good pastoral country, and is a tributary of the head of the Snowy River.

CRAWFORD RIVER is a W. tributary of the Myall River, in the county of Gloucester, falling into the main stream at Bullah-Delah. It is a small stream, and the country through which it flows of indifferent quality.

CROOKED RIVER is a small stream, in the county of Camden, falling into the ocean at the N. end of the 4-mile beach, and close under Blackhead, 2 miles S. of Gerringong. It has a bed of shifting sand at its lower end, over which is a crossing place, on the coast road from Gerringong to Shoalhaven, dangerous in some states of the tide.

CROOKHAVEN RIVER is to the S., about 3 miles, of the entrance to the Shoalhaven River, in the county of St. Vincent. It is a small stream draining the flat agricultural land to the S. of the lower part of the Shoalhaven River, and very difficult of navigation even for small boats.

CROOKWELL RIVER is the dividing boundary between the counties of King and Georgiana, and takes its rise in the W. slope of the Australian Alps, about 3 miles S. of the township of Crookwell. It has a course of about 60 miles through good country, and past the townships of Binda and Crookwell, into the upper part of the Lachlan River. It is fed by the Binda, Kangaloola, Patten, Julong, Burrawinda, and Whooo Creeks.

CUDGEGONG RIVER takes its rise in Mount Binben, a peak of the Australian Alps, and flows through the counties of Bligh, Roxburgh, Phillip, and Wellington into the Macquarie River, at the Burrandong gold-fields. It is a fine auriferous stream, and waters the Merinda gold-fields, and the townships of Tawinbang, Dabee, Rylstone, Cudgegong, Mudgee, and Wiadero in its course, and is fed by the Cooroongooba, Gunguddy, Cop's, Carwell's, Mullamuddy, Cudgegong, Lawson's, Burrardulla, Bumberra, Eurundurry, Eurudgere, Wialdra, Puggoon, Sandy, Goobma, Prainbong, Warrobil, Uamy, Bun Buckley, Ungula, Mullinarran, Warradugga, Dinney, Meroo, and Gunnel Creeks. The country through which it flows is rugged and scrubby.

CULGOA RIVER takes its rise in Queensland, and flows between the counties of Culgoa and Narran in this colony, and is the principal head of the Darling, joining this river about 20 miles N.E. of Fort Bourke. It was discovered by Mitchell in 1845. It was found by him to be a deep but narrow stream, lined with fine timber, having abundant water, and banks 40 feet high. The country around consists of loose sand, and at present not well suited for pastoral purposes. The Culgoa is fed by Bow, Noorooma, and Burbar Creeks, and by Gooroomero, Sandy, and Tooloomi Springs.

DARLING RIVER is a noble stream formed by the confluence of the Bogan, Barwon, Bokhara, and Culgoa Rivers. It was discovered by Captain Sturt in 1829, who traced it for a short distance only. Sir Thomas Mitchell, in his exploration tour down the Murray in 1835, discovered its embouchure into that river, and, voyaging up it, found that it was the same river spoken of by Sturt as the Darling. It flows through or along the counties of Cowper, Livingstone, Menindee, Perry, Windeyer, and Wentworth and is fed by the Clover, Ana Branch, Tallyawalka, Teryaweynya, Woytchugga, Pammumaroo, Lawley's Ponds, Undealke, and Coonalhugga Ana Branch Creeks. The townships of Bourke, Menindee, Perry, and Wentworth are situated on this river. Mr. Coghlan, in his very valuable work on the " Wealth and Progress of New South Wales," says of this river :—" Of all the tributaries of the Murray, the Darling drains the largest area, extending as it does over the greater portion of the western district of New South Wales, and embracing nearly all southern Queensland. From its confluence with the Murray at Wentworth up to its junction with the Culgon, a few miles above Bourke, the Darling receives only two tributaries, the Paroo and Warrego. For over 1,000 miles this great river holds its solitary course, Nile like, feeding the thirsty plains of the south with water falling many hundred miles distant on the downs of Queensland. The course of the river is tortuous in the extreme; in many places a narrow neck of land, a mile or two across, separates parts of the river 20 miles distant if the stream were followed. The Darling is navigable, in times of freshets, as far as the township of Walgett, 1,758 miles from its confluence with the Murray; thence to the sea the distance is 587 miles, making a total length of navigable water from Walgett to the sea 2,345 miles, and it therefore ranks high amongst the rivers of the world as estimated by navigable length." The whole exténf of the country through which the Darling flows is occupied, more or less, by immense sheep-walks, and is the outlet for produce of great value.

DARLING ANA BRANCH takes its rise in the county of Windeyer, and flows through the counties of Tara and Wentworth to its confluence with the Murray to the W. of the township of Wentworth, and waters rich pastoral country, all of which is taken up by pastoralists.

DAWSON'S RIVER takes its rise in the county of Macquarie, and is a small northern tributary of the lower end of the Manning River, falling into the main stream near Cundletown; there is some good land through which it flows.

DELEGETE RIVER takes its rise in the Delegete Range, in the colony of Victoria, and is an important S. tributary of the Bombala River in the county of Wellesley, flowing in a N. direction through the Delegete Plain and the Little Plain gold-field. It is fed by the Little Plain River.

DEUA RIVER. [See "MORUYA RIVER."]

DRY RIVER.—This river takes its rise in the South Coast Range, in the county of Dampier, between the Tuross and Brogo Rivers, about 20 miles N.E. of the township of Bega. Its course is through rugged and scrubby country for about 20 miles, and reaches the ocean at Jerimbul, a few miles to the S. of Bermagui. There are some good patches of land through which the Dry River flows, and it is a considerable sized stream.

DUMARESQ RIVER is a noble stream, taking its rise in Queensland, and is a tributary to the Macintyre. It forms the northern boundaries of the counties of Clive, Arrawatta, and Stapylton on the Queensland border. With the Macintyre and Barwon the Dumaresq really becomes the Upper Darling. Its course for 100 miles forms the dividing line between this Colony and Queensland, and first strikes the New South Wales border at Ekin's Flat, in the county of Clive, flowing through good pastoral country, and becomes a confluent of the Macintyre River about half-way between Bengalla and Boggabilla. It is fed by numerous streams over the border, and by the Mole River and Tenterfield Creek in this colony.

DYKE RIVER is a small stream rising in the rugged mountainous country in the county of Dudley, flowing N. in the Macleay River, of which it is an affluent.

EAST BRANCH RIVER has its rise in a spur of the Australian Alps at Mount Kosciusko, in the county of Selwyn, and is one of the heads or sources of the Murray River. Its course is about 25 miles through very rugged and mountainous country, and joins the main stream at Mount Indi. It is fed by numerous small mountain creeks, and its principal tributaries are the Kancobin, the Swampy Plains, and the Youngal Creeks. The scenery along this stream is highly romantic, and well timbered and grassed.

EDWARDS or HYALITE RIVER is a very important river, and, with the Wakool River, is navigable for over 400 miles, as far as the important town of Deniliquin. In the counties of Wakool, Townsend, and Urana, through which these rivers flow, there are a perfect cobweb of streams increasing the bulk of waters until the confluence with the Murray is reached, and which takes place about 15 miles S.E. of the confluence of the Murray and Murrumbidgee Rivers. The principal townships on the Edward are Deniliquin and Moulamein ; and the principal tributary streams are Ballatale, Gerapna, Gulpa, Coligon, Alloe's Tarangile, Coonambidgal, and Billabung Creeks, and the Wakool River. The course of the Edward is through very rich and highly productive country, occupied by pastoralists and agriculturists on an extensive scale of operations.

ELLENBOROUGH RIVER is an affluent of the Bannoo River, taking its rise in Botumboin Mountain, in the county of Macquarie, and is a fine S. tributary of the Hastings River, flowing through the rugged cedar country to the W. of Comboyne and Botumboin Mounts.

ENDRICK RIVER takes its rise in the N.W. slopes of the Tatalerang Mountains, in the county of St. Vincent, and is an auriferous stream flowing in a N.W. direction through the township of Nerriga into the Shoalhaven River of which it is an affluent. It flows through some good grazing country.

ERSKINE RIVER takes its rise in the Liverpool Range to the N.E. of Taree, in the counties of Lincoln and Bligh, and is an affluent of the Coolaburragundy River. Its course is through Talbragar and Cobborah, into the main stream a few miles N. of Dubbo, and is fed by Spicer's, Solitary, Mitchell's, and Plain Creeks.

ESK RIVER takes its rise to the E. of Mount Doubleduke. It is a fine stream, and is fed by Yorkie's Creek. The course of the Esk is nearly parallel with the seaboard, and through rather broken and scrubby country, emptying into the estuary of the Clarence River.

EUCUMBENE RIVER.—This important auriferous stream flows through the county of Wallace in a S. direction, taking its rise in the Kiandra gold-fields. Its course is about 64 miles through rugged country, with the Snowy River, near Jindabyne, flowing in its tortuous course through the townships of Kiandra and Denison. The Eucumbene passes through some good pastoral country, and is fed by the Fryingpan and Goorudee Creeks.

FISH RIVER takes its rise in the W. slope of the Australian Alps, and forms the E. head of the Macquarie River, in the counties of Westmoreland and Roxburgh. It flows through the townships of Mutton Falls, Kenlis, and O'Connell, and is fed by the Fish, Binda, Slippery, Fish River Branch, Waterfall, Sidmouth Valley, Solitary, Dixon's and Frying-pan Creeks, and joins the main stream about 4 miles S. of Bathurst. It flows through good agricultural and pastoral land, much of which is taken up by settlers. A portion of the Fish River forms the division between the counties of Roxburgh and Westmoreland. It is on this river the Jenolan Caves were discovered; and gold was discovered in 1823 by Mr. Surveyor O'Brien at Sidmouth Valley, on the Fish River, and recorded by him, and was allowed to rest unvisited until 1851.

GEORGE'S RIVER has its rise on the E. slope of the ranges in the county of Cumberland, and is fed by the Dahlia, Bunbury, Curran, Prospect, Orphan School, Saltpan, Cabramatta, and Deadman's Creeks. Its course is through somewhat indifferent country, but is occupied by small settlers, flowing past the townships of Campbelltown and Liverpool, and emptying into the head of Botany Bay, near Sans-Souci.

GILGIL RIVER is an affluent of the Macintyre River, joining it at the confluence of that river with the Barwon to the N. of Caidmurra, in the county of Benarba. The Gilgil is a stream of good water, and takes its rise in the W. slopes of Mount Mosquito, in the county of Burnett, and about 20 miles N.N.W. of Warialda. Its course is about 100 miles through indifferent sterile country, and it is fed by the Bullala and Wallon Creeks.

GLOUCESTER RIVER takes its rise in Mounts Paterson and Allyn, in the county of Durham, flowing across the county of Gloucester in an E. direction into the Manning River, of which it is an important tributary, about 16 miles N. of the township of Gloucester on the river. It is fed by the Berico, Barrington, Cathill, and Macarthur Creeks.

GOOD GOOD RIVER or BERUDBA is a fine stream flowing in the rugged and mountainous country in the S. part of the Monaro district.

GOODRADIGBY RIVER has its rise in the W. slope of Mount Murray, in the counties of Cowley and Buccleuch. It has a course of about 70 miles, and separates the two counties named, and enters the Murrumbidgee River near Barren Jack Hill in the county of Harden. It is fed by the Peppercorn, Sandy Flat, Flea, Limestone, Micalong, Weejasper, Cookbundoon, Sugar Loaf, and Native Dog Creeks. The Goodradigbee is a large and important stream, flowing through rugged mountainous districts of limestone formation where there are some cavernous underground channels. The tops of the mountains are, for many months in the year, covered with snow; it however passes through some good pastoral land; although diversified in character of soil, is suitable for cultivation.

GOULBURN RIVER is a fine stream flowing in the counties of Hunter, Brisbane, Bligh, and Phillip, taking its rise in Mount Moolarben, flowing in an E. direction through good pastoral and agricultural country, falling into the Hunter River near the township of Denman. Its tributaries are Widden Brook and Krui River, and it is fed by Munmurra, Wollar, Bow, Bylong, Keerabbee, Merriwa, Wybong, Baerann, Gungall, Worondi, and Giant's Creeks.

GROSE RIVER is a fine affluent of the Hawkesbury River, taking its rise in the mountainous districts in the county of Cook. Its course is through deep ravines of the wildest magnificence. The upper part of this mountain stream is 3,000 feet above sea-level. Sir Thomas Mitchell, in his account of the discovery of the Grose River, says that his progress up the valley was arrested by water-worn pebbles as large as houses in the bed of the stream; and on the upper part of the basin it is a magnificent level, miles in width.

GUDGENBY RIVER is a tributary of the Murrumbidgee River, in the county of Cowley, and is a fine stream taking its rise in Gudgenby Hill. Its course is about 25 miles through broken and undulating pastoral country, and it joins the Murrumbidgee at the township of Tharwa. It is fed by numerous tributaries, the principal of which are the Naas Valley, Rendezvous, Nursery, Orraral, and Mount Tennant Creeks. It flows in some parts of its course between hills of schist and granite.

GUNGARLIN RIVER takes its rise in the Muniong Range, in the county of Wallace, and is a mountain stream flowing into the head of the Snowy River, of which it is an affluent. It has a course of about 20 miles through good pastoral country. It is liable to floods from its snow-fed tributaries.

GUY FAWKES RIVER has a course of about 50 miles, taking its rise in the N.W. part of the county of Raleigh, flowing N. through rough pastoral and well-timbered country into the Sara River, the two forming the Boyd River, and becoming an affluent of that river and a tributary of the Clarence River before entering the ocean.

GWYDIR RIVER.—This noble river takes its rise in the county of Hardinge by several heads in the W. slopes of the Australian Alps, in the neighbourhood of the Rocky River gold-fields. It has a course of about 450 miles, and flows through the counties of Hardinge, Murchison, Burnett, Courallie, and Benarba, where it enters the Barwon at Pockataroo; and passes the townships of Nundle, Bingera, and Moree, in its course. The head of the

Gwydir is fed by the confluence of the Rocky River and Honeysuckle Creek; and by the Nundle, Five-Mile, Two-Mile, Barlow's, Cameron's, Smashem's, King John's, Baker's, George's, Clark's, New Valley, Churchyard, Allen's, Cope's, Keera, Angula, Bingara, Horton, Myall, Warialda, Mosquito, Miah-Miah, and Weah-Waa Creeks. The whole course of the river is very productive, and is taken up for pastoral and agricultural purposes, and for which it is eminently adapted; and some of the numerous tributaries are also highly auriferous, and surrounded by large and extensive gold-producing country. The lower portion of the river below Bingera is well-wooded and clothed with gum forests.

GYRA RIVER takes its rise in the Great Dividing Range, near Ben Lomond, in the county of Sandon. It has a course of about 50 miles, and flows S. past the township of Falconer to its junction with the Filibuster Ponds, near the Great Falls, the two forming the Macleay River. This river flows through splendid country and is well timbered.

HASTINGS RIVER has a course of about 70 miles, and flows across the county of Macquarie, having its embouchure at the head of Port Macquarie, near the township of Sancrox. It takes its rise in Mounts Sea View and Jasper, and has for its tributaries the rivers Forbes, Ellenborough, Kinder Brook, Wilson, and Maria. The Hastings flows through rich country, and finely timbered with cedar and mahogany, and in parts the river opens into reaches of great width and beauty. It was discovered and named by Mr. Oxley in honour of the Governor-General of India at that time. It is fed by the Poppinbarra, Stony, Rawdon, Limeburners', Narran, Yeppin-Yeppin, and Thone Creeks. The township of Port Macquarie is situated on the S. side of the entrance to the river.

HAWKESBURY RIVER has a course of 330 miles, flowing, with its tributaries, through the counties of Cumberland, Camden, Cook, Westmoreland, and Argyle, before its embouchure in Broken Bay, where it reaches the ocean. It is formed, in the first instance, by the Wollondilly, and its S. branch, the Mulwaree, in the county of Argyle, not far from Goulburn, and was named by Governor Phillip after Lord Hawkesbury. It is a continuation of the Nepean River after the junction of the latter with the Grose River, issuing from the Blue Mountains, near Richmond. Along the base of these mountains the Hawkesbury flows in a N. direction, fed by numerous tributary mountain torrents, descending from narrow gorges, and becomes exceedingly tortuous in its W. course. The distance of the town of Windsor from the sea in a direct line is only 35 miles; but, by the windings of the river, is 140 miles. The Hawkesbury is navigable for vessels of 100 tons for 4 miles above Windsor; but its navigation is impeded by shallows after being joined by the Nepean. The rise of tide is 4 feet only at Windsor, and the water fresh 40 miles below it. It has for its tributaries the Wollondilly, Mulwaree, Macdonald, Cox, Grose, Colo, Cowpasture, Nepean, and Warragamba Rivers; and the Mangrove, Breakfast, Gunderman, Myrtle, Billong, Currency, Cattai, South, and Rickaby's Creeks. The scenery is highly picturesque and beautiful on this river, and is the scene of much enjoyment and festivity continually.

HENRY RIVER takes its rise in the E. slopes of Mount Mitchell, in the county of Gough. It is a small stream flowing E. into the Boyd River, near Barney's Hill, and thence into the Clarence River.

HORTON RIVER is a tributary of Horton Creek, having its rise in the county of Murchison, and flowing in a N. direction into the Gwydir River, in the county of Burnett, and with it reaches the Barwon at Pockataroo. Its course is through rugged country, some of which is highly auriferous, and is fed by the Cobbadah, Noocera, and Rocky creeks. The geological formation of the country through which it flows is upper palæozoic, connected with serpentine charged with chromate of iron.

HUNTER RIVER has its source in the Liverpool Range, and flows through the counties of Durham, Gloucester, Hunter, and Northumberland, and pursues a course of 300 miles, and disembogues at Port Hunter, on the shores of which is situated the City of Newcastle. It was discovered and named by Mr. Shortland in 1797, in honour of Governor Hunter, during whose administration the river was discovered. It is navigable for ocean-going vessels as far as Morpeth, 34 miles from the sea, and is one of the most important rivers of New South Wales. Its principal tributaries are the Williams and the Paterson, with their numerous tributaries; the one is navigable 18 miles, and the other 20 miles. The Williams divides the counties of Gloucester and Durham, and is the head of the navigation of the Hunter. It is fed by numerous streams, the principal of which, besides the Williams and Paterson, are the Goulburn and Page Rivers, the Branch, Omadale, Bells, Munimbah, Greig's, Jump-up, Rix's, Black, Lamb's Valley, Wallis', and Doyle's Ironbark Creeks; and the Stewart's, Dart, Rouchel, St. Hillier's, Muscle, Foy, Fal, Wollombi West, and Glendon Brooks, the whole, with their small tributaries, draining an area of 10,000 square miles of country, much of which is of the richest description, and is taken up by farmers and settlers who are employed, not only in grazing but in agricultural pursuits; hence these districts are the finest in the Colony. Through its lower course the river drains the largest and most important coal-fields of Australia, whose emporium is Newcastle, the second city of the Colony in shipping and commerce. The lower part of the Hunter is divided into two streams by a number of islands, the principal of which is known as Ash Island. These two streams, however, reunite near its mouth, forming the fine capacious harbour called Port Hunter. The geological formation of the district is mostly carbonaceous sandstone, overlying the invaluable coal-beds of the Colony.

INDI RIVER.—This important river takes its rise on the Snowy Mountains, in the county of Selwyn. Its course is on the W. side of this county, and forms the boundary-line between Victoria and this Colony. The Indi becomes an affluent of the Murray a few miles to the S. of Welaregang; the district through which it flows is very rugged and mountainous, but it passes patches of good country for pastoral pursuits.

ISABELLA RIVER is a tributary of the Abercrombie River. It is a fine stream, taking its rise in the W. slopes of Mount Werong, in the county of Georgiana, flowing into the Lachlan above the confluence of the Crookwell with that river. Its confluence with the Abercrombie is at the village of Bingham, and to the N.E. of the Tuena gold-fields. The Isabella flows through good pastoral country.

ISIS RIVER takes its rise in the Liverpool Range, near Downey's Pass, in the county of Brisbane. It is a fine stream flowing into the Page River, of which it is an affluent, and into which it falls at Gundy Gundy, and becomes a tributary of the Hunter River.

2 A

JACOB'S RIVER takes its rise in the E. slopes of the Snowy Mountains, in the county of Selwyn, and flows in a S.E. direction across the county of Wallace, and becomes a tributary of the Snowy River to the N. of the Pilot Mountain. The course of this river is through very rugged and mountainous country, but suitable for grazing purposes, and is fully occupied as such.

JOHN'S RIVER takes its rise in the county of Macquarie. It is a small stream, and flows into Watson Taylor's Lake, on the E. seaboard of the South Pacific Ocean.

KANGAROO RIVER commences its course in the W. slope of the Cambewarra Range, near Jamberoo, in the S. part of the county of Camden, and is a tributary of the Shoalhaven River. It traverses about 30 miles through the thickly-timbered brush country known as the Kangaroo Ground, exceedingly rugged, and in many places totally inaccessible. It is fed by the Yarringa, Mergla, and Bundanoon Creeks. The soil is very rich through which this river flows.

KARUAH RIVER takes its rise in the Mount Royal Range, and is a fine stream flowing from N. to S. through the centre of the county of Gloucester, and emptying itself into the head of Port Stephens. It flows past the township of Stroud, and is fed by the Deep, Lawler, Telegaree, Serpent, Pipeclay, and Limeburners' Creeks. The course of the Karuah is about 45 miles, and the country through which it flows is taken up by settlers for agricultural and pastoral purposes. The township of Stroud lies on the E. of this river, about 25 miles from its mouth.

KRUI RIVER takes its rise in the Liverpool Range, to the S. of Mount Mooan, in the county of Bligh, and is a N. tributary of the upper end of the Goulburn River. Its course is in a S. direction, and it flows through the township of Ailsa, and is fed by the Lorimer, Berrenderry, and Bella-Leppa Creeks.

KUMBALINE RIVER takes its rise in the S. slopes of Mount Kippora, in the county of Macquarie, and is a tributary of the Wilson River, which flows into the Hastings River at Port Macquarie.

KYBEAN RIVER is a tributary of the Umaralla River, in the county of Beresford, taking its rise in the W. slopes of the Australian Alps. Its course is about 20 miles N.W. with the main stream, 4 miles S.E. of Umaralla township. It flows through fine pastoral country, much of it highly suitable for agricultural settlement.

LACHLAN RIVER.—This very important river is the chief tributary of the Murrumbidgee, having its source in the Main Dividing Range, Mandonen or Cullarin, about 12 miles S.W. of Gunning, in the Yass Plains. Its course is over 700 miles, flowing through or separating the counties of King, Georgiana, Monteagle, Forbes, Bathurst, Ashburnham, Gipps, Cunningham, Blaxland, Darling, Franklin, Nicholson, Waradgery, and Waljeers. Upon it are situated the townships of Dalton, Cowra, Wangan, Forbes, Caradjery, Condobolin, Murrin, Booligal, Tegorohoke, Oxley, and Twopruck, and the Lachlan gold-fields; and it is fed by the Belubula, Crookwell, Abercrombie, and Burrowa Rivers, and the Jerrawa, Oolong,

Cullarin, Kildare, Blakeney's, Lampton, Grabben Gullen, Old Man's, Mulgowrie, Glengarry, Brahma, Graham's, Sandy, Oakey, Milburn, Spring, Hovell, Wangoola, Crowther, Kangarooby, Byrne's, Ooma, Goobang, Mitchell's, Kalingabungagay, Willandra, Billabong, Middle Billabong, and Gonowlia Creeks. This fine river pursues an exceedingly tortuous course, and its basin has an area of about 27,000 square miles, embracing an immense tract of excellent pastoral country in the S. and central parts of the Colony. The confluence of the Lachlan with the Murrumbidgee is in the counties of Caira and Waradgery, in a flat country covered with swamps, which Oxley, who discovered the river, met with, and was stopped by, in his first exploring expedition in 1817. The whole length of this Nile-like river is now taken up for pastoral purposes, and producing rich returns to the enterprising pastoral tenants of the Crown who occupy it.

LANE COVE RIVER takes its rise near Pennant Hills, in the county of Cumberland, and is a N. branch of the Parramatta River. Its course is about 12 miles through a well cultivated district, taken up, for the most part, by small settlers. It is fed by the Blue Gum, Swaine's, and Stringybark Creeks. All kinds of fruit are successfully cultivated in the district of the river, and the orange is particularly attended to by successful settlers, who supply the Sydney and other markets with fruit.

LANSDOWNE RIVER is an affluent of the Manning River, taking its rise in the county of Macquarie. It is a fine stream, flowing from the N.W. into the N. mouth of the Manning, about 6 miles W. of the entrance, and to the E. of Jones' Island. The course of the Lansdowne is through good agricultural country, and the land is taken up by thriving settlers.

LITTLE RIVER is a tributary of the Macquarie River, falling into it at Murrumbidgerie Falls, in the county of Gordon. It takes its rise on the E. slope of the Gingham Gap Range, and flows N. into the Macquarie, watering very good pastoral country, and passing through the township of Obley. It is fed by the Dilgar, Rocky Ponds, Hervy Range, and Buckinbar Creeks.

LITTLE PLAIN RIVER is an affluent of the Delegate River, flowing across the county of Wellesley, and joining the main stream at its confluence with the Snowy River. The Little Plain River takes its rise in the Delegete Range over the border line of Victoria, flowing N. near the W. road from Bombala to Gippsland. This stream flows through the diggings known as the Little Plain, and to the E. of the Delegete Range. Its course is through good pastoral country.

LOST RIVER takes its rise in the W. slope of the Australian Alps, in the county of King, a few miles S. of the township of Crookwell. It is a small stream flowing W. about 10 miles into the Wheoo Creek, through the N.E. portion of Yass Plains. Its course is through good pastoral and agricultural land, occupied by thriving settlers and pastoralists.

MACARTHUR RIVER is a tributary of the Gloucester River, flowing into it at the township of Gloucester, in the county of that name. It is but a small stream, watering the N.W. portion of the county, where settlers have small holdings and cultivate for agricultural purposes.

**MACDONALD RIVER** is a tributary of the Hawkesbury, dividing the counties of Hunter and Northumberland, and having its confluence with the main stream at Sackville Reach. It is an important affluent of the Hawkesbury, and is navigable for some distance above its confluence with that river. It flows through the township of St. Albans, watering some good agricultural country, and is fed by the Yengo and Wright's Creeks.

**MACINTYRE RIVER** is a continuation of the Barwon River, in the county of Benarba. It is joined by the Dumaresq in the extreme N. of the Colony, the two rivers separating the colonies of Queensland and New South Wales. It receives the waters of the Bombi, the Whalan, and the Gilgil, to the N. of Cnidmurra, where its confluence with the Barwon takes place. The Macintyre is a noble river, having a course of 350 miles, taking its rise in Mount Lomond, in the Australian Alps, about 16 miles S. of the township of Stonehenge, in the county of Gough, and flowing through the counties of Gough, Arrawatta, Stapylton, and Benarba, and the townships of Newstead, Inverell, Byron, Yetman, and Boggabilla. It is fed by the Severn and Dumaresq Rivers, and the Moredan, Querra, Paradise, Newstead, Middle, Swan, Rob Roy, Byron, Gramen, Redbank, Erna, Mundoe, Trigamon, and Oxley's Creeks. In the N. portion of its course the Macintyre flows through land of great fertility, with undulating flats and open forest, suitable for pastoral and agricultural pursuits.

**MACLEAN RIVER** takes its rise in the county of Gloucester, on the W. side, and flows across the county into Wallis' Lake, lying on the E. seaboard. It is a small stream, and the land through which it flows is of an indifferent character.

**MACLEAY RIVER** is a magnificent stream, taking its rise in the W. slopes near Ben Lomond, and has a course of about 200 miles through very rich and splendidly timbered country in the counties of Dudley, Sandon, and Vernon, emptying itself into the ocean at Trial Bay, a distance of about 80 miles N. of Port Macquarie. There is a bar across the entrance, and this river is only capable of admitting small steamers and coasting vessels, but is, however, navigable for more than 50 miles, as far as the town of Greenhills, a few miles above Kempsey. The Macleay is formed by the confluence of the Guyra River and the Tilbuster Ponds, and flows past the townships of East and West Kempsey and Fredericktown, and is fed by the Apsley, Styx, and Dyke Rivers, the Mihi, Kunderang, George's, Comara, Peedee, Nulla-Nulla, Parabel, Hickey's, Munga, Bococo, Christmas, Clybucca, Kinchela, and Darkwater Creeks, and the Oreen, Warbro, and Yessaba Brooks. Much of the land is of excellent quality, and is taken up by settlers, and under cultivation.

**MACQUARIE RIVER** is an important affluent of the Darling River, and takes its rise in the county of Roxburgh, about 8 miles S. of Bathurst, in the Blue Mountain Range. It was discovered by Mr. Evans in 1813, the then Deputy Surveyor-General. Mr. Oxley, the Surveyor-General, in 1818 was unsuccessful in his exploration of this river. Sturt also made a futile attempt to trace it. Sir Thomas Mitchell, however, subsequently followed it to its confluence with the Barwon, which takes place at Boree, in the county of Clyde. The course of the Macquarie is through 750 miles of magnificent country, flowing past the townships and villages of Bathurst, Burrendong, Wellington, Dubbo, Narromine, Gimerabunga, Gingi, and Cowalong, and being fed by the Fish and Campbell's Rivers, the Turon, Bell,

Cudgegong, Little, and Erskine Rivers, and the Queen Charlotte Vale, Princess Charlotte Vale, Neal's Water-hole, Swallow, Winburndale, Tambaroora, Coolamin, Pyramul, Curragurra, Section, Trianbil, Muckerwa, Burrandong, Stockyard, Eagle Beagle, Dreel, Hamgery, Wylandra, Coolbaggie, Brummagem, Budd, Ewenmair, and Martaguy Creeks. It divides the counties of Roxburgh and Bathurst, Oxley, Wellington, and Gordon, and flows through Lincoln, Ewenmar, Gregory, and Clyde, and waters the Macquarie, Tambaroora, Pyramul, Burrendong, and Muckerwa gold-fields. The principal falls in its course are Butler's and the Macquarie Cataract, the former about 4 miles S. of Dubbo, and the latter near the village of Gingi. The upper part of the Macquarie flows in a winding gravelly bed, with beautifully verdant banks, through extensive level plains of deep, fine, rich soil. Lower down the country is generally open forests, with rich flats on either side of the stream. The whole of the country through which the river flows is taken up for pastoral and agricultural purposes.

MACQUARIE RIVULET is a small stream flowing from near the E. end of the Wingecarribee Swamp into Lake Illawarra, in the county of Camden. It is fed by Johnstone's Creek.

M'LAUGHLIN RIVER takes its rise in the W. slopes of the Coast Range, in the county of Wellesley, flowing S. into the Snowy River, at the confluence of the Delegete with that river. It has a course S.E. for about 50 miles through the Monaro Plains, and is fed by the Springflat Creek. It flows through good pastoral country, and the stream is partially auriferous.

MANILLA RIVER is an affluent of the Namoi River, taking its rise in the Nandewar Range, in the county of Darling. It is a fine auriferous stream, flowing into the Namoi River at the township of Manilla. Its course is about 65 miles S.E. and S.S.E. through the township of Barraba and the Ironbark gold-field, and is fed by the Hawkins, Connor's, Barraba, Naugahra, Eumur, Hoskinson's, Tarporley, and Borah Creeks. The Manilla River waters fine undulating pastoral country.

MANNING RIVER takes its rise in the Main Dividing Range, near Omadale, flowing E., forming the N. boundary of the county of Gloucester, and from which it separates the counties of Hawes and Macquarie on the N., and it enters the ocean by two main entrances, known as Harrington Inlet to the N., and Farquar Inlet to the S., the delta lying between consisting of Oxley's and Mitchell's Islands. The Manning is a fine large river, having a course of about 100 miles through magnificent agricultural country, much of it taken up by thriving settlers. It is fed by the Barnard, Gloucester, Nowendoc, Dawson, and Lansdowne Rivers, and by the Khatambu, Woolshed, Dingo, Pahpoo, Dickenson's, Waramba, Berady, Milbai, Fattorini, Burril, and Belbora Creeks. The back country is densely timbered with valuable trees of various kinds, cedar being found in considerable quantities. The river is navigable for over 20 miles from its mouth for ocean-going vessels—as far as Wingham.

MARIA'S RIVER is a small stream taking its rise in Mount Kippara, on the N. boundary of the county of Macquarie, flowing through the village of Mariaville, in a S.E. direction, into the Wilson River. Marias River flows through good agricultural country, much of which is under cultivation.

MITCHELL RIVER is a fine stream, taking its rise in the E. slope of the Great Dividing Range, in the county of Gough, flowing in an E. direction across the county of Drake, where it becomes a tributary of the Nymboi River, and enters the Clarence River.

MOLE RIVER takes its rise on the W. slope of the Doctor's Nose Hill and the high bluffs near the township of Bolivia, in the county of Clive. It is a fine stream, flowing N.W. over 50 miles through good pastoral and agricultural country into the Dumaresq River at Mingoola, on the Queensland border. It is fed by the Deepwater Creek, where there are open forests and grassy downs. The Mole abounds in very fine fish, the Murray cod being an especial favourite.

MOLONG RIVER is a small auriferous tributary of the Bell River, rising on the W. side of the county of Wellington, and flowing N. into the main stream. It waters good country.

MOLONGLO RIVER takes its rise in the W. slope of the Australian Alps, in the county of Murray. It is a large and important stream, taking a N.W. course, and flowing over 50 miles before entering the Murrumbidgee River, near Big Hill. It is an affluent of the Queanbeyan River, and receives the waters of the Bellallala, Yandyganulla, Primrose Valley, Yarrow, and Jerabombera Creeks. The Molonglo waters the extensive rich grassy flats known as the Molonglo and the Limestone Plains, and flows through the township of Queanbeyan, where it is joined by the Queanbeyan River.

MONGARLO RIVER is an important auriferous tributary of the Shoalhaven River, taking its rise in the mountains near the township of Monga, on the W. side of the county of St. Vincent. It flows through the township of Marlow and the Mongarlo gold-fields. The course of this river is in a N. direction, flowing about 60 miles to its confluence with the Shoalhaven River, and it is fed by several small creeks, more or less auriferous.

MOONIE RIVER is a tributary of the Gwydir River, before that river's confluence with the Barwon at Pockataroo, in the county of Benarba. It has a course of about 25 miles through scrubby plains, with occasional swamps and reed beds, before entering the main stream.

MORUYA RIVER forms the boundaries between the counties of St. Vincent and Dampier, and takes its rise in the mountainous districts of Araluen, in the county of St. Vincent, flowing in a S.E. direction past the townships of Kiora and Moruya into the ocean, by a wide estuary, at Toragy Point. The course of the Moruya River is about 80 miles, through splendid country for agricultural and dairy purposes, and is an important outlet by water for the produce of the Araluen and Braidwood districts, with their gold-fields. The land is well taken up by prosperous settlers, and is highly productive.

MOWAMBA RIVER takes its rise in the W. slope of the Snowy Mountains, in the county of Wallace, and is a small tributary of the upper part of the Snowy River, flowing into it past Mount Mowamba and below Jindabyne. Its course is through good, pastoral country.

MUMMEL RIVER takes its rise in the county of Macquarie, and is a small N. tributary of the Cooperacurraba and Nowendoc River, falling into the Manning River, near the township of Nowendoc. Its course is through fairly good country.

MURRABINE RIVER is a small stream taking its rise to the S. of Mount Dromedary, in the county of Dampier. Its course is through rugged country, and falls into the ocean at Marruna.

MURRAY RIVER takes its rise in the Snowy Mountains, in the S.E. portion of New South Wales, and adjoining that of the sister colony, Victoria. It has three sources, from which it commences to spread out its waters, which orm the magnificent water-course known as the Murray or Hume—they are he Indi, the Tooma, and the Hume. The first of these has the longest course, rising in the Pilot Mountain, at an elevation of 5,000 feet above the sea-level; the other two heads take their rise in the N. and W. slopes of Mount Kosciusko. From the confluence of these three rivers the Murray has a course of 1,719 miles before falling into the ocean in South Australia, 1,132 of which are within the Colony of New South Wales, and it flows through and waters the counties of Auckland, Wellesley, Wallace, Selwyn, Goulburn, Hume, Denison, Townsend, Cadell, Wakool, Caira, Taila, Wentworth, and Tara; and is fed by the E. branch Tooma, Edward, Murrumbidgee, Darling, and Rufus Rivers, and the Pilot Hill, Ram's Head, Leather-jacket, Snowy, Springflat, Coppabella, Dora, Sugarloaf, Mullanjandra, Ournane, Jingellec, Seven-mile, Burrongo, Genapna, Merang, Tuppal, Tittara, Nolyango, Taila, Bengallow, Moontong, Ana-branch, Tharbry, and Bundawingee Creeks. It flows through the following townships:—Wellaregang, Jingellee, Dora, Albury, Wahgunyah, Howlong, Corowa, Duanarangownie, Mowarry, Weinmunar, Mulwalla, Belubula, Moama, Euston, Luidattul, Calludwug, Tarracama, Morquong, Wentworth, and Moorna. The following are the crossing-places from New South Wales into Victoria:— Albury (by railway), N. Wahgunyah or Corowa, Moama (by railway), Swan Hill, Euston, and Wentworth, and at these places there are Custom-houses, and officers for the collection of border duties. The whole of the country bordering the river is essentially a pastoral one, and the land is generally well grassed and watered. The Murray has been navigated as far as the Ournie gold-field, about 150 miles above Albury, and 1,590 miles from its mouth. The course of this river is extremely tortuous; measured circuitously it has an immense mileage, and it drains an area of 270,000 square miles. According to Mr. Acheson's table of discharges, its width from Albury to Moama at summer level varies from 200 to 240 feet. The upper part of the river, particularly the Indi branch, flows through high rocky cliffs, where the celebrated Murray Gates (a perpendicular chasm in the mountains) overhang the infant stream 3,000 feet. The timber grown on the banks of the river are of the most valuable kind, and for ornamental furniture not to be equalled in quality for usefulness or the beauty of its grain. The mallee scrub is most valuable in its power of retaining water in the driest season, and renders the pasture valuable wherever it abounds.

MURRUMBIDGEE RIVER has a course of 1,350 miles, flowing almost due E. and W. from its rise in the county of Buccleuch until its confluence with the Murray in the counties of Caira and Taila on the southern border of the Colony. The source of this fine and magnificent river rises from two heads in the mountainous regions of the County of Buccleuch, where an altitude is attained of over 5,000 feet above sea-level—the one is from Peppercorn Hill, a detached mountain lying about 10 miles N.E. of the township of Yarrangobilly, and the other is in the N. slope of Mount Tantangora, about 3 miles from the township of Kiandra. Both these mountains, although detached from the main chain, belong to the Snowy Mountains. After the junction of the heads of these two sources, the Murrumbidgee flows through very rugged and scrubby country for over 100 miles until its confluence with the Yass River. It then takes a W. course, being fed by numerous important streams through a vast extent of fine country, its principal tributaries being the Umaralla, Bredbo, Gudgenby, Molonglo, Cottor, Yass, Goodradigbee, Tumut, and Lachlan Rivers; and the Gulf, Yaouk, Back, Alum, Wambrook, Coolringdon, Stacks, Colyer's, 6-Mile, Micalago, Stoney, Guise's, Bulgar, Swamp, Tinker's, Waterhole, Oakey, Dam, Brassil, Warroo, Mountain, Macpherson's Swamp, Jeremiah, Rocky Bedding, Matchems, Oak, Limestone, The Oak, Crowpal, Jugiong, Spring, Muttama, Adelong, Native Dog, Nakie-Nakie, Nargus, Jetting, Billabong, Yaven Yaven, Tarcutta, Houlahan's, Kiambla, Bullenbung, Yanko, and Morrool Creeks ; and the following townships are situated on the Murrumbidgee River, viz. :—Bolaira, Colinton, Tharwa, Jugiong, Aura, Wantabadgery, Gundagai, Wagga Wagga, Narrandera, Yanko, Bunandara, Turambola, Bringalgee,, Liordonga, Currattfoot, Mulburraga, Benbola, Waradgery, Hay, Murthurgugala, Bungah, Rapaula, Maude, and Balranald. In its course the river flows through or by the following counties, viz. :—Wallace, Beresford, Cowley, Murray, Buccleuch, Harden, Clarendon, Wynyard, Mitchell, Bourke, Cooper, Boyd, Sturt, Waradgery, and Caira ; and in its course waters several fertile and agricultural plains, and passes through the Kiandra, Gulf, and Adelong gold-fields. The area of the basin of the Murrumbidgee is estimated at 25,725 square miles, all of which is occupied, either for pastoral, agricultural, or other purposes by an enterprising and thriving population. Captain J. C. Cadell opened up the navigation of the Murrumbidgee in his steamboat "Albury" as far as Gundagai, in 1858, since which a fleet of small river steamers have been plying to and from Adelaide.

MYALL RIVER takes its rise in the county of Gloucester, to the S.E. of the township of Gloucester. It is a fine stream, and flows through country well suited for agricultural purposes, and it empties into the lagoon known as the Broadwater. It is fed by the Crawford River, which falls into it at Bullah Delah, and then flows into the N.E. part of Port Stephens.

NAMBUCCA RIVER takes its rise in the coastal range in the county of Raleigh, and is fed by the Algomera and Dargan Creeks. It is a fine mountain stream, watering good country, well timbered with cedar and other valuable woods. Its embouchure with the ocean is by a narrow rocky channel, lying between the Clarence and Trial Bay. This river is navigable by small craft only, trading in timber and other produce of the district.

NAMOI RIVER is an affluent of the Darling River, taking its rise in the Moonbi Range, in the county of Inglis, and flowing N.W. over 600 miles before its confluence with the Barwon, above Walgett. It is fed by innumerable tributary streams, among which are the Manilla, Mulucrindie, and Cockburn Rivers ; and Smith's, Ingleba, Bald, Black Spur, Surveyor's, Congi, Carlyle's, Mount Lowry, New England, and Hall's, Wombramarg, Nundle, Hanging Rock, Duncan's, Ogunbil, Goonoo Goonoo, Moore, and Sandy Creeks. The Namoi flows through or divides the counties of Inglis, Parry, Buckland, Pottinger, Darling, Jamison, Baradine, White, and Denham ; and flows through the townships of Bendemeer, Carroll, Burburgate, Gunnedah, Gulligal, Boggabri, Wallah, Narrabri, Wee Waa, and Walgett. The upper part of the river is through very rocky and rugged country ; but in its lower course it opens up very fine and rich country, known as the Liverpool Plains District, first discovered by Oxley in 1818, and named by him after Lord Liverpool ; and subsequently further explored by Sir Thomas L. Mitchell on his voyage down the Namoi River in 1831.

NARRAN RIVER takes its rise in Queensland, and enters this Colony, dividing the counties of Narran and Finch in its course, to its confluence with the Barwon, at the township of Geera, in the county of Clyde. It has a course of about 125 miles through very swampy country before it reaches and joins the Barwon. This river was discovered by Sir Thomas L. Mitchell in 1845.

NATTAI RIVER is a tributary of the Wollondilly River, taking its rise near Berrima. It is a fine stream, and joins the main river at the township of Burragorang. It is fed by the Jellore River, and the township of Nattai lies near the banks of the river.

NEPEAN RIVER.—This river takes its rise in the county of Camden, in the mountainous district around Berrima, and is an important affluent of the Hawkesbury, flowing into this river between Penrith and Richmond at the confluence of the Grose River with the main stream. The Nepean is, in fact, only another name for the upper end of the Hawkesbury. It is a fine stream, and is fed by the Wattle, Mount Hunter, Stonequarry, and the Warragamba, Bargo, Cordeaux, and Cataract Rivers; and flows past the townships of Picton, Riversford, and Camden. The Nepean flows through rich and highly cultivated country. Camden Estate, the seat of the Macarthurs, lies upon this stream.

NOWENDOC RIVER is a tributary of the Manning River, taking its rise in the E. slope of the mountain range, near the Basaltic Column, in the county of Hawes. It is a fine stream, flowing past the township of Nowendoc, and watering very good country, through which it flows. The Mummel, Cooperacurraba, and Rowley's Rivers are tributary streams to the Nowendoc, and enter the Manning by one stream.

NYMBOI RIVER is a tributary of the Clarence River, taking its rise in the counties of Drake, Gresham, and Fitzroy, and is formed by the confluence of the Don Dorrigo and Cloud's Creeks, near Nymboida. It is a fine affluent of the Clarence, and is fed by the Blaxland's, Boyd, Boundary, Doughboy, and Cunglebung Creeks, and the Boyd and Mitchell Rivers.

ORARA RIVER is the dividing line between the counties of Clarence and Fitzroy, and takes its rise near Bagowa, flowing N.W. into the Clarence River, through good country.

ORRORAL RIVER is a tributary of the Murrumbidgee River, taking its rise in the county of Cowley, and flowing through undulating pastoral country for about 20 miles, passing between Mount Tennant and the Bunberi Ranges.

PADDY'S RIVER takes its rise in the county of Camden, and is a tributary of the Wollondilly River, flowing at an elevation of 1,856 feet above sea-level. It is fed by the Uringalla Creek, and flows through the township of Murrimba.

PADDY'S RIVER is a small stream in the county of Gordon, taking its rise at the head of Wylandra Creek, in that county. The country is good through which it flows.

PAGE RIVER is a tributary of the Hunter River, taking its rise in Mount Murulla, in the county of Brisbane. It is a fine stream, flowing past the townships of Scone and Murrurundi, and the Boxtree Flat. It is fed by the Isis River and Warland's Creek, and flows through good country, suitable for grazing and agricultural pursuits.

PANBULA RIVER takes its rise in the Wolumla Peak, in the county of Auckland, and flows into the sea by the Toallo Lake. It is a tidal river, and is navigable to within a mile of Panbula wharf at high tide for vessels of 60 or 70 tons burden. The township of Panbula is situated on its banks, and the river abounds with fish and aquatic birds.

PAROO RIVER takes its rise in Queensland, flowing S., dividing the counties of Thoulcanna and Irrara, Ularara and Barrona, Fitzgerald and Killara, where, at the latter place, its confluence with the Darling takes place. The Paroo has an ana branch (known as the Calbaoro Billabong), and has a course of about 200 miles through some available sheep country, which is mostly taken up by tenants of the Crown.

PARRAMATTA RIVER is the name applied to the W. arm of Port Jackson, extending for about 18 miles inland. There are steamboats running almost hourly to Parramatta, which is the head of the navigation, passing the villages of Hunter's Hill and Gladesville, and the township of Ryde, places celebrated for the beauty of the scenery it affords to pleasure seekers, and for the splendid quality of its orangeries and orchards. The stream beyond Parramatta is not worthy the name of a river. The land, however, is very good along the course of this creek, and most of it is well cultivated.

PATERSON RIVER is a very important affluent of the Hunter River, and is navigable for 20 miles above its confluence with that river at Hinton. It takes its rise in the Mount Royal Range, and flows through rich agricultural and grazing land, mostly taken up by flourishing settlers, and is fed by the Allyn River and Plumby Creek. In its course it flows past the townships of Lostock, Gresford, Gostwych, and Paterson. The district through which it flows is well grassed and finely timbered.

PEEL RIVER takes its rise in the Liverpool Range, between Hanging Rock and Crawney Pass, in the counties of Brisbane and Parry, and flows about 80 miles through the townships of Nundle, Dungowan, Woolomin, Tamworth, Bective, and Somerton, below which it joins the N. head of Muluerindie River, and has for its tributaries the Conadilly River, and Turraberle, Maules, Brigalow, Calathora, Pian, and Baradine Gully Creeks, and flows into the main stream, or Namoi River proper. The Peel River and its tributaries are more or less auriferous, and the country is good grazing land through which it flows.

PINCH RIVER takes its rise in the lofty Snowy Mountains, in the county of Wallace. It is a fine stream, and its course is about 30 miles into the Snowy River, flowing through good grazing country.

QUEANBEYAN RIVER is a tributary of the Molonglo River, rising in the W. slope of the Australian Alps, in the county of Murray. Its course is about 30 miles through good undulating country, much of it being under cultivation, but the greater part taken up for pastoral purposes. It flows past the townships of Queanbeyan and Jingery, and is fed by the Tinderry and Burra Creeks.

REDBANK RIVER takes its rise near the coast-line, in the county of Fitzroy, and is fed by the Dirty Creek. It is a small stream falling into the ocean opposite the Red Rock.

RICHMOND RIVER separates the counties of Rous and Richmond for the greater part of its course, taking its rise in the Macpherson Range, on the Queensland border, flowing S.E. for about 120 miles through the county of Richmond to its embouchure in the estuary at Richmond Heads. It is fed by the N. Richmond and S. Richmond Rivers, and the Emigrant, Macguire's, Duck, Dungarabbee, Rocky Mouth, Deep, Derubba, and Eden Creeks, and flows past the townships of Casino, Codrington, Wardell, and Ballina. The mouth of the Richmond is obstructed by a sand bar, but is navigable for sea-going steamers and other vessels for about 30 miles, on to the junction of the S. Richmond River with the main stream at Coraki Junction. The N. arm on N. Richmond River flows past the townships of Lismore and Gundurimba, and is fed by the Leycester's, Boatharbour, Boseri, Pelican, and Wilson's Creek. Ballina Head, the N. head of the estuary, is 32 miles N. of Shoal Bay. The course of this river is through very rich land, well grassed, and finely timbered with cedar and other valuable trees, and there is a great and increasing trade on the river.

ROCKY RIVER takes its rise in the N. slope of Harnham Hill, about 6 miles S. of Uralla, in the counties of Hardinge and Sandon, flowing through the Rocky River gold-fields and the township of Uralla into the Gwydir, a few miles S. of Nundle. The Rocky River is a fine auriferous stream, and forms one of the bends of the Gwydir River, and has for its tributaries Kentucky Ponds, Honey's, Kennedy's, and Boorolong Creeks. In its course the Rocky River has several fine waterfalls, notably in the parish of Elton, a few miles below Uralla, and also some high granite rocks known as The Wallabies.

ROWLEY'S RIVER is a small stream rising in the county of Macquarie, and watering good agricultural land. It is a N. tributary of the lower end of the Nowendoc River, flowing into the Manning River.

RUFUS RIVER takes its rise near the South Australian border, in the county of Taila. It is a small stream, watering a sterile country, flowing through Hawdon's Plains.

SANDON RIVER takes its rise in the county of Clarence, and is a small stream flowing into the ocean at Plover Island. It flows through good country, abounding in cedar, and is fed by the Toumbaal and Condole Creeks.

SEVERN RIVER is a tributary of the Macintyre River, taking its rise in the W. slope of the Australian Alps, in the county of Clive. It is fed by the Beardy Waters, Wellingrove, Cameron, Arrawatta, Spring, Sandy, Frazers, and Myall Creeks, and flows through the counties of Gough and Arrawatta, and the townships of Severn and Strathbogie. Its course is about 80 miles through good pastoral country, with plains of fine rich land, and suitable for agricultural purposes. Its confluence with the Macintyre is at the Great Falls, in the county of Arrawatta.

SHOALHAVEN RIVER takes its rise in the coastal range called Coromboro, at an elevation of 2,801 feet above sea-level, under the main range, in the county of Dampier, and has a course of 260 miles in length, being fed by numerous tributaries, the principal of which are the Kangaroo, Endrick, Corang, and Mongarlow Rivers, and the Broughton's, Bumberra, Nowra, Bungalee, Yerriong, Yalwall, Borimbadal, Barbers, Jerrara, Bungonia, Nerrimungo, Bindi, Ningee Nambla, Durran Durra, Gillimatong, Modbury, Jembaicumbene, Oranmeir, Wiabene, Jerrabalgulla, Yiarranbene Creeks, flowing N. through the townships of Ballababa, Larbert, Nowra, Numba, and Terara, into the ocean by a fine wide estuary at Greenwell Point. The Shoalhaven is the largest and most important river on the coast side of the dividing range, on the S. of Sydney, and forms the boundaries between the counties of Camden, St. Vincent, and Argyle; and its upper part is highly auriferous. Its course is through deep gullies and wild and magnificent scenery, with terrific glens from 500 to 1,500 feet in height; and in its lower part it flows through rich, low-lying agricultural land, and considered the richest and most productive in the country. The navigation of this river is limited, not extending many miles inland, and confined to small steamers which ply from its mouth upwards.

SNOWY RIVER has its rise in the Munion Range of mountains in the counties of Wallace and Wellesley, and which counties its waters divide, and after a course of 360 miles enters the ocean near Bass' Straits, in the colony of Victoria. It is fed by numerous streams, the principal of which are the Gungarlin, Barranbugge, Crackenback, Eucumbene, Wollonaby, Mowamba, Beloka, Wullwye, Bobundara, McLaughlin, Bombala, Matong, Murrumboola, Tongara or Jacobs, and Pinch Rivers or Creeks. This river is snow fed, and its flow liable to sudden changes on the melting of the snow in the ranges by which it is encompassed. Its course is through rugged but good grazing country in places, and the soil and climate suitable for agriculture and the growth of European fruits and vegetables.

STYX RIVER, taking its rise in Oakey Creek, in the county of Dudley, is a small stream and a tributary of the Macleay River, flowing through good country.

TIA RIVER is a S. tributary of the Apsley River, in the county of Vernon, flowing into the Macleay. The course of this river is through very rough, rugged country, and its confluence with the main stream is about 12 miles below Apsley Falls.

TIMBARRA RIVULET has its source from the mountainous regions to the E. of the township of Severn, in the county of Drake, flowing into the upper part of the Clarence River, and is fed by the Demon, West, and East Creeks. The lower part of this river is auriferous, and waters good country, flowing through the Timbarra gold-fields.

TOMAGO RIVER takes its rise in the county of St. Vincent, between Bateman's Bay and Broulee, and is a small stream falling into the sea at Tomago Inlet.

TOOLOOM RIVULET is an affluent of the upper part of the Clarence River, taking its rise near the S. Obelisk, in the counties of Buller and Rous, and flowing S. through the Tooloom gold-fields. It is a fine auriferous stream, and flows through well grassed and finely-timbered country.

TOOMA RIVER has its source in the Snowy Range of the Australian Alps to the N.E. of Mount Kosciusko, in the county of Selwyn. It is a fine stream flowing near Big Bogong Peak, and after a course of about 35 miles it falls into the river Murray at Welaregang. It waters a large tract of good pastoral country. The Tooma River is fed by numerous tributaries, the principal of which are the Tumberumba and Wolumla Creeks.

TOWAMBA RIVER takes its rise in the S. coast range, opposite Catchcart, in the county of Auckland, and after a course of about 40 miles through fine pastoral and agricultural country, empties itself into the S. arm of Twofold Bay. It is an important stream, and is fed by the Perica, Wog-Wog, Jingo, and Matagana Creeks. The township of Boyd stands near this river at its estuary.

TUMUT RIVER is an important affluent of the Murrumbidgee River, and takes its rise in the Big Bogong or Mane's Range and the Snowy Mountains, and forms the division between the counties of Buccleuch on the E., and Wynyard on the W. Its course is for about 80 miles through rugged scrubby country until it falls into the Murrumbidgee, about 8 miles N.E. of Gundagai, and is fed by numerous streams, the principal of which are the Yarrongobilly, Waterfall, Joanama, Black, Sandy, Blowering, Logbridge, Gooburragandra, Gilmore, Bumboloo, Killimicat, Brungle, and the Adjungbilly Creeks; and it flows through the townships of Talbingo, Tumut, and Mingery, and the Adelong gold-fields. This river flows through very good country, adapted for cultivation as well as for pastoral purposes.

TURON RIVER is an important auriferous affluent of the Macquarie River, taking its rise in the W. slope of the Australian Alps, N. of the Cullen Bullen township, and in the parish of Ben Bullen and county of Roxburgh. It has a course of about 50 miles, forming the largest of the western gold-fields—the Turon. Its tributaries are the Crown Ridge, Williwa, Coolamigal, Round Swamp, Arthur's, Oaky, Little Oaky, Sheep Station, Insolvent, Tanwarra, and Cunningham Creeks. This river flows through rugged well-timbered country, and all its tributaries and creeks are more or less auriferous. Most extensive alluvial diggings have been worked on the river, and well-known as the Cullen Bullen, Palmer's or Oakey Creek, Wattle Flat or Sofala, and Tambaroora.

TUROSS RIVER takes its rise in the Barren Jumbo Mountain in the county of Dampier, having a course of 60 miles before reaching its embouchure, which is by a wide open estuary into the South Pacific Ocean, having, however, a bar at its mouth. This river flows during its course through the Gulf or Tuross gold-fields, and crosses the road from Bega to Moruya, about 6 miles S. of Coila, a small town on the N. bank of the estuary; and is fed by the Bambo, Gulph, and Wadbilliga Creeks. The country through which the Tuross flows is of the richest and finest quality for cultivation and is splendidly grassed and timbered.

TWEED RIVER is the most northerly in the Colony, being on the Queensland boundary-line. It takes its rise in Mount Warung, in the county of Rous, taking a course of about 30 miles into the South Pacific Ocean at Point Danger, and flowing through rich semi-tropical country. This river is navigable for small craft only; it has a bar across its entrance, and is exposed to the ocean swell.

UMARALLA RIVER is a tributary of the Upper Murrumbidgee River, taking its rise in the W. of the Australian Alps, about 12 miles to the E. of Nimmitibel, in the county of Beresford. It has a course of about 80 miles through good pastoral and agricultural country, and is a fine stream and an important affluent of the Murrumbidgee. The Umaralla flows past the township of that name and has many tributary streams flowing into it: the principal ones are the Bigbadja and Kibeyan Rivers, and the Winifred, Granny's Flat, and Cooma Creeks. This river waters a great part of the celebrated Monaro Plains, and is liable to overflow from the melting of the snow in the ranges by which it is encompassed.

WAKOOL RIVER flows through and has its origin in the counties of Wakool, Townsend, and Cadell, and waters a great part of the district known as Riverina. This river is, in fact, a S. branch of the Edward, and the two rivers together are navigable for over 400 miles, as far as the important town of Deniliquin from their confluence with the Murray River, in the county of Caira. The Wakool flows to the W. of Deniliquin, about 6 miles, and through the village of Wakool and the township of Jegur, and is fed by the Merribul, Cobul, Merang, and Neimur Creeks. Its course is through rich land and flat pastoral country well grassed; and the branches of the Edward and the Wakool Rivers form a most complete network of creeks.

WALLAMUMBI RIVER is an affluent of the Macleay River, taking its rise in the Great Dividing Range near Ben Lomond, in the county of Clarke. It joins the Chandler River before its confluence with the Macleay. Its course is through good pastoral and agricultural country.

WARAMBA RIVER takes its rise in the county of Gloucester, and is a small tributary of the S. mouth of the Manning River.

WARRAGAMBA RIVER takes its rise in the county of Westmoreland, and is a tributary of the Nepean River and joins the Cox River before its confluence with the main stream. Its course is about 20 miles through rugged and scrubby country, and it is fed by the Werriberri Creek.

WARREGO RIVER takes its rise in the high table-land in the colony of Queensland; flowing S. into this Colony it separates and flows through the counties of Irrara and Culgoa, Barrona, Landsborough, and Gunderbooka. It is an important tributary of the Darling River, and has a course of 125 miles before its confluence with this noble stream, at the township of Ouraweria, in the county of Landsborough. The Warrego is fed by the Irrara Creek, but its flow is through poor, sandy, and stony country, with belts of myall scrub.

WHALAN RIVER takes its rise in the county of Stapylton, on the Queensland border, and is an overflow from the Macintyre River, and before its confluence with the Barwon it is joined by the Bombi and the Gilgil. Its course is through open and scrubby plains, arid in summer and swampy in winter.

WOLGAN RIVER is a small stream rising in the county of Cook, flowing through what is known as the Valley of the Wolgan into the Colo River, and of which it is a tributary.

WOLLOMBA RIVER takes its rise in the county of Gloucester, flowing through the township of Wollomba into Wallis Lake. It is a small stream.

WOLLONDILLY RIVER takes its rise in the S. coast range, in the county of Camden, to the W. of Wollongong, and with its tributary streams the Cataract and Cordeaux form the source from which Sydney obtains its water supply. In its tortuous course it flows through the valley of Burragorang, and waters portions of the counties of Camden, Argyle, and Westmoreland. After a course of about 90 miles it flows through the township of Goulburn, and joins Cox's River at the junction of the counties of Cook and Westmoreland before entering the Nepean. The Wollondilly flows through exceedingly rich country, well grassed and highly adapted for agriculture, watering among other places the celebrated Goulburn Plains. It is fed by the Mulwaree

Ponds, Bullamalita, Pejar, Burnaby, Guinecor, Murruin, Wingecarribee, Joortland, Tinkettle, and Bob Higgin's Creeks, and the Cookbundoon, Paddy's, and Nattai Rivers.

WOOLI-WOOLI RIVER is a small stream rising in the S. part of the county of Clarence, flowing into the South Pacific Ocean, opposite the well known N. rocks on the coast.

WORONORA RIVER flows into Botany Bay, near the estuary of George's River, in the county of Cumberland. It is a small stream rising in the coast range. The land is rich through which this small river flows.

WILLIAMS RIVER is an important affluent to the Hunter River, taking its rise in the Liverpool Range at the Hanging Rock, in the county of Hawes, flowing through the counties of Brisbane, Durham, and Gloucester, dividing these two latter counties in its course, and is navigable from its confluence with the Hunter at Raymond Terrace for about 20 miles. It flows through fine agricultural and pastoral country, much of it highly cultivated, and is fed by the Chichester River, and the Myall, Carowery, Wangi, Wallarobby, Uwarabin, Nolan, Doggrel, and Wattle Creeks. It flows through the townships of Forsterton, Dungog, Clarencetown, and Seaham.

WILSON'S RIVER takes its rise in Mount Kippara, in the county of Macquarie, and is an affluent of Maria's River, having its embouchure in Lake Macquarie. It flows past the village of Ballengara through good agricultural and pastoral country.

WINBURNDALE RIVER takes its rise in the county of Roxburgh, and is a tributary of the Macquarie River. It flows through fine land, and rich auriferous country, and is fed by the Kirkconnell, St. Anthony's, Clear, Duramana, Cheshire, Rover's, and Millah-Murrah Creeks. In its course it waters the Kirkconnell and Glanmire gold-fields, the Cheshire Creek, the Wattle Flat, and Macquarie gold-fields. The course of the Winburndale is about 60 miles to its confluence with the Macquarie.

WULLWYE RIVER takes its rise in the Snowy Mountains, in the county of Wallace. It is a tributary to the Snowy River, and its confluence with that river is near Buckley's crossing-place. It is fed by the Arable Creek, and has a course of about 36 miles through good pastoral country.

YARROW RIVER takes its rise in the Great Dividing Range, in the county of Gough, and is a tributary to the Mitchell River which flows into the Clarence River. It is a small stream and flows through rugged country.

YASS RIVER takes its rise in the W. slope of the S. Coast Range, near Mount Ainslie, and flows through or borders the counties of Harden, King, and Murray. It is a large and important stream, and is a valuable tributary to the Murrumbidgee River. In its tortuous course the Yass River flows through the townships of Gundaroo and Yass, and the fertile Yass Plains. It is fed by M'Laughlin's, Shinglehouse, Gundaroo, Nelsonglade, Five-mile, Murrumbatemen, Manton's Bango, Derringellan, and Bowning Creeks. The course of the Yass River is through very rich pastoral and agricultural land, and copper ore is largely developed throughout the district in which it flows.

*This concludes the Rivers of the Colony.*

RIVERSTONE (*Co. Cumberland*), a postal village, 28 miles W. of Sydney, with mail twice daily. It is a railway station on the Windsor and Richmond line.

RIX'S CREEK (*Co. Durham*), a postal village, 150 miles N. of Sydney, with daily mail. A railway station on the northern line.

RIX'S CREEK (*Co. Durham*), a small northern tributary of the Hunter River, flowing into it at the village of Auckland.

RIX'S LAGOON (*Co. Sandon*), a waterhole, lying about 6 miles W. of Armidale, in the parish of Broker.

ROBERTSON (*Co. Camden*), a postal village, 102 miles S. of Sydney, with mail twice daily. Telegraph and money-order offices, and Government savings bank. The nearest railway station is Moss Vale, on the southern line.

ROBERTSON'S POINT (*Co. Cumberland*), a narrow rocky promontory, on the N. shore of Port Jackson, lying between Shell Cove on the W. and Mossman's Bay on the E. It was the paternal residence of the late Hon. John Robertson, K.C.M.G., but is perhaps better known as "Cremorne."

ROBINSON, a county in the Western Division of the Colony. [See "COUNTIES."]

ROBINSON'S MOUNT (*Co. Cowley*), a lofty hill, overhanging the upper part of the Murrumbidgee River. The highest point in this range attains an elevation of 4,192 feet above sea-level.

ROBINSVILLE (*Co. Camden*), a postal village, about 40 miles S. of Sydney, with daily mail. A railway station on the Illawarra and South Coast line.

ROB ROY (*Co. Murray*), a railway station, 210 miles S. of Sydney, on the Goulburn and Cooma line.

ROB ROY (*Co. Gough*), a postal village, 73 miles N. of Sydney, with mail twice a week. The nearest railway station is Glen Innes, 45 miles, on the northern line.

ROB ROY CREEK (*Co. Gough*), a small western tributary of the Macintyre River, falling into it at the township of Byron.

ROCK, THE (*Co. Nandewar*), a small settlement, lying a short distance from the township of Narrabri.

ROCK FLAT (*Co. Beresford*), a postal receiving-office, 267 miles S. of Sydney, with mail four times a week. The nearest railway station is Cooma, 10 miles, on the Goulburn and Cooma line. It is a rocky flat to the N. of Nimmitibel.

ROCK FLAT CREEK (*Co. Beresford*), a tributary of the Cooma Creek, rising on the Jinny Brother Peak of the Kiandra Ranges.

ROCK'S CREEK (*Co. Evelyn*), a small tributary of Neale's Waterholes, in the parish of Vittoria.

ROCKDALE (*Co. Cumberland*), a postal suburb, 6 miles S. of Sydney, with mail twice daily. Telegraph and money-order office, and delivery by letter-carriers. A railway station on the Illawarra and South Coast line. It was proclaimed a municipal district in 1871, with eight aldermen and a mayor.

ROCKGEDGIEL (*Co. Napier*), a township on the boundary-line of county of Napier.

ROCKLEY (*Co. Georgiana*), a postal village, 166 miles W. of Sydney, with daily mail. Telegraph and money order offices, and Government savings bank. The nearest railway station is George's Plains, 15 miles, on the western line, situated on Pepper's Creek, at an elevation of 2,000 feet above sea-level, in the parish of Rockley. The Campbell is within 3 miles E., and the district is principally agricultural.

ROCKWELL (*Co. Yancowinna*), a postal town, 951 miles S. of Sydney, with mail therefrom four times a week.

ROCKY BEDDING CREEK (*Co. Bucclench*), a southern tributary of the Murrumbidgee River, rising in the Parson Hill.

ROCKY BIGHT (*Co. Cumberland*), a small opening in the cliffs of the coast, about 5 miles S. of the entrance to Port Jackson.

ROCKY BRIDGE CREEK (*Cos. Georgiana and Bathurst*), a northern tributary of the Abercrombie River, rising in a swamp about 5 miles S.E. of the township of Somers, on the Rocky and Cowra Road, and flowing S.W. about 30 miles.

ROCKY CREEK (*Co. Evelyn*), is a southern tributary of the Evelyn Creek, flowing in a S.E. direction.

ROCKY CREEK (*Co. Courallie*), a western tributary of the Horton River, rising in Mount Lindsay, in the Nandewar Range, and flowing past the village of Carega.

ROCKY FALLS (*Co. Clarence*), a waterfall on the Clarence River, in the parish of Copmanhurst. There are other falls about the same place known as Smith's, Tindal's, Bullock, and Double Channel Falls.

ROCKY FORD (*Co. Clyde*), is a passage over the upper part of the Narran River, on the road from Bourke to Queensland.

ROCKY GLEN (*Co. White*), a postal village, 351 miles N. of Sydney, with mail three times a week. The nearest railway station is Gunnedah, 40 miles, on the north-western line.

ROCKY HALL (*Co. Wallace*), a postal village, 339 miles S. of Sydney, with mail twice a week. The nearest railway station is Cooma, 74 miles, on the Goulburn and Cooma line.

ROCKY MOUTH (*Co. Clarence*), is the postal village of the village of Maclean (which see). It is 323 miles to the N. of Sydney, and is a very fertile district, abounding in native game of every description, and the lakes abound in fish.

ROCKY MOUTH CREEK (*Co. Richmond*), a small southern tributary of the S. arm of the Clarence River, falling into it opposite Maclean.

ROCKY PINNACLE (*Co. Wynyard*), a high hill lying between Tarcutta and Umbang Creek, about 10 miles S. of the township of Umutbee.

ROCKY PLAIN (*Co. Wallace*), a postal village, 288 miles S. of Sydney, with mail once a week. The nearest railway station is Cooma, 28 miles, on the Goulburn and Cooma line.

ROCKY PLAINS (*Co. Wallace*), a tract of flat country, affording good pasturage, but covered with snow during the winter months, lying on the N. bank of the Giandarra River, between the township of Kiandra and Denison.

ROCKY PONDS (*Co. King*), a railway station, 166 miles S. of Sydney, on the southern line.

ROCKY RIVER (*Co. Sandon*), a postal village, 348 miles N. of Sydney, with mail three times a week. The nearest railway station is Uralla, 4 miles, on the northern line, situated in the parish of Yarrowick, about 2 miles S.E. from the township of Uralla, and 12 miles N.E. from Armidale. The dividing range reaches an elevation of 4,000 feet above sea-level. Gold-mining is the chief interest of the district, principally alluvial workings.

ROCKY RIVER (*Co. Hardinge*). [*See* "RIVERS."]

ROLLANDS PLAINS (*Co. Macquarie*), a postal village, 310 miles N. of Sydney, with mail three times a week, and telegraph office. The nearest railway station is Hexham, 164 miles, on the northern line. Situated on Wilson's River, about 20 miles N.W. of Port Macquarie, and consists of fine, open, grazing country, and good alluvial land, suitable for agricultural pursuits.

ROOKWOOD (*Co. Cumberland*), a postal village, 10 miles W. of Sydney, with mail twice daily. Telegraph and money-order offices, and Government savings bank. It is a railway station on the suburban line.

ROOKWOOD (*Co. Cumberland*).—The mortuary for the city and suburbs of Sydney.

ROOTY HILL (*Co. Cumberland*), a postal village, 25 miles W. of Sydney, with mail twice daily, and money-order office. A railway station on the western line. A small village, lying about 6 miles from Blacktown.

ROPE'S CREEK (*Co. Cumberland*), a small agricultural village, situated on Rope's Creek, an eastern tributary of South Creek, 3 miles W. of Hebersham, or Eastern Creek.

ROSE BANK (*Co. Clarence*), a postal village, 380 miles N. of Sydney, with mail per Clarence and Richmond River steamers.

ROSE BAY (*Co. Cumberland*), a beautiful bay on the S. shore of Port Jackson, about 1 mile across from E. to W. The head of the bay consists of a lovely sandy beach, along the border of which the new road to Sydney to the South Head runs, in a semicircle, for about a mile and a half, being one of the most delightful drives in the neighbourhood of the metropolis.

ROSEBROOK (*Co. Durham*), a postal receiving-office, 130 miles N. of Sydney, with mail twice a week. The nearest railway station is West Maitland, on the northern line.

ROSEDALE (*Co. Beresford*), a postal village, 306 miles S. of Sydney, with mail twice a week. The nearest railway station is Cooma, on the Goulburn and Cooma line.

ROSEHILL CREEK (*Co. Rous*), a small tributary of the Leycester Creek.

ROSE'S LAGOON (*Co. Argyle*), a small lake of permanent fresh water, lying about 9 miles of Lake George, and 3 miles N. of Spring Valley.

ROSEMOUNT (*Co. Buccleuch*), a postal receiving-office, 306 miles S. of Sydney, with mail three times a week.

ROSE VALLEY (*Co. Beresford*), a grassy valley, on the N.E. of the Urumalla River, to the N.E. of Bunyan.

ROSEWOOD (*Co. Wynyard*), a postal village, 387 miles S. of Sydney, with mail three times a week.

ROTHBURY (*Co. Durham*), a postal village, 140 miles N. of Sydney, with mail three times a week. The nearest railway station is Branxton, 12 miles, on the northern line.

ROUCHEL BROOK (*Co. Durham*), an eastern tributary of the Upper Hunter, fed by Davis and Dry Creeks. It falls into the main stream about 6 miles N.E. of Aberdeen.

ROUCHEL BROOK (*Co. Durham*), a postal village, 199 miles N. of Sydney, with mail twice a week. The nearest railway station is Aberdeen, 12 miles, on the northern line.

ROUMALLA CREEK (*Co. Harden*), a western tributary of the Honeysuckle Creek. It is auriferous, the gold being found as at Uralla or Rocky River gold-fields.

ROUND HILL (*Co. Harden*), a lofty peak, lying about 6 miles S.W. of Jugiong, and on the N. bank of the Murrumbidgee River.

ROUND HILL (*Co. Yancowinna*), a postal receiving-office, 917 miles S. of Sydney, with mail five times a week. The nearest railway station is Hay, 410 miles, on the south-western line.

ROUND MOUNTAIN (*Co. Wallace*), a peak of the Crackenback Mountain, in the Bald or Snowy Mountain Range of the Muniongs. It is near the head of the Mowamba River.

ROUND SWAMP CREEK (*Co. Roxburgh*), an auriferous tributary of the Turon River, rising in the Cherrytree Hill.

ROUND SWAMP (*Co. Roxburgh*), a postal receiving-office, 134 miles W. of Sydney, with mail three times a week.

ROUS.—A county in the Eastern Division of the Colony. [*See* "COUNTIES."]

ROUS (*Co. Rous*), a postal village, 357 miles N. of Sydney, with mail per Clarence and Richmond Rivers steamers.

ROUS MILL (*Co. Rous*), a post-office, 359 miles N. of Sydney, with mail therefrom per Clarence and Richmond Rivers steamers. Telegraph and money-order offices.

ROUSE HILL (*Co. Cumberland*), a postal village, 29 miles W. of Sydney, with mail twice daily. The nearest railway station is Riverstone, 4 miles, on the Windsor and Richmond line, situated on the Cattai Creek in the parish of Gwydir. The district is agricultural, and abounds with fine clay.

ROUSEVILLE (*Co. Cumberland*), a railway station on the Hornsby-St. Leonards line.

ROVER'S CREEK (*Co. Roxburgh*), a small tributary of the Winburndale Rivulet, rising on the high ranges in the parish of Waltham.

ROWLEY RIVER (*Co. Macquarie*). [*See* "RIVERS."]

ROXBURGH. A county in the Eastern Division of the Colony. [*See* "COUNTIES."]

ROZELLE BAY (*Co. Cumberland*), a wide arm at the head of Johnstone's Bay, lying between the Glebe, Glebe Island, and the isthmus of the Balmain peninsula.

RUFUS RIVER (*Co. Tara*). [*See* "RIVERS."]

RUGGED PEAK (*Co. Wynyard*), a high peak in the range to the N.E. of the township of Tarcutta, on the N.E. bank of the Yaven-Yaven Creek.

RUMBEE MOUNT (*Co. Clive*) is the second highest peak in the New England range of mountains, attaining an elevation of 4,947 feet above sea-level. It lies near the head of the Mole River.

RUMKER'S PEAK (*Co. Phillip*) is the name given to the highest peak of a double-headed detached mountain, lying on the E. side of the road from Dabee to Merriwa.

RUNNING CREEK (*Co. Parry*), a small eastern tributary of the Bald Creek.

RUSH'S (*Co. Camden*), a railway station, 74 miles S. of Sydney, on the southern line.

RUSHCUTTERS' BAY (*Co. Cumberland*) is one of the bays on the south shore of Port Jackson, lying about 2 miles to the E. of Sydney, and receiving the waters of Rushcutters' Creek. It lies between Darling and Potts Points, and is ¾ of a mile long from N. to S. On its western shore is a curious rock, known as the Horse's Head or the Kangaroo, from a supposed resemblance to one or the other of these objects.

RUSHCUTTERS' CREEK (*Co. Cumberland*), a small stream rising at the head of the valley of Lacroza, to the east boundary of the city of Sydney, and across the Lower South Head Road.

RYAN'S CREEK (*Co. Beresford*), a small stream flowing into Tinderry Creek to the N. of Bredbo River.

RYDAL (*Co. Cook*), a postal village, 111 miles W. of Sydney, with mail twice daily. Telegraph and money-order offices, and Government savings bank. A railway station on the western line. Situated in the parish of Lisdale, on the Solitary Creek. The district is agricultural and pastoral.

RYDALMERE (*Co. Cumberland*), a postal receiving-office, 18 miles W. of Sydney, with daily mail. The nearest railway station is Ryde, 2 miles, on the Ryde and Hawkesbury River line.

RYDE (*Co. Cumberland*), a postal village, 12 miles W. of Sydney, with mail twice daily. Telegraph and money-order offices, Government savings bank, and delivery by letter-carriers; and a railway station on the Ryde and Hawkesbury River line. Situated on the N. bank of the Parramatta River, in the parish of Hunter's Hill. The nearest point of the Lane Cove River is 2 miles E. from Ryde, and its junction with the Parramatta River is at Onion's Point. There is a good steamer's wharf at Ryde, where the Parramatta to Sydney boats call. The district is very fertile. It was proclaimed a municipal district in 1870, with a council of eight aldermen and a mayor.

RYE PARK (*Co. King*), a postal village, 198 miles S. of Sydney, with mail three times a week. The nearest railway station is Binalong, 34 miles, on southern line.

RYLSTONE (*Co. Roxburgh*), a postal town, 149 miles W. of Sydney, with daily mail. Telegraph and money-order offices, and Government savings bank. A railway station on the western line. Situated on the left bank of the Cudgegong River. The district is principally pastoral. Gold has been found in nearly all the watercourses.

# S

SACKVILLE REACH (*Cos. Cook and Cumberland*), a postal village, 44 miles W. of Sydney, with mail three times a week. The nearest railway station is Windsor, 12 miles, on the Richmond line. Situated on both sides of the Hawkesbury River, in the parish of Maroota. The district is an agricultural one.

SADLEIR'S FLAT (*Co. Buccleuch*), a small plain, lying to the N. of Adjungbilly Creek, and at the S. foot of Paddy's Rock Hill.

ST. ALBAN'S (*Co. Northumberland*), a postal village, 70 miles W. of Sydney. Telegraph and money-order offices, with mail twice a week. The nearest railway station is Windsor, 36 miles, on the Richmond line. Situated on the Macdonald River, and police district of the same. The district is an entirely agricultural one.

ST. ANTHONY'S CREEK (*Co. Roxburgh*), a small auriferous tributary of the Winburndale Rivulet, flowing N.W. through the new Glanmire gold workings.

ST. CLAIR (*Co. Durham*), a postal village, 166 miles N. of Sydney, with mail twice a week. The nearest railway station is Singleton, 20 miles, on the northern line.

ST. GEORGE'S BASIN (*Co. St. Vincent*), a postal receiving-office, 141 miles S. of Sydney, with mail three times a week. The basin is a coast lake or lagoon, lying to the N.W. of Sussexhaven.

ST. GEORGE'S CAPE (*Co. St. Vincent*), a rock promontory, on the peninsula forming the south head of Jervis Bay. At a distance of 2 miles N. of this cape is a white stone tower erected, and on which a light is exhibited, called the Cape St. George light, 224 feet above sea-level. It is a revolving light, exhibiting at intervals of 30 seconds a red, green, and white light alternately.

ST. HILLIER'S BROOK (*Co. Durham*), an eastern tributary of the Hunter River, falling into it to the N. of Musclebrook.

ST. IVES (*Co. Cumberland*), a postal receiving-office, 12 miles north of Sydney, with daily mail.

ST. JOHN'S PARK (*Co. Cumberland*), a postal receiving-office, 23 miles S. of Sydney, with daily mail.

ST. LEONARD'S (*Co. Cumberland*). [See "NORTH SYDNEY."]

ST. LEONARD'S CREEK (*Co. Parry*), a postal receiving-office, 367 miles N. of Sydney, with mail once a week. This creek is a small tributary of the Inglebah Creek flowing from Watch Hill.

ST. MARKS (*Co. Cumberland*), a suburb of Sydney, in the parish of Alexandria, municipality of Paddington, and police district of Sydney. It lies on the new South Head Road, between Rushcutters' and Double Bay, about 2 miles east of the city of Sydney, and the communication to the city of Sydney is by vehicular traffic, and which is abundantly supplied.

ST. MARYS (*Co. Cumberland*), a postal village, 29 miles W. of Sydney, with mail twice daily. Telegraph and money-order offices, and Government savings bank. A railway station on the western line. Situated on Rope's Creek. The district is an agricultural one. It was incorporated a municipal district in 1890, with a council of five aldermen and a mayor.

ST. PETERS (*Co. Cumberland*), a suburban postal village, 4 miles S. of Sydney, with mail twice daily. Telegraph and money-order offices, Government savings bank, and delivery by letter-carriers. It is situated about 1 mile N.E. of Cook's River, in the parish of Petersham, and police district of Sydney, and adjoins Newtown and Kingston. It was incorporated in 1871 a municipal district with a council of eight aldermen and a mayor.

ST. THOMAS (*Co. Cumberland*), a postal village, 9 miles S. of Sydney, with mail twice daily.

ST. VINCENT. A country in the Eastern Division of the Colony. [*See* "COUNTIES."]

SALISBURY (*Co. Durham*), a postal village, 176 miles N. of Sydney, with mail three times a week.

SALISBURY PLAINS (*Co. Sandon*), a postal receiving-office, 356 miles N. of Sydney, with mail twice a week. The nearest railway-station is Kentucky, 7 miles, on the northern line. The plains comprise a good tract of pastoral country, in the parishes of Salisbury, Mihi, Blacknote, and Gostwyche.

SALISBURY WATERS (*Co. Sandon*), a fine stream flowing from the Ohio Peak through Salisbury Plains into the Mihi Creek, a little below Dangar's Falls.

SALLY'S FLAT (*Co. Wellington*), a postal receiving-office, 169 miles W. of Sydney, with mail three times a week.

SALLY'S FLAT (*Co. Wellington*), an auriferous flat, forming part of the Tambaroora gold-field, about 6 miles N.W. of the township of Sofala.

SALLY'S FLAT CREEK (*Co. Buccleuch*), a small tributary of Peppercorne Creek, rising on the E. of Peppercorne Hill.

SALLY'S FLAT CREEK (*Co. Wellington*), a small auriferous tributary of Green Valley Creek, lying to the E. of the Tambaroora gold-field.

SALT ASH (*Co. Gloucester*), a postal village, 99 miles N. of Sydney, with mail once a week. An agricultural settlement, lying about 13 miles E. of Raymond Terrace.

SALTPAN CREEK (*Co. Cumberland*), a small northern boundary of the lower end of George's River. Also a small creek flowing into Long Bay, a western arm of Middle Harbour.

SALTWATER CREEK (*Co. Durham*), a small stream flowing into the southern part of Port Stephens.

SANCRO (*Co. Macquarie*), a proclaimed village, on the Hastings River, near Port Macquarie.

SANDON.—A county in the Eastern Division of the Colony. [*See* "COUNTIES."]

SANDON RIVER (*Co. Clarence*). [*See* "RIVERS."]

SANDGATE (*Co. Northumberland*), a railway station, 6 miles from Newcastle, on the Newcastle, Maitland, and Singleton line.

SANDRINGHAM (*Co. Cumberland*), a suburb of Sydney, 4 miles to the south of the city. The nearest railway-station is Kogarah, 4 miles, on the Illawarra and South Coast line.

SANDY CREEK (*Co. Auckland*), a small southern tributary of the Bembooka River, rising in the South Coast Range, and flowing through good pastoral country.

SANDY CREEK (*Co. Camden*), a small stream flowing into the sea near Black Head, at the N. end of Four-mile Beach, about 1 mile S. of Gerringong.

SANDY CREEK (*Co. Georgiana*), a small eastern tributary of the Lachlan River, rising near the village of Bigga.

SANDY CREEK (*Co. Gough*), a small southern tributary of the Severn River, rising in the N.E. slope of Tower Hill, on the Glen Innes and Warialda Road.

SANDY CREEK (*Co. Hardinge*), a small tributary creek of the Eragerra Creek, crossing the road from Armidale to Inverell.

SANDY CREEK (*Co. Parry*), a small southern tributary of the Peel River, flowing to the S.W. of Bective township.

SANDY CREEK (*Co. Urana*), a small eastern tributary of the Urana Creek.

SANDY CREEK (*Co. Wynyard*), a railway station, 318 miles S. of Sydney, on the southern line.

SANDY CREEK (*Co. Wynyard*), a small western tributary of the Tumut River, flowing into it N. of and near the township of Talbingo.

SANDY CREEK NORTH (*Co. Sandon*), a village, 358 miles N. of Sydney. The nearest railway station is Armidale, 22 miles, on the northern line.

SANDY FLAT (*Co. Clive*), a postal village, 465 miles N. of Sydney, with daily mail. A railway station on the northern line.

SANDY FLAT CREEK (*Co. Buccleuch*), a western tributary of the Goodradigbee River, flowing S. of the Yass Plains.

SANDY HILL (*Co. Clive*), a postal village, 510 miles N. of Sydney, with daily mail.

SANDY WATERHOLE CREEK (*Co. Goulburn*), a small eastern tributary of the Coppabella Creek.

SANS-SOUCI (*Co. Cumberland*), a township, 7 miles S. of Sydney. The nearest railway station is Kogarah, 2 miles, on the Illawarra and South Coast Line. It is a pleasant spot, lying on the George's River, and is a favourite place for picnic parties.

SARA RIVER (*Co. Gresham*), a fine stream, rising in Mount Mitchell, to the N. of the Oban diggings, and flowing into the Guy Fawkes River, the two forming the Boyd River.

SASAFRAS (*Co. St. Vincent*), a postal receiving-office, 246 miles S. of Sydney, with mail twice a week. It is on the road from Shoalhaven to Braidwood.

SAUMAREZ (*Co. Sandon*), a proclaimed village, near the northern railway, to the S. of Tamworth.

SAUMAREZ CREEK (*Co. Sandon*), a fine stream rising on the ranges to the W. of Armidale and flowing into the Salisbury waters.

SAVERNAKE (*Co. Urana*), a postal receiving-office, 469 miles S. of Sydney, with mail once a week.

SAWYERS (*Co. Wynyard*), a mining village, situated on the Sawyers' Creek, about 10 miles from the township of Adelong.

SCHNAPPER ISLAND (*Co. Cumberland*), a small island, in the Parramatta River, at the mouth of Long Cove, about half a mile from Cockatoo Island.

SCHONE'S PADDOCK (*Co. Wellington*), a small alluvial diggings on the Burrendong gold-fields.

SCOFIELDS (*Co. Cumberland*), a railway station, 27 miles W. of Sydney, on the Windsor and Richmond line.

SCONE (*Co. Brisbane*), a postal village, 194 miles N. of Sydney, with mail twice daily. Telegraph and money-order offices, and Government savings bank. A railway station on the northern line. Situated in the parish of St. Luke, on the Kingdon Ponds, about 7 miles S.E. of the Hunter River. The district is agricultural and pastoral. It was proclaimed a municipal district in 1888 with a council of five aldermen and a mayor.

SCOTCHMAN'S (*Co. Wallace*), a peak in the Monaro Range, overhanging the Snowy River, about 16 miles below Buckley's Crossing-place.

SCOTLAND ISLAND (*Co. Cumberland*), a small rocky and well-wooded island in Pittwater, and parish of Narrabeen.

SCOTT'S CREEK (*Co. Macquarie*), a small drainage creek flowing into the Manning River.

SCOTT'S FLAT (*Co. Northumberland*), a postal village, 159 miles N. of Sydney, with mail twice a week. The nearest railway station is Singleton, 5 miles, on the northern line.

SCROPE RANGE, a chain of low sandstone hills to the W. of the Darling River, near the dividing line with South Australia.

SCRUMBO MOUNT (*Co. Durham*), a peak of the Mount Royal Range, lying near the junction of the Rouchel Brook and Davis' Creek.

SEAHAM (*Co. Durham*), a postal town, 130 miles N. of Sydney, with daily mail. The nearest railway station is Morpeth, 8 miles, on the East Maitland and Morpeth line. In the parish of Seaham, on a peninsula formed by the Williams and Hunter Rivers. The district is an agricultural one.

SEAL ROCKS (*Co. Gloucester*), a cluster of rocky islets, lying off the coast opposite Sugarloaf Point.

SEAVIEW MOUNT (*Co. Hawes*), a lofty mountain attaining an altitude of 6,000 feet above sea-level, and a prominent landmark for vessels sailing up the N. coast, lying near the head of the Hastings River.

SEBASTOPOL (*Co. Clarendon*), a postal village, 312 miles S. of Sydney, with mail twice a week. The nearest railway station is Junee, 25 miles, on the southern line.

SECTION CREEK (*Co. Wellington*), a western tributary of the Macquarie River, rising on the south-eastern slope of Mount Vernon.

SEDGEFIELD (*Co. Durham*), a postal village, 129 miles N. of Sydney, with mail twice a week. The nearest railway station is Singleton, on the northern line.

SELWYN.—A county in the Eastern Division of the Colony. [*See* "COUNTIES."]

SENTRY-BOX BEACH (*Cos. Cumberland and Northumberland*), a part of the Hawkesbury River, in the parish of Spencer.

SENTRY-BOX MOUNT (*Co. Selwyn*), a lofty peak of the Bogong Ranges.

SERPENT CREEK (*Co. Gloucester*), a small stream falling into the estuary of the Karuah River, on its N. bank.

SERPENTINE CREEK (*Co. Hume*), a southern tributary of the Billabong Creek.

SEVEN HILLS (*Co. Cumberland*), a postal village, 20 miles W. of Sydney, with mail twice daily. A railway station on the western line.

SEVEN-MILE CREEK (*Co. Goulburn*), a tributary of the Murray River, to the S.E. of Jergyle Mountain. Also a small tributary of the Billabong Creek. Also a name for the head of Woomargarma Creek. Also a small tributary of the head of Thurgonia Creek.

SEVEN OAKS (*Co. Dudley*), a small agricultural settlement, a few miles from Kempsey, on the Macleay River.

SEVERN (*Co. Gough*), a proclaimed village, situated on the Severn River, in the parish of Severn, and police district of Wellingrove. The district is a pastoral and agricultural one.

SEVERN RIVER (*Co. Arrawatta*). [*See* "RIVERS."]

SEYMOUR (*Co. Wallace*), situated on the slope of a hill about 3 miles from the Eucumbene River, in the parish of Adaminaby, 329 miles to the S. of Sydney. Adaminaby is the postal town [which *see*.] The district is auriferous.

SHAKING BOG (*Co. Buccleuch*), a tract of swampy country, near the head of the Adjunbilly Creek.

SHANNON MOUNT (*Co. Tongowoko*), a peak of the Grey Range.

SHANNON VALE (*Co. Gough*), a tract of fine pastoral country, lying about 12 miles W. of Glen Innes, over the ranges.

SHARK CREEK (*Co. Clarence*), a small southern tributary of the S. arm of the Clarence River, falling into it to the S.W. of Maclean.

SHARK ISLAND (native name, BAAMBILLY) (*Co. Cumberland*), a well-known island in Port Jackson, opposite Rose Bay, about 2 miles S.W. of the inner South Head.

SHARK POINT (*Co. Cumberland*), forms the eastern head of Rose Bay, on the S. side of Port Jackson. Also, a bold rocky promontory on the coast, about 6 miles S. of the entrance of Port Jackson.

SHAW (*Co. Bathurst*), a postal village, 184 miles W. of Sydney, with mail three times a week. The nearest railway station is Blayney, 12 miles, on the Blayney and Murrumburrah line.

SHEA'S CREEK (*Co. Cumberland*), a small watercourse, flowing from the Waterloo Swamp into the head of the N. arm of Botany Bay.

SHEARERS' SPRINGS (*Co. Culgoa*), a township, to the W. of Culgoa River, on the Queensland border.

SHEEHAN'S HILL (*Co. Buccleuch*), a peak, lying on the S. bank of the Murrumbidgee River, and to the E. of Gundagai, near the head of the Yellow Clay Creek.

SHEEP STATION CREEK (*Co. Gough*), a small western tributary of the Yarrow River.

SHEEP STATION CREEK (*Co. Roxburgh*), a small auriferous tributary of the Turon River, flowing into it at the township of Sofala.

SHEEP STATION GULLY CREEK (*Co. Buckland*), a small tributary of the Kangaroo Station Creek.

SHEET OF BARK (*Co. Bathurst*), a village, 210 miles S. of Sydney. The nearest railway station is Woodstock, 1 mile, on the Blayney-Murrumburrah line.

SHEET OF BARK CREEK (*Co. Buckland*), a small creek, draining some good agricultural land, flowing into the Binni Creek.

SHELL COVE (*Co. Cumberland*), a well-known and favourite beach on the N. shore of Port Jackson, lying opposite Woolloomooloo Bay. Also a wide bight on the W. side of the Middle Harbour, to the S. of the sandspit.

SHELLHARBOUR (*Co. Camden*), a postal town, 66 miles S. of Sydney, with mail twice daily. A railway station on the Illawarra and South Coast line. It is about 4 miles N.E. of Jamberoo, and the same distance N. of Kiama. The district is highly productive for dairy-farming. It was proclaimed a municipality in 1859, with a council of eight aldermen and a mayor.

SHEPHERD'S (*Co. Wellington*), a tributary of the Curragurra Creek, flowing to the S. of the Stony Creek gold-field.

SHEPHERD'S RANGE (*Co. Wellesley*), a ridge of hills to the S.W. of Nimmitabel, the highest peak of which is One-Tree Hill.

SHEPHERD'S TOWN (*Co. Wellington*), a postal village, 305 miles S. of Sydney, with daily mail. The nearest railway station is Gundagai, 21 miles, on the Cootamundra-Gundagai line.

SHERBROKE (*Co. Camden*), a postal town, 65 miles S. of Sydney, with mail therefrom three times a week.

SHERWOOD (*Co. Macquarie*), a postal town, 223 miles N. of Sydney, with mail three times a week. The nearest railway station is Hexham, 111 miles, on the northern line.

SHINGLE-HOUSE CREEK (*Co. Murray*), an eastern tributary of the Yass River, rising to the W. of Lake George, and flowing into the main stream, near Gundaroo.

SHOAL BAY (*Co. Clarence*) is the estuary of the Clarence River. The coast from Shoal Bay trends N.E. 50 miles to Cape Byron, and is mostly low and sandy.

SHOALHAVEN (*Co. St. Vincent*), situated on the Shoalhaven River, is one of the principal towns in the district, lying about 120 miles S. of Sydney. It was incorporated a municipality in 1878, with a council of five aldermen and a mayor. The land is very fertile, and dairy-farming is pursued very successfully.

SHOALHAVEN RIVER (*Cos. Dampier, Argyle, Camden, and St. Vincent*). [*See* "RIVERS."]

SHORTER'S HILL (*Co. Parry*), a postal receiving-office, 155 miles W. of Sydney, with mail twice a week.

SIDMOUTH VALLEY CREEK (*Co. Westmoreland*), a small southern tributary of the Fish River, rising to the S. of Mutton Falls, and flowing between it and Kenlis. This valley is exceedingly fertile.

SILENT GROVE (*Co. Parry*), a village, 281 miles to the N. of Sydney. The nearest railway station is Tamworth, on the northern line.

SILVERTON (*Co. Yancowinna*), a postal town, 822 miles S.W. of Sydney, with mail five times a week. Telegraph and money-order offices, Government savings bank, and delivery by letter-carrier. The nearest railway station is Hay, 400 miles, on the south-western line. It was proclaimed a municipal district in 1886, with a council of eight aldermen and a mayor. Population, about 1,800. Courts of petty sessions and district courts are held here periodically.

SIMPSON MOUNT (*Co. Northumberland*), a high peak, in the parish of Lockyer, about 9 miles S. of Wollombi.

SIMPSON'S PASS (*Co. Northumberland*), a gap in the Dowling Range, near Mount Lockyer, about 16 miles S. of Wollombi, and 72 N. of Sydney.

SIMS' GAP (*Co. Cooper*), a gap in the Cocopara range of hills.

SINGLETON (*Co. Northumberland*), a postal town, 148 miles N. of Sydney, with daily mail. Telegraph and money-order offices, Government savings bank, with delivery by letter-carrier. A railway station on the northern line. Situated on the Hunter River, in the parish of Singleton. The district is highly productive. It was proclaimed a municipality in 1866, with a council of eight aldermen and a mayor. Population, about 1,000. Courts of petty sessions and district courts are held here periodically.

SIRIUS COVE (AND LITTLE SIRIUS COVE) (*Co. Cumberland*).—These two bays now form Mossman's Bay, which see.

SISTER'S BAY (*Co. Cumberland*), a small bight on the western shore of Long Cove.

SKELTON CREEK (*Co. Gough*), a small northern tributary of the Mitchell River, falling into it at Shannon Vale.

SKILLION FLAT (*Co. Macquarie*), a postal village, 323 miles N. of Sydney, with mail three times a week.

SLAPDASH CREEK (*Co. Bligh*), a northern tributary of the Wialdra Creek. The road from Cooyal to Mendooran runs alongside the creek to its head.

SLATHERUM SWAMP (*Co. Sandon*), a swampy piece of land in the parish of Arding, lying about half-way between Uralla and Armidale.

SLAUGHTER-HOUSE CREEK (*Co. Wellesley*), a small northern tributary of the Bombala River, flowing into the Snowy River.

SLIPPERY CREEK (*Co. Westmoreland*), a postal receiving-office, 132 miles W. of Sydney, with daily mail therefrom. The creek is a western tributary of the Fish River, rising to the south of Mutton Falls.

SMALL PLAINS (*Co. Clyde*), a tract of flat pastoral country, to the N. of the Barwon River.

SMART'S CREEK (*Co. Wellington*), a small mining village in the district of Adelong, situate about 8 miles distant from the township.

SMASHEM'S CREEK (*Co. Hardinge*), a small eastern tributary of the Gwydir River, rising near the village of Alington.

SMITH'S CREEK (*Co. Hardinge*), a small auriferous tributary of the Gwydir River, falling into it near the village of Nundle.

SMITH'S CREEK (*Co. Wellington*), a tributary of the Black Willow Creek, rising to the W. of the Louisa Creek gold-field.

SMITH'S CREEK (*Co. Parry*), a small creek, at the head of the Mulucrindie River, rising near the Basaltic Column, at the junction of the Australian Alps and the Moombi Range.

SMITH'S FALLS (*Co. Clarence*). [*See* "ROCKY FALLS AND COPMANHURST."]

SMITHFIELD (*Co. Cumberland*), a postal village, 20 miles S. of Sydney, with mail twice daily. Telegraph and money-order offices. The nearest railway-station is Fairfield, 2 miles, on the southern line. Situated on the Prospect Creek, in the parish of St. Luke. The neighbourhood is agricultural and fruit-growing, and very fertile. It was proclaimed a municipality in 1888, with a council of eight aldermen and a mayor.

SMITH'S RIVULET (*Co. Brisbane*). [*See* "MERRIWA CREEK."]

SMITHTOWN (*Co. Macquarie*), a postal town, 324 miles N. of Sydney, with mail three times a week, and per steamer. Telegraph and money-order offices. The nearest railway station is Hexham, 206 miles, on the northern line.

SMOKY CAPE (*Co. Dudley*), a prominent rocky headland, to the S. of Trial Bay, on the entrance of the Macleay River. It received its name from Captain Cook, from seeing dense volumes of smoke rising from it as he passed.

SNAIL'S BAY (*Co. Cumberland*), a small bight, on the S. side of Port Jackson, in the suburb of Balmain.

SNAKE VALLEY (*Co. Beresford*), a grassy valley, on the E. of Slack's Creek and the Murrumbidgee River, and to the S.W. of the township of Bunyan.

SNODGRASS BAY (*Co. Gloucester*), a small bay, on the Myall Lakes. This bay is not in any way affected by the tides of the ocean, nor is the water salt, but brackish; the cattle, however, use it, but it is not fit for domestic purposes.

SNODGRASS VALLEY (*Co. Northumberland*), a valley, lying about 25 miles S. of Wollombi, and 12 miles N. of Wiseman's Ferry.

SNOWY CREEK (*Co. Selwyn*), a small creek rising in the N. of Mount Kosciusko, and flowing S.W. into the Upper Murray, near Grogan's Hill.

SNOWY MOUNTAINS (*Cos. Wallace and Selwyn*). [*See* "BALD MOUNTAINS."]

SNOWY PLAINS (*Co. Wallace*), an extensive tract of country, lying between the Muniong or Snowy Ranges on the W. and the Eucumbene River on the E.

SNOWY RIVER (*Cos. Wallace* and *Wellesley*). [*See* "RIVERS."]

SOBRAON (*Co. Hardinge*), a postal-receiving office, 391 miles N. of Sydney, with mail therefrom twice a week.

SODWALLS (*Co. Roxburgh*), a railway station, 114 miles from Sydney, on the western line.

SOFALA (*Co. Roxburgh*), a postal town, 166 miles W. of Sydney, with daily mail. Telegraph and money-order offices and Government savings bank. The nearest railway station is Bathurst, 30 miles, on the western line. Situated on the Turon River, in the parish of Sofala. In its immediate neighbourhood are Palmer's Oakey, Big Oakey, Little Oakey, Spring, Bell's, and Crudine Creeks, all of which are more or less auriferous.

SOLANDER CAPE (*Co. Cumberland*), the southern head of the entrance to Botany Bay.

SOLFERINO (*Co. Drake*), a proclaimed village, on the banks of the Clarence.

SOLITARY CREEK (*Co. Lincoln*), a southern boundary of the Erskine River, crossing the road from Dubbo to Mendooran.

SOLITARY CREEK (*Cos. Roxburgh* and *Westmoreland*), a northern tributary of the Fish River, having its rise in the Honeysuckle Hill, in the parish of Polnash, flowing into the main stream at Mutton Falls. The township of Rydal is situated on this creek.

SOLITARY ISLES (*Co. Fitzroy*), a series of islets lying off the coast, about 60 miles S. of Shoal Bay. They are small and rocky, and the two largest, and farthest away from the land, are from 60 to 80 feet high. They are conspicuous objects at sea.

SOMERS (*Co. Bathurst*), a proclaimed village, to the S. of Lyndhurst, in the same county.

SOMERTON (*Co. Inglis*), a postal town, 301 miles N. of Sydney, with daily mail, and money-order office. The nearest railway station is Tamworth, 25 miles, on the northern line, situated on the Peel River, about 12 miles N.E. of Carroll.

SOPHIA CREEK (*Co. Brisbane*), the eastern head of the Guangua Creek.

SOUTH BOWENFELLS (*Co. Cook*), a postal village, 100 miles W. of Sydney, with daily mail, and money-order office.

SOUTH BROKEN HILL (*Co. Yancowinna*), a postal receiving-office, 943 miles S. of Sydney, with mail five times a week.

SOUTH CLIFTON (*Co. Camden*), a railway station, 36 miles S. of Sydney, on the Illawarra and South Coast line.

SOUTH COAST RANGE (*Cos. Auckland, Beresford, and Wellesley*), a chain of hills running suddenly from the Monaro Range to the Munion Range, with the spurs of which they appear to interlace. The highest peak is 3,712 feet above the sea-level.

SOUTH COLAH (*Co. Cumberland.*) [*See* "HORNSBY."]

SOUTH CREEK (*Co. Cumberland*), a fine stream rising near Narellan, and flowing N.W. about 45 miles into the Hawkesbury River, near Windsor. It flows past the villages of Cabramatta and St. Mary's, and the township of Windsor.

SOUTHGATE (*Co. Clarence*), a postal village, 358 miles N. of Sydney, with mail by steamers therefrom.

SOUTH GRAFTON (*Co. Clarence*). [*See* "COUNTIES."]

SOUTH HEAD, INNER (*Co. Cumberland*), a rocky promontory, lying between the ocean on the E. and Port Jackson on the W., and is, as its name imports, the south rounding point of the entrance to that harbour. On it stands the Hornby lighthouse, where a bright white light is exhibited from sunset to sunrise.

SOUTH HEAD, OUTER (*Co. Cumberland*) a bold, perpendicular cliff, to the S. of Port Jackson from the entrance to the harbour. On it is erected the Macquarie Lighthouse, at an elevation of 344 feet above sea-level, and a revolving light is exhibited, emitting its greatest brightness at intervals of one minute and a half.

SOUTH MOUNT HOPE (*Co. Dowling*), a postal receiving-office, 418 miles W. of Sydney, with mail twice a week.

SOUTH PARK (*Co. Northumberland*), a large tract of alluvial flat land on the W. of West Maitland, and watered by the Wallis Creek.

SOUTH-WEST ARM (*Co. Cumberland*), a long creek, on the S. side of Broken Bay, extending about 10 miles S.W., to near the head of Lane Cove River.

SOUTH WOODBURN (*Co. Richmond*), a postal town, 336 miles N. of Sydney, with mail per Clarence and Richmond River steamers. Telegraph and money-order offices, and Government savings bank.

SOW AND PIGS (*Co. Cumberland*), a shoal of rocks, lying in the fairway of the entrance to Port Jackson. A lightship is moored at this dangerous spot, from which is exhibited, from sunset to sunrise, two fixed white lights, as a guide to mariners on entering the port.

SPARKES' LAGOON (*Co. Nandewar*), a fine permanent sheet of water, supplying the township of Gulligal. It is fed by the Namoi River.

SPARROW HILL (*Co. Wellington*), an auriferous hill, on the Green Valley Creek, and forming part of the Tambaroora gold-field.

SPECTACLE ISLAND (*Co. Cumberland*), a well-known series of rocks in the Parramatta River, to the westward of Cockatoo Island.

SPECTACLE ISLAND (*Co. Northumberland*), situated in the estuary of the Hawkesbury River, at the confluence of Mooney-Mooney Creek. Also an island in the Hunter River, lying to the S. of Mosquito Island.

SPENCER'S CREEK, a postal village, 341 miles N. of Sydney, with mail three times a week.

SPICER'S CREEK (*Co. Lincoln*), a postal village, 273 miles W. of Sydney, with mail four times a week. A southern tributary of the Erskine River.

SPIT, THE (*Co. Cumberland*), a well-known spot in Middle Harbour, where the ferry crosses to Manly and Pittwater from North Sydney.

SPORTSMAN'S CREEK (*Co. Clarence*), a small northern tributary of the N. arm of the Clarence River, joining it at Lawrence.

SPRING, THE (*Co. Wallace*), a hill in the ranges to the E. of the Wullwye River.

SPRING COVE (*Co. Cumberland*), a small bay on the E. side of the N. harbour of Port Jackson. The quarantine station and reserve lie on the S.E. side of this bight.

SPRING CREEK (*Co. Ashburnham*), a small northern tributary of Bourimbla Creek, rising in the W. of Canobolas.

SPRING CREEK (*Co. Baradine*), a tributary of the head of Baradine Creek, rising in Mount Boolemdilly, in the Warrabungle Ranges.

SPRING CREEK (*Co. Bathurst*), a northern tributary of the Lachlan River, flowing into it S.E. of Cowra.

SPRING CREEK (*Co. Buccleuch*), a southern tributary of the lower part of the Oak Creek, rising on the western slope of Paddy's Rock Hill. Also a tributary of the Adjungbilli Creek, rising in Mount Tummorrama, flowing through the Shaking Bog.

SPRING CREEK (*Co. Gordon*), a tributary of the head of the Buckinbar Creek.

SPRING CREEK (*Co. Gough*), a northern tributary of the Severn River, about 16 miles E. of Avisford.

SPRING CREEK (*Co. Harden*), a stream of good water, rising between the Burrowa and Cunningham Plains.

SPRING CREEK (*Co. Inglis*), a small auriferous northern tributary at the head of Carlyle's Creek.

SPRING CREEK (*Co. Monteagle*), a small stream near the township of Young, in the Burrangong gold-field, flowing into Burrangong Creek.

SPRING CREEK (*Co. Murray*), a tributary of the Brassil Creek, flowing through part of Yass Plains.

SPRING CREEK (*Co. Phillip*), a small tributary of the Wollan Creek.

SPRING CREEK (*Co. Roxburgh*), a small western tributary of Arthur's Creek, flowing in the Oakey Creek gold-field.

SPRING CREEK (*Co. Wellington*), an auriferous tributary of the Stockyard Creek, flowing in the Burrendong gold-fields. Also a tributary at the head of the Kingarragan Creek.

SPRING CREEK DIGGINGS (*Co. Murchison*), an alluvial gold workings in the Bingera gold-field, lying 2 miles S. of the township of Bingera.

SPRING CREEK DIGGINGS (*Co. Roxburgh*) forms part of the Turon diggings, about 1 mile distant from the township of Sofala.

SPRING FLAT (*Co. Selwyn*), lying between Mount Dargal and its spurs on the E. and the Murray River on the W. It abounds in springs of pure water, affording excellent pasturage for cattle.

SPRING FLAT CREEK (*Co. Selwyn*), a small creek rising in the western slope of Mount Dargal, and flowing into the Murray River, about 5 miles N. of the head of that river, and 8 miles S.E. of Welaregang.

SPRING FLAT CREEK (*Co. Wallace*), a tributary of the M'Laughlin River, rising in Mount Cooper.

SPRING GULLY CREEK (*Co. Buckland*), a small tributary of the Kangaroo Station Creek.

SPRING HILL (*Co. Bathurst*), a postal village, 184 miles W. of Sydney, with daily mail. Telegraph and money-order offices, and Government savings bank. A railway station on the western line.

SPRING HILLS (*Co. Goulburn*), a high peak lying about 6 miles N.W. of the town of Albury.

SPRING RIDGE (*Co. Buckland*), a village, 272 miles N. of Sydney. The nearest railway station is Quirindi, 30 miles, on the northern line.

SPRING VALLEY (*Co. Argyle*), a village, 146 miles S. of Sydney; Goulburn, 19 miles N.; and Collector, 7 miles W. In the parish of Spring Vale. The neighbourhood is auriferous in parts, the soil fertile, Lake George being about 6 miles distant to the S., and Rose's Lagoon about 3 miles to the N.

SPRINGS (*Co. Wellington*), a postal village, 241 W. of Sydney, with daily mail. A railway station on the western line.

SPRING'S CREEK (*Co. Buckland*), an eastern tributary of Chilcott's Creek, falling into it at Doughboy Hollow Creek.

SPRING'S CREEK (*Co. Wynyard*), a tributary of the Black Creek, flowing N. a few miles.

SPRINGSIDE (*Co. Ashburnham*), a postal village, 194 miles W. of Sydney, with mail therefrom twice a week. The nearest railway station is Orange, 4½ miles, on the Orange and Molong line.

SPRINGWOOD (*Co. Cook*), a postal village, 48 miles W. of Sydney, with mail three times daily. Telegraph and money-order offices, Government savings bank, and delivery by letter-carriers. A railway station on the western line.

STACK'S CREEK (*Co. Beresford*), a southern tributary of the Upper Murrumbidgee River, rising in the E. of Stack's Hill, in the Kiandra Range.

STANBOROUGH (*Co. Hardinge*), a postal town, 408 miles N. of Sydney, with mail three times a week. The nearest railway station is Uralla, 60 miles, on the northern line.

2 c

STANHOPE (*Co. Northumberland*), an agricultural settlement, lying on the banks of the Hunter River, about 6 miles from Branxton.

STANLEY RANGE (*Albert District*), a chain of sandstone hills to the W. of the Darling River, lying near the boundary-line of the Colony from South Australia.

STANMORE (*Co. Cumberland*), a suburb, 4 miles W. of Sydney, with daily mail therefrom. Telegraph and money-order offices, Government savings bank, and delivery by letter-carriers. A railway station on the suburban line.

STANNIFER (*Co. Gough*), a postal village, 425 miles N. of Sydney, with mail three times a week. The nearest railway station is Guyra, 49 miles, on northern line.

STAPYLTON, a county in the Central Division of the Colony. [*See* "COUNTIES."]

STAPYLTON LAKE (*Co. Taila*), a series of lagoons lying on the N. bank of the Murray River, about 20 miles E. of Euston.

STEINBROOK (*Co. Clive*), a postal village, 485 miles N. of Sydney, with mail twice a week. The nearest railway station is Tenterfield, 5 miles, on the northern line.

STEPHEN CREEK (*Co. Yancowinna*), a stream rising in the Barrier Range, and flowing in a S.E. direction.

STEPHENS CREEK (*Co. Durham*) is the S. head of Port Stephens, on which the lighthouse stands. Distant 77 miles from the N. head of Port Jackson.

STEWART'S BROOK (*Co. Durham*), a postal village, 229 miles N. of Sydney, with mail twice a week. The nearest railway station is Scone, 35 miles, on the northern line. The brook is an eastern tributary of the upper part of the Hunter River.

STEWART'S RIVER (*Co. Macquarie*), a drainage creek, flowing into the S. end of Watson Taylor's Lake.

STINGAREE POINT (*Co. Northumberland*), a point on the western shore of Lake Macquarie, where the Dora Creek flows into it.

STOCKDALE POINT (*Co. Northumberland*). [*See* "LAKE MACQUARIE."]

STOCKINBINGAL (*Co. Clarendon*), a postal receiving-office, 267 miles S. of Sydney, with mail twice a week. Situated about 15 miles W. of Coramundria. The district is fertile.

STOCKTON (*Co. Northumberland*), a postal town, 76 miles N. of Sydney, with daily mail. Telegraph and money-order offices, Government savings bank, and delivery by letter-carrier. The nearest railway station is Newcastle, 1 mile, on the Sydney and Newcastle line. It was proclaimed a municipal district in 1889, with a council of eight aldermen and a mayor.

STOCKYARD CREEK (*Co. Clarence*), a postal village, 586 miles N. of Sydney, with mail per Grafton steamers. The creek is a western tributary of the White Man's Creek.

STOCKYARD CREEK (*Co. Gough*), a western tributary of the Yarrow River.

STOCKYARD CREEK (*Co. Wellington*), an auriferous creek, flowing through the Burrandong gold-fields into the Macquarie River, at Burrandong.

STOKE'S ISLAND (*Co. St. Vincent*), a rocky islet, lying off the coast 11 miles S. of Ulladulla.

STONEHENGE (*Co. Gough*), a postal town, 416 miles N. of Sydney, with mail five times a week. The nearest railway station is Glen Innes, 6 miles, on the northern line.

STONEQUARRY (*Co. Camden*), the original name of the district round Picton.

STONEQUARRY CREEK (*Co. Camden*), a tributary of the Nepean River, joining it at the township of Picton.

STONYBATTER CREEK (*Co. Hardinge*), an auriferous tributary of the head of the Nundle Creek, rising in Mount Lowry, and falling into it at the village of Stonybatter.

STONY CREEK (*Co. Phillip*), a postal village, 200 miles W. of Sydney, with mail twice a week. The nearest railway station is Mudgee, 10 miles, on the western line. The creek is a tributary of the Cooyal Creek, into which it flows at Cooyal, which rises at Mount Bara.

STONY CREEK (*Co. Harden*), a tributary of the Bogolong Creek, flowing into it near Bookham.

STONY CREEK (*Co. Macquarie*), a northern tributary of the Hastings River.

STONY CREEK (*Co. Monteagle*), a western tributary of the Burrowa River.

STONY CREEK (*Co. Murchison*), a western tributary of Maule's Creek, flowing through rich pastoral country.

STONY CREEK (*Co. Murray*), an eastern tributary of the Upper Murrumbidgee River, draining the rich country between the townships of Jingery and Queanbeyan.

STONY CREEK (*Co. Northumberland*), an eastern tributary of Black Creek, crossing the Maitland and Wollombi Road at Bishop's Bridge.

STONY CREEK (*Co. Roxburgh*), and eastern tributary of the Macquarie River, rising in the ranges in the parish of Waltham.

STONY CREEK (*Co. Vernon*), a southern tributary of the Apsley River, falling into it near the Apsley Falls.

STONY CREEK (*Co. Wellington*), an auriferous southern tributary of the Bodaldura Creek.

STONY CREEK (*Co. Westmoreland*), an eastern tributary of the Campbell Creek, rising in the northern slope of Bushrangers' Hill.

STONY CREEK (*Co. Wynyard*), an auriferous tributary of the Gilmore Creek, flowing N. through the Upper Adelong gold-fields.

STONY CREEK GOLD-FIELD (*Co. Wellington*), a tract of auriferous country, situated on the eastern tributaries of the Bell River. The gold extracted from this gold-field in 1864 amounted to £69,925 4s.

STONY CROSSING (*Co. Caira*), a postal receiving-office, 621 miles S. of Sydney, with mail three times a week.

STORE CREEK (*Co. Wellington*), a postal town, 222 miles W. of Sydney, with daily mail therefrom. A railway station on the western line.

STORM CREEK (*Co. Gresham*), a southern tributary of the Sara River.

STOTT'S CREEK (*Co. Wellington*), a postal receiving-office, 425 miles N. of Sydney, with mail three times a week.

STRATHFIELD (*Co. Cumberland*), an important suburb of Sydney, 7 miles S. of the city, with mail therefrom three times daily. Telegraph office and delivery by letter-carriers. A railway station on the suburban line. It was proclaimed a municipal district in 1885, with a council of five aldermen and a mayor.

STRINGY BARK CREEK (*Co. Cumberland*), an eastern tributary of the Lane Cove River.

STRINGYBARK, SPRING CREEK (*Co. Wynyard*), a drainage creek rising near Plum Pudding Hill, on the road from Wagga Wagga to Albury, flowing into the Murrumbidgee River, in the parish of Wagga Wagga.

STRONTIAN PARK (*Co. Clarence*), an agricultural settlement on the Clarence River, lying at the mouth of Alum Creek, opposite the township of Ulmarra.

STROUD (*Co. Gloucester*), a postal town, 146 miles N. of Sydney, with daily mail. Telegraph and money-order offices and Government savings bank. The nearest railway station is Hexham, 12 miles, on the northern line, situated between Mill's Creek and Smith's Creek. The district is both agricultural and pastoral, and abounds in minerals. The Australian Agricultural Company have large possessions here.

STUART TOWN (formerly IRONBARKS) (*Co. Wellington*), a postal town 229 miles W. of Sydney, with daily mail. Telegraph and money-order offices, and a railway station, on the western line, situated on the Ironbark Creek. The district is exclusively a mining one, both quartz and alluvial.

STUART'S MOUNT (*Co. Tongowoko*), a peak of the Grey Range.

STUART'S POINT (MACLEAY RIVER HEADS) (*Co. Clarence*), a postal, receiving, and telegraph office, N. of Sydney, with mail by steamer to the Macleay. Situate on Macleay River Heads.

STUBBO CREEK (*Co. Bligh*), an eastern tributary of the Slapdash Creek. It is crossed by the road from Cooyal to Mendooran.

STURT, a county in the Central Division of the Colony. [*See* "COUNTIES."]

STURT (*Co. Auckland*), an agricultural village on the Towamba River, about 10 miles E. of Eden.

STYX RIVER (*Co. Dudley*). [*See* "RIVERS."]

SUGARLOAF (*Co. Bathurst*), a high solitary hill, near the junction of the Lachlan and Abercrombie Rivers.

SUGARLOAF (*Co. Buccleuch*), a lofty peak in the northern portion of the Blowering Mountains, in which the Log Bridge Creek has its rise.

SUGARLOAF (*Co. Cumberland*), two considerable hills, distinguished as Little and Big, in the parish of Willoughby, lying near the head of Middle Harbour.

SUGARLOAF CREEK (*Co. Cowley*), a tributary of the Goodradigbee River, rising in the Narangullen Hill, and flowing N.W. across the Yass and Kiandra Road.

SUGARLOAF CREEK (*Co. Goulburn*), a tributary of the Murray River, rising in the Sugarloaf Hill, and flowing about 10 miles S.

SUGARLOAF CREEK (*Co. Wellington*), an auriferous western tributary of the Molong River.

SUGARLOAF MOUNT (*Co. Argyle*), a lofty peak in the parish of Turallo, on the W. bank of the Tarlo Creek, about 6 miles N.W. of the village of Tarlo.

SUGARLOAF MOUNT (*Co. Wynyard*), two high conical peaks, lying to the S. of Tarcutta, and divided by Kiambla Creek.

SUGARLOAF POINT (*Co. Gloucester*), usually called Seal Rock Point, is a projection of the mainland into the ocean, and a well-known land-mark at sea.

SUGARLOAF RANGE (*Co. Northumberland*), a chain of hills, lying to the N.W. of Lake Macquarie, and about 12 miles S. of Maitland, from which township they form a prominent land-mark.

SUMMER ISLAND (*Co. Dudley*), a postal village, 334 miles N. of Sydney, with mail three times a week, and money-order office. The nearest railway station is Hexham, 212 miles, on the northern line. Situated on the Macleay River, the nearest township being Darkwater, 2 miles, and Kempsey, 10 miles; from the latter there is steamboat communication with Sydney.

SUMMERHILL (*Co. Cumberland*), a suburb of Sydney, about 5 miles W. of the city, with mail therefrom three times daily. Telegraph and money-order offices, Government savings bank, and delivery by letter-carriers. A railway station on the suburban line.

SUMMERHILL (*Co. Bathurst*), a detached hill, about 3 miles E. of Orange township, on the W. bank of the Frederick's Valley Creek.

SUNNY CORNER (*Co. Roxburgh*), a postal village, 124 miles W. of Sydney, with daily mail. Telegraph and money-order offices, Government savings bank, and delivery by letter-carriers. The nearest railway station is Rydal, 14 miles, on the western line.

SUNNYSIDE *(Co. Clive)*, a postal receiving-office, 486 miles N. of Sydney. with mail twice a week. A railway station on the western line.

SUNTOP *(Co. Lincoln)*, a postal receiving-office, 254 miles W. of Sydney, with mail twice a week.

SURRY HILLS *(Co. Cumberland)*, a suburb of Sydney with mail therefrom three times daily. Telegraph and money-order offices, and delivery by letter-carriers. It lies to the S. of the city.

SURVEYOR'S CREEK *(Co. Inglis)*, a village, 320 miles N. of Sydney. The nearest railway station is Walcha Road, 4 miles, on the northern line.

SURVEYOR'S CREEK *(Co. Gough)*, a southern tributary of the Mitchell River, falling into it near the junction of the Yarrow River.

SURVEYOR'S CREEK *(Co. Inglis)*, a small eastern tributary of the Muluerindie River.

SUSAN ISLAND *(Co. Clarence)*, a small island in the Clarence River, lying on the S.W. of the town of Grafton, distant about 5 miles.

SUSSEX HAVEN *(Co. St. Vincent)*, a bight on the S. side of Cape George on the southern coast.

SUTHERLAND *(Co. Cumberland)*, a postal village, 15 miles S. of Sydney, with daily mail, and money-order office. A railway station on the Illawarra and South Coast line.

SUTHERLAND POINT *(Co. Rous)*, a rocky promontory on the coast to the N. of Sydney, lying about 10 miles S. of Point Dangar.

SUTTON *(Co. Argyle)*, a postal receiving-office, 191 miles S. of Sydney, with daily mail. The nearest railway station is Gunning, 18 miles, on the southern line.

SUTTON FOREST *(Co. Camden)*, a postal village, 89 miles S. of Sydney, with mail twice daily. Telegraph and money-order offices, and Government savings bank. The nearest railway station is Moss Vale, 3 miles, on the southern line. Situated on the Medway Creek, in the parish of Sutton Forest and police district of Berrima.

SWAINE'S CREEK *(Co. Cumberland)*, a small eastern tributary of Lane Cove River.

SWALLOW CREEK *(Co. Cowley)*, a western tributary of the Macquarie River, rising near the township of Guyong.

SWALLOW'S NEST *(Co. Bathurst)*, a postal village, 185 miles W. of Sydney, with mail once a week. The nearest railway station is George's Plains, 32 miles, on the western line.

SWAMP CREEK *(Co. Cowley)*, a western tributary of the Murrumbidgee River, rising in the south-western slopes of Big Hill.

SWAMP CREEK *(Co. Phillip)*, a northern tributary of Lawson's Creek.

SWAMP OAK *(Co. Inglis)*, a village, 292 miles N. of Sydney. The nearest railway station is Moonbi, 3½ miles, on the northern line.

SWAMPY CREEK (*Co. Vernon*), a stream of fine water flowing into the head of the Apsley River, about 12 miles S. of Walcha.

SWAMPY FLAT CREEK (*Co. Selwyn*), an eastern tributary of the eastern branch of the Murray River, rising in Mount Dargal, and flowing S.W. about 15 miles through rich pastoral country.

SWAN BAY (*Co. Clarence*), a postal village, 342 miles N. of Sydney, with mail therefrom per Clarence River steamer.

SWAN CREEK (*Co. Clarence*), a southern tributary of the Clarence River, flowing into the main stream near Grafton.

SWAN CREEK (*Co. Gough*), a fine stream, rising in a detached hill called Fletcher's Nob, and flowing W. past Swan Peak into the Macintyre River, S. of the township of Byron.

SWAN PEAK (*Co. Gough*), a high hill on the Swan Creek, about 12 miles S.W. of the township of Wellingrove.

SWANSEA (*Co. Northumberland*), a postal village, 98 miles N. of Sydney with mail three times a week. Telegraph and money-order offices, and Government savings bank. The nearest railway station is Cockle Creek, 15 miles, on the Newcastle and Lake Macquarie line.

SWAN VALE (*Co. Gough*), a postal town, 454 miles N. of Sydney, with daily mail. The nearest railway station is Glen Innes, 20 miles, on the northern line.

SWATCHFIELD (*Co. Bathurst*), a village about 18 miles from Rockly and the same distance from Bathurst.

SWEENY CREEK (*Co. Clarence*), a western tributary of the Coldstream River, flowing through good agricultural land.

SYDNEY (*Co. Cumberland*), 33° 51' 41" S. latitude, 151° 11' 30" E. longitude, in the parishes of Alexandria and Petersham, and the metropolis of New South Wales and the seat of Government. The entire continent of Australia was founded by the British Government in the reign of George III, and the first fleet arrived in Port Jackson on the 26th January, 1788, under the command of Arthur Phillip, R.N., who was the first Governor. The city is most picturesquely situated on the southern shores of Port Jackson, on the sandstone formation overlying the coal measures which crop out at Newcastle in the N. and Bulli on the S. The city cannot be said to have been *laid out*, but only main thoroughfares adopted, running in a direct line S. to N., with streets at right angles. The port, however, is without an equal in any part of the world. Steamers of the largest tonnage afloat come up to the centre of the city and lie alongside the Circular Quay, in Sydney Cove. The western side of the city, Darling Harbour, possesses equal facilities with the Circular Quay for the shipping requirements it affords, with the addition that the railway terminus for heavy goods is situated in Darling Harbour. The magnificent edifices erected within the city testify to the value of the building stone upon which the city stands. Sydney is the central terminus of all the lines in Australia—Brisbane on the N.; Melbourne and South Australia on the S. and S.W.; and its telegraphic arrangements are simply perfect. Government House and grounds are within the city, having an aspect and view of the harbour quite enchanting, and with the beautiful Botanic Gardens, Hyde

Park, and Cook Park, give a charm which the citizens and visitors thoroughly appreciate. Commercially, Sydney is a hive of industry. Garden Island, in Sydney Harbour, is now a Naval Depot for the Imperial Service. Sheers capable of lifting 160 tons are erected, and all the recent appliances necessary for war service are centred there. The magnificent dock accommodation and unrivalled strategical position of the harbour alike justify the selection. The facilities for docking and repairing steamers and ships in Sydney are unsurpassed in any port in the world, Sydney claiming the distinction of owning the largest graving-dock ever constructed, its length being 635 feet, breadth, 108 feet, and depth over the sill, 32 feet. It has been named the Sutherland Dock, in patriotic remembrance of the late Honorable John Sutherland. [*See also* "PORT JACKSON," under "PORTS, HARBOURS, &c."]

SYDNEY COVE (*Co. Cumberland*) lies between Battery Point on the E. and Dawes' Point on the W. side. At the head of the Cove is the Circular Quay, and was the spot selected by Governor Phillip, on the 23rd January, 1788, as the site for the new settlement, and the name was given in honor of Thomas Townsend, Viscount Sydney.

SYLVANIA (*Co. Cumberland*), a postal village, 13 miles S. of Sydney, with daily mail. The nearest railway station is Kogarah, 5 miles, on the Illawarra and South Coast line.

# T

TABLETOP CREEK (*Co. Goulburn*), a northern tributary of the Bowna Creek, rising in a peak of the Piney Range, called the Table.

TABLETOP MOUNTAIN (*Co. Wallace*), a high peak of the Muniong, or Snowy Range, about 8 miles S. of Kiandra and 10 miles W. of Denison.

TABRABUCCA CREEK (*Co. Roxburgh*) is the name of the N. head of Cunninghame's Creek.

TABRABUCCA SWAMP (*Co. Roxburgh*), a tract of marshy land lying on the N. bank of the Tabrabucca Creek, on the road from Sofala to Rylstone, about 12 miles S.W. of the latter place.

TABRATONG (*Co. Narromine*), a township on the S. branch of the Bogan River.

TABULAM (*Co. Buller*), a postal town, 530 miles N. of Sydney, with mail four times a week. Telegraph and money-order offices and Government savings bank. The nearest railway station is Tenterfield, 54 miles, on the northern line. Situated on the Clarence River and the Timbarra Rivulet, in the parish of Tabulam. The district is a pastoral and mining one.

TABULAM RIVULET (*Co. Richmond*), an auriferous stream flowing W. into the Clarence River at Tabulam.

TACKING POINT (*Co. Macquarie*), a rocky promontory, lying about $2\frac{1}{2}$ miles S. of Port Macquarie.

TAILA, a county in the Western Division of the Colony. [*See* "COUNTIES."]

TAILA LAKE (*Co. Taila*). [*See* "BENANEE LAKE."]

TAJARI CREEK (*Co. Camden*), a tributary of the Nepean River, flowing within 4 miles of the village of Menangle.

TALATERANG MOUNT (*Co. St. Vincent*), a lofty peak of the Budawang Range, lying on the banks of the Clyde River.

TALAWANTA (*Co. Narran*), a township, 456 miles W. of Sydney. The nearest railway station is Byrock, 186 miles, on the western line.

TALAWUNG CREEK (*Co. Bligh*), a western tributary of the Slapdash Creek.

TALBINGO (*Co. Buccleuch*), a proclaimed village on the E. bank of the Tumut River; a mining population.

TALBINGO HILL (*Co. Buccleuch*), a lofty peak in the Tumut Range, lying about 4 miles S. of the village of Talbingo, on the E. bank of the Tumut River.

TALBRAGAR (*Cos. Lincoln and Bligh*). [*See* "ERSKINE RIVER."]

TALERANG PIC (*Co. Murray*), a lofty peak in the Gourock Range of mountains, lying on the W. bank of the Shoalhaven River, about 8 miles W. of Braidwood. It attains a height of about 3,500 feet above sea-level.

TALGARNA (*Co. Goulburn*), a township on the Murray River, to the E. of Albury.

TALLEWANG (*Co. Bligh*), a postal village, 225 miles W. of Sydney, with mail three days a week. The nearest railway station is Mudgee, 30 miles, on the western line.

TALMO CREEK (*Co. Harden*), a tributary of the head of the Jugiong Creek, falling into it near Bookham.

TALMO WATERFALL (*Co. Harden*), a cataract on the Talmo Creek, in the parish of Talmo, about 6 miles S. of Bookham.

TALOUMBI (*Co. Clarence*), a postal receiving-office, 321 miles N. of Sydney, with mail twice a week.

TALTINGAN (*Co. Yancowinna*), a proclaimed township, in the county of Yancowinna.

TALYAWALKA CREEK (*Co. Landsborough*), a creek flowing from Mount Guntpermucko into the Darling River on its W. side.

TALLY-HO (*Co. Buckland*), a township, 242 miles N. of Sydney. The nearest railway station is Quirindi, 55 miles, on the northern line.

TAMBAR SPRINGS (*Co. Pottinger*), a postal village, 336 miles N. of Sydney, with mail three times a week. Money-order office and Government savings bank. The nearest railway station is Gunnedah, 43 miles, on the north-western line.

TAMBAROORA *(Co. Wellington)*, a postal town, 206 miles W. of Sydney, with mail three times a week, and money-order office. The nearest railway station is Bathurst, 61 miles, on the western line. Situated on the Tambaroora Creek, and distant about 10 miles from the Macquarie River. The district is entirely a mining one, both alluvial and quartz.

TAMBAROORA CREEK *(Co. Wellington)*, an auriferous northern tributary of the Macquarie River, rising in and flowing through the Tambaroora goldfield.

TAMBOURINE BAY *(Co. Cumberland)*, a well-known bight on the N. side of the Lane Cove River, near its fall into the Parramatta River.

TAMWORTH *(Co. Parry)*, a postal village, 282 miles N. of Sydney, with daily mail. Telegraph and money-order offices, Government savings bank, and delivery by letter-carrier. A railway station on the northern line. Situated on the Peel and Cockburn Rivers, and the district is both mining and agricultural. It was proclaimed a borough in 1876, with a council of eight aldermen and a mayor. Sittings of the supreme court, courts of quarter sessions, and district courts are held at Tamworth periodically during each year.

TANBERRY *(Co. Perry)*, a township on the E. bank of the Darling River, above Wentworth.

TANDANANGALO CREEK *(Co. Auckland)*, one of the heads of the Candelo Creek.

TANDANGO CREEK *(Co. Narromine)*, a western tributary of the head of the Bogan River.

TANDENALOGY *(Co. Livingstone)*, a township on the E. bank of the Darling River.

TANDORA, a county in the Western Division of the Colony. [*See* "COUNTIES."]

TANGERIN *(Co. Durham)*, a lofty hill, near the junction of the Hunter River and the Glendon Brook, about 9 miles E. of Singleton.

TANGMANGAROO *(Co. Harden)*, a postal town, 206 miles S. of Sydney, with mail three times a week. The nearest railway station is Browning, 12 miles, on the southern line.

TANJA *(Co. Auckland)*, a postal village, 340 miles S. of Sydney, with mail twice a week. The nearest railway station is Cooma, 84 miles, on the Goulburn and Cooma line.

TANLANGARA MOUNT *(Co. Wallace)*, a high peak, lying on the N.E. of the town of Kiandra.

TANNAN CREEK *(Co. Wellington)*. [*See* "LOUISA CREEK."]

TANTAWANGLO *(Co. Auckland)*, a postal receiving-office, 360 miles S. of Sydney, with mail once a week.

TANWARRA CREEK *(Co. Roxburgh)*, an auriferous southern tributary of the Turon River, flowing to the S.W. of Sofala, and past the western foot of Mount Tanwarra.

TANWARRA MOUNT (*Co. Roxburgh*), a peak in the hills on the Turon River, near the township of Sofala, at the head of Insolvent Creek.

TARA, a county in the Western Division of the Colony. [*See* "COUNTIES."]

TARAGO (*Co. Argyle*), a postal village, 157 miles S. of Sydney, with daily mail. Telegraph and money-order offices, and Government savings bank. A railway station on the Goulburn and Cooma line. Situated on the Mulwaree Ponds, close to Lake Bathurst.

TARAGO LAKE (*Co. Argyle*), a small lake, lying in the parish of the same name, and to the S. of the village reserve of Tarago.

TARALGA (*Co. Argyle*), a postal town, 164 miles S. of Sydney, with daily mail. Telegraph and money-order offices. The nearest railway station is Goulburn, 30 miles, on the Goulburn and Cooma line.

TARANA (*Co. Bathurst*), a postal village, 120 miles W. of Sydney, with daily mail. Telegraph and money-order offices. A railway station on the western line.

TARANGILE CREEK (*Co. Townsend*), a small branch of the Edward River, at Deniliquin. This creek and the main stream form a small island, which is reserved for public recreation.

TARBAN (*Co. Cumberland*), is the name of the village of Gladesville. It is also the name of the lunatic asylum, situated in that village, and on the S. bank of Tarban Creek and northern side of the Parramatta River.

TARBAN CREEK (*Co. Cumberland*) a small fresh water creek, flowing on the eastern side of the village of Gladesville into the Parramatta River.

TARCOOLA (*Co. Perry*), a township on the E. bank of the Darling River to the S. of Pooncarie.

TARCUTTA (*Co. Wynyard*), a postal village, 324 miles S. of Sydney, with daily mail. Telegraph and money-order offices. The nearest railway station is Gundagai, 30 miles, on the Cootamundra and Gundagai line. Situated on the Tarcutta Creek, 15 miles S. of the Murrumbidgee.

TARCUTTA CREEK (*Co. Wynyard*), a fine stream, rising in Mane's Range, and flowing by a tortuous course, generally N.W., into the Murrumbidgee River, about 7 miles E. of the township of Wagga Wagga. It flows through the township of Nimilbee and Tarcutta, where it expands into the Umbango Swamp.

TARCUTTA HILL (*Co. Wynyard*), a lofty peak in the range of mountains, lying to the N.E. of the township of Tarcutta.

TAREE (*Co. Macquarie*), a postal village, 224 miles N. of Sydney, with daily mail, and by steamer. Telegraph and money-order offices, Government savings bank, and delivery by letter-carrier. The nearest railway station is Hexham, 113 miles, on the northern line. Situated on the N. bank of the Manning River, 20 miles from the heads. The district is agricultural and pastoral, having rich soil on the banks of the rivers and creeks. It was proclaimed a municipal district in 1885, with a council of five aldermen and a mayor. Population, about 700. Courts of quarter sessions and district courts are held here periodically.

TAREENA *(Co. Tara)*, a postal village, 796 miles S. of Sydney, with mail twice a week.

TARLO *(Co. Argyle)*, a postal village, 142 miles S. of Sydney, with mail three times a week. The nearest railway station is Goulburn, 8 miles, on the southern line. Situated on the river Tarlo or Cookbundoon, in the parish of Tarlo. The district is an agricultural and pastoral one.

TARLO RIVER *(Co. Argyle)*, a stream rising in the Carnbungla Flats, flowing through the township of Tarlo, and after a circuitous course of about 50 miles falls into the Wollondilly.

TARPORLEY CREEK *(Co. Darling)*, a western tributary of the Manilla River, and fed by the Oaky Creek.

TARRAGAL LAKE *(Co. Northumberland)*, an inlet from the sea, about a mile square, lying in the parish of Kincumber, nearly 6 miles E. of Gosford.

TARRO *(Co. Northumberland)*, a postal town, 109 miles N. of Sydney, with daily mail. A railway station on the northern line.

TARRUNGA *(Co. Camden)*, a newly settled agricultural district, forming part of the celebrated Yarrah-Wah Brush. The land is exceedingly fertile.

TATAILA *(Co. Cadell)*, a postal village, 582 miles S. of Sydney, with mail therefrom twice a week, near Moama.

TATHAM *(Co. Clarence)*, a postal town, 368 miles N. of Sydney, with mail per Clarence River steamers.

TATHRA *(Co. Auckland)*, a postal town 328 miles S. of Sydney, with mail twice a week, and telegraph office. The nearest railway station is Cooma, 124 miles, on the Goulburn and Cooma line. Situated at the mouth of the Bega River, in the parish of Tathra. Steamers call here to and from Sydney.

TATHRA BAY *(Co. Auckland)*, an indentation in the land, sheltered from S. and S.W. winds, situate about 24 miles N. of Eden light.

TAWINGBANG *(Co. Phillip)*, a proclaimed village on the Cudgegong River.

TAWINGBANG CREEK *(Co. Roxburgh)*, a tributary of the upper part of the Cudgegong River, into which it flows at the village reserve of Tawingbang.

TAYAN PIC *(Co. Roxburgh)*, a lofty peak of the Blue Mountain Range, lying at the head of the Capertee River, 25 miles S.E. of Rylstone. This mountain attains an elevation of 4,000 feet above sea-level.

TAYLOR'S ARM *(Co. Raleigh)*, a postal receiving-office, 356 miles N. of Sydney, with mail once a week.

TAYLOR'S BAY *(Co. Cumberland)*, a sandy bay on the N. shore of Port Jackson, to the E. of Bradley's Head, and about 2 miles from the entrance.

TAYLOR'S CREEK (OR BIRREBOOLA) *(Co. Buckland)*, an eastern tributary of the Yarrimanbah Creek, rising in Mount Many.

TAYLOR'S CREEK (*Co. Murray*), a stream rising in the western slope of the Australian Alps, and flowing into the eastern part of Lake George.

TAYLOR'S POINT (*Co. Cumberland*), a rocky promontory, forming the S. head of Careel Bay, in Pittwater.

TEA-GARDENS (*Co. Gloucester*), a postal town, 147 miles N. of Sydney, with mail three times a week.

TEAPOT SWAMP (*Co. Bathurst*), an agricultural settlement on the old Lachlan Road, lying 20 miles W. of Bathurst.

TEA-TREE CREEK (*Co. Clarence*), an eastern tributary of the Orara River, crossing the road from Grafton to Nymboida.

TEESDALE (*Co. Bathurst*), a village, 150 miles W. of Sydney, in the parish of Neville. Situated near the old Lachlan Road, midway between Bathurst and Cowra. The district is agricultural and pastoral.

TELARAREE (*Co. Gloucester*), a proclaimed village, on the Karuah River.

TELARAREE BROOK (*Co. Gloucester*), a small stream, flowing into the Karuah River, near the township of Stroud.

TELEGHERRY (*Co. Gloucester*), a postal receiving-office, 152 miles N. of Sydney, with daily mail. The nearest railway station is Hexham, 16 miles, on the northern line.

TELEGRAM CREEK (*Co. Dudley*), a small western tributary of the Comars Creek.

TELEGRAPH, THE (*Co. Wellesley*), a lofty peak, between the Camelong and Native Dog Creeks, about 18 miles N. of Bombala.

TELEGRAPH POINT (*Co. Macquarie*), a postal village, 287 miles N. of Sydney, with daily mail. The nearest railway station is Hexham, 179 miles, on the northern line.

TELLA LAKE (*Co. Caira*), a lagoon, lying on the E. bank of the Murrumbidgee River, about 8 miles N.E. of Balranald.

TEMI MOUNT (*Co. Buckland*), a peak of the Liverpool Range, about 12 miles from the townships of Wallabadah and Murrurundi, and attaining an elevation of 4,000 feet above sea-level.

TEMORA (*Co. Bland*), a postal town, 342 miles S. of Sydney, with daily mail. Telegraph and money-order offices, and Government savings bank. The nearest railway station is Cootamundra, 35 miles, on the Cootamundra and Gundagai line. Courts of quarter sessions and district courts are held here periodically during each year.

TEMPE (*Co. Cumberland*), a postal village, 7 miles S. of Sydney, with mail twice daily. Money-order office. A railway station on the Illawarra and South Coast line. Situated on the N. side of Cook's River.

TEMPLE COURT (*Co. Buckland*), a railway station, 218 miles N. of Sydney, on the northern line.

TENANDRA (*Co. Bathurst*), a postal village, 358 miles W. of Sydney, with mail three times a week. The nearest railway station is Nevertire, 15 miles, on the western line.

TENANDRA CREEK (*Co. Bathurst*), a tributary of the Belubula River, in the parishes of Tenandra and Chaucer.

TENANT MOUNT (*Co. Cowley*), a lofty peak, lying on the W. bank of the Murrumbidgee River, near the village of Thurwa. It belongs to the Murrumbidgee Range, although it is partially detached from them.

TEN-MILE CREEK (*Co. Goulburn*), a tributary of the Billabong Creek, rising in Mount Pleasant, and flowing about 16 miles into the main stream.

TEN-MILE CREEK (*Co. Macquarie*), a drainage creek, flowing through rugged cedar country into Lake Innes.

TEN-MILE CREEK (*Co. Narromine*), an eastern tributary of the Upper Bogan River, rising in Hervey's Range, near Gingham Gap, flowing in a western direction through good country.

TENNYSON, MOUNT (*Co. Auckland*), a solitary high mount on the Victoria border.

TENT HILL (*Co. Clive*), a postal village, 457 miles N. of Sydney, with daily mail. The nearest railway station is Deepwater, 14 miles, on the northern line.

TENTERFIELD (*Co. Clive*), a postal town, 480 miles N. of Sydney, with daily mail. Telegraph and money-order offices, Government savings bank, and delivery by letter-carrier. A railway station on the northern line. Situated on the Tenterfield Creek, and in the police district of Tenterfield. It is the most northerly large township of the Colony, lying within 12 miles of the nearest point in Queensland. The district is agricultural, pastoral, and mining. It was proclaimed a municipal district in 1871, with a council of eight aldermen and a mayor. Population, about 1,000. Courts of quarter sessions and district courts are held here periodically.

TENTERFIELD CREEK (*Co. Clive*), a southern tributary of the Dumaresq River, rising in the western slopes of the Australian Alps, flowing past the township, and joining that river, in the colony of Queensland, about 6 miles over the border line.

TERABEILE (*Co. Gowen*), a proclaimed township in this county.

TERABEILE CREEK (*Co. Gowen*), a creek draining the flat pastoral country to the E. of the township of Terabeile, flowing into the Castlereagh River.

TERALBA (*Co. Northumberland*), a postal village, 89 miles N. of Sydney, with daily mail. Telegraph and money-order offices. A railway station on the Newcastle and Lake Macquarie line.

TERALGA (*Co. Argyle*), a township, 153 miles S. of Sydney, situated in the parish of Teralga, on the Teralga Creek, the Abercrombie River being 12 miles N.

TERAMBI (*Co. Gloucester*), a proclaimed village in the county.

## NEW SOUTH WALES.

TERANG CREEK (*Co. Northumberland*), an eastern tributary of the head of Wyong Creek.

TERARA (*Co. Camden*), a postal village, 126 miles S. of Sydney, with daily mail. Telegraph and money-order offices, and Government savings bank. The nearest railway station is Moss Vale, 41 miles, on the southern line.

TERILBAH (*Co. Northumberland*), is the opening from the sea into Tuggerah Beach Lake.

TERMEIL (*Co. St. Vincent*), a postal town, 176 miles S. of Sydney, with mail once a week.

TERRA BELLA (*Co. Wellington*), a postal receiving-office, 268 miles W. of Sydney, with mail four times a week. The nearest railway station is Wellington, 23 miles, on the western line.

TERREL MOUNT (*Co. Buckland*), a peak of the Liverpool Range, lying between Merriwa and Breeza, about 24 miles W. of Murrurundi. It has an altitude of 4,000 feet above sea-level.

TERRERGEE MOUNT (*Co. Courallie*), a precipitous peak of the Nandewar Range of mountains, lying to the N.E. of Narrabri, and W. of Horton River.

TERRIANA CREEK (*Co. Rous*), a tributary of the N. arm of the Richmond River, flowing into it about 6 miles N.W. of Lismore.

TERRIARO (*Co. Nandewar*), a small agricultural village, lying a few miles from Narrabri.

TERRIGONG SWAMP (*Co. Camden*), a large tract of swampy land, lying near Kiama.

TERRYAWEYNYA CREEK (*Co. Livingstone*), a small creek, flowing into the Terryaweynya Lake.

TERRYAWEYNYA LAKE (*Co. Livingstone*), an expansion of the creek of the same name, and of the Talwynwalka Ana Branch of the Darling River.

TEVEN (*Co. Rous*), a proclaimed village in this county.

TEXAS (*Co. Arrawatta*), a postal village, 551 miles N. of Sydney, on the Queensland border, with mail once a week.

THACKARINGA (*Co. Yancowinna*), a postal village, 974 miles S. of Sydney, with mail five times a week. Telegraph and money-order offices, and Government savings bank. The nearest railway station is Hay, 400 miles, on the south-western line.

THALABA (*Co. Georgiana*), a postal receiving-office, 169 miles S. of Sydney, with mail three times a week.

THALABA CREEK (*Co. Denham*), a creek rising in the N. of the district, and flowing into the Barwon or Upper Darling River.

THARWA (*Co. Cowley*), a postal receiving-office, 211 miles S. of Sydney, with mail three times a week. The nearest railway station is Queanbeyan, 16 miles, on the Goulburn and Cooma line.

THE BULGA (*Co. Northumberland*), a postal village, 165 miles N. of Sydney, with mail three times a week. The nearest railway station is Singleton, on the northern line.

THE GULF (*Co. Phillip*), a postal receiving-office, 487 miles N. of Sydney, with mail once a week. The nearest railway station is Deepwater, 35 miles, on the northern line.

THE LAGOON (*Co. Bathurst*), a postal village, 162 miles W. of Sydney, with mail twice a week. The nearest railway station is George's Plains, 7 miles, on the western line.

THE REEFS (*Co. Clarendon*), a postal village, 298 miles S. of Sydney, with mail twice a week. The nearest railway station is Junee, 8 miles, on the southern line.

THE ROCK (*Co. Mitchell*), a postal village, 327 miles S. of Sydney, with daily mail. Telegraph and money-order offices. A railway station on the southern line.

THEROLONONG (*Co. Murray*), is the highest peak of the Cullarin Range, attaining an altitude of 3,108 above sea-level.

THE VALLEY HEIGHTS (*Co. Cook*), a postal village, 46 miles W. of Sydney, with mail twice daily. A railway station on the western line.

THIERWILLAR (*Co. Thoulcanna*), a township on the W. bank of the Paroo River, on the Queensland border.

THIRLMERE (*Co. Camden*), a postal village, 57 miles S. of Sydney, with daily mail. A railway station on the southern line.

THOMAS MOUNT (*Co. Sandon*), a detached peak, lying about 3 miles S.W. of Armidale, in the parish of Butler.

THOMPSON (*Co. Vernon*), a small settlement, about 20 miles N.E. of Walcha.

THOMPSON'S CREEK (*Co. Brisbane*), a western tributary of the Dartbrook.

THOMPSON'S CREEK (*Co. Georgiana*), a fine auriferous stream, rising to the N.E. of the Tuena gold-fields, flowing into the Abercrombie River, at Bombah.

THONE CREEK (*Co. Macquarie*), a southern tributary of the Hastings River.

THOOLABOOL MOUNT (*Co. Killara*), a flat-topped hill, lying on the W. bank of the Darling River, to the S.W. of Bourke.

THORNLEIGH (*Co. Cumberland*), a postal village, 18 miles N. of Sydney, with daily mail. A railway station on the Ryde and Hawkesbury River line.

THORNTHWAITE (*Co. Brisbane*), a village, 166 miles N. of Sydney. Situated on the Dartbrook, on the line of road from Scone to Merriwa.

THORNTON (*Co. Northumberland*), a postal receiving-office, 112 miles N. of Sydney, with daily mail. A railway station on the northern line.

THOULCANNA, a county in the Western Division of the Colony. [*See* "COUNTIES."]

THREE BROTHERS (*Co. Bathurst*), a triple-peaked detached mountain, at the head of the Fitzgerald's, Queen Charlotte's Vale, and Caloola Creeks, about 10 miles S.E. of the township of Blayney.

THREE BROTHERS (*Co. Cumberland*), three rocks on the N. side of the Parramatta River, opposite Fig-tree Bay, and between Five Dock Point and the Bedlam ferry.

THREE BROTHERS (*Co. Macquarie*), three remarkable hills contiguous to each other, extending from 1 to 5 miles in shore, about 33 miles from Cape Hawke. It is an excellent land-mark out at sea.

THREE HILLS (*Co. Goulburn*), a group of detached hills to the W. of Mullanjandra Reserve, in the parish of that name.

THREE HILLS (*Co. Wellington*), a part of the Stoney Creek gold-field, a few miles W. of Ironbarks.

THREE-MILE CREEK (*Co. Wynyard*), a drainage creek, flowing W. into the head of Tarcutta Creek.

THREE-MILE CREEK (*Co. Durham*), a village, 178 miles N. of Sydney. The nearest railway station is Muswellbrook, on the northern line.

THREE-MILE FLAT (*Co. Auckland*), a tract of good pastoral land on the upper part of the Bemboka River, about 30 miles W. of Bega.

THUDDUNGRA (*Co. Monteagle*), a postal village, 266 miles S. of Sydney, with mail twice a week.

THURGOONA CREEK (*Co. Goulburn*), a postal village, 392 miles S. of Sydney, with mail twice a week. The nearest railway station is Albury, 4 miles, on the southern line.

THURNAPATCHA (*Co. Irrara*), a township on the E. bank of the Paroo River, near the Queensland boundary.

THURROWA (*Co. Urana*), a township on the banks of the Yanco Creek, to the N.W. of the Junee-Jerilderie railway line.

THYRA (*Co. Cadell*), a postal receiving-office, 524 miles S. of Sydney, with mail once a week.

TIA (*Co. Vernon*), a village on the N.W. bank of the Tia River, near Apsley Falls.

TIA RIVER (*Co. Vernon*). [*See* "RIVERS."]

TIANJARA (*Co. St. Vincent*), an agricultural village, lying on the head of the Yalwall Creek, and on the road from Nowra to Nerriga.

TIBOOBURRA (*Co. Tongowoko*), a township on the borders of Queensland and near that of South Australia.

TIBOOBURRA *(Co. Evelyn)*, a postal village, 892 miles S.W. of Sydney, with mail twice a week. Money-order office. The nearest railway station is Hay, 370 miles, on the south-western line.

TICHBOURNE *(Co. Ashburnham)*, a postal receiving-office, 284 miles W. of Sydney, with daily mail. The nearest railway station is Borenore, 82 miles, on the Orange and Molong line.

TIDBINBILLA CREEK *(Co. Cowley)*, a tributary of the Cotter River rising in Mount Tidbinbilla, falling into the Cotter, near its confluence with the Murrumbidgee River.

TIDBINBILLA *(Co. Cowley)*, a high hill lying to the W. of the Molonglo River, the Cotter River separating it from the Murrumbidgee Range.

TIGHE'S HILL *(Co. Northumberland)*, a postal village, 81½ miles N. of Sydney, with daily mail, and money-order office. The nearest railway station is Hamilton, 1 mile, on the Newcastle and Lake Macquarie line.

TILBA TILBA *(Co. Dampier)*, a postal village, 249 miles S. of Sydney, with daily mail and telegraph office. The nearest railway station is Tarago, 118 miles, on the Goulburn and Cooma line.

TILBA TILBA CREEK *(Co. Dampier)*, a small inlet of the sea, lying about a mile S. of Barbinga Head.

TILBUSTER PONDS *(Co. Sandon)*, a series of waterholes, rising near the Devil's Waterholes, on the main road from Armidale to the N., and flowing to the E. until its junction with the Gyra River, near the Great Falls, and flowing into the Macleay River.

TILLARA CREEK *(Co. Durham)*, a small tributary of the Murray River, flowing from the western slopes of Mount Waldania.

TILLIGERRY CREEK *(Co. Durham)*, a small stream flowing into the southern part of Port Stephens.

TILPA *(Co. Landsborough)*, a postal village, 636 miles W. of Sydney, with mail therefrom twice a week, and telegraph office. The nearest railway station is Bourke, 133 miles, on the western line.

TILRINGO CREEK *(Co. St. Vincent)*, a southern tributary of the Endrick River, flowing into it a few miles N.W. of Nerriga.

TIMBARRA *(Co. Drake)*, a postal village, 497 miles N. of Sydney, with mail twice a week. The nearest railway station is Tenterfield, 117 miles, on the northern line.

TIMBARRA GOLD-FIELDS *(Co. Drake)*, an alluvial diggings, lying on the Demon and Timbarra Creeks, about 20 miles S.W. of Tabulam.

TIMBARRA RIVULET *(Co. Drake)*. [*See* "RIVERS."]

TIMBERY RANGE *(Co. Beresford)*, a postal town, 301 miles S. of Sydney, with mail once a week. The nearest railway station is Cooma, 24 miles, on the Goulburn and Cooma line.

TIMBILICA *(Co. Auckland)*, a postal village, 316 miles S. of Sydney, with mail by Eden steamers. The nearest railway station is Cooma, 141 miles, on the Goulburn and Cooma line.

TIMBRIEBUNGIE (*Co. Ewenmar*), a postal village, 308 miles W. of Sydney, with mail twice a week. The nearest railway station is Narramine, 9 miles, on the western line.

TIMOR (*Co. Brisbane*), a postal village, 225 miles N. of Sydney, with mail twice a week. The nearest railway station is Blandford, 17 miles, on the northern line.

TIMOR MOUNT (*Co. Leichhardt*), a high peak of the Warrabungle Range, at the head of the Castlereagh River, about 4 miles W. of Coonabarabran.

TINAGROO MOUNT (*Co. Buckland*), a peak of the Liverpool Range, about 10 miles W. of Murrurundi, attaining an altitude of 4,000 feet above sea-level.

TINANDRY CREEK (*Co. Gowen*), a tributary of the Baronne Creek, rising in Mount Boreable.

TINDERRY (*Co. Beresford*), a township, 226 miles S. of Sydney. Situated on Colyer's Creek, in the police district of Cooma, 10 miles S. of Michelago.

TINDERRY CREEK (*Cos. Murray and Beresford*), a tributary of the Queanbeyan River, flowing from the Tindery Peak, and forms part of the boundary between the two counties. It is also a northern tributary of the Bredbo River.

TINDERRY RANGE (*Cos. Murray and Beresford*), a chain of lofty mountains, running from N. to S., in the northern part of Beresford and the S. of Murray, running about 4 miles N.E. of the village of Bredbo, and the N. point known as the Twins, or Tinderry Pic, into the Queanbeyan River.

TINGARAJAH CREEK (*Co. Northumberland*), a small tributary of the Mangrove Creek.

TINGHA (*Co. Hardinge*), a postal town, 418 miles N. of Sydney, with daily mail. Telegraph and money-order offices, and Government savings bank. The nearest railway station is Guyra, 42 miles, on the northern line.

TINKER'S CREEK (*Co. Cowley*), a western tributary of the Murrumbidgee River, flowing past the N. foot of Pig Hill.

TINKETTLE CREEK (*Co. Cumberland*), a small stream flowing near Cabramatta.

TINKETTLE CREEK (*Co. Westmoreland*), a western tributary of the Wollondilly River, rising near Mount Colong.

TINONEE (*Co. Gloucester*), a postal town, 208 miles N. of Sydney, with daily mail. Telegraph and money-order offices. The nearest railway station is Hexham, 107 miles, on the northern line. Situated on the S. bank of the Manning River, in the parish of Wingham. The district is an agricultural one.

TINTENBAR (*Co. Rous*), a postal village, 371 miles N. of Sydney, with mail per Clarence and Richmond steamers.

TINTINHUL (*Co. Inglis*), a postal village, 288 miles N. of Sydney, with mails three times a week. A railway station on the northern line.

**TIPPERARY GULLY** (*Co. Sandon*), the name of a gold diggings on the Rocky River gold-fields.

**TIRRANDUBUNDEBA MOUNT** (*Co. Macquarie*), a high point on the Hastings Range, lying at the head of the Huntingdon Creek.

**TIURRA CREEK** (*Co. Vernon*), a southern tributary of the Apsley River, falling into it and below the Apsley Fall.

**TNONONGA** (*Co. Sturt*), a township, to the N. of the Murrumbidgee River. A station on the south-western railway line.

**TOALLO POINT** (*Co. Auckland*), a rocky promontory, lying a few miles S. of Murrimbula, forming the S. head of the Panbula River.

**TOCUMWAL** (*Co. Denison*), a postal village, 449 miles S. of Sydney, with mail four times a week. Telegraph and money-order offices. The nearest railway station is Jerilderie, 37 miles, on the Junee and Jerilderie line.

**TODE'S CREEK** (*Co. Wynyard*), an eastern tributary of the Kyambla Creek, rising near Mount Coreinbob.

**TOLEHAMBAH** (*Co. Northumberland*), a narrow neck of sandy land, between the ocean and Tuggerah Beach Lake. The village of Norah, or Cabbage-tree Harbour, and Bungaree Norah Point are on this point. The S. point is called Karagi, and forms the N. head of the lake.

**TOLGA MOUNT** (*Co. Cunningham*), a lofty solitary hill on the N. bank of the Lachlan River, near Condobolin.

**TOLLGATE ISLANDS** (*Co. St. Vincent*).—Several small rocky islets, lying on the S. side of the entrance to Bateman's Bay.

**TOM THUMB'S LAGOON** (*Co. Camden*), an inlet of the sea, lying about 3 miles S. of Wollongong. It is named after the small boat in which Bass and Flinders made their discoveries in 1796.

**TOMAGO RIVER** (*Co. St. Vincent*), a stream rising between Bateman's Bay and Broulee, falling into the sea at Tomaga Inlet. [*See* "RIVERS."]

**TOMAGO** (*Co. Durham*), a postal village, 108 miles N. of Sydney, with daily mail. The nearest railway station is Hexham, 3 miles, on the northern line. Situated on the N. bank of the Hunter River, in the parish of Stockton, and is an agricultural and coal-mining district.

**TOMAH MOUNT** (*Co. Cook*), a lofty peak of the Blue Mountain Range, lying on the S. side of the road from Hartley to Richmond, and on the N. bank of the Grose River. The peak attains an elevation of 3,240 feet above sea-level, and is distinctly seen from the neighbourhood of Sydney.

**TOMAKIN** (*Co. St. Vincent*), a postal receiving-office, 210 miles N. of Sydney, with mail once a week, and telegraph office.

**TOMBOY** (*Co. Murray*), a postal receiving-office, 218 miles S. of Sydney, with mail twice a week. The nearest railway station is Tarago, 39 miles, on the Goulburn and Cooma line.

TOMERONG (*Co. St. Vincent*), a postal village, 137 miles S. of Sydney, with daily mail and telegraph office. The nearest railway station is Kiama, 39 miles, on the Illawarra and South Coast line. Situated on the Ulladulla Road, in the parish of Tomerong. The district is an agricultural one, and the soil very good.

TOMINGLEY (*Co. Narromine*), a township, 278 miles W. of Sydney. The nearest railway station is Dubbo, 30 miles, on the western line.

TOMINGLEY CREEK (*Co. Narromine*), an eastern tributary of the upper part of the Bogan River, rising in Hervey's Range, in the flat country to the N.W. of Obley.

TONABUTTA (*Co. Wellington*), a village lying 2 miles N.W. of the township of Cudgegong.

TONGA (*Co. Wynyard*), an agricultural settlement, on the Tarcutta Creek, lying about 4 miles S. of Tarcutta.

TONGARO or JACOB'S RIVER (*Co. Wallace*), a fine stream rising in the Snowy Mountains, and flowing into the Snowy River.

TONGBONG GAP (*Co. Phillip*), a passage between two high points in the mountainous range on the road between Dabee and Dungaree, in the parish of Loue.

TONGOWOKO, a county in the Western Division of the Colony. [*See* "COUNTIES."]

TONGUL (*Co. Waradgery*), a township on the N. bank of the Murrumbidgee River, and to the W. of Hay.

TOOGONG (*Co. Wellington*), a postal village, 226 miles W. of Sydney, with daily mail. The nearest railway station is Borenore, 23 miles, on the Orange and Molong line.

TOOLAMANANG CREEK (*Co. Wellington*), an auriferous northern tributary of the Pyramul Creek, rising in the Toolamanang Mountains.

TOOLEBUCK (*Co. Wakool*), a township on the banks of the Murray River.

TOOLOOM (*Co. Drake*), a postal village, 570 miles N. of Sydney, with mail twice a week. The nearest railway station is Tenterfield, 56 miles, on the northern line. Situated on the Tooloom Creek.

TOOLOOM GOLD-FIELD (*Co. Drake*), an alluvial diggings lying on both sides of the Tooloom Creek, 8 miles N. of Tabulam.

TOOLOOM RIVULET (*Cos. Buller and Rous*). [*See* "RIVERS."]

TOOLOOMBI CREEK (*Co. Richmond*), an eastern tributary of the head of the Clarence River.

TOOLEYBUCK (*Co. Wakool*), a township on the N. bank of the Murray River, 450 miles S.W. of Sydney. The nearest railway station is Hay, 150 miles, on the south-western line.

TOOMA (*Co. Hume*), a postal town, 490 miles S. of Sydney, with mail twice a week. The nearest railway station is Wagga Wagga, 85 miles, on the southern line.

TOOMA RIVER (*Co. Selwyn*). [*See* "RIVERS."]

TOOMEREE HEAD (*Co. Durham*).—The S. head of Port Stephens, which rises abruptly to a conspicuous summit at an elevation of 440 feet above sea-level.

TOONGABBIE (*Co. Cumberland*), a postal village, 23 miles W. of Sydney, with daily mail. A railway station on the western line. It is one of the original districts of the county.

TOORALE (*Co. Gunderbooka*), a township at the confluence of the Darling and Warrego Rivers, below Bourke.

TORAGY CREEK (*Co. Dampier*) is the S. head of the Moruya River.

TORINGTON (*Co. Gough*), a postal town, 460 miles N. of Sydney, with mail twice a week. The nearest railway station is Deepwater, 17 miles, on the northern line.

TORONTO (*Co. Northumberland*), a postal town, 89 miles N. of Sydney, with daily mail.

TORRENS (*Co. Bathurst*), a proclaimed township, to the N. of Blayney.

TORRENS' CREEK (*Co. Blaxland*), a small stream, rising in Mount King, a peak of the Grey Range.

TOUMBAAL CREEK (*Co. Clarence*), a small northern tributary of the mouth of the Sandon River.

TOWAMBA (*Co. Auckland*), a postal town, 298 miles S. of Sydney, with mail twice a week. The nearest railway station is Cooma, 124 miles, on the Goulburn and Cooma line.

TOWAMBA or KIAH RIVER (*Co. Auckland*). [*See* "RIVERS."]

TOWARRI (*Co. Buckland*), a peak of the Liverpool Range, lying about 16 miles W. of Murrurundi, attaining an altitude of 4,000 feet above sea-level.

TOWER HILL (*Co. Arrawatta*), a lofty solitary hill, lying on the E. bank of Frazer's Creek, near Bukkulla.

TOWINBANG (*Co. Roxburgh*), a peak in the spur of the Blue Mountain Range, on the S. bank of the Cudgegong River.

TOWNSEND, a county in the Central Division of the Colony. [*See* "COUNTIES."]

TOWPRUCK (*Co. Caira*), a township, on the N. bank of the Lachlan River, lying to the S. of Oxley.

TOWRANG (*Co. Argyle*), a postal town, 124 miles S. of Sydney, with daily mail. A railway station on the southern line.

TOWRANG MOUNT (*Co. Argyle*), a high peak on the E. of the Goulburn Plains.

TRABA CREEK (*Co. Forbes*), a tributary of the head of the Ooma Creek.

TRABUNDIE CREEK (*Co. Darling*), an auriferous creek, flowing through the Ironbark gold-field into the Nangabra Creek.

TRAGONG CREEK (*Co. Forbes*), a northern tributary of the Burrangong Creek.

TRANGIE (*Co. Wellington*), a postal village, 320 miles W. of Sydney, with daily mail. Telegraph, and money-order offices, and Government savings bank. A railway station on the western line.

TRAVELLERS' REST (*Co. Richmond*), an agricultural settlement on the Tenterfield and Tabulam Road, 30 miles S.W. of Grafton.

TREACHERY HEAD (*Co. Gloucester*), a rocky promontory, lying about 20 miles N.E. of Port Stephens.

TREVALLYN (*Co. Durham*), a postal town, 135 miles N. of Sydney, with daily mail therefrom. The nearest railway station is East Maitland, 26 miles, on the Morpeth line.

TRIAL BAY (*Co. Dudley*) is an estuary of the Macleay River, situated on the N.W. side of Smoky Cape, and affords good anchorage during S. winds for small vessels.

TRIANBIL CREEK (*Co. Wellington*), an eastern tributary of the Macquarie River, rising to the S. of the Louisa Creek gold-fields.

TRIJAMON CREEK (*Co. Arrawatta*), a western tributary of the Macintyre River, S. of the township of Yetman.

TRINIDAD CREEK (*Co. Vernon*), a southern tributary of the Apsley River.

TRUNDLE LAGOON (*Co. Ashburnham*), a postal receiving-office, 314 miles W. of Sydney, with mail twice a week. The nearest railway station is Borenore, 112 miles, on the Orange and Molong line.

TRUNKEY CREEK (*Co. Bathurst*), a postal town, 182 miles W. of Sydney, with daily mail. Telegraph and money-order offices, and Government savings bank. The nearest railway station is Newbridge, 18 miles, on the western line.

TUBBAL (*Co. Monteagle*), a postal receiving-office, 267 miles S. of Sydney, with mail once a week.

TUCABIA (*Co. Clarence*), a proclaimed township to the N. of Grafton.

TUCKERIMBA (*Co. Clarence*), a postal receiving-office, 353 miles N. of Sydney, with mail by Clarence and Richmond steamers.

TUEKÜ-TUEKÜ (*Co. Richmond*), a village, situated on the Richmond River, about 12 miles S. from the township of Lismore by water.

TUENA (*Co. Georgiana*), a postal town, 197 miles W. of Sydney, with daily mail. Telegraph and money-order offices, and Government savings bank. The nearest railway station is Newbridge, 36 miles, on the western line. Situated on the Tuena Creek, in the police district of Carcoar. The district is agricultural and mining, and produces in perfection both cereals and fruits. Minerals also abound.

TUENA CREEK (*Co. Georgiana*), a southern auriferous tributary of the Abercrombie River, rising to the N. of Binda, and flowing through the Tuena gold-fields.

**TUGGA PLAINS** (*Co. Goulburn*), an alluvial flat, near the Cookardinia and Billabong Creeks, about 4 miles from Carabobala.

**TUGGERAH BEACH LAKE** (*Co. Northumberland*), a series of large lagoons, opening into the sea by a narrow channel at a point on the eastern coast called Tuggerah. These lagoons are three in number, the most southerly one being the largest—about 8 miles long by 4 miles broad—and which receives the waters of Wyong and Ourimbah Creeks. The shores of the lagoons are sandy. The narrow neck of land which lies between the lake and the sea is called Toleambah, upon which is situated the village of Norah and Cabbage-tree Harbour.

**TUGGERNONG** (*Co. Murray*), a postal village, 207 miles S. of Sydney, with mail therefrom three times a week. A railway station on the Goulburn and Cooma line.

**TUGLOW CAVES** (*Co. Westmoreland*), the name given to several chasms on the E. side of the Blue Mountain Range, at the head of the Tuglow Creek.

**TULLIMBAR** (*Co. Camden*), a postal village, 82 miles S. of Sydney, with daily mail and money-order office. The nearest railway station is Kiama, 18 miles, on the Illawarra and South Coast line.

**TUMANWONG MOUNT** (*Co. Murray*), a lofty peak of the Gourock Range, attaining an elevation of 3,500 feet above sea-level. It lies to the S. of Bullalaba.

**TUMBALONG** (*Co. Wynyard*), a village, lying 4 miles S. of Gundagai.

**TUMBERUMBAH** (*Co. Wynyard*), a postal town, 358 miles S. of Sydney, with mail four times a week. Telegraph and money-order offices. The nearest railway station is Culcairn, 68 miles, on the southern line. Situated on the creek and parish of the same name. The district is pastoral and alluvial mining.

**TUMBULGUM** (*Co. Rous*) a postal town, 421 miles N. of Sydney, with daily mail. Telegraph and money-order offices, and Government savings bank.

**TUMUT** (*Co. Buccleuch*) a postal town, 254 miles S. of Sydney, with daily mail. Telegraph and money-order offices, Government savings bank, and delivery by letter-carrier. The nearest railway station is Gundagai, 20 miles, on the Cootamundra and Gundagai line. Situated on the S. bank of the Tumut River. It is essentially an agricultural district, producing the finest cereals and fodder for cattle. It was proclaimed a municipal district in 1887, with a council of eight aldermen and a mayor. Population, about 400. Courts of quarter sessions and district courts are held here periodically.

**TUMUT RANGE** (*Co. Buccleuch*), a spur from the Muniong Range, dividing the waters of the Tumut from those of the Goodradigbee Rivers.

**TUMUT RIVER** (*Cos. Buccleuch and Wynyard.*) [*See* "RIVERS."]

**TUNGO CREEK** (*Albert District*), a small creek, rising in the Monolon Mountains, and flowing into the swamp to the E.

**TUNK'S CREEK** (*Co. Cumberland*), a small creek, flowing near the village of Dural, on the N. road from Parramatta to Wiseman's Ferry.

TUNNABIDGEE (*Co. Wellington*), a southern auriferous tributary of the Pyramul Creek, rising in the eastern part of the Tambaroora gold-fields.

TUNNY'S SWAMP (*Co. Buccleuch*), a tract of marshy country, to the E. of the Honeysuckle Ranges, and the S. of the Adjungbilly Creek.

TUPPAL (*Co. Townsend*), a proclaimed village, on Tuppal Creek.

TUPPAL CREEK (*Cos. Townsend and Denison*), a watercourse, connecting the Murray and Edward Rivers, flowing near the township of Tocumwal, and joining the latter river near Deniliquin.

TURA POINT (*Co. Auckland*), a rocky promontory, standing boldly out on the coast, about 3 miles N. of Murrimbula.

TURALLO CREEK (*Co. Murray*), a small stream, rising in the Molonglo Plains, about 8 miles S. of Bungendore, through which township it flows, and empties into Lake George at its southern point.

TUREE CREEK (*Co. Bligh*) a postal receiving-office, 262 miles N. of Sydney, with mail once a week. The nearest railway station is Muswellbrook, 80 miles, on the northern line. The creek is a tributary of the Erskine River, flowing through Turee. The district is an agricultural and pastoral one.

TURILL CREEK (*Co. Bligh*), a tributary of the head of the Munmurra Creek.

TURIMELLA HEAD (*Co. Cumberland*), a rocky promontory, lying about 2 miles N. of the Narrabeen Lagoon.

TURI MOUNT (*Co. Buckland*), a peak of the Peel Range, to the N. of Currabubula, attaining an altitude of 2,972 feet above sea-level.

TURKEY ISLAND (*Co. Clarence*), an island, lying in the Clarence River, between Palmer's and Harwood Islands.

TURLINJAH (*Co. Murray*), a postal receiving-office, 252 miles S. of Sydney, with daily mail. The nearest railway station is Tarago, 52 miles, on the Goulburn and Cooma line.

TURON (*Co. Roxburgh*) a township, 145 miles W. of Sydney. A railway station on the western line.

TURON, LOWER (*Co. Roxburgh*), a gold workings on the Turon River, forming part of the Turon diggings, about 21 miles from the township of Sofala.

TURON DIGGINGS (*Co. Roxburgh*), include the whole of the extensive workings on the Turon River and its auriferous tributaries, of which Sofala is the chief town on these diggings.

TURON RIVER (*Co. Roxburgh*), a fine auriferous stream, rising in the cleared hill in the western slope of the Australian Alps, N. of Cullen-Bullen township, and in the parish of Ben-Bullen. The whole course is auriferous, forming the Turon, the largest of the western gold-fields. [See "RIVERS."]

TUROSS RIVER (*Co. Dampier*), an important river, rising in the Barren Jumbo Mountains, and flowing into the sea by a fine, wide, open estuary, having, however, a bar at its mouth. This river flows through the Gulf, or Tuross gold-fields, and crosses the road from Bega to Moruya, about 6 miles S. of Coila, a small town on the N. bank of the estuary.

TURRABEILE CREEK (*Co. Pottinger*) a fine stream, rising on the western extremity of the Liverpool Range of the Australian Alps, and flowing N. into the Namoi River at Boggabri, and it forms the western boundary of the county.

TURRAWAN (*Co. White*), a proclaimed township and a railway station, 338 miles to the N.W. of Sydney, on the north-western line.

TWEED HEADS (*Co. Rous*), a postal village, 427 miles N. of Sydney, with daily mail. Telegraph and money-order offices.

TWEED RIVER (*Co. Rous*). [*See* "RIVERS."]

TWICKENHAM MEADOWS (*Co. Brisbane*) is the name of the beautiful and fertile country near the junction of the Goulburn and Hunter.

TWOFOLD BAY (*Co. Auckland*) is the principal harbour on the southern part of the coast of the Colony. It was discovered by Mr. Bass in 1727, and lies 280 miles S. of Sydney. Twofold Bay is the port of the Monaro district, and the flourishing town of Eden is built on its northern bank. The lighthouse is built on the southern extremity of Lookout Point, 102 feet above the level of the sea.

TWO-MILE CREEK (*Co. Gordon*), a small western tributary of the Bell River.

TWO-MILE CREEK (*Co. Harden*), a small drainage creek of the low hills to the south of Young, flowing into the Connaughtman's Creek.

TWO-MILE CREEK (*Co. Hardinge*), an auriferous northern tributary of the Gwydir River, flowing through rugged country.

TWO-MILE CREEK (*Co. Roxburgh*), an auriferous tributary of the Four-mile Creek, rising in the Cherry-tree Hills.

TWO-MILE FLAT (*Co. Wellington*), a postal village, 288 miles W. of Sydney, with mail four times a week. The nearest railway station is Mudgee, 31 miles, on the western line.

TWORALE (*Co. Gunderbooka*), a township, 503 miles to the N.W. of Sydney, and 45 miles from Bourke, the nearest railway station on the western line.

TWYONG CREEK (*Co. Wynyard*), a western tributary of the Kiambla Creek, flowing to the S. of the Murrumbidgee River, near Wagga Wagga.

TYAGONG CREEK (*Co. Monteagle*), a small creek, a tributary to the Lachlan River.

TYNDALE (*Co. Clarence*), a postal town, 344 miles N. of Sydney, with mail per Clarence and Richmond steamers.

TYRAMAN (*Co. Durham*), a village, 146 miles to the N. of Sydney, on the Paterson River.

TYRAMAN MOUNT (*Co. Durham*), a peak of the Mount Royal Range, lying on the W. bank of the Paterson River, about 4 miles S. of Gresford.

# U

UAMBY CREEK (*Co. Bligh*), a small northern tributary of the Cudgegong River, flowing into the main stream near Wiadere.

UARBRY (*Co. Bligh*), a postal village, 238 miles W. of Sydney, with mail twice a week. The nearest railway station is Mudgee, 45 miles, on the western line.

UARDRY (*Co. Sturt*), a railway station, 427 miles S.W. of Sydney, on the south-western line.

UCAYARRA (*Co. Cowley*), a small creek, draining into lagoon formed at the S. foot of the Big Nile by the expansion of the Swamp Creek.

ULAN (*Co. Bligh*), a postal receiving-office, 204 miles W. of Sydney, with mail twice a week.

ULARARA, a county in the Western Division of the Colony. [*See* "COUNTIES."]

ULARARA (*Co. Barrona*), a township, on the E. bank of the Paroo River, to the S. of Monkilmoultha.

ULCENDAH ISLAND (*Co. Clarence*), a small island in the Clarence River, opposite the town of Ashby.

ULIMAMBRA CREEK (*Co. Gowen*), an eastern tributary of the upper part of the Castlereagh River, rising to the S.W. of the Kerewally Springs.

ULLADULLA (*Co. St. Vincent*), a postal town, 164 miles S. of Sydney, with daily mail. Telegraph and money-order offices and Government savings bank. A seaport town, situate about 18 miles S. of Jervis Bay. The harbour is one of the safest in New South Wales; it is surrounded on three sides by high land, with rocky bluffs at the entrance, and plenty of depth of water. The district is very fertile, and dairy-farming is extensively carried on. It was proclaimed a municipal district in 1874, with a council of eight aldermen and a mayor.

ULMAMBRA MOUNT (*Co. Baradine*), a high peak of the Warrabungle Range, lying about 4 miles N.E. of the township of Coonabarabran.

ULMARRA (*Co. Clarence*), a postal village, 342 miles N. of Sydney, with mail twice a week, and per Clarence steamers. Telegraph and money-order offices, and Government savings bank. Situated on the Clarence River, in the parish of Ulmarra. The land is very fertile, and produces large crops of maize. Grafton lies about 9 miles S.W., where steam communication with Sydney is constant. It was proclaimed a municipal district in 1871, with a council of eight aldermen and a mayor.

ULTIMO (*Co. Cumberland*), a postal suburb of Sydney, with mail four times daily. Telegraph and money-order offices, and Government savings bank. It lies between Parramatta-street and Pyrmont, Blackwattle Cove and Darling Harbour.

ULUMBIE (*Co. Mossgiel*), a township, to the N. of the Willandra Billabong and the main thoroughfare to Wilcannia.

ULUPNA (*Co. Denison*), a proclaimed village within this county.

UMARALLA (*Co. Beresford*), a proclaimed village, on the river of the same name, and a railway station, 254 miles S. of Sydney, on the Goulburn and Cooma line.

UMARALLA RIVER (*Co. Beresford*). [See "RIVERS."]

UMBANGO CREEK (*Co. Wynyard*), a western tributary of the Tarcutta Creek, falling into it at the Umutbee Swamp, and draining good pastoral country to the N. of main range.

UMBERUMBERKA (*Co. Yancowinna*), a postal receiving-office, 824 miles S.W. of Sydney, with mail five times a week.

UMUTBEE SWAMP (*Co. Wynyard*) lies to the S.E. of the township of Umutbee, and is an expansion of the Tarcutta Creek, and receives the waters of the Umbango Creek and its tributaries. It is an alluvial morass.

UNANDERRA (*Co. Camden*), a postal village, 52 miles S. of Sydney, with mail twice daily. A railway station on the Illawarra and South Coast line.

UNDEALKA CREEK (*Co. Menindie*), a small creek, flowing to the S. of Menindie, out of the Murray River, into a swamp on its eastern side.

UNDERBANK (*Co. Durham*), a postal village, 147 N. of Sydney, with mail three times a week. A settlement on the Upper Williams River, near Bandon Grove. The nearest railway station is Morpeth, 51 miles, on the Maitland and Morpeth line.

UNDERCLIFF (*Co. Cumberland*), a small village lying on Cook's River, to the W. of the dam.

UNDOO CREEK (*Co. Beresford*), a southern tributary of the Bigbadja River, falling into it near its confluence with the Umaralla River.

UNDOWAH CREEK (*Co. Wellesley*), a small tributary of the head of the Bombala River.

UNDOW HEIGHTS (*Co. Wellesley*), a lofty group of mountains, lying between the Undowah River and Native Dog Creek, about 16 miles N. of Bombala.

UNGARIE (*Co. Gipps*), a postal town, 444 miles S. from Sydney, with mail therefrom twice a week.

UNGULA CREEK (*Co. Bligh*), a northern tributary of the Cudgegong River, falling into it near the Merindi Gold-field.

UNIVERSITY OF SYDNEY (*Co. Cumberland*).—The University, with its suffragan colleges—St. Paul's (Church of England), St. John's (Church of Rome), and St. Andrew's (Church of Scotland)—stands on a most beautiful undulating piece of land, known as Grose Farm, comprising an area of about 150 acres in extent. It is situated close to the W. boundary of the City of Sydney, and the main trunk line of railway skirts its S. border. Grose Farm, having been highly cultivated in the early days of the Colony, was almost entirely denuded of its indigenous forest trees, which is to be regretted, but since the establishment of the University and its suffragan colleges it has had substituted an arboretum more congenial to the eye, as well as giving greater protection for shade during the summer months of the year. These institutions are well filled with students, and presided over by competent masters.

UNUMGAR (*Co. Clarence*), a postal town, 435 miles N. of Sydney, with mail per Clarence River steamers.

UPPER ARALUEN (*Co. St. Vincent*), a township, 157 miles S. of Sydney. The nearest railway station is Tarago, 20 miles, on the Goulburn and Cooma line. Situated on the Araluen Creek, and surrounded by alluvial diggings.

UPPER BANKSTOWN (*Co. Cumberland*), a postal village, 12½ miles S. of Sydney, with daily mail.

UPPER BINGARA (*Co. Murchison*). [*See* "BINGARA."]

UPPER BOTOBOLA (*Co. Cook*), a postal village, 185 miles W. of Sydney, with mail once a week.

UPPER BURROGORANG (*Co. Camden*), a postal town, 66 miles S. of Sydney, with mail twice a week. The nearest railway station is Picton, 30 miles, on the southern line.

UPPER CHICHESTER (*Co. Gloucester*), a postal receiving-office, 158 miles N. of Sydney, with mail twice a week.

UPPER COLDSTREAM (*Co. Clarence*), a postal village, 318 miles N. of Sydney, with mail by steamers twice a week.

UPPER COLO (*Co. Cook*), a postal town, 66 miles W. of Sydney, with mail therefrom twice a week.

UPPER FOREST CREEK (*Co. Goulburn*), a small western tributary of the Little Billabong Creek.

UPPER GILMORE (*Co. Wynyard*), a postal receiving-office, 325 miles S. of Sydney, with mail twice a week.

UPPER GUNDAROO (*Co. King*), a postal village, 187 miles S. of Sydney, with daily mail. The nearest railway station is Gunning, 24 miles, on the southern line.

UPPER LANSDOWN (*Co. Macquarie*), a postal receiving-office, 244 miles N. of Sydney, with mail twice a week.

UPPER LOSTOCK (*Co. Durham*), a postal receiving-office, 159 miles N. of Sydney, with mail twice a week. The nearest railway station is East Maitland, 58 miles, on the East Maitland and Morpeth line.

UPPER MACDONALD (*Co. Northumberland*), a postal village, 76 miles N. of Sydney, with mail twice a week. The nearest railway station is Hawkesbury on the Sydney and Newcastle line.

UPPER MANILLA (*Co. Darling*), a postal village, 317 miles N. of Sydney, with daily mail. The nearest railway station is Manilla, 33 miles, on the northern line.

UPPER MYALL RIVER (*Co. Gloucester*), a postal village, 165 miles N. of Sydney, with mail twice a week. The nearest railway station is Hexham, 57 miles, on the northern line.

UPPER NORTH CREEK (*Co. Richmond*), a postal receiving-office, 371 miles N. of Sydney, with mail once a week.

UPPER ORARA (*Co. Clarence*), a postal receiving-office, 593 miles to the N. of Sydney, with mail per Clarence River steamers.

UPPER PYRAMUL (*Co. Wellington*), a postal village, 161 miles W. of Sydney, with mail four times a week, and money-order office. The nearest railway station is Mudgee, 32 miles, on the Mudgee line.

UPPER QUINBURRA (*Co. Wellesley*), a postal receiving-office, 344 miles S. of Sydney, with mail once a week.

UPPER ROLLANDS PLAINS (*Co. Macquarie*), a postal receiving-office, 317 miles N. of Sydney, with mail three times a week.

UPPER RUN (*Co. Westmoreland*), a postal village, 92 miles W. of Sydney, with mail three times a week.

UPPER SOUTH ARM (*Co. Clarence*), a postal village, 376 miles N. of Sydney, with mail therefrom once a week.

UPPER TUMBERUMBA (*Co. Wynyard*), a postal receiving-office, 353 miles S. of Sydney, with mail twice a week.

UPPER TURON (*Co. Roxburgh*), a postal village, 184 miles W. of Sydney, with mail twice a week. The nearest railway station is Bathurst, 30 miles, on the western line.

UPRIGHT POINT (*Co. St. Vincent*), a lofty rocky headland, at the N. of the estuary of the Benandra Creek, a few miles N. of Bateman's Bay.

URALBA (*Co. Rous*), a proclaimed township to the S. of Lismore.

URALLA (*Co. Sandon*), a postal town, 344 miles N. of Sydney, with daily mail. Telegraph and money-order offices, Government savings bank, and delivery by letter-carriers. A railway station on the northern line. Situated on the Rocky River, in the parish of Uralla. The district is agricultural, pastoral, and mining. It was proclaimed a municipal district in 1882, with a council of five aldermen and a mayor.

URAMAGAMBALA MOUNT (*Co. Wynyard*), a double peak lying to the W. of Kyamba Creek, and about 7 miles N.W. of the village of Kyamba.

URANA (*Co. Urana*), a postal town, 393 miles S.W. of Sydney, with mail four times a week. Telegraph and money-order offices, and Government savings bank. The nearest railway station is Widgiewa, 18 miles, on the Junee and Jerilderie line. Situated on the Urana Creek, in the parish of Urana, and is a pastoral district.

URANA CREEK (*Co. Urana*), lying to the N. of Morven and Wallandoon, and, after a course of about 36 miles, falling into Lake Urana near the township.

URANA, a county in the Central Division of the Colony. [*See* "COUNTIES."]

URANA LAKE (*Co. Urana*), a large lagoon formed by the expansion of the Urana and Coonong Creeks. It lies about 2 miles W. of the township.

URANBEEN (*Co. Murray*), a lofty peak of the Gourock Range, attaining an elevation of 3,800 feet above sea-level.

URANGELINE (*Co. Urana*), a postal village, 366 miles S. of Sydney, with mail three times a week.

URANGELINE CREEK (*Co. Urana*), a creek tributary to the Urana Creek, to the W. of Morven.

URANQUINTY (*Co. Wynyard*), a postal receiving-office, 318 miles S. of Sydney, with daily mail.

URAWILKIE (*Co. Leichhardt*), a village, 415 miles N.W. of Sydney. The nearest railway station is Dubbo, 96 miles, on the western line.

URIARRA (*Co. Murray*), a postal village, 221 miles S. of Sydney, with mail twice a week. The nearest railway station is Queanbeyan, 26 miles, on the Goulburn and Cooma line.

URINGALLA CREEK (*Co. Camden*), a small southern tributary of the Paddy's River.

UROPE (*Co. Harden*), a lofty solitary hill, near the junction of the Limestone Creek and the Murrumbidgee River, about 8 miles S.W. of Bookham.

URUMWALLA CREEK (*Co. King*), a small western tributary of the Blakeney's Creek, flowing E. in the Yass Plains.

UWARABIN CREEK (*Co. Durham*), a western tributary of the Williams' River, falling into it between Clarence Town and Dungog.

# V

VACY (*Co. Durham*), a postal village, 130 miles N. of Sydney, with daily mail and money-order office. The nearest railway station is East Maitland, 18 miles, on the East Maitland and Morpeth line. Situated on the confluence of the Paterson and Allyn Rivers, in the parish of Houghton. It is an agricultural and pastoral district, and parts of it very fertile and well cultivated.

VALE OF CLWYDD (*Co. Cook*), a postal village, 95 miles W. of Sydney, with daily mail. The nearest railway station is Eskbank, 1 mile, on the western line.

VAUCLUSE BAY (*Co. Cumberland*), a rocky bight, with a sandy beach at its head, lying about 2 miles inside from the inner S. head of Port Jackson. A remarkable rock, called the Bottle and Glass, is at the entrance to this bay.

VAUDEVILLE (*Co. Camden*), a township to the N. of the town of Camden. [*See* "OAKES."]

VEGETABLE CREEK (*Co. Gough*). [*See* "EMMAVILLE."]

VENGOAN MOUNT (*Co. Wellington*), a lofty peak, lying to the E. of the Stony Creek Gold-field, and at the head of the Boduldura Creek.

**VERMONT** (*Co. Camden*), an agricultural settlement, lying about 8 miles from Camden and Cobbity. The district is very fertile and well cultivated.

**VERNON**, a county in the Eastern Division of the Colony. [*See* "COUNTIES."]

**VERO** (*Co. Northumberland*), a postal village, 149 miles N. of Sydney, with daily mail. The nearest railway station is Singleton, 12 miles, on the northern line.

**VERY DEEP CREEK** (*Co. Cowley*), a small tributary of the Naas Valley Creek, flowing N.W. from Booth's Hill.

**VETERAN'S PEAK** (*Co. Wynyard*), a lofty eminence, to the S. of the Murrumbidgee River, and to the S.W. of Gundagai.

**VICTORIA LAKE** (*Co. Tara*), a large swampy lagoon, about 36 miles W. of Wentworth, on the road to Adelaide, and on the N. bank of the Murray River.

**VICTORIA MOUNT** (*Co. Cook*), a lofty peak of the Blue Mountain Range, about 10 miles S.E. of Hartley and 70 miles W. from Sydney.

**VICTORIA-STREET** (*Co. Northumberland*), a railway station, 17 miles from Newcastle, on the northern line.

**VINCENT'S HOLE** (*Co. Roxburgh*) a remarkable sunk valley in the Blue Mountain Range. It lies in the parish of Clandulla, on the W. bank of the Capertee River, and about 4 miles from it.

**VINEGAR HILL** (*Co. Cumberland*), a steep ascent on the road between Parramatta and Windsor.

**VITTORIA** (*Co. Bathurst*), a postal village, 183 miles W. of Sydney, with mail twice a week. The nearest railway station is Blayney, 11 miles, on the Blayney-Murrumburrah line.

# W

**WAAHMA MOUNT** (*Co. Auckland*), a hill, lying about 2 miles from the boundary-line between New South Wales and Victoria, and near the Yambulla Creek.

**WADBILLIGA CREEK** (*Co. Dampier*), a small southern tributary of the upper part of the Tuross River.

**WADDI** (*Co. Cooper*), a township on the N. bank of the Murrumbidgee River, and to the S. of the south-western railway at Witton.

**WADDIWONG** (*Co. Leichhardt*), a township, to the S. of the junction of the Barwon and Namoi Rivers.

**WAGGA WAGGA NORTH** (*Co. Clarendon*), a proclaimed township, on the opposite side of the Murrumbidgee River to Wagga Wagga South.

WAGGA WAGGA SOUTH (*Co. Wynyard*), a postal town, 300 miles S. of Sydney, with mail twice daily, telegraph and money-order offices, Government savings bank, and delivery by letter-carriers; a railway station on the southern line; situated on the S. bank of the Murrumbidgee River. It lies in the midst of a fine pastoral country. It was proclaimed a borough in 1870, with a council of eight aldermen and a mayor. Population, about 3,000. Courts of quarter sessions and district courts are held here periodically.

WAGONGA (*Co. Dampier*), a postal village, 272 miles S. of Sydney, with daily mail. The nearest railway station is Tarago, 102 miles, on the Goulburn and Cooma line. Situated on the Wagonga River; a small agricultural settlement, and the nearest township is Urobodalla, distant 10 miles.

WAGONGA HEADS (*Co. Dampier*), a postal village, 272 miles S. of Sydney, with daily mail.

WAGONGA INLET (*Co. Dampier*), a small inlet, lying on the coast about 10 miles S. of the estuary of the Tuross River. The village of Wagonga lies near the head of the inlet.

WAGRA (*Co. Goulburn*), a postal village, 416 miles S. of Sydney, with mail therefrom twice a week. The nearest railway station is Albury, 30 miles, on the southern line.

WAHGUNYAH NORTH (*Co. Hume*), a township, 400 miles S. of Sydney, in the parish of Corowa. It lies on the N. bank of the Murray River, opposite the township of Wahgunyah (Victoria). The district is pastoral and agricultural.

WAKOOL, a county in the Central Division of the Colony. [*See* "COUNTIES."]

WAKOOL RIVER (*Cos. Wakool and Townshend*). [*See* "RIVERS."]

WALBUNDRIE (*Co. Hume*), a postal village, 418 miles S. of Sydney, with mail three times a week. The nearest railway station is Gerogery, 20 miles, on the southern line.

WALCHA (*Co. Vernon*), a postal town, 332 miles N. of Sydney, with daily mail, telegraph and money-order offices, and Government savings bank. The nearest railway station is Walcha Road, 12 miles, on the northern line. Situated on the Apsley River, in the parish of Walcha. The district is an agricultural one, but surrounded by mountains. It was proclaimed a municipal district in 1889, with a council of five aldermen and a mayor.

WALCHA HILLS (*Co. Hawes*), a lofty peak of the New England Range, lying at the head of the Apsley River, about 16 miles S.E. of Walcha.

WALCHA ROAD (*Co. Vernon*), a postal village, 320 miles N. of Sydney, with daily mail, money-order offices, and Government savings bank. A railway station on the northern line.

WALDAIRE LAKE (*Co. Caira*), a lagoon, on the road from Balranald to Wentworth, about 12 miles W. of the former place, and on the N. bank of the Murray River.

WALGETT (*Co. Denham*), a postal town, 476 miles N. of Sydney, with mail three times a week, telegraph, money-order offices, and Government savings bank. The nearest railway station is Narrabri, 130 miles, on the north-western line. Situated at the junction of the Barwon and Namoi Rivers. The district is strictly a pastoral one. Courts of quarter sessions and district courts are held here periodically.

WALHALLOW (*Co. Pottinger*), a township to the W. of the Moola River and Werris Creek, on the northern railway.

WALJEERS, a county in the Western Division of the Colony. [*See* "COUNTIES."]

WALKER MOUNT (*Co. Cook*), a lofty peak of the Blue Mountain Range, lying between Hartley and Rydal.

WALLA WALLA (*Co. Hume*), a postal village, 375 miles S. of Sydney, with mail three times a week. The nearest railway station is Gerogery, 13 miles, on the southern line.

WALLABADAH (*Co. Buckland*), a postal village, 253 miles N. of Sydney, with daily mail and money-order office. The nearest railway station is Quirindi, 9 miles, on the northern line. Situated on the Quirindi Creek, in the parish of Wallabadah. The surrounding country is suitable for agricultural and pastoral pursuits.

WALLABY CREEK (*Co. Roxburgh*), a small western tributary of the Tanwarra Creek, flowing through rugged country.

WALLABY ROCKS (*Co. Roxburgh*), a number of large granite boulders on the S. bank of the Turon River, about 2 miles W. of Sofala.

WALLACE, a county in the Eastern Division of the Colony. [*See* "COUNTIES."]

WALLACE (*Co. Clarendon*), a proclaimed village within this county.

WALLACE (*Co. Cumberland*), a postal receiving-office, 42 miles W. of Sydney, with daily mail.

WALLAGOOT LAKE (*Co. Auckland*), a swampy, saline lake, lying on the coast, in the parish of Wallagoot, about 6 miles S.E. of the township of Bega.

WALLAH (*Co. Nandewar*), a township, on the banks of the Namoi River to the E. of Narrabri.

WALLAMBINE SWAMP (*Co. Northumberland*), a tract of marshy land lying on the E. bank of the Macdonald River, near its junction with the Hawkesbury, in the parish of Wallambine.

WALLAMBURRAWONG CREEK (*Co. Gowen*), a northern tributary of the Castlereagh River, rising by two heads in Mount Cowang, and flowing S.W. through the village of Wallamburrawong.

WALLAMUMBI RIVER (*Co. Clarke*). [*See* "RIVERS."]

WALLANDOON HILL (*Co. Hume*), a high hill, on the N. bank of the Billabong Creek, about 30 miles S.W. of the township of Urana.

WALLAN BILLAN (*Co. Narromine*), a postal receiving-office, 336 miles W. of Sydney, with mail twice a week.

WALLANDRY (*Co. Ashburnham*), a postal receiving-office, 384 miles S. of Sydney, with mail once a week.

WALLANGARA (*Co. Clive*), a postal village, 486 miles N. of Sydney, with daily mail. A railway station on the northern line.

WALLANGRA (*Co. Burnett*), a postal village, 446 miles N. of Sydney, with mail four times a week.

WALLANIAGO CREEK (*Co. Gough*), a small northern tributary of the Mitchell River.

WALLANTHRY (*Co. Franklin*), a township, 392 miles S. of Sydney, situated on the S. side of the Lachlan River, 5 miles S.W. of the Wabbalong range of hills, and in a purely pastoral district.

WALLAROBBA (*Co. Durham*), a postal town, 140 miles N. of Sydney, with mail three times a week. The nearest railway station is East Maitland, 24 miles, on the East Maitland and Morpeth line. A fine grazing district between the rivers Patterson and Williams.

WALLAROBBA CREEK (*Co. Durham*), a small western tributary of the Williams River, falling into it at Clarence Town and Dungog.

WALLAROY MOUNT (*Co. Dowling*), a solitary hill, lying on the vast plain between the Lachlan and the Murrumbidgee Rivers, a few miles S. of Condobolin.

WALLAWANDRA CREEK (*Co. Wellington*), a small tributary of the Waramagallon Creek, joining it in the Louisa Creek gold-field.

WALLENDBEEN (*Co. Harden*), a postal village, 241 miles S. of Sydney, with daily mail. Telegraph and money-order offices and Government savings bank. A railway station on the southern line.

WALLERAWANG (*Co. Cook*), a postal village, 105 miles W. of Sydney, with mail twice daily. Telegraph and money-order offices and Government savings bank. A railway station on the Mudgee line.

WALLI (*Co. Bathurst*), a postal village, 203 miles W. of Sydney, with mail twice a week. The nearest railway station is Mandurama, 15 miles, on the Blayney-Murrumburrah line.

WALLIS CREEK (*Co. Northumberland*), a southern tributary of the Hunter River, rising in Mount Vincent, flowing N. and separating the townships of East and West Maitland. This creek waters rich agricultural land known as South Park.

WALLIS CREEK (*Co. Bathurst*), a small northern tributary of the Princess Charlotte Vale Creek, flowing in the parish of Malmsbury.

WALLIS ISLAND (*Co. Gloucester*), a small island, lying in Wallis Lake, opposite the entrance to Wollumba River. Alluvial deposit. Also a small sandbank lying on the W. side of Fullerton Cove, and separated from the main land by a narrow channel.

WALLIS LAKE (*Co. Gloucester*), a large saltwater lake, formed by the expansion of the estuary of the Maclean and Wollomba Rivers. The lake is divided from the sea by the peninsula of which Cape Hawke forms the most prominent point.

WALLIS PLAINS (*Co. Northumberland*), a tract of flat country, lying on the S. bank of the Hunter River, on which the town of Maitland now stands.

WALLON (*Co. Courallie*), a postal village to the N. of Sydney, with mail twice a week.

WALLON CREEK (*Co. Stapylton*), a small southern tributary of the Gil Gil River.

WALLSEND (*Co. Northumberland*), a postal village, 107 miles N. of Sydney, with daily mail. Telegraph and money-order offices and Government savings bank. A railway station on the Newcastle and Wallsend line. Situated on the Ironbark Creek. The district is a coal-mining one. It was proclaimed a borough in 1874, with eight aldermen and a mayor.

WAMBACK LAGOON (*Co. Harden*), a swampy waterhole, lying in the parish of Wambat.

WAMBANGALONG CREEK (*Co. Gordon*), a small tributary of the Wylandra Creek.

WAMBANUMBA (*Co. Monteagle*), a small hamlet, lying about 10 miles from Murringo.

WAMBARUMBAH (*Co. Monteagle*), a township, to the N. of the town of Young, on the Blayney and Murrumburrah railway.

WAMBAT (*Co. Harden*), a gold-field lying on the Back, Wambat, and Demondrille Creeks, about 9 miles N.W. of Murrumboola.

WAMBAT CREEK (*Co. Harden*), a small tributary of the head of the Demondrille Creek.

WAMBERAL (*Co. Northumberland*), a postal village, 58 miles N. of Sydney, with mail three times a week. The nearest railway station is Gosford, 9 miles, on the Sydney and Newcastle line.

WAMBERAL LAKE (*Co. Northumberland*), a small lagoon, or inlet from the sea, lying in the parish of Kincumber, about 6 miles E. of Gosford.

WAMBO PONDS (*Co. Hunter*), a small creek, rising in Mount Wambo, and flowing E. into the Wollombi Brook.

WAMBOOL RIVER.—The native name of the Macquarie River [which *see*.]

WAMBROOK CREEK (*Co. Wallace*), a tributary of the Upper Murrumbidgee River, flowing from the S.W. of Coolringdon, on the Kiandra Ranges. There is a picturesque waterfall on the N. head of the creek.

WANAARING (*Co. Irrara*), a postal village, 616 miles W. of Sydney, with mail once a week. Telegraph and money-order offices, and Government savings bank. The nearest railway station is Bourke, 113 miles, on the western line.

WANDABADURY MOUNT (*Co. Wellington*), a peak, lying to the north of the Merinda gold-field, and on the S. bank of the Cudgegong River.

WANDANDIAN (*Co. St. Vincent*), a postal village, 140 miles S. of Sydney, with daily mail. The nearest railway station is Kiama, 46 miles, on the Illawarra and South Coast line. Situated on the Wandandian Creek, and in the parish of the same name. It is partly agricultural and partly pastoral.

WANDARTILLO (*Co. Livingstone*), a township on the E. bank of the Darling River, 33° 30′ S. lat.

WANDAWANDONG CREEK (*Co. Gordon*), a small tributary of the Hervey's Range Creeks.

WANDAWANDIAN CREEK (*Co. St. Vincent*), a fine mountain stream, rising to the N. of Tianjura and flowing in the St. George's Basin.

WANDELLA (*Co. Wellesley*), a postal village, 304 miles S. of Sydney, with mail twice a week. The nearest railway station is Cooma, 99 miles, on the Goulburn and Cooma line.

WANDERA (*Co. Arrawatta*), a proclaimed village in this county.

WANDSWORTH (*Co. Hardinge*), a postal village, 405 miles N. of Sydney, with mail three times a week, and money-order office. The nearest railway station is Guyra, 16 miles, on the northern line.

WANGANDERY CREEK (*Co. Camden*), a small tributary of the Wingecarribee Creek.

WANGANELLA (*Co. Townsend*), a postal village, 510 miles S. of Sydney, with daily mail. The nearest railway station is Hay, 54 miles, on the south-western line. Situated in the parish of Wanganella, on the Billabong Creek, the surrounding district being a totally pastoral one.

WANGAT (*Co. Durham*), a postal village, 174 miles S. of Sydney, with mail therefrom once a week.

WANGI CREEK (*Co. Gloucester*), a small eastern tributary of the Williams River.

WANGOOLA CREEK (*Co. Bathurst*), a northern tributary of the Lachlan River, flowing into it at Cowra.

WANIORA POINT (*Co. Camden*), a rocky promontory, lying between Bellambi and Bulli, on the coast, about 6 miles N. of Wollongong.

WANSTEAD (*Co. Cumberland*), a postal suburb, 4 miles S. of Sydney, with mail twice daily.

WANTABADGERY (*Co. Clarendon*), a township on the N. bank of the Murrumbidgee River, to the E. of Wagga Wagga.

WAPENGO (*Co. Auckland*), a postal town, 351 miles S. of Sydney, with mail once a week.

WARADGERY, a county in the Central Division of the Colony. [*See* "COUNTIES."]

WARADGERY (*Co. Waradgery*), a township, 446 miles S.W. of Sydney. A railway station on the south-western line.

WARAMAGALLON CREEK (*Co. Wellington*), an auriferous tributary of the Blackwillow Creek, draining the western part of the Louisa Creek gold-field.

WARAMBA RIVER (*Co. Gloucester*). [*See* "RIVERS."]

WARATAH (*Co. Northumberland*), a postal village, 103 miles N. of Sydney, with daily mail. Telegraph and money-order offices, Government savings bank, and delivery by letter-carrier. A railway station on the Newcastle and Wallsend line. Situated in the parish of Waratah. Coal-mining is the principal occupation of the district, some large mines being in active work in the neighbourhood. It was proclaimed a municipal district in 1871, with a council of eight aldermen and a mayor.

WARBROBROOK (*Co. Dudley*), a small southern tributary of the Macleay River.

WARBURTON (*Co. Bligh*), a township on the Cudgegong River, to the N. of Wellington.

WARDELL (*Co. Richmond*), a postal village, 353 miles N. of Sydney, with mail by Clarence and Richmond River steamers. Money-order office and Government savings bank. Situated on the N. bank of the Richmond River.

WARD'S RIVER (*Co. Gloucester*), a postal receiving-office, 170 miles N. of Sydney, with daily mail therefrom. The nearest railway-station is Hexham, 30 miles, on the northern line.

WARENG MOUNT (*Co. Northumberland*), a lofty peak of the Hunter Range of mountains, lying on the E. bank of Wareng Creek, and in the parish of Burton, attaining an altitude of 2,500 feet above sea-level.

WARGE ROCK (*Co. Pottinger*), a postal receiving-office, 326 miles W. of Sydney, with mail once a week.

WARGEILA (*Co. King*), a postal receiving-office, 203 miles S. of Sydney, with mail therefrom once a week.

WARIALDA (*Co. Burnett*), a postal village, 406 miles N. of Sydney, with daily mail. Telegraph and money-order offices, and Government savings bank. The nearest railway station is Glen Innes, 80 miles, on the northern line. Situated on the Warialda Creek, in the parish of the same name. It is partly agricultural, pastoral, and mining.

WARIALDA CREEK (*Co. Burnett*), an auriferous stream, flowing through the township of Warialda into the Gwydir River.

WARKTON (*Co. Napier*), a postal village, 285 miles W. of Sydney, with mail three times a week.

WARKWORTH (*Co. Northumberland*), a postal village, 159 miles N. of Sydney, with mail three times a week. The nearest railway station is Singleton, 10 miles, on the northern line. Situated on the Wollombi Brook, in the parish of Warkworth.

WARLAND'S CREEK (*Co. Brisbane*), a tributary of the head of the Page River, rising in the Liverpool Range and falling into the main stream at Murrurundi.

WARNE (*Co. Wellington*), a postal village, 218 miles W. of Sydney, with daily mail. A railway station on the northern line.

WARNETON (*Co. Dudley*), a postal village, 318 miles N. of Sydney, with mail three times a week and per steamer. The nearest railway station is Hexham, 180 miles, on the northern line, situated in the parish of Yarravil, and on the N. bank of the Macleay River, about 6 miles above East Kempsey.

WARNING MOUNT (*Co. Rous*), a lofty peak, lying at the head of the Tweed River. It is a well-known land-mark for coasting vessels, rising 3,353 feet about sea level, and is visible in fine weather fully 60 miles distant.

WARNOOK CREEK (*Co. Denison*), a small creek watering pastoral country, and flowing N. into Tuppal Creek.

WAROO (*Co. Gipps*), a postal village, 301 miles W. of Sydney, with mail three times a week.

WARPUSTAH (*Co. Irrara*), a township on the Warrego River, near the Queensland boundary.

WARRABUNGLE RANGE, Liverpool Plains, the western prolongation of the Liverpool Range. It consists of a series of steep and lofty peaks; the highest point is Mount Exmouth, which attains an elevation of 3,000 feet above sea-level. Numerous springs are found in this range. The prevailing rocks are trap and granite, and the surrounding soil is of excellent quality.

WARRAGAMBA RIVER (*Co. Westmoreland*). [*See* "RIVERS."]

WARRADUGGA CREEK (*Co. Wellington*), a southern tributary of the Cudgegong River, rising in Mount Yannuin, and flowing through the northern part of the Merinda Gold-field.

WARRAH CREEK (*Co. Buckland*), a southern tributary of the Borambil Creek, rising near the Cedar Brush Gap, on the road from Scone to Quirindi.

WARRAH HILL (*Co. Buckland*), a spur of the Liverpool Range, running N. from near Mount Towarri.

WARRAH RIDGE (*Co. Buckland*), a postal village, 229 miles N. of Sydney, with mail twice a week. The nearest railway station is Quirindi, 10 miles, on the northern line.

WARREGO RIVER (*Co. Irrara*). [*See* "RIVERS."]

WARRELL CREEK (*Co. Dudley*), a postal receiving-office, 351 miles N. of Sydney, with mail once a week.

WARREN (*Co. Oxley*), a postal town, 353 miles W. of Sydney, with mail five times a week. Telegraph and money-order offices and Government savings bank. The nearest railway station is Nevertire, 12 miles, on the western line. Courts of quarter sessions and district courts are held here periodically during each year.

WATERFALL (*Co. Cumberland*), a postal village, 24 miles S. of Sydney, with daily mail. A railway station on the Illawarra and South Coast line.

WATERLOO (*Co. Cumberland*), a postal suburb of Sydney, with mail twice daily. Telegraph and money order offices, Government savings bank, and delivery by letter-carriers. It was proclaimed a municipality in 1860, with a council of eight aldermen and a mayor.

WATERLOO SWAMP (*Co. Cumberland*), a tract of marshy land in the parish of Alexandria and suburban municipality of Waterloo. It lies to the S. of Sydney, the Botany tram-line running through it.

WATERVIEW BAY (*Co. Cumberland*), a small bay on the south side of Port Jackson, in the suburb of Balmain. At the head of the bay is situated Mort's Dry Dock and ship-engineering establishment.

WATSON'S BAY (*Co. Cumberland*), a postal suburb, 7 miles E. of Sydney, with mail twice daily, and delivery by letter-carrier. Situated in the parish of Alexandria. It is a sandy bight just inside the inner South Head of Port Jackson, and is a very favourite resort of the citizens of Sydney. The celebrated Gap, close where the ill-fated "Dunbar" was wrecked, August 20th, 1857, is here situated. The bay will be made memorable by the long residence of the veteran the late Hon. Sir John Robertson, K.C.M.G., at Clovelly.

WATSON TAYLOR'S LAKE (*Co. Macquarie*) is the southern part of the Camden Haven.

WATTA RIVER, one of the native names of the Darling River.

WATTAMOLLA (*Co. Camden*), a postal village, 110 miles S. of Sydney, with mail twice a week. The nearest railway station is Moss Vale, 29 miles, on the southern line.

WATTAWA CREEK (*Co. Wellington*), a small tributary of the head of the Triambil Creek.

WATTLE CREEK (*Co. Camden*), a small tributary of the Nepean River.

WATTLE CREEK (*Co. Durham*), a small western tributary of the Williams River, falling into it at its lower end.

WATTLE CREEK (*Co. Wynyard*), a small tributary of the head of the Tarcutta Creek, flowing to the north of Mane's Range.

WATTLE CREEK (*Co. King*), a southern tributary of the Grabben Gullen Creek, rising in the western slopes of the Australian Alps.

WATTLE FLAT (*Co. Roxburgh*), a postal village, 161 miles W. of Sydney, with daily mail. Money-order office and Government savings bank. The nearest railway station is Bathurst, 25 miles, on the western line. Situated on a table-land, lying 2,000 feet above the sea-level. The district is a mining one, alluvial and quartz. The Turon River runs about 7 miles N., and Sofala, 7 miles.

WATTLE PONDS (*Co. Durham*), a small northern tributary of the Hunter River.

WAUCHOPE (*Co. Macquarie*), a postal village, 288 miles north of Sydney, with mail three times a week.

WAURDONG CREEK (*Co. Wellington*), a northern auriferous tributary of the Pyramul Creek, rising in the Louisa Creek.

WAVERLEY (*Co. Cumberland*), a postal branch office of Sydney, 4 miles east, with mail three times daily. Telegraph and money-order offices, Government savings bank, and delivery by letter-carriers. The tram-line passes through it to and from Sydney. Situated on the South Head Road, in the parish of Alexandria, and police district of Sydney. It was proclaimed a municipality in 1859, with a council of eleven aldermen and a mayor.

WAYO MOUNT (*Co. Argyle*), a high detached mountain, lying in the parish of Wayo, about 10 miles N.W. of Goulburn.

WEAH-WAA CREEK (*Co. Courallie*), a fine stream flowing from the Nandewar Range into the Gwydir River, about 12 miles W. of Moree, and passing through the village of Tyemah.

WEANDRE CREEK (*Co. Wellington*), an eastern auriferous tributary of the Stony Creek.

WEATHERBOARD (*Co. Cook*), a village, 59 miles W. of Sydney, situated on the Weatherboard Creek. The Nepean River lies to the E. and Cox and Lett Rivers to the W. The surrounding country is elevated more than 3,000 feet above sea-level. The great Darwin, in his "Naturalist's Voyage" speaks as follows of this part of the country :—

About a mile and a half from the little inn called the "Weatherboard," an immense gulf unexpectedly opens through the trees, which borders the pathway at the depth of perhaps 1,500 feet. Walking on a few yards one stands at the brink of a vast precipice, and below one sees a grand bay or gulf—for I know not what other name to give to it—thickly covered with forest. The point of view is situate as if at the head of a bay, the line of cliff diverging on each side, and showing headland behind headland, as on a low sea-coast. These cliffs are composed of horizontal strata of whitish sandstone, and are so absolutely vertical that in many places a person standing on the edge and throwing down a stone can see it strike the trees in the abyss below. So unbroken is the line of cliff that, in order to reach the foot of the waterfall formed by the little stream, it is said to be necessary to go sixteen miles round. About five miles distant in front another line of cliff extends, which then appears completely to encircle the valley; hence the name of bay is justified as applied to this grand amphitheatrical depression. If we imagine a winding harbour, with its deep waters surrounded by bold cliff-like shores, to be laid dry and a forest to spring up upon its sandy bottom, we should then have the appearance and structure here exhibited.

WEBBER'S CREEK (*Co. Durham*), a small tributary of the head of Glendon Brook.

WEBIMBLE AND MYRABLUEN (*Co. Brisbane*), two peaks of a forked mountain, lying on the W. bank of Wybong Creek, and to the N.E. of the township of Merriwa.

WEDDIN MOUNTAINS (*Co. Monteagle*), a range of hills lying between the Lachlan and Murrumbidgee Rivers, in a flat rugged country.

WEDDIN (*Co. Monteagle*), a postal village, 286 miles S. of Sydney, with daily mail. The nearest railway station is Young, 12 miles, on the Blayney-Murrumburrah line.

WEDDIN MOUNT (*Co. Monteagle*), a lofty peak in the ranges near the junction of the Tragong and Burrangong Creeks, to the N.W. of Young.

WEE WAA (*Co. Jamison*), a postal town, 376 miles N. of Sydney, with mail three times a week. Telegraph and money-order offices, and Government savings bank. The nearest railway station is Narrabri, 25 miles, on the north-western line. Situated on a lagoon of the same name, about a mile distant from the Namoi River, and in the parish of Wee Waa. The district is purely a pastoral one.

WEEHO CREEK (*Co. King*), a fine stream rising in the western slopes of the Australian Alps, and flowing N.W. through good country into the Crookwell River. It runs through the township of Weeho.

WEEJASPER (*Co. Buccleuch*), a postal village, 219 miles S. of Sydney, with mail once a week.

WEEJASPER CREEK (*Co. Buccleuch*), a small creek receiving the drainage of the N. side of Weejasper Hill, and falling into the Goodradigbee River.

WEEJASPER HILL (*Co. Buccleuch*), a high peak lying on the W. bank of the Goodradigbee River, between Weejasper and Micalong Creeks.

WEEKES (*Co. Raleigh*), a township, 363 miles N. of Sydney, on the Bellinger River.

WEETALABA (*Co. Napier*), a small pastoral village, on the road from Coonabarabran to Coola and Cassilis. It lies at the confluence of the Weetalaba and Oaky Creeks.

WEETALABA CREEK (*Co. Napier*), a drainage creek, rising in the Booyamurra Plains and flowing into the Castlereagh River at its upper end.

WEIR CREEK (*Co. Benarba*), a small western tributary of the Lower Macintyre River, falling into it near Burrondoon.

WEIMBY (*Co. Caira*), a proclaimed township, at the junction of the Lachlan and Murray Rivers.

WELAREGANG (*Co. Selwyn*), a township, 385 miles S. of Sydney. Situated on the head of the Murray River, in the parish of Welaregang.

WELCOME PONDS (*Co. Jamison*), a chain of ponds flowing into the Namoi River, near Narrabri.

WELCOME REEF (*Co. St. Vincent*), a postal town, 147 miles S. of Sydney, with mail therefrom twice a week.

WELLAR (*Co. Phillip*), a township, on the Goulburn River.

WELLESLEY, a county in the Eastern Division of the Colony. [*See* "COUNTIES."]

WELLESLEY (*Co. Wellesley*), a proclaimed village in this county.

WELLINGROVE (*Co. Gough*), a postal town, 439 miles N. of Sydney, with mail four times a week. The nearest railway station is Glen Innes, 16 miles, on the northern line. Situated on the Wellingrove Creek, in the parish of the same name, and is a pastoral district.

WELLINGROVE CREEK (*Co. Gough*), a southern tributary of the river Severn, rising on a detached hill, called Fletcher's Nob, about 10 miles W. of Glen Innes.

WELLINGTON, a county in the Eastern Division of the Colony. [*See* "COUNTIES."]

WELLINGTON (*Co. Wellington*), a postal town, 248 miles W. of Sydney, with daily mail. Telegraph and money-order offices, Government savings bank, and delivery by letter-carriers. A railway station on the western line. Situated on the Macquarie River, the township of Montefiores being on the opposite side. The district is agricultural, mining, and pastoral, and all kinds of fruit grow in perfection. It was proclaimed a municipal district in 1879, with a council of eight aldermen and a mayor. Population, about 1,500. Courts of quarter sessions and district courts are held here periodically.

WELLINGTON VALLEY (*Co. Wellington*), a valley discovered by Oxley. It is situated at the junction of the Bell and Macquarie Rivers.

WELL'S CREEK (*Co. St. Vincent*), an auriferous stream on the Araluen diggings.

WELUMLA CREEK (*Co. Selwyn*), a small tributary of the Tooma River, rising near Mount Dargal.

WEMEN (*Co. Taila*), a township on the banks of the Murray River, below Euston.

WENTWORTH, a county in the Western Division of the Colony. [*See* "COUNTIES."]

WENTWORTH (*Co. Wentworth*), a postal town, 720 miles S. of Sydney, with mail three times a week. Telegraph and money-order offices, Government savings bank, and delivery by letter-carriers. The nearest railway station is Hay, 260 miles, on the south-western line. Situated on the river Darling, at the junction of that river with the Murray, in the parish of Wentworth. It is an exclusively pastoral district. It was proclaimed a municipal district in 1879, with a council of two aldermen and a mayor. Population, about 800. Courts of quarter sessions and district courts are held here periodically.

WENTWORTH FALLS (*Co. Cook*), a postal village, 62 miles W. of Sydney, with mail therefrom twice daily. A railway station on the western line.

WENTWORTHVILLE (*Co. Cumberland*), a railway station, 16 miles W. of Sydney, on the western line.

WEROMBIE (*Co. Camden*), a postal village, 48 miles S. of Sydney, with mail therefrom three times a week. The nearest railway station is Camden, 11 miles, on the southern line.

WERONERA MOUNT (*Co. Wellington*), a solitary hill, lying on the north bank of the Grattai Creek.

WERONG CREEK (*Co. Northumberland*), a small western tributary of the Wollombi Creek.

WERRIBERRI CREEK *(Co. Westmoreland)*, a small southern tributary of the Warragamba River, flowing from the N. of Picton, past the western slope of Brownlow Hill.

WERRIS CREEK *(Co. Buckland)*, a chain of lagoons flowing from the E. into the Corradilly River, S. of Morbi township.

WERRIS CREEK *(Co. Buckland)*, a postal village, 254 miles N. of Sydney, with daily mail. Telegraph and money-order offices. A railway station on the north-western line.

WERTERANNA *(Co. Thoulcanna)*, a township on the Paroo River, near the Queensland boundary.

WERUNDA, a county in the Western Division of the Colony. [*See* "COUNTIES."]

WERUNDA *(Co. Killara)*, a township on the N.W. bank of the Darling River.

WERUNG MOUNT *(Co. Georgiana)*, a lofty peak in the dividing range, at the head of the Werung branch of the Abercrombie River.

WESTBROOK *(Co. Durham)*, a postal village, 156 miles N. of Sydney, with mail twice a week. The nearest railway station is Singleton, 8 miles, on the northern line.

WESTBROOK *(Co. Durham)*, a fine stream rising to the N. of Camberwell and flowing into Glendonbrook, near its junction with the Hunter River.

WEST CAMBEWARRA *(Co. Camden)*, a postal village, 118 miles S. of Sydney, with mail twice a week.

WEST CREEK *(Co. Clive)*, a small western tributary of the Timbarra Rivulet, through pastoral country.

WEST DENISON *(Co. Cowley)*, lies on the Eucumbene River, the Murray River being 9 miles E., forming part of the Kiandra gold-field. The township of Kiandra lies 9 miles E.

WEST KEMPSEY *(Co. Dudley)*, a postal town, 312 miles N. of Sydney, with daily mail, and per steamer direct. Telegraph and money-order offices, and Government savings bank. The nearest railway station is Hexham, 185 miles, on the northern line.

WESTMEAD *(Co. Cumberland)*, a railway station, 15 miles W. of Sydney, on the western line.

WEST MITCHELL *(Co. Cook)*, a postal town, 125 miles W. of Sydney, with mail three times a week.

WEST TAMWORTH *(Co. Parry)*, a postal town, 280 miles N. of Sydney, with daily mail. Telegraph and money-order offices and Government savings bank. A railway station on the northern line.

WEST TEMORA *(Co. Bland)*, a postal receiving-office, 302 miles S. of Sydney, with mail twice a week.

WEST WALLSEND *(Co. Northumberland)*, a postal village, 92 miles N. of Sydney, with daily mail.

WESTMORELAND, a county in the Eastern Division of the Colony. [*See* "COUNTIES."]

WET LAGOON (*Co. Argyle*), a small lagoon, lying to the S. of the Third Bredalbane Plain, in the parish of Milbang.

WHALAN (*Co. Stapylton*), a township on the banks of the Whalen River, near the Queensland boundary.

WHALAN RIVER (*Co. Stapylton*).  [*See* "RIVERS."]

WHAMBEYAN CAVES (*Co. Georgiana*), lying on the Bannaby Creek, about 125 miles from Laggan. The entrance to these caves is about 200 feet high, and resembles a gothic window in form. The walls are of marble, interspersed with mica, and abounding in stalactites.

WHEALBAH (*Co. Franklin*), a postal village, 455 miles W. of Sydney, with mail three times a week. The nearest railway station is Hay, 85 miles, on the south-western line.

WHEENEY CREEK (*Co. Cook*), situated in the parish of Kurrajong, and police district of Windsor. The Hawkesbury River is distant about 5 miles, and the township of Richmond 7 miles to the E., and is the termination of the Windsor and Richmond railway.

WHEEO (*Co. King*), a postal village, 160 miles S. of Sydney, with mail three times a week. The nearest railway station is Goulburn, 26 miles, on the southern line, situated on the Wheeo Creek, in the parish of the same name.

WHERRAL FLAT (*Co. Gloucester*), a postal village, 243 miles N. of Sydney, with mail twice a week. The nearest railway station is Hexham, 133 miles, on the northern line.

WHINSTONE VALLEY (*Co. Beresford*), a postal town, 306 miles S. of Sydney, with mail twice a week. The nearest railway station is Cooma, 40 miles, on the Goulburn and Cooma line.

WHITE, a county in the Central Division of the Colony. [*See* "COUNTIES."]

WHITE BAY (*Co. Cumberland*), a small bay, lying on the W. side of Johnstone's Bay, and between Glebe Island and the suburbs of Balmain.

WHITE COW HILL (*Co. Sandon*), a detached hill in the parish of Dangarsleigh, on the S. bank of Saumarez Creek, 5 miles S.W. of Armidale.

WHITE ROCK (*Co. Roxburgh*), a postal village, 149 miles W. of Sydney, with daily mail. The nearest railway station is Bathurst, 6 miles, on the western line.

WHITE SWAMP (*Co. Drake*), a postal receiving-office, 595 miles W. of Sydney, with mail once a week.

WHITE'S CREEK (*Co. Cumberland*), a small stream rising in the suburb of Sydenham, and flowing into the western head of Rozella Bay.

WHITE'S CREEK (*Co. Camden*), a small tributary of the Midway Rivulet, flowing in Sutton Forest.

WHITEHORSE POINT (*Co. Cumberland*), a bold promontory on the E. side of Parramatta River and the W. side of Balmain, opposite Cockatoo Island.

WHITEMAN CREEK (*Co. Clarence*), a postal village, 580 miles N. of Sydney, with mail twice a week per Grafton steamer.

WHITEMAN'S CREEK (*Co. Clarence*), a fine stream rising in Mount Lardner, flowing through the village of Coalbale into the Clarence River at Moleville.

WHITING BEACH (*Co. Cumberland*), a sandy beach on the N. shore of Port Jackson, to the W. of Bradley's Head, and opposite Rushcutters' Bay.

WHITTON (*Co. Cooper*), a postal village, 375 miles S.W. of Sydney, with mail five times a week. Telegraph and money-order offices, and Government savings bank. A railway station on the south-western line,

WIADERE (*Co. Phillip*), a small village situated on the Cudgegong Creek, and police district of Mudgee, about 12 miles distant. The district is an agricultural one, and very fertile.

WIAGDON CREEK (*Co. Roxburgh*), an auriferous stream flowing from the Mount Wiagdon into the Cheshire Creek.

WIAGDON MOUNT (*Co. Roxburgh*), a lofty peak of the Limekiln spur of the Blue Mountains, near the village of Wiagdon, and on the Wattle Flat gold-field.

WIALDRA CREEK (*Cos. Phillip and Bligh*), a northern tributary of the Cudgegong Creek, rising in the western slope of the Australian Alps, and flowing into the main stream near Guntawang.

WIAMBENE CREEK (*Co. St. Vincent*), a small tributary of the head of the Shoalhaven River. This creek abounds in fossils of the Silurian general

WIANNAMATTA CREEK (*Co. Cumberland*), the original name of South Creek [which *see*].

WICKETYWEES (*Co. Hunter*), an agricultural settlement, lying about 12 miles from Singleton.

WICKHAM (*Co. Brisbane*), an agricultural settlement, situated on the Gungal, or Hall's Creek, about 15 miles from Merriwa. It was proclaimed a municipal district in 1871, with a council of eight aldermen and a mayor.

WICKHAM (*Co. Northumberland*), a postal town, 104 miles N. of Sydney, with daily mail. Telegraph and money-order offices, Government savings bank, and delivery by letter-carrier. The nearest railway station is Honeysuckle Point, on the Newcastle and Wallsend line.

WIDDEN (*Co. Phillip*), a postal receiving-office, 232 miles north of Sydney, with mail twice a week.

WIDDINBROOK (*Cos. Phillip and Hunter*), a southern tributary of the Goulburn River, rising in the Blue Mountains, and joining the main stream above Denman.

WILANWITAL CREEK (*Co. Durham*), a small creek following into the western part of Port Stephens.

WILBERFORCE (*Co. Cook*), a postal town, 38 miles W. of Sydney, with daily mail. The nearest railway station is Windsor, 4 miles, on the Richmond line. Situated on the Hawkesbury River, in the parish of Wilberforce.

WILBERTREE (*Co. Phillip*), a village, 158 miles W. of Sydney, situated on the Pipeclay Creek, the Mudgee River running 3 miles W., and in the police district of Mudgee. Wilbertree is an agricultural, pastoral, and mining district. Mudgee is 5 miles E.

WILCANNIA (*Co. Young*), a postal town, 708 miles S. of Sydney, with mail four times a week. Telegraph and money-order offices, Government savings bank, and delivery by letter-carrier. The nearest railway station is Hay, 260 miles, on the south-western line. It was proclaimed a municipal district in 1883, with a council of eight aldermen and a mayor. Population, about 1,800. Courts of quarter sessions and district courts are held here periodically.

WILD CATTLE CREEK (*Co. Fitzroy*), a small eastern tributary of the Don Dorrigo River.

WILD'S MEADOWS (*Co. Cook*), a postal village, 98 miles S. of Sydney, with daily mail. The nearest railway station is Moss Vale, 10 miles, on the southern line.

WILE'S GULLY (*Co. Buckland*), a deep chasm on the road from Wallabadah to Tamworth, about 4 miles N. of the former place.

WILGA VALE (*Co. Narromine*), a postal receiving office, 311 miles W. of Sydney, with mail once a week.

WILLANDRA BILLABONG CREEK (*Co. Franklin and Blaxland*), a fine and important tributary of the Lachlan River, but liable to great droughts and sudden inundations.

WILLANTHRY (*Co. Waradgery*), a postal village, 405 miles W. of Sydney, with mail three times a week. Money-order office and Government savings bank. The nearest railway station is Hay, 113 miles, on the south-western line.

WILLAWILLINGBAH (*Co. Narran*), a township, 456 miles W. of Sydney. The nearest railway station is Byrock, 200 miles, on the western line.

WILLERO CREEK (*Co. Argyle*), a small creek, rising in the parish of Currawang, and flowing into Lake George, near the village of Kenny's Point.

WILLEROON (*Co. Canbelego*), a township, 397 miles W. of Sydney. The nearest railway station is Nyngan, 50 miles, on the western line.

WILLIAM TOWN (*Co. Northumberland*), a postal village, 92 miles N. of Sydney, with mail three times a week. The nearest railway station is Hexham, on the northern line.

WILLIAMS RIVER (*Cos. Durham and Gloucester*). [See "RIVERS."].

WILLIAMS CROSSING (*Co. Monteagle*), a postal receiving-office, 297 miles S. of Sydney, with mail twice a week.

WILLIAMSDALE (*Co. Murray*), a postal receiving-office, 205 miles S. of Sydney, with mail twice a week.

WILLIWAH CREEK (*Co. Roxburgh*), a southern auriferous tributary of the head of the Turon River, rising in the Badger Brush, flowing through the Cullen Bullen diggings.

WILLOUGHBY (*Co. Cumberland*), a suburb of North Sydney, about 9 miles N. of the city of Sydney. It was incorporated a municipality in 1865, with a council of eight aldermen and a mayor.

WILLOUGHBY CREEK (*Co. Cumberland*), a small stream, rising in the high ground of St. Leonards, and flowing into the south head of Long Bay, in Middle Harbour, over a waterfall, which is considerable in a rainy season. It is known as Willoughby Falls.

WILLOUGHBY POINT (*Co. Northumberland*), a rocky headland, lying between Broken Bay and the entrance to Tuggarah Beach Lake.

WILLOW-TREE (*Co. Buckland*), a postal village, 232 miles N. of Sydney, with mail twice daily. A railway station on the northern line.

WILLY WALLY (*Co. Brisbane*), a postal receiving-office, 249 miles N. of Sydney, with mail four times a week.

WILLYAMA (*Co. Yancowinna*), a proclaimed township in this county.

WILPENDALE MOUNT (*Co. Phillip*), a high peak in a spur of the Blue Mountain Range, lying on the bank of the Wilpinjong Creek, and on the E. side of the road from Mudgee to Cassilis.

WILPINJONG CREEK (*Co. Phillip*), a western tributary of Wallar Creek.

WILSON (*Co. Urana*), a postal village, 427 miles S. of Sydney, with mail three times a week.

WILSON (*Co. Raleigh*), a proclaimed township, to the S. of Nambucca.

WILSON'S CREEK (*Co. Rous*), a small tributary of the N. arm of the Richmond River.

WILSON'S CREEK (*Co. Vernon*), a small southern tributary of the Apsley River.

WILSON'S DOWNFALL (*Co. Clive*), a postal village, 506 miles N. of Sydney, with mail twice a week, and money-order office. The nearest railway station is Tenterfield, 26 miles, on the northern line.

WILSON'S PEAK (*Co. Buller*), a lofty peak in the Macpherson Range, lying at the head of the Cooreele Creek and the Condamine River.

WILSON'S RIVER (*Co. Macquarie*). [*See* "RIVERS."]

WILTON (*Co. Camden*), a postal town, 53 miles S. of Sydney, with daily mail, and money-order office. A railway station on the southern line.

WILWORREL MOUNT (*Co. Phillip*), a peak of the Blue Mountain Range, near the N. head of the Cudgegong River.

WIMBLEDON (*Co. Bathurst*), a postal town, 158 miles W. of Sydney, with daily mail. A railway station on the western line.

WINBINYAH (*Co. Fitzgerald*), a township, to the W. of the Paroo River.

WINBURNDALE (*Co. Roxburgh*), a township, 145 miles W. of Sydney. The nearest railway station is Bathurst, 7 miles, on the western line.

WINBURNDALE RIVULET (*Co. Roxburgh*). [*See* "RIVERS."]

WINDANG ISLAND (*Co. Camden*), a small islet, lying at the mouth of the Illawarra Lake.

WINDELLA MOUNT (*Co. King*), a lofty mountain, lying on the S. of the Crookwell River, and at the head of the Burrawinda Creek.

WINDELLAMA (*Co. Argyle*), a postal village, 138 miles S. of Sydney, with mail twice a week. The nearest railway station is Marulan, 18 miles, on the southern line. Situated in the parish of Christchurch.

WINDELLEWA CREEK (*Co. Argyle*), a south-western tributary of the head of the Nerrimungo Creek, flowing through the Goulburn Plains.

WINDER'S HILL (*Co. Northumberland*), a peaked hill, overhanging the Hunter River, about 2 miles N.E. of Lochinvar.

WINDERMERE (*Co. Northumberland*), an agricultural village, lying within half-a-mile of Lochinvar.

WINDEYER, a county in the Western Division of the Colony. [*See* "COUNTIES."]

WINDEYER (*Co. Wellington*), a postal town, 179 miles W. of Sydney, with mail four times a week, and money-order office. The nearest railway station is Mudgee, 25 miles, on the Wallerawang and Mudgee line. Situated on the Meroo River, and police district of Mudgee, and is the centre of an important mining district.

WINDSOR (*Co. Cumberland*), a postal town, 34 miles W. of Sydney, with mail twice daily. Telegraph and money order offices, Government savings bank, and delivery by letter-carriers. A railway station on the Windsor and Richmond line. Situated on the Hawkesbury River, in the parish of St. Matthew. A rich and extensive agricultural district, producing in abundance all kinds of cereals and farm produce. It was proclaimed a borough in 1871, with a council of eight aldermen and a mayor. Population, about 1,000. Courts of quarter sessions and district courts are held here periodically.

WINDUELLA (*Co. King*), a postal town, 164 miles S. of Sydney, with mail three times a week.

WINGECARRIBBEE (*Co. Camden*), situated on the Wingecarribbee Creek, and police district of Berrima. Lying between Berrima on the W. and the Illawarra coast range on the E., and on elevated country, attaining an altitude of 2,500 feet above sea-level; the soil is highly productive for all kinds of farming produce.

WINGECARRIBBEE CREEK (*Co. Camden*), a small stream, rising in the Wingecarribbee Swamp, and flowing into the Wollondilly River

2 F

WINGECARRIBBEE SWAMP (*Co. Camden*), a large tract of marshy land near the townships of Bong-Bong and Kangaloon. The land is exceedingly rich from the mixture of decomposed vegetable matter with the soil, and roots and tubers grow abundantly.

WINGELLO (*Co. Camden*), a postal village, 105 miles S. of Sydney, with daily mail. A railway station on the southern line. Situated near the Uringelly Creek, and in the police district of Berrima. It lies 5 miles S. of the township of Murrumbah, and 6 miles N. of Marulan.

WINGEN (*Co. Brisbane*), a postal village, 204 miles N. of Sydney, with mail twice daily, and telegraph office. A railway station on the northern line. Situated at the junction of the Petwyn and Kingdon Ponds Creek, in the parish of Wingen.

WINGEN, MOUNT (*Co. Brisbane*), known as the Burning Mountain, is on a range about 12 miles from Scone. There is a constant emission of smoke and vapour from the underground fire, produced by the burning coal-seams beneath the surface, and at a considerable depth below. Nothing definite is known as to the position of the seam or seams of coal thus ignited. There are abundant impressions on the shales of the ferns and flora peculiar to the carboniferous deposits to be found.

WINGHAM (*Co. Macquarie*), a postal town, 232 miles N. of Sydney, with daily mail, and per steamer. Telegraph and money-order offices, Government savings bank, and delivery by letter-carrier. The nearest railway station is Hexham, 112 miles, on the northern line. Situated on the banks of the Manning River, in the parish of Wingham. Tinonee is about 6 miles distant, and Taree 8 miles. It was proclaimed a municipal district in 1889, with a council of five aldermen and a mayor.

WINIFRED CREEK (*Co. Beresford*), a small southern tributary of the Umaralla River, crossing the road from Panbula to Nimmitibel, about 3 miles E. of the latter place.

WINIFRED PEAK (*Co. Beresford*), a high peak in the Monaro Range, N.E. of Nimmitibel. It attains an altitude of 3,700 feet above sea-level.

WINTERBOURNE (*Co. Vernon*), a township, to the S. of the Macleay River.

WISEMAN'S CREEK (*Co. Westmoreland*), a postal village, 146 miles W. of Sydney, with mail twice a week.

WISEMAN'S FERRY (*Co. Northumberland*), a postal village, 59 miles W. of Sydney, with mail four times a week. Telegraph and money-order offices, and Government savings bank. The nearest railway station is Windsor, 26 miles, on the Richmond line. Situated on the Hawkesbury River, in the parish of Nelson.

WITTINGHAM (*Co. Northumberland*), a postal village, 144 miles N. of Sydney, with daily mail. A railway station on the northern line.

WIVEOR (*Co. Sturt*), a township, to the N. of the south-western railway, and the Murrumbidgee River.

WODONGA (*Colony of Victoria*), on the S. side of the Murray River, opposite Albury, 389 miles S. of Sydney.

WOHIMIN MOUNT (*Co. Clarence*), a lofty detached hill, lying on the E. side of the road from Yamba to Grafton. This is the peaked hill of Captain Cook.

WOLGAN RIVER (*Co. Cook*). [*See* "RIVERS."]

WOLLANGAMBE CREEK (*Co. Cook*), a southern tributary of the Colo River.

WOLLAR (*Co. Phillip*), a postal village, 254 miles W. of Sydney, with mail twice a week, and money-order office. The nearest railway station is Mudgee, 31 miles, on the Wallerawang and Mudgee line.

WOLLEMI CREEK (*Co. Hunter*), a northern tributary of the Colo River.

WOLLOMBA (*Co. Gloucester*), a proclaimed village, to the W. of Forster.

WOLLOMBA RIVER (*Co. Gloucester*). [*See* "RIVERS."]

WOLLOMBI (*Co. Northumberland*), a postal town, 156 miles N. of Sydney, with mail three times a week. Telegraph and money-order offices, and Government savings bank. The nearest railway station is East Maitland, 34 miles, on the East Maitland and Morpeth line. Situated on the Wollombi Creek, in the parish of Wollombi.

WOLLOMBI BROOK (*Cos. Northumberland and Hunter*), a fine stream rising near Mount Simpson, and flowing past the township of Wollombi into the Hunter at Singleton.

WOLLOMBI ROAD (*Co. Northumberland*), a village near Farley, 22 miles from Newcastle, the nearest railway station on the northern line.

WOLLOMOMBI (*Co. Sandon*), a postal town, 394 miles N. of Sydney, with mail three times a week. The nearest railway station is Armidale, 24 miles, on the northern line.

WOLLONABY CREEK (*Co. Wallace*), a small southern tributary of the head of the Snowy River, flowing into it at the crossing of the road from Cooma to Gippsland.

WOLLONDILLY CREEK (*Co. Bland*), a small western tributary of the Narraburra Creek.

WOLLONDILLY RIVER (*Cos. Argyle, Camden, and Westmoreland*). [*See* "RIVERS."]

WOLLONGBAR (*Co. Clarence*), a postal town, 366 miles N. of Sydney, with mail per Clarence River steamer.

WOLLONGONG (*Co. Camden*), a postal town, 48 miles S. of Sydney, with mail three times daily. Telegraph and money-order offices, Government savings bank, and delivery by letter-carrier. A seaport town, situated on the Macquarie Rivulet, and on the head of the harbour, in the parish of Wollongong. It is justly celebrated for the beauty of its scenery and the salubrity of its climate. It was proclaimed a municipality in 1859, with a council of eight aldermen and a mayor. Population, about 2,000. Courts of quarter sessions and district courts are held here periodically.

WOLLONGOUGH (*Co. Gipps*), a township, 365 miles S. of Sydney. The nearest railway station is Young, 122 miles, on the Murrumburrah and Blayney line.

WOLOGORONG LAKE (*Co. Argyle*), a swampy lake, lying to the S. of the second Bredalbane Plain.

WOLOMBON (*Co. Narromine*), a township, on the S. bank of the Bogan River.

WOLUMLA (*Co. Auckland*), a postal village, 326 miles S. of Sydney, with mail four times a week. Telegraph and money-order offices, and Government savings bank. The nearest railway station is Cooma, 84 miles, on the Goulburn and Cooma line. Situated on the Wolumla Creek, in the parish of the same name.

WOLUMLA CREEK (*Co. Auckland*), a southern tributary of the Bega River, rising in the northern slope of the Wolumla Peak.

WOLUMLA PEAK (*Co. Auckland*), the highest elevation in the centre of the county, attaining an elevation of 2,220 feet above the sea-level, at the head of the Panbula River.

WOMBALLAWAY MOUNT (*Co. St. Vincent*), a lofty peak of the Buddawang Range, lying on the banks of the Clyde River.

WOMBAT (*Co. Monteagle*), a postal village, 241 miles S. of Sydney, with daily mail, and money-order office. The nearest railway station is Murrumburrah, 9 miles, on the Murrumburrah and Blayney line.

WOMBAT BRUSH (*Co. Camden*), a tract of fertile land, lying on the road from Berrima to Tarlo, in an elevated position of 2,128 feet above sea-level.

WOMBOO (*Co. Cadell*), a postal receiving-office, 561 miles S. of Sydney, with mail twice a week. The nearest railway station is Hay, 130 miles, on the south-western line.

WOMBOOTA (*Co. Cadell*), a postal receiving-office, 607 miles S. of Sydney, with mail twice a week. The nearest railway station is Hay, 130 miles, on the south-western line.

WOMBRAMARCA CREEK (*Co. Parry*), an auriferous tributary of the head of the Peel River, rising in the Australian Alps, near Crawney Pass.

WOMPAH (*Co. Tongowoko*), a township on the Queensland border.

WONDALGA (*Co. Wynyard*), a proclaimed township, on the creek of the same name.

WONDALGA CREEK (*Co. Wynyard*), a small tributary of the Adelong Creek, on the Adelong gold-fields.

WONDOWONDA MOUNT (*Co. Hunter*), a peak of the Hunter Range, lying near the Tupa Creek.

WONDOWYEE CREEK (*Co. Wynyard*), an auriferous creek, rising in the county between Adelong and Tumut, flowing into the Gilmore Creek.

WONIORA (*Co. Cumberland*), a township, 7 miles S. of Sydney. The nearest railway station is Kogarah, 4 miles, on the Illawarra and South Coast line.

WOOD HALL (*Co. Macquarie*), a postal receiving-office, 316 miles N. of Sydney, with mail three times a week.

WOOD'S FLAT CREEK (*Co. Bathurst*), a tributary of the Wangoola Creek, falling into it between Cowra and Carcoar.

WOOD'S MOUNT (*Co. Wellington*), a lofty peak, lying in the W. bank of the Macquarie River, between the Stony Creek and the Tambaroora gold-fields.

WOOD'S REEF (*Co. Darling*), a postal receiving-office, 438 miles N. of Sydney, with mail once a week. Situated on the Nangahra Creek.

WOODBURN (*Co. Richmond*), a postal village, 337 miles N. of Sydney, with mail per Clarence and Richmond Rivers steamers. Telegraph and money-order offices, and Government savings bank.

WOODBURN (*Co. St. Vincent*), an agricultural settlement, lying about 9 miles W. of Ulladulla, in the midst of fine land.

WOODFORD (*Co. Cook*), a railway station, 54 miles W. of Sydney, on the western line.

WOODFORD BAY (*Co. Cumberland*), a small bay, on the N. bank of the Lane Cove River, near its fall into the Parramatta River.

WOODFORD LEIGH (*Co. Clarence*), a postal village, N. of Sydney, with mail per Clarence River steamers.

WOODHILL (*Co. Camden*), a postal village, 128 miles S. of Sydney, with mail three times a week. The nearest railway station is Kiama, 26 miles, on the Illawarra and South Coast line.

WOODHOUSELEE (*Co. Argyle*), a postal village, 144 miles S. of Sydney, with mail three times a week. The nearest railway station is Goulburn, 14 miles, on the southern line. Situated on the Pejar Creek, in the parish of the same name.

WOODLANDS (*Co. Brisbane*), a postal village, 209 miles N. of Sydney, with mail twice a week. The nearest railway station is Scone, 18 miles, on the northern line.

WOODSIDE (*Co. Gloucester*), a postal village, 248 miles N. of Sydney, with mail three times a week. The nearest railway station is Hexham, 137 miles, on the northern line.

WOODSTOCK (*Co. Bathurst*), a postal village, 206 miles W. of Sydney, with daily mail and telegraph office. A railway station on the Murrumburrah and Blayney line.

WOODVILLE (*Co. Durham*), a postal village, 121 miles N. of Sydney, with daily mail. The nearest railway station is East Maitland, 5 miles, on the northern line. Situated on the Paterson River, the Hunter River being about 3 miles to the E.

WOOGOOLA (*Co. Fitzroy*), a proclaimed village in this county.

WOOLA CREEK (*Co. St. Vincent*), a small eastern tributary of the Drua, or upper part of the Moruya River.

WOOLACHLAN CREEK (*Co. Wellington*), an auriferous southern tributary of the Meroo Creek, rising in the Upper Waurdong Range, and flowing through the Louisa Creek gold-field.

WOOLAMBA (*Co. Gloucester*), a township to the E. of Forster, 227 miles N. of Sydney.

WOOLGOOLGA (*Co. Clarence*), a pastoral village, 391 miles N. of Sydney, with mail per Clarence River steamers.

WOOLLI (*Co. Richmond*), a village on the Clarence River, about 12 miles S.W. of the Clarence River Heads.

WOOLLI CREEK (*Co. Cumberland*), a small watercourse, falling into the estuary of Cook's River, on the S. side of Unwin's Bridge.

WOOLI WOOLI RIVER (*Co. Clarence*). [*See* "RIVERS."]

WOOLONORA (*Co. Cumberland*), a village, lying about 5 miles S. of Kogarah.

WOOLOOLA MOUNT (*Co. Buckland*), a spur of the Peel Ranges, lying to the N.E. of the township of Carroll.

WOOLOOMIN (*Co. Parry*), a postal village, 271 miles N. of Sydney, with mail three times a week. The nearest railway station is Tamworth, on the northern line.

WOOLSHED CREEK (*Co. Macquarie*), a small northern tributary of the Manning River, falling into it near Mount Khanghat.

WOOLLAHRA (*Co. Cumberland*), a postal suburb of Sydney, with mail twice daily. Telegraph and money-order offices, Government savings bank, and delivery by letter-carrier. It lies between the Old and New South Head Roads, on the eastern side of the city, and forms part of the Point Piper Estate. It was proclaimed a municipality in 1860, with a council of eleven aldermen and a mayor.

WOOLLOOMOOLOO (*Co. Cumberland*), an eastern suburb of Sydney, lying within the city boundary. [*See* "SYDNEY."]

WOOLLOOMOOLOO BAY (*Co. Cumberland*), forms a part of the eastern portion of the city of Sydney. The wharf at the head of the bay affords accommodation for a large fleet of vessels, and the district is very populous.

WOOMARGAMA (*Co. Goulburn*), a postal village, 404 miles S. of Sydney, with daily mail. The nearest railway station is Albury, 21 miles, on the southern line. It lies in the parish and on the creek of the same name.

WOOMARGAMA CREEK (*Co. Goulburn*), a tributary of the Billabung Creek, rising in Mount Jergyle, and passes through the township of that name, and is fed by the Native Dog and Boundary Creeks.

WOOMARGAMA MOUNTAIN (*Co. Goulburn*), a range of high schistose hills, lying to the S. and E. of the village of Woomargama.

WOOMBAH (*Co. Clarence*), a proclaimed village, in this county.

WOONONA (*Co. Camden*), a postal town, 60 miles S. of Sydney, with mail twice daily. Money-order office and Government savings bank. The nearest railway station is Bulli, 1 mile, on the Illawarra and South Coast line. Situated in the parish of Northern Illawarra, and lies between the Illawarra Range and the sea, and the range attains an altitude of 1,300 feet above sea-level. On the face of the escarpment, which is almost perpendicular, the various coal-seams crop out, and are worked, and are known as the southern collieries. Iron ore also abounds in the range.

WOORE, a county in the Western Division of the Colony. [*See* "COUNTIES."]

WOORE (*Co. Argyle*), a postal village, 142 miles S. of Sydney, with mail three times a week. The nearest railway station is Goulburn, 14 miles, on the southern line.

WOORE'S HILL (*Co. Denison*), a lofty mountain, lying on the N. bank of the Murray River, about 12 miles N. of Mulwala.

WORENDO MOUNT (*Co. Rous*), a peak of the Macpherson Range, about 30 miles W. of Point Danger.

WORENGY (*Co. Roxburgh*), a village reserve on the Capertee River, near the junction of the Umbiella Creek, on the road from Rylstone to Bowenfels.

WORINDI RIVULET (*Co. Brisbane*), a northern tributary of the Goulburn River.

WORONDI MOUNT (*Co. Bligh*), a high hill, situated on the bank of the Goulburn River, about 6 miles S. of Wickham.

WORONORA CREEK (*Co. Cumberland*), a small stream, rising in the coast range, and flowing N. into Botany Bay, near the estuary of George's River.

WORRIGAL CREEK (*Co. Baradine*), a small eastern tributary of the Baradine Creek, falling into that creek at the township of Baradine.

WOWAGIN *(Co. Argyle)*, a postal town, 171 miles S. of Sydney, with weekly mail.

WOY WOY (*Co. Northumberland*), a railway station, 45 miles N. of Sydney, on the Sydney and Newcastle line.

WOY WOY BAY (*Co. Northumberland*), the western arm of Brisbane Water. There is abundance of fine timber in the district.

WOY WOY CREEK (*Co. Auckland*), a southern tributary of the Towamba River, rising in the eastern slope of Mount Coolangubra, and flowing into the main stream near Sturt Town.

WOYTCHUGGA CREEK (*Co. Young*), a small western tributary of the Darling River.

WREN'S NEST CREEK (*Co. Georgiana*), a western tributary of the Tuena Creek, flowing to the S.W. of Tuena gold-fields.

WRIGHT'S CREEK (*Co. Brisbane*), a western tributary of the Dart Brook.

WRIGHT'S CREEK (*Co. Northumberland*), a small eastern tributary of the Macdonald River, joining it near St. Albans.

WRIGHT'S (*Co. Wellesley*), a postal receiving-office, 337 miles S. of Sydney, with mail once a week.

WUDYONG (*Co. Cumberland*), a point lying to the N.E. of Kirribilli Point, and forming the western head of Careening Cove and Neutral Bay.

WULLWYE MOUNT (*Co. Wallace*), a peak lying to the E. of the Wullwye Creek, near its fall into the Snowy River.

WULLWYE RIVER (*Co. Wallace*), a tributary of the upper part of the Snowy River, rising to the W. of the Eucumbene River, falling into the Snowy River, near Buckley's crossing-place.

WUMPA (*Co. Perry*), a township on the E. bank of the Darling River, in S. lat. 33°.

WUNLUMAN (*Co. Lincoln*), a postal receiving-office, 269 miles W. of Sydney, with mail once a week.

WYALDRA (*Co. Phillip*), a proclaimed village in this county.

WYAGDON (*Co. Bathurst*), a township, 145 miles W. of Sydney. The nearest railway station is Bathurst, 17 miles, on the western line.

WYBONG (*Co. Brisbane*), a postal town, 172 miles N. of Sydney, with mail twice a week. The nearest railway station is Muswellbrook, 10 miles, on the northern line.

WYBONG CREEK (*Co. Brisbane*), a northern tributary of the Goulburn River, falling into it a few miles W. of Denman. It rises in the Liverpool Range.

WYEE (*Co. Northumberland*), a postal receiving-office, and a railway station on the Sydney and Newcastle line, 71 miles N. of Sydney, with daily mail.

WYEE FLAT (*Co. Northumberland*), a tract of flat alluvial land, in the parish of Morrisset, lying at the S. end of Lake Macquarie.

WYLANDRA CREEK (*Co. Gordon*), a southern tributary of the Macquarie River, falling into it about 6 miles S.E. of Dubbo.

WYNDHAM (*Co. Auckland*), a postal village, 358 miles S. of Sydney, with mail twice a week. Money-order office and Government savings bank. The nearest railway station is Cooma, 84 miles, on the Goulburn and Cooma line.

WYNYARD, a county, partly in the Central and Eastern Divisions of the Colony. [*See* "COUNTIES."]

WYONG (*Co. Northumberland*), a postal village, 6 miles N. of Sydney, with daily mail. A railway station on the Sydney and Newcastle line. The creek is a fine stream, rising in Mount Warrawolong, and flowing into the Tuggerah Beach Lake.

WYONG HILL (*Co. Northumberland*), a high hill lying on the N. bank of the Wyong Creek, near its fall into the Tuggerah Beach Lake.

WYONG PLAINS (*Co. Northumberland*), a large tract of swampy land, lying to the N. of Wyong Hill.

WYRALLAH (*Co. Clarence*), a postal town, 349 miles N. of Sydney, with mail per Clarence and Richmond River steamers. Telegraph office.

# Y

YAARANUNG MOUNT (*Co. Phillip*), a peak in a northern spur of the Blue Mountain Range, lying about 2 miles E. of the township of Barigan.

YACAABA HEAD (*Co. Gloucester*), the N. head of the entrance to Port Stephens. It is a peaked hill, 810 feet in height.

YACCO PIC (*Co. Gordon*), a lofty hill, lying on the Rocky Ponds, at the head of the Little River.

YAGOBIE (*Co. Burnett*), a postal receiving-office, 405 miles N. of Sydney, with mail twice a week.

YALAMA (*Co. Townsend*), a township to the N. of Mathoura.

YALCOGRIN (*Co. Dowling*), a township, 290 miles W. of Sydney. The nearest railway station is Hay, 116 miles, on the south-western line.

YALGOGORING MOUNT (*Co. Cooper*), a solitary hill, lying on the vast plains between the Lachlan and Murrumbidgee Rivers.

YALLAH (*Co. Camden*), a railway station, 59 miles S. of Sydney, on the Illawarra and South Coast line.

YALTOLKA (*Co. Windeyer*), a township on the E. bank of the Darling River, in lat. 33° S.

YALWAL (*Co. St. Vincent*), a postal village, 149 miles S. of Sydney, with mail twice a week. The nearest railway station is Kiama, 56 miles, on the Illawarra and South Coast line.

YALWAL CREEK (*Co. St. Vincent*), a fine, large stream, rising between Narriga and Tianjara, and flowing into the Shoalhaven River, W. of Nowra.

YAMBA (*Co. Clarence*), a postal village, 307 miles N. of Sydney, with mail per Clarence steamer. Telegraph and money-order offices.

YAMBLA (*Co. Goulburn*), a postal village, 377 miles S. of Sydney, with daily mail and telegraph office. A railway station on the southern line.

YAMMATREE (*Co. Clarendon*), a township, 283 miles S. of Sydney. The nearest railway station is Bethungra, 15 miles, on the southern line.

YAMMIM MOUNT (*Co. Wellington*), a peak on the S. bank of the Cudgegong River, N. of Meringo gold-field.

YANCORRINA GLEN CREEK (*Co. Yancowinna*), a stream, rising on the Barrier Range, and flowing in an easterly direction.

YANCOWINNA, a county in the Western Division of the Colony. [*See* "COUNTIES."]

YANDA, a county in the Western Division of the Colony. [*See* "COUNTIES."]

YANDA (*Co. Cowper*), a township, on the Darling River, below Bourke.

YANDARLO (*Co. Young*), a postal town, 786 miles S. of Sydney, with mail twice a week.

YANDYGANRILLA CREEK (*Co. Murray*), a tributary of the upper portion of the Molonglo River, flowing from the Australian Alps across the Molonglo Plains.

YANGO CREEK (*Co. Northumberland*), a small western tributary of the Wollombi Brook.

YANKO (*Co. Cooper*), a railway station, 361 miles S.W. of Sydney, on the south-western line.

YANKO CREEK (*Co. Cooper*), a watercourse dividing the counties of Boyd and Mitchell, and flowing through the county of Urana. It leaves the Murrumbidgee River, at the village of Yanko, near Narrandera township, and flows through the village of Cudgel into the Billabung Creek, at Conargo.

YANTABULLABULLA (*Co. Irrara*), a township, near the Queensland border, to the N.W. of the Warrego River.

YANTARA, a county in the Western Division of the Colony. [*See* "COUNTIES."]

YAOUK CREEK (*Co. Cowley*), a tributary creek to the head of the Murrumbidgee River, rising between Gudjenby Hill and Mount Murray, and flowing past Yaouk Bill's Peak.

YAOUK BILL'S PEAK (*Co. Cowley*), a high peak of the S. part of the Murrumbidgee Range, lying about 12 miles N. of Bolairo.

YAPPA (*Co. Gloucester*), a small agricultural settlement, lying on the Manning River, near Wingham.

YARDOWINDIDJA CREEK (*Co. Taulora*), a small creek rising in the Monolon Mountains.

YARENAIGH CREEK (*Co. Wellington*), an auriferous western tributary of the Molong River.

YARIMBA CREEK (*Co. Baradine*) is the western head or tributary of the Brigalow Creek. It rises in the Warabungle Range, near Coonabarabran.

YARRA (*Co. Argyle*), a postal village, 140 miles S. of Sydney, with daily mail. A railway station on the southern line.

YARRAFORD (*Co. Gough*), a railway station, 420 miles N. of Sydney, on the northern line.

YARRAHAPINNI MOUNT (*Co. Dudley*), a solitary hill on the sea-coast, about 4 miles N. of Trial Bay, at the mouth of the Macleay River.

YARRALOW CREEK (*Co. Argyle*), a fine stream, rising in the eastern part of the Goulburn Plains, flowing into the Merrimungo Creek, about 12 miles from Bungonia.

YARRAMALONG (*Co. Northumberland*), a postal village, 71 miles N. of Sydney, with mail three times a week. The nearest railway station is Wyong, 9 miles, on the Sydney and Newcastle line.

YARRAMAN (*Co. Pottinger*), a postal village, 278 miles N. of Sydney, with mail three times a week. The nearest railway station is Quirindi, 35 miles, on the northern line.

YARRA MUNDA (*Co. Cook*), a village, situated on the Hawkesbury River, about 2 miles S.W. of Richmond.

YARRAN (*Co. Wakool*), a small watercourse connecting the Edward River with the Neimur Creek.

YARRANBENE CREEK (*Co. Murray*), a western tributary of the head of the Shoalhaven River.

YARRANGOBILLY (*Co. Selwyn*), an agricultural village on the Yarrangobilly Creek, 22 miles S. of Tumut.

YARRANGOBILLY CREEK (*Co. Buccleuch*), a stream rising on the N. of the Snowy or Bald Mountains, near the village of Yarrangobilly, flowing into the upper part of the Tumut River, at Lob's Hole.

YARRARA (*Co. Hume*), a postal receiving-office, 400 miles S. of Sydney, with mail twice a week. The nearest railway station is Culcairn, 35 miles, on the southern line.

YARRAS (*Co. Macquarie*), a postal village, 314 miles N. of Sydney, with mail three times a week. The nearest railway station is Hexham, 196 miles, on the northern line.

YARRA WAH BRUSH (*Co. Camden*) is in the western slope of the range dividing the Illawarra district from that of Berrima and Sutton Forest.

YARRA-YARRA CREEK (*Co. Goulburn*), a southern tributary of the Billabung Creek, rising to the N.E. of Jergyle, and flowing into the main stream at the township of Billabung, where it is crossed by the main road from Albury to Sydney.

YARREN-YARREN CREEK (*Co. Wynyard*), a fine stream, rising in the N. of Mane's Range, and flowing into the Murrumbidgee River.

YARRIBIL CREEK (*Co. Bligh*), a small northern tributary of the Cudgegong River.

YARRIGUAN (*Co. Leichhardt*), a peak of the Warribungle Range, lying at the head of Baradine Creek, N.W. of Coonabarabran.

YARRIMANDA CREEK (*Co. Buckland*), an eastern tributary of the Conadilly River, rising in Mount Palmer, flowing through the Australian Agricultural Company's grant of 249,000 acres.

YARRINGA CREEK (*Co. Camden*), a tributary of the Kangaroo River, rising in the Wingacarribee Swamp.

YARROW CREEK (*Co. Murray*), a tributary of the Molonglo River, rising on Yarrow Peak, and flowing into the Molonglo Plains.

YARROW PEAK (*Co. Murray*), a high peak, lying to the S.W. of Molonglo Plains, between the Molonglo and Queanbeyan Rivers.

YARROW RIVER (*Co. Gough*). [*See* "RIVERS."]

YARROWITCH (*Co. Vernon*), a postal receiving-office, 340 miles N. of Sydney, with mail twice a week. The nearest railway station is Walcha, 35 miles, on the northern line.

YARROWITCH CREEK (*Co. Vernon*), a small southern tributary of the Apsley River.

YARROWYCH (*Co. Hardinge*), a postal village, 379 miles N. of Sydney, with mail twice a week.

YARROWYCH MOUNT (*Co. Hardinge*), a lofty peak of the New England Range, on the N. bank of the Rocky River, about 16 miles W. of Armidale.

YARRUNGA (*Co. Cook*), a township, 86 miles W. of Sydney. The nearest railway station is Moss Vale, 6 miles, on the southern line.

YASS (*Co. King*), a postal town, 190 miles S. of Sydney, with daily mail. Telegraph and money-order offices, Government savings bank, and delivery by letter-carrier. A railway station on the southern line. Situated on the N and S. banks of the river of the same name, the Murrumbidgee River flowing about 10 miles distant, S. The surrounding district is very fertile, and is highly cultivated for agricultural purposes. It was proclaimed a municipal district in 1873, with a council of eight aldermen and a mayor. Population, about 1,800. Sittings of the supreme court, courts of quarter sessions, and district courts are held here periodically.

YASS PLAINS (*Cos. Murray and King*), a fine tract of pastoral land, lying on the E. and S. of Yass River, and to the S. of the township of Yass. They are well watered and grassed, and afford excellent grazing for cattle. They were discovered by Messrs. Hovell and Hume, in 1828.

YASS RIVER (*Cos. Harden, King, and Murray*). [See " RIVERS."]

YATHONG (*Co. Urana*), a railway station, 399 miles S. of Sydney, on the Narrandera and Jerilderic line.

YATHELLA (*Co. Clarendon*), a postal receiving-office, 299 miles S. of Sydney, with mail once a week.

YATTEYATAH (*Co. St. Vincent*), a postal village, 153 miles S. of Sydney, with daily mail.

YAVEN GAP (*Co. Wynyard*), a passage between two hills, lying N. of the Yaven-Yaven reserve, and through which the creek flows.

YAVEN-YAVEN CREEK (*Co. Wynyard*), a tributary of the Nacka-Nacka Creek, flowing through the village of Yaven.

YAYPO BRUSH (*Co. Macquarie*), a small agricultural settlement on the Manning River.

YELLOW CLAY CREEK (*Co. Buccleuch*), a tributary of the Oak Creek, rising in the southern slope of Crowpal Hill.

YELLOW JACKET CREEK (*Co. Gough*), a small southern tributary of the Mitchell River.

YELLOW ROCK MOUNT (*Co. Northumberland*), a rocky hill in the Hunter range of mountains, lying to the S.E. of the township of Broke, and on the E. bank of the Wollombi Brook.

YENGO CREEK (Co. Northumberland), the name of the eastern head of the Macquarie River.

YENGO MOUNT (Co. Northumberland), a peak of the Hunter range of mountains, lying on the E. bank of the Macdonald River, and 16 miles W. of Wollombi.

YEOVAL (Co. Gordon), a postal town, 248 miles W. of Sydney, with mail four times a week.

YEO-YEO CREEK (Cos. Bland and Gipps), a stream which rises in the S. of the township of Yeo-Yeo, and flowing into the Cowal Lake.

YEO-YEO (Co. Bland), a village, 350 miles to the S.W. of Sydney.

YEPPIN-YEPPIN CREEK (Co. Macquarie), a small southern tributary of the lower end of the Hastings River.

YERNEA (Co. Irrara), a township on the banks of the Paroo River, on the Queensland border.

YERONERA MOUNT (Co. Wellington), a detached mountain, lying at the head of the Grattai Creek, to the S.W. of the township of Mudgee.

YERONG CREEK (Co. Mitchell), a postal village, 336 miles S. of Sydney, with daily mail and telegraph office. A railway station on the southern line.

YERONG MOUNT (Co. Mitchell), a lofty range of mountains, lying near the head of Pulletop Creek.

YERRIRONG CREEK (Co. St. Vincent), a southern tributary of the lower end of the Shoalhaven River.

YETHOLME (Co. Roxburgh), a postal village, 127 miles W. of Sydney, with mails three times a week. The nearest railway station is Rydal, 16 miles, on the western line.

YETMAN (Co. Arrawatta), a postal village, 547 miles N. of Sydney, with mail twice a week, and telegraph office. The nearest railway station is Tamworth, 195 miles, on the northern line.

YONGA LAKE (Co. Cairo), a lagoon, lying on the E. bank of the Murrumbidgee River, about 8 miles S.E. of Balranald.

YORK MOUNT (Co. Cook), a lofty peak of the Blue Mountain Range, 72 miles from Sydney. Its summit is 3,442 feet above sea-level, and was first reached in 1813 by Messrs. Lawson, Wentworth, and Blaxland.

YORKIE'S CREEK (Co. Clarence), a small western tributary of the Esk River.

YOUNG, a county in the Western Division of the Colony. [See "COUNTIES."]

YOUNG (*Co. Monteagle*), a postal town, 256 miles S. of Sydney, with daily mail. Telegraph and money-order offices, Government savings bank, and delivery by letter-carrier. A railway station on the Murrumburrah and Blayney line. Situate on the Burrangong Creek, on the main line of road from Yass to Forbes. The Burrangong gold-fields, which are alluvial, are 30 miles in extent. The surrounding country is elevated with open ridges of rich, red loam, suitable for the growth of grain of all kinds, the district being one of the richest in the Colony. Young was proclaimed a borough municipality in August, 1882, with eight aldermen and a mayor. Population, about 2,400. Sittings of the supreme court, courts of quarter sessions, and district courts are held here periodically.

YOUNGAL CREEK (*Co. Selwyn*), a western tributary of the E. branch of Murray River, rising in Mount Youngal.

YOWACA (*Co. Auckland*), a small agricultural settlement, lying near Panbula.

YOWACKA CREEK (*Co. Auckland*), a southern tributary of the Panbula River, falling into it at the township of Panbula.

YUGGLAMAH (*Co. Auckland*), a village reserve, lying on the Towamba River, about 12 miles S. of Catchcart.

YUGLO CREEK (*Co. Gipps*), a stream caused by the overflow of a swamp called Morris' Lagoon, and flowing into Yeo Yeo Creek.

YULUNDRY (*Co. Wellington*), a township, 216 miles W. of Sydney. The nearest railway station is Molong, 21 miles, on the Orange and Molong line.

YUNGNULGRA, a county in the Western Division of the Colony. [*See* "COUNTIES."]

YURRUNGA (*Co. Camden*), a postal village, 93 miles S. of Sydney, with daily mail.

# Z

ZANDVLIET (*Co. Cumberland*), at Watson's Bay, in the parish of Alexandria, 8 miles E. of Sydney.

ZIGZAG (*Co. Cook*), a railway station, 92 miles W. of Sydney, on the western line. The Zigzag railway crossing the Blue Mountains ranks as one of the most substantial works in the world. The series of zigzags commences at Lapstone Hill, 50 miles distant from Sydney, and continues its course until it reaches its highest point at 91 miles from Sydney, at an elevation of 3,362 feet above the sea-level. After passing two viaducts and through a short tunnel, it reaches the lowest point of the Zigzag at an elevation of 3,261 feet, and thence descends into Bathurst, a distance of 145 miles from Sydney, at an elevation of 2,153 feet. This gigantic work was constructed at a cost of £812,000, under Mr. John Whitton, the Engineer-in-Chief for Railways in the Colony.

# ADVERTISEMENTS.

BY THE SAME AUTHOR.   DEMY 8VO., PRICE 21S.

# THE PASTORAL POSSESSIONS OF NEW SOUTH WALES,

ALPHABETICALLY ARRANGED IN THE EASTERN, CENTRAL, AND WESTERN DIVISIONS,

WITH THE NAMES OF THE PASTORAL HOLDERS OF THE CROWN, THE LAND DISTRICT AND COUNTY IN WHICH EACH HOLDING IS SITUATED, THE AREA IN ACRES, THE ANNUAL RENT AND LICENSE FEE, THE RATE PER ACRE AND PER SECTION FOR EACH LEASEHOLD AND RESUMED AREA RESPECTIVELY, WITH COPIOUS INDICES AND A MAP.

BY WILLIAM HANSON, A.L.S., LOND., EX-GOVERNMENT PRINTER OF NEW SOUTH WALES.

SYDNEY: TURNER & HENDERSON, HUNTER-STREET.—1889.

### ABRIDGED NOTICES AND OPINIONS.

"I have found the work characterised by accuracy, with sufficient fulness of detail, without unnecessary diffuseness."—THE HON. SIR HENRY PARKES, G.C.M.G., Premier of New South Wales.

"The book must be found to be of great value, as its contents are ample and accurate in almost every case."—THE HON. THOMAS GARRETT, M.P.

"I feel justified in saying that, to all having any interest in our public lands—and who has not—it is a most valuable work."—THE HON. SIR JOHN ROBERTSON, K.C.M.G.

"We think it will be conceded by those who know the Land question that he (Mr. Hanson) has provided a useful directory of the Pastoral Lands, and one which will serve fairly the purposes he has set forth in his introduction. He has supplemented his volume by a very complete index of Registered Pastoral Holders."—*Sydney Morning Herald.*

"Mr. Hanson's 'Pastoral Possessions' must of necessity become, from its birth, a standard volume in the statistical library of the country. It will be the most valuable companion of its kind a speculator in station property can have at his elbow."—*Daily Telegraph.*

"To intending speculators in land, especially, the book must prove invaluable, as it indicates what territory is available."—*The Bathurst Free Press.*

"Land legislation during the last seven years has brought many phases of the great land question prominently to the fore, but the information was disjointed. There was a lack of the concentration which Mr. Hanson has brought to bear."—*Sydney Mail.*

"Mr. Hanson is to be commended for the diligence and pains which have led him to put out a valuable work of reference."—*Maitland Mercury.*

"The work is one of the most valuable references on an important subject which has been issued for a long time."—*Pastoral Times.*

"The work supplies in a handy and attractive form a vast amount of information."—*The Clarence and Richmond Examiner.*

"The curious land student will find much food for reflection in going through the pages of this apparently dry catalogue of leasehold areas."—*Freeman's Journal.*

"'The Pastoral Possessions of New South Wales.'—So many Victorians have become interested in pastoral properties in New South Wales that a publication just issued in Sydney, giving complete and readily acceptable information respecting them, is likely to meet with a ready sale in this Colony."—*The Age,* Melbourne.

"The volume bespeaks a great deal of research, and is certain to prove indispensable to those owning or who contemplate owning land in New South Wales."—*The Leader,* Melbourne.

"If the public perused this work they would know where to obtain homestead leases and selections. He would like to see a copy of the work sent to every School of Arts in the country."—T. M. SLATTERY, ESQ., M.P. for Burrowa.

"It contains a fund of information of benefit to any person seeking to take up a homestead lease or a conditional purchase. They would be able to form from this book a good idea of the character of the land."—W. C. WALL, ESQ., M.P. for Mudgee.

"He regarded the book as an invaluable compilation in the interests of the public who desired to settle upon the land."—O. O. DANGAR, Esq., M.P. for the Macleay.

"To business men, bankers, and merchants this is a most valuable compilation. It enables one to find out the number of squatters in the country, the persons who occupy the land, and the acreage of their holdings."—J. TORPY, Esq., M.P. for Orange.

"The list of runs, showing at a glance the area of land 'not under occupation license' and therefore virtually commonage, ought to be of special interest. All persons who intend to take up land in the Colony will do well, as a preliminary step, to obtain a copy of this work."—*The Albury Banner.*

"One of the most useful and carefully compiled works which we have ever seen is the 'Pastoral Possessions of New South Wales' by Mr. Hanson."—*Central Australian and Bourke Telegraph.*

"'The Pastoral Possessions of New South Wales' is a useful addition to the statistical works of the Colony, and should find a place on every station and in every reference library, as well as in the counting houses of all business men interested in the land question."—*Town and Country Journal.*

# THE
# Equitable Life Assurance Society
## OF THE UNITED STATES.

Head Office: 120, BROADWAY, NEW YORK.

THE **Equitable Society** is:—

1.—The **strongest Company,** holding a larger cash surplus than any other assurance organization in the world.

2.—The **largest Company,** having the greatest volume of Outstanding Assurance.

3.—The **most popular Company,** having for many years transacted the largest annual business.

4.—The **safest to patronise,** as every policy becomes absolutely **incontestable,** and cannot, then, like the policies of many Companies, be contested, or compromised for part of its face value.

5.—**Of all Companies the most prompt.** As soon as a policy becomes incontestable it is payable, not after the usual delay of sixty days, but immediately upon the receipt of "Proofs of Death." Of 1,999 death claims paid in 1890, nearly **two-thirds** (1,259) were paid **the very day** "Proofs of Death" were received; while more than **four-fifths** of the whole were paid within ten days.

6.—The **most progressive Company,** having been the pioneer in all the reforms which have made American life assurance famous throughout the world.

7.—The **most liberal Company,** issuing a policy which combines more guarantees and advantages than any other company can offer under a single contract of assurance.

8.—The **most remunerative Company,** having not only accumulated a larger surplus for the future benefit of policy-holders, but having devised the Tontine method of assurance under which larger profits have been paid to policy-holders than under any form of assurance ever introduced.

---

SYDNEY BRANCH: JUNCTION OF PITT, O'CONNELL, AND HUNTER STREETS.

Brisbane Office: Edward-street.

**R. HOPE ATKINSON,** *Manager.*

# Bank of New South Wales.

ESTABLISHED 1817.

| | |
|---|---|
| AUTHORISED CAPITAL | £3,000,000. |
| PAID-UP CAPITAL | 1,250,000. |
| RESERVE FUND | 990,000. |

*Directors:*
THOMAS BUCKLAND, Esq., *President*; ROBERT CAMPBELL CLOSE, Esq.; JAMES THOMAS WALKER, Esq.; JAMES RICHARD HILL, Esq.; THOMAS CADELL, Esq.; CHARLES SMITH, Esq.

*Auditors:* GEORGE M. MERIVALE, Esq.; ALFRED G. MILSON, Esq.

*General Manager:* GEORGE MILLER.

### HEAD OFFICE, SYDNEY.
THOMAS HUNT IVEY, Manager.

### LONDON OFFICE, OLD BROAD-STREET.

*Directors:*
DONALD LARNACH, Esq., *Chairman*; SIR DANIEL COOPER, BART.; FREDERICK TOOTH, Esq.; DAVID GEORGE, *Manager*.

*London Bankers:*
THE BANK OF ENGLAND.  THE LONDON JOINT STOCK BANK.

### MELBOURNE BOARD.
HON. DAVID MOORE, ESQ.   F. A. WALSH, ESQ.

**Branches in New South Wales.**—J. RUSSELL FRENCH, *Chief Inspector*.

SYDNEY—Bathurst-st., Pitt-st., William-st., Sussex-st., Parramatta-st., Haymarket.

COUNTRY—Adelong, Albury, Araluen, Armidale, Ashfield, Balmain, Balmain West, Bathurst, Bega, Bingara, Bombala, Bourke, Braidwood, Brewarrina, Broken Hill, Bungendore, Burrowa, Burwood, Camden, Campbelltown, Casino, Coolamon, Cooma, Coopernook, Cootamundra, Corowa, Cowra, Crookwell, Deniliquin, Dubbo, Dungog, (Agency East Maitland) Forbes, Glen Innes, Goulburn, Grafton, Grenfell, Gulgong, Gundagai, Gunnedah, Hay, Inverell, Jerilderie, Junee, Lismore, Liverpool, Maclean, Maitland, Millthorpe, Moama, Moree, Mornya, Mudgee, Murrumburrah, Narandera, Narrabri, Newcastle, Newcastle West, Newtown, Orange, Parramatta, Penrith, Port Macquarie, Queanbeyan, Richmond, Ryde, Scone, Singleton, Sofala, St. Leonards, Tamworth, Taralga, Taree, Temora, Tenterfield, Thornleigh, Tocumwal, Tumut, Uralla, Urana, Vegetable Creek, Wagga Wagga, Walgett, Warialda, Warren, Waverley, Wellington, Windsor, Wollongong, Yass, Young.

**Branches in Victoria.**—HENRY NORMAN, *Assistant Inspector*.

Ararat, Bairnsdale, Ballarat, Beechworth, Benalla, Bendigo, Brunswick, Castlemaine, Chiltern, Creswick, Eaglehawk, E. Collingwood, Echuca, Elmore; Flinders-st., W. Melbourne; Fitzroy, Geelong, Inglewood, Kyneton, Linton, Maldon, Malmsbury, Mansfield, Melbourne, Richmond, Rochester, St. Arnaud, Tallangatta, Wangaratta, Warragul, Warrnambool, Wodonga.

**Branches in Queensland.**—E. J. FINCH, *Inspector*.

Barcaldine, Beaudesert, Blackall, Bowen, Brisbane, Bundaberg, Cairns, Charters Towers, Clermont, Cooktown, Croydon, Fortitude Valley, Georgetown, Goondiwindi, Gympie, Ipswich, Longreach, Maryborough, Nerang, Normanton, Port Douglas, Rockhampton, Roma, South Brisbane, Stanthorpe, St. George, Toowoomba, Townsville, Warwick, Winton.

**Branches in New Zealand.**—W. G. RHIND, *Inspector*.

Amberley, Ashburton, Auckland, Blenheim, Bulls, Charleston, Christchurch, Dannevirke, Dunedin, Geraldine, Gisborne, Greymouth, Hastings, Hawera, Hokitika, Invercargill, Kumara, Lawrence, Masterton, Napier, Naseby, Nelson, New Plymouth, Oamaru, Ophir, Patea, St. Bathans, Temuka, Thames, Timaru, Wanganui, Wellington, Westport.

**Branches in South Australia.**—Adelaide, Port Adelaide.

**Branch in Western Australia.**—Perth.

**Agency Within the Colonies**—TASMANIA: The Commercial Bank of Tasmania (Limited).

### Agencies beyond the Colonies.

SCOTLAND.—The Royal Bank of Scotland.  IRELAND.—The National Bank.  MANCHESTER.—The Manchester and Liverpool District Bank.  BIRMINGHAM.—Lloyd's Bank (Limited).  HUDDERSFIELD.—West Riding Union Banking Co. (Limited).  LIVERPOOL.—The North and South Wales Bank.  BRISTOL AND WEST OF ENGLAND.—Stuckey's Banking Co.  HAMBURG.—Messrs. H. J. Merck & Co.  NEW YORK.—The Bank of British North America.  SAN FRANCISCO.—The London and San Francisco Bank (Limited).  INDIA AND CHINA.—The Chartered Mercantile Bank of India, London, and China; The Chartered Bank of India, Australia, and China.  MANILLA.—Messrs. Ker & Co.  RIO JANEIRO.—The English Bank of Rio de Janeiro.  AFRICA.—The Standard Bank of South Africa (Limited).

The Bank allows interest on Deposits, if lodged for fixed periods, at rates which may be ascertained at its various offices. Collects for its customers dividends on Shares in public companies, and interest on debentures. Invests Money on their behalf in Colonial Securities or those of Great Britain. Issues DRAFTS, CIRCULAR NOTES and LETTERS OF CREDIT, and negotiates approved bills, payable at any of the above-named places, and undertakes the agency of other banks on such terms as may be agreed upon.

# The Australian Joint Stock Bank.

INCORPORATED BY ACT OF COUNCIL, 1853.

| | |
|---|---:|
| CAPITAL (AUTHORISED) | £1,000,000. |
| PAID-UP | 704,394. |
| RESERVE FUNDS | 517,660. |

*Directors:*
THE HON. JEREMIAH B. RUNDLE, ESQ., M.L.C., *Chairman*; GEO. A. MURRAY, ESQ.; WALTER FRIEND, ESQ.; LOUIS PHILLIPS, ESQ.; THE HON. W. A. LONG, ESQ., M.L.C.; CHAS. H. MYLES, ESQ.

*Auditors:* DR. A. K. MORSON AND JOHN S. DUNLOP, ESQ.

*Solicitors:* MESSRS. FISHER, RALPH, & MACANSH; MESSRS. STEPHEN, JACQUES, & STEPHEN.

*Directors, London Office:*
WILLIAM MORT, ESQ.; WM. HEMMANT, ESQ.; JAS. E. OWEN DALY, ESQ.; SIR SAUL SAMUEL, K.C.M.G.

*Auditor:* A. H. J. BAASS, ESQ.

*Bankers:* THE NATIONAL PROVINCIAL BANK OF ENGLAND (LIMITED).

## HEAD OFFICE, GEORGE AND KING STREETS, SYDNEY.

FRANCIS ADAMS, *General Manager (absent on leave).* BARTON LODGE, *Acting General Manager.* GREGORY G. BLAXLAND, *Manager.* WILLIAM REID, *Secretary.* HENRY T. WEBSTER, *Accountant.* HENRY WILLIAM WALTON, *Branch Accountant.* ISAAC TOOLE, JUN., *Sub-Accountant.*

### LONDON OFFICE, 2 KING WILLIAM-STREET, E.C.
*Manager:* ALEXANDER B. BAXTER. *Accountant:* GEORGE J. GROUND.

### Branches in New South Wales.
B. LODGE, *Chief Inspector.* C. DENHAM, *Acting Chief Inspector.* A. J. GREVILLE, *Assistant Inspector.* B. B. RODD, *Assistant Inspector.*
*Relieving Officers:* FRANK HARGRAVE AND H. L. APPERLEY.

CITY AND SUBURBAN—Ashfield, Botany, Burwood, Camperdown, Darling Point, Enmore, Exchange Office, Glebe, Gordon, Granville, Haymarket, Hunter's Hill, Hurstville, Leichhardt, Manly, Miller's Point, Milson's Point, Newtown, Paddington, Petersham, Pyrmont, Randwick, Redfern, Rockdale, Summer Hill, Surry Hills, Sussex-street, Waterloo, Woollahra.

COUNTRY—Albury, Armidale, Ballina, Balranald, Bathurst, Bega, Berry, Binalong, Blayney, Bellingen, Boggabri, Bombala, Bowraville, Bourke, Branxton, Brewarrina, Broken Hill, Bulli (with agency at Helensburgh), Bullahdelah, Byerock, Cargo, Casino, Cassilis, Castle Hill, Clarence Town, Cobar, Cobargo, Colombo-Lyttleton, Condobolin, Cooma, Coonabarabran, Coonamble, Coraki, Cowra, Crookwell, Cumnock, Deepwater, Deniliquin, Drake, Dubbo, East Maitland, Eden, Forbes, Fredericton, Germanton, Gerringong, Glen Innes, Gosford (with agency at Wyong), Goulburn, Grafton, Grenfell, Greta, Gulgong, Gundagai, Gunnedah, Gunning, Guym, Harden, Haydonton, Hay, Hill End, Hillgrove, Hillston, Hinton, Inverell, Katoomba (with agencies at Blackheath and Mount Victoria), Kempsey, Kiama, Lake Cudgellico, Lambton, Lawrence, Lismore, Macksville, Maclean, Mandurama, Meniudie, Merriwa, Milton (with agency at Ulladulla), Mitchell (Sunny Corner), Moama, Molong, Moree, Morpeth, Moulamein, Mudgee, Murwillumbah, Muswellbrook, Narrandera, Narrabri, Newbridge, Newcastle (with agencies at Adamstown, Carrington (Bullock Island), and Merewether), Nowra, Nymagee, Nyngan, Oberon, Orange, Pambula, Parkes, Parramatta, Parramatta North, Peak Hill, Penrith, Quirindi, Raymond Terrace, Richmond, Rockley, Rylstone, Scone, Singleton, Smithfield, Smithtown, South Grafton, Stockton, St. Mary's, Tamworth, Tenora, Tenterfield, Tumut, Uhuarra, Uralla, Urana, Wagga Wagga, Walcha, Walgett, Wallsend (with agencies at Minmi and West Wallsend), Wardell, Warren, Wauchope, Wentworth, West Maitland, Whitton, Wickham (with agency at Hamilton), Wilcannia, Windsor, Wingham, Wollongong (with agency at Dapto), Wolumla, Woodburn, Wyndham, Yass.

### Branches in Queensland.
H. P. ABBOTT, *Manager, Brisbane, and Inspector for Queensland.* A. KERR, *Assistant Manager, Brisbane, and Assistant Inspector for Queensland.*

Brisbane, Allora, Bowen, Charters Towers, Clermont, Croydon, Gladstone, Gympie, Ipswich, Killarney North, Mackay, Maryborough, Normanton, Queenton, Ravenswood, Rockhampton, Stanthorpe, Toowoomba, Townsville, Warwick.

### Agents and Correspondents in the Colonies.
VICTORIA—The Bank of Victoria, Limited; The E. S. and A. Chartered Bank; The National Bank of Australasia. TASMANIA—The Commercial Bank of Tasmania, Limited. SOUTH AUSTRALIA—The National Bank of Australasia; The E. S. and A. Chartered Bank. WESTERN AUSTRALIA—The National Bank of Australasia. NEW ZEALAND—The Bank of New Zealand; The National Bank of New Zealand. FIJI—The Bank of New Zealand.

### In Great Britain and Foreign Places.
LONDON—The Australian Joint Stock Bank, 2 King William-street, E.C.; *Bankers*—National Provincial Bank of England, Limited. SCOTLAND—The Royal Bank of Scotland. IRELAND—The Provincial Bank of Ireland. INDIA AND CHINA—Chartered Mercantile Bank of India, London, and China; Chartered Bank of India, Australia, and China; Hongkong and Shanghai Banking Corporation; Comptoir Nationale D'Escompte de Paris. AMERICA—Messrs. Brown Bros. & Co., New York, Philadelphia, and Boston; Messrs. Alex. Brown & Sons, Baltimore; Chas. F. Hoffman, Esq., New Orleans; The Merchants' Loan and Trust Company, Chicago; Agency of the Bank of British North America. San Francisco and New York; The Anglo Californian Bank, Limited, San Francisco; The Bank of British North America, Canada; London, Paris, and American Bank, Limited, New York and San Francisco. And correspondents in the principal cities in Europe and Africa.

**Circular Notes issued for the use of Travellers.**

www.ingramcontent.com/pod-product-compliance
Lightning Source LLC
Chambersburg PA
CBHW051853300426
44117CB00006B/373